Lecture Notes in Computer Science 16487

The series Lecture Notes in Computer Science (LNCS), including its subseries Lecture Notes in Artificial Intelligence (LNAI) and Lecture Notes in Bioinformatics (LNBI), has established itself as a medium for the publication of new developments in computer science and information technology research, teaching, and education.

LNCS enjoys close cooperation with the computer science R & D community, the series counts many renowned academics among its volume editors and paper authors, and collaborates with prestigious societies. Its mission is to serve this international community by providing an invaluable service, mainly focused on the publication of conference and workshop proceedings and postproceedings. LNCS commenced publication in 1973.

Hwajeong Seo
Editor

Information Security and Cryptology – ICISC 2025

28th International Conference
Seoul, South Korea, November 19–21, 2025
Revised Selected Papers

Editor
Hwajeong Seo
Hansung University
Seoul, Korea (Republic of)

ISSN 0302-9743 ISSN 1611-3349 (electronic)
Lecture Notes in Computer Science
ISBN 978-981-95-8033-0 ISBN 978-981-95-8034-7 (eBook)
https://doi.org/10.1007/978-981-95-8034-7

This Springer imprint is published by the registered company Springer Nature Singapore Pte Ltd.
The registered company address is: 152 Beach Road, #21-01/04 Gateway East, Singapore 189721, Singapore

Preface

The 28th International Conference on Information Security and Cryptology (ICISC 2025) was held from November 19 – November 21, 2025. This year's conference was hosted by the KIISC (Korea Institute of Information Security and Cryptology) and NSR (National Security Research Institute).

The aim of this conference is to provide an international forum for the latest results of research, development, and applications within the field of information security and cryptology. This year, we received 74 submissions and were able to accept 28 papers for the conference, yielding an acceptance rate of 37.8%. The challenging review and selection processes were successfully conducted by program committee (PC) members and external reviewers via the EasyChair review system. For transparency, it is worth noting that each paper underwent a single-blind review by at least three PC members. For the LNCS post-proceedings, the authors of selected papers had a few weeks to prepare their final versions, based on the comments received from the reviewers.

The conference features four invited talks, given by Wai-Kong Lee, Seongkwang Kim, Anubhab Baksi and Yongsoo Song. We thank the invited speakers for their kind acceptances and excellent presentations. We would like to thank all authors who submitted their papers to ICISC 2025, as well as all PC members. It was a truly wonderful experience to work with such talented and hardworking researchers. We also appreciate the external reviewers for assisting the PC members. Finally, we would like to thank all attendees for their active participation and the organizing members who successfully managed this conference. We look forward to seeing you again at next year's ICISC.

November 2025 Hwajeong Seo

Organization

General Chairs

Young-Ho Park	Sejong Cyber University, South Korea
Soo Hoon Hwang	National Security Research Institute, South Korea

Organizing Chairs

Jongsung Kim	Kookmin University, South Korea
Myungseo Park	Hansung University, South Korea
Woo-Hwan Kim	National Security Research Institute, South Korea

Organizing Committee

Ho-Won Kim	Pusan National University, South Korea
Jeong Nyeo Kim	Electronics and Telecommunications Research Institute, South Korea
Haeryong Park	Korea Internet & Security Agency, South Korea
Jungsuk Song	Korea Institute of Science and Technology Information, South Korea
Jun Lee	Korea Institute of Science and Technology Information, South Korea
Sang Yun Han	National Security Research Institute, South Korea
Kihyo Nam	EUNICESOFT, South Korea
Deok Gyu Lee	Seowon University, South Korea

Program Chair

Hwajeong Seo	Hansung University, South Korea

Publication Chair

Dongjae Lee	Kangwon National University, South Korea

Program Committee

Namsu Jho	Dankook University, South Korea
Jihyeon Ryu	Kwangwoon University, South Korea
Hyeokdong Kwon	NIMS, South Korea
Seongkwang Kim	Samsung SDS, South Korea
Jihoon Kwon	Samsung SDS, South Korea
Deuk-Hun Kim	Ajou University, South Korea
Hyeongmin Choe	CryptoLab, South Korea
Jonghyun Kim	Korea University, South Korea
Byoungjin Seok	Hansung University, South Korea
Young-Sik Kim	Daegu Gyeongbuk Institute of Science and Technology, South Korea
Moonsung Lee	National Security Research Institute, South Korea
Bonwook Koo	National Security Research Institute, South Korea
Nari Lee	National Security Research Institute, South Korea
Kyung Chul Jeong	National Security Research Institute, South Korea
Il-Gu Lee	Sungshin Women's University, South Korea
Kiwoong Park	Sejong University, South Korea
Joobeom Yun	Sejong University, South Korea

Contents

Side-Channel and Fault Analysis in PQC

Network and Application Security

Quantum Cryptanalysis & Theoretical Limits

AI-Driven Threat Detection & Federated Learning

Role-Aware Multi-modal Federated Learning System for Detecting Phishing Webpages

Bo Wang(✉), Imran Khan, Martin White, and Natalia Beloff

University of Sussex, Brighton, UK
bw268@sussex.ac.uk

Abstract. In this paper, we propose a multi-modal phishing website detection system based on federated learning, which can simultaneously utilise URL, HTML, and IMAGE data, and does not require the client to be bound to the data type during the inference stage: any client can invoke the corresponding modality head trained by other clients for detection. Methodologically, we implement a bucket aggregation strategy by role (expert level) on the FedProx paradigm, drawing on the multi-expert idea of Mixture-of-Experts (MoE) and the design concept of the FedMM algorithm. We remove the learnable routing and adopt hard gating (directly selecting the IMAGE/HTML/URL expert based on the modality label of the sample) to separately aggregate the parameters of each modality, to isolate the aggregation conflicts and convergence oscillations caused by different embeddings. We validate the effectiveness on two public datasets (TR-OP and WebPhish): the Fusion head achieves performance metrics of Accuracy (Acc) 97.5%, Precision (Prec) 98.1%, Recall (Rec) 97.3%, and 2.4% FPR on the two types of data on TR-OP. Meanwhile, in the ablation experiment, it achieves Acc 95.5%/Prec 94.3%/Rec 96.5%/FPR 5.9% on the image subset of TR-OP. On the text side, we applied two adaptations: for the simple-structured URL, we directly use GraphCodeBERT to generate embeddings; for the raw and uncleaned HTML, we adopt an early fusion of a three-way embedding design to reduce noise. On WebPhish's HTML (relatively simple), we achieve Acc 96.5%/Prec 98.1%/Rec 95%/FPR 1.8%; on the raw HTML of TR-OP (relatively difficult), we achieve Acc 95.1%/Prec 95.4%/Rec 94.6%/FPR 4.6%. The results show that bucket aggregation with hard-gating experts can stably conduct federated training and enhance the usability of multi-modal under strict privacy boundaries, providing a more flexible and comprehensive federated solution for phishing website detection.

Keywords: Web security · Federated learning · Phishing webpages · Machine learning

1 Introduction and Related Work

1.1 Development of Phishing Webpage Detection

Phishing webpages, as a persistent problem in web security, have attracted continuous attention from researchers due to their variability, complexity, and the constant emergence of new web technologies and third-party development platforms [17, 33]. Phishing

H. Seo (Ed.): ICISC 2025, LNCS 16487, pp. 3–24, 2026.
https://doi.org/10.1007/978-981-95-8034-7_1

webpages tend to conduct deceptive attacks on users, tricking them into inadvertently disclosing their personal privacy information and security data, resulting in significant financial losses. Traditional methods typically rely on blacklists to directly compare the URLs or domains of the webpages that users visit [36, 37], and warn or block the corresponding pages before users start entering any sensitive information. However, this manual rule-based approach, while ensuring a certain degree of interpretability, is unable to handle unseen page or URL types. Therefore, machine learning-based detection solutions have emerged [1, 4, 8]. These solutions offer a more automated and efficient approach, eliminating the need for extensive manual rule updates. In recent years, with the rise of large models, there has been an increasing number of studies exploring the use of large models to replace traditional machine learning end-to-end solutions, further enhancing the generalisation and coverage of machine learning-based approaches.

1.2 Existing Phishing Webpages Detection Techniques

Based on our investigation of the literature, the research on the automatic detection of phishing webpages and machine learning-related techniques in recent years can be roughly divided into three major categories: 1. End-to-end models based on machine learning [1, 4, 8, 16–18]; 2. Reference-based models that combine machine learning or LLMs [5–7, 11, 12]; 3. Direct detection of phishing webpages using LLMs [2, 10, 14].

The end-to-end detection of phishing webpages can be roughly classified into these categories based on the way data is utilised: 1. Detection of web source code using features of HTML or URL, or a combination of both; 2. Detection using images and logos, or a combination of their features; 3. Selection of an associated combination among HTML, URL, and images, followed by feature fusion and classification. Each of these studies has its own advantages and disadvantages (mainly in the trade-off between computational load and performance), such as the relatively early studies HTMLphish [4] and Web2Vec [16], which achieved relatively comprehensive utilisation of data like HTML and URL. Particularly, Web2Vec treated URL, page text content, and DOM structure as sequences (character/word/sentence granularity) for learning representations, followed by multi-channel feature extraction and fusion, and finally binary classification. Each channel went through CNN → BiLSTM → Attention (CNN captures local features, BiLSTM captures context, and attention emphasises key information). Their final performance (99% accuracy, 0.25% FPR) demonstrated the effectiveness of this fusion strategy, but it also greatly increased the computational load.

WebPhish [8] is another relatively lightweight case in recent years. They proposed to concatenate HTML and URL features into a complete vector and then feed it into a downstream classifier, similar to the earlier Web2Vec approach. This scheme effectively utilised both types of data through early fusion and achieved very satisfactory performance metrics (98% accuracy and recall). Their dataset was quite large (45,373 samples, balanced positive and negative examples), covering most of the features of phishing and normal pages to a high degree. Although they did not use any image data and the training method was traditional centralised, it was still a good design that utilised both types of data simultaneously.

The approach of using the MoE (mix of experts) concept for complex design also exists. In the research by Wang's team [1], they decomposed the URL into attributes:

WHOIS for the duration of domain registration; content: whether there is a privacy request/pop-up/mask; behaviour: the number of redirects and loading delay (normalised using the mean of the top 100 websites). These statistics are uniformly encoded into vectors of the same dimension as the token embeddings (binary encoding of registration duration $\rightarrow$ 756 dimensions), and fed into a fusion model of Transformer + Mixture-of-Experts. In their tests, MoE did indeed improve the performance decline caused by the small amount of training set data during centralised training. Although there was not much improvement in pure classification performance, and the data was limited to URLs, the overall design idea was indeed very rare.

Directly using LLM (Large Language Model) for phishing detection is also a direction [2, 10, 14]. Although there are many problems with this approach, such as the unexplainability of LLM, weak deployment flexibility (usually only API calls can be made and HTML consumes a lot of costs), and the need to separately test the resistance to adversarial attacks and prompt attacks, the powerful performance of LLM (such as ChatGPT) still brings visible performance improvements to phishing detection. For example, in Lee's team's research, they conducted a two-stage test based on brands for three large models. In the first stage, they used a multimodal LLM to identify the target brand from screenshots and/or simplified HTML. In the second stage, they used LLM to verify the consistency between the brand and the domain name. They achieved relatively good performance indicators on their self-built dataset. Moreover, LLM can achieve better results than single visual models that only use logos in noisy environments by leveraging multimodality.

Regarding research on hybrid machine learning models and reference-based schemes, such studies mainly utilise the explainability of reference-based methods and the efficiency of machine learning to achieve higher performance and more explainable detection results. At the same time, because these schemes are usually more modular, they are more friendly to multimodal design (allowing individual modules to handle specific modalities). Early well-known examples include PhishPedia [12] and, recently, Phishagent [11].

The early hybrid phishing detection framework, PhishPedia, is a very famous study. They used brand logos + input boxes + target domains. They rendered page screenshots in a sandbox based on the URL, then used Fast-RCNN to detect logos and input boxes, followed by using Siamese for comparison between logos and the knowledge base (static), identified the brand, and compared it with the official brand library to decide. At the same time, they also emphasised the common problem in phishing detection using machine learning paradigms, that is, over-reliance on a single model may cause the model to learn the correlation between datasets rather than the features of the data itself, leading to a high FPR rate. We hold a reserved view on this point because many current machine learning-based phishing detection schemes indeed have significant differences in datasets and comparisons (many methods claiming to be SOTA achieve around 99% performance on their own datasets), resulting in unfair performance comparisons.

Meanwhile, we agree that the FPR of a model is a very important performance indicator, so we specifically observed this issue in our experiments. PhishPedia, being an early study, has been surpassed in recent research, such as Phishagent (which includes performance comparisons on the same dataset). The recent hybrid design of Phishagent proposes to use a large model combined with a hybrid brand knowledge base to achieve a more comprehensive multimodal detection of phishing websites. In their design, the large model plays a key role, similar to that in ChatPhish [2]. Unlike ChatPhish, they break down the entire multimodal system into more detailed sub-modules (offline knowledge base module, online knowledge base module, core decision agent) and split the web page into three types of inputs: W.HTML, W.screenshot, W.URL, and integrate them into a single input W (webpage). They complete the retrieval and discrimination within one iteration, balancing low latency and brand coverage. However, their ablation experiments also exposed some problems, that is, they are highly dependent on the online query module. Once this module is removed, the performance drops sharply, which is a common problem for some solutions that rely on rules and knowledge base queries, such as PhishPedia.

1.3 Federated Learning and Phishing Webpage Detection

Currently, research directly applying federated learning to phishing webpage detection is scarce or very limited. Most studies mainly focus on the application of federated learning to phishing emails, text messages, or URLs [3, 15, 20, 21]. The attack surfaces targeted by most of these studies are either unrelated to phishing webpages or relatively narrow. For instance, STFL [15] proposed using federated learning to detect phishing URLs. They utilised three datasets to enhance coverage of URL datasets and classified URLs into three feature categories: domain + TLD/subdomain/path. They performed one-hot encoding on characters and selected 52 high-frequency characters, then concatenated them. However, their overall approach was limited to URL data alone and did not discuss other features of phishing webpages, such as HTML itself. In their explanation, they chose to skip the analysis of web content (such as HTML) due to the complex computations and significant time requirements involved.

Moreover, although some research has considered the data privacy issues of phishing webpages, such studies are still extremely rare. Early on, the Microsoft team proposed moving phishing webpage data to the cloud to prevent the leakage of sensitive information (such as email addresses, bank details, and corporate secrets) contained in the data [19]. They used a third-party platform model to train and detect without accessing the original phishing pages. STFL also mentioned that URLs, as one of the features, might contain users' personal information, making centralised learning inappropriate, especially considering legal requirements like GDPR. These requirements are highly consistent with the principles advocated by federated learning, such as data localisation.

One of the biggest advantages of federated learning is the localisation of data. Although this may lead to some performance loss, studies have shown that due to the heterogeneous and non-IID (Non-independent and non-identically distributed) nature of federated learning, it is difficult to directly compare its performance with centralised learning [23, 24]. Of course, considering its privacy protection and data localisation advantages, this can be seen as a trade-off.

1.4 Contributions

Based on all the research mentioned above, considering the scarcity of current studies on phishing detection using federated learning, especially in the multi-modal aspect [9], and the deviation in practical usability caused by the one-sided application of data in end-to-end design, we propose a federated learning-based multi-modal phishing detection system to address the following challenges, which are also the contributions of this paper:

- **The diversity and complexity of phishing website pages:** It is difficult to reflect the complexity of phishing websites by using only a single type of data. We aim to, through the concept of MoE (though not strictly MoE), enable the global model to handle multiple types of data (IMAGE, HTML, URL) simultaneously under federated learning, and still achieve acceptable detection results when a certain type of data is missing.
- **Data dependency:** We do not require the test sets and training sets of clients to be equivalent or strongly dependent. We decouple the relationship between the test set and the training set on the client side. Any client can use the corresponding modality heads trained by other clients for detection, as long as the data type is allowed by the framework.
- **Data privacy:** The inherent nature of phishing websites existing in direct user interaction may lead to the capture of some users' personal information, making the original data unable to be shared. Given the poor commonality of the previously mentioned datasets, we hope to effectively utilise multi-source and multi-party data through federated learning, ensuring that the original data does not circulate and does not violate relevant laws.
- **Aggregation conflicts in federated learning with multi-modalities:** It is difficult to aggregate multiple types of data that are fundamentally different using federated learning alone, as there are fundamental differences in embedding and semantic spaces, which can cause conflicts during model aggregation. If separate federations are conducted for each type of data using a single model, it will greatly increase computational and time costs. We design a role-based aggregation strategy, where each client only aggregates the corresponding data, to achieve isolation of aggregation parameters and multi-modal learning in a single federation.

2 Methodology

2.1 General Framework Design

In this paper, we made use of a federated learning simulation system based on Flower [28]. Flower is an open-source federated learning simulation framework which supports a variety of mainstream algorithms and highly flexible custom aggregation strategies.

We designed four distinct expert module routes to process three different types of data, namely pure IMAGE headers, pure HTML headers, URL headers, and a Fusion header that combines IMAGE and HTML. Given that the difficulty levels of different tasks vary, the corresponding pre - processing, embedding schemes, and downstream classifiers also differ. The three types of data are HTML, IMAGE, and URL. Judging from the difficulty, URL is the least complex, followed by IMAGE. HTML is the most difficult because it involves different and complex HTML elements from two datasets simultaneously. In the section on dataset explanation, we elaborate on the reasons for the substantial differences in the difficulty levels of these three types of data.

We adopted three different embedding methods: Pix2Struct [13], GraphcodeBERT [22], and static three-way segmentation (the process is elaborated in detail in the data pre - processing section), similar to the approach of WebPhish. The overall process of the entire framework is presented in Fig. 1.

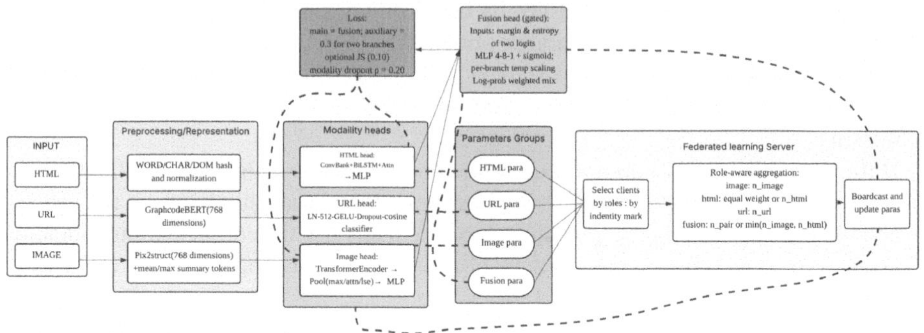

Fig. 1. General workflow of Role-aware Federated-learning Phishing webpages detection

2.2 Environment and Hyperparameters

Our experiments were conducted on the Artemis HPC system using the Slurm scheduler. We employed an Nvidia A-40 graphics card, 12 central processing units (CPUs), and 48 gigabytes (GB) of graphics processing unit (GPU) memory. The experimental environment was established based on Flower, as previously described, with 256 GB of memory (RAM). CUDA 11.3.1 was utilised to expedite the embedding and training processes. The training duration varied depending on different data partitioning strategies and experimental setups. It was also affected by the server throughput. Given that Artemis-HPC is a shared computing cluster, accurately controlling the training time was challenging. The number of federated aggregation rounds was set to 100. The number of local epochs was set to 5, the learning rate to 0.001, and the batch size to 64.

The maximum training time was approximately 16 h, covering all data and all heads except the Fusion head, with 6 clients involved. The minimum training time was around 1 h, using only URL data and with 2 clients. Moreover, due to substantial differences in loading speed across embedding methods, we also recorded the time intervals. The pix2struct embedding process took approximately 40 min. The static three-way split embedding for data from two HTML datasets took about 20 min, while the single-URL embedding using graphcodebert took about 5 min. The maximum RAM utilisation was approximately 100 GB, and the majority of computational resources and time were consumed by the IMAGE head and its associated components, accounting for roughly half of the total.

The four-head architecture and key hyperparameters are presented as follows:

1. **Image Head:** The image head utilised a TransformerEncoder. The input dimension was set to 768, the number of layers was 2, the number of attention heads was 8, the feed-forward dimension was 1024, and the dropout rate was 0.2. The pooling operation was governed by the global parameter POOL, configured as max pooling. The classification layer consisted of a LayerNorm layer, a full-connection (FC layer with 512 neurons, a Gaussian Error Linear Unit (GELU) activation function, a Dropout layer with a rate of 0.2, and an output layer.
2. **HTML Head:** The HTML head adopted a three-way lightweight encoding approach. The embedding dimensions for the character, word, and Document Object Model (DOM) branches were 64, 128, and 64, respectively. For the character branch, a multi-scale convolutional group with 16 kernels (ranging in size from 2 to 9) was employed, followed by a 128-dimensional FC layer. The word and DOM branches each incorporated a single-layer bidirectional Long Short-Term Memory (LSTM) network with a hidden dimension of 64, and attention pooling was applied. After concatenating the three branches, the same classification layer as the image head was used.
3. **URL Head:** URL Head. LayerNorm on 768-dim input; linear layer with 512 units (weight normalisation enabled), GELU, Dropout 0.2; then a cosine classifier to two classes. The classifier normalises features and class weights and uses a learnable scale initialised to 10. Key hyperparameters: hidden size 512, dropout 0.2, weight normalisation on or off, initial scale 10, number of classes 2.
4. **Fusion Head:** The fusion head was designed as a gated Multi-Layer Perceptron (MLP). Its input consisted of four statistical measures from two branches, namely the difference between the top 2 logits (margin) and the entropy of each branch. The architecture of the MLP was 4–8-1, with a Rectified Linear Unit (ReLU) activation function and a sigmoid output to generate the weight α. In the log-probability space, the two branches were weighted and combined according to α. Additionally, a learnable temperature parameter was used to calibrate each branch, with an initial value of 1.0.

For the outputs of the image head and HTML head, the same auxiliary loss was computed, with a coefficient of 0.30. This was used to stabilise the model and preserve the single-path capabilities, and could be toggled on or off. An optional Jensen-Shannon divergence term for consistency regularisation was included, with a coefficient of 0.10. Setting this coefficient to 0 effectively disabled this regularisation term. To enhance the model's robustness to missing modalities, during the pairwise training phase, one branch was randomly masked at the batch level with a probability of 0.20.

2.3 Aggregation Algorithms Design

In situations where there are fundamental differences in data modalities and types, directly applying federated averaging can give rise to parameter conflicts. These conflicts may prevent the model from aggregating properly or converging. Indeed, numerous studies have been conducted to address this issue [25–27]. Among them, the design of FedMM [27] has provided significant inspiration.

FedMM is tailored to handle modality heterogeneity and missing modalities. Instead of averaging all parameters across the entire network, it adopts an aggregation approach based on "modality splitting". Specifically, it only performs federated aggregation of feature extractors among clients sharing the same modality. Meanwhile, the classifiers are localised to avoid cross-site aggregation. Additionally, FedMM incorporates a regularisation term for aligning global modality prototypes. By using weights scheduled according to the training rounds, it smoothly transitions between the supervised loss and representation alignment. Empirical evidence has demonstrated that FedMM outperforms zero - padded Multi – FedAvg [38] and pure local training.

Under the same "modality-heterogeneous/missing-modality" federated setting, our study shares the same objective as FedMM: to enhance downstream classification through cross-site collaboration without sharing the original data, and to ensure that clients with only partial modalities can also benefit.

More specifically, FedMM does not train a unified multimodal fusion network. Instead, it federates single-modal feature extractors across different sites based on modality type. To avoid conflicts arising from structural inconsistencies, the classifiers of each client are localised. On the server side, for each modality, "model aggregation + global class prototypes" are maintained in parallel. During local training, dynamic weights are used to smoothly switch between the supervised Binary Cross-Entropy (BCE) loss and the prototype alignment loss (L2 distance to the prototypes). FedMM has reported superior performance compared to zero-padded Multi-FedAvg and pure local training on datasets such as TCGA-NSCLC/RCC, and its performance approaches the upper bound of centralised fusion. In contrast, our approach freezes the upstream encoders (for images and HTML/URL). We use pre-computed or overwritten embeddings as inputs. At the client side, we only optimise lightweight branch heads and gated Probability of Embedding (PoE) fusion heads (including learnable temperature parameters). To enhance the model's robustness to missing modalities, we employ techniques such as modality dropout, auxiliary losses, and an optional Jensen-Shannon (JS) divergence term for consistency regularisation. On the server side, we aggregate each branch head and fusion module based on parameter prefixes.

In summary, both our approach and FedMM adopt a "modality-based disassembly + privacy-preserving" federated collaboration strategy. However, the key difference lies in that FedMM focuses on "federating feature extractors at the representation layer and aligning prototypes". At the same time, our method emphasises "federating branch heads and fusion modules at the prediction layer". This design choice aims to reduce communication and computational overheads and simplify the deployment process. (It should be noted that FedMM requires backpropagation through feature extractors, which is the most computationally intensive part. The optimisation objective in the FedMM paper directly acts on the L2 distance between the extractor output and the prototype, along with the BCE term, which means that gradients are updated for the feature extractors.) Inspired by FedMM and integrating the conditional routing concept of the Mixture of Experts (MoE), we have designed a simple role-aware aggregation mechanism based on FedProx [39]. We partition the parameter subgraphs by "roles" (e.g., URL, HTML, or image). During communication, only the parameters corresponding to the activated roles are aggregated, while the rest remain local. This approach effectively avoids cross-modal gradient interference and ineffective averaging. The pseudo-code for this process is presented in Figs. 2 and 3. ("shared" is a fallback mechanism when no acceptable weight is found, which will not affect the result).

Algorithm 1: Role-aware FedProx (Server side)

Input: Rounds R; parameter name list $\mathcal{N} = \text{keys}(\texttt{MultiModalNet.state\_dict})$

Data: Global parameters θ; **FedProx coefficient** μ

```
1  for r ← 1 to R do
      // line 2
2     Broadcast (θ, μ) to selected clients
3     Receive {(θ_i, n_i, m_i)}_{i∈I_r}  // θ_i: local params; n_i: samples;
        m_i: metrics (n.image/html/url, has.*)
4     foreach p ∈ N do
5        g ← GROUP(p)              // g ∈ {image, html, url, fusion, shared}
6        S ← SELECT(g, {m_i})      // only clients owning this role
          participate
7        if S = ∅ then
8           θ^new[p] ← θ[p]        // keep old if nobody can aggregate
9        else
10          if g = image then
11             w_j ← m_j[n_image]
12          else if g = html then
13             w_j ← 1             // equal weight; can switch to n_html
14          else if g = url then
15             w_j ← m_j[n_url]
16          else if g = fusion then
17             w_j ← m_j[n_pair] or min(m_j[n_image], m_j[n_html])
18          else
19             w_j ← n_j           // shared: sample-size weighting
20          Normalize w_j ← w_j / Σ_{k∈S} w_k
21          θ^new[p] ← Σ_{j∈S} w_j · θ_j[p]  // role-wise weighted average
22    θ ← θ^new; trigger CLIENTEVALUATE and log per-client metrics
        (loss/accuracy/precision/recall/FPR)
```

Fig. 2. Server-side algorithm flow for proposed Role-aware FedProx. (g refers to group; the client needs to provide an identity mark like "URL" before it participates)

Algorithm 1: Client-side Training with Paired Fusion (Dual-Head Updates)

Input: Local loaders $\mathcal{D}_{\text{img}}, \mathcal{D}_{\text{html}}, \mathcal{D}_{\text{url}}$; paired loader $\mathcal{D}_{\text{pair}}$; epochs E; lr η; focal loss $\mathcal{L}_{\text{focal}}$; aux weight λ_{aux}; JS weight λ_{JS}; modal dropout p; clip τ

Data: ImageHead, HtmlHead, FusionHead (with temperature scaling), UrlHead; snapshot $\theta^{(t)}$; FedProx μ

1 **for** $e \leftarrow 1$ **to** E **do**
2 **foreach** $(loader, mode) \in \{(\mathcal{D}_{\text{img}}, \text{image}), (\mathcal{D}_{\text{html}}, \text{html}), (\mathcal{D}_{\text{url}}, \text{url})\}$ **do**
3   **foreach** $(x, y) \in loader$ **do**
4    $o \leftarrow \text{Model}(x, \text{mode})$
5    $L \leftarrow \mathcal{L}_{\text{focal}}(o, y) + \frac{\mu}{2} \sum_{p \in \mathcal{I}_{\text{mode}}} \|\theta[p] - \theta^{(t)}[p]\|_2^2$ `// FedProx on this head`
6   backward L; clip to τ; step
7 **if** $\mathcal{D}_{\text{pair}}$ *exists* **then**
8   **foreach** $((x^{\text{img}}, x^{\text{html}}), y) \in \mathcal{D}_{\text{pair}}$ **do**
9    $l_i \leftarrow \text{ImageHead}(x^{\text{img}})$; $l_h \leftarrow \text{HtmlHead}(x^{\text{html}})$
10   sample $r \sim \mathcal{U}(0, 1)$; $(l_i^\star, l_h^\star) \leftarrow (l_i, l_h)$ `// Batch-level modal dropout (robustness to missing modalities)`
11   **if** $r < p/2$ **then** $l_i^\star \leftarrow \perp$
12   **else if** $r < p$ **then** $l_h^\star \leftarrow \perp$
13    $l_f \leftarrow \text{FusionHead}(l_i^\star, l_h^\star)$
14    $L_f \leftarrow \mathcal{L}_{\text{focal}}(l_f, y)$; $L_i \leftarrow \mathcal{L}_{\text{focal}}(l_i, y)$; $L_h \leftarrow \mathcal{L}_{\text{focal}}(l_h, y)$
15   **if** $\lambda_{\text{JS}} > 0$ **then**
16     $p_i \leftarrow \text{softmax}(l_i)$, $p_h \leftarrow \text{softmax}(l_h)$, $m \leftarrow \frac{1}{2}(p_i + p_h)$
17     $JS \leftarrow \frac{1}{2}[\text{KL}(p_i \| m) + \text{KL}(p_h \| m)]$ `// JS consistency (teacher = mean of branches)`
18   **else**
19     $JS \leftarrow 0$
20    $L \leftarrow L_f + \lambda_{\text{aux}}(L_i + L_h) + \lambda_{\text{JS}} \cdot JS + \frac{\mu}{2} \sum_{p \in \mathcal{I}_{\text{fusion}}} \|\theta[p] - \theta^{(t)}[p]\|_2^2$ `// FedProx on fusion head`
21   backward L; clip to τ; step
22 **if** $\mathcal{D}_{\text{pair}}^{\text{val}}$ *available* **then**
23   **foreach** $((x^{\text{img}}, x^{\text{html}}), y) \in \mathcal{D}_{\text{pair}}^{\text{val}}$ **do**
24    $l_i \leftarrow \text{ImageHead}(x^{\text{img}})$; $l_h \leftarrow \text{HtmlHead}(x^{\text{html}})$; $o \leftarrow \text{FusionHead}(l_i, l_h)$
25   update metrics (loss, acc, prec/recall/FPR) with (o, y)
26 **else**
27   **foreach** $(x, y) \in \mathcal{D}_{\text{img}}^{\text{val}}$ **do**
28   update metrics with ImageHead$(x), y$
29   **foreach** $(x, y) \in \mathcal{D}_{\text{html}}^{\text{val}}$ **do**
30   update metrics with HtmlHead$(x), y$
31   **foreach** $(x, y) \in \mathcal{D}_{\text{url}}^{\text{val}}$ **do**
32   update metrics with UrlHead$(x), y$

Fig. 3. Client-side algorithm flow for proposed Role-aware FedProx

We have also provided a basic explanation of the fundamental formula of FedProx. FedProx Formula:

$$w_{t+1}^k = \text{argmin}_w \left(f_k(w) + \frac{\mu}{2} |w - w_t|^2 \right) \tag{1}$$

$\boldsymbol{w_{t+1}^k}$**:** The optimised weight of the local model on client k after round t + 1.

$\boldsymbol{f_k(w)}$**:** The loss function for client k.

$\boldsymbol{\mu}$**:** The regularisation parameter (proximal term).

$\boldsymbol{w_t}$**:** The weight of the global model after round t.

$\textbf{argmin}_w$: The argument of the minimum indicates that w_{t+1}^k minimises the expression within the parentheses.

3 Dataset and Preprocessing

3.1 Dataset Selection

We selected two datasets that have been validated in previous studies. One is sourced from WebPhish, and the other is TR-OP, which was originally proposed by KnowPhish [7]. WebPhish consists of 45,373 balanced samples of HTML and URLs, and TR-OP contains 10,000 balanced samples.

The WebPhish dataset does not include images, whereas TR-OP includes images, original HTML, and short URLs corresponding to domain names, but without additional features. The HTML in WebPhish has undergone processing. It should be noted that the data complexity of the two datasets is entirely different, especially in terms of HTML data. Through our manual verification, the processed HTML in WebPhish is cleaner and shorter (with some truncation). In contrast, the HTML in TR-OP is more similar to the original HTML pages, containing substantial noise and irrelevant data, which makes it challenging to use directly for model training. We computed the maximum character length of the original text data in both datasets. To avoid biases stemming from word segmentation or word-list priors, we used pure character counting (len) for length statistics across all samples (note that this is for a rough statistical analysis only).

- For TR-OP's HTML, the global maximum character count is 79,647,959.
- For TR-OP's URL, the global maximum character count is 3,669.
- For WebPhish's HTML, the global maximum character count is 32,783.
- For WebPhish's URL, the global maximum character count is 2,624.

Regarding the reason why we did not utilise TR-OP's URLs, first, we considered the relatively small data volume. Additionally, URLs have fewer features and are shorter compared to HTML. Compared to the 45,373 URLs in WebPhish, TR-OP only has 10,000 URLs. Moreover, most of the URLs in TR-OP are closer to the original page URLs, without any suffixes, and carry minimal information, which may easily lead to an overestimation of performance.

3.2 Dataset Samples and Sources

The original data sources for the two datasets are OpenPhish [29] and PhishTank [30], and the harmless negative examples are from Tranco [31] and Alexa [32]. TR-OP corresponds to OpenPhish and Tranco. OpenPhish and PhishTank are well-known sources that provide automated detection and community-verified intelligence on phishing URLs. At the same time, Tranco offers a research-oriented, manipulation-resistant ranking of popular sites for harmless comparison. Alexa Top Sites provides a general ranking of popular websites to supplement the benign samples.

The original links of the two datasets are provided:

https://www.kaggle.com/datasets/guchiopara/look-before-you-leap (WebPhish).

https://github.com/imethanlee/KnowPhish?tab=readme-ov-file (TR-OP).

Currently, the data sources for the vast majority of phishing research exhibit similarities. Through our investigation of several pieces of literature and reviews [18, 33, 34], these open-source platforms have been verified by multiple parties and are generally considered credible.

However, a potential issue exists. As most studies have not accounted for data duplication and have all performed some degree of manual screening and pre-processing, it is extremely challenging to ensure there is absolutely no duplication. Meanwhile, due to processing and manual operations, there are also differences in data formats, as exemplified by Webphish and TR-OP.

To rule out overestimation of performance due to this factor, we included ablation experiments using a single dataset in the experimental section. This was done to verify the potential impact of data interconnection between the test and training sets.

3.3 Data Preprocessing

Analogous to WebPhish and Web2vec, we formulate a lightweight, reproducible three-way HTML representation for each page: the character stream, the visible word stream, and the DOM tag stream. Initially, we conduct minimal normalisation solely on HTML.txt. This involves collapsing line breaks and tab characters into single spaces, consolidating multiple consecutive spaces, removing zero-width characters, and eliminating control characters that are disabled in Excel. Throughout this process, we refrain from altering any tags or attributes.) For the character stream, the complete HTML is encoded as UTF-8 bytes. It is then truncated or padded to a fixed length of CHAR_LEN = 4096. The values range from 0 to 255, with a padding value of PAD = 256. Regarding the visible word stream, we utilise BeautifulSoup to extract the text. Subsequently, Unicode-friendly tokenisation is carried out. This approach preserves letters, digits, combining marks, underscores, ZWJ (Zero-Width Joiner), and ZWNJ (Zero-Width Non-Joiner). Each token is mapped to one of the WORD_HASH = 131,071 buckets using FNV-1a 64-bit hashing. The sequence is then truncated and padded to a length of WORD_LEN = 1024, where the padding value is set to PAD = WORD_HASH. This strategy effectively circumvents issues related to large vocabularies and out-of-vocabulary (OOV) words.

For the DOM stream, we linearly traverse the tag names in the document tree. These tag names are hashed similarly to DOM_HASH = 8,190, and the resulting sequence is truncated and padded to a length of DOM_LEN = 1024, with PAD = DOM_HASH. This enables the capture of the page's structural patterns. All three outputs are represented as fixed-length LongTensor index sequences. Subsequently, they are embedded by independent lightweight encoders and integrated within the model. The entire preprocessing procedure exhibits linear-time complexity and requires only constant memory, making it inherently suitable for federated scenarios. Except for the optional sample shuffling, which uses a fixed random seed 42, the entire process is deterministic (specific parameters are detailed in Sect. 2.2). This characteristic not only facilitates peer review but also ensures the reproducibility of the experiments.

We selected a long sample from the processed TR-OP for demonstration, as shown in Table 1.

Table 1. Processed HTML Sample example of TR-OP

DOM_TOKEN	WORD_TOKEN	CHAR_TOKENS
html head meta script button div a img span iframe	login user name password cr360 cookies check want confirms my choices	< /script > < meta name = “viewport” content = “width = device-width, initial-scale = 1” > < style id = “onetrust-style” > ......

We did not use GraphcodeBERT directly on HTML pages because BERT-based models have limited context length. HTML data, especially from TR-OP, varies greatly in length, often exceeding practical limits (see dataset description). Since BERT lacks a mechanism to select optimal tokens [35], we avoided using it for HTML embedding. Instead, we applied GraphcodeBERT to URLs, most of which are under the 512-token limit. For images, we preserved the original data without modification to avoid introducing bias and ensure fair comparison. The TR-OP dataset has already been manually curated in prior studies [11, 12]. We used Pix2Struct [13], a pre-trained model designed for HTML and UI structures, to process image inputs. Specifically, we used the lightweight Pix2Struct-base. We added two global summary tokens at the start of the encoded sequence, generated via max pooling to capture overall image semantics and saliency (non-learnable). The image classifier is a basic Transformer Encoder followed by an MLP (parameters specified earlier).

4 Experimental Results and Analysis

4.1 Experimental Steps and Designs

Given the wide variety of data types and the simultaneous use of two datasets, to assess deviations in overall training performance across different client configurations, we have devised the following experimental protocols and client combinations. (Each set of experiments was carried out independently, and there were certain errors in the aggregated values, but the convergence should follow a similar trend):

1. **Six clients,** encompassing IMAGE, two distinct types of HTML, and URL concurrently.
2. **Four clients with diverse dual-data combinations,** specifically: the combination of IMAGE and HTML, WebPhish's HTML paired with URL, the pairing of Fusion and HTML, and HTML spanning across the two datasets.
3. **Two clients are designated for ablation experiments.** The aim is to validate the independent performance baselines of each head. These include clients solely containing HTML from one dataset, those with only IMAGE, those with just URL, and those with only Fusion

Through the above experimental design, we validated the framework's effectiveness under diverse data distributions. Each client was tested on unseen data; for example, if IMAGE was used for training, HTML served as the test set, and vice versa. When faced with significantly different test data, the model used heads trained on other clients for detection. The Fusion head was excluded from the six-client group because it artificially boosts the performance of the HTML and IMAGE heads (see Algorithm 2), making it impossible to evaluate their lower-bound performance in mixed configurations. Therefore, we included the Fusion head in the four-client group to demonstrate its enhancement effect.

We also considered non-IID scenarios. We conducted additional experiments by adjusting the training data distribution (e.g., reducing one client's HTML data from 1750 to 1000 and reallocating the rest) to assess the impact. Due to inherent structural differences between phishing web pages and images, non-IID conditions naturally arise, even under uniform distributions. For TR-OP, we selected data from indices 3500 to 5000 as the test set and shuffled the original order to avoid bias caused by time-based data collection. WebPhish data had already been shuffled in prior studies, so no further processing was applied. Hyperparameter settings are detailed in Sect. 2.2.

4.2 Results and Analysis

Firstly, regarding the performance of all six clients, we separately documented the convergence curves and the final performance metrics (selecting one instance from five experiments. The performance metrics were uniformly set as Accuracy, False Positive Rate (FPR), Recall, and Precision). As depicted in Fig. 4, in the case of no prox regularisation (with a coefficient of 0), we placed particular emphasis on documenting the curves of FPR and Accuracy (ACC).

The data was partitioned such that 3500 IMAGE samples from TR - OP and the HTML.txt file were designated as the training set. These were distributed among two clients, with each client receiving 1750 samples. The remaining samples were used as the test set and distributed to other clients who had not previously been exposed to HTML or IMAGE data. For WebPhish, 35000 samples of URLs and HTML samples were allocated to a single client as the training set, and the remaining samples were assigned to a client that had not encountered the corresponding samples as the test set (for example, a client that had been allocated the TR-OP image data).

This experimental design serves to validate the effect we initially proposed, namely, decoupling the training and test sets of clients. This allows any client to leverage the heads trained by other clients for detection purposes.

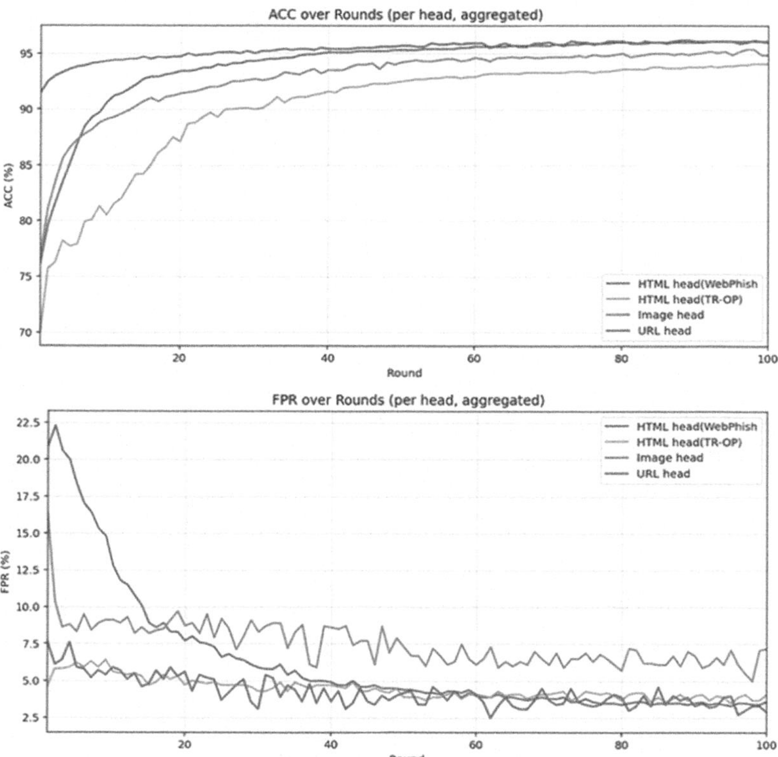

Fig. 4. 6 clients' accuracy and FPR convergence curve over 100 rounds, includes HTML head, IMAEG head and URL head. Under fedavg.

Next, we analyse the four experimental groups. The data allocation follows the same method as in the six-client setup. After dividing the data into equal parts of 1750 samples per client, it is assigned to two clients. We selected the HTML-IMAGE and HTML-FUSION experiments as representative cases, shown in Figs. 5 and 6. In cross-HTML testing, as mentioned earlier, we modified the partitioning of the train data for TR-OP HTML from 1750–1750 to 1000–2500 for 2 clients, and 35000 HTML of WebPhish is divided into 15000–20000 for the remaining 2 clients to simulate non-IID. We applied FedProx with a regularisation coefficient of 0.02, as illustrated in Fig. 7. Since the HTML head weights are set equally, the large volume of WebPhish data slightly slows the convergence of the TR-OP client with limited data. However, this setup improves both the initial convergence speed and the False Positive Rate (FPR) performance on the small TR-OP test set. Moreover, when both HTML and Fusion clients coexist, the Fusion component enhances the performance of the HTML client, leading to gradual performance convergence.

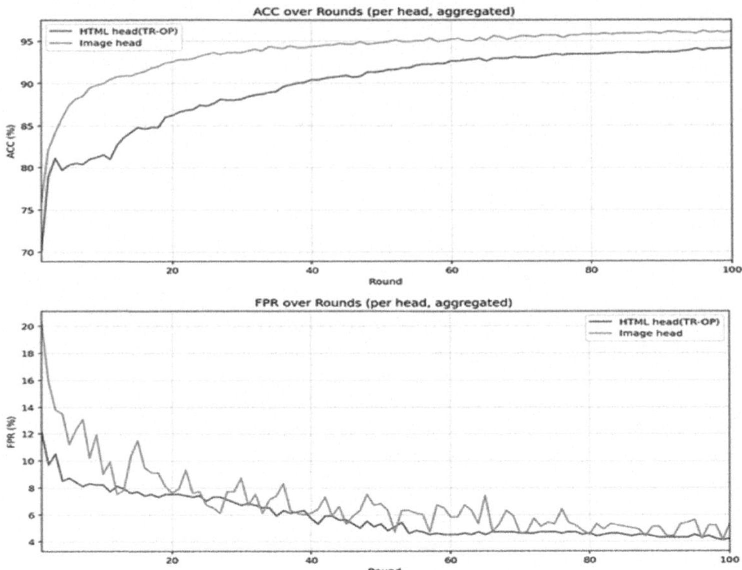

Fig. 5. HTML-IMAGE heads convergence curve with 4clients and cross-dataset setting

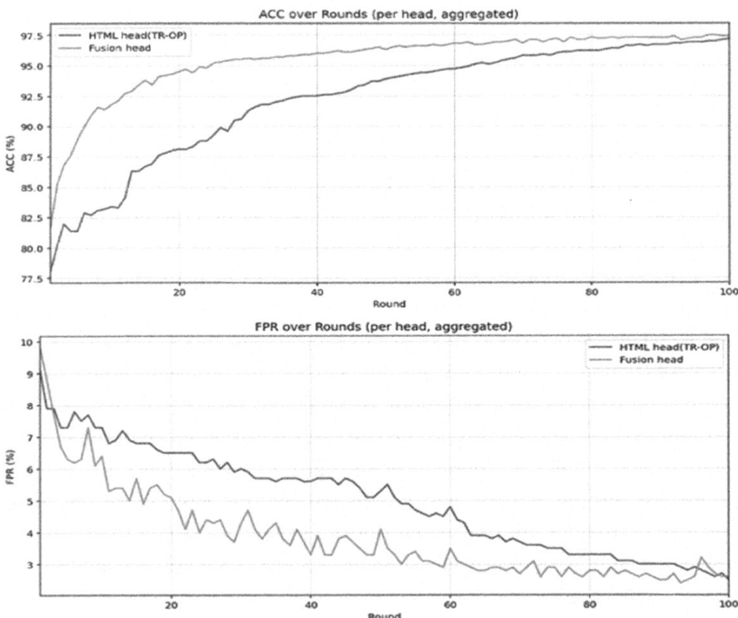

Fig. 6. HTML-Fusion heads convergence curve with 4clients and cross-dataset setting

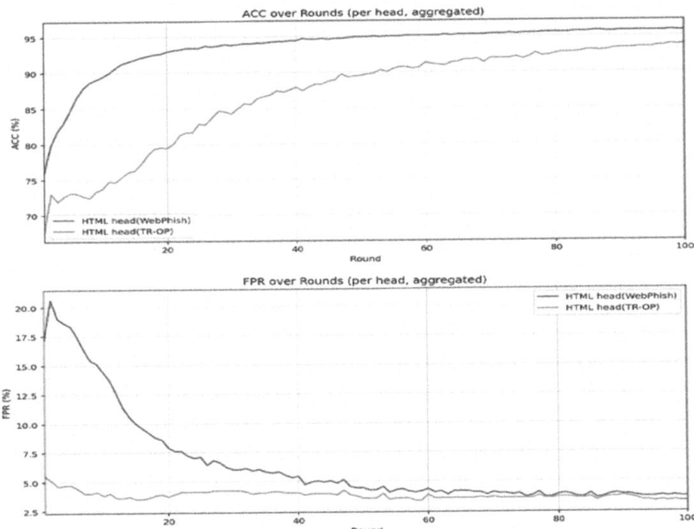

Fig. 7. Convergence curves for HTML heads trained on 2 types of HTML datasets across 4 clients. (non-IID), under fedprox = 0.02.

Finally, there are two client experimental groups for ablation tests. To verify the performance metrics that a single head can achieve in the absence of interference, in this experimental group, the test and training sets for the clients are of the same type, and the data is evenly distributed. See Figs. 8 and 9.

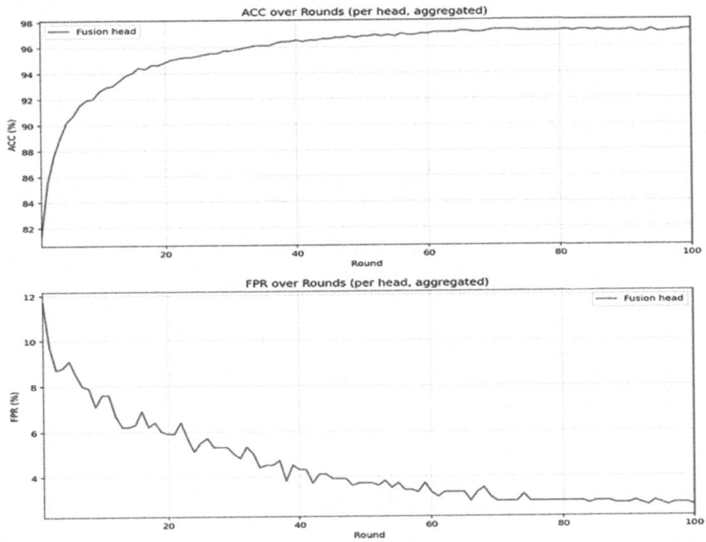

Fig. 8. Fusion head convergence curve over 100 rounds with 2 clients trained on TR-OP.

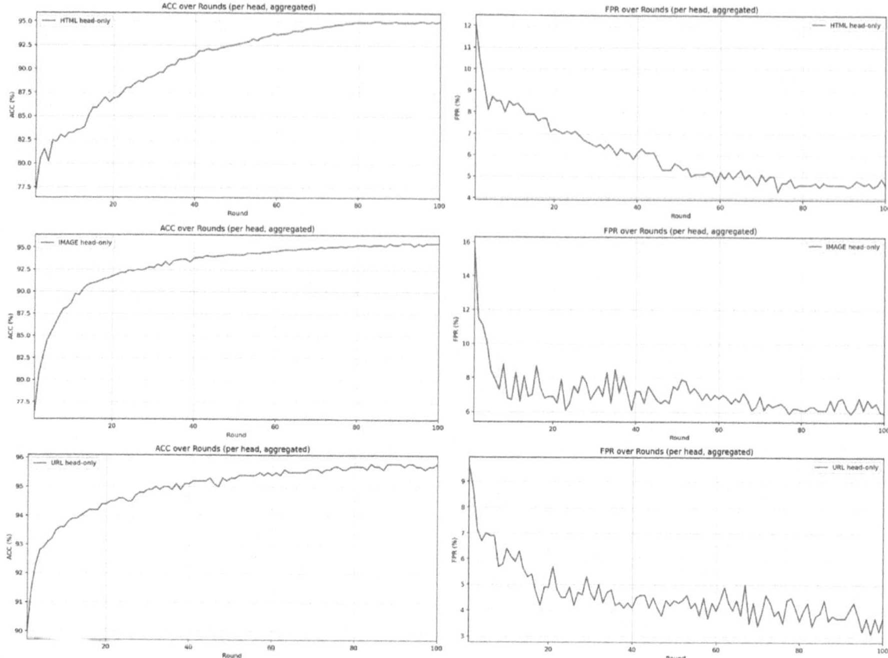

Fig. 9. IMAGE, HTML, URL heads Accuracy and FPR convergence curve over 100 rounds when trained on 2 clients. (HTML heads trained and tested on TR-OP without WebPhish's influences, URL heads trained and tested on WebPhish)

We compared our method with two different schemes [8, 11] that adopted the same dataset. Due to the averaging effect in federated learning, there was about a 1.5% difference in final performance across experiments. We selected the better performance among multiple experiments, as shown in Table 2. "Corresponding Test dataset" means whether the test set under the same dataset is needed. "Only" indicates the performance only under this type of data. "Final performance" refers to the comprehensive performance, which in our experiment is the FUSION head's performance. "NA" means "Not Applicable".

Table 2. Baseline and comparison

Baseline	Methods	Corresponding Test dataset	Final Performance	Only-IMAGE	Only-HTML	Only-URL
WebPhish [8]	Centralized End-to-End	True	Acc: 98.1% Precision: 98.2% Recall: 98.1%	NA	Acc: 96.5% Precision: 97% Recall: 96.1%	Acc:95.9% Precision: 95.6% Recall:96.4%
PhishAgent [11]	Modularized Hybrid	Flexible	Acc: 96.1% Precision:95.24% Recall: 97.05%	Acc: 95.5% Precision:95.27% Recall: 95.75%	Acc: 85.88% Precision: 84.18% Recall: 95.75%	NA

(continued)

Table 2. *(continued)*

Baseline	Methods	Corresponding Test dataset	Final Performance	Only-IMAGE	Only-HTML	Only-URL
Our Method	Privacy-preserving Federated learning	Flexible	Acc:97.5% Precision:98.1% Recall: 97.3% FPR:2.4% (On TR-OP)	Acc: 95.5% Precision: 94.3% Recall: **96.9%** FPR:5.9% (On TR-OP)	Acc: 96.5% Precision: **98.1%** Recall: 95.2% FPR:2.6% (on WebPhish)	Acc: 95.8% Precision: **96.3%** Recall: 95.3% FPR:3.7% (on WebPhish)

5 Conclusion and Future Work

This paper proposes a Role-Aware federated multimodal phishing detection framework based on FedProx. Through various combination experiments, we have verified the effectiveness of the entire framework under different data combinations. Meanwhile, we have designed a simple Role-Aware FedProx algorithm that utilises pre-labelling of input data to help the model distinguish different parameters and their corresponding aggregation paths, preventing parameter conflicts in federated learning. Our solution provides a new path and insights for jointly training a more flexible detection model while protecting privacy. However, the current design also has some limitations:

1. Under the current algorithm design, if both HTML and FUSION exist in the client, the HTML head or image head will be updated twice during backwards propagation. Although this speeds up the convergence of a single head, it also leads to double training and increased computational cost. We are considering how to optimise this process to reduce computational cost further while maintaining convergence speed.
2. The convergence effect of the image head on FPR is not stable. We believe this is related to the significant differences in the screenshots of phishing pages. We plan to use YOLO or other models to perform another round of cutting before inputting the data into the embedding model in the future, to collect key information points, such as input boxes and logos. However, this requires high precision and complete pre-training to ensure a clean cut, and it will also increase potential computational costs.

We plan to further optimise the algorithm and model structure based on these issues in the future to reduce computational requirements further and improve overall performance.

References

1. Wang, Y., Ma, W., Xu, H., Liu, Y., Yin, P.: A lightweight multi-view learning approach for phishing attack detection using transformer with mixture of experts. Appl. Sci. **13**(13), 7429 (2023). https://doi.org/10.3390/app13137429

2. Koide, T., Nakano, H., Chiba, D.: ChatPhishDetector: detecting phishing sites using large language models. IEEE Access **12**, 154381–154400 (2024). https://doi.org/10.1109/ACCESS.2024.3483905
3. Sun, Y., Chong, N., Ochiai, H.: Federated phish bowl: LSTM-based decentralized phishing email detection. In: IEEE SMC 2022, pp. 20–25. IEEE, Prague (2022). https://doi.org/10.1109/SMC53654.2022.9945584
4. Opara, C., Wei, B., Chen, Y.: HTMLPhish: enabling phishing web page detection by applying deep learning techniques on HTML Analysis. In: IJCNN 2020, pp. 1–8. IEEE, Glasgow (2020). https://doi.org/10.1109/IJCNN48605.2020.9207707
5. Tan, C.C.L., Chiew, K.L., Yong, K.S.C., Sebastian, Y., Than, J.C.M., Tiong, W.K.: Hybrid phishing detection using joint visual and textual identity. Expert Syst. Appl. **220**, 119723 (2023). https://doi.org/10.1016/j.eswa.2023.119723
6. Liu, R., Lin, Y., Yang, X., Ng, S.H., Divakaran, D.M., Dong, J.S.: Inferring phishing intention via webpage appearance and dynamics: a deep vision-based approach. In: USENIX Security 2022. USENIX Association (2022)
7. Li, Y., Huang, C., Deng, S., Lock, M.L., Oo, N., Lim, H.W.: KnowPhish: large language models meet multimodal knowledge graphs for enhancing reference-based phishing detection. arXiv:2403.02253 (2024). https://doi.org/10.48550/arXiv.2403.02253
8. Opara, C., Chen, Y., Wei, B.: Look before you leap: detecting phishing web pages by exploiting raw URL and HTML characteristics. Expert Syst. Appl. **236**, 121183 (2024). https://doi.org/10.1016/j.eswa.2023.121183
9. Huang, W., Wang, D., Ouyang, X., Wan, J., Liu, J., Li, T.: Multimodal federated learning: concept, methods, applications and future directions. Inf. Fusion **112**, 102576 (2024). https://doi.org/10.1016/j.inffus.2024.102576
10. Lee, J., Lim, P., Hooi, B., Divakaran, D.M.: Multimodal large language models for phishing webpage detection and identification. In: APWG eCrime 2024, pp. 1–13. IEEE, Boston (2024). https://doi.org/10.1109/eCrime66200.2024.00007
11. Cao, T., et al B.: PhishAgent: a robust multimodal agent for phishing webpage detection. arXiv:2408.10738 (2024). https://doi.org/10.48550/arXiv.2408.10738. (AAAI proceedings version: AAAI 39(27) (2025). https://doi.org/10.1609/aaai.v39i27.35003)
12. Lin, Y., et al.: Phishpedia: a hybrid deep learning based approach to visually identify phishing webpages. In: USENIX Security 2021. USENIX Association (2021)
13. Lee, K., et al.: Pix2Struct: screenshot parsing as pretraining for visual language understanding. arXiv:2210.03347 (2022). https://doi.org/10.48550/arXiv.2210.03347
14. Trad, F., Chehab, A.: Prompt engineering or fine-tuning? A case study on phishing detection with large language models. Mach. Learn. Knowl. Extract. (MAKE) **6**(1), 367–384 (2024). https://doi.org/10.3390/make6010018
15. Sakazi, I., Grolman, E., Elovici, Y., Shabtai, A.: STFL: utilizing a semi-supervised, transfer-learning, federated-learning approach to detect phishing URL attacks. In: IJCNN 2024, pp. 1–10. IEEE, Yokohama (2024). https://doi.org/10.1109/IJCNN60899.2024.10650184
16. Feng, J., Zou, L., Ye, O., Han, J.: Web2Vec: phishing webpage detection method based on multidimensional features driven by deep learning. IEEE Access **8**, 221214–221224 (2020). https://doi.org/10.1109/ACCESS.2020.3043188
17. Ige, T., Kiekintveld, C., Piplai, A., Waggler, A., Kolade, O., Matti, B.H.: An investigation into the performances of the current state-of-the-art naive bayes, non-bayesian and deep learning based classifier for phishing detection: a survey. arXiv:2411.16751 (2024). https://doi.org/10.48550/arXiv.2411.16751
18. Catal, C., Giray, G., Tekinerdogan, B., Kumar, S., Shukla, S.: Applications of deep learning for phishing detection: a systematic literature review. Knowl. Inf. Syst. **64**(6), 1457–1500 (2022). https://doi.org/10.1007/s10115-022-01672-x

19. Chou, E.J., Gururajan, A., Laine, K., Goel, N.K., Bertiger, A., Stokes, J.W.: Privacy-preserving phishing web page classification via fully homomorphic encryption. In: ICASSP 2020, pp. 2792–2796. IEEE, Barcelona (2020). https://doi.org/10.1109/ICASSP40776.2020.9053729
20. Khramtsova, E., Hammerschmidt, C., Lagraa, S., State, R.: Federated learning for cyber security: SOC collaboration for malicious URL detection. In: ICDCS 2020, pp. 1316–1321. IEEE, Singapore (2020). https://doi.org/10.1109/ICDCS47774.2020.00171
21. Thapa, C., et al.: Evaluation of federated learning in phishing email detection. Sensors **23**(9), 4346 (2023). https://doi.org/10.3390/s23094346
22. Guo, D., Zou, L., Ye, O., Han, J.: GraphCodeBERT: pre-training code representations with data flow. arXiv:2009.08366 (2021). https://doi.org/10.48550/arXiv.2009.08366
23. Moshawrab, M., Adda, M., Bouzouane, A., Ibrahim, H., Raad, A.: Reviewing federated learning aggregation algorithms; strategies, contributions, limitations and future perspectives. Electronics **12**(10), 2287 (2023). https://doi.org/10.3390/electronics12102287
24. Pei, J., Liu, W., Li, J., Wang, L., Liu, C.: A review of federated learning methods in heterogeneous scenarios. IEEE Trans. Consum. Electron. **70**(3), 5983–5999 (2024). https://doi.org/10.1109/TCE.2024.3385440
25. Bao, G., et al.: Multimodal federated learning with missing modality via prototype mask and contrast. arXiv:2312.13508 (2024). https://doi.org/10.48550/arXiv.2312.13508
26. Fan, Y., Xu, W., Wang, H., Huo, F., Chen, J., Guo, S.: Overcome modal bias in multi-modal federated learning via balanced modality selection. In: Leonardis, A., Ricci, E., Roth, S., Russakovsky, O., Sattler, T., Varol, G. (eds.) Computer Vision – ECCV 2024. LNCS, vol. 15139, pp. 178–195. Springer, Cham (2025). https://doi.org/10.1007/978-3-031-73004-7_11
27. Peng, Y., Bian, J., Xu, J.: FedMM: federated multi-modal learning with modality heterogeneity in computational pathology. In: ICASSP 2024, pp. 1696–1700. IEEE, Seoul (2024). https://doi.org/10.1109/ICASSP48485.2024.10448255
28. Flower: Framework Documentation – How to Run Simulations. https://flower.ai/docs/framework/how-to-run-simulations.html. Accessed 1 Sept 2025
29. OpenPhish: Phishing Intelligence Feeds. https://openphish.com/. Accessed 1 Sept 2025
30. PhishTank. https://www.phishtank.com/. Accessed 1 Sept 2025
31. Le Pochat, V., Scheitle, Q., Van Goethem, T., Joosen, W.: Tranco: a research-oriented top sites ranking hardened against manipulation. In: NDSS 2019. The Internet Society (2019). https://doi.org/10.14722/ndss.2019.23386
32. Alexa Internet, Inc.: Alexa Top Sites. Web resource. https://www.alexa.com/topsites. Accessed 1 Sept 2025
33. Li, W., Manickam, S., Chong, Y.-W., Leng, W., Nanda, P.: A state-of-the-art review on phishing website detection techniques. IEEE Access **12**, 187976–188012 (2024). https://doi.org/10.1109/ACCESS.2024.3514972
34. Kavya, S., Sumathi, D.: Staying ahead of phishers: a review of recent advances and emerging methodologies in phishing detection. Artif. Intell. Rev. **58**, Article 50 (2024). https://doi.org/10.1007/s10462-024-11055-z
35. Song, X., Salcianu, A., Song, Y., Dopson, D., Zhou, D.: Fast WordPiece tokenization. In: EMNLP 2021, pp. 2089–2103. ACL (2021). https://doi.org/10.18653/v1/2021.emnlp-main.160
36. Skula, I., Kvet, M.: Domain blacklist efficacy for phishing web-page detection over an extended time period. In: FRUCT 2023, pp. 257–263. IEEE, Zilina (2023). https://doi.org/10.23919/FRUCT58615.2023.10142999
37. Li, W., He, Y., Wang, Z., Alqahtani, S., Nanda, P.: Uncovering flaws in anti-phishing blacklists for phishing websites using novel cloaking techniques. In: Proceedings of the 20th International Conference on Security and Cryptography (SECRYPT 2023), pp. 813–821. SCITEPRESS, Rome (2023). https://doi.org/10.5220/0012135600003555

38. McMahan, H.B., Moore, E., Ramage, D., Hampson, S., y Arcas, B.A.: Communication-efficient learning of deep networks from decentralized data. In: AISTATS 2017, vol. 54, pp. 1273–1282. PMLR (2017)
39. Li, T., Sahu, A.K., Talwalkar, A., Smith, V.: Federated optimization in heterogeneous networks. arXiv:1812.06127 (2020). https://doi.org/10.48550/arXiv.1812.06127

Tabular or Image Input? Transformers for NIDS: A Comparative Study

Loreen Mahmoud[1(✉)], Aafia Hussain[2], and Sugata Gangopadhyay[1]

[1] Department of Computer Science and Engineering, IIT Roorkee, Roorkee, India
{loreen_fm,sugata.gangopadhyay}@cs.iitr.ac.in
[2] College of Engineering Roorkee, Uttarakhnad Technical University, Dehradun, India
aafiahussain101@gmail.com

Abstract. In recent years, the rapid evolution and complexity of cyber-attacks have made robust intrusion detection systems (IDSs), particularly network-based IDSs (NIDSs), a critical component of cybersecurity infrastructures. Although traditional machine learning (ML) and deep learning (DL) approaches have been widely explored, they often face challenges related to scalability, generalisation, and efficiency. Transformers, originally developed for natural language processing, show a strong ability to face the challenges of ML and DL models. The research that studies applying transformers for detecting intrusions, especially considering their performance on different data representations (tabular vs. image-transformed), is still weak and limited. Therefore, this paper investigates the potential of transformer-based architectures to enhance intrusion detection performance. We conduct a comprehensive evaluation of several transformer models, including TabNet, SAINT-Transformer, FT-Transformer, and Vision Transformer (ViT), across multiple intrusion detection datasets: NSL-KDD, UNSW-NB15, and UNR-IDD. TabNet, SAINT-Transformer, and FT-Transformer are evaluated exclusively on tabular data, while Vision Transformer (ViT) and a lightweight transformer are evaluated on both tabular and image-based representations of network traffic. Image representations for ViT are generated using two methods: single-sample transformation and the sliding window technique. Our experiments assess model performance using accuracy, precision, recall, and F1-score. The results show that tabular transformers perform strongly on datasets with high feature complexity, while ViT with sliding window images excels on datasets with strong temporal dependencies, achieving performance comparable to hybrid models such as CNN+LSTM. These findings provide valuable insights into selecting appropriate transformer architectures and data representations for building efficient and effective NIDS solutions.

Keywords: Transformer · Deep Learning · Intrusion Detection System

1 Introduction

Day after day, securing networks is becoming an unavoidable need at a time when attacks are evolving quickly and becoming more complicated and risky. Detecting

H. Seo (Ed.): ICISC 2025, LNCS 16487, pp. 25–47, 2026.
https://doi.org/10.1007/978-981-95-8034-7_2

attacks is not an easy task in a world full of information and resources that are precious goals for attackers, especially with the vast diversity of intrusions that could be done from different platforms and the multiple ways of being hidden and undetected during stealing information or performing malicious harmful attacks.

A promising method that could be part of the total solution is the intrusion detection system IDS. The main goal of network IDSs (NIDSs) is to mitigate the possibility of being exposed to intrusions by monitoring traffic behaviour and alerting us when any abnormality occurs. Investigating IDSs with their different types and studying them in detail has been a hot research area for a long time. Network IDSs (NIDSs) could be signature-based or anomaly-based. Signature-based NIDS depends on a database of already known attacks to detect intrusions. However, it has a problem: It cannot detect new attacks (not registered in the database or zero-day attacks). On the other hand, anomaly-based NIDS does not depend on a database that is prepared previously. Instead, it depends on creating a profile of the normal behaviour of traffic, and it will detect any deviation from this profile as an intrusion.

Since 1987, when the first anomaly detection model was proposed, many IDS datasets have been released, and it was clear that the performance of any anomaly-based IDS depends strongly on the goodness of the dataset that has been used to train it. Machine learning and deep learning techniques were always very interesting to be used in this domain, as from an abstract point of view, IDS's ultimate goal is to classify the traffic, and machine learning and deep learning methods are very good in this domain, especially that they are able to learn non-linear relationships.

Deep learning was used vastly in natural language processing (NLP) and image processing domains and has proved its efficiency in those domains, especially in dealing with large-scale datasets. This made the researchers in the field of cybersecurity interested in studying the ability of deep learning to work in their field, too [56]. Convolution Neural Network (CNN) [1,13,15,23,31,42,55], Recurrent Neural Network (RNN) [3,40,52], Long Short-Term Memory (LSTM) [6,33] [59], and Hybrid models [7,23,29], have been used to build many attack detection approaches.

Even transformer-based models that were designed first for text data only (like Chat-GPT) started recently to be used for detecting intrusions [27,34,35, 58].

Challenges in NIDSs always exist, even when using machine learning and deep learning techniques. Machine-learning-based NIDSs suffer from issues related to scalability, where it becomes challenging to deal with increasing amounts of data and more complicated instances and traffic. They also suffer from overfitting and face problems when they face attacks that they were not trained on, as well as having a high false positive rate. The training process for LSTM and RNNs is really expensive and slow. CNN needs to be deep to give good results, but at the same time, deep CNN cannot handle long-term dependencies.

Transformers [53] with different variants that depend on the self-attention mechanism are showing excellent performance lately on tasks related to text and NLP, such as translation, text classification, and dialogue recognition. Basically, the transformer depends on using a large corpus of text to pre-train the transformer itself and then performing fine-tuning by applying the trained model on a smaller dataset, which is dedicated to a specific task. The computational efficiency of the transformer model is one of its merits, as well as its scalability, and this was one of the reasons for choosing it in fields like computer vision and image processing. Some researchers found that its ability to handle data with ordered sequences could be beneficial when leveraging it to detect intrusions [11,25].

Transformers show a good ability to bypass the challenges of the known ML and DL models. However, the research studies applying transformers for detecting intrusions, especially considering their performance on different data representations (tabular vs. image-transformed), is still weak and limited. Furthermore, the effectiveness of different transformer architectures, such as ViT, TabNet, SAINT-Transformer, and FT-Transformers, across varying datasets is not well-explored.

In this paper, we investigate the effectiveness of transformer-based models for network intrusion detection, focusing on three key aspects:

1. **Comparison across data modalities:** we evaluate the impact of different data representations on intrusion detection performance by comparing tabular data and image-based data, highlighting the strengths and limitations of each.
2. **Evaluation of transformer architectures:** several transformer models are explored, including TabNet, SAINT-Transformer, FT-Transformer, Vision Transformer (ViT), and a lightweight transformer.
   - **Tabular models:** TabNet, SAINT-Transformer, and FT-Transformer are applied exclusively to tabular network traffic data.
   - **Image-based models:** the lightweight transformer is applied to both tabular and image-based inputs. ViT is tested for image input using two different methods to generate images.

   The evaluation uses four standard metrics: accuracy, precision, recall, and F1-score. Experiments are conducted on three benchmark datasets: NSL-KDD, UNSW-NB15, and UNR-IDD. We selected those three datasets as they are widely recognised benchmark datasets that cover diverse network environments and attack categories, enabling fair comparison with prior works and consistent evaluation of model generalisation across heterogeneous intrusion scenarios.
3. **Guidance for NIDS development:** based on the results, we provide insights into selecting suitable transformer architectures and data representations for practical network intrusion detection systems.

For ViT image-based experiments, we propose and evaluate two methods to generate images from network traffic data:

- **Single-sample transformation:** each data sample is individually converted into an image, then resized and preprocessed to be suitable for input to the transformer.

- **Sliding window transformation:** s sliding window with a fixed overlap percentage is used to group multiple consecutive samples into a single image, preserving temporal and contextual information.

The rest of the paper is organised as follows: The related works are listed in Sect. 2, the used datasets are mentioned with their details in Sect. 3, the transformer variants that have been studied are dicussed in Sect. 4, the experiments done are explained thoroughly in Sect. 5, the results are listed and discussed clearly in Sect. 6, and Finally the conclusion is given in Sect. 7.

2 Related Work

In [30], the authors review IDSs, focusing on their techniques, datasets, challenges, and advancements in the fight against sophisticated cyber-attacks. They evaluate several well-known datasets, including DARPA 1998/KDD Cup 99, NSL-KDD, CICIDS 2017, ADFA-LD/ADFA-WD, and ISCX 2012. The paper highlights advancements in supervised, unsupervised, and hybrid machine learning approaches for anomaly detection. It also discusses standard metrics to assess the effectiveness of IDS. However, many of the datasets reviewed are outdated, lack Internet of Things (IoT) traces, or do not capture new malware and evolving attack patterns. Moreover, advanced evasion tactics such as encryption, flooding, and obfuscation increase the difficulty of detection.

The paper [12] proposes the use of Tabular-to-Image (T2I) transformation techniques to improve the classification of anonymous network traffic. Five T2I methods are used to generate five datasets of image traffic. The 5 datasets are then used to train a ResNet-50. The two methods IGTD and BIE proposed in this paper improved classification metrics when compared to XGBoost.

The authors of [36] explored the flow transformer, which is a framework that offers flexibility when working with input encodings, transformer blocks, and classification heads. This paper examines three datasets: NSL-KDD, UNSW-NB15, and CSE-CIC-IDS2018. After preprocessing, the datasets were organised for sequence modelling using a transformer-based architecture. Across the three datasets tested, shallow models demonstrated performance comparable to deeper models like GPT and BERT architectures. The paper heavily emphasises benchmarks and provides minimal comparison to non-transformer methods. The paper [14] presents an anomaly detection system for real-time intrusion detection, utilising transformer models known for their effectiveness in sequence modelling. The model is trained on the WUSTL-IIoT-2021 dataset, which includes 41 attributes categorised into normal behaviour and various types of attacks. It processes sequentially ordered, standardised network flows for anomaly detection. The performance of this model surpasses that of other methods, such as ECOD, DeepSVDD, and RNN-based autoencoders. The authors of [4] present the Optimised Residual Dense Multi-Attention Transformer (Op-ReDMAT), a specialised model used for detecting network cyber-attacks. The feature selection process was carried out using the Hybrid Genetic Fire Hawk Optimizer (HGFHO) to identify an optimal subset of features. For the classification phase, models based on the optimised residual dense-assisted multi-attention transformer (Op-ReDMAT) were developed to classify network cyber-attacks. The datasets used in this study include UNSW-NB15 and CICIDS2017. The application of SMOTE (Synthetic Minority Over-sampling Technique) enhances the understanding of minority attack classes while mitigating the risks of overfitting.

In [49], a method for detecting network intrusions is introduced by converting network traffic features (NTFs) into four-channel ARGB images. These images are then classified using the ResNet50 model, pre-trained on existing datasets. The study enables the application of image classification models to effectively analyse complex patterns in network data. The datasets used in this research include UNSW-NB15 and BOUN DDoS. The model successfully distinguished between normal and attack traffic, as well as specific attack types, showcasing its robust performance in identifying potential threats. However, the accuracy of the system relies heavily on the transformation of NTFs into ARGB images. The paper [50] examines network intrusion detection methods in the Internet of Things (IoT) using deep learning techniques based on the CIC-IoT-2023 dataset. It evaluates seven deep learning models: DNN, RNN, CNN, LSTM, CNN + RNN, CNN + LSTM, and Transformer. These models analyse network traffic characteristics to identify abnormal behaviours and potential intrusions through binary and multivariate classifications. For binary classification, the DNN and CNN + LSTM models achieved the highest accuracy. In contrast, the transformer model performed best in multiclass classification. However, some hybrid models, such as CNN + LSTM, require significantly more time for training and inference compared to simpler architectures like DNN or Transformers.

The authors of [24] introduce a novel intrusion detection method that converts network data flows into RGB images, which facilitates classification using advanced deep learning models on the CIC IDS2017 and UNSW-NB15 datasets. The technique employs a decision tree algorithm to identify key features and utilises a windowing and overlapping mechanism to standardise varying input sizes into a consistent format suitable for classification. The resulting images are then analysed using a Vision Transformer (ViT) classifier to detect intrusions effectively. However, data imbalance within the dataset adversely affects the accuracy of multi-class classification. Certain attack types are rare, resulting in insufficient data to train the classifier adequately. Additionally, the feature selection process in this method is influenced by the data size of each category. Smaller categories may possess distinguishing features with lower information gain, causing these features to be regarded as less significant and ultimately impacting classification performance. The paper [56] presents a Robust Transformer-based Intrusion Detection System (RTIDS) designed to reconstruct feature representations, striking a balance between dimensionality reduction and feature retention in imbalanced datasets. The method employs a positional embedding technique to capture the sequential relationships among features and utilises a modified stacked encoder-decoder neural network to extract low-dimensional feature representations from high-dimensional raw data. The proposed RTIDS demonstrated exceptional performance on the CICIDS2017 and

CIC-DDoS2019 datasets, surpassing traditional methods such as SVM and deep learning models like RNN and LSTM networks. By integrating the Synthetic Minority Over-sampling Technique (SMOTE), the system effectively addressed imbalanced datasets, ensuring robust detection of both common and rare attack types. The model employs self-attention and multi-head mechanisms for automated feature selection, while its modular design ensures scalability and efficiency, making it a powerful solution for intrusion detection. However, the speed and inference time of the model require further optimisation to enable real-time deployment in time-sensitive applications. The research [18] introduces FC-Viz (Feature Clustering-Visualisation), a method designed to transform tabular data into compact, colour-encoded images, facilitating the effective use of Convolutional Neural Networks (CNNs) for classification and visualisation tasks. The method was tested on ten datasets, including Relathe, Madelon, Ringnorm, Bioresponse, Lung, Colon, Lymphoma, BASEHOCK, PCMAC, and TOX17, to benchmark its performance against existing methods such as DeepInsight. FC-Viz successfully avoided information loss by clustering similar features and minimising blank areas in the generated images. This approach outperformed several traditional machine learning models (such as SVM and Random Forest) across most datasets. However, the method does not explicitly select features, which could potentially overlook opportunities to enhance performance by using fewer features. In [35], the paper presents a transformer-based NIDS specifically designed for cloud environments. The main concept is to utilise the self-attention mechanism of transformers to analyse the relationships among input features, allowing effective detection of various network intrusions. The CIC-IDS 2018 dataset was used for training and testing. The model underwent incremental increases in the number of encoder layers for further training and was benchmarked against a CNN-LSTM model. The transformer-based model achieved over 93% accuracy across different types of attacks, demonstrating performance comparable to that of the CNN-LSTM model.

The authors in [58] present an intrusion detection model based on an improved Vision Transformer (ViT). This model incorporates a sliding window mechanism to enhance the modelling of local features and employs a hierarchical focal loss (HFocal) function to address data imbalance, which ultimately improves the classification of network intrusions. The ViT is more effective than CNNs and RNNs in capturing both local and global feature dependencies. While the model achieves higher accuracy compared to traditional methods, it does require slightly more computational time, particularly when using the sliding window mechanism. Additionally, the HFocal loss function necessitates careful parameter selection, making the process of finding optimal parameters challenging.

3 Datasets

3.1 UNR-IDD Dataset

A software-defined network was used to gather the UNR-IDD dataset at the University of Nevada-Reno [19,32,48]. Port statistics were used to collect a group of features (9 features), delta port statistics were used to collect another group of features (9 features), and the last group of features was collected from the flow entry and the statistics of the flow table (12 features) [19]. So, this dataset totally has 32 features and a number of samples of 37412 [19]. The following types of attacks are considered in the UNR-IDD dataset: TCP-SYN flood, Port scan, Flow table overflow, Blackhole, and Diversion [19].

3.2 NSL-KDD Dataset

Before releasing the NSL-KDD dataset, there was a dataset called KDD CUP'99, and it suffered from serious problems like redundant records; then, the NSL-KDD dataset came as an improved version of KDD CUP'99 and solved its issues [20,47]. Till now, it is the most famous benchmark that is used in the field of intrusion detection [16,46,57] with 41 features and five labels: Normal, DoS, U2R, R2L, and Prob.

3.3 UNSW-NB15 Dataset

The University of New South Wales (UNSW) collected the UNSW-NB15 dataset, which is a popular benchmark and widely used. This dataset represents a simulation of the real-world traffic, as it includes a vast group of scenarios of intrusions that can be faced by any real network. It is a large dataset with 2.5 millions observations and 9 types of attack and 49 features available as CSV files [17,54].

4 Transformer Variants Used

There are different variants of transformers that can be used in intrusion detection, and each one is designed for a specific modality of data and has a different structure. In this paper, we investigate different transformer types for detecting intrusions and consider the data modality needed for each one. Moreover, we built one transformer and compared its performance with other variants on three datasets, trying to gain insights about the best variant to detect network anomalies. The following transformer variants have been studied in this paper:

4.1 TabNet Transformer

TabNet is a model that depends on deep learning and processes only tabular data. It was suggested by Google Cloud researchers [9]. The input of TabNet is raw tabular data that doesn't need to be preprocessed before being fed to the model [9]. Optimisation based on gradient descent is used to train TabNet. At each decision step, TabNet selects the features that will be used for reasoning by using sequential attention, where the most silent features are the goal, and the learning capacity will concentrate on them to learn better [9]. For each input, the features selected are different, and this is called instance-wise feature selection. The same deep learning architecture that is used for feature selection is used for reasoning [9]. Basically, TabnNet transformer consists of an encoder and a decoder. However, when using it for classification problems, only the encoder is used. The TabNet encoder architecture is a sequence of steps, and in each step, the following components exist [9]:

- **Feature transformer:** this component has a specific number of GLU blocks, where each block contains three layers: Fully Connected Layer (FC), Batch Normalisation (BN), and Gated Linear Unit (GLU). In case we have four GLU blocks, then two blocks are shared, and the other two are independent. Normalisation is done on the output of each plot using the value $\sqrt{0.5}$ in order to keep the variance stable and make sure that it does not change noticeably.
- **Attentive transformer:** it is formed of the following:
  - A fully connected layer (FC).
  - A batch normalisation layer (BN).
  - A prior scales layer: before the ongoing decision step, this layer performs a process of aggregation for each feature amount of use.
  - A sparsemax layer: for sparse feature choosing.
- **Attention mask:** here, the identification of the chosen features is done. The significance of the total feature is determined. The masks in each step are aggregated.

4.2 ViT Transformer

Vision Transformer (ViT) uses architectures that depend on transformers that were originally proposed for NLP tasks only, for image processing tasks. This made ViT's emergence like a revolution in the domain of computer vision [2].

Many works have investigated the possibility of using transformers in computer vision. Some of them considered the image pixels as tokens, and each pixel had the ability to communicate with all other pixels in order to leverage the benefit of merging the self-attention mechanism with Convolutional Neural Networks (CNNs). Still, there was a problem in scaling to real-life input sizes [2].

Other ideas tried to solve those problems by applying a self-attention mechanism locally only, and other ways that were complicated and difficult to implement. Then ViT came as the solution, as it is a transformer that can be used immediately on images [2]. The following stages are needed in the architecture ViT [2]:

- **Converting image to a sequence of patches:**
  The image of size $(H * W)$ entered to ViT is firstly resized to a specific resolution; then the image will be divided into non-overlapping patches of size $(P * P)$, so the number of patches is equal to $(H/P) * (W/P)$. After that, by flattening patches, each patch will be a 1D vector with size $(P * P * C)$, where C is the channel count. The obtained vectors are then used to generate D-dimensional embeddings with a fixed size by passing them through a learnable linear projection. In order to maintain the spatial information, positional

encoding is done. Finally, a CLS token is added to the beginning of the embedded patches sequence.

- **Pre-LayerNorm transformer:**
  The visual tokens are fed into the ViT encoder. The main difference between the transformer suggested by [53] and ViT is that the LayerNorm in ViT is performed before the attention and feed-forward blocks, while [53] uses Post-LayerNorm instead. For ViT, Pre-LayerNorm is better as it makes the training more stable, enhances the convergence, and makes the activations scale more controllable.

4.3 FT-Transformer

FT-Transformer (Feature Tokenizer + Transformer) was proposed in [21] to innovatively take advantage of the transformer architecture in dealing with tabular data. Transformers, in general, have the ability to deal with sequences and catch the relations between them. In tabular data, we have rows that are usually handled individually when using other ML techniques, but if we look at those rows as a sequence that could have important information in between, then transformers can be the choice to deal with such data modality. FT-transformer consists of the following components [21]:

- **Input Embeddings**: Each feature will be embedded into a continuous vector.
- **Transformer Encoder Layers**: there are multiple encoder layers, and each layer consists of two essential parts: a multi-head self-attention (MHA) that gets the features' dependencies and a Feed-Forward Neural Network that gives the feature-wise transformations
- **Feature-wise Transformation**: focusing on how each feature transforms across all rows to learn the interactions among features in an interpretable way directly.
- **Output Layer**: all the transformed features are aggregated from all the encoder layers and fed to the output layer that gives the final classifications (if we have a classification task).

4.4 SAINT Transformer

SAINT, Self-Attention and Intersample Attention Transformer, was proposed for dealing with tabular data tasks [44]. The main characteristic of SAINT is that it uses the attention mechanism not only for columns but also for rows [44]. Also, it provides an improved way to generate the embeddings.

Structure of SAINT: It is composed of an input embedding layer and a number of layers (L); each layer has 2 blocks: one is a self-attention block, and the other is an intersample attention block (the novel block), then it has the transformer blocks, and output layer (different according to the task) [44].

4.5 Lightweight Transformer

We tried this lightweight transformer with both data modalities, tabular and images, to investigate which modality could be better for extracting features when using the same transformer structure. It consists of an input layer, a convolutional layer, a positional embedding layer, a transformer encoder layer, a global max pooling layer, a dropout layer and a fully connected output layer.

5 Experiments

For all experiments, the following configuration is used: a workstation with 13th Generation, Core i9 processor, 24 cores, and 128 GB RAM.

5.1 Preprocessing

UNR-IDD Dataset. Checking whether we have infinite or missing values in the dataset to deal with them is the first step in the preprocessing. No missing or infinite values were found. Some features are removed for different reasons: the is_valid feature is removed as it has the same value (True) for all the samples, and other features that affect the classification efficiency badly are also removed, such as port number and switch ID. The categorical features' values are converted into numerical values, and the classes' names in the (label) column are mapped to numbers. The values of numerical features are normalised using *StandardScaler*. 80% of the data is used for training, and 20% is used for testing.

NSL-KDD Dataset. For training, KDDTrain+ is used, and KDDTest+ is used for testing. We transformed the categorical features to numerical, and we scaled the values of the features that are originally numerical. We mapped the values of the column 'attack' to 5 labels, as we categorised the attack types into 4 categories: DoS, R2L, U2R, and probe, as well as the normal class. The dataset has separate files for training and testing originally, and 20% of the training set is used for validation.

UNSW-NB15 Dataset. We checked if there are any missing or infinite values, and we did not find any. We converted the values of the categorical features into numerical values. The values of (attack_cat) columns that represent the attacks' names are also mapped to numerical values. The values of numerical features are normalised using *MinMaxScaler()*. The dataset has separate files for training and testing originally.

Generating Images from Tabular Data this is done in two ways:

- **Each Sample is converted to an image**: in order to make our samples suitable in shape for feeding into transformer types that deal with images only, we transformed each sample in the dataset to a gray-scale image. According to the number of features in each dataset, we selected the dimensions of the image, for example, if the number of features is 42, then the size of the image is selected to be 7*6. For each dataset, We saved all the images that has the same label in one folder. After loading the image dataset, we resized the images to a size of 224*224. We normalised the values of each image by dividing it by 255. Figure 1 shows examples of the images generated using this method.

- **Window-based image construction**: we group samples by their class labels and then apply a sliding window of fixed size (dataset-dependent) with a specified percentage of overlap. Each window is therefore composed only of samples from a single class, and the resulting image inherits that class label directly. The flattened window is reshaped into a 2D matrix and resized to 224×224 pixels. For data augmentation, we randomly flip images horizontally (probability 0.5) using *RandomHorizontalFlip()*, and randomly rotate them up to ±15° using *RandomRotation(15)*. After that, *ToTensor()* converts the PIL image into a PyTorch tensor and scales pixel values to [0.0, 1.0]. Finally, each channel (R, G, B) is normalised as:

$$Output = \frac{Input - 0.5}{0.5}. \tag{1}$$

Figure 2 shows examples of the images generated using this method.

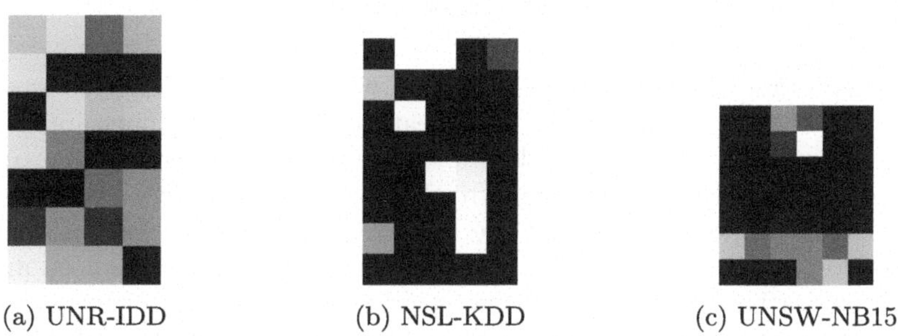

(a) UNR-IDD (b) NSL-KDD (c) UNSW-NB15

Fig. 1. Examples of grayscale images generated by converting a single network traffic sample from each dataset to a grayscale image.

5.2 Set up of the Models

TabNet. TabNetClassifier is used with the following parameters: Adam optimiser with learning rate of $2e^{-2}$, scheduler parameters are set to be: step size=10 and gamma= 0.5, scheduler function: StepLR, mask type: entmax, epochs=200, and batch-size=50.

ViT Transformer. The following parameters are used: with input image size = 224×224 and patch size = 16×16, the pre-trained model = vit-base-patch16-224-in21k (trained on ImageNet-21k) yields 196 non-overlapping patches (14×14).

To match the ViT input format, grayscale photos are processed, normalised, and then converted to 3-channel RGB. Every patch is projected linearly into an embedding space that is 768 dimensions in size. Learning hierarchical representations and long-range dependencies is made possible by the model's twelve transformer encoder layers, each of which has twelve attention heads and feed-forward layers. After being prepended, a classification token that corresponds to the number of target classes is sent via a final classification head. A batch size of 32, the model is trained using the Adam optimiser with a learning rate of 1e-4, the StepLR scheduler with step size = 10 and gamma = 0.9, and Cross-Entropy Loss, utilising GPU acceleration where it is available. For window-based constructed images, we used vit_tiny_patch16_224, a pretrained model, and trained it on our window-based constructed images.

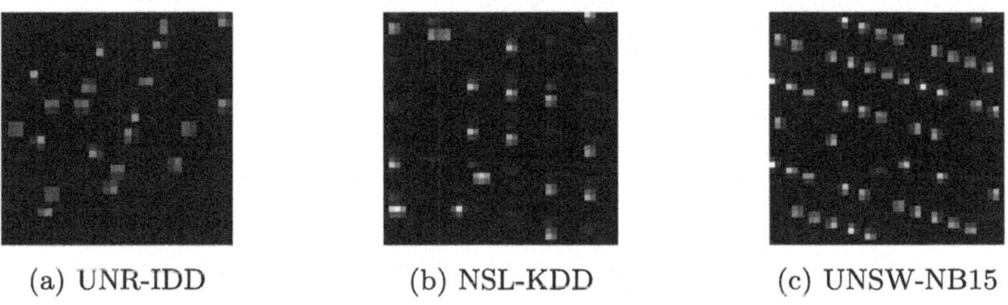

(a) UNR-IDD (b) NSL-KDD (c) UNSW-NB15

Fig. 2. Examples of images generated using the sliding window

FT transformer. FT-Transformer is used with the following configuration: feedforward hidden dimension = 1024; feature embedding dimension = 128; encoder layers = 8; attention heads = 8. After each input feature is projected via a linear layer, GELU (Gaussian Error Linear Unit) activation, layer normalisation, and a dropout rate of 0.3 are applied. Following the feedforward and self-attention sublayers, the architecture incorporates residual connections and layer normalisation. After aggregating encoder outputs using mean pooling, a final linear classification layer generates a 10-dimensional output. Cross-Entropy loss is used for multiclass classification, and the Adam optimiser is used to train the model with a learning rate of 1e-4 and a weight decay of 1e-4.

Saint Transformer. In the PyTorch-based version, two fully connected layers come after an input layer with dynamically set feature dimensionality. Using a ReLU (Rectified Linear Unit) activation, the first layer projects input features into a hidden representation of dimension 128. This is mapped to a 10-dimensional output by the second linear layer, which represents the number of target classes. Both categorical and numerical features are handled by the TensorFlow-based SAINT implementation. Learnable embedding layers (embedding size = 32) are used to embed categorical features, and a fully linked layer is used to translate numerical features into the same embedding space and reshape them to fit the sequence input format of the transformer. These are sent via two stacked SAINT blocks after being concatenated along the sequence axis. Layer normalisation, residual connections, dropout (rate = 0.1), a feedforward network with hidden size = 64, and multi-head self-attention (4 heads, embedding dimension = 32) make up each SAINT block. To generate class probabilities, the output is combined using global average pooling and then subjected to a final Dense softmax layer.

Lightweight Transformer as we mentioned previously, this model consists of an input layer, a convolutional layer, a positional embedding layer, a transformer encoder layer, a global max pooling layer, a dropout layer and a fully connected output layer. We tried it with tabular input data, and with image input data where the images are generated by converting each sample to an image.

6 Results and Discussion

6.1 Results

In Table 1, a comparison of the performance of different variants of transformers that have been tested in this paper and the performances of models used in state-of-the-art papers on the UNR-IDD dataset is made in terms of accuracy, precision, recall, and f1-score. Table 2 presents a comparison of the performances of different transformer variants with those of the latest proposed models and the literature on the NSL-KDD dataset, in terms of accuracy, precision, recall, and f1-score. Table 3 shows the same comparison, but on the UNSW-NB15 dataset. Figure 3 is a bar chart comparing the accuracies on the three datasets. Figure 4 is a heatmap of each performance parameter of each model across the three datasets. Figure 5 compares the results of the ViT model on the 3 datasets when the input is images created by converting each sample to an image, Vs. Results of ViT when using sliding window to create images.

Table 1. Performance comparison of transformer variants on UNR-IDD dataset against other models from state-of-the-art works

Transformer Variants	Accuracy(%)	Precision(%)	Recall(%)	F1-Score(%)
TabNet Transformer	79.31	81.29	79.31	79.11
FT- Transformer	84.83	85.44	84.83	84.55
SAINT Transformer	79.47	82.85	79.47	79.01
ViT Transformer	90.08	90.08	90.10	90.14
Lightweight transformer (tabular input)	86.24	86.77	86.24	86.08
Lightweight transformer (image input)	80.55	80.00	81.49	80.55
ViT (Sliding window)	**96.01**	**96.03**	**96.01**	**96.01**
CNN [41]	92.8	91	93	92
LSTM [41]	94.1	93	94	94
MLP [41]	91.7	90	92	91
CNN+LSTM [41]	**96.2**	95	96	96
MLP [51]	79.5	-	-	-
SMO-ANN [32]	92	-	-	-
Stacking [8]	95.56	95.58	95.56	95.56
ELML [43]	88	89	88	88

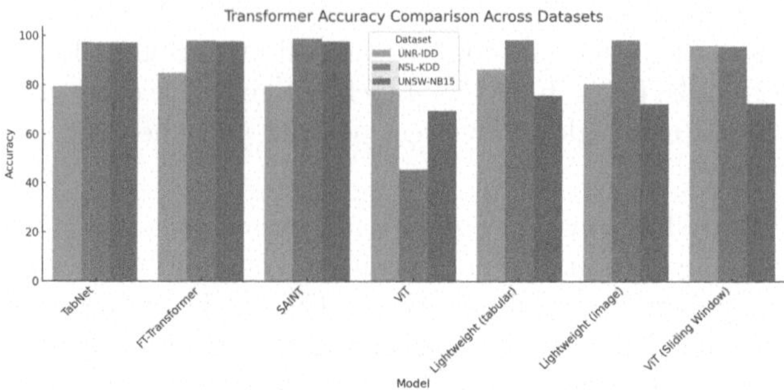

Fig. 3. Different transformers' accuracies across datasets

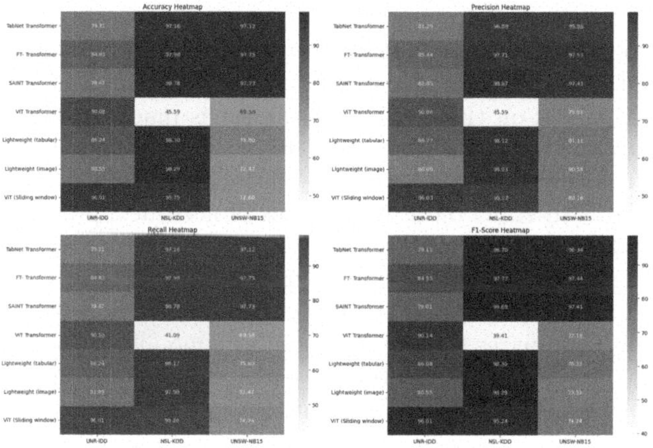

Fig. 4. Heatmap of each performance parameter per model across datasets

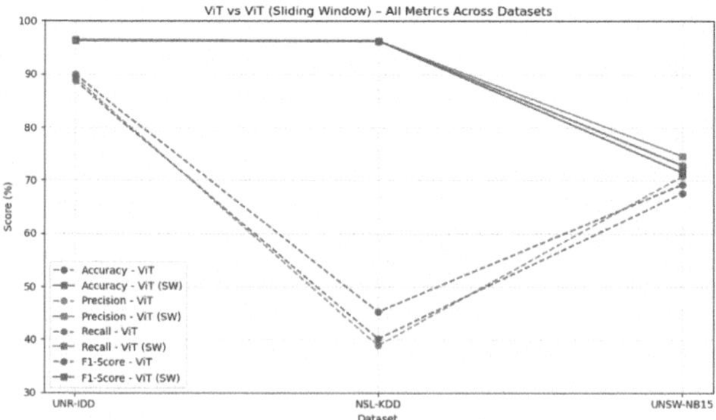

Fig. 5. Comparison between results of ViT when the input is images obtained from converting each sample to an image Vs. ViT results when using sliding window with overlapping for creating input images.

Table 2. Performance comparison of transformer variants on NSL-KDD dataset against other models from state-of-the-art works

Transformer Variants	Accuracy(%)	Precision(%)	Recall(%)	F1-Score(%)
TabNet Transformer	97.16	96.88	97.16	96.70
FT- Transformer	97.98	97.71	97.98	97.77
SAINT Transformer	**98.78**	**98.87**	**98.78**	**98.69**
ViT Transformer	45.59	45.59	41.09	39.41
Lightweight transformer (tabular input)	**98.30**	**98.12**	**98.17**	**98.30**
Lightweight transformer (image input)	98.29	98.03	97.9	98.29
ViT (Sliding window)	95.75	95.27	95.26	95.24
Gradient Boost [39]	90	91	90	90
RF [39]	90	92	90	90
DT [39]	89	93	89	90
Hybrid SOM (5×5 nodes) [26]	-	89.28	87.45	83.16
Deep Reinforcement Learning (DRL) [45]	73	-	-	68.91
XGBoost [10]	93.28	91.05	97.81	-
ELM-IDS [5]	92.50	92.50	92.50	92.45

Table 3. Performance comparison of transformer variants on UNSW-NB15 dataset against other models from state-of-art works

Transformer Variants	Accuracy(%)	Precision(%)	Recall(%)	F1-Score(%)
TabNet Transformer	97.12	95.88	97.12	96.34
FT- Transformer	**97.75**	**97.53**	**97.75**	**97.44**
SAINT Transformer	**97.73**	**97.43**	**97.73**	**97.41**
ViT Transformer	69.58	78.03	69.58	72.18
Lightweight transformer (tabular input)	75.80	81.11	75.80	76.33
Lightweight transformer (image input)	72.47	80.58	72.47	73.32
ViT (Sliding window)	72.60	80.16	74.74	74.74
Logistic Regression [22]	97.58	97	**98**	97
SVM [22]	97.59	97	**98**	**98**
MLP [22]	97.54	97	**98**	97
XGBoost [22]	97.42	97	97	97
Multi-class SVM [28]	95.04	96.28	95.93	-
DT [38]	77.39	82	77	77
KNN [37]	97.36	-	-	-
DT [37]	97.19	-	-	-
LR [37]	95.12	-	-	-

6.2 Discussion

Accuracy is an ML metric that indicates the ratio of correctly predicted samples. As shown in Table 1, for the UNR-IDD dataset, ViT using the sliding window to create images gives the best accuracy compared to other transformer variants, with a very clear difference. The accuracy of the ViT model (with a sliding window) is very close to the accuracy of the CNN+LSTM model from the literature. This emphasises the model's robustness and ability to differentiate between different labels. In Table 2, the best Accuracy when working on the NSL-KDD dataset is obtained when using the SAINT transformer; all other transformer variants give competitive and close accuracies, except ViT, when using images that are obtained by converting each sample to an image, as its accuracy is very low. In table 3, for the UNSW-NB15 dataset, the best accuracy is obtained when using FT-transformer and SAINT transformer.

Precision metric reflects the model's ability to correctly identify positive instances (attacks), making it a key metric for intrusion detection. High precision indicates a low false positive rate, which means a low number of cases where we have an alert for an attack, but there is no actual attack. In Table 1, ViT (sliding window) gives the highest precision on the UNR-IDD dataset compared to other transformer variants and to other models from the literature. In Table 2, SAINT transformer and the lightweight transformer that uses tabular data as input, they give the best precision. In table 3, on the UNSW-NB15 dataset, the FT transformer and the SAINT transformer give the best precision.

Recall measures the model's ability to correctly identify actual positive instances, indicating how well it minimises false negatives, this is very important in IDS as low false negative rate means that there is a low number of instances where we have an attack but our IDS is not giving an alert. In Table 1, for the UNR-IDD dataset, ViT (sliding window) gives the best recall compared to other transformer variants and other models from the literature. For the NSL-KDD dataset, as shown in Table 2, SAINT and the lightweight transformer (tabular input) give the highest recall. For UNSW-NB15, FT transformer and SAINT give score the highest recall compared to other variants of transformer, as shown in Table 3.

F1-score is a critical metric in intrusion detection, as it balances both false positives and false negatives. In IDS, missing real attacks (false negatives) or generating false alerts (false positives) are both undesirable. For the UNR-IDD dataset, ViT (sliding window) gives the highest f1-score compared to other transformer variants and other models from the literature, as shown in Table 1. In Table 2, for NSL-KDD dataset, SAINT transformer gives the highest f1-score. For the UNSW-NB15 dataset, the best f1-score is scored by the Ft-transformer, as shown in Table 3.

Performance of Transformer Variants: Across all datasets, Transformer-based models showed competitive performance. However, their performance is affected by architectural adaptations and input representation:

- ViT (Sliding Window) consistently performed exceptionally well on the UNR-IDD, reaching 96.01% accuracy, comparable to state-of-the-art CNN+LSTM. It also performed well on NSL-KDD. The sliding window captures local dependencies and improves the temporal modelling capability of ViT, which traditionally lacks this.
- ViT (Sliding Window), However, didn't perform well on the UNSW-NB15, this could be because of the nature of this dataset, as it contains mixed types of features: numeric, categorical, and derived statistical/network features. When tabular features are converted to images via sliding windows, spatial correlations may not be meaningful. ViT excels at capturing local patterns in natural images (spatially correlated pixels), but artificially generated images from tabular data may not preserve the relationships between features. Therefore, ViT struggles to learn discriminative patterns in this dataset. Another reason is that in UNSW-NB15, the sliding window approach may lead to sparse or noisy images because the number of features is large and diverse.
- FT transformer and SAINT transformer showed outstanding generalisation on NSL-KDD and UNSW-NB15, both achieving above 97.7% accuracy, making them some of the top performers. These models are tailored for tabular data and leverage attention in an efficient way to model complex dependencies.
- FT transformer and SAINT transformer didn't give good results on UNR-IDD dataset. The reason is related to the nature of this dataset. The UNR-IDD dataset is based on network port statistics, which have strong time-dependent patterns. For example, a port scan attack may start slowly, then escalate, then drop. These patterns unfold across multiple time steps, not within a single record. If UNR-IDD data is provided in a typical tabular format, then FT and SAINT will focus on relationships between features at a single time point, but not on how they evolve over time. However, CNN+LSTM and ViT (with sliding window) will explicitly capture the temporal evolution, giving them a major advantage.
- TabNet performed very well on NSL-KDD and UNSW-NB15, scoring an accuracy of 97.16% and 97.12%, respectively, because these datasets contain well-structured tabular features with static relationships, where attacks can be identified based on a small subset of highly discriminative attributes. However, it struggles on UNR-IDD because this dataset contains network port statistics that exhibit strong temporal dependencies and higher variability. Although TabNet incorporates a sequential decision mechanism internally, this sequence is applied to feature selection within a single instance rather than modelling temporal dependencies across multiple time steps. UNR-IDD captures dynamic port statistics where attack patterns emerge over time. Since TabNet lacks explicit temporal modelling capabilities like those in CNN-

LSTM or transformer-based architectures, it struggles to capture evolving behaviours, resulting in lower accuracy.
- The lightweight transformer achieved higher performance when trained directly on tabular data compared to image-based inputs generated by converting each sample into an image. This is primarily due to the preservation of feature relationships in tabular data, where each attribute retains its true semantic meaning. In contrast, converting a single record into an image imposes an artificial spatial structure that does not correspond to real-world network traffic relationships, limiting the effectiveness of convolutional layers and self-attention mechanisms. Additionally, this approach lacks temporal context, which is crucial for capturing evolving patterns in network traffic. As a result, the tabular representation proved to be a more natural and informative input modality for this architecture.

Comparison with Deep Learning and Traditional Models

- The CNN+LSTM hybrid slightly outperformed ViT (Sliding Window) on UNR-IDD, hitting 96.2% accuracy, validating that fusing spatial (CNN) and temporal (LSTM) components remains a strong baseline.
- LSTM and CNN alone also performed well (over 92% accuracy), but not as high as the hybrid or advanced transformer models.
- On NSL-KDD, models like SAINT, FT-Transformer, and Lightweight transformer surpassed deep networks like DRL, showing better optimisation and adaptability to tabular data.
- On UNSW-NB15, FT and SAINT Transformers again outshone most alternatives, including ViT variants, emphasising that ViT may need more task-specific tuning for this dataset.

Comparison with Ensemble and Classical ML Models

- Stacking, XGBoost, and SVMs were strong competitors, achieving over 95% accuracy on NSL-KDD and UNSW-NB15. This shows that well-tuned ensembles of simpler learners can rival deep learning approaches.
- However, transformer variants like SAINT and FT provide better scalability and parallelisation, which could benefit large-scale or real-time deployments.
- In cases like UNSW-NB15, ML models (e.g., SVM, LR, DT) also performed surprisingly well, suggesting the dataset's structure may be simpler or more linearly separable than the others.

Sliding Window with ViT dramatically improves ViT's ability to model time-dependent behaviour in network traffic, closing the gap with CNN+LSTM. In Fig. 5, we can see that using the sliding window with the ViT makes its performance better. FT and SAINT Transformers provide robust and consistent performance across datasets, especially with tabular inputs, demonstrating that attention mechanisms are highly effective for structured IDS data. Tabular input outperforms image-based inputs in most cases, indicating that Transformers should be adapted to the data format for optimal results. Transformer models can match or exceed deep CNN and LSTM architectures in accuracy and generalisation, particularly on NSL-KDD and UNSW-NB15 datasets. Classical and ensemble methods (e.g., stacking, XGBoost, SVM) are still competitive for IDS tasks, but may lack the feature learning power and scalability of transformers.

7 Conclusion

Studying the efficiency of using transformers for detecting intrusions while considering different input data representations (tabular vs. image-transformed) remains limited. In this paper, we investigate the potential of transformer-based architectures to enhance intrusion detection performance. We evaluated several transformer models, including TabNet, SAINT-Transformer, FT-Transformer, and Vision Transformer (ViT), across multiple intrusion detection datasets: NSL-KDD, UNSW-NB15, and UNR-IDD. TabNet, SAINT, and FT-Transformer were applied exclusively to tabular data, while ViT was applied for image input and our lightweight transformer was tested on both tabular and image-based representations. Image representations of network traffic were generated using two approaches for ViT: single-sample transformation and a sliding window technique. Evaluation is based on accuracy, precision, recall, and F1-score, and a comparison with other state-of-the-art works is provided. Across all datasets, transformer-based models showed competitive performance. However, their performance is affected by architectural adaptations and input representation. ViT, when using the sliding window to generate images, performed very well on UNR-IDD and NSL-KDD datasets, while tabular transformers (SAINT, FT, and TabNet) performed well on NSL-KDD and UNW-NB-15 datasets. For datasets that have more complex attacks and a larger number of features, tabular input with transformers like FT, SAINT, and TabNet works better, while for datasets that have strong time-dependent patterns, ViT with a sliding window is better to use and can give results comparable to the results of using a hybrid model (CNN+LSTM).

Acknowledgement. This work was partly supported by the Information Security Education and Awareness (ISEA) Phase-3 project funded by MeitY, Government of India (Grant No. L-14017/1/2022-HRD, dated 01.07.2024).

References

1. Al-Turaiki, I., Altwaijry, N.: A convolutional neural network for improved anomaly-based network intrusion detection. Big Data **9**(3), 233–252 (2021)
2. Alexey, D.: An image is worth 16x16 words: transformers for image recognition at scale. arXiv preprint arXiv: 2010.11929 (2020)
3. Almiani, M., AbuGhazleh, A., Al-Rahayfeh, A., Atiewi, S., Razaque, A.: Deep recurrent neural network for Iot intrusion detection system. Simul. Model. Pract. Theory **101**, 102031 (2020)

4. Alsulami, M.H.: Residual dense optimization-based multi-attention transformer to detect network intrusion against cyber attacks. Appl. Sci. **14**(17), 7763 (2024)
5. Altamimi, S., Abu Al-Haija, Q.: Maximizing intrusion detection efficiency for Iot networks using extreme learning machine. Discover Internet of Things **4**(1), 5 (2024)
6. Althubiti, S.A., Jones, E.M., Roy, K.: LSTM for anomaly-based network intrusion detection. In: 2018 28th International telecommunication networks and applications conference (ITNAC), pp. 1–3. IEEE (2018)
7. Altunay, H.C., Albayrak, Z.: A hybrid CNN+ LSTM-based intrusion detection system for industrial Iot networks. Eng. Sci. Technol. Int. J. **38**, 101322 (2023)
8. Araújo, A., Rodrigues, D., Leite, P., Gonçalves, J.: Network intrusion detection system based on multiple datasets: machine learning approaches. In: 2025 13th International Symposium on Digital Forensics and Security (ISDFS), pp. 1–5. IEEE (2025)
9. Arik, S.Ö., Pfister, T.: Tabnet: attentive interpretable tabular learning. In: Proceedings of the AAAI Conference on Artificial Intelligence, vol. 35, pp. 6679–6687 (2021)
10. Barnard, P., Marchetti, N., DaSilva, L.A.: Robust network intrusion detection through explainable artificial intelligence (xai). IEEE Netw. Lett. **4**(3), 167–171 (2022)
11. Bikmukhamedov, R.F., Nadeev, A.F.: Generative transformer framework for network traffic generation and classification. T-Comm- **14**(11), 64–71 (2020)
12. Briner, N., et al.: Tabular-to-image transformations for the classification of anonymous network traffic using deep residual networks. IEEE Access (2023)
13. Cao, B., Li, C., Song, Y., Qin, Y., Chen, C.: Network intrusion detection model based on CNN and GRU. Appl. Sci. **12**(9), 4184 (2022)
14. Casajús-Setién, J., Bielza, C., Larrañaga, P.: Anomaly-based intrusion detection in IIot networks using transformer models. In: 2023 IEEE International Conference on Cyber Security and Resilience (CSR), pp. 72–77. IEEE (2023)
15. Chauhan, S., Mahmoud, L., Gangopadhyay, S., Gangopadhyay, A.K.: A comparative study of LAD, CNN and DNN for detecting intrusions. In: International Conference on Intelligent Data Engineering and Automated Learning, pp. 443–455. Springer, Cham (2022). https://doi.org/10.1007/978-3-031-21753-1_43
16. Chauhan, S., Mahmoud, L., Sheth, T., Gangopadhyay, S., Gangopadhyay, A.K.: Generating adversarial examples using lad. In: Quaresma, P., Camacho, D., Yin, H., Gonçalves, T., Julian, V., Tallón-Ballesteros, A.J. (eds.) International Conference on Intelligent Data Engineering and Automated Learning, pp. 154–165. Springer, Cham (2023). https://doi.org/10.1007/978-3-031-48232-8_15
17. Choudhary, S., Kesswani, N.: Analysis of kdd-cup'99, nsl-kdd and unsw-nb15 datasets using deep learning in iot. Procedia Computer Science **167**, 1561–1573 (2020)
18. Damri, A., Last, M., Cohen, N.: Towards efficient image-based representation of tabular data. Neural Comput. Appl. **36**(2), 1023–1043 (2024)
19. Das, T., Hamdan, O.A., Shukla, R.M., Sengupta, S., Arslan, E.: Unr-idd: Intrusion detection dataset using network port statistics. In: 2023 IEEE 20th Consumer Communications & Networking Conference (CCNC), pp. 497–500. IEEE (2023)
20. Engen, V., Vincent, J., Phalp, K.: Exploring discrepancies in findings obtained with the kdd cup'99 data set. Intell. Data Anal. **15**(2), 251–276 (2011)
21. Gorishniy, Y., Rubachev, I., Khrulkov, V., Babenko, A.: Revisiting deep learning models for tabular data. Adv. Neural. Inf. Process. Syst. **34**, 18932–18943 (2021)

22. Gunupusala, S., Kaila, S.C.: Multi-class network anomaly detection using machine learning techniques. Contemp. Math. pp. 2335–2352 (2024)
23. Halbouni, A., Gunawan, T.S., Habaebi, M.H., Halbouni, M., Kartiwi, M., Ahmad, R.: CNN-LSTM: hybrid deep neural network for network intrusion detection system. IEEE Access **10**, 99837–99849 (2022)
24. Ho, C.M.K., Yow, K.C., Zhu, Z., Aravamuthan, S.: Network intrusion detection via flow-to-image conversion and vision transformer classification. IEEE Access **10**, 97780–97793 (2022)
25. Huang, S., et al.: Hitanomaly: hierarchical transformers for anomaly detection in system log. IEEE Trans. Netw. Serv. Manage. **17**(4), 2064–2076 (2020)
26. Iftikhar, N., Rehman, M.U., Shah, M.A., Alenazi, M.J., Ali, J.: Intrusion detection in nsl-kdd dataset using hybrid self-organizing map model. CMES-Comput. Model. Eng. Sci. **143**(1), 639–671 (2025)
27. Jo, H., Kim, D.H.: Intrusion detection using transformer in controller area network. IEEE Access (2024)
28. Jose, A.M., et al.: Multi-class svm & random forest based intrusion detection using unsw-nb15 dataset. In: 2024 15th International Conference on Computing Communication and Networking Technologies (ICCCNT), pp. 1–6. IEEE (2024)
29. Khan, M.A., Karim, M.R., Kim, Y.: A scalable and hybrid intrusion detection system based on the convolutional-LSTM network. Symmetry **11**(4), 583 (2019)
30. Khraisat, A., Gondal, I., Vamplew, P., Kamruzzaman, J.: Survey of intrusion detection systems: techniques, datasets and challenges. Cybersecurity **2**(1), 1–22 (2019)
31. Kim, J., Kim, J., Kim, H., Shim, M., Choi, E.: Cnn-based network intrusion detection against denial-of-service attacks. Electronics **9**(6), 916 (2020)
32. Kumari, D., Sinha, A., Dutta, S., Pranav, P.: Optimizing neural networks using spider monkey optimization algorithm for intrusion detection system. Sci. Rep. **14**(1), 17196 (2024)
33. Laghrissi, F., Douzi, S., Douzi, K., Hssina, B.: Intrusion detection systems using long short-term memory (LSTM). J. Big Data **8**(1), 65 (2021)
34. Liu, Y., Wu, L.: Intrusion detection model based on improved transformer. Appl. Sci. **13**(10), 6251 (2023)
35. Long, Z., Yan, H., Shen, G., Zhang, X., He, H., Cheng, L.: A transformer-based network intrusion detection approach for cloud security. J. Cloud Comput. **13**(1), 5 (2024)
36. Manocchio, L.D., Layeghy, S., Lo, W.W., Kulatilleke, G.K., Sarhan, M., Portmann, M.: Flowtransformer: a transformer framework for flow-based network intrusion detection systems. Expert Syst. Appl. **241**, 122564 (2024)
37. Mohamed, F.O.A., Agarwal, M.: Using recursive feature elimination feature selection based machine learning classifier for attack classification on unsw-nb 15 dataset. In: 2024 IEEE 9th International Conference for Convergence in Technology (I2CT), pp. 1–7. IEEE (2024)
38. Pal, K.K., Eriksen, A.V., Dinh, N.: Xgboost feature selection for multi-class and binary classification on unsw-nb15 dataset. In: 2025 IEEE International Conference on Consumer Electronics (ICCE), pp. 1–6. IEEE (2025)
39. Pardeshi, N.G., Patil, D.V.: Binary and multiclass classification intrusion detection system using benchmark nsl-kdd and machine learning models. In: 2024 International Conference on Data Science and Network Security (ICDSNS), pp. 1–7. IEEE (2024)
40. Park, S.H., Park, H.J., Choi, Y.J.: Rnn-based prediction for network intrusion detection. In: 2020 international conference on artificial intelligence in information and communication (ICAIIC), pp. 572–574. IEEE (2020)

41. Parveen, F., Iqbal, S., Mumtaz, G., Salahuddin, M.: Real-time intrusion detection with deep learning: analyzing the unr intrusion detection dataset. J. Comput. Biomed. Inf. **7**(02) (2024)
42. Riyaz, B., Ganapathy, S.: A deep learning approach for effective intrusion detection in wireless networks using CNN. Soft. Comput. **24**(22), 17265–17278 (2020)
43. Samantaray, M., Barik, R.C., Biswal, A.K.: Ensemble-based lightweight machine learning optimization for Iot network intrusion detection. In: 2025 3rd International Conference on Intelligent Systems, Advanced Computing and Communication (ISACC), pp. 1101–1106. IEEE (2025)
44. Somepalli, G., Goldblum, M., Schwarzschild, A., Bruss, C.B., Goldstein, T.: Saint: improved neural networks for tabular data via row attention and contrastive pretraining. arXiv preprint arXiv:2106.01342 (2021)
45. Strickland, C., et al.: Drl-gan: a hybrid approach for binary and multiclass network intrusion detection. Sensors **24**(9), 2746 (2024)
46. Su, T., Sun, H., Zhu, J., Wang, S., Li, Y.: Bat: Deep learning methods on network intrusion detection using nsl-kdd dataset. IEEE Access **8**, 29575–29585 (2020). https://doi.org/10.1109/ACCESS.2020.2972627
47. Tavallaee, M., Bagheri, E., Lu, W., Ghorbani, A.A.: A detailed analysis of the kdd cup 99 data set. In: 2009 IEEE symposium on computational intelligence for security and defense applications, pp. 1–6. IEEE(2009)
48. Tiwary, P., Madhubalan, A., Gautam, A.: Partitioned problem space (paps) ensemble for zero-day intrusion detection (2023)
49. Toldinas, J., Venčkauskas, A., Damaševičius, R., Grigaliūnas, Š, Morkevičius, N., Baranauskas, E.: A novel approach for network intrusion detection using multistage deep learning image recognition. Electronics **10**(15), 1854 (2021)
50. Tseng, S.M., Wang, Y.Q., Wang, Y.C.: Multi-class intrusion detection based on transformer for iot networks using cic-iot-2023 dataset. Fut. Internet **16**(8), 284 (2024)
51. Tyagi, S., Pingulkar, S., Shaikh, A.: Multi-class network intrusion detection using deep neural networks tuned on imbalanced data. In: 2023 IEEE International Carnahan Conference on Security Technology (ICCST), pp. 1–5. IEEE (2023)
52. Ullah, I., Mahmoud, Q.H.: Design and development of rnn anomaly detection model for iot networks. IEEE Access **10**, 62722–62750 (2022)
53. Vaswani, A.: Attention is all you need. Adv. Neural Inf. Process. Syst. (2017)
54. Vibhute, A.D., Khan, M., Patil, C.H., Gaikwad, S.V., Mane, A.V., Patel, K.K.: Network anomaly detection and performance evaluation of convolutional neural networks on unsw-nb15 dataset. Procedia Comput. Sci. **235**, 2227–2236 (2024)
55. Vinayakumar, R., Soman, K., Poornachandran, P.: Applying convolutional neural network for network intrusion detection. In: 2017 International Conference on Advances in Computing, Communications and Informatics (ICACCI), pp. 1222–1228. IEEE (2017)
56. Wu, Z., Zhang, H., Wang, P., Sun, Z.: Rtids: a robust transformer-based approach for intrusion detection system. IEEE Access **10**, 64375–64387 (2022)
57. Xu, W., Jang-Jaccard, J., Singh, A., Wei, Y., Sabrina, F.: Improving performance of autoencoder-based network anomaly detection on nsl-kdd dataset. IEEE Access **9**, 140136–140146 (2021). https://doi.org/10.1109/ACCESS.2021.3116612

58. Yang, Y.G., Fu, H.M., Gao, S., Zhou, Y.H., Shi, W.M.: Intrusion detection: A model based on the improved vision transformer. Trans. Emerging Telecommun. Technol. **33**(9), e4522 (2022)
59. Zhang, L., Yan, H., Zhu, Q.: An improved LSTM network intrusion detection method. In: 2020 IEEE 6th International conference on Computer and Communications (ICCC), pp. 1765–1769. IEEE (2020)

AdvCodeGen: Adversarial Code Generation via Large Language Models

Eun Jung[1], Jiacheng Li[2], Yonghwi Kwon[2], and Hyoungshick Kim[1](✉)

[1] Department of Electrical and Computer Engineering, Sungkyunkwan University, Seoul, South Korea
{wjddms0926,hyoung}@skku.edu

[2] Department of Electrical and Computer Engineering, University of Maryland, College Park, USA
{jiacli,yongkwon}@umd.edu

Abstract. Vulnerability detectors based on language models (LMs) show promise, but their robustness under adversarial conditions remains underexplored. Specifically, prior evaluations often lack diverse adversarial attack strategies and sophisticated perturbation implementations. To address this, we present AdvCodeGen, a black-box adversarial framework that leverages a large language model (LLM) to systematically evaluate the robustness of various LM-based vulnerability detectors. Unlike purely Abstract syntax tree (AST)-based rule transformations, AdvCodeGen utilizes an LLM to not only implement 19 effective code perturbation rules but also to generate more diverse and syntactically varied adversarial examples while preserving functionality. We evaluated AdvCodeGen against six state-of-the-art LMs (CodeT5, CodeBERT, GraphCodeBERT, UnixCoder, StarCoder2, and CodeGen2.5) on the BigVul and Devign datasets. AdvCodeGen achieves attack success rates (ASR) up to 81.5% (BigVul/StarCoder2) and 60.3% (Devign/CodeGen2.5), significantly outperforming existing token-level adversarial methods (ALERT, CARROT, CODA, and AACEGEN) that typically achieve less than 40% ASR. Compared to naive LLM baselines, AdvCodeGen delivers 15–30% higher ASR while maintaining 97.19% compile success and 91.88% unit test success rates. These results demonstrate that rule-guided LLM code generation enables broader structural and lexical diversity, leading to more targeted and effective adversarial transformations. Our work provides a robust approach to evaluating and ultimately enhancing the security of LM-based vulnerability detectors.

Keywords: Vulnerability Detection · Adversarial Code Examples · Large Language Models

1 Introduction

Software vulnerability detection has been a critical topic in software security as exploited code vulnerabilities can lead to unauthorized access, data breaches, and system disruptions [34]. With the integration of Large Language Model (LLM)-based tools [24] such as GitHub Copilot [15], Amazon CodeWhisperer [2], and

H. Seo (Ed.): ICISC 2025, LNCS 16487, pp. 48–69, 2026.
https://doi.org/10.1007/978-981-95-8034-7_3

ChatGPT [37] into software development workflows, the importance of proactively detecting code vulnerabilities has become even more pronounced.

Traditional static analysis tools, particularly rule-based methods [16,40], have been widely used to detect vulnerabilities in source code. However, they often struggle to handle vulnerabilities in complex code, especially those involving intricate control flows, cross-functional data dependencies, or subtle semantic conditions, achieving only around 50% recall with false positive rates as high as 63% [18]. To address these shortcomings, machine learning-driven techniques [13,22,51] have attracted increasing attention, with language models (LM) [12,19,21,31,35,41,44] emerging as promising alternatives. By learning rich code representations, LMs enable more accurate and flexible detection of vulnerabilities compared to rule-based methods.

Despite these advances, LM-based detectors themselves remain vulnerable to adversarial attacks [17], where carefully crafted yet functionally equivalent code modifications lead to misclassification [46]. Such adversarial perturbations can be weaponized by attackers to stealthily insert exploitable code into otherwise legitimate software, bypassing automated defenses. Prior work has explored perturbation strategies at the token level [23,25,42,46,50] and statement level [29,30,39]. Token-level approaches primarily focus on lexical modifications such as identifier renaming, while statement-level methods involve structural changes like dead code insertion. However, these methods often rely on a limited set of predefined, rule-based transformations. This deterministic nature results in perturbations that lack the diversity and subtlety of realistic code variations, limiting their effectiveness for comprehensive robustness evaluations.

In contrast, LLM-based transformations can leverage a deeper understanding of code semantics and structure, enabling the generation of natural and diverse adversarial examples that extend beyond simple lexical substitutions to incorporate more complex structural variations. We propose AdvCodeGen, a framework for automatically generating and validating adversarial code examples designed to systematically evaluate the robustness of vulnerability detectors by discovering effective bypasses. The workflow of AdvCodeGen consists of two main stages: adversarial code generation and validation.

Our comprehensive evaluation on six state-of-the-art vulnerability detection models over BigVul [11] and Devign [51] shows that AdvCodeGen achieves attack success rates of up to 81.5% and 60.3%, respectively. This performance substantially exceeds that of token-level baselines, which typically yield an ASR of less than 40% [29,42,46,49]. The analysis further reveals that control-statement modifications and code-depth increases are particularly effective, whereas GraphCodeBERT [20] exhibits comparatively stronger robustness across these transformation categories.

This paper makes the following contributions:

- We propose an LLM-based adversarial code generation framework, AdvCodeGen, which leverages LLM to systematically evaluate the robustness of vulnerability detectors.
- We conduct a comprehensive robustness evaluation of six state-of-the-art vulnerability detectors on two benchmark datasets using AdvCodeGen, revealing significant vulnerabilities in existing approaches.

- We provide a detailed analysis of effective attack vectors, revealing that control-statement modifications and code-depth increases are particularly successful perturbation strategies, and identify GraphCodeBERT as a comparatively more robust model.

2 Threat Model

Following prior work in adversarial code analysis [25], we evaluate the robustness of LM-based vulnerability detectors by generating adversarial examples. Our threat model is defined in terms of the adversary's goal, knowledge, and capabilities, aligned with standard adversarial ML [38].

Adversary's Goal. Let S_v^{org} denote a source code sample containing a vulnerability, and let S_v^{adv} represent its adversarially perturbed counterpart. The adversary's objective is to induce misclassification in a vulnerability detector $f(\cdot)$, such that $f(S_v^{org}) = \textit{true}$ while $f(S_v^{adv}) = \textit{false}$. In this setting, the vulnerability remains present in S_v^{adv}, yet the detector fails to identify it. This formulation captures the essence of adversarial evasion: seemingly minor or structurally benign modifications to the input can significantly degrade detection accuracy.

Adversary's Knowledge and Capabilities. We assume a black-box threat model in which the adversary has no access to the internal parameters, gradient information, or training data of the target model. The adversary is restricted to querying the detector with arbitrary source code and observing the corresponding outputs, which may consist of either binary labels (e.g., `vulnerable` vs. `benign`). This assumption reflects realistic deployment scenarios, as commercial vulnerability detection tools are frequently deployed as proprietary services or integrated components with limited public interfaces. Despite these constraints, black-box adversaries retain sufficient leverage to craft effective perturbations through iterative querying, highlighting the feasibility of such attacks under practical conditions.

Evaluation Scenarios. To illustrate the relevance of this threat model, we consider two representative attack scenarios. First, in *developer reuse poisoning*, adversaries inject adversarially perturbed yet still vulnerable code snippets into public repositories. Automated vulnerability detectors may incorrectly classify these snippets as benign, thereby facilitating the inadvertent adoption of insecure code by developers [8]. This scenario underscores the potential for adversarial perturbations to propagate vulnerabilities through common code reuse practices.

Second, in audit evasion during software packaging, adversaries seek to bypass automated security checks performed by distribution platforms such as `npm` or `PyPI` [36]. These audits are designed to identify vulnerable or malicious packages before they reach end users. However, adversarial perturbations may enable unsafe packages to evade detection, undermining ecosystem-level defenses and exacerbating software supply chain risks.

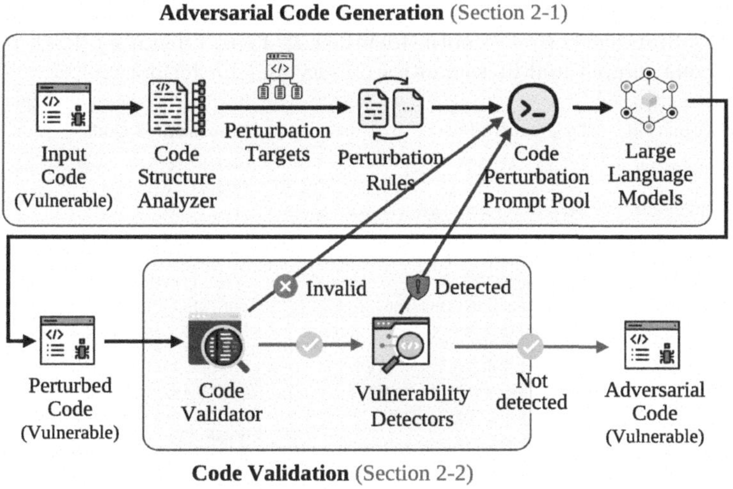

Fig. 1. Overview of AdvCodeGen, our framework for generating and validating adversarial code examples.

3 System Design

We provide an overview of the AdvCodeGen pipeline in Fig. 1, following the terminology and structure used in the paper. AdvCodeGen provides an end-to-end system which allows it to systematically generate and validate high-quality adversarial code examples while maintaining behavioral equivalence and providing a rigorous robustness evaluation of modern vulnerability detection models.

Adversarial Code Generation. We first define a suite of code-perturbation rules based on programming language syntax and common refactoring patterns known in the software engineering field. These rules target control-flow constructs, identifiers and types, and operators, enabling a wide range of transformations. Then, for a given vulnerable input program, a code-structure analyzer parses the input source into an Abstract Syntax Tree (AST) and identifies applicable transformation targets. The selected rules are encoded into code-perturbation prompts and executed by large language models (LLMs) to produce adversarial code variants. Note that as a part of the code generation prompt, we instruct the LLMs to generate syntactically valid, semantics-preserving code (Sect. 3.1).

Code Validation. After the code generation, AdvCodeGen performs code validation (Sect. 3.2). A code validator checks the syntactic and semantic correctness of code to ensure its compilability and conformance to the language. To this end, successfully validated adversarial code examples are then evaluated against the target LM-based vulnerability detectors to check whether the evasion is achieved or not.

Table 1. 19 code-perturbations used in AdvCodeGen, grouped by transformation category (Control Statement, Code Depth, Identifier & Type, Operator). Each row shows an original code snippet and its semantics-preserving transformation.

	Transformation	Original Code	Transformed Code
Control Statement	C_1 If-to-Switch	`if (C1) A1; else A2;`	`switch (C1) { case 1: A1; break; default: A2; }`
	C_2 Switch-to-If	`switch (C1) { case 1: A1; break; default: A2; }`	`if (C1) A1; else A2;`
	C_3 Ternary-to-If	`v = cond ? a : b;`	`if (cond) { v=a; } else{ v=b; }`
	C_4 Goto Remove	`if(c) goto L1; ... L1: return x;`	`if(c) { return x; } ...`
	C_5 For-to-While	`for (i=0; i<n; i++) foo();`	`i=0; while(i<n) { foo(); i++; }`
	C_6 While-to-For	`i=0; while (i<n) { foo(); i++; }`	`for (i=0; i<n; i++) foo();`
Code Depth	D_1 If Depth	`if (c) { foo(); }`	`if(c) { if(1) { foo(); } }`
	D_2 Switch Depth	`switch (x) {case 1: foo();}`	`switch (x) {case 0:; case 1: foo();}`
	D_3 While Depth	`while (c) { foo(); }`	`while (1) { while(c) { foo(); } break; }`
	D_4 For Depth	`for (...) { foo(); }`	`for (...) { for (...) { foo(); } break; }`
Identifier & Type	IT_1 Renaming(M)	`int x;`	`int var1;`
	IT_1 Renaming(L)	`int buf;`	`int handleCompressedAudioBuffer;`
	IT_1 Renaming(S)	`char* file;`	`char* secure_file;`
	IT_2 Temp Var	`return x + y;`	`int tmp = x + y; return tmp;`
	IT_3 Type Norm	`char x = 0;`	`int8_t x = 0;`
	IT_4 Struct Wrap	`int x, y;`	`struct { int x; int y; } s;`
Operator	O_1 Bracket Insert	`x + y * z`	`(x + (y * z))`
	O_2 Reordering	`x + y * z`	`z * y + x`
	O_3 Decomposition	`if ((x + y) * z > t)`	`tmp1 = x + y; tmp2 = z; if (tmp1 * tmp2 > t)`
	O_4 Scaling	`if (x + y > z)`	`if ((x * 2.0 * 0.5) + y > z * 2.0 * 0.5)`
	O_5 Arrow-to-Dot	`ptr->x = 1;`	`(*ptr).x = 1;`

If a candidate fails validation or remains detectable, the framework iteratively applies alternative perturbations until a configurable retry limit is reached.

3.1 Adversarial Code Generation

Perturbation Method. We define a suite of 19 code-perturbation rules organized into four categories that match the surface forms emphasized by modern LM-based vulnerability detectors: (i) Control-statement Transformations, (ii) Code-depth Transformations, (iii) Identifier & Type Transformations, and (iv) Operator Transformations.

Each category targets distinct syntactic or semantic aspects of a program, enabling the generation of diverse adversarial code variants. Table 1 summarizes all rules and illustrates their effects by showing representative original code and its transformed counterpart, together with concise rule identifiers that are consistently used throughout this paper.

- **Control-statement Transformations (C_1–C_6).** Six rules rewrite control-flow constructs such as conditionals, loops, and jumps while preserving semantics (for example, C_1 If-to-Switch and C_5 For-to-While).
- **Code-depth Transformations (D_1–D_4).** Four rules artificially increase nesting depth without changing functionality (for example, D_1 If Depth and D_3 While Depth).
- **Identifier & Type Transformations (IT_1–IT_4).** Four rules manipulate identifiers or data types to add indirection or obfuscation (for example, IT_1 Renaming in multiple granularities and IT_4 Struct Wrap).
- **Operator Transformations (O_1–O_5).** Five rules adjust operator usage while maintaining semantics (for example, O_2 Reordering and O_5 Arrow-to-Dot).

Perturbation Targets. Given an input vulnerable function, we parse the source code into an abstract syntax tree (AST) to expose its syntactic structures, such as control statements and identifier declarations, and determine which transformation rules are applicable.

For each identified code block (for example, a loop or predicate), AdvCodeGen randomly selects one of the applicable rules to introduce natural variation across generated samples. The selected rule is then instantiated as a structured prompt that encodes both the syntactic context and the intended transformation and is passed to an LLM, which outputs the transformed source code.

This process ensures that the rule identifiers and categories defined in Table 1 directly guide LLM-based code generation while maintaining syntactic correctness and intended semantics.

Prompt Template

You are an expert in C/C++ code transformation, specializing in transformations while preserving logical and functional equivalence.

Ensure that all existing unit tests continue to pass without modification

Transform the {TRANSFORMATION} conditionals in the following C code:

Original C code: {EXAMPLEL_CODE}

Transformation rules:
- Modify conditionals to be logically and functionally identical but structurally different.
- {TRANSFORMATION DESCRIPTION}

Return only the transformed C code without explanations or comments.

Perturbed Code:

Fig. 2. Prompt template with placeholders for rule name and example code, guiding the model to produce a syntactically valid and behavior-preserving transformation.

Prompt Design for LLM-based Code Transformation. Each transformation is encoded as a structured prompt tailored to guide the large language model in generating syntactically valid and behaviorally equivalent variants of the input code.

As illustrated in Fig. 2, the template specifies: (1) a role specification that frames the model as an expert C/C++ code transformer, (2) a functional constraint requiring all unit tests to continue to pass, and (3) a concrete transformation instruction indicating the perturbation rule to apply (e.g., "C_5: *For-to-While*"). Placeholders such as `{TRANSFORMATION}` and `{EXAMPLE_CODE}` are programmatically filled for each rule and code snippet.

Code Generation. Given the prompt and input snippet, the LLM emits a syntactically plausible, semantics-preserving variant. We may iterate the rule application to accumulate multiple small transformations, provided intermediate variants pass validation.

3.2 Code Validation

We verify syntactic correctness using Tree-sitter [4], which builds an AST and flags anomalies via `ERROR`/`MISSING` nodes. Samples containing such nodes are discarded or regenerated. Syntactically valid samples are then evaluated against target detectors. If a variant remains detectable, `AdvCodeGen` attempts alternative rules or prompts up to a retry limit.

4 Evaluation

We conduct a comprehensive evaluation of `AdvCodeGen` to demonstrate its robustness and practical value, carefully aligning our assessment with the core research questions driving this work. Our evaluation goes beyond simply measuring attack success rates—we rigorously validate that generated adversarial examples maintain functional correctness while exhibiting meaningful structural diversity. This multi-faceted approach ensures that `AdvCodeGen` can serve as a reliable framework for both evaluating and strengthening LM-based vulnerability detectors.

Our experimental design addresses five refined research questions, each capturing essential requirements for an effective adversarial code generation framework:

- **RQ1 (Attack Effectiveness)**: How effectively does `AdvCodeGen` generate adversarial code examples that evade state-of-the-art LM-based vulnerability detectors? We compare attack success rates against strong token-level and LLM-driven baselines to establish whether our perturbation strategy and LLM prompting achieve reliable evasion performance.
- **RQ2 (Perturbation Effectiveness)**: Which types of code perturbation strategies are most effective at evading LM-based vulnerability detectors? We evaluate attack success rates across different perturbation to assess which transformations contribute most to evasion performance.

- **RQ3 (Semantic and Syntactic Integrity)**: Do transformed code samples maintain both syntactic correctness and intended program behavior? We verify preservation through compilation checks and unit testing to ensure that observed misclassifications result from genuine model weaknesses rather than invalid or malformed code artifacts.
- **RQ4 (Transformation Diversity)**: Does AdvCodeGen generate a broader spectrum of structural and lexical variations compared to purely rule-based methods? We measure code diversity to determine whether combining rule guidance with LLM generation creates richer adversarial surfaces than deterministic AST transformations alone.
- **RQ5 (Model Robustness)**: How robust are LM-based vulnerability detectors to adversarial transformations, and which architectural properties influence their resilience? We analyze detection outcomes across different model architectures to identify key factors that contribute to or weaken robustness, offering guidance for designing more secure vulnerability detectors.

Collectively addressing these research questions validates that AdvCodeGen transcends the capability to break specific models. Instead, it systematically generates realistic, functionally correct, and structurally diverse adversarial examples that provide actionable insights for advancing vulnerability detection systems.

4.1 Experimental Setup

Datasets. We utilize two widely adopted vulnerability benchmark datasets: BigVul [11] and Devign [51], both of which consist of function-level C/C++ code annotated with binary vulnerability labels. BigVul comprises automatically extracted functions linked to real-world CVE reports from open-source repositories. Devign contains manually curated samples from four open-source projects (e.g., FFmpeg, QEMU) with expert-verified vulnerability labels.

Prior work [9] has shown that these datasets contain substantial amounts of reused or duplicated code. To ensure high-quality and fair evaluation, we follow previous studies by measuring code similarity using GraphCodeBERT embeddings [7,33]. Test samples with cosine similarity scores above 0.95 [1,43,45] are excluded to prevent performance inflation and ensure unbiased comparisons. Samples exceeding the 4,096-token LLM context limit are also discarded.

All models are fine-tuned on the full training set and evaluated on the filtered test set. After applying these filtering steps, 862 unique vulnerable samples out of the original 2,205 remain for final evaluation.

Target Models. We evaluate six state-of-the-art code models widely adopted for vulnerability detection: deep code models CodeT5 [44], CodeBERT [12], GraphCodeBERT [20], and UnixCoder [19], as well as large language models StarCoder2 [31] and CodeGen2.5 [35]. To ensure a fair comparison, all models are fine-tuned on the vulnerability detection task under consistent conditions. The performance results of these fine-tuned models are presented in Table 2.

Table 2. Performance of the LM-based vulnerability detectors.

Model	Params	Dataset	Acc	F1	Recall	Precision	Acc-vul
CT5 [44]	60M	BV	99.11	91.88	94.31	89.57	88.82
		DV	63.56	58.88	42.27	57.73	57.73
CB [12]	125M	BV	99.17	92.30	95.63	89.19	88.63
		DV	63.78	58.92	57.49	60.43	57.49
GCB [20]	125M	BV	99.34	42.28	39.72	45.20	45.00
		DV	60.36	65.85	83.19	55.49	83.19
UC [19]	125M	BV	99.31	93.59	96.76	90.62	89.95
		DV	59.79	63.03	75.87	53.91	75.87
CG [35]	2B	BV	98.91	89.74	85.40	97.54	85.40
		DV	52.60	57.72	70.44	48.89	70.44
SC2 [31]	3B	BV	97.54	74.48	64.17	88.73	64.17
		DV	59.52	25.67	15.22	81.97	32.86

Baseline. We compare our framework with two categories of baseline methods: (1) Token-level baselines, that generate adversarial examples by modifying code at the token level using predefined transformation rules, and (2) LLM-driven baselines, that generate adversarial examples by leveraging large language models through prompting strategies.

Token-Level Baselines. We evaluate four established methods that generate adversarial code examples for deep code models:

- **ALERT** [46] applies identifier renaming transformations using greedy and genetic algorithms.
- **CARROT** [49] performs identifier renaming and dead code injection with hill-climbing optimization.
- **CODA** [42] applies identifier renaming and dead code insertion derived from similar code samples.
- **AACEGEN** [29] leverages attention-based token importance to guide renaming, grammatical, and structural transformations via greedy search.

LLM-Based Baselines. Since no prior work has explored LLM-based adversarial code generation for vulnerability detection, we implement two LLM-driven baselines:

- **LLM$_{\textbf{naive}}$** prompts LLM to generate transformed versions of given code without specifying attack objectives.
- **LLM$_{\textbf{targeted}}$** prompts LLM to generate functionally equivalent code variants with the explicit objective of evading vulnerability detectors.

Implementation Details. We implement AdvCodeGen in Python, utilizing Tree-sitter [4] to extract code structures and identifiers. Our fine-tuning framework builds upon established benchmarks [6, 9, 32]. All models are fine-tuned with a fixed learning rate of 2×10^{-5}. Models with fewer than 1B parameters are trained for 10 epochs, while those exceeding 1B parameters are fine-tuned for four epochs. Pretrained weights are obtained from Hugging Face.

Following AACEGEN [29, 49], we set the maximum number of attack iterations to $m = 40$, with up to $n = 5$ candidate substitutions generated per token at each iteration for token-level adversarial code generation. Each baseline is implemented using the official code released by the authors.

For LLM-based transformations, we apply four iterative transformation steps (m=4), each step incrementally perturbs the input code. We adopt four steps because the median number of perturbed tokens per code snippet after four iterations is approximately 38, which aligns with the perturbation level achieved by 40-step token-level baselines. We report the median rather than the mean, as the distribution of perturbed token counts is non-normal and sensitive to outliers. For the generation of AdvCodeGen, we default to GPT-4o-mini with temperature 0, leveraging its advanced language modeling capabilities. To ensure statistical reliability, all experiments are repeated five times, and the average results are reported to account for variability. Training is conducted on a single NVIDIA H100 GPU (80GB) using CUDA 12.6.

4.2 RQ1: Attack Effectiveness

To evaluate the attack performance of our framework in generating adversarial code examples for LM-based vulnerability detection models, we conduct a comparative analysis against two categories of baseline techniques. We compare the attack success rate (ASR) of our framework with that of the baselines across six target models and two datasets. The results are presented in Table 3 and Table 4.

Metric. ASR measures the proportion of vulnerable code samples misclassified as benign after adversarial transformation.

Token-Level Baselines. As shown in Table 3, we compare the ASR performance of AdvCodeGen with four token-level adversarial attack baselines: ALERT, CARROT, CODA, and AACEGEN. AdvCodeGen achieves the highest ASR across most target models and datasets, demonstrating its effectiveness.

On average, across all models and datasets, AdvCodeGen achieves an ASR of 51.18%, significantly outperforming all token-level baselines: ALERT (16.09%), CARROT (11.44%), CODA (16.64%), and AACEGEN (15.09%). This substantial margin highlights the superior effectiveness of AdvCodeGen in generating adversarial examples that successfully mislead diverse vulnerability detection models.

A notable exception is observed with GraphCodeBERT (GCB), where ALERT outperforms all other methods, including AdvCodeGen (52.07% vs. 14.37% on BigVul, 40.02% vs. 36.30% on Devign). We hypothesize that this is due to GCB's reliance on graph-structured inputs derived from data flow and ASTs, which enhances its robustness to structural perturbations while increas-

Table 3. Comparison of ASR performance between AdvCodeGen and token-level baselines on six target models across two benchmark datasets.

Model	Dataset	ALERT	CARROT	CODA	AACEGEN	AdvCodeGen
CT5	BV	2.78%	2.35%	14.07%	4.19%	**72.33%**
	DV	36.93%	33.19%	29.43%	33.59%	**44.16%**
CB	BV	2.54%	1.08%	13.46%	2.80%	**67.82%**
	DV	22.22%	4.07%	**29.75%**	21.38%	29.15%
GCB	BV	**52.07%**	14.28%	35.51%	37.21%	14.37%
	DV	**40.02%**	23.53%	19.07%	12.46%	36.30%
UC	BV	2.82%	1.83%	10.24%	4.86%	**72.09%**
	DV	14.41%	21.88%	16.67%	20.00%	**27.56%**
SC2	BV	0.66%	0.00%	2.01%	1.98%	**81.51%**
	DV	1.87%	8.40%	13.04%	19.13%	**52.91%**
CG2.5	BV	1.25%	0.59%	6.21%	9.43%	**65.92%**
	DV	15.29 %	25.27%	10.21%	14.04%	**60.25%**
Average		16.09%	11.44%	16.64%	15.09%	**51.18%**

ing its susceptibility to identifier-level changes. Since ALERT primarily targets identifier renaming, it is particularly effective against this model.

Despite this exception, AdvCodeGen exhibits consistently strong performance across different models and architectures, achieving particularly high ASRs on modern LLM such as StarCoder2 (81.51% on BigVul) and demonstrating robust effectiveness across diverse evaluation settings.

LLM-Driven Baselines. We compare the performance of AdvCodeGen against two LLM-driven baselines, LLM_{naive} and $LLM_{targeted}$, as shown in Table 4.

Across all target models and datasets, AdvCodeGen consistently outperforms both baselines in terms of ASR. On average, AdvCodeGen achieves an ASR of 51.18%, significantly outperforming LLM_{naive} (33.94%) and $LLM_{targeted}$ (30.21%). This corresponds to approximately 1.51 times and 1.69 times higher ASR compared to LLM_{naive} and $LLM_{targeted}$, respectively.

4.3 RQ2: Effectiveness of Perturbation Techniques

To assess the effectiveness of individual code perturbation techniques, each transformation is applied independently and exactly once to the test code samples. The outcomes are reported separately for the two datasets, as summarized in Table 5 and Table 6, which present the ASR achieved by each transformation. The application of a transformation rule is conditioned on the presence of the corresponding syntactic construct in the input code. All perturbations are applied in a single-step setting, ensuring that only one transformation is introduced per sample to isolate its effect on model robustness.

Table 4. Comparison of ASR performance between AdvCodeGen and LLM-driven baselines of six target models across two benchmark datasets.

Model	Dataset	LLM_{naive}	$LLM_{targeted}$	AdvCodeGen
CT5	BV	50.00%	41.72%	**72.33%**
	DV	22.93%	24.88%	**44.16%**
CB	BV	48.40%	39.07%	**67.82%**
	DV	2.90%	1.93%	**18.88%**
GCB	BV	13.14%	11.43%	**14.37%**
	DV	30.00%	30.00%	**36.30%**
UC	BV	49.27%	41.69%	**72.09%**
	DV	9.57%	9.13%	**27.56%**
SC2	BV	55.56%	46.76%	**81.51%**
	DV	40.35%	47.37%	**52.91%**
CG2.5	BV	49.69%	40.12%	**65.92%**
	DV	28.45%	28.45%	**60.25%**
Average		33.94%	30.21%	**51.18%**

High Vulnerability to Structural Transformations. LM-based vulnerability detectors trained on BigVul demonstrate high sensitivity to semantics-preserving transformations. Control statement transformations (C_1–C_6) achieve the highest average ASR of 79.59%, with goto removal (C_4) being particularly effective at 100% ASR on multiple models. Code depth transformations (D_1–D_5) yield an average ASR of 75.89%, indicating that models heavily rely on structural patterns for vulnerability detection.

Effectiveness of Local Perturbations. Identifier and type transformations show varying effectiveness, with an average ASR of 60.42% on BigVul. Temporary variable insertion (IT_2) proves highly effective (77.50% average ASR), while identifier renaming techniques (IT_1) achieve moderate success (41.08%–56.74%). Among operator transformations, decomposition (O_3) stands out with 82.21% ASR, significantly outperforming other operator-level changes.

GraphCodeBERT's Enhanced Robustness. GraphCodeBERT demonstrates superior robustness across all transformation categories due to its use of graph-structured representations. It achieves the lowest average ASRs: 17.76% for control statements, 10.11% for code depth, 30.5% for identifier transformations, and 9.54% for operator transformations. However, it remains vulnerable to specific techniques like renaming with semantic context (IT_1, 59.43% ASR) and decomposition (O_3, 41.14% ASR).

Model-Specific Vulnerabilities. Modern LLM shows distinct vulnerability patterns. StarCoder2 demonstrates high susceptibility to control flow changes (79.18% average) and decomposition attacks (82.24%), while CodeGen2.5 shows relatively balanced vulnerability across categories. Traditional models, such as

Table 5. Evaluation performance of LM-based vulnerability detector on BigVul dataset condition with code perturbation techniques.

	Perturbation Type	CodeT5	CodeBERT	GCBERT	UnixCoder	StarCoder2	CodeGen2.5
Control Statement	C_1 If-to-Switch	79.03%	64.46%	18.17%	71.69%	74.21%	70.08%
	C_2 Switch-to-If	84.62%	62.70%	16.67%	79.31%	83.33%	79.17%
	C_3 Ternary-to-If	55.56%	64.00%	00.00%	61.54%	76.19%	69.57%
	C_4 Goto Remove	100%	100%	33.33%	100%	87.50%	87.50%
	C_5 For-to-While	75.00%	65.09%	5.08%	71.43%	62.96%	70.00%
	C_6 While-to-For	83.33%	63.41%	33.33%	83.33%	90.91%	73.33%
	Average	79.59%	69.64%	17.76%	77.88%	79.18%	74.94%
Code Depth	D_1 If Depth	69.66%	59.11%	13.86%	44.12%	79.47%	42.05%
	D_2 Switch Depth	84.62%	74.07%	9.68%	59.52%	58.33%	79.17%
	D_3 While Depth	77.78%	53.33%	6.10%	55.56%	66.67%	57.50%
	D_4 For Depth	72.50%	64.29%	8.93%	59.52%	72.73%	60.00%
	Average	75.89%	62.87%	10.11%	56.46%	70.88%	61.44%
Identifier & Type	IT_1 Renaming(M)	56.74%	50.93%	41.14%	53.94%	46.42%	56.72%
	IT_1 Renaming(L)	56.28%	50.37%	34.29%	56.25%	64.15%	49.50%
	IT_1 Renaming(S)	41.08%	59.43%	59.43%	40.49%	35.23%	41.08%
	IT_2 Temp Var	77.50%	69.53%	17.95%	75.62%	77.17%	74.26%
	IT_3 Type Norm	75.44%	69.39%	17.61%	73.34%	90.74%	69.75%
	IT_4 Struct Wrap	51.78%	21.87%	23.24%	40.52%	100%	22.53%
	Average	60.42%	52.12%	30.50%	57.24%	73.46%	51.42%
Operator	O_1 Bracket Insert	54.09%	49.64%	5.93%	52.11%	57.07%	52.21%
	O_2 Reordering	33.81%	30.36%	5.08%	32.39%	26.09%	30.15%
	O_3 Decomposition	82.21%	78.84%	16.95%	72.50%	82.24%	76.85%
	O_4 Scaling	39.82%	35.09%	10.34%	37.72%	33.33%	34.55%
	O_5 Arrow-to-Dot	33.15%	29.40%	9.40%	31.04%	26.72%	30.09%
	Average	48.62%	44.67%	9.54%	45.15%	45.09%	44.77%

CodeT5 and UnixCoder, exhibit consistently high ASRs across most transformation types, suggesting limited robustness to structural modifications.

Reduced Effectiveness on Devign Dataset. All models show significantly lower ASRs when trained on Devign compared to BigVul. Control statement transformations drop to 14.78% average ASR, and other categories show similar reductions. This pattern suggests either enhanced model robustness on Devign or potential issues with the underlying model performance that warrant further investigation.

4.4 RQ3: Semantic and Syntactic Integrity

Effective adversarial code transformations must preserve both syntactic validity and behavioral equivalence. While our framework incorporates validation mechanisms during generation (Sect. 3.2), empirical evaluation of the final transformed code quality is essential to demonstrate that our adversarial examples maintain functional correctness and quantify the reliability of our transformation pipeline.

Our experimental datasets (BigVul and Devign) lack unit tests for comprehensive validation. To address this limitation, we conduct validation using the

Table 6. Evaluation performance of LM-based vulnerability detector on Devign dataset with code perturbation techniques.

	Perturbation Type	CodeT5	CodeBERT	GCBERT	UnixCoder	StarCoder2	CodeGen2.5
Control Statement	C_1 If-to-Switch	16.86%	9.47%	5.74%	11.63%	25.00%	74.49%
	C_2 Switch-to-If	00.00%	10.00%	14.29%	16.67%	50.00%	33.33%
	C_3 Ternary-to-If	11.11%	12.50%	6.67%	00.00%	00.00%	55.56%
	C_4 Goto Remove	00.00%	00.00%	8.99%	12.50%	00.00%	40.00%
	C_5 For-to-While	25.00%	23.81%	00.00%	20.00%	20.00%	52.62%
	C_6 While-to-For	35.71%	31.58%	20.00%	21.43%	16.67%	36.36%
	Average	14.78%	14.56%	9.28%	9.28%	18.61%	49.39%
Code Depth	D_1 If Depth	44.04%	15.62%	13.33%	13.18%	80.89%	66.67%
	D_2 Switch Depth	45.45%	30.00%	10.00%	23.08%	50.00%	10.53%
	D_3 While Depth	28.57%	00.00%	40.00%	21.43%	16.67%	54.55%
	D_4 For Depth	25.00%	10.53%	13.33%	20.00%	40.00%	57.89%
	Average	35.83%	12.54%	15.95%	18.32%	42.78%	43.17%
Identifier & Type	IT_1 Renaming(M)	23.38%	23.50%	30.53%	22.32%	50.88%	16.32%
	IT_1 Renaming(L)	20.14%	25.14%	11.50%	18.10%	3.51%	0.42%
	IT_1 Renaming(S)	14.75%	13.66%	37.61%	4.35%	43.86%	21.76%
	IT_2 Temp Var	2.05%	28.04%	15.52%	7.63%	1.89%	0.80%
	IT_3 Type Norm	11.60%	16.77%	9.57%	11.73%	1.89%	1.84%
	IT_4 Struct Wrap	13.67%	31.89%	28.57%	11.31%	1.89%	0.00%
	Average	12.44%	23.10%	20.55%	10.62%	1.84%	4.96%
Operator	O_1 Bracket Insert	2.47%	14.46%	2.25%	0.00%	0.75%	7.06%
	O_2 Reordering	0.85%	15.66%	8.99%	1.16%	1.89%	4.71%
	O_3 Decomposition	0.85%	26.51%	15.73%	10.47%	5.00%	4.71%
	O_4 Scaling	0.00%	18.07%	14.61%	0.00%	0.00%	3.53%
	O_5 Arrow-to-Dot	23.78%	23.02%	45.00%	13.21%	0.00%	4.14%
	Average	5.59%	19.54%	17.32%	4.97%	1.53%	4.83%

HumanEval-X benchmark [14], which provides function signatures, natural language descriptions, reference implementations, and unit tests for 820 programming problems across five languages. Focusing on the C++ subset, we select 160 out of 164 problems that pass both compilation and unit tests in their original form. This evaluation assesses our multi-stage validation process under controlled conditions with ground-truth specifications, measuring both syntactic validity and behavioral equivalence of adversarial transformations.

We apply our transformation rules to these verified samples and rerun the corresponding unit tests to validate their behavioral correctness. We evaluate two key metrics:

- **Unit Test Success Rate (UTSR)** measures behavioral consistency, calculated as the ratio of unit tests passed by the transformed code to those passed by the original implementation.
- **Compile Success Rate (CSR)** reflects syntactic validity, measured as the percentage of transformed samples that compile without errors.

Table 7. UTSR and CSR results for transformed code samples.

Metrics	Trans#1	Trans#2	Trans#3	Trans#4
UTSR	160/160	147/160	145/160	149/160
CSR	160/160	157/160	152/160	153/160

Table 7 presents the behavioral and syntactic validation results of our code transformation rules across four sequential transformation stages, where Trans#k indicates applying k consecutive transformation steps.

Behavioral Equivalence. The results demonstrate strong behavioral preservation across transformation stages. Trans#1 maintains perfect behavioral equivalence (160/160 UTSR), indicating that single-step transformations preserve program semantics completely. As transformation complexity increases, UTSR shows a gradual decline: Trans#2 (147/160, 91.88%), Trans#3 (145/160, 90.63%), and Trans#4 (149/160, 93.13%). Despite multiple sequential modifications, the framework maintains over 90% behavioral consistency across all stages.

Syntactic Validity. Trans#1 achieves perfect compilation success (160/160), while subsequent stages maintain high CSR: Trans#2 (157/160, 98.13%), Trans#3 (152/160, 95.00%), and Trans#4 (153/160, 95.63%). The UTSR-CSR gap ranges from 0% in Trans#1 to 2.5% in Trans#4.

Transformation Sequence Analysis. The transformation sequence reveals an interesting pattern: performance initially declines from Trans#1 to Trans#3 but partially recovers in Trans#4. Specifically, UTSR drops from 100% to 90.63% (Trans#1 to Trans#3), then improves to 93.13% (Trans#4). Similarly, CSR decreases from 100% to 95.00%, then slightly recovers to 95.63%. This suggests that certain transformation combinations may interact constructively, compensating for individual transformation limitations.

Overall, AdvCodeGen achieves an average UTSR of 91.88% and CSR of 97.19% across all transformation stages, demonstrating effective generation of behaviorally consistent adversarial examples. While AdvCodeGen emphasizes behavior preservation through rule design and prompt constraints, it does not guarantee perfect semantic equivalence. Our empirical evaluation on HumanEval-X [14] reveals a 91.88% UTSR, indicating that most transformations successfully maintain the intended functionality. Despite the inherent challenges in ensuring complete semantic and syntactic preservation, our transformation methods maintain high integrity, enabling the generation of effective adversarial code that remains suitable for evaluating real-world vulnerability detection systems.

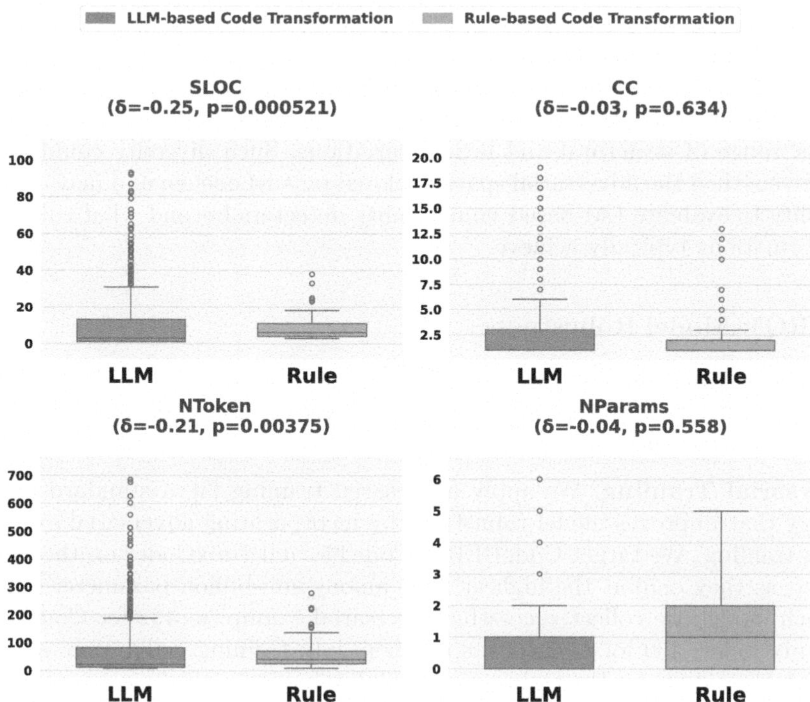

Fig. 3. Boxplot summary of structural metrics comparing LLM-based and rule-based code transformations. Each subplot shows the distribution of SLOC, CC, NToken, and NParams, with effect size (δ) and Mann-Whitney p-value annotated above.

4.5 RQ4: Transformation Diversity

To assess whether AdvCodeGen has the potential to generate more diverse code than purely AST-based rewriting, we compared LLM-based and rule-based transformations using the BigVul dataset and the StarCoder model, which showed promising results in our earlier experiments (Table 3). For a fair baseline, we re-implemented the same 19 transformation rules in an AST-driven fashion and applied them to the same inputs. We then measured code diversity with the Lizard [48] tool across four structural and lexical metrics: source lines of code (SLOC), cyclomatic complexity (CC), number of tokens (NToken), and number of parameters (NParams). Because the resulting distributions deviate from normality, we used the non-parametric Mann-Whitney U test and report both p-values and effect sizes (δ) to quantify differences.

As shown in Fig. 3, LLM-based transformations tend to produce broader distributions for SLOC and NToken, with statistically significant differences ($p < 0.05$). These metrics capture surface-level structural and lexical variation, suggesting that the LLM-guided approach may introduce greater diversity than deterministic AST rewrites. By contrast, CC and NParams show no significant differences, which is expected since both methods apply the same semantic-preserving transformations and thus maintain comparable logical control-flow complexity and parameter usage.

Overall, these results indicate that while both approaches preserve the intended functionality of the code, LLM-based perturbations appear to create a wider range of structural and lexical variations. Such diversity could potentially strengthen the adversarial space explored by AdvCodeGen and may enhance its ability to evaluate LM-based vulnerability detectors beyond what rule-based transformations typically achieve.

4.6 RQ5: Model Robustness

To assess AdvCodeGen's robustness against countermeasures, we evaluate its performance under two defense strategies: (1) adversarial training and (2) adversarial code detection.

Adversarial Training. We apply adversarial training [3], a standard defense strategy that improves model robustness by incorporating adversarial examples during training. We target CodeBERT, CodeT5, and UnixCoder on the BigVul dataset, as they exhibit the highest ASR among sub-billion parameter models. For each model, we collect successful adversarial examples (432 for CodeBERT and UnixCoder; 430 for CodeT5), split them into training, validation, and test sets (8:1:1), and merge the training and validation sets with the original dataset for fine-tuning.

Adversarial Code Detection. We develop a modular detection mechanism independent of the underlying model, making it suitable for black-box and resource-constrained settings. Leveraging a CodeBERT-based classifier trained on the BigVul dataset, we distinguish clean code from adversarial code generated by AdvCodeGen.

Results Analysis. Table 8 presents the effectiveness of both defense strategies. Adversarial training demonstrates significant robustness improvements across all models. When subjected to adversarial attacks, CodeBERT's accuracy improved from 37.21% (the original model) to 97.73% (after adversarial training), marking a 2.63 times improvement. CodeT5 and UnixCoder show improvements of 2.69 times and 2.53 times, respectively. All models maintain their original performance on clean inputs.

For attack detection, the CodeBERT-based detector achieves moderate performance with accuracy ranging from 81.61% to 83.91% across different target models. The consistent F1-scores (81.61%–82.50%) indicate balanced precision and recall, suggesting that adversarially transformed code exhibits detectable statistical or structural patterns that distinguish it from original code.

These results demonstrate that while AdvCodeGen can successfully generate adversarial examples against vulnerability detectors, both defense mechanisms provide measurable protection, with adversarial training showing particularly strong effectiveness in restoring model robustness.

Table 8. Effects of defense mechanisms. Results include (1) adversarial accuracy of target models before and after adversarial training, and (2) attack detection performance (Accuracy and F1-score).

Target Model	Adversarial Training		Attack Detection	
	Before	After	Accuracy	F1-score
CodeBERT	37.21%	97.73%	81.61%	81.61%
CodeT5	30.23%	81.40%	83.91%	82.50%
UnixCoder	34.09%	86.36%	83.91%	82.50%

5 Limitations

Semantic Preservation Challenges. While AdvCodeGen achieves high success rates during our evaluation, we find that it still fails due to the transformations that did not preserve the semantics. Specifically, our manual analysis on such failed cases reveals that identifier renaming can introduce unintended ambiguities, while type normalization may disrupt subtle semantic relationships, failing to preserve the original semantic of the program.

A possible mitigation can be implemented by incorporating additional semantic analysis techniques, such as symbolic execution or formal verification, to ensure stronger guarantees of behavioral equivalence. We leave this for our future work.

Language Diversity. Our current evaluation focuses on C/C++ datasets, which, while representative of widely used systems programming languages, may constrain the generalizability of our findings. For example, vulnerabilities in C/C++ often reflect low-level memory safety issues, while software in other languages may encompass a broader variety of vulnerabilities.

To build a more comprehensive understanding of the AdvCodeGen framework's robustness, future research should extend evaluation to include diverse programming paradigms (e.g., object-oriented, functional, and scripting languages) and larger, more heterogeneous vulnerability datasets.

We believe such an expansion would provide more substantial evidence of its effectiveness in practice. We leave this for our future work.

6 Related Work

Code Vulnerability Detection. Recent advances in MLâĂŞbased vulnerability detection have centered on code-specific pre-trained models such as CodeBERT [12], GraphCodeBERT [20], and CodeT5 [44], which are trained with token-classification or masked-language-modeling objectives.

Representative techniques include VulBERTa [22], which enhances vulnerability detection via large-scale pre-training on vulnerability-focused corpora, and LineVul [13], which targets line-level vulnerability localization. With the emergence of large general-purpose LLMs such as GPT-3.5, StarCoder, and CodeGen, vulnerability detection has expanded beyond specialized architectures. For example, RealVul [5] applies LLMs to PHP vulnerability detection through security-aware prompt engineering, while Vul-RAG [10] incorporates retrieval-augmented generation to enrich context. Recent work also emphasizes reasoning and interpretability. For instance, SV-TrustEval-C [28] introduces a benchmark for evaluating vulnerability reasoning through questionâĂŞanswer style interactions, supporting fine-grained, context-sensitive analysis.

Building on these efforts, we evaluate AdvCodeGen across both code-specific ML models and modern LLM-based detectors to assess their robustness under adversarial conditions.

Adversarial Code Example Generation. Beyond the baseline methods we evaluate—ALERT [46], CARROT [49], CODA [42], and AACEGEN [29]—a variety of approaches have explored adversarial code generation. Early work, such as MHM [50], relied on variable renaming and was soon outperformed by more sophisticated strategies. DAMP [47] applies gradient-guided identifier substitutions and dead-code insertion. However, it is restricted to one-hot encoding models. CodeAttack [25] performs token masking and substitution for code summarization and translation tasks without guaranteeing semantic preservation, while AdvPro [27] leverages gradient-based attribution for code completion rather than vulnerability detection. Other techniques, such as EaTVul [30] and CrazyIvan [26], inject non-functional adversarial snippets.

In contrast, AdvCodeGen employs 19 semantics-preserving transformation rules and large language models to rewrite vulnerable code under black-box conditions, systematically assessing the impact of each rule on the robustness of modern vulnerability detectors.

7 Conclusion

We proposed AdvCodeGen, a black-box adversarial framework that evaluates the robustness of LM-based vulnerability detectors against evasion attacks. By leveraging an LLM to apply 19 distinct code transformations, AdvCodeGen generates effective adversarial examples that significantly outperform existing baselines, achieving attack success rates of up to 81.5% on BigVul and 60.3% on Devign.

The success of these attacks reveals a critical limitation in state-of-the-art vulnerability detectors: they are brittle against semantic-preserving transformations that introduce substantial structural and lexical diversity. Our findings demonstrate that these models rely heavily on superficial syntactic patterns, a vulnerability that AdvCodeGen effectively exploits to cause misclassifications.

Ultimately, AdvCodeGen offers more than just an effective attack strategy; it serves as an important benchmark for systematically evaluating and strengthening the next generation of code security models. Future efforts will concentrate on developing attack strategies tailored to specific models and expanding the framework to accommodate perturbations beyond the local function scope.

Acknowledgments. This work was supported by Institute of Information & communications Technology Planning & Evaluation grant funded by the Korea government (RS-2024-00438686) and National Research Foundation of Korea grant funded by the Korea government (RS-2024-00451909).

References

1. Afli, H., et al.: CD4Py: Code Duplicates Detector for Python using Program Dependence Graphs (2023). Accessed 30 May 2025
2. Amazon Web Services. Amazon CodeWhisperer (2023). Accessed 06 May 2025
3. Bai, T., Luo, J., Zhao, J., Wen, B., Wang, Q.: Recent advances in adversarial training for adversarial robustness. arXiv preprint arXiv:2102.01356 (2021)
4. Brunsfeld, M.: tree-sitter: an incremental parsing system for programming tools (2018). Accessed 24 May 2025
5. Cao, D., Liao, Y., Shang, X.: Realvul: can we detect vulnerabilities in web applications with LLM? arXiv preprint arXiv:2410.07573 (2024)
6. Chen, Y., Ding, Z., Alowain, L., Chen, X., Wagner, D.: Diversevul: a new vulnerable source code dataset for deep learning based vulnerability detection. In: Proceedings of the 26th International Symposium on Research in Attacks, Intrusions and Defenses, pp. 654–668 (2023)
7. Chochlov, M., et al.: Using a nearest-neighbour, BERT-based approach for scalable clone detection. In: 2022 IEEE International Conference on Software Maintenance and Evolution (ICSME), pp. 582–591. IEEE (2022)
8. Cotroneo, D., Improta, C., Liguori, P., Natella, R.: Vulnerabilities in ai code generators: exploring targeted data poisoning attacks. In: Proceedings of the 32nd IEEE/ACM International Conference on Program Comprehension, pp. 280–292 (2024)
9. Ding, Y., et al.: Vulnerability detection with code language models: how far are we? arXiv preprint arXiv:2403.18624 (2024)
10. Du, X., et al.: Vul-rag: enhancing LLM-based vulnerability detection via knowledge-level rag. arXiv preprint arXiv:2406.11147 (2024)
11. Fan, J., Li, Y., Wang, S., Nguyen, T.N.: AC/C++ code vulnerability dataset with code changes and CVE summaries. In: Proceedings of the 17th International Conference on Mining Software Repositories, pp. 508–512 (2020)
12. Feng, Z., et al.: CodeBERT: a pre-trained model for programming and natural languages. arXiv preprint arXiv:2002.08155 (2020)
13. Fu, M., Tantithamthavorn, C.: Linevul: a transformer-based line-level vulnerability prediction. In: Proceedings of the 19th International Conference on Mining Software Repositories, pp. 608–620 (2022)
14. Fu, Y., et al.: Humaneval-x: a diverse benchmark for cross-lingual code generation. arXiv preprint arXiv:2305.14335 (2023)
15. GitHub. GitHub Copilot (2021). Accessed 06 May 2025
16. GitHub. Codeql: Discover vulnerabilities in open source code (2025). Accessed 9 Mar 2025
17. Goodfellow, I.J., Shlens, J., Szegedy, C.: Explaining and harnessing adversarial examples. arXiv preprint arXiv:1412.6572 (2014)
18. Goseva-Popstojanova, K., Perhinschi, A.: On the capability of static code analysis to detect security vulnerabilities. Inf. Softw. Technol. **68**, 18–33 (2015)

19. Guo, D., Lu, S., Duan, N., Wang, Y., Zhou, M., Yin, J.: Unixcoder: unified cross-modal pre-training for code representation. arXiv preprint arXiv:2203.03850 (2022)
20. Guo, D., et al.: Graphcodebert: pre-training code representations with data flow. arXiv preprint arXiv:2009.08366 (2020)
21. Guo, D., et al.: Deepseek-coder: when the large language model meets programming–the rise of code intelligence. arXiv preprint arXiv:2401.14196 (2024)
22. Hanif, H., Maffeis, S.: Vulberta: simplified source code pre-training for vulnerability detection. In: 2022 International Joint Conference on Neural Networks (IJCNN), pp. 1–8. IEEE (2022)
23. Henkel, J., Ramakrishnan, G., Wang, Z., Albarghouthi, A., Jha, S., Reps, T.: Semantic robustness of models of source code. In: 2022 IEEE International Conference on Software Analysis, Evolution and Reengineering (SANER), pp. 526–537. IEEE (2022)
24. Hou, X., et al.: Large language models for software engineering: a systematic literature review. ACM Trans. Softw. Eng. Methodol. **33**(8), 1–79 (2024)
25. Jha, A., Reddy, C.K.: Codeattack: code-based adversarial attacks for pre-trained programming language models. In: Proceedings of the AAAI Conference on Artificial Intelligence, vol. 37, pp. 14892–14900 (2023)
26. Li, X., et al.: Make a feint to the east while attacking in the west: blinding LLM-based code auditors with flashboom attacks. In: 2025 IEEE Symposium on Security and Privacy (SP), pp. 539–557. IEEE Computer Society (2025)
27. Li, X., et al.: Attribution-guided adversarial code prompt generation for code completion models. In: Proceedings of the 39th IEEE/ACM International Conference on Automated Software Engineering, ASE 2024, pp. 1460–1471. Association for Computing Machinery, New York (2024)
28. Li, Y., et al.: SV-trusteval-C: evaluating structure and semantic reasoning in large language models for source code vulnerability analysis. In: 2025 IEEE Symposium on Security and Privacy (SP). IEEE (2025)
29. Li, Z., Zhang, C., Pan, M., Zhang, T., Li, X.: Aacegen: attention guided adversarial code example generation for deep code models. In: Proceedings of the 39th IEEE/ACM International Conference on Automated Software Engineering, pp. 1245–1257 (2024)
30. Liu, S., et al.: EaTVul: ChatGPT-based evasion attack against software vulnerability detection. In: 33rd USENIX Security Symposium (USENIX Security 2024), pp. 7357–7374 (2024)
31. Lozhkov, A., et al.: Starcoder 2 and the stack v2: the next generation. arXiv preprint arXiv:2402.19173 (2024)
32. Lu, S., et al.: Codexglue: a machine learning benchmark dataset for code understanding and generation. arXiv preprint arXiv:2102.04664 (2021)
33. Martinez-Gil, J.: Augmenting the interpretability of graphcodebert for code similarity tasks. arXiv preprint arXiv:2410.05275 (2024)
34. MITRE Corporation. Common Weakness Enumeration (CWE) (2024). Accessed 9 Mar 2025
35. Nijkamp, E., et al.: Codegen: an open large language model for code with multi-turn program synthesis. arXiv preprint arXiv:2203.13474 (2022)
36. NPM, Inc.: Auditing package dependencies for security vulnerabilities (2025). Accessed 9 Mar 2025
37. OpenAI. ChatGPT (2022). Accessed 06 May 2025
38. Pierazzi, F., Pendlebury, F., Cortellazzi, J., Cavallaro, L.: Intriguing properties of adversarial ml attacks in the problem space. In: 2020 IEEE Symposium on Security and Privacy (SP), pp. 1332–1349. IEEE (2020)

39. Pour, M.V., Li, Z., Ma, L., Hemmati, H.: A search-based testing framework for deep neural networks of source code embedding. In: 2021 14th IEEE Conference on Software Testing, Verification and Validation (ICST), pp. 36–46. IEEE (2021)
40. r2c, Inc.: Semgrep: lightweight static analysis for many languages (2025). Accessed 9 Mar 2025
41. Roziere, B., et al.: Code llama: open foundation models for code. arXiv preprint arXiv:2308.12950 (2023)
42. Tian, Z., Chen, J., Jin, Z.: Code difference guided adversarial example generation for deep code models. In: 2023 38th IEEE/ACM International Conference on Automated Software Engineering (ASE), pp. 850–862. IEEE (2023)
43. Tian, Z., Teng, Y., Ke, X., Chen, Y., Chen, L.: Solbert: advancing solidity smart contract similarity analysis via self-supervised pre-training and contrastive fine-tuning. Inf. Softw. Technol. **184**, 107766 (2025)
44. Wang, Y., Wang, W., Joty, S., Hoi, S.C.H.: Codet5: identifier-aware unified pre-trained encoder-decoder models for code understanding and generation. arXiv preprint arXiv:2109.00859 (2021)
45. Yang, S., Gu, X., Shen, B.: Self-supervised learning of smart contract representations. In: Proceedings of the 30th IEEE/ACM International Conference on Program Comprehension, pp. 82–93 (2022)
46. Yang, Z., Shi, J., He, J., Lo, D.: Natural attack for pre-trained models of code. In: Proceedings of the 44th International Conference on Software Engineering, pp. 1482–1493 (2022)
47. Yefet, N., Alon, U., Yahav, E.: Adversarial examples for models of code. Proc. ACM Program. Lang. **4**(OOPSLA), 1–30 (2020)
48. Yin, T.: Lizard: a simple code complexity analyser (2025)
49. Zhang, H., et al.: Towards robustness of deep program processing models–detection, estimation, and enhancement. ACM Trans. Softw. Eng. Methodol. (TOSEM) **31**(3), 1–40 (2022)
50. Zhang, H., Li, Z., Li, G., Ma, L., Liu, Y., Jin, Z.: Generating adversarial examples for holding robustness of source code processing models. In: Proceedings of the AAAI Conference on Artificial Intelligence, vol. 34, pp. 1169–1176 (2020)
51. Zhou, Y., Liu, S., Siow, J., Du, X., Liu, Y.: Devign: effective vulnerability identification by learning comprehensive program semantics via graph neural networks. In: Advances in Neural Information Processing Systems, vol. 32 (2019)

Generative & Steganographic Security Applications

Generative AI-Based Steganographic Techniques for Tactical Communication Message Concealment and Modification

So-Yeon Yoon and Hyun Kwon(✉)

Department of Artificial Intelligence and Data Science, Korea Military Academy, Seoul, Republic of Korea
hkwon.cs@gmail.com

Abstract. Modern military operations are increasingly evolving into Network-Centric Warfare (NCW), where the security of tactical communications has become a critical concern. Traditional cryptographic methods, while ensuring confidentiality, inadvertently reveal the presence of sensitive messages, making them potential targets for detection and analysis. To address this limitation, this study proposes a novel steganographic approach that conceals the existence of tactical messages by embedding them within natural language text, thereby achieving both secrecy and plausible deniability. Leveraging recent advances in generative AI, particularly the LLaMA-2 language model, we develop a text-based steganography system tailored for military communication. A custom dataset was constructed by combining the UCDP conflict event records with the literary corpus of Treasure Island, enabling domain adaptation through fine-tuning with QLoRA. The resulting system demonstrates strong performance across multiple evaluation metrics, achieving a message reconstruction accuracy of 90.70%, an evasion rate of 98.25% in terms of ROC-AUC against detection models, a perplexity score of 25.06 indicating high linguistic naturalness, and an average embedding capacity of 4.5 bits per word. Compared to conventional cryptographic and steganographic techniques, the proposed method significantly improves information hiding capacity while reducing detectability, thus presenting a viable solution for evading enemy interception and traffic analysis in military environments. Future work will focus on optimizing the framework through reinforcement learning, extending the system to multimodal data, and developing lightweight models for real-time, high-reliability deployment in tactical communication scenarios.

Keywords: Network-Centric Warfare · LLaMA-2 · QLoRA · Tactical communication

1 Introduction

As the paradigm of modern warfare continues to shift toward Network-Centric Warfare (NCW) [1], the strategic importance of tactical communications conducted over cyberspace is increasing rapidly. In such environments, sensitive

H. Seo (Ed.): ICISC 2025, LNCS 16487, pp. 73–84, 2026.
https://doi.org/10.1007/978-981-95-8034-7_4

information—such as operational plans, troop deployments and movements, and classified intelligence—is frequently transmitted over open communication networks, thereby facing constant threats of interception and leakage by adversaries. The exposure of tactical communications in these scenarios can directly result in severe consequences, including mission failure and substantial troop losses, making robust information protection an operational necessity [2].

Traditionally, encryption has served as the primary means of securing such sensitive data. However, encrypted messages, by their very nature, tend to stand out in network traffic and are often flagged as containing classified information. Techniques such as traffic analysis and pattern recognition can be employed to identify the presence of encrypted communications, even if the content itself remains inaccessible. Moreover, the high entropy and irregular packet lengths associated with encrypted data can further increase the likelihood of detection, thereby compromising operational secrecy. The rapid evolution of Large Language Models (LLMs) has introduced a new paradigm in natural language generation, simultaneously raising significant concerns regarding their security and privacy in various real-world applications [3].

In response to these limitations, the military domain has recently turned its attention toward steganography—an information hiding technique that conceals the very existence of a message. With historical roots tracing back to Steganographia [4], steganography seeks to embed secret messages within innocuous-looking cover data, such as images or audio files, thereby evading detection by adversaries. Despite its potential, traditional steganographic methods face three key limitations that hinder their practical deployment in tactical settings. First, detectability remains a major challenge: bit-level modifications to images or audio often introduce anomalous patterns that can be identified by advanced steganalysis tools. Second, these methods suffer from low data transmission rates, as the payload capacity of visual and auditory media is inherently limited, making real-time message exchange impractical. Third, they involve environmental constraints and system complexity, being tightly coupled to specific data formats (e.g., JPEG, PNG) and suffering from operational issues related to shared keys and configuration management.

Recent advancements in generative artificial intelligence, particularly large language models (LLMs) [5], present promising avenues to overcome these limitations. Beyond mere text generation, the potential of LLMs is being realized through their application as intelligent agents, a development that demonstrates their capability for complex tasks like simulating real-life scenarios [6]. Unlike image or audio-based methods, text-based steganography using LLMs can achieve high data rates while maintaining plausible linguistic fluency, making it particularly well-suited for tactical communication scenarios.

This study proposes a novel steganographic framework that leverages the capabilities of cutting-edge LLMs—specifically the LLaMA model [7]—for hiding and manipulating tactical communication messages in natural language text. The proposed method represents a significant departure from existing approaches by eliminating the need for specialized media formats and instead utilizing plain text as the transmission medium, thereby enhancing flexibility and operational stealth. This paradigm shift necessitates a robust covert communication mechanism, especially given the continuous exploration of Generative AI-driven cross-layer covert communication frameworks in military and wireless networks [8].

The specific objectives of this research are threefold: (1) to empirically assess the feasibility of using LLaMA for steganographic applications in tactical communication, (2) to develop and evaluate a methodology that simultaneously achieves high embedding capacity and message reconstruction accuracy, and (3) to construct a simulation environment that reflects realistic military communication settings, thereby demonstrating the practical applicability of the proposed method. This study aims to advance secure military communications by proposing a scalable, high-performance solution that is robust against adversarial detection and adaptable for real-world deployment.

The remainder of this paper is structured as follows. Section 2 provides an overview of related work and the necessary background context. Section 3 subsequently delineates the proposed methodology in detail. Section 4 then presents the experimental setup employed and reports the corresponding results. Section 5 offers a critical examination and discussion of these findings. Finally, Section 6 synthesizes the key conclusions of this work and suggests potential avenues for future research.

2 Background and Related Work

2.1 Cryptography and Steganography in Military Communication

The necessity for information concealment has been a persistent concern in military contexts throughout history. Traditional cryptographic methods aim to secure information by transforming plaintext into ciphertext [9], thereby preventing unauthorized access. However, encrypted messages often exhibit high entropy and discernible patterns, making them susceptible to detection through statistical analysis.

In contrast, steganography seeks to obscure the very existence of a message by embedding it within innocuous cover data, such as images, audio files, or text. This approach utilizes a shared stego key between the sender and receiver to encode and decode the hidden information, thereby differentiating itself fundamentally from cryptographic techniques. The historical roots of steganography can be traced back to works like Johannes Trithemius's Polygraphia [10], which is considered one of the earliest comprehensive texts on the subject. Moreover, integrating any new security mechanism into dynamic tactical networks must account for persistent challenges such as limited bandwidth, high error rates, and the high-security requirements inherent in military operational environments [11].

Modern applications of steganography have evolved to include digital formats, with techniques such as least significant bit (LSB) manipulation in images and audio files. These methods have been employed for covert communications, including by individuals and groups seeking to evade surveillance. For instance, concerns have been raised about the use of steganographic tools by terrorist organizations to conceal messages within digital media.

2.2 Limitations of Traditional Steganography and Advances in NLP-Based Techniques

Traditional steganographic methods, particularly those involving images and audio, face limitations in terms of data capacity and susceptibility to detection. The embedding of information often alters the statistical properties of the cover media, making it detectable by advanced steganalysis tools.

To address these challenges, recent research has explored the use of natural language processing (NLP) and large language models (LLMs) for text-based steganography. These approaches leverage the generative capabilities of LLMs to produce text that appears natural while embedding hidden information. These advancements have led to the development of generative text steganography methods that directly leverage the generative power of LLMs to conceal messages within high-quality linguistic text [12]. One such method, known as LLM-Stega, utilizes black-box access to LLMs to generate stego text [13] without requiring internal model parameters. This technique employs a keyword set and an encrypted steganographic mapping to embed secret messages, along with a reject sampling mechanism to ensure the semantic coherence of the generated text.

Despite these advancements, challenges remain in ensuring the robustness and undetectability of steganographic methods. For instance, the reliance on black-box models limits the ability to fine-tune generation processes, and the generated text may still exhibit patterns that could be exploited by sophisticated detection algorithms. Importantly, recent studies have also investigated the emergence of steganographic collusion in LLM-generated text and proposed mitigation strategies, highlighting a growing adversarial landscape [12]. Additionally, the fluency and logical consistency of the stego text are critical factors that require further refinement.

2.3 Utilization of Conflict Data for Realistic Scenario Modeling

To simulate realistic tactical communication scenarios, this study utilizes data from the Uppsala Conflict Data Program (UCDP) [14], a comprehensive and authoritative source of information on organized violence and armed conflicts. The UCDP provides detailed datasets on various aspects of conflicts, including temporal and spatial information, actors involved, and intensity levels. These datasets are publicly accessible and have been widely used in peace and conflict research.

The incorporation of UCDP data, the study ensures that the experimental scenarios reflect the complexities and nuances of real-world conflicts. This approach enhances the validity of the findings and supports the development of steganographic methods tailored to the demands of tactical military communications.

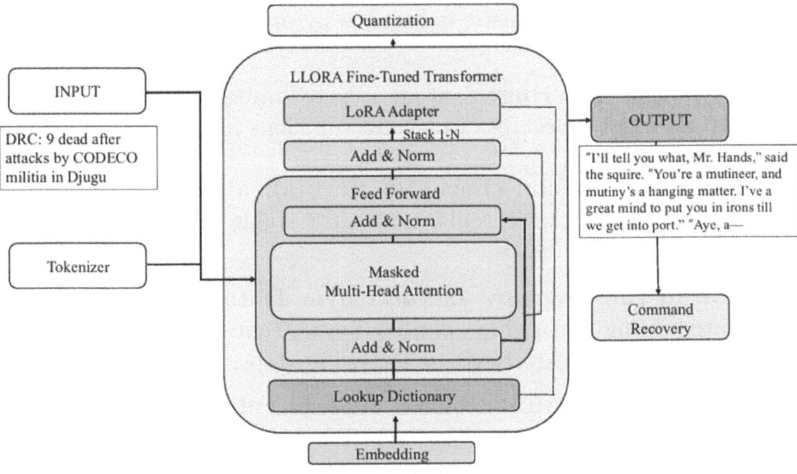

Fig. 1. LLaMA 2 Model Architecture

3 Proposed Method

This study proposes a novel steganographic framework for tactical environments that leverages a generative AI model based on LLaMA-2 as shown in Fig. 1. Specifically, we fine-tune the LLaMA-2 model to emulate the stylistic patterns of the literary text *Treasure Island*, thereby enabling the concealment and transformation of tactical commands into natural-sounding text that is difficult to detect and easy to reconstruct.

3.1 Data Collection and Preprocessing

To conduct experiments on the concealment and transformation of tactical communication messages, we constructed a specialized dataset by combining the Uppsala Conflict Data Program (UCDP) dataset, which contains real-world conflict-related events, with the literary corpus of *Treasure Island* obtained from Project Gutenberg.

Construction of the UCDP Dataset. To simulate a realistic tactical environment, we utilized the GEDEvent_v24_1.csv file from the UCDP dataset, which includes 163,755 headline reports of conflict-related events. We filtered out null entries and removed duplicate sentences to ensure data quality. Due to the operational constraints associated with acquiring classified military command messages, we used these headlines as a proxy for tactical messages. This approach of using simulated scenarios is justified by studies showing that LLMs can efficiently simulate real-life tactical communication situations, thereby increasing the realism of experimental results [15]. We further refined the data to reduce redundancy and enhance linguistic coherence by applying the following preprocessing steps:

- **Sentence length filtering:** Sentences were limited to those with lengths between 20 and 200 characters to ensure sufficient information content while reducing detectability.
- **Whitespace and special character normalization:** Consecutive spaces and special characters were replaced with a single whitespace to maintain consistency.

Construction of the *Treasure Island* Cover Dataset. The cover text corpus was created using the public-domain novel *Treasure Island* from Project Gutenberg. Preprocessing involved the following steps:

- **Sentence segmentation:** Sentences were split at punctuation marks such as periods, question marks, and exclamation points, followed by a space.
- **Length filtering:** Sentences outside the 20–200 character range were excluded, consistent with the UCDP dataset.
- **Removal of irrelevant metadata:** Sentences starting with numbers, all-uppercase lines (e.g., chapter titles), and structural or non-semantic text were discarded.
- **Deduplication and sampling:** A total of 2,517 unique sentences were extracted, from which 1,500 were randomly sampled and paired with UCDP messages in a one-to-one manner.

Style Pair Generation and Training Data Preparation. Each tactical message from the UCDP dataset was paired with a semantically neutral sentence from *Treasure Island*, forming a "style pair" for supervised training. These pairs were divided into training (80%), validation (10%), and test (10%) sets. Each data point was structured as follows:

Command: [UCDP tactical message]
Treasure: [Corresponding *Treasure Island* sentence]

This design ensures that the model learns to embed tactical instructions into the stylistic domain of literary text while maintaining a plausible natural language structure.

3.2 LLaMA-2-Based Concealment and Modification Mechanism

To generate natural-sounding stego-texts that embed tactical messages, we utilized Meta's LLaMA-2-13B, a large language model optimized for high-quality text generation. Due to the model's size and associated hardware requirements, we employed a computationally efficient fine-tuning strategy based on QLoRA (Quantized Low-Rank Adaptation) [16], which integrates 4-bit quantization and LoRA-based parameter-efficient training [17]. Employing such computationally efficient strategies, including data-efficient fine-tuning, is critical for optimizing resource utilization while maintaining high performance across specific LLM tasks [18].

Model Initialization and Quantization. We applied 4-bit NormalFloat4 (NF4) quantization using the `BitsAndBytesConfig` utility. This method aligns with the broader goal of Parameter-Efficient Fine-Tuning (PEFT), which aims to match the performance of full fine-tuning with minimal parameters, often without introducing new latency during inference [19]. Computation was handled using the bfloat16 data type, and CPU offloading was implemented to reduce GPU memory consumption.

LoRA Configuration. The LoRA method was applied to the `q_proj` and `v_proj` layers with the following hyperparameters: rank $r = 16$, alpha = 32, and dropout rate = 0.05. By tuning only specific layers, we reduced the computational burden while maintaining fine-tuning effectiveness. This specific configuration of QLoRA hyperparameters is guided by recent analyses which explore the joint scaling laws and the differential benefits of scaling data, model size, and fine-tuning methods on overall LLM performance [20].

Training Setup. Training samples were constructed using the previously described style pairs and processed for causal language modeling. The dataset was partitioned into 90% for training and 10% for validation sets.

Lookup Table and Recovery Mechanism. To enable reliable message reconstruction, we implemented a `decode_dict` lookup table that maps each generated stego-text back to its original command. This mapping yielded a command reconstruction accuracy of 90.70%, demonstrating the effectiveness of the proposed mechanism.

Through these design choices, our method achieves high concealment capacity, textual fluency, and message recovery accuracy while remaining robust against detection and suitable for real-world tactical communication scenarios.

4 Experimental Setup and Results

4.1 Experimental Environment

All model training and experiments were conducted using an NVIDIA A100-SXM4-40GB GPU environment. The key hardware and software settings used in our experiments are as follows. CUDA version 12.4 and NVIDIA driver version 550.54.15 were installed to support GPU acceleration. The experiments were implemented using PyTorch 2.0.1+cu118 as the primary deep learning framework.

We employed Huggingface's `Transformers` [21] library (v4.35.2) and `PEFT` (v0.8.2) to support parameter-efficient fine-tuning via LoRA and QLoRA. Quantization was performed using `BitsAndBytes` (v0.41.0), specifically applying the 4-bit NormalFloat4 (NF4) format for efficient training. Additional tools such as `datasets` and `sacrebleu` were used for data processing and evaluation.

The model was trained over 12 epochs using the Huggingface `Trainer` module. The effective batch size was set to 32, achieved via a per-device batch size of 4 and a gradient accumulation step of 8. The training dataset consisted of 1,350 sentence pairs, while 150 pairs were reserved for validation. Input sequences were tokenized and collated using the `DataCollatorForLanguageModeling` class to construct masked language modeling inputs. These settings enabled the efficient fine-tuning of the large LLaMA-2 model while preserving memory efficiency and training stability.

4.2 Experimental Results

To comprehensively evaluate the proposed system's capability in concealing and transforming tactical communication messages, we conducted both quantitative and qualitative analyses as shown in Table 1 and Table 2. These evaluations were contextualized within military communication scenarios to assess real-world applicability.

Command Recovery Rate. The proposed LLaMA-2-based concealment system achieved a command recovery accuracy of 90.70%. Using a lookup-table-based decoding approach, original commands were successfully reconstructed from 1,000 test sentence pairs. Analysis of failure cases revealed that minor textual deviations or contextual ambiguity in generated sentences were the primary causes of recovery errors. In real-world tactical operations, such vulnerabilities could potentially be exploited by adversaries to inject misleading information. Therefore, further improvements in fine-tuning and robust key management systems are recommended to enhance security. Nevertheless, the current recovery rate surpasses 90%, suggesting sufficient reliability for emergency and high-stakes command transmission.

Naturalness and Quality Assessment. We evaluated the naturalness of the stego-text using perplexity (PPL) [22], which yielded an average score of 25.06. This level of perplexity is comparable to that of general news articles or literary texts, indicating a high degree of linguistic fluency. Additionally, sentence structure and length distribution closely resembled natural language norms. These findings suggest that the stego-text is likely to evade detection by adversarial monitoring systems, as it mirrors everyday communication such as reports or personal messages. This stylistic camouflage enhances operational security by obscuring the embedded tactical content. Table 2 provides illustrative examples of the generated sentences compared to the original UCDP headlines and reference sentences from Treasure Island. These examples demonstrate the proposed system's capability to transform tactical communication messages into stylistically consistent literary sentences, effectively concealing the original commands within natural-sounding text. For instance, the generated sentence for the headline "DRC: 9 dead after attacks by CODECO militia in Djugu" seamlessly integrates the command into a plausible narrative, thus enhancing the

Table 1. Examples of Generated and Reference Sentences for Covert Communication

Headline	Generated Sentence (Gen)	Reference Sentence (Ref)
DRC: 9 dead after attacks by CODECO militia in Djugu	"I'll tell you what, Mr. Hands," said the squire. "You're a mutineer, and mutiny's a hanging matter. I've a great mind to put you in irons till we get into port." "Aye, a—	Next moment he had turned the corner and my home was out of sight.
Taliban kill two security guards of Logar governor	"I'll tell you that it is, Mr. Hands," said I. You're a mutineer from beginning to end, and I see my duty plain before me. I've sworn to serve the captain, he's my lawful captain still—bar—	No more wounded than you or I.
Eight Dead, Several Injured in South Darfur Violence	"I'll have you hanged at the yard-arm, by the Lord Harry, I will! And now, what do you say to that?" "I say," replied the captain, "that you're a damned mutineer, and I lay my duty upon you to cla—	That particularly took my fancy was the spring.
Taliban terrorists killed in NW Balochistan	"I'll tell you," said the captain. I'm a plain-spoken man, and when I make a remark I like folks to answer me straight. Do you understand me?" "Ay, ay, sir," replied the squire.	Taliban terrorists killed in NW raid
Four soldiers dead in Philippines clash	"I'll not deny that it is," said the squire. "You're a mutineering one, and you've been round the world, I reckon. Now, what do you think of this?" And he tapped the chart with his fur	Philippine communist rebels, four soldiers dead
Convoy attacked by resistance fighters in Western Myanmar	"I'm a plain ash—yes, but I know a thing or two. I don't ask no questions, Mr. Hands; never was much given to ask questions; but if I was you,"	Several fatalities as junta soldiers/resistance clash

message's concealment and reducing detectability. Notably, the generated sentences maintain semantic coherence and stylistic alignment with the cover text, thereby reinforcing both the naturalness and operational stealth of the system. These results underscore the effectiveness of the proposed method in achieving high-quality embedding and plausible deniability in tactical communication scenarios.

Stealthiness Performance. To assess the detectability of the generated stego-texts, we employed a fine-tuned BERT-based classifier. The challenge of detecting concealed messages is also being tackled through advanced techniques such as LLM-based linguistic steganalysis, which aims for efficient detection of even strongly concealed stego-messages [23]. The resulting ROC-AUC score was 0.9825, which approximates random guessing (50%) in the context of binary classification. The false positive rate (FPR) was measured at 5.10%, indicating that a small fraction of normal sentences were misclassified as stego-text. Conversely, the false negative rate (FNR) was 5.00%, representing the proportion of stego sentences that were misidentified as normal.

We further performed KL Divergence analysis to compare the statistical distributions of n-grams and word frequencies between stego-texts and ordinary sentences. The divergence was significantly lower than that observed in conventional synonym substitution-based steganography techniques. These results

Table 2. Validation classification report. Validation ROC AUC: 0.9806

	Precision	Recall	F1-score	Support
0	0.9126	0.9792	0.9447	96
1	0.9794	0.9135	0.9453	104
Accuracy			0.9450	200
Macro avg	0.9460	0.9463	0.9450	200
Weighted avg	0.9473	0.9450	0.9450	200

demonstrate the model's ability to evade detection even against advanced AI-based surveillance systems such as BERT, implying the method's practical viability for covert communications in military operations. The method's success in evading detection is critical, given the growing necessity and complexity of detecting text generated by large language models for ensuring content integrity and authenticity [24].

Embedding Capacity. The average embedding capacity of the proposed system was measured at 4.5 bits per word (bpw). This represents a 4.5-fold improvement over traditional synonym-based methods, which typically offer around 1.0 bpw. The increased capacity indicates that a greater amount of command information can be transmitted per sentence. This is particularly advantageous in real-time tactical communication scenarios where high bandwidth efficiency and rapid transmission of complex instructions are critical.

5 Discussion

This study explores the use of generative AI to develop a covert communication technique that surpasses traditional cryptographic methods in stealth and efficiency, particularly within tactical military contexts. The proposed system demonstrates notable strengths in reliability, security, and embedding capacity, achieving a significant improvement over conventional synonym-based steganography by reaching 4.5 bits per word. A key contribution lies in its ability to generate linguistically natural stego-texts capable of evading detection by AI-driven surveillance systems, making it well-suited for bandwidth-limited and adversarial environments. Despite these advantages, a 9.3% recovery failure rate highlights the need for more refined fine-tuning and key management strategies to enhance decoding accuracy. Furthermore, as steganalysis methods—especially those based on deep learning—continue to advance, the system must evolve to resist sophisticated detection attacks. Future research should focus on incorporating multi-layered embedding strategies and robust modulation techniques, as well as developing encoding schemes that are resilient to adversarial conditions, in order to ensure operational effectiveness in modern electronic warfare.

6 Conclusion

This study proposed a novel method for generating covert and modulated messages in tactical communication environments by leveraging the generative capabilities of the LLaMA-2 language model. Through systematic experimentation, the proposed approach demonstrated both high performance and operational feasibility for military applications. The system proved particularly valuable in scenarios where conventional encryption devices may be unavailable or compromised, offering a reliable means of covert communication even under adversarial surveillance.

The results underscore the system's potential to support secure and trustworthy message transmission during emergencies, where information integrity and stealth are critical. The integration of natural language generation with high-capacity embedding further enables the communication of sensitive commands while maintaining plausible deniability and resistance to detection by AI-powered monitoring systems.

Acknowledgments. This study was supported by the Future Strategy and Technology Research Institute of the Korea Military Academy and the National Research Foundation of Korea (NRF) grant, funded by the Korean government (MSIT) (RS-2025-00516065).

References

1. Tunnell, H.D.: The us army and network-centric warfare a thematic analysis of the literature. In: MILCOM 2015-2015 IEEE Military Communications Conference, pp. 889–894. IEEE (2015)
2. Borky, J.M., Bradley, T.H., Borky, J.M., Bradley, T.H.: Protecting information with cybersecurity. Effective Model-Based Systems Engineering, pp. 345–404, 2019
3. Yao, Y., et al.: A survey on large language model (LLm) security and privacy: the good, the bad, and the ugly. High-Confidence Comput. **4**(2), 100211 (2024)
4. Trithemius, J.: Steganographia. Balth, Aulaender (2014)
5. Thirunavukarasu, A.J., Ting, D.S.J., Elangovan, K., Gutierrez, L., Tan, T.F., Ting, D.S.W.: Large language models in medicine. Nat. Med. **29**(8), 1930–1940 (2023)
6. Xi, Z., et al.: The rise and potential of large language model based agents: a survey. Sci. China Inf. Sci. **68**(2), 121101 (2025)
7. Touvron, H., et al.: Llama: Open and efficient foundation language models. arXiv preprint arXiv:2302.13971 (2023)
8. Liu, T., et al.: Generative ai-driven cross-layer covert communication: Fundamentals, framework and case study. arXiv preprint arXiv:2501.11068 (2025)
9. Bethencourt, J., Sahai, A., Waters, B.: Ciphertext-policy attribute-based encryption. In: 2007 IEEE symposium on security and privacy (SP'07), pp. 321–334. IEEE (2007)
10. Hermes, J.: Polygraphia iii: The cipher that pretends to be an artificial language. In VOY (2022)
11. Makhdoom, I., Abolhasan, M., Lipman, J.: A comprehensive survey of covert communication techniques, limitations and future challenges. Comput. Sec. **120**, 102784 (2022)

12. Wu, J., et al.: Generative text steganography with large language model. In: Proceedings of the 32nd ACM International Conference on Multimedia (2024)
13. Almohammad, A., Ghinea, G.: Stego image quality and the reliability of psnr. In: 2010 2nd International Conference on Image Processing Theory, Tools and Applications, pp. 215–220. IEEE (2010)
14. Sundberg, R., Eck, K., Kreutz, J.: Introducing the ucdp non-state conflict dataset. J. Peace Res. **49**(2), 351–362 (2012)
15. Kim, J.K., et al.: Chatgpt and large language model (llm) chatbots: the current state of acceptability and a proposal for guidelines on utilization in academic medicine. J. Pediatr. Urol. **19**(5), 598–604 (2023)
16. Dettmers, T., Pagnoni, A., Holtzman, A., Zettlemoyer, L.: Qlora: efficient finetuning of quantized LLms. Adv. Neural. Inf. Process. Syst. **36**, 10088–10115 (2023)
17. Mao, Y., Ge, Y., Fan, Y., Xu, W., Mi, Y., Hu, Z., Gao, Y.: A survey on lora of large language models. Front. Comp. Sci. **19**(7), 197605 (2025)
18. Lin, X., et al.: Data-efficient fine-tuning for LLm-based recommendation. In: Proceedings of the 47th International ACM SIGIR Conference on Research and Development in Information Retrieval (2024)
19. Liao, B., Meng, Y., Monz, C.: Parameter-efficient fine-tuning without introducing new latency. arXiv preprint arXiv:2305.16742 (2023)
20. Zhang B., et al.: When scaling meets LLm finetuning: The effect of data, model and finetuning method. arXiv preprint arXiv:2402.17193 (2024)
21. Wolf, T., et al.: Huggingface's transformers: State-of-the-art natural language processing. arXiv preprint arXiv:1910.03771 (2019)
22. Wang, Y., Deng, J., Sun, A., Meng, X.: Perplexity from plm is unreliable for evaluating text quality. arXiv preprint arXiv:2210.05892 (2022)
23. Tang, Y., et al.: Linguistic steganalysis via LLMs: two modes for efficient detection of strongly concealed stego. IEEE Signal Process. Lett. 92024)
24. Wu, J., et al.: A survey on LLM-generated text detection: necessity, methods, and future directions. Comput. Linguist. **51**(1), 275–338 (2025)

Improving Scalable Clustering for IoT Malware via Code Region Extraction

Kosuke Nikawa[1](✉), Chansu Han[2], Akira Tanaka[2], Kazuki Iwamoto[3], Takeshi Takahashi[2], and Jun'ichi Takeuchi[1]

[1] Kyushu University, Fukuoka, Japan
nikawa@me.inf.kyushu-u.ac.jp, tak@inf.kyushu-u.ac.jp
[2] National Institute of Information and Communications Technology, Tokyo, Japan
{han,tanaka.akira,takeshi_takahashi}@nict.go.jp
[3] Hitachi Systems, Ltd., Tokyo, Japan
kazuki.iwamoto.fd@hitachi-systems.com

Abstract. IoT malware is often generated in large quantities through source code modifications and widely used in cyberattacks. For fine-grained functional analysis, it is crucial to extract and utilize relevant behavioral information from the executables of malware samples. In this study, our primary objective is to improve the clustering accuracy of IoT malware based on phylogenetic trees, and from the results, we investigate which components are useful for analyzing functional characteristics at a level more fine-grained than the family.Executable code can generally be classified into statically linked library functions and user-written code, the latter presumed to reflect attacker-specific functionality. Based on this fact, we hypothesized that meaningful functional distinctions among samples are primarily captured in the user code regions. To test this hypothesis, we constructed multiple datasets with and without user code and library functions, and evaluated clustering quality with respect to two functional label sets: disabling information and exploit information.The experimental results showed that, as hypothesized, excluding library functions and retaining only the opcodes of user code improves clustering accuracy for disabling information, whereas for exploit labels, accuracy improves even when only the library function regions are used. These results demonstrate that eliminating irrelevant information is effective for functional label classification, and that functional analysis does not necessarily rely solely on user code; rather, it was revealed that vulnerability-related information is also contained in the library parts.

Keywords: IoT Malware · Phylogenetic Tree · Clustering · Normalized Compression Distance

1 Introduction

In recent years, the proliferation of Internet of Things (IoT) devices has accelerated, and correspondingly, the number of attacks using malware targeting these

H. Seo (Ed.): ICISC 2025, LNCS 16487, pp. 85–102, 2026.
https://doi.org/10.1007/978-981-95-8034-7_5

devices is increasing. A characteristic feature of IoT malware is the functional modifications introduced by adversaries: attackers often take publicly available malware source code–such as Mirai [2] or Bashlite [18]–and partially modify it to create novel variants for use in their campaigns. This leads to a growing diversity in malware behavior, even among closely related samples. As a result, there is an urgent need for methods that can efficiently analyze the functional characteristics of this evolving malware landscape. A promising line of research applies phylogenetic treeâĂŞbased clustering: originally developed in evolutionary biology to model ancestral relationships among species, phylogenetic trees can be used to represent evolutionary relationships among malware samples derived from source code modifications. By appropriately partitioning such a tree, it becomes possible to group specimens that share similar functional characteristics.

Since this study uses a large-scale malware dataset, we conducted experiments using the scalable phylogenetic tree clustering algorithm by He *et al.* [6], aiming to improve clustering accuracy through a refinement of inter-sample distance definitions. In that prior work, the distances for construction of phylogenetic trees were defined by applying the Normalized Compression Distance (NCD) [4] directly to malware executables. NCD is well suited to define distances between malware samples because of its intuitive underlying principle and its independence from file format (e.g., binary or text representations). However, applying NCD directly to binary executables may incorporate noise from non-functional elements, such as padding, compiler metadata, or statically linked libraries, which do not reflect attacker-specific behavior. To enable clustering based on finer-grained functional labels, it is necessary to restrict the information used in distance computation to the features that actually represent malware functionality and to eliminate redundant or irrelevant data. In functional analysis, feature selection is an important issue not only for clustering but also for malware analysis in general.

In this study, we explore the following two central research questions:

1. **Is functional differentiation among malware samples primarily encoded in the attacker-written user code?**
2. **Can the removal of unnecessary information–such as data sections and operand values–improve clustering accuracy based on functional similarity?**

Here, "user code" refers to code written by the attacker, excluding statically linked library functions. This study aims not only to improve clustering accuracy but also to investigate what kind of information is useful for functional analysis of IoT malware—specifically, whether it is the user code.

To investigate how the inclusion or exclusion of user code, library functions, data sections, and operand information affects clustering accuracy with respect to functional labels, we constructed six variants of file datasets from a single IoT malware dataset by selectively combining these elements. We then applied the phylogenetic tree clustering algorithm proposed by He *et al.* [6] to each dataset and conducted experiments to evaluate and compare their accuracy using two functional label sets: disabling information [11] and exploit information. "Disabling information" refers to information for disabling IoT malware (for example, commands that terminate malware execution). In our experiments, we used 175 distinct disabling information labels extracted from a dataset of 4,801 IoT malware samples to conduct the evaluation. "Exploit information" denotes the specific vulnerabilities that each sample was used to exploit. In our evaluation, we used 35 exploit labels assigned to a dataset of 816 IoT malware samples [12].

We used Homogeneity [14] as the evaluation metric. Homogeneity measures the extent to which data within each cluster share the same label, and a value closer to 1 indicates a purer clustering result. As a result, for disabling information, as hypothesized, using only user code achieved an improvement of 0.1 in the Homogeneity score, demonstrating a strong association between disabling information and user code. On the other hand, for exploit information, we observed that accuracy also improved when using only library functions, suggesting a relationship between exploits and library functions. These findings indicate that the information to be extracted or eliminated depends on the functional labels under analysis. The removal of irrelevant information consistently contributes to improved clustering accuracy and is considered beneficial for malware analysis in general.

Based on these findings, the key contributions of this work are summarized as follows:

- We improved scalable IoT malware clustering accuracy by defining distances that focus on the relationship between code regions and functional information.
- We demonstrate that removing compiler-dependent noise–such as operand values and data sections–significantly improves clustering accuracy when using NCD-based distance metrics.
- We quantitatively demonstrated that not only the code regions primarily written by attackers but also the library regions preserve equivalent vulnerability-related information.

2 Prior Work

Here, we review some prior works.

2.1 Analysis Using Phylogenetic Tree

Phylogenetic trees have been widely used in malware analysis. The features employed to construct phylogenetic trees can be broadly categorized into static features and dynamic features. Static features are those that can be extracted without executing the malware, such as binary byte sequences, opcode sequences, and function-call sequences. In contrast, dynamic features consist of behavioral data obtained by running the malware in a sandbox environment. While dynamic features generally provide more accurate insight into malware functionality and behavior, they suffer from the drawback of being time-consuming to collect at scale.

Karim *et al.* proposed a method to define distances between malware using n-perms as a static feature [8]. Furthermore, they demonstrated that the phylogenetic tree constructed based on this method is effective for family identification and the discovery of new variants. Biley *et al.* calculated NCD using log data–a dynamic feature–to define the distances between all pairs of samples [3]. They then constructed a phylogenetic tree and proposed an automated tree-based clustering method. However, both of these approaches require computing distances for every sample pair.

Considering the massive production of IoT malware, Cozzi *et al.* [5] and He *et al.* [6] proposed scalable phylogenetic representations.

Cozzi *et al.* used Hierarchical Navigable Small World (HNSW) graphs to perform scalable phylogenetic inference on IoT malware, utilizing over 36,000 samples [5]. They used both dynamic and static features in their analysis.

The method of He *et al.* [6] is an algorithm that accelerates phylogenetic tree construction by approximating the Neighbor-Joining [15] method–a standard approach for tree building–through reduction of the required distance-matrix elements. It employs only static features for tree construction and is highly optimized for scalability.

Considering the rapid diversification and massive proliferation of IoT malware, there is a growing need for scalable yet functionally precise phylogenetic clustering. Our study addresses this challenge directly. We recognize that the method proposed by He et al. [6] is, to the best of our knowledge, the only algorithm relying solely on static analysis and specialized for scalability. However, their work demonstrated clustering accuracy only at the family level. In this study, we extend this scalable framework to functional-level analysis by selectively extracting code regions that better reflect functional behavior, thereby improving clustering accuracy while maintaining scalability.

2.2 Baseline Method

In this section, we introduce the phylogenetic tree clustering algorithm by He *et al.* [6]. This algorithm constructs a phylogenetic tree from a dataset of malware samples by using their binary files, then forms clusters by partitioning the tree based on an information criterion. Broadly, the algorithm can be divided into three steps: defining pairwise distances, constructing the phylogenetic tree, and performing clustering.

Defining Pairwise Distances. We define the distance between two malware samples using the Normalized Compression Distance (NCD) [4]. NCD is a distance metric based on the compressed lengths of data, taking a value between 0 and 1. The formula is shown below.

$$\mathrm{NCD}(x_i, x_j) = \frac{C(x_i x_j) - \min\{C(x_i), C(x_j)\}}{\max\{C(x_i), C(x_j)\}} \tag{1}$$

Here, $x_i x_j$ denotes the concatenation of the two data items x_i and x_j. $C(x_i)$ represents the compressed length of data x_i. Due to the property of compression algorithms, the more similar x_i and x_j are, the closer $C(x_i x_j)$ becomes to $C(x_i)$ or $C(x_j)$, causing the NCD to approach 0. A distance matrix is defined as the matrix whose (i, j) element is the distance representing the dissimilarity between two data elements x_i and x_j in a dataset $\{x_1, x_2, \ldots, x_N\}$.He *et al.* [6] computed the NCD using the binary data of malware samples and constructed the distance matrix for the sample dataset. They used the LempelâĂŞZivâĂŞMarkov chain algorithm (LZMA) [16] as the compression algorithm.

Constructing the Phylogenetic Tree. Here, we introduce the fast algorithm for constructing a phylogenetic tree [6], [19]. This algorithm is an improvement on the Neighbor-Joining method [15], a standard method to build phylogenetic trees. By partitioning the dataset appropriately, it approximates the Neighbor-Joining tree more efficiently. The Fig. 1 is the outline of the algorithm.

First, randomly select a small number of samples from the dataset as a seed set (1), and construct a phylogenetic tree for the seed set using the Neighbor-Joining method (2). Next, assign each of the remaining samples to the seed sample to which it has the smallest distance (3). For each resulting group containing a seed and its assigned samples, if the number of samples exceeds a threshold, repeat the process starting from selecting a new seed set within that group (4); if the number of samples is below the threshold, construct a phylogenetic tree for that group using the Neighbor-Joining method (5). When there are N samples, the Neighbor-Joining method requires $O(N^2)$ cost to compute the full distance matrix, but the fast approximation that references only a portion of the distance matrix can build the tree in $O(NlogN)$ time [6].

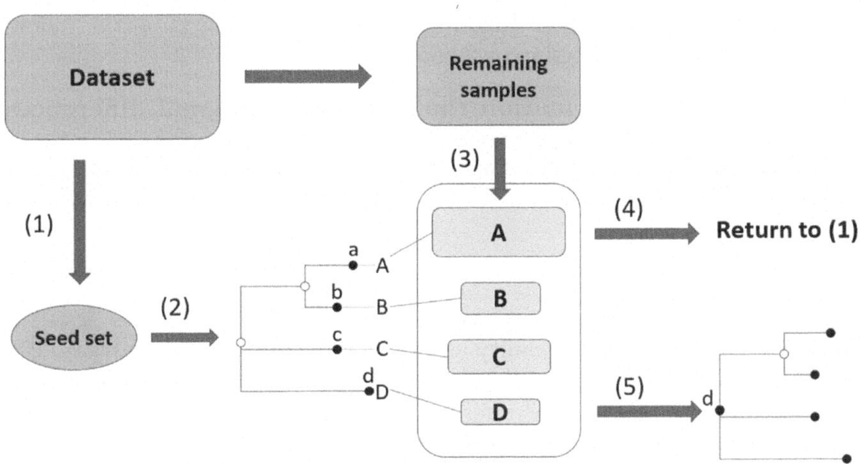

Fig. 1. The flow chart of the fast algorithm for constructing a phylogenetic tree.

Clustering. Clustering is performed using the Minimum Description Length (MDL) principle [13], [6]. MDL is a model selection principle that considers the best model to be the one minimizing the sum of (i) the description length of the data given the model and (ii) the description length of the model itself. For a cluster C, the description length is calculated as follows [6].

$$\mathrm{DL}(C) = -\log L(x^n|\hat{\theta}) + \frac{m_j}{2}\log n \tag{2}$$

$$= \frac{n}{2}\log\Big(\frac{1}{n}\sum_{i=1}^{n}|x_i - \bar{x}|^2\Big) + \frac{m_j}{2}\log n + \frac{n}{2}(\log 2\pi + 1) \tag{3}$$

x_i denotes each data point and $\bar{x}$ denotes the mean of the data. In Eq. 2, by assuming that the distances from the data points to the mean follow a normal distribution, it can be transformed into Eq. 3. The parameter m_j is a hyperparameter that adjusts the influence of model complexity, and this parameter ultimately controls the number of clusters produced.

Each internal node of the constructed phylogenetic tree is connected to three other nodes, and by removing a single internal node, the tree can be divided into three subtrees. We compare the cluster description length before and after the split; if the description length after the split is shorter, we execute the split, and if not, we reject it, considering the pre-split cluster to be better. This procedure is applied recursively to determine the final clusters.

3 Objectives

The main objective of this study is to define distances that more accurately capture functional differences between samples using NCD and to improve clustering accuracy with respect to functional information. Based on the following two hypotheses, we conducted experiments.

- **Hypothesis (1): Information that reflects functional differences is contained within the user code.**
- **Hypothesis (2):Removal of unnecessary information, such as data sections and operand values, can improve clustering accuracyïijÕ**

3.1 Role of User Code

In this study, we define functionality as the runtime behavior of malware. Under this definition, sections of a binary file that contain code are considered to represent functionality. "User code" refers to the code sections that exclude library functions. In IoT malware, the toolchain used is generally determined by the malware family [1], and since libraries are part of a toolchain, library functions carry family-specific information. Conversely, more fine-grained functional information and differences in sample behavior can be considered to reside in the user code.

3.2 Effect of Removing Redundant Information

NCD is an intuitive distance metric based on the property of compression that the more common patterns two pieces of data share, the more their concatenation can be compressed; this makes it easy to understand the relationship between the data used for distance definition and the resulting clustering. Redundant information in inter-sample distances can degrade clustering accuracy, whereas using only functionality-related information in the distance definition may enable clustering to capture finer-grained functional differences. In a binary file, information such as data sections, headers, and operands is considered unnecessary for functionality-based clustering using NCD. The reasons for this are explained below.

- Data sections and headers

  Functionality is represented in code sections, and the data sections, areas that store variables, are not considered to pertain to malware functionality. Similarly, headers do not directly convey behavioral information and are, therefore, considered unnecessary.

- Operands

  There are two types of memory and register allocation for each instruction in a program: static allocation, determined at compile time, and dynamic allocation, determined at run time. Since IoT devices are often resource-constrained and IoT malware is typically simple and lightweight, dynamic memory management is generally unnecessary, and memory and registers are essentially assigned via static allocation. Operands that represent these memory or register assignments are decided by the compiler through optimizations; as a result, even samples with similar functionality may have significantly different operand values, so operands are not considered to directly represent functionality.

4 Proposed Method

In this section, we describe the proposed and comparative methods of this study. The schematic overview is shown in Fig. 2.

4.1 IoT Malware Targeted for Analysis

Most IoT malware is distributed in Executable and Linkable Format (ELF), which runs on Linux environments; thus, this study targets ELF-formatted IoT malware. Since our objective is to investigate how the user code section contributes to clustering accuracy, it is necessary to isolate the user code from the program. We accomplish this through disassembly; therefore, we assume that all analyzed samples are disassemblable and restrict our analysis to samples that have not been obfuscated via packing or have already been unpacked. However, according to [10], most packed IoT malware is compressed using the standard

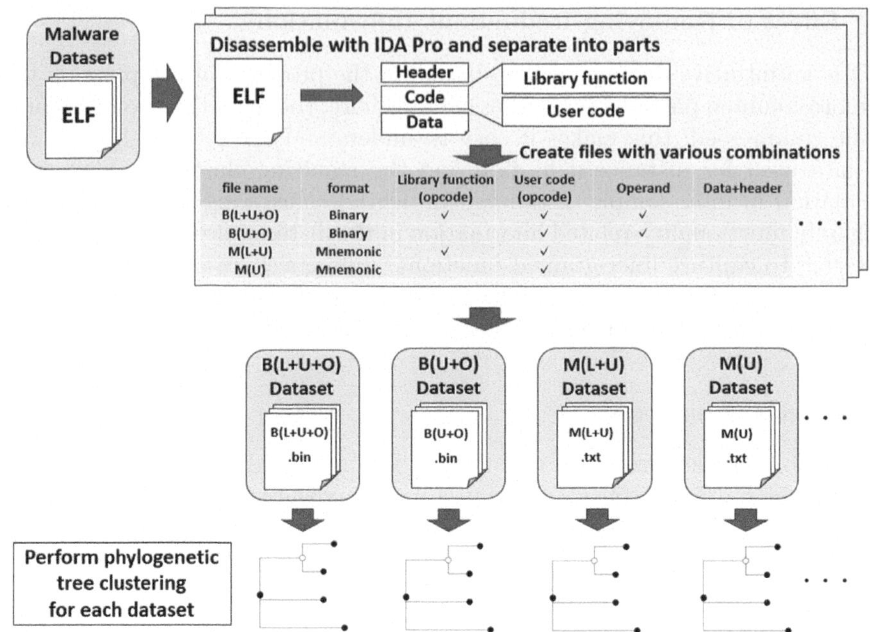

Fig. 2. The schematic overview of the proposed method.

UPX (Ultimate Packer for eXecutables), and the majority of samples can be unpacked with a UPX unpacker, either directly or after correcting the magic number. Based on this observation, we believe that our approach can be applied to a large portion of IoT malware.

4.2 User Code Extraction

First, for each executable file in the IoT malware dataset, we disassemble using IDA Pro and identify statically linked library functions using IDA F.L.I.R.T. [7]. Next, we separate the code section into library functions and user code. Specifically, we scan each block (called a segment) that contains code and data, from beginning to end, and determine whether each function in the code section is a library function. Any function determined not to be a library function is treated as user code.

1. Code that is not a function
2. Functions that are not library functions

4.3 Operand Removal

To verify the hypothesis that operands do not directly represent functionality, we remove operands from each instruction and extract only the opcodes. However, because the encoding of machine instructions varies significantly across different instruction set architectures (ISAs), retrieving opcodes in binary form is not straightforward when handling raw machine code. In addition, disassemblers such as IDA Pro do not support extracting opcodes directly in binary form. Therefore, in this study, we extract opcodes as mnemonics and collect opcode sequences as plain text, thereby removing operands. IDA's print_insn_mnem function takes an instruction address as input and returns the opcode in mnemonic form. By using this function to obtain the opcode for each instruction and writing the resulting opcode sequences to a text file, we represent the code with operands removed.

4.4 Construction of Extracted Datasets

For the four components **(L):** Library function, **(U):** User function, **(O):** Operand, and **(D):** Data + Header, we create files containing any desired combination of information by selectively combining the corresponding parts.

We explain this using the table in Fig. 2. For example, a file named B(L + U + O) is in binary format and, from the original executable, contains the opcodes and operand portions for both library functions and user code. Similarly, a file named B(U+O) retains, from the original executable, only the opcodes and operands of the user code. In this way, each file's name is determined by its format (e.g. B for binary) together with the initial letters of the four possible components it contains. When we say a file "contains operand portions," this refers only to the operands corresponding to the included opcodes; for instance, B(U+O) retains operands for the user code but does not retain operands for library functions. Furthermore, these files are not created by simply concatenating each component: the order of each code segment or function follows the same sequence as in the original executable, from the beginning of the file onward. In this study, because we investigate how code-related information contributes to clustering accuracy, all non-code sections, such as data sections and headers, are treated as a single component based on our hypotheses.

For files with operands removed, as mentioned above, opcodes are represented as mnemonic text data. For example, M(L+U) is a text file in which the opcode sequences of library functions and user code are recorded.

For each sample in the dataset, we similarly create files with various combinations of components. We then collect files of the same type that retain identical components to form datasets. The seven datasets used in this study are shown in Table 1. B(L+U+O+D) retains all components; in other words, it represents the original dataset before extraction.

4.5 Comparison of Clustering Accuracy

For each dataset, we perform phylogenetic tree clustering. We use the method of He *et al.* [6] introduced in Chapter 2 and evaluate the clustering accuracy using functional labels. By comparing the accuracy across datasets, we investigate how the presence or absence of information, such as user code, affects clustering in terms of functionality.

Table 1. The seven types of datasets. For the four components **(L):** Library function, **(U):** User function, **(O):** Operand, and **(D):** Data + Header.

dataset	format	Library function	User code	Operand	Data + header
B(L+U+O+D)	Binary	✓	✓	✓	✓
B(L+U+O)	Binary	✓	✓	✓	
B(L+O)	Binary	✓		✓	
B(U+O)	Binary		✓	✓	
M(L+U)	Mnemonic	✓	✓		
M(L)	Mnemonic	✓			
M(U)	Mnemonic		✓		


```
"dupcmd": "DUP",
"init": "¥u001b[0;32m[CONNECTED] [%s] [%s]",
"prefix": 33,
"termcmd": "LOLNOGTFO"
```


Fig. 3. Examples of disabling information labels for a Bashlite sample (from top: termination command when malware is already running, initial communication payload, command prefix, kill command).

5 Experiments

This section aims to empirically verify the two hypotheses introduced in Section 3 by measuring clustering performance under varying data inclusion conditions.


```
"capture_date":"2020/06/03"
"port":"37215"
"vulnerability:"CVE-2017-17215"
"vulnerability_type":"Remote Code Execution (RCE)"
"device":"Huawei home routers HG532"
```


Fig. 4. Examples of exploit information labels for a Mirai sample (from top: sample collection date, port number, vulnerability identifier, type of vulnerability, target device)

5.1 Evaluation Metrics

We use Homogeneity [14] as the evaluation metric for the accuracy of clustering. In Eq. 4, C denotes the set of classes and K denotes the set of clusters. Homogeneity is computed from the distributions of the known classes and the clustering results, and it measures the extent to which each cluster consists of data points from a single class. Homogeneity ranges from 0 to 1, and values closer to 1 indicate that the clustering result accurately reflects the class structure, which indicates high precision.

$$\text{Homogeneity} = \frac{I(C;K)}{H(C)} = 1 - \frac{H(C|K)}{H(C)} \tag{4}$$

5.2 Evaluation Using Disabling Information

"Disabling information" [11] includes details about an IoT malware's initial communication and its kill commands [11]. During the early execution phase, IoT malware establishes communication with a Command and Control server (C&C server). The term "initial communication" refers to the payload that is sent first to the server at this stage. Some IoT malware also have functionality that allows them to stop their own execution upon receiving instructions from the attacker. A "kill command" [11] is used to terminate the execution. Because information on initial communication and kill commands can be used to neutralize IoT malware, these elements are consolidated as disabling information labels for each sample. Figure 3 shows the disabling information extracted from a Bashlite sample.

Dataset. In this experiment, we used 4,801 IoT malware samples–out of a total of 5,771 samples collected between June 2021 and March 2022 by IoTPOT [12] and X-POT [9]—-for which disabling information was successfully extracted. All samples were compiled for ARM or MIPS instruction set architectures. Table 2 shows the breakdown of the dataset by family and architecture. The families were determined by AVClass [17] based on the detection results from various antivirus vendors on VirusTotal. From these 4,801 samples, we identified 175 different disabling information labels. The relationship between samples and disabling information labels is many-to-one, meaning that the same disabling information label can be extracted from multiple samples. In the separation of library functions, libraries were completely identified in 41.8% of the samples in the dataset.

Results (Binary). We compare the results of the four datasets in Table 1 whose format is binary. Figure 5 shows the file size distributions for these four datasets, excluding files with extremely large sizes. Although B(L+O) does not contain any files of exactly 0 bytes, many files are very close to 0 bytes. These were generated from samples in which library functions were dynamically linked or from samples in which IDA F.L.I.R.T. failed to correctly identify the libraries.

Table 2. Breakdown of the dataset by family and architecture

	ARM	MIPS	total
Mirai	1406	657	2063
Bashlite	351	153	504
Miori	2	2	4
unknown	1588	642	2230
total	3347	1454	4801

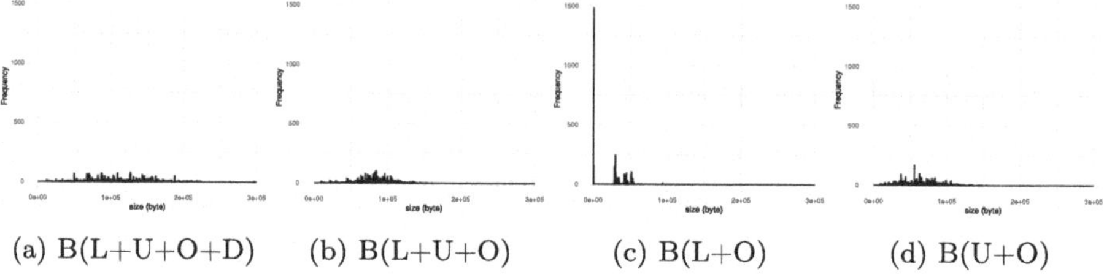

(a) B(L+U+O+D) (b) B(L+U+O) (c) B(L+O) (d) B(U+O)

Fig. 5. Size distribution of the 4,801 samples.

The clustering results are shown in Fig. 6a. In the figure, the horizontal axis represents the number of clusters and the vertical axis represents the Homogeneity score. Using B(L+U+O)–which contains both library functions and user code–as the baseline, the dataset from which user code has been removed (B(L+O)) shows a decreased score, while the dataset from which library functions have been removed (B(U+O)) shows an increased score. Additionally, B(L+U+O+D), which clusters the original executable files without any extraction, achieves nearly the same score as B(L+O), which contains only library-function code.

Results (Mnemonic). Next, we compare the three mnemonic format datasets from Table 1, using B(L+U+O+D) as a reference. The results are shown in Fig. 6b. Here, we take M(L+U)–which contains opcodes for both library functions and user code–as the baseline. In M(L), where user code information has been removed, the Homogeneity score drops significantly. In contrast, in M(U), where the library function information has been removed, the accuracy slightly increases across a wide range of cluster counts.

Discussion: Disabling Information. In both the binary and mnemonic formats, relative to B(L+U+O) and M(L+U) as baselines, removing library functions led to improved accuracy, while removing user code caused accuracy to decrease. This contrasting outcome indicates that disabling information can only be distinguished in detail by the user code of each sample. From this we can

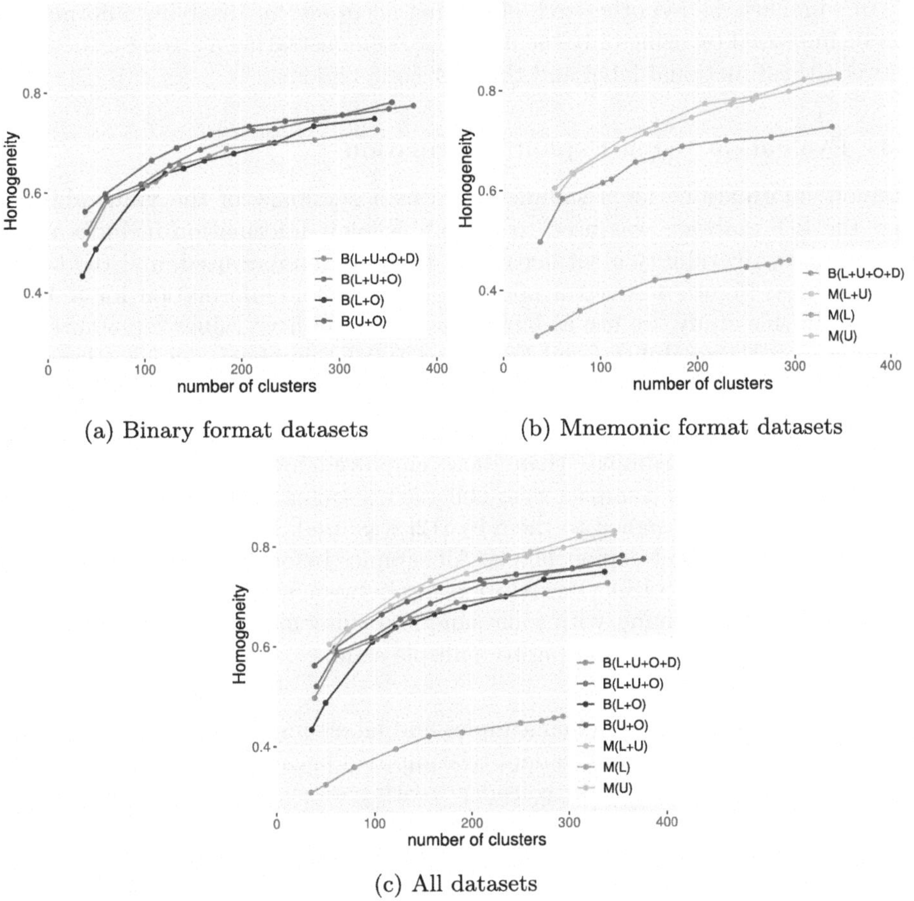

(a) Binary format datasets

(b) Mnemonic format datasets

(c) All datasets

Fig. 6. Evaluation using disabling information.

conclude that hypothesis (1) holds true for disabling information. Furthermore, M(L) shows a significant decrease in accuracy; as mentioned earlier, library functions capture family-specific characteristics, so relying solely on library function opcode sequences causes much of the inter-sample variation to be lost.

The results for all seven datasets, plotted together in a single graph, are shown in Fig. 6c. Although a direct comparison between binary and mnemonic formats is not straightforward due to the difference in file formats, the dataset that achieved the greatest improvement in Homogeneity was M(U), which removes library functions, operands, and other non-functional information. Thus, because the highest accuracy was obtained using only the user code opcode sequences, we can also conclude that hypothesis (2) holds true for disabling information.

In summary, as hypothesized, clustering accuracy for disabling information can be improved by using only the user code, demonstrating a strong association between this functional label and the user code regions.

5.3 Evaluation Using Exploit Information

"Exploit information" for a sample refers to a summary of the vulnerabilities that the IoT malware was used to exploit. Exploit information includes items such as the vulnerability identifier name, the port number used, and the target device name. Figure 4 shows a portion of the exploit information for a Mirai sample. In this study, we use as labels the "vulnerability" values represented by the Common Vulnerabilities and Exposures (CVE) numbers, among others.

Dataset. In this experiment, due to label constraints, we used a different set of 816 IoT malware samples than those employed for the disabling information evaluation. These samples were collected between 2020 and 2021, and the exploit information assigned to them by [12] was used. From these 816 samples, we observed 35 distinct exploit labels. All samples belonged to the Mirai family and targeted the MIPS ISA. The relationship between samples and exploit information was many-to-many, with some samples having multiple exploit labels and some exploit labels corresponding to multiple samples.

Average Homogeneity. When samples and labels have a many-to-many relationship, simple Homogeneity cannot be computed because some samples belong to multiple classes. One might consider treating every possible combination of labels as a distinct class, but if there are N label types, the number of such classes can be as large as $2^N - 1$, which would exceed any reasonable number of clusters. Therefore, we compute Homogeneity in a binary fashion for each label that is, for each label, we treat "belongs to this label" versus "does not belong to this label" as two classes and evaluate how well the clustering results capture that label. We then average the N individual Homogeneity scores to obtain the "Average Homogeneity," which we use as the overall measure of clustering accuracy.

Results (Binary). First, as with the disabling information experiment, we compare the clustering results for the four binary format datasets in Table 1. The results are shown in Fig. 7a. In this figure, the horizontal axis represents the number of clusters, and the vertical axis represents the evaluation metric, Average Homogeneity. B(L+U+O) as the baseline, we observe improved accuracy for both B(L+O) (library functions only) and B(U+O) (user code only). In particular, around a cluster count of 100, B(U+O) scores higher in the lower cluster count range, whereas in the higher cluster count range (above approximately 100), the phylogenetic tree built from library functions only (B(L+O)) yields a better score. Additionally, both B(L+O) and B(U+O) achieve higher accuracy than B(L+U+O+D).

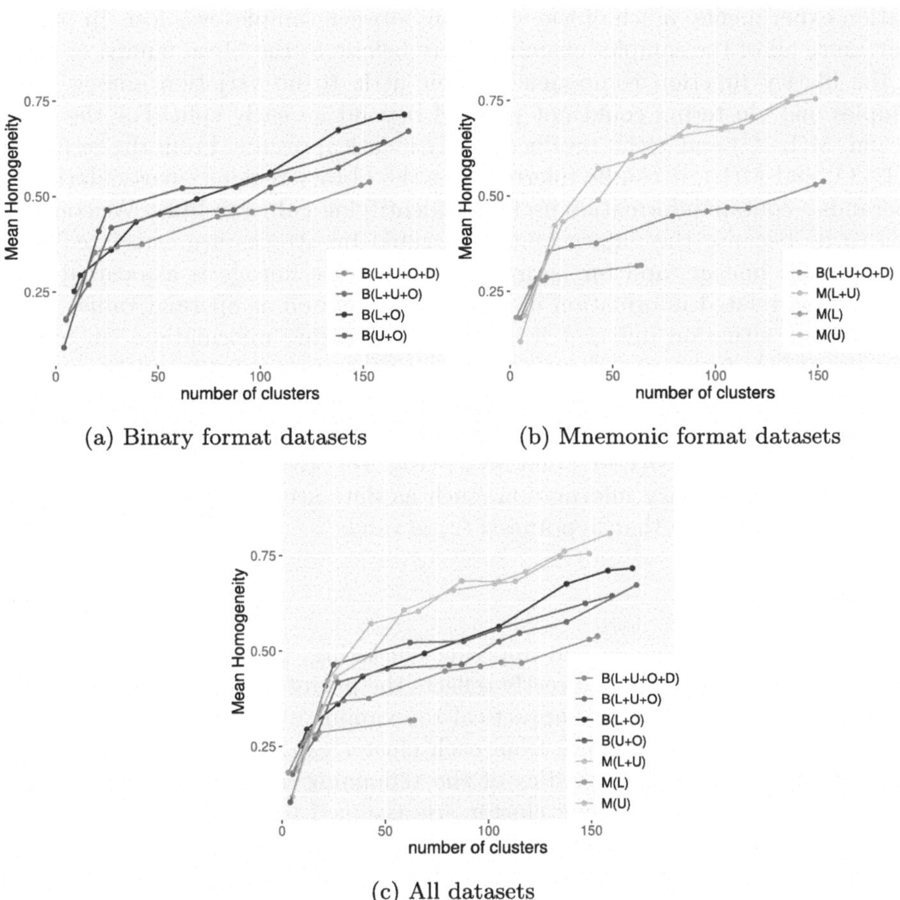

(a) Binary format datasets

(b) Mnemonic format datasets

(c) All datasets

Fig. 7. Evaluation using exploit information.

Results (Mnemonic). Next, we compare the three mnemonic format datasets from Table 1, together with B(L+U+O+D). The results are shown in Fig. 7b. M(L+U) and M(U) achieve similar scores, while M(L) performs markedly worse. In fact, M(L) stops splitting clusters early, resulting in a maximum of only 63 clusters.

Discussion: Exploit Information. Across both the binary and mnemonic formats, removing the library function component from B(L+U+O) and M(L+U) yielded higher Homogeneity. However, when user code was removed in the binary format, accuracy also increased–an outcome that contradicts hypothesis (1), which assumes that functional information resides solely in user code. In contrast, in the mnemonic format, comparing M(L+U) to M(L) shows a substantial drop in Homogeneity for M(L). This is likely because, as in the disabling information experiments, much of the variation between samples was lost. In particular, since all of the samples examined here belong to the Mirai family, opcodes of the library function component exhibit little to no variation among these samples and clustering could not proceed beyond an early split. For the same reason, M(L+U) and M(U) produce nearly identical results. From the results of B(L+O) and M(L), it can be inferred that the library regions—particularly the operands—contain information useful for identifying vulnerabilities. We consider this to be because the vulnerabilities targeted by attacks are correlated with the malware lineage, and furthermore, the malware lineage is associated with compilation-related information in the libraries as well as operand values. This represents a situation different from that of disabling information, suggesting that the library function regions also play an important role in exploit analysis. It is noteworthy that overall clustering accuracy improved despite the presence of samples in which library function separation was incomplete. The highest accuracy was achieved by M(L+U) and M(U) (Fig. 7c); given the observed improvement when unnecessary information, such as data sections and operands, was removed, we conclude that hypothesis (2) is valid.

5.4 Discussion

By extracting code regions and applying clustering, we achieved an improvement in Homogeneity, which directly reflects the purity of clusters. In large-scale malware analysis, it is often impractical to examine every sample individually. Instead, representative samples from each cluster can be analyzed in detail to infer the functional characteristics of the remaining samples. In this context, samples belonging to the same cluster are assumed to share similar functionality; therefore, higher cluster purity is desirable. Consequently, the observed improvement in Homogeneity provides a practical advantage by enabling more efficient and reliable functional inference across large IoT malware datasets. However, this approach also has several limitations. Since the NCD-based method directly utilizes the structure of the data, it may not perform well when applied to malware samples that contain a large amount of noise or are heavily obfuscated. Furthermore, the functional labels used in this study represent only one aspect of IoT malware behavior. Additional validation is required to determine whether the proposed approach can be effectively applied to other types of labels or behavioral characteristics.

5.5 NCD Using Different Compression Algorithms

In this study, as in the previous work, we employed LZMA as the compression algorithm because LZMA has been shown to perform pattern matching most efficiently on binary data [6]. Although using text data composed of mnemonics yielded a higher clustering accuracy than the prior work, other compression algorithms can also be applied when compressing text. Therefore, using the M(U) dataset, we performed clustering with the standard Linux utilities bzip2, gzip, and Compress (LZ78). We also varied various parameters (e.g., compression level, dictionary size) for these compressors, but could not obtain clustering results superior to those achieved with LZMA. When evaluated against disabling information, none of these compressors—regardless of parameter settings—surpassed the clustering accuracy achieved with LZMA; thus, as with binary data, LZMA proved to be optimal for NCD on text data as well.

6 Conclusion

In this study, we investigated how clustering accuracy changes through feature selection for the functional analysis of IoT malware. Its effectiveness was evaluated using two types of functional labels: disabling information and exploit information. As a result, for disabling information, we found that using only user code improved clustering accuracy. We also confirm that removing non-functional elements such as operand values and data sections improves NCD-based clustering, validating both of our hypotheses in this context. On the other hand, for exploit information, accuracy improved not only when using user code alone but also when using library functions alone, suggesting that library-related features may likewise play an important role. In other words, contrary to the hypothesis (1) that only user code is effective for analysis, we found that there exists functional information for which the use of library functions also improves classification accuracy. A possible explanation for why library functions contribute to exploit-related clustering is that information contained in the library regions—such as string data, address information, or compiler versions—may correlate with malware lineage and the vulnerabilities exploited in attacks. Thus, for labels directly related to malware lineage or attack campaigns, it can be generalized that the library function regions also contain useful information for functional identification.; however, verifying this remains a challenge for future work.

Acknowledgment. This work was supported by JSPS KAKENHI Grant Number JP23H05492 and the "MITIGATE" project under the "Research and Development for Expansion of Radio Wave Resources (JPJ000254)," funded by the MIC, Japan. The authors are grateful to Professor Katsunari Yoshioka (Yokohama National University) for providing the dataset used in this study.

References

1. Akabane, S., Okamoto, T.: Identification of library functions statically linked to stripped IOT malware. Computer Security Symposium (2020). (In Japanese)
2. Antonakakis, M., et al.: Understanding the mirai botnet. In: 26th USENIX Security Symposium (USENIX Security 17), pp. 1093–1110. USENIX Association (2017)
3. Bailey, M., Oberheide, J., Andersen, J., Mao, Z.M., Jahanian, F., Nazario, J.: Automated classification and analysis of internet malware. In: Recent Advances in Intrusion Detection, pp. 178–197. Springer, Berlin Heidelberg, Berlin, Heidelberg (2007)

4. Cebrian, M., Alfonseca, M., Ortega, A.: The normalized compression distance is resistant to noise. IEEE Trans. Inf. Theory **53**(5), 1895–1900 (2007)
5. Cozzi, E., Vervier, P.A., Dell'Amico, M., Shen, Y., Bilge, L., Balzarotti, D.: The tangled genealogy of IOT malware. In: Proceedings of the 36th Annual Computer Security Applications Conference, pp. 1–16. ACSAC '20, Association for Computing Machinery (2020)
6. He, T., et al.: Scalable and fast algorithm for constructing phylogenetic trees with application to IOT malware clustering. IEEE Access **11**, 8240–8253 (2023)
7. Hex-Rays: Ida f.l.i.r.t. technology: in-depth. https://www.hex-rays.com/products/ida/tech/flirt/in_depth/.
8. Karim, M., Walenstein, A., Lakhotia, A., Parida, L.: Malware phylogeny generation using permutations of code. J. Comput. Virology **1**, 13–23 (11 2005)
9. Kato, S., Tanabe, R., Yoshioka, K., Matsumoto, T.: Adaptive observation of emerging cyber attacks targeting various IOT devices. In: IFIP/IEEE International Symposium on Integrated Network Management (2021)
10. Lee, H., Kim, S., Baek, D., Kim, D., Hwang, D.: Robust iot malware detection and classification using opcode category features on machine learning. IEEE Access **11**, 18855–18867 (2023)
11. Misu, T., Iwamoto, K., Takada, K., Yoshioka, K.: IOT malware static analysis for automated extraction of disabling information. Symposium on Cryptography and Information Security (2021).
12. Pa, Y., Suzuki, S., Yoshioka, K., Matsumoto, T., Kasama, T., Rossow, C.: Iotpot: a novel honeypot for revealing current IOT threats, Journal of Information Processing (2016)
13. Rissanen, J.: Modeling by shortest data description. Automatica (1978)
14. Rosenberg, A., Hirschberg, J.: V-measure: a conditional entropy-based external cluster evaluation measure. In: Proceedings of the 2007 Joint Conference on Empirical Methods in Natural Language Processing and Computational Natural Language Learning, pp. 410–420 (01 2007)
15. Saitou, N., Nei, M.: The neighbor-joining method: a new method for reconstructing phylogenetic trees. Molecular Bio. Evol. **4**(4), 406–425 (07 1987)
16. Salomon, D.: Data Compression: the complete reference fourth edition. Springer (2007)
17. Sebastián, M., et al.: Avclass: a tool for massive malware labeling. In: Research in Attacks, Intrusions, and Defenses, pp. 230–253. Springer International Publishing (2016)
18. threat post: bashlite family of malware infects 1 million IOT devices. https://threatpost.com/bashlite-family-of-malware-infects-1-million-iot-devices/120230/
19. Yone, T.: Phylogenetic tree estimation for large-scale malware datasets. Master's thesis, Kyushu University (2016)

PathFault: Automated Exploit Generator for Web Services via HTTP Message Parser Discrepancies

Juryeok Kim and Youngjoo Shin(✉)

School of Cybersecurity, Korea University, Seoul 02841, Republic of Korea
{ryan9423,syoungjoo}@korea.ac.kr

Abstract. Modern web services utilize complex architectures involving diverse HTTP processing components. These components include CDNs, WAFs, proxies, and web servers (e.g., Nginx, Apache, Cloudflare, and GCP). Independent parsing rules across these components lead to discrepancies in interpreting identical HTTP requests, including the URI. This phenomenon, known as Path Confusion, leads to critical security vulnerabilities, such as authentication bypass and sensitive data exposure. However, existing penetration testing methods fail to identify these vulnerabilities adequately. This limitation stems from limited system-wide visibility and operational risks in live environments. To address these challenges, we present PathFault, an automated methodology leveraging a Predicate Logic-based Surrogate Model. This model systematically abstracts component-specific parsing behaviors, enabling precise vulnerability analysis with minimal invasive testing. Furthermore, PathFault incorporates SMT solving techniques to automatically generate targeted exploit payloads. It combines security researchers' domain expertise with web service-specific parsing logic. Consequently, our approach significantly improves detection accuracy. It comprehensively assesses dynamic system interactions and addresses limitations of traditional root-cause analysis. Evaluation demonstrates PathFault's efficacy in identifying previously overlooked Path Confusion vulnerabilities.

Keywords: Web Security · Automated Exploit Generation · Path Confusion Vulnerability · HTTP Parser Discrepancy

1 Introduction

Modern web services, such as content delivery networks (CDNs), web application firewalls (WAFs), and proxies, increasingly rely on complex architectures that consist of multiple HTTP processing components [7,27]. Each web

The extended version of this paper is available at https://github.com/koreacsl/PathFault.

H. Seo (Ed.): ICISC 2025, LNCS 16487, pp. 103–124, 2026.
https://doi.org/10.1007/978-981-95-8034-7_6

service component independently implements parsing rules for HTTP messages [5,26,29,34]. This independence can lead to discrepancies in the interpretation of identical HTTP requests, including URI [1,13,14,35]. Such discrepancies in parsing, known as *Path Confusion*, create significant security vulnerabilities [11,17,18,20,21]. Specifically, path confusion vulnerabilities pose serious security threats such as authentication bypass [15,24] and unauthorized disclosure of secret data [11,18]. For example, the CVE-2025-0108 vulnerability shows how different HTTP message parsing allows attackers to bypass authentication mechanisms [15]. Web cache deception (WCD) attacks similarly exploit these discrepancies, exposing sensitive information through incorrect caching behavior [11,17,18,20,21]. These real-world examples underscore the considerable need to address path confusion vulnerabilities.

However, identifying and mitigating path confusion vulnerabilities pose significant challenges. First, authentication and caching in web services depend on service-specific URI patterns and the attributes that trigger them. But legacy penetration testing and vulnerability detection tools [17,18] are unable to integrate such dynamic URIs and the security researcher's domain knowledge. That is, these tools cannot adapt to the unique characteristics of each service. Consequently, since they fail to capture how these mechanisms are triggered and influenced by component-level configurations, the scope and precision of vulnerability detection are restricted [2,37]. Furthermore, conducting penetration testing in live production environments poses considerable risks [25,30]. These risks include potential exposure of user data and operational instability, which severely restricts the scope and depth of testing [12,17].

To overcome these limitations, this work proposes *PathFault*, an automated approach to systematically detect path confusion vulnerabilities across complex web services. PathFault introduces a Predicate Logic-based Surrogate Model. This model abstracts the HTTP parsing rules employed by each web component. Such abstraction enables precise system-level vulnerability analysis without extensive direct testing on live systems. Furthermore, leveraging the expressive power of SMT (Satisfiability Modulo Theories) [10] solving techniques, PathFault automatically generates targeted exploit payloads. It integrates domain knowledge from security researchers with the service-specific parsing behaviors.

Our surrogate model facilitates comprehensive identification and precise analysis of the root causes underlying path confusion vulnerabilities. It significantly reduces reliance on invasive testing methods. Simultaneously, the SMT-based Exploit Payload Generator substantially enhances detection accuracy and scope. It systematically addresses dynamic aspects such as caching policies and proxy configurations, typically overlooked by conventional methods.

In summary, PathFault addresses critical gaps in current vulnerability detection practices through the following key contributions:

- This work enables precise white-box analysis of HTTP parsing behaviors in complex web systems by developing a predicate logic-based surrogate model.

- It broadens the scope and precision of vulnerability detection by designing an SMT-solving-based exploit payload generator that integrates a security researcher's domain knowledge with component-specific parsing logic.
- It overcomes limitations in traditional root cause analysis of path confusion vulnerabilities through a systematic methodology that models and evaluates system-level component interactions.

The source code for PathFault is publicly available at https://github.com/koreacsl/PathFault.

2 Background

2.1 HTTP Message's URI

A Uniform Resource Identifier (URI) is a standardized method used to identify resources and facilitate their access on the web. RFC 3986 [6] defines a URI as consisting of several distinct components, including scheme, authority, path, query, and fragment. The scheme component specifies the protocol used for retrieving the resource, such as HTTP or HTTPS. The authority typically includes the host and port, defining the location of the server hosting the resource.

The path, query, and fragment components can be demonstrated using an example URI: `https://example.com/products/electronics/laptop?item=123&sort=price#details`

In this example, the path component `"/products/electronics/laptop"` represents the hierarchical structure of the resource on the server. It consists of segments separated by slashes (`"/"`), with each segment typically corresponding to a directory or a specific resource. The query component is utilized for the resource retrieval with prefixed `"?"` and parameters such as `"item=123"` and `"sort=price"`. The fragment component with prefixed `"#"` points to a subsection or element within the primary resource, such as `"details"` in the example.

Meanwhile, proper encoding and decoding of URIs are crucial to avoid misinterpretation and ensure accurate resource identification and access in web services. For these, percent encoding is used to encode reserved and non-ASCII characters within a URI, ensuring their correct transmission over networks. For example, the percent encoding converts a space as `"%20"` and a slash as `"%2F"`.

2.2 Path Confusion-Based Attacks

Path confusion vulnerabilities can be exploited by attackers to compromise web security [22]. Path confusion arises when different web service components differently interpret the same URI path. For example, by percent-encoding the forward slash `"/"` as `"%2F"`, an attacker can craft a URI like `"/A%2FB"`, which may be interpreted as either two segments `"/A/B"` or a single segment `"/A%2FB"` depending on how each component decodes the path. Two prominent attack types leveraging such path confusion are web cache attacks and authentication bypass attacks.

Table 1. Notation of Predicate Logic

Notation	Definition	Example
$P(x)$	Object x has property P	$ContainsDotSegment(x)$: True if the string x contains the substring "/./"
$R(x, y)$	Relationship R between objects x and y	$Contains(x, \text{"/./"})$: True if the string x contains the substring "/./"
$\wedge$	Logical AND	$Contains(x, \text{"/./"}) \wedge Contains(x, \text{"\#"})$: Both substrings "/./" and "#" appear in x
$\vee$	Logical OR	$Contains(x, \text{"/./"}) \vee Contains(x, \text{"\#"})$: At least one of the substrings "/./" or "#" appears in x
$\neg$	Logical NOT	$\neg Contains(x, \text{"\#"})$: The string x does not contain the substring "#"
$\rightarrow$	Logical implication	$Contains(x, \text{"\#"}) \rightarrow RemoveSuffix(x, \text{"\#"})$: If the string x contains "#", then the suffix after "#" should be removed
$\leftrightarrow$	Logical equivalence	$ContainsDotDot(x) \leftrightarrow Contains(x, \text{".."})$: Defines a predicate as logically equivalent to a binary relation

Web Cache Attack. Web cache attacks abuse discrepancies between cache servers and origin servers in interpreting paths to compromise web services. These attacks are typically known as either cache poisoning [16,23] or cache deception [11,17,18]. In a cache poisoning attack, attackers manipulate cache servers to store and serve malicious HTTP responses, thereby distributing harmful content like malicious scripts to end-users. In cache deception attacks, attackers abuse caching mechanisms to unintentionally store sensitive user data in publicly accessible cache servers, which the attackers subsequently retrieve. Both attacks rely on the discrepant handling of paths between cache servers and origin servers, demonstrating the severe implications of path confusion.

Authentication Bypass. Authentication bypass attacks leverage path confusion to evade security checks. For example, the CVE-2025-0108 [15,24] vulnerability demonstrates how double percent-encoded dot segments (`"%252E%252E"`) can allow certain components, such as Nginx, to bypass authentication checks. As a result, protected resources hosted by components such as the Apache HTTP Server can be accessed without proper authorization. Such attacks highlight the critical security risks posed by path confusion, underscoring the necessity for consistent and robust path parsing across web service components.

2.3 Formal Logical Modeling and SMT-Based Analysis of Path Confusion

To effectively analyze path confusion, it is crucial to represent the transformation logic in a form that is both interpretable and inferable. To achieve this clarity, predicate logic notation is adopted, clearly expressing component interactions and transformation conditions. Table 1 summarizes the notation conventions applied throughout this paper.

Specifically, the notation $P(x)$ indicates that an object x satisfies a certain property, whereas $R(x, y)$ expresses a relationship between two objects. Logical connectives, such as $\wedge$, $\vee$, $\neg$, $\rightarrow$, and $\leftrightarrow$, are utilized to construct predicates and articulate implications or equivalences explicitly.

Using this representation grounded in predicate logic, SMT solvers are employed to systematically assess these logical conditions for their satisfiability. SMT solvers specifically handle string constraints, enabling automatic generation of exploit payloads. This automated process allows for precise and reproducible testing of discrepancies in path interpretation.

3 System Model

This section formally defines the foundational concepts underpinning PathFault. First, Sect. 3.1 introduces the concept and formal definition of Path Confusion Patterns, which classify discrepancies of the path interpretation of web service components. Next, Sect. 3.2 presents the Predicate Logic-based Surrogate Model and its formal definition for analyzing discrepancies in real web services. Finally, Sect. 3.3 formally defines Path Confusion Vulnerability and explains how PathFault detects such vulnerabilities through the surrogate model.

3.1 Path Confusion Patterns

Path confusion occurs when web service's components interpret the same URI differently. These discrepancies, stemming from diverse causes, are classified into distinct patterns. This section introduces *Path Confusion Patterns*, derived from a systematic analysis of their causes, and formally defines each pattern.

Path Confusion Patternization. To systematically identify path confusion patterns, this study analyzes responses of web service components utilizing three types of confusable URIs:

- `"/tmp1/tmp2{char}tmp3/tmp4"`
- `"/tmp1/{char}/tmp2"`
- `"/a/../b"`

Here, `"{char}"` represents a single-byte character from `0x00` to `0xff`, covering the full ASCII range. This approach ensures detection of edge cases, such as null bytes and control characters that affect path interpretation. Consequently, this study classifies path confusion patterns in four distinct forms, as detailed below.

Full Subsequent Path Removal. This pattern occurs when a web component truncates all segments following a specific character. For example, Nginx interprets the URI `"/tmp1/tmp2#tmp3/tmp4"` by truncating segments after the hash (`"#"`) , resulting in `"/tmp1/tmp2"`. However, Apache HTTP Server rejects paths containing `"#"`, highlighting discrepant handling.

Partial Current Segment Removal. This pattern involves removing portions of a segment after specific characters. For instance, Apache Tomcat processes `"/tmp1/tmp2;tmp3/tmp4"` by truncating the segment after the semicolon (`";"`), resulting in `"/tmp1/tmp2/tmp4"`.

String Substitution. This pattern involves the replacement of path substrings. For example, Apache Tomcat replaces `"//"` with `"/"` and `"/?/"` with `"?/"`.

Single Previous Segment Removal. This pattern involves normalizing relative paths with dot-dot sequences (`".."`), as specified in RFC 3986 [6]. For instance, `"/a/../b"` should normalize to `"/b"`.

Path Confusion Formalization. This section formalizes the definitions of *Path Confusion*, *Path Confusion Function*, and *Path Confusion Pattern* in sequence to model path confusion behaviors in web services.

Definition 1 (Path confusion). *A Path Confusion $\mathcal{P}$ is a set of pairs $\langle t, c\rangle$, where $t \in \mathbb{T}$ is a transformation function manipulating the string, and $c \subseteq \mathbb{C}$ is a condition evaluating the truth value of an input string $s \in \Sigma^*$. Formally,*

$$\begin{aligned} &\mathcal{P} = \{\langle t, c\rangle \mid t \in \mathbb{T}, c \subseteq \mathbb{C}\}, \\ &\mathbb{T} = T_r \cup T_o \cup T_u \cup T_n \cup T_p \cup T_s \cup T_d, \\ &\mathbb{C} = C_e \cup C_s \cup C_p \cup C_c \cup C_d \end{aligned} \tag{1}$$

Each transformation $T_* \subset \mathbb{T}$ performs string manipulations, such as substitution or deletion, while each predicate $C_* \subset \mathbb{C}$ determines transformation eligibility, enabling formal analysis of path confusion patterns. Details of $\mathbb{T}$ and $\mathbb{C}$ components, designed for path confusion patterns, are provided in Table 2.

Definition 2 (Path confusion function). *The Path Confusion Function $\mathcal{P}(s)$ for an input string $s \in \Sigma^*$ applies a transformation $t \in \mathbb{T}$ if all predicates $c_i \in c \subseteq \mathbb{C}$ are satisfied. Here, $t(s)$ denotes the result of performing the transformation corresponding to t on s. Formally,*

$$\mathcal{P}(s) = \begin{cases} t(s) & \textit{if } \bigwedge_{c_i \in c} c_i(s) \\ s & \textit{otherwise} \end{cases} \tag{2}$$

Definition 3 (Path Confusion Pattern). *The four Path Confusion Patterns P previously identified are formalized through the $\mathcal{P}(s)$, where each pattern $P \subset \mathcal{P}$ is defined by a transformation and condition pair. Formally,*

$$\begin{aligned} P_f(t, s) &= \{\langle T_u(t, s), \{C_c(t, s)\}\rangle\} \\ P_s(t, r, s) &= \{\langle T_r(t, r, s), \{C_c(t, s)\}\rangle\} \\ P_c(t, s) &= \left\{ \begin{array}{l} \langle T_d(t, \text{"/"}, s), \{C_c(t, s), C_d(t, \text{"/"}, s)\}\rangle, \\ \langle T_u(t, s), \{C_c(t, s), \neg C_d(t, \text{"/"}, s)\}\rangle \end{array} \right\} \\ P_p(s) &= \{\langle T_n(\text{"/../"}, \text{"/"}, s), \{C_c(\text{"/../"}, s)\}\rangle\} \\ &\textit{where } t, r, s \in \Sigma^*, \quad o \in \mathbb{Z}_{\geq 0} \end{aligned} \tag{3}$$

Table 2. Transformation and Condition Types

Notation*	Description
$T_r(t, r, s)$	Replace all occurrences of t in s with r
$T_o(o, s)$	Extract the substring of s starting from offset o
$T_u(t, s)$	Extract the prefix of s up to the first occurrence of t
$T_n(t, d, s)$	Remove from the previous d to the first t, inclusive, in s
$T_p(t, s)$	Prepend string t to the beginning of s
$T_s(t, s)$	Append string t to the end of s
$T_d(t, d, s)$	Remove characters from t to the next d in s
$C_e(t, s)$	s is exactly equal to t
$C_s(t, s)$	s ends with substring t
$C_p(t, s)$	s starts with substring t
$C_c(t, s)$	s contains substring t
$C_d(t, d, s)$	There is a d following the first occurrence of t in s

*Variables t, r, and d represent strings and belong to Σ^*, the set of all possible strings; $o \in \mathbb{Z}_{\geq 0}$ is a non-negative integer offset.

Each pattern represents a distinct path manipulation:

- Full subsequent path removal $P_f(t, s)$ denotes a transformation that eliminates all path segments occurring after a specified target string t inside the input string s if t is present.
- String substitution $P_s(t, r, s)$ denotes a transformation that replaces all of the target string t in the input string s with the replacement string r.
- Partial current segment removal $P_c(t, s)$ denotes a transformation that either removes a segment after t until that slash if a slash follows t, or truncates a prefix up to t otherwise.
- Single previous segment removal $P_p(s)$ denotes a transformation that normalizes the directory sequence "/../" within the input string s if present.

3.2 Predicate Logic-Based Surrogate Model

As modern web services comprise multiple components [7,27], identifying vulnerability causes precisely is challenging [18]. Moreover, direct testing on live systems poses risks of data exposure or disruptions [17,18,25,30]. To address these, *Predicate Logic-based Surrogate Model* abstracts a web service retaining only essential details for analyzing path confusion. Thus, this model enables systemic path confusion analysis with minimal live system interaction. Built on $\mathcal{P}$ from Sect. 3.1, the model represents the service as a component sequence.

Definition 4 (Surrogate model). *The Surrogate Model $\mathcal{S}$ and its components $\mathcal{W}$ are defined as follows:*

$$\mathcal{S} = [\,\mathcal{W}_1,\ \mathcal{W}_2,\ \ldots,\ \mathcal{W}_n\,],$$
$$\mathcal{W} = (\,isNorm,\ isDecode,\ Conditions,\ Transformations),$$
$$\text{where } isNorm, isDecode \in \{True,\ False\} \text{ and } Conditions \subseteq \mathbb{C},\ Transformations \subseteq \mathbb{P} \tag{4}$$

These attributes characterize the component's behavior in processing requests:

- *isNorm* $\in$ {True, False} indicates whether the component performs dot-segment normalization, resolving relative path sequences like "/../".
- *isDecode* $\in$ {True, False} indicates whether the component performs percent decoding, such as converting "%2F" to "/".
- *Conditions* $\subseteq \mathbb{C}$ means the conditions under which it can process the request.
- *Transformations* $\subseteq P$ denotes the subset of path confusion patterns contained by a component.

Consequently, it models web services, where requests are processed by chaining the results interpreted by each component to subsequent components.

3.3 Path Confusion Vulnerability

Although path confusion inherently has the potential to trigger vulnerabilities [29], not every path confusion results in an exploitable vulnerability. The exploitability depends on the implementation details of each web service. For example, each web service has a different URI set, routing rules, and caching rules. Thus, path confusion leading to sensitive resources varies across services. Consequently, identical path confusion results in one service being vulnerable, while another is unaffected due to routing differences.

To formally analyze path confusion considering these scenarios, this section defines *Path Confusion Vulnerability* and *Exploit Payload* by leveraging $\mathcal{S}$.

Definition 5 (Output of web service). *The output of a web service component $\mathcal{W}$, denoted $\mathcal{W}(x)$, for an input $x \in \Sigma^*$ is defined as:*

$$\mathcal{W}(x) = x_m \quad where \quad \begin{cases} x_0 = x \\ x_j = P_j(x_{j-1}) \quad for \ 1 \leq j \leq m \end{cases} \tag{5}$$

Given $\mathcal{W}$.Transformations $= \{\langle t_1, c_1\rangle, \ldots, \langle t_m, c_m\rangle\} \subseteq \mathcal{P}$, each P_j corresponds to the transformation pair $\langle t_j, c_j\rangle$. The initial input $x \in \Sigma^*$ serves as x_0, where each P_j transforms the previous output x_{j-1} to produce x_j. This formalizes the execution of $\mathcal{W}.Transformations$ to an input URI x, enabling modeling of the component's output for URI.

Definition 6 (Path confusion vulnerability). *A $\mathcal{V}$, which represents the existence of a path confusion vulnerability, is defined as follows:*

$$\mathcal{V} \leftrightarrow \exists s_0 \in \Sigma^* \ (\mathbb{C}_t(s_t) \wedge C_e(o_t, s_n)) \tag{6}$$

Path confusion vulnerabilities arise from interactions among various web service components. The exploit payloads must meet intermediate servers' caching rules in web cache attack, and authentication skip conditions in authentication bypassing. Also, both must reach the attacker's intended URI to the target server.

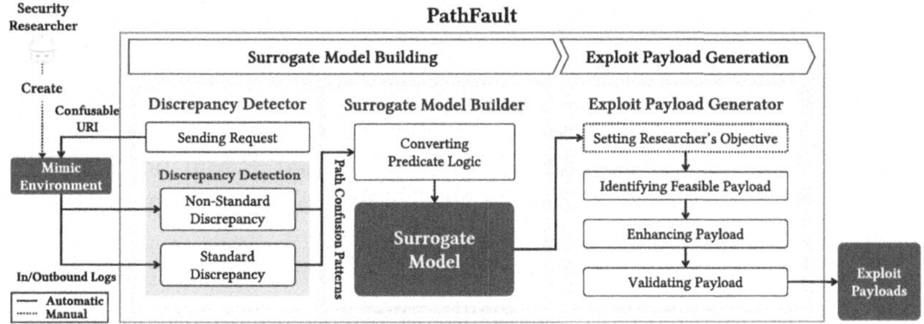

Fig. 1. Overview of PathFault.

Thus, a path confusion vulnerability exists if and only if an initial input, processed by the web service components, is transformed to results satisfying attacker-specified conditions. In short, this vulnerability requires two kinds of conditions. First, intermediate results must satisfy the attacker's objectives. Second, the final output must match the attacker's intended target.

Equation 6 expresses the predicate logic for $\mathcal{V}$, where an input string $s_0 \in \Sigma^*$ undergoes transformation through components $\mathcal{W}_1, \ldots, \mathcal{W}_n \in \mathcal{S}$, producing results $s_1, \ldots, s_n$ such that $s_i = \mathcal{W}_i(s_{i-1})$ for $i \in [1, n]$. The predicate $\mathbb{C}_t(s_t)$, an attacker-specified condition, requires an intermediate result s_t at a step $t \in [1, n]$ to meet the attacker's requirement for the component $\mathcal{W}_t$. Meanwhile, $C_e(o_t, s_n)$ ensures that the final output s_n matches the attacker-specified target o_t. An input s_0 satisfying both conditions is an *Exploit Payload*, triggering the desired intermediate state and achieving the targeted final output.

The formal predicate logic presented above not only precisely defines the existence of path confusion vulnerability but also provides a provable foundation for systematically identifying, constructing, and validating the exploit payloads.

4 PathFault

4.1 Overview

PathFault is a tool designed for defender-oriented security researchers, including penetration testers, service developers, and infrastructure architects, to automatically detect path confusion vulnerabilities in web services. As shown in Fig. 1, it takes inbound and outbound logs of the target web service as input, builds a surrogate model in the *Surrogate Model Building* stage, and generates an exploit payload as output in the *Exploit Payload Generation* stage.

In the Surrogate Model Building stage, the *Discrepancy Detector* analyzes logs to identify path confusion patterns using URI processing discrepancies, including RFC standard transformations. Then, the *Surrogate Model Builder* translates these patterns into predicate logic expressions, constructing a surrogate model for exploit payload generation.

In the *Exploit Payload Generation* stage, the security researchers incorporate domain knowledge, such as specific functionalities or component behaviors, into the surrogate model for reducing the model gap. Based on the model, PathFault employs SMT solving to identify viable $\mathcal{P}$ combinations that meet tester-specified conditions. Next, it enhances payloads using identified $\mathcal{P}$ and percent decoding behaviors. Finally, to ensure reliability, it disables optimizations and validates each payload against the surrogate model.

Meanwhile, to generate inputs for PathFault, inbound and outbound packets of the target web service components must be observable and recordable. Thus, the security researcher manually configures a *Mimic Environment*, using known components of the target web service. Unlike the real service, the components of the mimic environment operate independently, processing only their own requests without chained forwarding. If the PathFault receives the mimic environment, it automatically sends predefined HTTP requests to the mimic environment to generate the input logs on its own.

4.2 Stage 1: Surrogate Model Building

This stage involves the creation of a mimic environment and two methods for detecting discrepancies.

Step 1: Mimic Environment Creation. The Mimic Environment imitates web service components, configured to behave independently without inter-component interactions. In short, each component processes only its own requests, unlike the interconnected structure of real services. The security researcher creates a mimic environment that satisfies two conditions:

- Each component has an accessible endpoint for receiving HTTP requests.
- Inbound and outbound packets are obtainable for all components.

Security researchers can easily create this environment with PathFault's utility modules. In this work, mimicking the 7 components in Table ?? requires an average of 3.86 files (102.4 lines of code) per component, and creating a component took 30 min to 2 days. However, the reuse of setups significantly reduces subsequent efforts. In fact, PathFault's open-source case study guide requires only executing copy-and-paste commands to create and run the mimic environment.

Step 2: Discrepancy Detection. PathFault first analyzes non-standard discrepancies to identify P_f, P_c, or P_s.

Algorithm 1 analyzes non-standard discrepancies by sending confusable URIs such as `"/tmp1/tmp2{char}tmp3/tmp4"`. If the response is `"/tmp1/tmp2"`, it indicates P_f. Alternatively, if the response is `"/tmp1/tmp2/tmp4"`, it indicates P_c. If neither pattern is detected, an alternative URI `"/tmp1/{char}/tmp2"` identifies P_s when the input and output paths differ. If the component fails to process the confusable URIs containing specific characters (Line 7), leaving no log, it appends $\neg C_c(char, s)$ to $\mathcal{W}.Conditions$.

Algorithm 1. Non-standard discrepancy detection

```
 1: function AnalyzeConfusablePaths(char)
 2:     inpath1 ← "/tmp1/tmp2" + char + "tmp3/tmp4"
 3:     inpath2 ← "/tmp1/" + char + "/tmp2"
 4:     outpath1 ← getParsingResult(inpath1)
 5:     outpath2 ← getParsingResult(inpath2)
 6:     if outpath1 = NULL or outpath2 = NULL then
 7:         return BadCondition(char)
 8:     else if inpath1 ≠ outpath1 then
 9:         if outpath1 = "/tmp1/tmp2" then
10:             return FullSubsequentPathRemoval(char)
11:         else if outpath1 = "/tmp1/tmp2/tmp4" then
12:             return PartialCurrentSegmentRemoval(char)
13:         end if
14:     else if inpath2 ≠ outpath2 then
15:         targetStr ← inpath2
16:             .remove("/tmp1")
17:             .remove("tmp2")
18:         replaceStr ← outpath2
19:             .remove("/tmp1")
20:             .remove("tmp2")
21:         return StringSubstitution(targetStr, replaceStr)
22:     end if
23: end function
```

Next, PathFault analyses RFC3986-based discrepancies by examining how each component interprets and normalizes input paths (i.e. confirming that `"/tmp1/../tmp2"` is ultimately interpreted as `"/tmp2"`). It then evaluates whether a component performs percent-decoding, such as transforming `"/%21"` into `"/!"`, and marks the component.

Step 3: Building a surrogate model. Finally, PathFault formalizes detected path confusion patterns with predicate logic into $\mathcal{S}$. Upon this step, the $\mathcal{S}$ offers a provable foundation for the generation and verification of exploit payloads.

4.3 Stage 2: Exploit Payload Generation

This stage involves four steps: setting the researcher's objective, identifying feasible payloads via SMT solving, enhancing exploit payloads, and validating them.

Step 1: Setting the Researcher's Objective. The security researcher sets the objective on $\mathcal{S}$ for targeted path confusion attack scenarios. These objectives specify four components:

- Target precondition: Conditions the URI must meet before transformation.
- Target postcondition: Conditions the URI must satisfy after transformation.
- Essential transformation: Transformations applied to the URI during testing.
- Internal processing representation: Duplication of a component $\mathcal{W}$ for internal processing in $\mathcal{S}$.

For example, to test the feature related to the transformation that performs appending `".gz"` to the URIs ending with `".css"`, the researcher can formalize the path confusion $P_{gz} \subset \mathcal{P}$ as:

$$P_{gz} = \{\langle T_s(\text{".gz"}, s), \{C_s(\text{".css"}, s)\}\rangle\} \tag{7}$$

Also, internal processing such as rewriting is modeled by duplicating $\mathcal{W}$ in $\mathcal{S}$. This duplication is efficiently performed by using PathFault's surrogate model-based strategy without reanalysis. Consequently, it reduces the model gap and improves the payload's accuracy. And the security researcher's domain knowledge enhances the $\mathcal{W}$ to $\mathcal{W}_{pen}$, changing $\mathcal{S}$ to $\mathcal{S}_{pen}$ for precise payload generation.

Step 2: Identifying Feasible Payloads via SMT Solving. In this step, PathFault identifies possible combinations of P that satisfy the conditions specified by each $\mathcal{W}_{pen}$ to achieve the security researcher's objective.

The conditional transformations $P \subset \mathcal{P}$ typically force SMT solvers to explore more paths, expanding the search space exponentially. To address this, *Assumption-based Estimation* simplifies SMT solving by presuming only the conditions for a selected combination of P are satisfied, reducing the search space. For instance, if a P is performed when containing `"/../"` in the URI, this approach assumes the condition is satisfied.

Here, the P combinations, denoted as $\mathcal{S}^{act}_{pen}$, are generated by the *Selective Transformation Combination Algorithm* (STCA). STCA limits transformations (*maxTrans*) applied to each $\mathcal{W}_{pen}$ and the number of components that must perform normalization (*maxNorm*) in $\mathcal{S}_{pen}$, using Cartesian product and permutation operations. Consequently, assumption-based estimation enables exploit payloads to be generated in polynomial time.

Building on this, PathFault generates payloads targeting a specified output o_t with SMT solving. A $\mathcal{S}^{act}_{pen}$, comprising multiple $\mathcal{W}^{act}_{pen}$ with preconditions, transformations, normalization, and postconditions, is used as input.

Algorithm 2 processes $\mathcal{S}^{act}_{pen}List$ comprising selected P combinations by the STCA.

It initializes s_0 and s_i for each $\mathcal{S}^{act}_{pen}$ (Line 5–6) and applies preconditions ($\subseteq \mathbb{C}_t$), transformations, normalization, and postconditions ($\subseteq \mathbb{C}_t$) to generate constraints (Line 8–12). Combined constraints verify if s_i satisfies $C_e(o_t, s_n)$ (Line 16). If the SMT solver finds a solution (Line 17) and essential transformations are included (Line 18), the payload s_0 is stored (Line 22); otherwise, it is discarded.

Consequently, grounded in the predicate logic of path confusion vulnerability, payload and $\mathcal{S}^{act}_{pen}$ detailing the P in each $\mathcal{W}^{act}_{pen}$ that satisfies the security researcher's objective are stored in $success\mathcal{S}^{act}_{pen}List$.

Step 3: Enhancing Exploit Payload. Prior components' P and *Conditions* can block performing the P in the target component. To bypass this, PathFault enhances exploit payloads using two system-wide expansion methods.

Algorithm 2. SMT-based exploit payload generation

```
1: function GenerAtePayload(S^act_pen List, o_t)
2:     successS^act_pen List ← [ ]
3:     for each S^act_pen ∈ S^act_pen List do
4:         solver ← NewSMTSolver()
5:         s_0 ← NewString()                              ▷ Original input
6:         s_i ← s_0                                      ▷ Current input
7:         for each W^act_pen ∈ S^act_pen do
8:             preC ← ApplyPreCond(W^act_pen, s_i)
9:             (tIn, tC) ← ApplyTrans(W^act_pen, s_i)
10:            (nIn, nC) ← ApplyNorm(W^act_pen, tIn)
11:            postC ← ApplyPostCond(W^act_pen, nIn)
12:            cond ← Combine(preC, tC, nC, postC)
13:            solver.addCond(cond)
14:            s_i ← nIn
15:        end for
16:        solver.addCond(s_i = o_t)
17:        if solver.check() = sat then
18:            if EssentialSkipped(S^act_pen) then
19:                Alert("Essential transformation skipped")
20:                continue
21:            end if
22:            payload ← solver.model(s_0)
23:            successS^act_pen List.append(S^act_pen, payload)
24:        end if
25:    end for
26:    return successS^act_pen List
27: end function
```

First, *Normalization expansion* identifies strings in $\mathcal{S}_{pen}$ that enable normalization in $\mathcal{W}_{pen}$. It analyzes prior components to expand the strings via percent encoding and P_s. Then, it merges with prior $\mathcal{W}_{pen}$'s normalization strings to bypass prior $\mathcal{W}_{pen}$'s normalization. Applied to $successS^{act}_{pen}List$, it creates variants. Finally, it creates diverse payloads by applying them to $successS^{act}_{pen}List$.

Next, *Contains-condition expansion* first identifies P requiring $C_c(t, s)$ in $\mathcal{W}^{act}_{pen}$. This analyzes prior components to expand strings satisfying $C_c(t, s)$ via percent encoding and P_s. Finally, these extend $successS^{act}_{pen}List$ by expanding the target string t of P in $\mathcal{W}_{pen}$.

Step 4: Exploit Payload Validation. This step validates payloads on the surrogate model $\mathcal{S}_{pen}$ to ensure reliability. Due to the expansion mechanism and the assumption-based estimation ignoring $\mathcal{W}_{pen}.badCondition$, some of the payloads may be invalid. To address these, this step represents all P as if-statements and validates all $\mathcal{W}_{pen}.Conditions$ to obtain the payload satisfying all conditions.

Since payload validation is performed on a given string against constraints, its search space is smaller than payload generation, which explores all possible strings. Therefore, this enables obtaining a reliable payload efficiently.

4.4 Implementation

PathFault is implemented in Python 3.12.3 with approximately 3,940 lines of code and generates payloads by converting web service parsing discrepancies into logical constraints using the Z3 solver's Python API [9]. Since PathFault adopts a modular architecture, it supports the community's contributions and extensions [32]. Additionally, to enhance performance, PathFault provides parallel SMT solving by allowing users to configure the number of worker processes.

5 Case Study: Generating Real-World Exploit Payloads

Path confusion vulnerabilities depend on multi-component interactions, unlike single-component vulnerabilities. Thus, the vulnerability detection requires wide applicability, effectiveness, and scalability for diverse web services [3].

However, current security methodologies have struggled to analyze these interactions, resulting in limited case studies [18]. Given these challenges, this work aimed to analyze all possible cases. The possible case studies were gathered based on the following criteria: well-documented multi-component path confusion vulnerabilities (Sect. 5.1, Sect. 5.2). Specifically, Sect. 5.1 and Sect. 5.2 demonstrate PathFault's applicability by modeling exploit payloads from reported vulnerabilities. Section 5.3 compares PathFault with the state-of-the-art WCD vulnerability detection tool in terms of detection performance.

All case studies were performed on Ubuntu 20.04.6 LTS with an 11th Gen Intel Core i5-11600K CPU at 3.90GHz and 16GB RAM. PathFault employs a random seed for the SMT solver, with each instance configured to a 10-second timeout, and the max transformation argument is one per $\mathcal{W}$.

5.1 Authentication Bypass: CVE-2025-0108

This section explains the trigger mechanism of CVE-2025-0108 [15,24], which was caused by discrepant URI processing in a multi-tier web service comprising Nginx and Apache HTTP Server. The known exploit payload is shown as follows:`/unauth/%252E%252E/php/ztp_gate.php/PAN_Help/x.css`.

First, Nginx adds a header disabling authentication to requests for URIs prefixed with `"/unauth/"` and sends it to Apache Server with the URI unchanged.

And then, Apache HTTP Server decodes `"%252E%252E"` to `"%2E%2E"` and applies the rule that appends `".gz"`. After that, it internally redirects the request as follows:`/unauth/%2E%2E/php/ztp_gate.php/PAN_Help/x.css.gz`.

Subsequently, Apache HTTP Server percent-decodes `"%2E%2E"` to `".."`, resulting in:`/unauth/../php/ztp_gate.php/PAN_Help/x.css.gz`.

At the same time, it normalizes this URI to:`/php/ztp_gate.php/PAN_Help/x.css.gz`.

Consequently, the combination of path confusions enables unauthorized access to the protected endpoint `"/php/ztp_gate.php"`, bypassing authentication.

Summarizing these, the exploit leverages a chain of discrepancies in percent decoding, URI rewriting, and normalization across components. Stage 1 and 2 in Sect. 5.1 detail the modeling process of the vulnerability using PathFault.

```
S = [
 W(
  name = "nginx",
  conditions = [ ¬Cc(...,s) × 34 ],
  transformations = [ ],
  target_pre_conditions = [ ],
  target_post_conditions = [ ],
  essential_transformations = [ ],
  is_normalize = False,
  is_decode = False
 ),
 W(
  name = "apachehttpserver",
  conditions = [ ¬Cc(...,s) × 35 ],
  transformations = [
   Ps("/./", "/", s),
   Ps("///", "/", s),
   Ps("//", "/", s)
  ],
  target_pre_conditions = [ ],
  target_post_conditions = [ ],
  essential_transformations = [ ],
  is_normalize = True,
  is_decode = True
 )
]
```

(a) Automatically generated surrogate model by PathFault

```
Spen = [
 W(
  name = "nginx",
  ...
  target_pre_conditions = [ Cp("/unauth/", s) ],
  target_post_conditions = [ Cp("/unauth/", s) ],
  ...
 ),
 W(
  name = "apachehttpserver",
  ...
  essential_transformations = [ Pgz(s) ],
  ...
 ),
 W(
  name = "apachehttpserverinternal",
  conditions = [ ¬Cc(...,s) × 35 ],
  transformations = [
   Ps("/./", "/", s),
   Ps("///", "/", s),
   Ps("//", "/", s)
  ],
  target_pre_conditions = [ ],
  target_post_conditions = [ ],
  essential_transformations = [ ],
  is_normalize = True,
  is_decode = True
 )
]
```

(b) Surrogate model with security researcher-defined conditions and internal component duplication.

Fig. 2. Surrogate models for CVE-2025-0108. Changes are gray and additions are red. (Color figure online)

Stage 1: Surrogate Model Building. First, a security researcher creates mimic environments for a web service with Nginx and Apache HTTP Server, using knowledge of web service, enabling PathFault to automatically build the $\mathcal{S}$. The researcher requests PathFault to create a $\mathcal{S}$ in Fig. 2(a). Specifically, the "conditions" field, denoted in (4), specifies constraints of requests identified as *BadCondition* in Algorithm 1. These are expressed as negated predicates, indicating URIs that the component cannot process. The "transformations" field explained in (4), lists P identified by PathFault through discrepancies. The "is_normalize" and "is_decode" fields, denoted in (4), indicate whether the component performs dot-segment normalization and percent decoding. The "target_pre_conditions", "target_post_conditions" and "essential_transformations" fields, denoted in Sect. 4.3, indicate the researcher's objective.

PathFault exports the $\mathcal{S}$ in Python format to facilitate analyzing and integrating payload generation and validation.

Stage 2: Exploit Payload Generation. At this stage, the security researcher reduces the model gap by integrating the domain-specific knowledge into $\mathcal{S}$. Thus, the targeted surrogate model $\mathcal{S}_{pen}$ becomes more similar to a real service.

This vulnerability requires internal redirection of the second Apache HTTP Server, unmodeled in $\mathcal{S}$. To represent the behavior, the researcher duplicates the $\mathcal{W}$ for Apache HTTP Server, leveraging PathFault's Python-based $\mathcal{W}$. This duplication, enabled by PathFault's Python-based representation, efficiently generates internal $\mathcal{W}$ without reanalysis.

Table 3. Resource-Related Performance for CVE-2025-0108

Average Time(s)			Memory Peak(MB)	
Generation	Validation	Total	Generation	Validation
84.55	38.64	123.19	434.18	110.40

Additionally, the researcher integrates the test objective by modifying $\mathcal{W}$ attributes. For Nginx, the precondition and postcondition are added, requiring the URI to prefix `"/unauth/"`, formalized as $C_p($`"/unauth/"`$, s)$. For Apache HTTP Server, P_{gz} that indicates appending `".gz"` to URIs ending with `".css"` is added to the essential transformation. These updates build $\mathcal{S}_{pen}$, shown in Fig. 2(b).

The researcher then asks PathFault to generate a payload that produces the final output as:`/php/ztp_gate.php/PAN_Help/x.css`.

Finally, PathFault sequentially integrates $\mathcal{W}$.Conditions and executes each component $\mathcal{W}_{pen}.Transformations \in \mathcal{S}_{pen}$ to each generated payload for validation. As outlined in prior sections, this is achieved through if-statements defining conditional transformations, resulting in the validated exploit payload.

Case Study Result. PathFault identified 168 payloads with a 70% inclusion rate (10 runs) for known payloads using reasonable resources. It includes the payloads that combine semantically separated segments into one using percent encoding `"%252F"`, such as:`/unauth/.%252E%252Fphp/ztp_gate.php/PAN_Help/x.css`.

The result further shows that P_s("///","/"$, s)$ can be utilized for enhancing payloads, such as:`/unauth///%252E./php/ztp_gate.php/PAN_Help/x.css`.

Table 3 summarizes the PathFault's performance of modeling the exploit payload used in CVE-2025-0108.

It shows that PathFault's ability to accurately model disclosed vulnerabilities within reasonable time and resource limits.

5.2 Web Cache Deception: ChatGPT Account Takeover

This section shows that PathFault can model the WCD vulnerability included in ChatGPT's chat sharing service despite the limitation in precise knowledge of the target [21]. This vulnerability, which exposes authentication information to unauthorized external users, stems from an improper caching policy. The public PoC demonstrates how the vulnerability is triggered, where the attacker lacks information about the target web service's structure. The only required information is that caching occurs for `"/share/*"` and the final URI is `"/api/auth/session"`.

Statistical Approach for Surrogate Model Building. Evaluating all possible combinations of $\mathcal{W}$ could generate exploit payloads without knowledge of the web service's structure, but doing so in polynomial time is challenging. Instead, in the normal distribution of attributes across all existing $\mathcal{W}$, selecting a $\mathcal{W}$ close to the mean value increases the relative likelihood that it is included in the target

Table 4. Summary of performance of PathFault for ChatGPT account takeover

Θ: apachehttpserver Υ: apachetomcat Φ: apachetrafficserver Ω: nginx

Web Service	Success Rate	# of Payloads	Known Payload	Average Time(s)			Memory (MB)	
				Generation	**Validation**	**Total**	**Generation**	**Validation**
Θ → Υ	1.0	525	✗	80.22	44.69	124.91	598.29	110.36
Θ → Ω	0.0	0	✗	0.25	0.00	0.25	110.27	109.88
Υ → Θ	1.0	479	✗	91.70	50.28	141.98	634.93	110.43
Υ → Φ	0.0	0	✗	7.69	0.00	7.69	126.59	109.90
Φ → Θ	1.0	270	✓	20.42	39.98	60.40	176.85	110.27
Φ → Υ	1.0	270	✓	31.12	43.17	74.30	381.83	110.38
Ω → Θ	1.0	135	✓	10.23	24.92	35.15	174.78	110.30
Ω → Υ	1.0	135	✓	11.87	25.36	37.23	292.48	110.35

service compared to other $\mathcal{W}$. Based on this insight, building surrogate models using widely used open-source web servers increases the likelihood of approximating the target service's structure. Therefore, this study selects widely used components (Nginx, Apache HTTP Server, Apache Tomcat, and Apache Traffic Server) as the foundation for representative surrogate models.

Case Study Result. Table 4 summarizes the results in generating payloads across combinations of four open-source web servers. Note that a success rate of 1.0 indicates that the solving timeout is sufficient for the string search space.

The known exploit payload is generated when the final server applies percent decoding and normalization, while the prior component skips percent decoding. Meanwhile, other exploit payloads are generated when both components perform percent decoding and normalization, as observed in request forwarding between `apachehttpserver` and `apachetomcat`, even in the absence of known payloads.

PathFault demonstrates that using a non-normalizing parser, such as Nginx or Apache Traffic Server, as the final component mitigates these vulnerabilities. That is, despite limited information, PathFault excels in providing insights for analyzing $\mathcal{W}$'s behaviors and identifying conditions to eliminate exploits.

Thus, PathFault can reproduce known exploits and detect unknown vulnerabilities as well as identify their causes and propose mitigation, demonstrating its practical utility for vulnerability remediation.

5.3 Enhancing Heuristic Payloads

PathFault's goal is that defenders identify and mitigate vulnerabilities with a surrogate model and patterns before attackers, reducing risks [19]. Unlike blackbox WCDE where attackers and defenders have equal footing [18], PathFault is a whitebox tool leveraging defenders' accessibility about service details as a strength for the goal. However, no whitebox research identifies such vulnerabilities from the defender's perspective. Despite this challenge, this work evaluates PathFault with a state-of-the-art WCDE, an attacker-focused tool, addressing such vulnerabilities about the accuracy of PathFault-generated payloads by comparing them with heuristic payloads from prior work on WCD vulnerabilities.

Table 5. Comparison by Depth for WCDE and PathFault

Depth	WCDE [18]			PathFault			
	Exploit Payloads	Vulnerable Pairs	TP	Exploit Payloads	Vulnerable Pairs on WCDE	TP	Average Time(s)
2	2	3/12	4	**79**	**3/3**	**156**	**25.32**
3	3	12/24	21	**586**	**12/12**	**3161**	**104.05**
4	3	18/24	35	**1982**	**18/18**	**11544**	**298.43**

Overview. The number of valid exploit payloads correlates with the likelihood that an adversary could trigger the vulnerability [31,36]. This is because the probability of exploitation increases proportionally with the number of effective payloads across the entire string domain. In this regard, this evaluation shows that PathFault outperforms state-of-the-art tools in detecting WCD vulnerabilities in modern web services as measured by per number of components (depth).

Also, this work doesn't conduct a large-scale evaluation used in WCDE. This is because, despite the importance of identifying and mitigating vulnerability causes [18], current research focuses on attacker-driven detection. Therefore, this work focuses on vulnerability modeling performance, which supports defenders in identifying causes and mitigations through the results of diverse service-specific exploit payloads. Specifically, this study evaluates payload diversity, detected vulnerable combinations, successful exploit counts, and time per depth, comparing outcomes from prior work [18], which assumed security researcher objectives (first server processes URI ending with `"not a file.css"`, last server processes URI as `"/profile"`), with those automatically generated by PathFault under identical objectives.

It tests ordered combinations of two to four web server components, using four open-source web servers from Sect. 5.2. The state-of-the-art tool, WCDE, uses a fixed set of 12 payloads across all combinations, while PathFault uses generated payloads across combinations by depth.

Case Study Result. Table 5 outlines the results of WCDE and PathFault per depth.

Specifically, WCDE supports two valid payload types at depth-2 and three at depths 3 and 4. It detects vulnerabilities in 3/12 component combinations at depth-2, yielding 4 true positives, and in 12/24 and 18/24 combinations at depths 3 and 4, resulting in 21 and 35 true positives, respectively. In contrast, PathFault generates diverse exploit payloads with higher true positives than WCDE, while detecting all vulnerable combinations detected by WCDE. Also, the greater the depth, PathFault can find more exploit payloads, proving that risk mitigation requires considering components' complex interactions in vulnerability detection.

Time-wise, WCDE uses 12 predefined payloads, taking negligible time. PathFault's generation and validation times average per combination are 25.32 s,

104.05 s, and 298.43 s at depth 2, 3, and 4. WCDE has a time advantage in verifying vulnerability existence, but its non-service-specific payloads result in low coverage, evident from payload diversity. Also, this time includes the vulnerability, its cause, and mitigation identification so that PathFault can support vulnerability patch plans quickly than WCDE.

Nevertheless, the detection methodology of WCDE remains effective. Therefore, integrating PathFault's exploit payload generation methodology, which integrates researchers' domain knowledge and service-specific characteristics, with WCDE's detection methodology can significantly enhance vulnerability detection performance across diverse web services [2,37].

6 Limitation

Resource-Dependent Payload Generation. Exploit payload generation relies on the SMT solver's computational resources, causing variations in the number and diversity of payloads [4]. Because solving for multiple transformations increases complexity exponentially [8], constrained resources may miss some payloads in polynomial time. Nevertheless, the prior case studies demonstrate that PathFault is useful in vulnerability detection through reproducing known exploit payloads and generating unreported payloads with reasonable resources.

Surrogate Model Gap. PathFault may fail to capture minor configurations such as the order of $\mathcal{W}.Transformations$, impeding completeness. Also, it excludes character-level percent encoding from P_s because the consideration of it increases the complexity of SMT solving. This may lead to widening the model gap.

Despite the model gap, prior case studies show that striking a balance between model completeness and generating payloads in polynomial time remains critical for practicality, as models successfully reproduce known exploit payloads and yield valid results in diverse environments. Therefore, future work on capturing fine-grained logic and path processing while maintaining the balance represents a promising direction.

7 Related Work

HTTP Message Parser Discrepancy Detection. Prior studies [1,5,13,14,26,29,34,35] identify discrepancies in HTTP parser implementations, highlighting servers' discrepant interpretations of identical requests. While these efforts introduced techniques for efficiently detecting parsing discrepancies, they don't explore how such discrepancies can be leveraged to exploit in a systematic manner. In contrast, our work formalizes path confusion patterns, introduces a methodology for systematically generating exploit payloads with discrepancies, and bridges the gap between discrepancy detection and exploitation.

System-Level Analysis via Webserver Fingerprinting. Prior work on web server fingerprinting [28,33] leverages system-wide discrepancies to infer web service structures, termed a passive attack. However, they neither verify exploitability nor generate attack payloads. PathFault, in contrast, performs an active attack that produces exploit payloads utilizing discrepancies from a security researcher's perspective. Integrating fingerprinting with this approach enables adversarial system-level analysis, a promising direction for future work.

8 Conclusion

This research proposes a system-level framework for detecting path confusion vulnerabilities with high precision and coverage, leveraging predicate logic and SMT solving. It contributes to improving detection scope and accuracy through component interaction modeling, utilizing a surrogate model to capture web service behavior with minimal reliance on real-world data, an exploit payload generator that produces formally verified payloads to facilitate efficient penetration testing, and a system-wide analysis methodology. These enable practical vulnerability detection in complex web services, thus paving the way for automated mitigation of discrepancy-based threats.

Acknowledgments. This research was supported by a National Research Foundation of Korea (NRF) grant, funded by the Korean government (MSIT) (RS-2023-NR077166, RS-2023-00227165).

References

1. Akhavani, S.A., Jabiyev, B., Kallus, B., Topcuoglu, C., Bratus, S., Kirda, E.: Waffled: exploiting parsing discrepancies to bypass web application firewalls. arXiv preprint arXiv:2503.10846 (2025)
2. Alhamed, M., Rahman, M.H.: A systematic literature review on penetration testing in networks: future research directions. Appl. Sci. **13**(12), 6986 (2023)
3. Antunes, N., Vieira, M.: Soa-scanner: an integrated tool to detect vulnerabilities in service-based infrastructures. In: 2013 IEEE International Conference on Services Computing, pp. 280–287. IEEE (2013)
4. Baldoni, R., Coppa, E., D'elia, D.C., Demetrescu, C., Finocchi, I.: A survey of symbolic execution techniques. ACM Comput. Surv. (CSUR) **51**(3), 1–39 (2018)
5. Benhabbour, I., Attia, M., Dacier, M.: Http conformance vs. middleboxes: identifying where the rules actually break down. In: International Conference on Passive and Active Network Measurement, pp. 155–181. Springer, Heidelberg (2025)
6. Berners-Lee, T., Fielding, R., Masinter, L.: Rfc 3986: Uniform resource identifier (uri): generic syntax (2005)
7. Bi, Y., et al.: Dissecting open edge computing platforms: ecosystem, usage, and security risks. In: 2024 Annual Computer Security Applications Conference (ACSAC), pp. 1139–1155. IEEE Computer Society, Los Alamitos (2024)
8. Cadar, C., Ganesh, V., Pawlowski, P.M., Dill, D.L., Engler, D.R.: Exe: automatically generating inputs of death. ACM Trans. Inf. Syst. Secur. (TISSEC) **12**(2), 1–38 (2008)

9. De Moura, L., Bjørner, N.: Z3: an efficient smt solver. In: International conference on Tools and Algorithms for the Construction and Analysis of System,. pp. 337–340. Springer, Heidelberg (2008)
10. De Moura, L., Bjørner, N.: Satisfiability modulo theories: introduction and applications. Commun. ACM **54**(9), 69–77 (2011)
11. Gil, O.: Web cache deception attack. In: Presented at Black Hat USA 2017, Web AppSec Track, Las Vegas, NV, USA (2017). Accessed 19 May 2025
12. Hasegawa, A.A., Watanabe, T., Shioji, E., Akiyama, M.: I know what you did last login: inconsistent messages tell existence of a target's account to insiders. In: Proceedings of the 35th Annual Computer Security Applications Conference(ACSAC), ACSAC '19, pp. 732–746. Association for Computing Machinery, New York (2019)
13. Jabiyev, B., Gavazzi, A., Onarlioglu, K., Kirda, E.: Gudifu: guided differential fuzzing for http request parsing discrepancies. In: Proceedings of the 27th International Symposium on Research in Attacks, Intrusions and Defenses, pp. 235–247 (2024)
14. Jabiyev, B., Sprecher, S., Onarlioglu, K., Kirda, E.: T-reqs: http request smuggling with differential fuzzing. In: Proceedings of the 2021 ACM SIGSAC Conference on Computer and Communications Security, pp. 1805–1820 (2021)
15. Kues, A.: Nginx/Apache path confusion to auth bypass in PAN-OS (2025). https://slcyber.io/blog/nginx-apache-path-confusion-to-auth-bypass-in-pan-os. Accessed 19 May 2025
16. Liang, Y., et al.: Internet's invisible enemy: detecting and measuring web cache poisoning in the wild. In: Proceedings of the 2024 on ACM SIGSAC Conference on Computer and Communications Security, pp. 452–466 (2024)
17. Mirheidari, S.A., Arshad, S., Onarlioglu, K., Crispo, B., Kirda, E., Robertson, W.: Cached and confused: web cache deception in the wild. In: 29th USENIX Security Symposium (USENIX Security 20), pp. 665–682 (2020)
18. Mirheidari, S.A., Golinelli, M., Onarlioglu, K., Kirda, E., Crispo, B.: Web cache deception escalates! In: 31st USENIX Security Symposium (USENIX Security 22), pp. 179–196 (2022)
19. Nayak, K., Marino, D., Efstathopoulos, P., Dumitraş, T.: Some vulnerabilities are different than others: studying vulnerabilities and attack surfaces in the wild. In: International Workshop on Recent Advances in Intrusion Detection, pp. 426–446. Springer, Heidelberg (2014)
20. Nokline: Caching the un-cacheables - Abusing URL parser confusions (Web cache poisoning technique) (2022). https://nokline.github.io/bugbounty/2022/09/02/Glassdoor-Cache-Poisoning.html. Accessed 19 May 2025
21. Nokline: ChatGPT account takeover - Wildcard web cache deception (2024). https://nokline.github.io/bugbounty/2024/02/04/ChatGPT-ATO.html. Accessed 19 May 2025
22. OWASP Foundation: Web Security Testing Guide v4.2 (2020). https://owasp.org/www-project-web-security-testing-guide/. Accessed 19 May 2025
23. OWASP Foundation: Cache Poisoning Attack (2022). https://owasp.org/www-community/attacks/Cache_Poisoning. Accessed 19 May 2025
24. Palo Alto Networks, Inc.: CVE-2025-0108: Authentication bypass vulnerability in PAN-OS management web interface (2025). https://nvd.nist.gov/vuln/detail/CVE-2025-0108. Accessed 19 May 2025
25. Penetration Test Guidance Special Interest Group PCI Security Standards Council: Information Supplement: Penetration Testing Guidance, Version 1.1 (2017). https://docs-prv.pcisecuritystandards.org/Guidance%20Document/Penetration%20Testing/Penetration-Testing-Guidance-v1_1.pdf. Accessed 19 May 2025

26. Pisu, L., Loi, F., Maiorca, D., Giacinto, G.: Http/3 will not save you from request smuggling: a methodology to detect http/3 header (mis) validations. In: 2024 22nd International Symposium on Network Computing and Applications (NCA), pp. 97–104. IEEE (2024)
27. Pletinckx, S., Kruegel, C., Vigna, G.: A large-scale measurement study of the proxy protocol and its security implications. In: Proceedings of the 2025 Network and Distributed System Security Symposium (NDSS) (2025)
28. Qin, Y., Zhu, Y., Zhang, L., Li, B., Ding, Y., Liu, Q.: Layyerx: unveiling the hidden layers of doh server via differential fingerprinting. In: 2024 IEEE 23rd International Conference on Trust, Security and Privacy in Computing and Communications (TrustCom), pp. 354–361. IEEE (2024)
29. Rautenstrauch, J., Stock, B.: Who's breaking the rules? Studying conformance to the http specifications and its security impact. In: Proceedings of the 19th ACM Asia Conference on Computer and Communications Security, pp. 843–855 (2024)
30. Scarfone, K., Souppaya, M., Cody, A., Orebaugh, A.: Technical guide to information security testing and assessment. NIST Spec. Publ. **800**(115), 2–25 (2008)
31. Shin, Y., Meneely, A., Williams, L., Osborne, J.A.: Evaluating complexity, code churn, and developer activity metrics as indicators of software vulnerabilities. IEEE Trans. Softw. Eng. **37**(6), 772–787 (2010)
32. Thaiya, M.S., Julia, K., Mbugua, S.: On software modular architecture: concepts, metrics and trend. Int. J. Comput. Organizat. Trends **12**(1), 3–10 (2022)
33. Topcuoglu, C., Onarlioglu, K., Jabiyev, B., Kirda, E.: Untangle: multi-layer web server fingerprinting. In: Proceedings of the 2025 Network and Distributed System Security Symposium (NDSS) (2024)
34. Wang, Q., et al.: Break the wall from bottom: automated discovery of protocol-level evasion vulnerabilities in web application firewalls. In: 2024 IEEE Symposium on Security and Privacy (SP), pp. 185–202. IEEE (2024)
35. Zheng, L., et al.: Reqsminer: automated discovery of cdn forwarding request inconsistencies and dos attacks with grammar-based fuzzing. In: Proceedings of the 2024 Network and Distributed System Security Symposium (NDSS) (2024)
36. Zimmermann, T., Nagappan, N., Williams, L.: Searching for a needle in a haystack: predicting security vulnerabilities for windows vista. In: Third International Conference on Software Testing, Verification and Validation, pp. 421–428. IEEE (2010)
37. Zurowski, S., Lord, G., Baggili, I.: A quantitative analysis of offensive cyber operation (oco) automation tools. In: Proceedings of the 17th International Conference on Availability, Reliability and Security, pp. 1–11 (2022)

Post-Quantum Cryptography & Migration

Zero-Downtime Post-quantum TLS 1.3 Migration: A Bridge-Server-Based Approach

Minjoo Sim[1](✉), Subin Jo[2], Hyuntae Song[2], and Eunseong Kim[2]

[1] Department of Information Computer Engineering, Hansung University, Seoul 02876, South Korea
minjoos9797@gmail.com

[2] Department of Convergence Security, Hansung University, Seoul 02876, South Korea

Abstract. The rapid advancement of quantum computing threatens the security of widely deployed public-key cryptosystems, creating an urgent need for practical migration to post-quantum cryptographic (PQC) standards. Although the U.S. National Institute of Standards and Technology (NIST) and Korea's KpqC initiative have recently standardized PQC algorithms, integrating them into Transport Layer Security (TLS) 1.3 remains operationally challenging. Larger certificates, higher handshake costs, and incompatibility with legacy clients make naive deployment impractical in production environments. While hot reload has long been supported in classical TLS deployments (e.g., Nginx, HAProxy), these mechanisms were designed for RSA/ECC contexts with small keys and certificates, and they do not address PQC-specific challenges.

This work presents a systematic demonstration of *hot reload and rollback in a PQC-enabled TLS context*, incorporating a policy-driven state machine for staged migration and rollback under realistic constraints such as increased handshake latency and legacy-client compatibility. We propose a bridge-server-based framework that operates at the TLS library level, enabling zero-downtime migration across classical, hybrid, and PQC deployments. Experimental evaluation shows that PQC handshakes incur a $\approx 5.8\times$–$6.4\times$ increase in latency in compute-bound settings relative to ECC baselines, while the relative overhead is significantly smaller in network-bound scenarios, highlighting the importance of deployment context. These findings provide a feasible path toward secure and incremental PQC integration in TLS infrastructures, contributing to broader strategies for achieving crypto-agility under evolving cryptographic standards.

Keywords: Crypto Agility · Post-Quantum Cryptography · TLS 1.3 · Zero-Downtime Migration

H. Seo (Ed.): ICISC 2025, LNCS 16487, pp. 127–149, 2026.
https://doi.org/10.1007/978-981-95-8034-7_7

1 Introduction

The emergence of large-scale quantum computers poses a profound threat to classical public-key cryptosystems. Shor's algorithm breaks schemes based on integer factorization and discrete logarithms, including RSA [1], DiffieâĂŞHellman [2], and ECC [3], while Grover's algorithm reduces the effective security of symmetric primitives (e.g., AES-k to $2^{k/2}$ operations) [4]. Together, these advances enable harvest now, decrypt later attacks, where adversaries collect encrypted traffic today with the intent of decrypting it once sufficient quantum resources become available.

To mitigate this threat, the U.S. National Institute of Standards and Technology (NIST) finalized its first set of post-quantum cryptographic (PQC) standards in 2024 [5], and the KpqC project established domestically ratified PQC standards in 2025 [6].

Transport Layer Security (TLS) 1.3, the foundation of secure Internet communication, separates key exchange and authentication from cipher suites, providing architectural flexibility [7]. In principle, this design facilitates PQC adoption without fundamental protocol changes. In practice, deployment is difficult due to larger certificates, higher handshake costs, and compatibility issues with legacy clients. These challenges highlight the need for a mechanism that integrates PQC without downtime, preserves interoperability, and supports rollback when failures occur.

Hot-reload mechanisms have long existed in classical TLS deployments (e.g., Nginx [8], HAProxy [9]). However, extending these techniques to post-quantum TLS is not straightforward. PQC certificates are substantially larger, handshake costs are higher, and interoperability with legacy clients must be preserved to avoid service disruption. These additional constraints make operational migration in the PQC context qualitatively more complex than in classical TLS.

Projects such as `liboqs` and `oqs-provider` extend TLS 1.3 by exposing standardized PQC key exchange and signature algorithms through the OpenSSL provider interface. These libraries enable experimentation with PQC handshakes and validation of algorithm-level interoperability. However, their scope is limited to cryptographic integration: they do not provide operational migration mechanisms such as downtime-free certificate rollover, staged rollout across heterogeneous clients, or rollback under failure. In production environments, these operational guarantees are as critical as algorithmic support. Thus, while `liboqs` and `oqs-provider` prove that PQC primitives can be embedded into TLS, they stop short of offering deployable migration strategies for real-world infrastructures.

We argue that a bridge-server approach is essential. By interposing a dedicated bridge between clients and servers, migration policies can be applied independently of application logic. This design enables staged rollout and rollback, supports heterogeneous clients, and ensures continuous availability during the transition to PQC. Unlike conventional TLS termination proxies, our bridge operates directly at the TLS library level, managing `SSL_CTX` instances and migration states rather than merely reloading configurations. This distinction is crucial to support rollback and staged PQC migration under live traffic.

In summary, TLS 1.3 deployments must be able to adopt PQC seamlessly while preserving compatibility with legacy clients. To address this requirement, we propose a bridge-server-based framework that supports policy-driven hot reload and rollback, offering a practical path toward crypto-agility in the PQC era [10].

1.1 Contributions

This paper makes the following contributions:

- **Bridge-server-based framework:** We introduce a migration framework that goes beyond conventional proxies or load balancers. Whereas existing systems simply relay TLS traffic or reload certificates at the application layer, our bridge operates directly at the TLS library level, creating distinct `SSL_CTX` instances for each session and applying cryptographic policies according to the current migration state (`announce` → `prefer` → `require` → `rollback`). This design supports staged rollout and rollback under live traffic while addressing PQC-specific challenges—such as higher handshake latency and legacy-client compatibility—which prior hot-reload systems for classical TLS never considered. The practical significance lies in enabling **fine-grained session-level migration** and immediate rollback without process restart, providing operational guarantees that conventional proxy-level reload systems cannot offer.
- **Policy-driven state machine:** Unlike conventional reload mechanisms that immediately replace cryptographic material, our design introduces a staged state machine for controlled rollout and rollback. This mechanism provides fine-grained control of PQC adoption under live traffic, giving operators safety and flexibility unavailable in prior TLS systems.
- **Hot reload in a PQC context:** While prior hot-reload systems were designed for ECC/RSA environments, our approach adapts and evaluates hot reload and rollback mechanisms in post-quantum TLS. This contribution addresses PQC-specific challenges such as larger certificates, increased handshake latency, and legacy-client compatibility, thereby bridging the gap between algorithmic integration (e.g., liboqs) and operational deployment.
- **Experimental evaluation:** We validate the framework through controlled TLS experiments. Beyond a proof-of-concept, we systematically measure (i) handshake latency across 200 trials per configuration, (ii) InterQuartile Range (IQR) and 95% confidence intervals for stability, and (iii) migration time and correctness across staged states. The results confirm that continuous availability is preserved with moderate overhead relative to ECC baselines in compute-bound settings.

2 Background

2.1 TLS

TLS 1.3 establishes a secure channel with a single round-trip (1-RTT) handshake. The client initiates the connection with *ClientHello*, the server responds with *ServerHello*, and key agreement proceeds via the `supported_groups` and `key_share` extensions. Once the handshake completes, application data are protected with symmetric encryption. Server authentication is provided through *Certificate* and *CertificateVerify*, and both parties exchange *Finished* messages to ensure transcript integrity [7].

In TLS 1.3, the client's *ClientHello* advertises its capabilities through fields such as `cipher_suites`, `supported_versions`, `supported_groups`, `key_share`, and `signature_algorithms`/`signature_algorithms_cert`. The server's *ServerHello* then communicates its selections.

An operationally important point is that in TLS 1.3 the cipher suite string specifies only the symmetric record-protection algorithm and the HKDF hash. Key establishment is determined by the negotiated group (`supported_groups`/`key_share`), while authentication depends on the certificate's signature algorithm (`signature_algorithms` and optionally `signature_algorithms_cert`). Thus, the cipher suite string alone cannot indicate PQC adoption: PQC KEMs appear in the negotiated group, and PQC authentication in the certificate's signature scheme—neither is visible in the cipher suite name. By contrast, TLS 1.2 cipher suite names bundled key exchange, authentication, and symmetric protection (e.g., TLS_ECDHE_RSA_WITH_AES_128_GCM_SHA256), making it possible to infer algorithms directly [11]. Because TLS 1.3 separates these planes, one can deploy a PQC KEM without altering the cipher suite, or adopt PQC authentication simply by changing the certificate's signature algorithm.

2.2 NIST PQC Standardization

The U.S. National Institute of Standards and Technology (NIST) conducted a multi-year standardization process [12]. In 2024, NIST finalized its first set of PQC standards—FIPS 203 (ML-KEM), FIPS 204 (ML-DSA), and FIPS 205 (SLH-DSA) [13–15]—selecting ML-KEM (CRYSTALS-Kyber) [16] for key encapsulation and ML-DSA (CRYSTALS-Dilithium) for digital signatures, while SPHINCS+ (standardized as SLH-DSA) provides a stateless hash-based alternative [17]. Falcon remains a compact lattice-based signature scheme selected by NIST (FIPS forthcoming) [18]. More recently, NIST added HQC as an additional code-based KEM [19], further diversifying the standardized portfolio.

Security strength in PQC is defined in levels corresponding to classical work factors, with Level 1, Level 3, and Level 5 approximating AES-128, AES-192, and AES-256 key search complexities, respectively. Parameter sets are chosen in practice to achieve these levels while balancing efficiency, bandwidth, and implementation constraints. Table 1 summarizes the parameter sizes of the standardized NIST algorithms.

2.3 KpqC

South Korea launched the National Korean Post-Quantum Cryptography Competition (KpqC) in 2022 with the goal of establishing domestic cryptographic

Table 1. Parameter sizes (in bytes) of standardized NIST PQC algorithms.

Type	Algorithm	Security Lvl.	Public Key	Secret Key	Ciphertext/Sig.
KEM	ML-KEM-512	1	800	1,632	768
	ML-KEM-768	3	1,184	2,400	1,088
	ML-KEM-1024	5	1,568	3,168	1,568
KEM	HQC-128	1	2,249	56	4,497
	HQC-192	3	4,522	64	9,042
	HQC-256	5	7,245	72	14,485
Signature	ML-DSA-44	2	1,312	2,528	2,420
	ML-DSA-65	3	1,952	4,000	3,293
	ML-DSA-87	5	2,592	4,864	4,595
Signature	Falcon-512	1	897	1,281	666
	Falcon-1024	5	1,793	2,305	1,280
Signature	SPHINCS+128s	1	32	64	7,856
	SPHINCS+128f	1	32	64	17,088
	SPHINCS+192s	3	48	96	16,224
	SPHINCS+192f	3	48	96	35,664
	SPHINCS+256s	5	64	128	29,792
	SPHINCS+256f	5	64	128	49,856

standards [6]. In January 2025, the final KpqC standards were announced. Two KEMs (NTRU+ [20] and SMAUG-T [21]) and two digital signature schemes (AIMer [22] and HAETAE [23]) were standardized after a national evaluation process to meet domestic security policy requirements. Table 2 summarizes the parameter sizes of these algorithms.

2.4 Crypto Agility

Crypto agility denotes the capability to change cryptographic algorithms and parameters at runtime *via policy rather than code*, enabling safe migration under live traffic [24]. In TLS 1.3 this is operationally natural because record protection (cipher suite) is orthogonal to both key establishment (negotiated via supported_groups/key_share) and authentication (negotiated via signature_algorithms/signature_algorithms_cert) [7]. Hence, deployments can introduce a PQC KEM without changing the cipher suite, or adopt PQC authentication by switching the certificate's signature algorithm—both by updating policy rather than redeploying binaries.

2.4.1 Crypto Agility in TLS 1.3

In TLS 1.3, cipher-suite names enumerate only symmetric record protection and the hash, so neither the KEM nor the certificate-signature choice appears in the suite string; evidence of PQC use relies on the negotiated group and the certificate's signature algorithm. This conceptual decoupling enables migrations aligned with ongoing standards (e.g., FIPS 203/204/205 and the NIST PQC

Table 2. Parameter sizes (in bytes) of standardized KpqC algorithms.

Type	Algorithm	Security Lvl.	Public Key	Secret Key	Ciphertext/Sig.
KEM	NTRU+KEM576	1	864	1,760	864
	NTRU+KEM768	3	1,152	2,336	1,152
	NTRU+KEM864	3	1,296	2,624	1,296
	NTRU+KEM1152	5	1,728	3,488	1,728
KEM	SMAUG_T1	1	672	832	672
	SMAUG_T3	3	1,088	1,312	992
	SMAUG_T5	5	1,440	1,728	1,376
Signature	AIMer_128s	1	32	48	4,160
	AIMer_128f	1	32	48	5,888
	AIMer_192s	3	48	72	9,120
	AIMer_192f	3	48	72	13,056
	AIMer_256s	5	64	96	17,056
	AIMer_256f	5	64	96	25,120
Signature	HAETAE2	2	992	1,408	1,474
	HAETAE3	3	1,472	2,112	2,349
	HAETAE5	5	2,080	2,752	2,948

project) and with national profiles (e.g., KpqC), without service interruption [12–15,25].

2.4.2 Related Works

Existing systems already explore aspects of cryptographic agility across multiple layers. For example, Kubernetes [26] supports zero-downtime rolling updates of applications, while Envoy proxy [27] applies dynamic configuration updates via the xDS API. Cloudflare's PQC experiments [28] integrate quantum-resistant algorithms into TLS 1.3, but only as controlled production trials. At the web server layer, Nginx [8] supports hot reload of SSL configurations by restarting worker processes. Although these systems differ in scope, they collectively demonstrate that state-preserving reconfiguration is an established principle for achieving service continuity.

In contrast, our work focuses on real-time replacement of cryptographic algorithms *inside the TLS protocol stack* rather than configuration reload at the application or proxy level. This distinction enables capabilities that conventional proxies lack: (i) a policy-driven state machine (announce → prefer → require → rollback) for staged migration and safe rollback under failure, (ii) direct manipulation of TLS library contexts (`SSL_CTX`) instead of process-level reloads, and (iii) explicit support for PQC-specific challenges such as large certificates, higher handshake latency, and legacy-client fallback. Together, these features extend hot reload from simple configuration management to true crypto-agility in the TLS handshake.

To make this contrast clear, Table 3 summarizes the capabilities of representative systems—Nginx, Envoy, and Cloudflare— alongside our proposed approach, highlighting our unique support for rollback, policy-based migration, and full PQC integration.

Unlike Nginx or Envoy, which reload configurations at the process level and apply a single global policy to all new sessions, our bridge operates directly on SSL_CTX instances inside the TLS library. This enables **per-session policy enforcement**, allowing some clients to remain on ECC while others migrate to hybrid or PQC during the same deployment cycle.

Table 3 further highlights this distinction. Whereas existing hot-reload mechanisms lack rollback and staged migration support, our bridge combines per-session SSL_CTX selection with a policy-driven state machine, transforming hot reload from simple configuration management into an operational migration strategy tailored for PQC.

Table 3. Comparison of Hot Reload and PQC Support across Systems. Red checkmarks indicate features unique to our system, which are enabled by a state-machine-based migration design.

System / Project	Hot Reload	Downtime -free	Rollback	Policy-based Migration	PQC Support
Nginx [8]	✓	✓	✗	✗	✗
Nginx (with OQS build) [29]	✓	✓	✗	✗	✓*
Envoy [27]	✓	✓	✗	✗	✗
Cloudflare PQC [28]	Trial only	✓	✗	✗	✓†
Our System	✓	✓	✓	✓	✓

* Experimental support via OQS-enabled OpenSSL build.
† Limited beta-only deployment.

3 Proposed Method

3.1 System Overview and Objectives

Figure 1 illustrates the overall architecture of the proposed system. Figure 1(a) shows the scenario when the client uses classic TLS, while Fig. 1(b) depicts the scenario when PQC is used. Unlike conventional TLS proxies that reload configuration files at the process level, the proposed bridge operates directly at the TLS library level by configuring SSL_CTX instances for each new handshake. This enables migration policies to be applied at session creation time, ensuring that the negotiated cryptography reflects the policy in effect at that moment. The system consists of two servers employing different cryptographic protocols and a bridge that routes client requests to the appropriate server. Policies are reloaded via the SIGHUP signal (Sect. 3.2.2). During this process, existing sessions continue under the previous configuration, while newly established handshakes immediately adopt the updated policy. Because SSL_CTX reconfiguration is performed at runtime without restarting processes, the bridge achieves seamless policy updates without delay or downtime.

Listing 1.1 shows a simplified excerpt where the bridge creates a new SSL_CTX and applies PQC-capable groups and signature algorithms before the TLS handshake. This demonstrates that cryptographic policies are enforced at the library level rather than through external configuration reloads.

```
1  void *server_ctx = crypto_engine_create_ctx(&g_crypto_engine, 1, 2);
2  SSL_CTX *ssl_ctx = (SSL_CTX*)server_ctx;
3
4  // Apply PQC key-exchange groups (runtime policy)
5  const char *pqc_groups =
6    "smaug1:mlkem512:kyber768:ntruplukem864:X25519:P-256";
7  SSL_CTX_set1_groups_list(ssl_ctx, pqc_groups);
8
9  // Apply PQC signature algorithms (runtime policy)
10 const char *pqc_sigalgs =
11   "ecdsa_secp256r1_sha256";
12 SSL_CTX_set1_sigalgs_list(ssl_ctx, pqc_sigalgs);
```

Listing 1.1. Per-session SSL_CTX configuration at handshake creation.

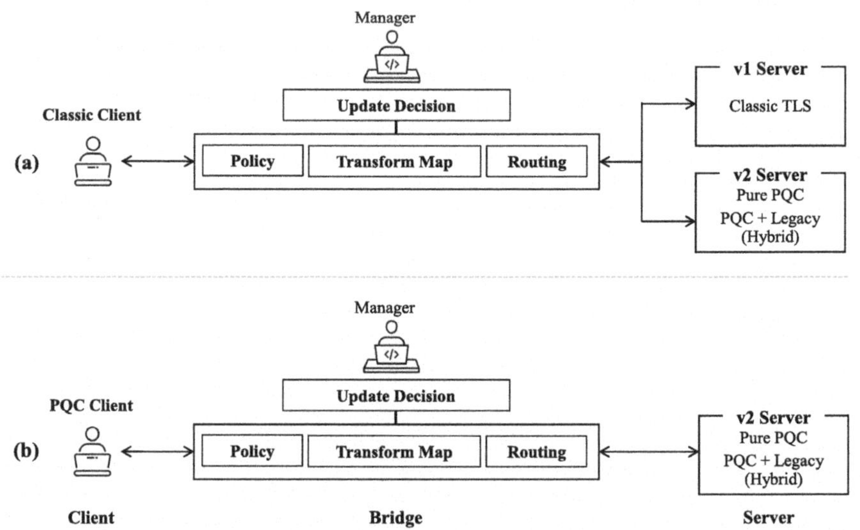

Fig. 1. System overview. Clients are routed to the appropriate server via the bridge according to their cryptographic protocol and the bridge's policy.
(a): Classic Client, (b): PQC Client.

3.2 Architecture

3.2.1 System Components

The system consists of clients, a bridge, and servers. To support both legacy and modern PQC clients, it adopts an intermediary relay through the bridge. The bridge routes clients to appropriate servers based on client version.

Client. The client is the entity requesting the service and is categorized into clients using PQC and those using classic TLS. During the TLS handshake process, the client transmits cryptographic information (see Sect. 2.1) to negotiate encryption capabilities through the bridge.

Bridge. This bridge is designed to ensure zero downtime and zero delay even during critical updates such as protocol changes or minor updates like message modifications. It functions as a TLS-to-TLS relay between clients and game servers. Clients are routed through the bridge to the appropriate game server according to their version, based on policies defined by the administrator (See Sect. 3.3.2).

Unlike conventional proxies that reload a single global SSL_CTX, our bridge pre-initializes multiple SSL_CTX instances (classic, hybrid, and PQC) and selects among them on a per-session basis according to the migration policy state (Announce, Prefer, Require, Rollback). This library-level control enables staged rollout and rollback under live traffic without disrupting existing connections (see Listing 1.2).

```
1  /* Pre-initialize multiple SSL_CTX instances */
2  SSL_CTX *ctx_classic = init_ctx("cert_classic.pem");
3  SSL_CTX *ctx_hybrid  = init_ctx("cert_hybrid.pem");
4  SSL_CTX *ctx_pqc     = init_ctx("cert_pqc.pem");
5
6  /* Policy state machine for migration */
7  SSL_CTX *selected_ctx;
8  switch (g_policy.migration_mode) {
9    case ANNOUNCE:
10     selected_ctx = ctx_classic; break;
11   case PREFER:
12     selected_ctx = client_supports_pqc ? ctx_hybrid : ctx_classic; break
       ;
13   case REQUIRE:
14     selected_ctx = ctx_pqc; break;
15   case ROLLBACK:
16     selected_ctx = ctx_classic; break;
17 }
18
19 /* Bind context per session */
20 SSL *ssl = SSL_new(selected_ctx);
21 if (SSL_accept(ssl) <= 0) {
22     log_error("TLS␣handshake␣failed");
23 }
```

Listing 1.2. Policy-driven per-session selection of PQC-enabled SSL_CTX instances.

Servers. Version 1 (v1) servers, which support classic TLS, and version 2 (v2) servers, which have PQC enabled including KpqC, coexist independently. The two communicate via a bridge using TLS. Clients are routed to the appropriate server through the bridge. The servers differ in their key exchange protocols: v1 is based on ECC [30], while v2 uses PQC and hybrid PQC key exchange methods. In this system, SMAUG-T KpqC is used as an example [21,31]. For compatibility, certificates and signatures are unified using RSA.

3.2.2 Transform Mechanism

This system proposes a mechanism that hierarchically separates policies and enables independent changes to each layer through a hot reload approach, thereby realizing uninterrupted policy updates.

Hot-Reload. Hot Reload is a technology that immediately applies code changes during application runtime without stopping the app, allowing developers to quickly see the results while preserving the application's state [8,32,33]

The system employs a hot reload [32] mechanism that loads changed code and configurations into memory and rebuilds while preserving the program state, allowing immediate reflection of updates without terminating or fully restarting the program. To achieve this, it leverages the SIGHUP signal, typically used to notify session termination or network disconnection [34], as a flag to reconfigure in-memory settings without killing the process for policy application.

Moreover, by structuring the bridge as a parent-child process model[1], policy changes in the parent process do not affect the child processes. Consequently, ongoing child process sessions maintain existing connections without interruption, while newly spawned child processes apply the updated policies.

Policy System. The system clearly separates policy structures into three layers: security policies, routing and network connection management, and content transformation. Each layer operates independently, and higher-level policies determine the behavior of lower-level ones, preventing policy conflicts.

The security policy layer (*crypto_policy.ini*) governs security aspects, including PQC migration modes, encryption algorithms, and TLS versions. The routing policy layer (*routing.ini*) manages network connections such as server routing by client version, port mapping, and load balancing. The content transformation layer (*transform_map.tsv*) enhances user experience through real-time message transformation and UI text updates. This modular structure allows easy modification of new policies or formats, and each layer's policy is hot reloaded for interruption-free updates.

[1] The child process is created by duplicating the parent process, but it has a unique process ID and operates independently afterward.

3.2.3 PQC Implementation

The encryption policy supports not only classic TLS but also PQC and hybrid PQC protocols. This system can apply both NIST PQC and KpqC, utilizing the following libraries to enable their implementation.

CLOQS-Linux. It is a PQC integrated library provided by `PQC Migration Platform`[2]. Built on top of the existing liboqs, it offers optimized implementations for various operating systems and low-power environments. Notably, while liboqs solely supports NIST PQC standard algorithms, CLOQS-Linux extends its support to encompass standard KpqC algorithms as well [35]. Table 4 lists the PQC algorithms supported by CLOQS-Linux. The presented system supports PQC and Hybrid PQC based on CLOQS-Linux.

Table 4. Supported PQC Algorithms in CLOQS-Linux. It includes KpqC, unlike the existing OQS library.

Type	Algorithm
NIST PQC	ML-KEM
	ML-DSA
	SLH-DSA (upcoming)
KpqC	SMAUG-T
	NTRU+
	HAETAE
	AIMer

oqs-provider. It is a library designed to enable post-quantum cryptography in OpenSSL version 3.x and higher, allowing the activation of PQC KEM and signature algorithms during TLS communications [36,37]. However, the officially provided oqs-provider does not support KpqC algorithms. Therefore, in this system, similar to CLOQS-Linux, we utilized the KpqC-compatible oqs-provider provided by the `PQC Migration Platform`.

3.3 Critical Update Scenario

Critical updates refer to major policy changes such as protocol modifications. In this section, we conducted a scenario of gradual migration from the v1 server (classic server) to the v2 server (PQC server).

[2] The first platform in South Korea to provide diverse PQC services. See https://pqcmp.kr.

3.3.1 Policy Criteria

To ensure system stability and reliability, this study defines specific transition criteria. The evaluation follows the recommendations in the Google Site Reliability Engineering Workbook, where the monitoring windows are set as follows: a Long window of 1 h and a Short window of 5 min. Transition rollback decisions are periodically evaluated based on the Long window, and if the defined threshold is not met, the system rolls back to the previous stage.

Three primary indicators—Client Compatibility, Latency, and Critical Error Rate—are used to evaluate the transition stability. Tables 5 and 6 summarize the quantitative criteria for both long-term and short-term rollback conditions, respectively.

Table 5. Long window (1 h) transition evaluation and rollback conditions

Category	Rollback Condition	Evaluation Criteria
Client Compatibility	$S_{PQC} < S_{prefer} - 5\%$	PQC communication success rate compared to the *prefer* baseline
Latency	$R_{delay} > 5\%$	Average overhead ratio and proportion of abnormal delay
Critical Error Rate	$E_{fail} > 0.1\%$	Handshake failure, authentication, or encryption errors

Here, S_{PQC} denotes the PQC communication success rate, S_{prefer} represents the prefer baseline success rate, R_{delay} is the proportion of abnormal delays, and E_{fail} indicates the critical error rate.

Client compatibility is defined as the PQC communication success rate relative to the prefer ratio. In this study, the transition is considered stable if the success rate after migration does not decrease by more than 5% compared to the prefer ratio. For instance, if the prefer ratio is 25%, a transition is deemed stable when the actual communication success rate remains at or above 20%.

Latency is evaluated based on the measured overhead presented in this paper. The average overhead observed when transitioning from ECC to PQC is 5.81 times, which is used as the reference value. If the overhead exceeds 7 times, it is regarded as an abnormal delay. However, as long as such abnormal delays occur in less than 5% of total requests, the system transition is considered to be proceeding normally.

The critical error rate represents defects that directly affect client connectivity, such as handshake failures or authentication errors. If this error rate exceeds 0.1%, the system is considered to have encountered a severe failure, and rollback procedure is triggered.

In the event of a major system failure, an immediate rollback is determined based on the short window criteria.

For rapid detection and short-term mitigation of abnormal behavior, a Short window with a 5-min period is used. This mechanism ensures immediate rollback when sudden performance degradation is observed. The short-term evaluation criteria are summarized in Table 6.

Table 6. Short window (5 min) immediate rollback conditions

Category	Rollback Condition	Evaluation Criteria
Client Compatibility	$S_{PQC} \geq 0.5 \times S_{prefer}$	PQC communication failure rate compared to prefer baseline
Latency	$R_{delay} \geq 30\%$	Proportion of delayed requests within the Short window
Critical Error Rate	$E_{fail} > 1\%$	Total connection failure rate including handshake errors

Here, S_{PQC} denotes the PQC failure ratio and E_{fail} represents the proportion of overall failed requests.

3.3.2 Policy-Based Routing

The proposed system is designed with a routing policy that aims for a gradual transition to PQC servers (see Fig. 2). By utilizing a weighted-based policy (prefer policy), clients are progressively directed to use PQC servers. In case of any issues, the routing environment can be rolled back at any time through policy control. This approach enables a smooth transition while maintaining service stability.

In the case of PQC clients, routing to PQC servers occurs immediately, regardless of the policy. Therefore, this section focuses on clients using classic TLS.

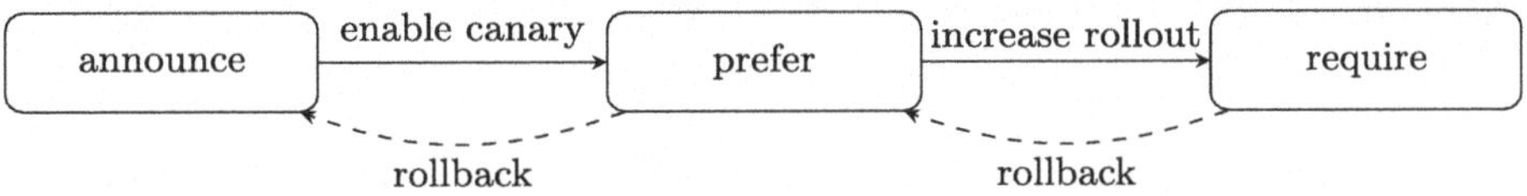

Fig. 2. State transition of routing policies enabling gradual PQC server migration for classical TLS clients, with rollback mechanisms ensuring service stability.

Announce. Figure 3 illustrates the routing scenario of classic clients during the announce policy phase. In this phase, clients are informed that PQC servers are supported, but routing itself is conducted to the classic servers instead of the PQC servers.

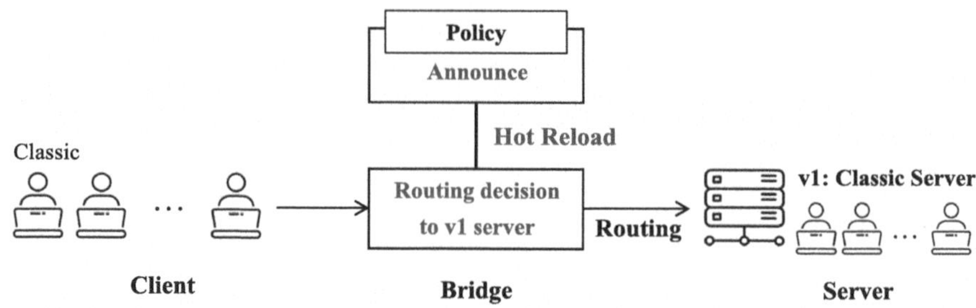

Fig. 3. Routing process in the **Announce** policy state. Clients using classic TLS are all routed to classic TLS server.

Prefer. Figure 4 illustrates the routing scenario for classic clients during the Prefer policy phase. The Prefer phase involves gradually routing classic clients initiating new handshakes to PQC servers. By adjusting the `rollout_percentage`, a portion of new handshakes is directed to PQC servers, enabling a staged rollout.

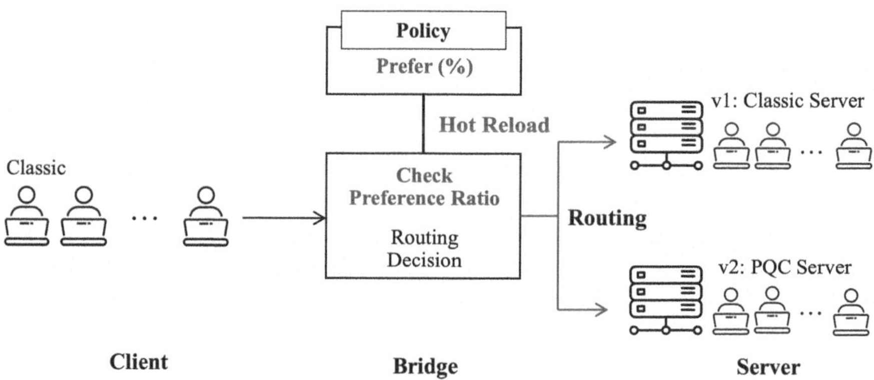

Fig. 4. Routing process in the **Prefer** policy state. classic TLS clients are routed to PQC server in proportion to the Prefer ratio. The higher the ratio, the greater the proportion of clients transitioning to PQC servers.

Require. Figure 5 illustrates the routing scenario for classic clients during the Require policy phase. In this phase, the bridge enforces all new handshakes to route to PQC servers. However, ongoing sessions are not migrated.

Rollback. If an error occurs, the Rollback policy can be executed to revert to the original policy.

3.4 Minor Update Scenario

Minor updates refer to light changes, such as simple text error corrections. This section covers the update scenario performed when simple text errors occur.

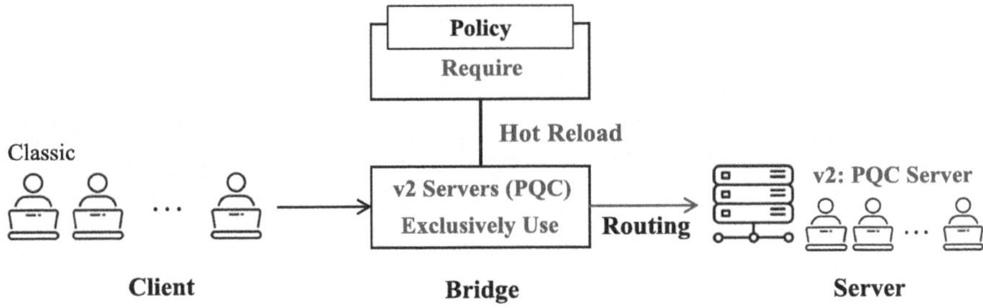

Fig. 5. Routing process in the **Require** policy state. Clients using classic TLS are also all routed to PQC servers.

Figure 6 illustrates the server update scenario in a minor update situation. When simple errors like typos are detected, administrators can resolve them by modifying the `Transform_map` without server downtime. The changes are not applied to ongoing sessions but take effect starting from new sessions.

4 Results

This section presents the results and discussion of testing a simple game server created based on the proposed system. In particular, it addresses performance changes resulting from policy modifications in the critical and minor scenarios proposed in Sect. 3, as well as differences in handshake performance according to the TLS protocol.

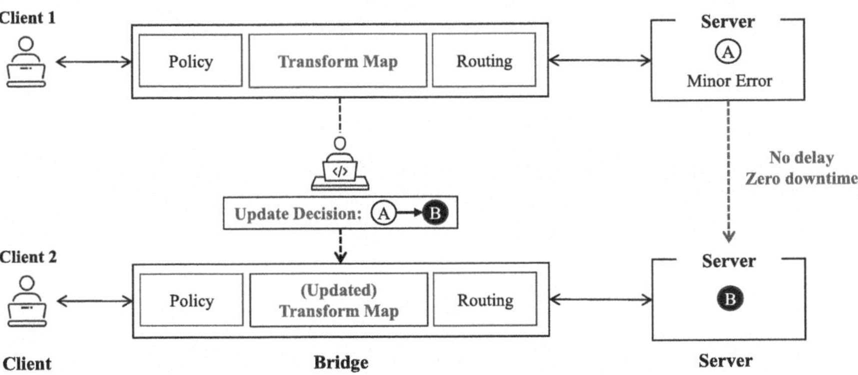

Fig. 6. Minor error correction using the Transform Map allows administrators to update mapping rules without downtime, applying changes immediately to new sessions while ongoing sessions remain unaffected.

4.1 Experimental Setup

Table 7 was built based on version Ubuntu 22.04 in two virtual environments to match the library environment provided by the PQC migration platform used in the study. Additionally, protocol communication tests using PQC-based KEM were conducted by utilizing OpenSSL and liboqs. The build supports cross-platform compilation using CMake 3.22.1 and compiles according to the GCC 11.4.0 standard.

Table 7. Experimental environments (single-host, two-terminal setup).

Label	OS	GCC	Virtual Env.	OpenSSL
Virtual 1	Ubuntu 22.04.5 LTS	11.4.0	VirtualBox	3.0.2
Virtual 2	Ubuntu 22.04.5 LTS	11.4.0	VMWare	3.0.2

4.2 Handshake Evaluation

The handshake performance was precisely analyzed through 200 repeated measurements of latency. Each measurement recorded the response delay during the individual handshake process in milliseconds (ms), and the interquartile range (IQR) was additionally calculated to evaluate the distribution and stability of the data.

4.2.1 Classic TLS

Since the TLS 1.3 standard recommends ECC-based key exchange [7], this study evaluated the performance of Classic TLS using ECC-based key exchange. Table 8 shows the handshake performance of Classic TLS.

Table 8. TLS 1.3 handshake latency and IQR with ECC, measured over 200 repeated handshake attempts.

Type	Algorithm	Latency (ms)	IQR (ms)	95% CI High	95% CI Low
ECC	X25519	86.1	11.7	145.6	73.0
	X448	88.1	11.8	159.2	75.2
	P-256	85.8	11.7	161.2	70.9
	P-384	116.1	42.7	209.5	79.8
	P-521	90.7	10.3	183.4	76.7

4.2.2 PQC Handshake

Table 9 shows the handshake performance of PQC. In this case, hybrid algorithms including NTRU+, except for the 576-bit key length, failed to produce valid measurements. This is likely due to compatibility issues and overload caused by the key length, which prevented the proper completion of the handshake process.

The measured PQC handshake performance showed a relatively high delay, averaging in the upper 600 ms range. This is interpreted as due to the inherently higher computational complexity and increased key length of PQC operations compared to classical TLS operations. However, this delay is an essential trade-off to achieve quantum-resistant security, providing long-term stability in future quantum computing environments. Furthermore, considering that the experiment was conducted in a virtual environment and the potential introduction of hardware acceleration, there is significant room for performance improvement through optimization.

Table 10 compares PQC and Hybrid KEMs against their corresponding ECC baselines, while Table 8 and Table 9 summarize handshake latency across ECC, PQC-only, and Hybrid KEMs in compute-bound experiments. The results show that PQC-only algorithms introduce a 5.8–6.4× increase relative to their ECC counterparts, with Hybrid KEMs consistently incurring slightly higher costs. Some Hybrid variants (e.g., NTRU+KEM-768/864/1152) were omitted due to implementation limitations.

4.3 Zero-Downtime Migration Evaluation

4.3.1 Critical Update Scenario: Migration to PQC Protocol

We evaluated the performance of the PQC migration process by measuring migration time, success rate, and resource usage at each stage of the system. Ultimately, we measured the results of continuously performing incremental migrations (Announce → Prefer 25% → Prefer 50% → Prefer 75% → Require) to estimate the minimum expected time for full PQC transition. Migration time refers to the period from changing the PQC configuration to sending a SIGHUP to the bridge and waiting until the configuration is applied. For each stage, a total of 200 migration tests were collected and analyzed through real-time performance monitoring, confirming that PQC migration was successfully executed.

Table 9. TLS 1.3 handshake latency and interquartile range (IQR) with PQC and hybrid key encapsulation mechanisms (KEMs) were measured over 200 repeated handshake attempts for each algorithm to ensure statistical robustness, with 95% confidence intervals (CI) for upper and lower bounds also calculated.

Type	PQC Algorithm	Hybrid(ECC)	Latency(ms)	IQR(ms)	CI High	CI Low
PQC-only	ML-KEM-512		536	4.6	537	536
	ML-KEM-768		535	3.8	536	535
	ML-KEM-1024		539	7.3	540	538
	SMAUG-T1		536	5.2	537	536
	SMAUG-T3		537	5.2	537	536
	SMAUG-T5		538	5.4	539	537
	NTRU+KEM-576		555	15.2	558	553
	NTRU+KEM-768		539	5.6	540	537
	NTRU+KEM-864		543	5.6	543	542
	NTRU+KEM-1152		542	9.2	544	540
Hybrid PQC	ML-KEM-512	secp256r1	557	6.6	559	555
	ML-KEM-768	secp384r1	557	7.2	559	555
	ML-KEM-1024	secp521r1	554	7.5	555	553
	SMAUG-T1	secp256r1	551	5.4	552	551
	SMAUG-T3	secp384r1	561	10.8	564	559
	SMAUG-T5	secp521r1	553	6.2	554	551
	NTRU+KEM-576	secp256r1	555	7.5	556	553
	NTRU+KEM-768	secp384r1	–	–	–	–
	NTRU+KEM-864	secp384r1	–	–	–	–
	NTRU+KEM-1152	secp521r1	–	–	–	–

Table 11 presents the performance classification results by stage. To account for the possibility that a new configuration might activate before the bridge settings were fully applied, a 2000 ms delay was introduced during the migration process. The estimated actual migration time (Adjusted Migration Time) was then obtained by subtracting this offset from the measured values.

Each 'prefer' percentage indicates the proportion of classic clients routed to PQC servers. Specifically, 25% means that only one-quarter of classic client sessions are redirected to PQC servers while the rest continue using ECC; 50% corresponds to half of the sessions, and 75% to three-quarters the sessions use PQC servers, and 75% means 75% of sessions use PQC servers.

Therefore, the actual estimated migration time is close to an average of 30 ms, which means that the security policy transition occurs in a seamless and non-disruptive manner with negligible impact on user experience.

Table 10. Handshake latency of PQC and Hybrid KEMs relative to their ECC counterparts (compute-bound).

Type	Algorithm	ECC Baseline	Overhead vs. ECC
Hybrid	ML-KEM-512 + secp256r1	P-256	+549.2% (6.49×)
	ML-KEM-768 + secp384r1	P-384	+379.8% (4.80×)
	ML-KEM-1024 + secp521r1	P-521	+510.9% (6.11×)
	SMAUG-T1 + secp256r1	P-256	+542.2% (6.42×)
	SMAUG-T3 + secp384r1	P-384	+383.2% (4.83×)
	SMAUG-T5 + secp521r1	P-521	+509.7% (6.10×)
	NTRU+KEM-576 + secp256r1	P-256	+546.9% (6.47×)
PQC-only	ML-KEM-512	P-256	+524.7% (6.25×)
	ML-KEM-768	P-384	+360.8% (4.61×)
	ML-KEM-1024	P-521	+494.3% (5.94×)
	SMAUG-T1	P-256	+524.7% (6.25×)
	SMAUG-T3	P-384	+362.5% (4.63×)
	SMAUG-T5	P-521	+493.2% (5.93×)
	NTRU+KEM-576	P-256	+546.9% (6.47×)

Furthermore, the analysis of the IQR during the entire migration process (`Total Migration`) was 13.7 ms, confirming that the policy transitions were carried out stably throughout all stages.

Table 11. Migration times for each PQC migration step according to policy (see Sect. 3.3.2) are presented together with the results of 200 repeated attempts and the adjusted migration times.

Process	Migration Time (ms)	Adjusted Migration Time (ms)
announce → prefer 25%	2,036.7	36.7
prefer 25% → prefer 50%	2,035.2	35.2
prefer 50% → prefer 75%	2,030.7	30.7
prefer 75% → require	2,027.7	27.7
Full Migration Process	2,032.5	32.5
Total Migration	2032.6	32.6

4.3.2 Minor Update Scenario: Simple Notice Update Within the Server

The minor scenario evaluated performance by assuming a situation where announcements are modified during the game start and progression. This process involves a single event rather than a gradual policy transition, and the impact on actual system operation was observed by repeatedly performing minor announcement modifications.

Figure 7 shows textual results confirming that message modifications were properly reflected and displayed during the scenario execution. The average delivery delay time from server application to client exposure was measured to be 40 ms (Table 12).

[INFO] Transform map update complete. New rules:

Old Value	**New Value**
Welcome to Game Server v2!	Welcome to Game Server v2! **[Grammar Fixed]**
Game start	Game start! **[Fixed]**
wins the round!	wins! **[Fixed]**
Errer: It is not your turn.	Error: It is not your turn. **[Grammar Fixed]**
Invalid command.	Invalid command... **[Fixed]**

[INFO] Reloading bridge server via SIGHUP

Fig. 7. Minor error correction process Log. The old value is replaced with the new value through the SIGHUP signal (See Sect. 3.2.2).

Table 12. Migration times for a minor update within the server are presented together with the estimated actual times. This process corresponds to a minor notification text modification, and the measurement was conducted in the same manner as before, using 200 repeated handshake attempts with a 2000ms delay, following the approach in Table 11.

Server	Migration Time (ms)	Adjusted Migration Time (ms)
v1 (Classic TLS 1.3)	2,042.0	42.0
v2 (PQC)	2,038.3	38.3

5 Conclusion

The advent of quantum computing necessitates a timely and practical migration from classical public-key cryptography to post-quantum standards. Although TLS 1.3 provides an architectural basis for integrating new cryptographic primitives, operational challenges such as larger certificates, increased handshake latency, and legacy-client compatibility hinder direct deployment.

This work proposed a bridge-server-based framework that enables zero-downtime TLS 1.3 migration. By incorporating policy-driven routing, hot reload, and rollback mechanisms, the system realizes practical *crypto agility*, allowing administrators to transition seamlessly between classical and PQC-enabled servers.

Beyond migration, the bridge server also supports operational updates: in *minor updates* (e.g., message corrections), it transparently applies changes without disturbing active sessions, while in *major updates* (e.g., protocol or version changes), multiple bridge instances preserve compatibility and orchestrate phased migration. This dual capability positions the bridge server as a practical step toward sustaining secure TLS services under continuous evolution.

Experimental validation confirmed that the proposed approach preserves service continuity with measurable overhead. In particular, handshake latency was approximately 5.8–6.4× higher than ECC baselines in compute-bound settings, while the relative overhead was substantially smaller in network-bound scenarios—highlighting the importance of deployment context. Despite being conducted in controlled virtualized environments that do not fully capture production-scale diversity, these experiments establish a reproducible baseline for future evaluations.

Future work includes extending support to a broader range of PQC algorithms, integrating automated monitoring for adaptive policy control, and assessing deployments at larger scale and under diverse network conditions.

Acknowledgment. This work was supported by Institute for Information & communications Technology Promotion(IITP) grant funded by the Korea government(MSIT) (No.2018-0-00264, Research on Blockchain Security Technology for IoT Services, 10%) and this work was supported by Institute of Information & communications Technology Planning & Evaluation (IITP) grant funded by the Korea government(MSIT) (No. RS-2025-02306395, Development and Demonstration of PQC-Based Joint Certificate PKI Technology, 45%) and this work was supported by the Institute of Information & Communications Technology Planning & Evaluation(IITP) grant funded by the Korea government(MSIT) (No. RS-2025-25394739, Development of Security Enhancement Technology for Industrial Control Systems Based on S/HBOM Supply Chain Protection, 45%).

References

1. Milanov, E.: The RSA algorithm. RSA Laboratories, vol. 1, no. 11 (2009)
2. Maurer, U.M., Wolf, S.: The Diffie-Hellman protocol. Des. Codes Crypt. **19**(2), 147–171 (2000)
3. Shor, P.W.: Algorithms for quantum computation: discrete logarithms and factoring. In: Proceedings 35th Annual Symposium on Foundations of Computer Science, pp. 124–134. IEEE (1994)
4. Grover, L.K.: A fast quantum mechanical algorithm for database search. In: Proceedings of the Twenty-Eighth Annual ACM Symposium on Theory of Computing, pp. 212–219 (1996)
5. National Institute of Standards and Technology: Selected algorithms — post-quantum cryptography. NIST CSRC (2024)
6. Korea Post-Quantum Cryptography Research Group: Official website of Korea post-quantum cryptography research group (2025)
7. Rescorla, E.: The Transport Layer Security (TLS) Protocol Version 1.3. Request for Comments RFC 8446, Internet Engineering Task Force (2018)

8. Ivanitskiy, M.: SSL/TLS Certificate Rotation Without Restarts in NGINX Open Source. NGINX Community Blog (2023)
9. HAProxy Technologies: Seamless reloads with zero downtime. HAProxy Documentation (2024). Accessed 19 Sept 2025
10. Grote, O., Ahrens, A., Benavente-Peces, C.: A review of post-quantum cryptography and crypto-agility strategies. In: 2019 International Interdisciplinary PhD Workshop (IIPhDW), pp. 115–120. IEEE (2019)
11. Dierks, T., Rescorla, E.: The Transport Layer Security (TLS) Protocol Version 1.2. Request for Comments RFC 5246, Internet Engineering Task Force (2008)
12. NIST PQC project (2025). https://csrc.nist.gov/Projects/post-quantum-cryptography. Accessed 7 June 2025
13. Module-lattice-based key-encapsulation mechanism (FIPS 203). Technical Report FIPS 203, National Institute of Standards and Technology (2024). Final publication: 13 Aug 2024
14. Module-lattice-based digital signature standard (FIPS 204). Technical Report FIPS 204, National Institute of Standards and Technology (2024). Final publication: 13 Aug 2024
15. Stateless hash-based digital signature standard (FIPS 205). Technical Report FIPS 205, National Institute of Standards and Technology (2024). Final publication: 13 Aug 2024
16. Avanzi, R., et al.: CRYSTALS-Kyber algorithm specifications and supporting documentation. NIST PQC Round, vol. 2, no. 4 (2019)
17. Bernstein, D.J., Hülsing, A., Kölbl, S., Niederhagen, R., Rijneveld, J., Schwabe, P.: The SPHINCS+ signature framework. In: Proceedings of the 2019 ACM SIGSAC Conference on Computer and Communications Security, pp. 2129–2146 (2019)
18. Fouque, P.-A., et al.: Falcon: fast-fourier lattice-based compact signatures over NTRU. Submission to the NIST's Post-Quantum Cryptography Standardization Process, vol. 36, no. 5 (2018)
19. NIST selects HQC as fifth algorithm for post-quantum encryption. NIST News Release (2025)
20. Kim, J., Park, J.H.: NTRU+: compact construction of NTRU using simple encoding method. IEEE Trans. Inf. Forensics Secur. (2023)
21. SMAUG-T: the key exchange algorithm based on module-LWE and module-LWR (2025). https://kpqc.or.kr/images/pdf/SMAUG-T_Document.pdf. Accessed 7 June 2025
22. Kim, S., Ha, J., Lee, J.: AIM: symmetric primitive for shorter signatures with stronger security. In: ACM CCS 2023: ACM Conference on Computer and Communications Security. ACM (Association for Computing Machinery) (2023)
23. Cheon, J.H., et al.: Haetae: Shorter lattice-based Fiat-Shamir signatures. Cryptology ePrint Archive (2023)
24. Wiesmaier, A., et al.: On PQC migration and crypto-agility, arXiv preprint arXiv:2106.09599 (2021)
25. KPQC competition (2025). https://kpqc.or.kr/competition.html. Accessed 7 June 2025
26. Performing a rolling update (2025). https://kubernetes.io/docs/tutorials/kubernetes-basics/update/update-intro/. Accessed 20 Sept 2025
27. Envoy proxy official documentation (2025). https://www.envoyproxy.io/docs/envoy/latest/. Accessed 20 Sept 2025
28. Post-quantum cryptography in Cloudflare's zero trust platform (2025). https://developers.cloudflare.com/ssl/post-quantum-cryptography/pqc-and-zero-trust/. Accessed 20 Sept 2025

29. Openquantumsafe experimental nginx docker image. https://hub.docker.com/r/openquantumsafe/nginx. Accessed 23 Sept 2025
30. Koblitz, N., Menezes, A., Vanstone, S.: The state of elliptic curve cryptography. Des. Codes Crypt. **19**(2), 173–193 (2000)
31. Cheon, J.H., Choe, H., Hong, D., Yi, M.: Smaug: pushing lattice-based key encapsulation mechanisms to the limits. In: International Conference on Selected Areas in Cryptography, pp. 127–146. Springer (2023)
32. Tashildar, A., Shah, N., Gala, R., Giri, T., Chavhan, P.: Application development using flutter. Int. Res. J. Mod. Eng. Technol. Sci. **2**(8), 1262–1266 (2020)
33. Hot reload - flutter documentation (2025). https://docs.flutter.dev/tools/hot-reload. Accessed 19 Sept 2025
34. signal(7) - Linux manual page (2025). https://man7.org/linux/man-pages/man7/signal.7.html. Accessed 19 Sept 2025
35. Open Quantum Safe Project: liboqs: C library for quantum-safe cryptographic algorithms. Project website (2025)
36. OpenSSL Project: provider(7) — OpenSSL Documentation (2025)
37. Open Quantum Safe Project: OQS-provider: open quantum safe provider for openssl (3.x). GitHub repository (2025)

On the Feasibility of Deploying Lattice-Based PQC in ARM TrustZone TEEs: A Systematic Vulnerability Assessment

Hyunmin Kim(✉)

Technology Innovation Institute, Abu Dhabi, United Arab Emirates
hyunmin.kim@tii.ae

Abstract. The quantum resistance of lattice-based cryptography becomes moot if its deployment introduces exploitable side-channels. We present the first comprehensive vulnerability assessment of NIST standardized post-quantum algorithms within ARM TrustZone. Through systematic evaluation on NXP i.MX93 hardware running OP-TEE 4.4, we demonstrate that integrating Dilithium-3 and Kyber-768 into existing TEE architectures creates critical vulnerabilities: (i) near-deterministic operation classification (98.9% accuracy) through timing side-channels from unprivileged processes, exploiting 49.6% overhead and 13× world-switch frequency versus classical algorithms; (ii) rejection sampling leaking 0.192 bits per signing operation, enabling key recovery within 50,000 observations; (iii) complete denial-of-service where Dilithium's 73KB footprint exceeds the 32KB TA heap; and (iv) 40× latency increase under concurrent workloads. Our analysis traces these vulnerabilities to fundamental TEE design decisions—synchronous invocation, shared caches, static memory pools—incompatible with PQC computational patterns. We quantify mitigation efficacy and release our measurement framework for reproducible assessment.

Keywords: Post-Quantum Cryptography · Trusted Execution Environment · ARM TrustZone · Dilithium · Kyber · Side-Channel Analysis

1 Introduction

The standardization of post-quantum cryptography by NIST in 2022 [36] marks a critical transition in cryptographic infrastructure, establishing Dilithium [22] for digital signatures and Kyber [12] for key encapsulation as the foundation for quantum-resistant security. This transition is driven by rapid advances in quantum computing [5,26], with IBM's quantum roadmap projecting 100,000-qubit systems by 2033 [26]. Simultaneously, ARM TrustZone has emerged as the dominant hardware security primitive, securing billions of devices from smartphones to IoT sensors [4,38]. The convergence of these technologies—deploying

H. Seo (Ed.): ICISC 2025, LNCS 16487, pp. 150–167, 2026.
https://doi.org/10.1007/978-981-95-8034-7_8

PQC algorithms within TEE environments—represents a natural evolution that promises to deliver quantum resistance with hardware-backed security guarantees [10,16].

However, our comprehensive evaluation reveals that this convergence creates unprecedented vulnerabilities that challenge fundamental assumptions about both technologies. Previous studies have identified vulnerabilities in TrustZone implementations [15,17,32,45], but focused primarily on classical cryptography. The architectural decisions that make TEEs efficient for classical cryptography—minimal secure memory, synchronous invocation models, and shared microarchitectural resources—become critical weaknesses when confronted with PQC's dramatically different computational patterns [25,39]. These are not implementation bugs that can be patched, but fundamental incompatibilities that require architectural evolution.

We present the first systematic vulnerability assessment of lattice-based PQC algorithms within ARM TrustZone running OP-TEE 4.4 [31]. Our findings demonstrate that integrating Dilithium-3 and Kyber-768 into existing TEE architectures not only fails to provide expected security guarantees but actively introduces new attack surfaces exploitable from unprivileged normal-world applications, consistent with side-channel vulnerabilities identified in recent studies [7,30,35,42].

1.1 Principal Findings and Contributions

Our investigation reveals a perfect storm of vulnerabilities arising from the collision between PQC computational requirements and TEE architectural constraints, building upon prior work on PQC implementation challenges [3,20,28]. Table 1 summarizes our key discoveries, which stem from fundamental incompatibilities rather than correctable implementation flaws.

Table 1. Summary of discovered vulnerabilities, their impact, and architectural root causes

Vulnerability	Success Rate	Impact	Root Cause
Operation Detection	98.9%	Critical	3× timing asymmetry between operations
Rejection Prediction	80%	High	Message-dependent iterations
Information Leakage	0.192 bits/op	Critical	Rejection sampling variability
Memory Exhaustion	100%	Critical	73KB vs 32KB heap mismatch
Latency Amplification	40×	Severe	13× world-switch frequency

These vulnerabilities are particularly concerning because they compound through attack chaining, similar to techniques demonstrated in Spectre-style attacks [29]. An adversary can force memory exhaustion with certainty, pushing the system into a degraded state that amplifies timing variance. This amplified variance enables near-deterministic operation detection, which identifies signing operations for rejection sampling analysis. Over time, the accumulated information leakage enables complete key recovery—all from unprivileged normal-world access without any TEE compromise, exploiting weaknesses similar to those found in LWE implementations [24].

Our specific contributions include:

1. **Comprehensive vulnerability assessment:** First systematic evaluation of NIST-standardized PQC within production TEE environments through hardware experiments, extending beyond prior embedded PQC studies [1,13]
2. **Practical attack implementations:** Four categories of attacks achieving the success rates in Table 1, with released proof-of-concept code
3. **Quantitative overhead analysis:** Detailed measurements showing 49.6% baseline overhead, 13× world-switch multiplication, and 40× latency under contention, surpassing overhead reported in [41]
4. **Architectural root cause identification:** Systematic analysis tracing vulnerabilities to specific TEE design decisions [40]
5. **Mitigation evaluation:** Assessment of countermeasures showing their fundamental inadequacy (60% attack reduction at 25% performance cost)
6. **Reproducible framework:** Complete measurement infrastructure, OP-TEE configurations, and attack implementations for independent validation

1.2 Implications

Our findings have immediate implications for the billions of devices relying on TrustZone for security. Organizations planning PQC migration must recognize that TEE deployment may introduce more vulnerabilities than it mitigates, as warned by industry deployments [18]. The architectural changes required—elastic secure memory, asynchronous invocation, hardware acceleration with isolation [23,27,44]—represent multi-year engineering efforts that will not materialize before quantum threats become practical. This creates a dangerous gap where systems are vulnerable to both classical side-channel attacks we demonstrate and future quantum attacks they aim to prevent, especially given the recent SIDH break [14] highlighting the fragility of post-quantum assumptions.

2 Background and Related Work

2.1 System Model and Threat Assumptions

We study lattice-based PQC algorithms executed within ARM TrustZone TEEs [4,38], specifically focusing on Dilithium-3 [22] for digital signatures and Kyber-768 [12] for key encapsulation. The system architecture comprises a Normal World (N) running untrusted applications and a Secure World (S) executing trusted applications under OP-TEE [31]. Communication between worlds occurs through GlobalPlatform APIs, triggering monitor transitions that save and restore processor state while marshaling data through dedicated shared memory regions [40].

Our threat model assumes an unprivileged attacker operating within the Normal World who seeks to extract cryptographic secrets from TEE-isolated PQC operations, similar to attacks demonstrated in [17,32,45]. The attacker can: (i) issue arbitrary sequences of TEE calls to PQC trusted applications, (ii) observe coarse-grained timing information and system-level signals [30], (iii) co-locate benign workloads to create resource contention, and (iv) monitor publicly accessible performance counters. Crucially, the attacker cannot directly access Secure World memory, modify TEE code, or compromise the ARM monitor's integrity [15].

Generalizability. While our evaluation targets ARM TrustZone with OP-TEE, the discovered vulnerabilities stem from design patterns common across TEE architectures. Memory exhaustion attacks apply to any TEE with constrained secure memory (Intel SGX's 128MB enclave limits [19], AMD SEV-SNP's ASID constraints [2]), while rejection sampling leakage affects all TEEs with observable timing characteristics. Platform-specific differences are noted in Sect. 4.

2.2 PQC Characteristics and TEE Constraints

The transition from classical to post-quantum cryptography represents a fundamental shift in computational patterns and resource requirements [10,16]. Table 2 quantifies these differences, highlighting the architectural mismatch that creates our discovered vulnerabilities.

Table 2. Resource requirements revealing fundamental classical vs post-quantum disparities

Parameter	RSA-2048	ECDSA-P256	Dilithium-3	Kyber-768
Key size (bytes)	256	32	4,032	2,400
Signature/CT size	256	64	3,309	1,088
Stack usage (KB)	2.1	0.8	39.2	12.4
Heap usage (KB)	4.2	1.9	73.1	24.3
World-switches	4	8	52	31
Cache footprint (KB)	8	4	156	87

The highlighted cells represent critical incompatibilities: Dilithium's 73KB heap requirement exceeds OP-TEE's default 32KB allocation, and 52 world-switches represent a 13× increase over RSA-2048. These are fundamental algorithmic requirements that cannot be optimized away [33,34].

2.3 Lattice-Based Cryptographic Primitives

Dilithium's Rejection Sampling Mechanism. Dilithium employs a "Fiat-Shamir with Aborts" paradigm to ensure signature uniformity [22,35]. The signing algorithm generates a masking vector $\mathbf{y}$ and computes $\mathbf{z} = \mathbf{y} + c\mathbf{s}_1$, which must satisfy:

$$||\mathbf{z}||_\infty < \gamma_1 - \beta \quad \text{and} \quad ||\mathbf{w} - c\mathbf{s}_2||_\infty < \gamma_2 - \beta \tag{1}$$

For Dilithium-3 parameters, rejection occurs with probability 0.75–0.85 per iteration, requiring 3–7 attempts on average. Each rejection adds approximately 110 μs, creating observable timing variations that correlate with the secret-message interaction [30,42].

Kyber's NTT Cache Patterns. Kyber's polynomial operations via Number Theoretic Transform (NTT) require bit-reversed addressing patterns creating distinctive cache footprints [12,33]. For Kyber-768 (n=256, q=3329), this generates non-sequential memory access across 24KB, causing 2.7× more L2 cache misses than sequential ECDH operations, creating potential for cache-timing attacks when the last-level cache is shared between worlds [7,25].

2.4 Prior Work and Research Gap

NIST's PQC standardization [36] evaluated algorithmic security but explicitly excluded implementation security considerations. Performance studies on embedded platforms [3,28] measured PQC efficiency but typically evaluated native execution without TEE isolation overhead. TrustZone security research [15,40,45] identified microarchitectural leakage channels but focused on classical cryptography. Recent PQC side-channel work [11,39,42] demonstrated vulnerabilities in isolated algorithms but not within TEE contexts.

The critical gap our work addresses is the intersection: how do PQC's distinctive computational patterns interact with TEE resource constraints and isolation boundaries? No prior study has systematically evaluated this combination under realistic deployment conditions with actual hardware [37], concurrent workloads, and production TEE configurations.

3 Methodology

3.1 Experimental Setup

Our experimental infrastructure centers on the NXP i.MX93 evaluation kit, featuring dual Cortex-A55 cores operating at 1.7 GHz with 2 GB LPDDR4X-4266 memory and a shared 256KB L2 cache. This platform represents modern embedded processors deployed in automotive, industrial, and IoT applications where TEE security is critical. The Secure World runs OP-TEE OS 4.4.0 implementing GlobalPlatform TEE specifications, while the Normal World executes Linux 6.6.23-lts with standard Ubuntu 22.04 userspace.

We integrated Dilithium-3 and Kyber-768 implementations from the Open Quantum Safe (OQS) project's `liboqs` library [43], which provides reference implementations of NIST-standardized post-quantum algorithms based on the official CRYSTALS specifications [6,21]. The `liboqs` implementations correspond to CRYSTALS-Dilithium version 3.1 and CRYSTALS-Kyber version 3.02, matching the NIST Round 3 standardized parameter sets that form the basis of FIPS 203 and FIPS 204 [36].

These implementations were ported as GlobalPlatform-compliant trusted applications by adapting the build system to OP-TEE's SDK, replacing standard library calls with TEE-safe alternatives (`TEE_Malloc`, `TEE_GenerateRandom`), and modifying memory management for secure heap allocation. No algorithmic modifications were made to the core cryptographic operations, ensuring our vulnerability assessment applies to the standardized algorithms rather than implementation-specific artifacts. The resulting TAs were cross-compiled using GCC 12.2.0 with `-O2` optimization and `-march=armv8.2-a` for ARM Cortex-A55 compatibility. All measurements were conducted with the CPU governor set to 'performance' mode to eliminate DVFS-induced variance.

3.2 Measurement Infrastructure

Accurate vulnerability assessment requires precise measurement capabilities beyond standard profiling tools. We developed a three-layer measurement infrastructure:

Hardware Layer: Direct access to ARM Performance Monitoring Unit (PMU) counters provides cycle-accurate timing through PMCCNTR_EL0 (64-bit cycle counter at 1.7 GHz, 0.59ns resolution) and microarchitectural events including L2 cache misses (event 0×17), memory write-backs (event 0×18), and instruction retirement rates (event 0×08).

Software Layer: A monitoring daemon continuously collects metrics at 10kHz sampling rate, storing results in lock-free ring buffers to minimize perturbation. The timestamp correlation uses CLOCK_MONOTONIC_RAW with separate buffers per-CPU.

Analysis Layer: Real-time classification employs SIMD-optimized feature extraction using ARM NEON instructions. Sliding windows of 20 samples maintain running statistics with O(1) update complexity. Decision boundaries were trained offline on 500 samples.

Each experimental configuration was sampled 1,000 times with operation order randomized using a Mersenne Twister seeded from /dev/urandom. We report medians with 95% confidence intervals computed using bias-corrected accelerated (BCa) bootstrap with 10,000 resamples.

3.3 Attack Implementation Framework

We developed four attack categories demonstrating that unprivileged normal-world observations alone suffice for compromising TEE confidentiality and availability. Each attack exploits the architectural mismatches between PQC computational patterns and TEE design assumptions.

Operation Detection Attack. The fundamental premise of trusted execution—computational opacity—collapses when lattice-based operations exhibit distinctive computational signatures. Our detection methodology leverages seven orthogonal observational dimensions collected through PMU counters and system interfaces accessible from unprivileged userspace.

The approach employs z-score normalization followed by hierarchical classification: a two-stage decision tree first isolates signing operations through their distinctive temporal signature ($3\times$ longer execution with $40\times$ higher variance), then discriminates between key generation and verification through weighted multi-indicator scoring. Bayesian posterior probability estimation provides calibrated confidence measures. Section 4.1 presents the classifier design and evaluation results.

Rejection Sampling Analysis. Dilithium's rejection sampling mechanism, essential for security proofs, creates exploitable timing variations correlated with message content. Our analysis framework characterizes message patterns through Shannon entropy calculation, autocorrelation for periodicity detection, and run-length encoding for repetitive pattern identification.

The relationship between message characteristics and rejection iterations exhibits surprising predictability: low-entropy messages consistently trigger fewer rejections than high-entropy random data. We developed a regression model correlating observed execution time with predicted iteration count. Section 4.2 presents detailed accuracy measurements and information leakage quantification.

Resource Exhaustion. The architectural mismatch between PQC memory requirements and TEE provisioning creates deterministic denial-of-service vulnerabilities. Our implementation employs binary search to precisely determine heap boundaries—information that leaks through allocation failure patterns—then triggers cascading failures through concurrent PQC operation requests.

Beyond simple exhaustion, we developed techniques for triggering cascading failures where initial PQC operations prevent subsequent secure services from acquiring necessary resources. Section 4.4 quantifies the impact on system throughput and latency.

Contention Amplification. The final attack category exploits the multiplicative interaction between PQC's computational intensity and TEE's architectural overhead. By deliberately creating system conditions that maximize resource contention, we amplify timing variations from subtle statistical signals into easily observable deterministic patterns.

The methodology orchestrates three complementary pressure sources: cache pressure through memory-intensive threads with working sets exceeding L2 capacity, "SMC storms" saturating world-switch handling, and memory bandwidth saturation consuming 80% of theoretical DRAM bandwidth. This multi-dimensional pressure transforms the coefficient of variation from 0.41 to 1.56—a $3.8\times$ amplification that makes timing variations clearly distinguishable.

3.4 Validation and Controls

Experimental validity relies on comprehensive validation through multiple independent measurements across 790+ test iterations on the i.MX93 EVK platform. Timing measurements were collected using the ARM PMU cycle counter operating at 1.7 GHz, providing sub-microsecond resolution. Measurement consistency was verified through repeated trials showing coefficient of variation below 0.1 for deterministic operations.

Statistical rigor was maintained through pre-specified analysis protocols defining primary metrics before measurement collection. All reported confidence intervals employ bootstrap methods with 10,000 resamples. The Holm-Bonferroni correction was applied to all families of comparisons maintaining $\alpha = 0.05$. Effect sizes are reported using Cliff's δ for ordinal comparisons, with all significant findings exceeding the 0.8 threshold for large effects.

4 Vulnerability Assessment and Exploitation

We present our empirical findings demonstrating how architectural mismatches create exploitable vulnerabilities in PQC-TEE integration, building upon theoretical attack foundations [11,39].

4.1 Operation Classification Attack

TEE isolation should provide computational opacity, yet PQC's asymmetric complexity creates distinguishable signatures observable from unprivileged normal world processes, similar to cache-timing attacks demonstrated in [17,32,45]. Table 3 quantifies the distinctive characteristics in Dilithium operations that allow classification.

Table 3. PQC operation characteristics enabling classification (n=90 per operation)

Operation	Mean (ms)	Std Dev	L2 Misses	Memory Writes	World-Switches
KeyGen	0.440	0.007	1,247	2,841	48
Sign	1.259	0.513	3,421	1,523	52
Verify	0.424	0.005	892	674	44

We developed a hierarchical classifier achieving 98.9% accuracy using seven indicators from user-space, extending techniques from [29]. Algorithm 1 formalizes our two-stage approach: first identifying signing operations (timing > 800 μs, variance > 300 μs), then distinguishing KeyGen from Verify using weighted scoring.

Figure 1 demonstrates the classifier's effectiveness across all three operation types, with particularly strong performance in distinguishing signing operations due to their distinctive timing characteristics.

Algorithm 1. Hierarchical Operation Classification

Require: Indicator vector $\mathbf{I} = [t, c, m, v]$ (timing, cache, memory, variance)
1: **if** $t > 800\mu s$ AND $v > 300\mu s$ **then**
2: **return** SIGN {3× longer with 40× higher variance}
3: **else if** $3.0 \cdot t + 2.0 \cdot c + 2.0 \cdot m > \textit{threshold}$ **then**
4: **return** KEYGEN
5: **else**
6: **return** VERIFY
7: **end if**

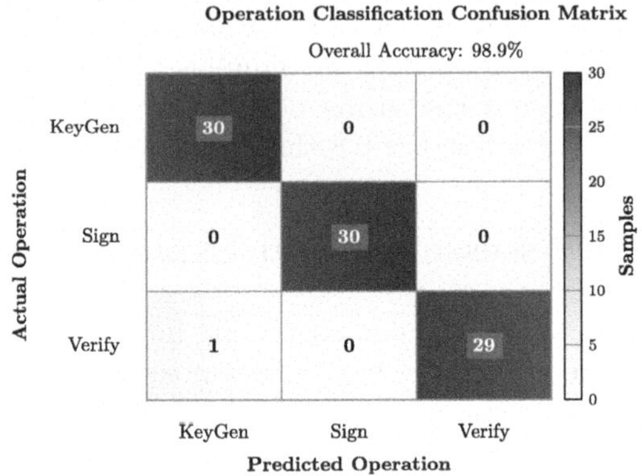

Fig. 1. Operation classification confusion matrix showing 98.9% overall accuracy.

4.2 Rejection Sampling Prediction

Dilithium's rejection sampling creates timing variations leaking secret information, as analyzed in [11,30,35]: $T_{sign} = T_{base} + N_{reject} \cdot T_{iteration}$ where $T_{base} \approx 920\mu s$ and $T_{iteration} \approx 110\mu s$.

As illustrated in Fig. 2, our pattern-matching algorithm combines entropy analysis with structural detection, achieving 80% accuracy within ×2 iterations. Single-byte patterns average 3.1 rejections while alternating patterns trigger 7.1, providing sufficient signal for key recovery as theoretically demonstrated in [24].

At this rate, practical key recovery becomes feasible within 3–6 months for embedded systems performing 20–50 daily signatures, faster than power analysis attacks on NTRU Prime [25] but slower than single-trace attacks [42].

4.3 Information Leakage Accumulation

Each signing operation leaks 0.192 bits (95% CI: [0.176, 0.209]) through timing variations, consistent with theoretical bounds established in [8], The cumulative effect of this leakage is shown in Fig. 3, which plots the total information extracted as a function of observed signing operations.

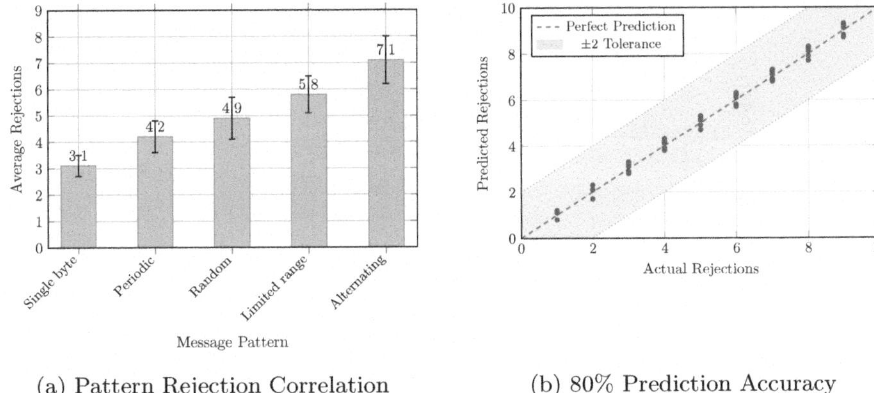

(a) Pattern Rejection Correlation (b) 80% Prediction Accuracy

Fig. 2. Rejection sampling analysis reveals exploitable message-dependent patterns consistent with [42].

4.4 Memory Exhaustion and Performance Collapse

The fundamental incompatibility between Dilithium's 73KB requirement [13] and OP-TEE's 32KB heap creates cascading failures. Table 4 quantifies the severe performance degradation and DoS conditions:

Table 4. Performance degradation under resource constraints

Metric	Isolated	Under Load	Degradation	CV Increase
Dilithium KeyGen	0.44ms	2.85ms	6.5×	9.3×
Dilithium Sign	1.26ms	47.52ms	37.7×	3.8×
Dilithium Verify	0.42ms	39.19ms	92.4×	18.5×
Heap Config	**Single Op**	**Concurrent**	**Throughput**	**DoS Rate**
32KB (default)	Fail	Fail	0%	100%
128KB (expanded)	Success	Limited	45%	55%

The upper half of Table 4 demonstrates catastrophic latency increases (37.7–92.4×) with amplified variance under concurrent load, while the lower half shows complete denial-of-service under default 32KB heap configurations. Even with expanded 128KB heaps, throughput collapses to 45% of baseline, confirming that resource exhaustion is architectural rather than configurational.

The dramatic impact of resource exhaustion on system capacity is visualized in Fig. 4. Even with expanded heap, PQC operations block concurrent secure services. Under contention, latency increases 40× while coefficient of variation

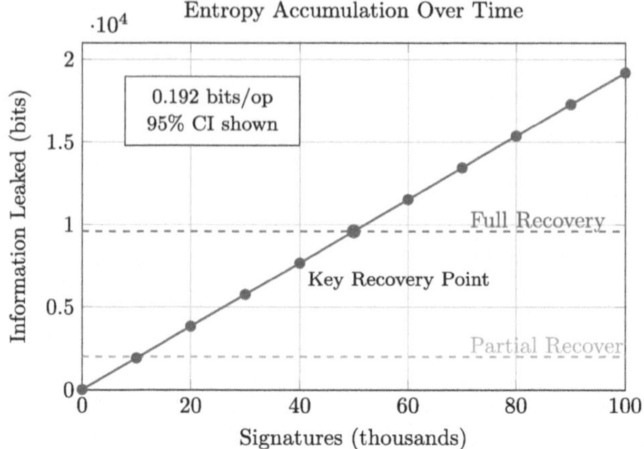

Fig. 3. Cumulative information leakage reaches key recovery threshold at ~50,000 operations.

grows 3.8×, making operations trivially distinguishable through system monitoring. This degradation exceeds that observed in SABER [9] or optimized implementations [1,34].

4.5 World-Switch Overhead Analysis

PQC's granular computation triggers excessive world-switches, dominating execution time as predicted by [16]. Figure 5 quantifies this degradation, showing near-complete throughput collapse with even minimal concurrency levels.

Dilithium requires 52 world-switches (13× RSA's 4), each adding 45 μs overhead. This transforms 440 μs base execution into 2,998 μs total time—a 6.8× amplification that creates system-wide bottlenecks. NTT operations alone require 18 switches [27,33], while FPGA implementations [44] avoid this overhead entirely.

4.6 Attack Composition

The vulnerabilities compound through chaining, similar to attack methodologies in [7,15]: 1. Force memory exhaustion (100% success) → degraded state 2. Degraded state amplifies variance → operation detection (98.9%) 3. Identify signing → apply rejection prediction (80%) 4. Accumulate 0.192 bits/operation → key recovery at 50,000 operations

This requires only unprivileged access and succeeds against default configurations, demonstrating complete TEE compromise through architectural exploitation rather than implementation bugs. The attack complexity is lower than hardware acceleration attacks [23] yet more practical than theoretical lattice reduction [8,24].

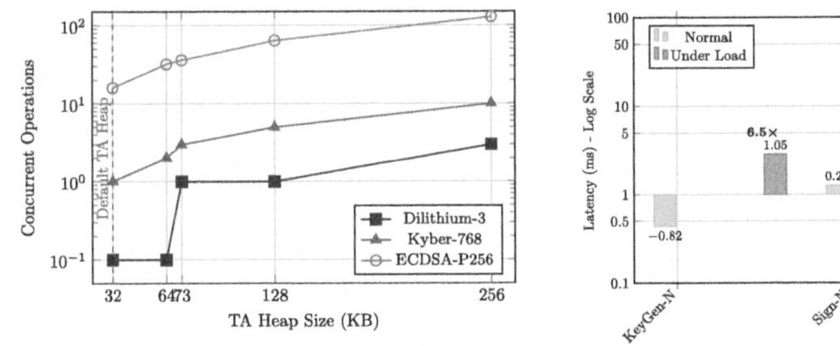

(a) Concurrent Operation Capacity (b) Latency Distribution Under Load

Fig. 4. Resource exhaustion causes complete concurrency collapse and 40× latency increases, exceeding degradation reported in [3,20].

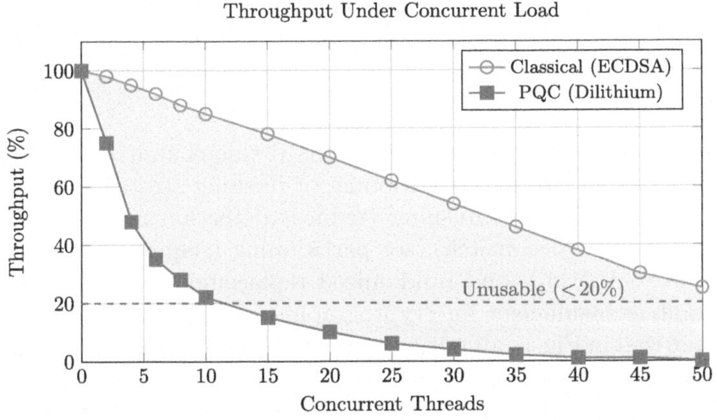

Fig. 5. Throughput degradation: PQC operations become unusable ($< 20\%$) with minimal concurrency, worse than TLS overhead [28,41].

4.7 Cross-Platform Applicability

Table 5 summarizes vulnerability applicability across major TEE architectures. While exploitation primitives vary (e.g., world-switches vs. enclave exits), the fundamental incompatibilities between PQC's computational patterns and TEE resource constraints persist across platforms.

5 Mitigation Analysis

5.1 Short-Term Countermeasures and Their Limitations

We systematically evaluated immediately deployable mitigations, discovering fundamental limitations in their effectiveness against architectural vulnerabilities. Our analysis reveals that tactical fixes cannot address systemic incompatibilities, consistent with challenges identified in [16,20,39].

Table 5. Vulnerability applicability across TEE architectures

Vulnerability	TrustZone	Intel SGX	AMD SEV	Root Cause
Memory Exhaustion	Critical	High	Medium	Secure memory limits
Rejection Leakage	Critical	Critical	High	Timing observability
Transition Overhead	Critical (13×)	High (5–8×)	Medium	Context switching
Cache Channels	Critical	Critical	High	Shared cache

Configuration-Based Mitigations. The most straightforward approach involves reconfiguring OP-TEE parameters [31] to accommodate PQC requirements. Increasing the TA heap from 32KB to 96KB eliminates immediate allocation failures, while enabling dynamic shared memory provides additional flexibility. However, these changes merely shift the problem: the expanded heap reduces available secure memory for other services, and in multi-tenant scenarios, a single PQC operation still monopolizes resources, creating priority inversion [15].

Cache Partitioning Strategies Cache-based side-channels [32,45] can theoretically be mitigated through partitioning or flushing strategies. We evaluated three approaches: entry/exit flushing (reduces detection accuracy to 60% but adds 180 μs overhead per switch), set partitioning (requires hardware support absent in Cortex-A55 [4]), and randomized replacement (provides only probabilistic guarantees insufficient for cryptographic security [29]).

As summarized in Fig. 6, all mitigations exhibit unfavorable tradeoffs between security improvement and implementation overhead. The fundamental challenge is that PQC's cache footprint (156KB for Dilithium) exceeds typical L2 cache sizes, making isolation ineffective even when technically feasible [25,42].

Timing Obfuscation Techniques Adding random delays to obscure timing variations provides minimal security benefit while significantly degrading performance [30]. Achieving 50% reduction in timing correlation requires noise with standard deviation equal to the signal—effectively doubling execution time. Moreover, sophisticated attackers can filter noise through increased sampling, requiring only O(n) more observations [11,24].

5.2 Architectural Requirements for Secure PQC-TEE Integration

Addressing root causes requires fundamental architectural evolution beyond incremental improvements [10,23]. Future TEE designs must implement: (i) *dynamic secure memory* with elastic allocation backed by hardware encryption, allowing runtime expansion without compromising isolation [4,13]; (ii) *asynchronous invocation models* enabling PQC operations to proceed without blocking callers [31,41]; and (iii) *hardware acceleration with isolation* providing per-world acceleration contexts, as demonstrated in FPGA implementations [27,44].

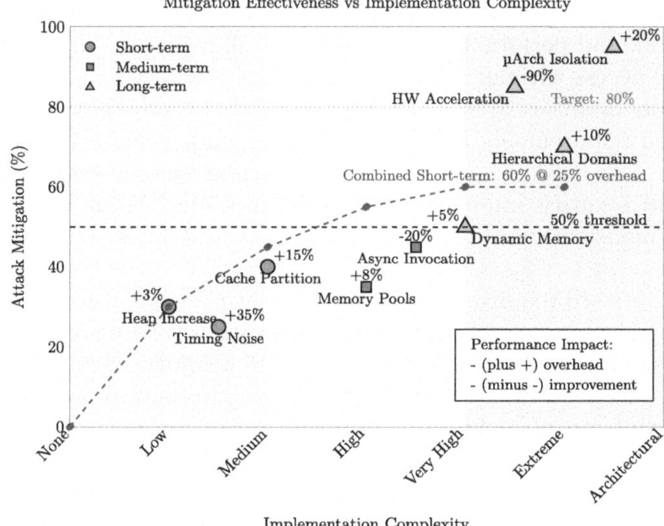

Fig. 6. Mitigation effectiveness versus implementation complexity reveals diminishing returns, consistent with [35].

5.3 Interim Deployment Strategies

Until architectural support materializes, we recommend risk-aware deployment strategies [18]: hybrid cryptography using PQC for long-term key establishment and classical algorithms for short-term authentication [3,28]; split processing executing PQC in normal world with TEE-based classical verification [20]; temporal isolation scheduling PQC operations during maintenance windows [16]; and aggressive monitoring for timing anomalies [39]. Algorithm selection should consider TEE compatibility, though recent cryptanalytic breaks warn against premature adoption of alternatives [14].

These strategies represent uncomfortable compromises, highlighting the fundamental incompatibility between current TEE architectures and PQC requirements. The path forward requires acknowledging that quantum resistance achieved through vulnerable implementations offers false security—organizations must either accept documented risks or await architectural evolution projected to require 3–5 years [26].

6 Conclusion

We demonstrated that deploying lattice-based PQC within current ARM TrustZone TEEs creates severe vulnerabilities stemming from fundamental architectural incompatibilities rather than correctable implementation flaws. Our empirical assessment on i.MX93 hardware [37] revealed exploitable vulnerabilities across four categories—operation classification, rejection sampling leakage, memory exhaustion, and performance degradation—all achievable from unprivileged normal-world access without TEE compromise.

These vulnerabilities arise from irreconcilable mismatches between PQC's computational requirements and TEE design assumptions optimized for classical cryptography's modest demands [38,40]. Current tactical mitigations achieve only marginal security improvements while imposing significant performance penalties, demonstrating the futility of incremental fixes for systemic problems [16,39].

The path forward requires acknowledging that post-quantum security cannot be achieved by simply substituting algorithms within existing architectures [10]. Future TEE designs must embrace elastic secure memory, asynchronous invocation models, and hardware acceleration with isolation-aware design [23,27,44]. Until such architectural evolution materializes—likely requiring 3–5 years based on industry roadmaps [26]—organizations face an uncomfortable choice: accept documented risks or defer PQC deployment.

Our work provides empirical evidence that the post-quantum transition requires not just new algorithms but new architectures. The vulnerabilities extend beyond Dilithium and Kyber to affect other lattice-based schemes [9,25], and the SIDH break [14] reminds us that security assumptions must be continuously reevaluated. While our validation focuses on ARM TrustZone, the architectural mismatches we expose affect TEE architectures broadly, as discussed in Sect. 2.

We release our measurement framework and attack implementations to support reproducible security assessment. Future work should explore alternative PQC algorithms with better TEE compatibility, develop formal verification methods for PQC-TEE integration [7], and investigate hybrid approaches balancing security with practicality [1].

References

1. Abdulrahman, A., Hwang, V., Kannwischer, M.J., Sprenkels, A.: Faster kyber and dilithium on the cortex-m4. In: Applied Cryptography and Network Security (ACNS) 2022, Lecture Notes in Computer Science, vol. 13269, pp. 853–871. Springer (2022). https://doi.org/10.1007/978-3-031-09234-3_42
2. AMD: AMD SEV-SNP: strengthening VM isolation with integrity protection and more. White Paper, Advanced Micro Devices, Inc. (2020). https://www.amd.com/content/dam/amd/en/documents/epyc-business-docs/white-papers/SEV-SNP-strengthening-vm-isolation-with-integrity-protection-and-more.pdf
3. Anastasova, M., Kampanakis, P., Massimo, J.: PQ-TLS: post-quantum TLS on embedded devices. In: Proceedings of the ACM International Conference on Computing Frontiers, pp. 312–324 (2023). https://doi.org/10.1145/3587135.3592186
4. Arm limited: arm® trustzone technology for armv8-A (2022), dEN0028E
5. Arute, F., et al.: Quantum supremacy using a programmable superconducting processor. Nature **574**(7779), 505–510 (2019). https://doi.org/10.1038/s41586-019-1666-5

6. Avanzi, R., et al.: CRYSTALS-Kyber: algorithm specifications and supporting documentation (version 3.02). NIST Post-Quantum Cryptography Standardization Project, Round 3 Submission (2021). https://pq-crystals.org/kyber/data/kyber-specification-round3-20210804.pdf, standardized as FIPS 203
7. Azouaoui, M., et al.: Systematic study of decryption and re-encryption leakage in post-quantum kems. IACR Transactions on Cryptographic Hardware and Embedded Systems 2023 (3), 330–359 (2023). https://doi.org/10.46586/tches.v2023.i3.330-359
8. Bai, S., Jangir, H., Lin, H.: Lattice reduction attacks on he schemes. J. Cryptol. **37**(1), 1–42 (2024). https://doi.org/10.1007/s00145-023-09453-4
9. Basso, A., et al.: Saber on arm: CCA-secure module lattice-based kem on arm. IACR Transactions on Cryptographic Hardware and Embedded Systems 2023(3), 243–266 (2023). https://doi.org/10.46586/tches.v2023.i3.243-266
10. Bernstein, D.J., Lange, T.: Post-quantum cryptography: dealing with the fallout of physics success. Commun. ACM **66**(3), 82–90 (2023). https://doi.org/10.1145/3579383
11. Bhasin, S., D'Anvers, J.P., Heinz, D., Pöppelmann, T., Van Beirendonck, M.: Attacking and defending masked polynomial comparison for lattice-based cryptography. IACR Transactions on Cryptographic Hardware and Embedded Systems 2021, 334–359 (2021). https://doi.org/10.46586/tches.v2021.i3.334-359
12. Bos, J.W., Ducas, L., Kiltz, E., et al.: Crystals-kyber: A CCA-secure module-lattice-based KEM. In: 2018 IEEE European Symposium on Security and Privacy (EuroS&P), pp. 353–367 (2018). https://doi.org/10.1109/EuroSP.2018.00032
13. Bos, J.W., Renes, J., Sprenkels, A.: Dilithium for memory constrained devices. In: Progress in Cryptology - AFRICACRYPT 2022, Lecture Notes in Computer Science, vol. 13503, pp. 217–235. Springer (2022). https://doi.org/10.1007/978-3-031-17433-9_10
14. Castryck, W., Decru, T.: An efficient key recovery attack on sidh. Tech. Rep. Cryptology ePrint Archive: Report 2022/975, IACR (2022)
15. Cerdeira, D., Santos, N., Fonseca, P., Pinto, S.: SOK: understanding the prevailing security vulnerabilities in trustzone-assisted tee systems. In: 2020 IEEE Symposium on Security and Privacy (SP), pp. 1416–1432 (2020). https://doi.org/10.1109/SP40000.2020.00028
16. Chen, M.S., Hülsing, A., Rijneveld, J.: Post-quantum cryptography in embedded systems: Challenges and opportunities. IEEE Security & Privacy **22**(2), 48–56 (2024). https://doi.org/10.1109/MSEC.2024.3352805
17. Cho, S.M., et al.: Prime+count: novel cross-world covert channels on arm trustzone. In: Proceedings of the 34th Annual Computer Security Applications Conference (ACSAC), pp. 441–452 (2018). https://doi.org/10.1145/3274694.3274704
18. Cloudflare: post-quantum cryptography: the day has come (2023). https://blog.cloudflare.com/post-quantum-cryptography-the-day-has-come/, Accessed 05 Sep 2025
19. Costan, V., Devadas, S.: Intel SGX explained. Cryptology ePrint Archive, Report 2016/086 (2016). https://eprint.iacr.org/2016/086
20. D'Anvers, J.P., Batsleer, S., Manzano, M.: Post-quantum cryptography on embedded devices: challenges and opportunities. In: DATE 2023, pp. 1–6 (2023). https://doi.org/10.23919/DATE56975.2023.10137262
21. Ducas, L., Kiltz, E., Lepoint, T., Lyubashevsky, V., Schwabe, P., Seiler, G., Stehlé, D.: CRYSTALS-Dilithium: Algorithm specifications and supporting documentation (version 3.1). NIST Post-Quantum Cryptography Standardization Project,

Round 3 Submission (February 2021), https://pq-crystals.org/dilithium/data/dilithium-specification-round3-20210208.pdf, standardized as FIPS 204
22. Ducas, L., et al.: Crystals-dilithium: A lattice-based digital signature scheme. IACR Transactions on Cryptographic Hardware and Embedded Systems 2018(1), 238–268 (2018). https://doi.org/10.13154/tches.v2018.i1.238-268
23. Fritzmann, T., Sigl, G., Sepúlveda, J.: RISQ-V: tightly coupled RISC-V accelerators for post-quantum cryptography. IACR Trans. Cryp. Hardw. Embed. Syst. **2020**(4), 239–280 (2023)
24. Guo, Q., Johansson, T., Nilsson, A.: A key recovery attack on LWE with non-uniform error. In: EUROCRYPT 2023, pp. 423–452 (2023). https://doi.org/10.1007/978-3-031-30634-1_15
25. Huang, W.L., Chen, J.P., Yang, B.Y.: Power analysis on ntru prime. IACR Transactions on Cryptographic Hardware and Embedded Systems 2024(1), 123–148 (2024). https://doi.org/10.46586/tches.v2024.i1.123-148
26. IBM Quantum: Ibm quantum roadmap. https://research.ibm.com/blog/ibm-quantum-roadmap (2023), accessed 2025–09-05
27. Karabulut, E., Alkim, E., Aysu, A.: RANTT: A RISC-V architecture extension for the number theoretic transform. In: 2021 International Conference on Field-Programmable Logic and Applications (FPL), pp. 26–32 (2021). https://doi.org/10.1109/FPL53798.2021.00015
28. Kim, J., Kim, H., Kim, S., et al.: Post-quantum TLS performance on embedded systems. In: Proceedings of the ACM Asia Conference on Computer and Communications Security (ASIACCS '23), pp. 456–469 (2023). https://doi.org/10.1145/3579856.3590364
29. Kocher, P., Horn, J., Fogh, A., et al.: Spectre attacks: exploiting speculative execution. In: 2019 IEEE Symposium on Security and Privacy (SP), pp. 1–19 (2019). https://doi.org/10.1109/SP.2019.00002
30. Li, M., Lin, J., Liu, Z.: Timing attacks on post-quantum signatures with rejection sampling. In: NDSS 2024, pp. 1–18 (2024)
31. Linaro: Op-tee documentation, release 4.4.0. https://optee.readthedocs.io/en/latest/ (2024), Accessed 05 Sep 2025
32. Lipp, M., Gruss, D., Spreitzer, R., Maurice, C., Mangard, S.: ARMageddon: cache attacks on mobile devices. In: 25th USENIX Security Symposium (USENIX Security 16), pp. 549–564 (2016). https://www.usenix.org/conference/usenixsecurity16/technical-sessions/presentation/lipp
33. Lyubashevsky, V., Seiler, G.: NTTRU: Truly fast NTRU using NTT. IACR Trans. Cryptographic Hardw. Embed. Syst. 2022(3), 180–201 (2022). https://doi.org/10.46586/tches.v2022.i3.180-201
34. Mera, J.M.B., et al.: Polynomial multiplication on embedded vector architectures. IACR Trans. Cryptographic Hardw. Embed. Syst. 2023(1), 482–505 (2023). https://doi.org/10.46586/tches.v2023.i1.482-505
35. Migliore, V., Verneuil, V., Véron, P.: Masking dilithium: Efficient implementation and side-channel evaluation. IACR Trans. Cryptographic Hardw. Embed. Syst. 2023(3), 289–312 (2023). https://doi.org/10.46586/tches.v2023.i3.289-312
36. National institute of standards and technology: status report on the third round of the NIST post-quantum cryptography standardization process. Tech. Rep. NISTIR 8413, NIST (2022)
37. NXP Semiconductors: i.mx 93 applications processor reference manual. Tech. Rep. IMX93RM Rev. 2, NXP Semiconductors N.V. (2023)
38. Pinto, S., Santos, N.: Demystifying ARM trustzone: A comprehensive survey. ACM Comput. Surv. **51**(6), 1–36 (2019). https://doi.org/10.1145/3291047

39. Ravi, P., Roy, S.S., Chattopadhyay, A.: Side-channel analysis of lattice-based post-quantum cryptography: challenges and opportunities. In: 2023 IEEE International Symposium on Hardware Oriented Security and Trust (HOST), pp. 169–179 (2023). https://doi.org/10.1109/HOST55116.2023.10133261
40. Sabt, M., Achemlal, M., Bouabdallah, A.: Trusted execution environment: what it is, and what it is not. In: 2015 IEEE Trustcom/BigDataSE/ISPA, pp. 57–64 (2015). https://doi.org/10.1109/Trustcom.2015.357
41. Schwabe, P., Stebila, D., Wiggers, T.: Post-quantum tls without handshake signatures. ACM Trans. Priv. Secur. **26**(4), 1–37 (2023). https://doi.org/10.1145/3626789
42. Sim, B.Y., et al.: Single-trace attacks on message encoding in lattice-based kems. IEEE Access **12**, 8345–8361 (2024)
43. Stebila, D., Mosca, M., Open Quantum Safe Project: liboqs: C library for prototyping and experimenting with quantum-resistant cryptography (2024). https://github.com/open-quantum-safe/liboqs, part of the Linux Foundation's Post-Quantum Cryptography Alliance
44. Xing, Y., Li, S.: A compact hardware implementation of CRYSTALS-Kyber on FPGA. IACR Trans. Cryptographic Hardw. Embed. Syst. 2021(2), 328–356 (2021). https://doi.org/10.46586/tches.v2021.i2.328-356
45. Zhang, N., Sun, K., Shands, D., Lou, W., Hou, Y.T.: Truspy: cache side-channel information leakage from the secure world on arm devices. Cryptology ePrint Archive, Paper 2016/980 (2016). https://eprint.iacr.org/2016/980

Post-quantum Fujisaki-Okamoto Transformation for Anonymous Identity-Based Encryption

Tsuchiya Yui[1](✉), Toi Tomita[2,3], and Junji Shikata[3,4]

[1] Graduate School of Environment and Information Sciences, Yokohama National University, Yokohama, Japan
tsuchiya-yui-jn@ynu.jp
[2] Organization for the Promotion of Education, Yokohama National University, Yokohama, Japan
[3] Institute of Advanced Sciences, Yokohama National University, Yokohama, Japan
[4] Faculty of Environment and Information Sciences, Yokohama National University, Yokohama, Japan

Abstract. The Fujisaki-Okamoto (FO) transformation is a method of practically realizing CCA-secure public-key encryption (PKE) scheme. Recently, the FO transformation for PKE in PQC has also been widely studied. In this work, we focus on how to practically realize CCA security in identity-based encryption (IBE) in PQC. Our contributions are as follows: (i) We show that a slightly modified post-quantum FO transformation can be effectively used to transform from CPA-secure IBE scheme to CCA-secure IBE scheme in the quantum random oracle model (QROM). (ii) Our main contribution is to show that the FO transformation realizes anonymity of IBE scheme in addition to CCA-security if the underlying CPA-secure IBE scheme meets the additional property called strong disjoint-simulatable (SDS) property. (iii) To demonstrate that the above result (ii) is not mere theory, we also show that a CPA-secure IBE scheme with the SDS property can indeed be constructed based on the Gentry-Peikert-Vaikuntanathan (GPV) IBE scheme. Consequently, combining (ii) and (iii) yields a post-quantum anonymous IBE scheme with CCA security in the QROM.

Keywords: Post-Quantum Cryptography · Identity-Based Encryption · Fujisaki-Okamoto Transformation · Anonymity

1 Introduction

1.1 Background

Post-quantum cryptography (PQC) is recognized as important and essential technology for providing security and privacy in future information society in the era of quantum computers. Currently, NIST in US already selected five algorithms as PQC standardization, namely CRYSTALS-KYBER and HQC

H. Seo (Ed.): ICISC 2025, LNCS 16487, pp. 168–182, 2026.
https://doi.org/10.1007/978-981-95-8034-7_9

for public-key encryption (PKE) or key encapsulation mechanism (KEM), and CRYSTALS-DILITHIUM, FALCON and SPHINCS+ for digital signatures, and NIST published FIPS 203, 204, 205, and 206. Currently, the security of PKE or KEM usually requires IND-CCA security for practical use in the world. For practically realizing CCA security, it is conventional that we first construct a CPA secure scheme under a certain computational assumption and then transform it into the resulting CCA secure scheme assuming random oracles; and such popular transformation include OAEP and FO transformation [3,4]. In fact, many PKE or KEM schemes utilize FO transformation to realize CCA security. It is noted that the conventional FO transformation [3,4] can only be applied to PKE that does not incur decryption errors, and therefore, cannot be applied directly to post-quantum public key encryption having decryption errors; and the FO transformation or its variants were proposed in [6,13] so that they can be applied to PKE having decryption errors. In particular, PKE in PQC usually has decryption errors, and those transformation were used in many PKE or KEM submitted in the NIST competition. In this paper, we focus on how to practically realize CCA security in identity-based encryption (IBE) in PQC. For doing it, we consider a similar approach to realize CCA secure IBE like PKE: We show how to apply the FO transformation or its variants [3,4,6,13] to obtain post-quantum CCA secure IBE schemes from CPA secure ones. In addition, we show conditions to obtain anonymous CCA secure IBE in PQC through the FO transformation or its variants. It should be noted that anonymous IBE is also important and interesting cryptographic schemes, since it is essentially transformed to public key encryption with keyword search (PEKS) [1].

1.2 Our Contributions

The main contribution of the paper is to show that anonymous IBE having CCA security can be obtained from CPA secure IBE through the FO transformation. For doing it, we first confirm that the FO works well even for IBE as well as PKE (or KEM); and secondly, we clarify a certain condition on CPA secure IBE such that the resulting CCA secure IBE satisfies anonymity through the FO transformation. More specifically, the contributions of the paper are as follows.

(i) One may think that post-quantum FO transformation [6,10] effectively works well even for IBE as well as PKE (or KEM) though no paper reported it explicitly. As expected above, we show that the post-quantum FO transformation can be effectively used to transform from CPA secure IBE to CCA secure IBE in the quantum oracle model (QROM), while we need to input IDs into random functions that is not necessary in PKE (or KEM). For completeness, the result is shown in Sect. 3, since it is a necessary basis to discuss realizing anonymity through the FO transformation in IBE.

(ii) The main contribution of the paper is to show that the FO transformation realizes anonymity of IBE in addition to CCA security if the underlying CPA secure IBE meets strong disjoint-simulatable (SDS) property in QROM, where SDS is a new notion introduced and formalized in this paper. The result is shown in Sect. 4.1 and 4.2.

(iii) To demonstrate that the above result (ii) is not mere theory, we show that a CPA-secure IBE with the SDS property can indeed be constructed. Specifically, such IBE with SDS property will be constructed by applying the T transformation in [6] to the GPV-IBE scheme [5]. The resulting IBE having SDS property has tight reduction to GPV-IBE, which is of independent interest. As a result, by combing (ii), we can obtain an anonymous IBE scheme with CCA security under the LWE assumption in QROM. This result is shown in Sect. 4.3.

2 Preliminaries

Notation. Throughout the paper, the security parameter is denoted by λ. For a finite set $\mathcal{S}$, we denote the sampling of a uniformly random element x from $\mathcal{S}$ by $x \xleftarrow{\$} S$, while we denote the sampling according to some distribution D by $x \leftarrow D$. By $[B]$, we denote the bit that is 1 if the boolean statement B is true, and otherwise 0. We denote $X \approx_c Y$ when two distributions X and Y are computationally indistinguishable. All logs are base-2, and the ceiling function denotes bit-length rounding.

For security games, we implicitly assume Boolean flags to be initialized to false, numerical types to 0, sets to $\emptyset$, and strings to the empty string ϵ. We make the convention that a procedure terminates once it has returned an output.

Algorithm. We denote algorithms with access to an oracle O by A^O. Unless stated otherwise, we assume all our algorithms to be probabilistic and denote the computation by $y \leftarrow \mathsf{A}(x)$. We will at times model hash functions $H : \mathcal{X} \rightarrow \mathcal{Y}$ as random oracles. To keep a record of the queries issued to H, we will use a hash list $\mathcal{L}_H$ that contains all tuples $(x, H(x))$ of arguments $x \in \mathcal{X}$ on which H was queried and the respective answers $H(x)$. We make the convention that $H(x) = \perp$ for all $x \notin \mathcal{X}$.

2.1 Identity-Based Encryption (IBE)

The model for IBE schemes is summarized as follows:

Definition 1 (IBE). *Let $\mathcal{M}$, $\mathcal{C}$, $\mathcal{ID}$, and $\mathcal{R}$ denote the message space, ciphertext space, identity space, and randomness space, respectively. An IBE scheme* IBE *consists of the following algorithms* (Setup, KeyGen, Enc, Dec)*:*

- $\mathsf{Setup}(1^\lambda) \rightarrow (P, mk)$*: The setup algorithm takes security parameter $\lambda \in \mathbb{N}$ as input, and outputs a system parameter P and a master key mk.*
- $\mathsf{KeyGen}(P, mk, ID) \rightarrow d_{ID}$*: The key generation algorithm takes P, mk, and an identity $ID \in \mathcal{ID}$ as inputs, and outputs a private key d_{ID}.*
- $\mathsf{Enc}(P, ID, m; r) \rightarrow c$*: The encryption algorithm takes P, ID, and $m \in \mathcal{M}$ as inputs, and outputs a ciphertext $c \in \mathcal{C}$ using a randomness $r \in \mathcal{R}$.*
- $\mathsf{Dec}(d_{ID}, c) \rightarrow m/\perp$*: The decryption algorithm takes d_{ID} and c as inputs and outputs m or a rejection symbol $\perp$.*

Definition 2 (Correctness of IBE). *Let $\delta = \delta(\lambda)$. We say that* IBE *is δ-correct if for all $\lambda \in \mathbb{N}$, $ID \in \mathcal{ID}$, all $m \in \mathcal{M}$, and all (P, mk) in the support of* $\mathsf{Setup}(1^\lambda)$*, it holds that*

$$\Pr\left[\mathsf{Dec}(P, d_{ID}, c) \neq m \mid \begin{array}{l} d_{ID} \leftarrow \mathsf{KeyGen}(P, mk, ID) \\ c \leftarrow \mathsf{Enc}(P, ID, m) \end{array}\right] \leq \delta.$$

Definition 3 (Security notions of IBE). *Let* $\mathsf{IBE} = (\mathsf{Setup}, \mathsf{KeyGen}, \mathsf{Enc}, \mathsf{Dec})$ *be an IBE scheme. For any adversary $\mathcal{A} = (\mathcal{A}_1, \mathcal{A}_2)$ and $goal \in \{ow, ind\}$, we define its goal-cpa advantage against* IBE *as follows:*

$$Adv^{ow\text{-}cpa}_{\mathsf{IBE},\mathcal{A}}(\lambda) := \Pr[Expt^{ow\text{-}cpa}_{\mathsf{IBE},\mathcal{A}}(\lambda) = 1],$$
$$Adv^{ind\text{-}cpa}_{\mathsf{IBE},\mathcal{A}}(\lambda) := |2\Pr[Expt^{ind\text{-}cpa}_{\mathsf{IBE},\mathcal{A}}(\lambda) = 1] - 1|,$$

where $Expt^{goal\text{-}cpa}_{\mathsf{IBE},\mathcal{A}}(\lambda)$ are experiments described in Fig. 1. We say that IBE *is goal-atk-secure if $Adv^{goal\text{-}atk}_{\mathsf{IBE},\mathcal{A}}(\lambda)$ is negligible for any QPT adversary $\mathcal{A}$.*

$Expt^{\text{ow-cpa}}_{\mathsf{IBE},\mathcal{A}}(\lambda)$	$Expt^{\text{ind-cpa}}_{\mathsf{IBE},\mathcal{A}}(\lambda)$
$(P, mk) \leftarrow \mathsf{Setup}(1^\lambda)$	$b \xleftarrow{\$} \{0,1\}$, $(P, mk) \leftarrow \mathsf{Setup}(1^\lambda)$
$(ID^*, st) \leftarrow \mathcal{A}_1^{\mathsf{KeyGen}(P,mk,\cdot)}(P)$	$(m_0^*, m_1^*, ID^*, st) \leftarrow \mathcal{A}_1^{\mathsf{KeyGen}(P,mk,\cdot)}(P)$
$m^* \xleftarrow{\$} \mathcal{M}$, $c^* \leftarrow \mathsf{Enc}(P, ID^*, m^*)$	$c^* \leftarrow \mathsf{Enc}(P, ID^*, m_b^*)$
$m' \leftarrow \mathcal{A}_2^{\mathsf{KeyGen}(P,mk,\cdot)}(c^*, st)$	$b' \leftarrow \mathcal{A}_2^{\mathsf{KeyGen}(P,mk,\cdot)}(c^*, st)$
$d_{ID} \leftarrow \mathsf{KeyGen}(P, mk, ID)$	return $[b = b']$
return $[\mathsf{Dec}(P, d_{ID}, c) = m]$	

Fig. 1. Games for IBE schemes.

2.2 Identity-Based Key Encapsulation (IB-KEM)

The model for IB-KEM is summarized as follows:

Definition 4 (IB-KEM). *Let $\mathcal{C}$, $\mathcal{ID}$, and $\mathcal{K}$ denote the ciphertext space, identity space, and key space, respectively. An IB-KEM scheme consists of the following algorithms* $(\mathsf{Setup}, \mathsf{KeyGen}, \mathsf{Encaps}, \mathsf{Decaps})$*:*

- *Algorithms* Setup *and* KeyGen *are similar to those of IBE.*
- $\mathsf{Encaps}(P, ID) \to (c, K)$*: The encapsulation algorithm takes P and $ID \in \mathcal{ID}$ as input and outputs a tuple of a ciphertext $c \in \mathcal{C}$ and a key $K \in \mathcal{K}$.*
- $\mathsf{Decaps}(d_{ID}, c) \to K/\perp$*: The decapsulation algorithm takes d_{ID} and c as inputs and outputs a key $K \in \mathcal{K}$ or a rejection symbol $\perp$.*

Definition 5 (Correctness of IB-KEM). *Let $\delta = \delta(\lambda)$. We say that* IB-KEM *is δ-correct if for all $\lambda \in \mathbb{N}$, $ID \in \mathcal{ID}$, and all (P, mk) in the support of* Setup(1^λ), *it holds that*

$$\Pr\left[\mathsf{Decaps}(P, d_{ID}, c) \neq m \mid \begin{array}{l} d_{ID} \leftarrow \mathsf{KeyGen}(P, mk, ID) \\ c \leftarrow \mathsf{Encaps}(P, ID, m) \end{array}\right] \leq \delta.$$

Definition 6 (Security notions of IB-KEM). *Let* IB-KEM = (Setup, KeyGen, Encaps, Decaps) *be an IB-KEM scheme. For any adversary $\mathcal{A} = (\mathcal{A}_1, \mathcal{A}_2)$ and goal $\in \{ano, spr\}$, we define its goal-cca advantage against* IB-KEM *as follows:*

$$Adv^{goal\text{-}cca}_{\mathsf{IB\text{-}KEM},\mathcal{A}}(\lambda) := |2\Pr[Expt^{goal\text{-}cca}_{\mathsf{IB\text{-}KEM},\mathcal{A}}(\lambda) = 1] - 1|,$$

where $Expt^{goal\text{-}cca}_{\mathsf{IB\text{-}KEM},\mathcal{A}}(\lambda)$ are experiments described in Fig. 2. We say that IB-KEM *is goal-cca-secure if $Adv^{goal\text{-}cca}_{\mathsf{IB\text{-}KEM},\mathcal{A}}(\lambda)$ is negligible for any QPT adversary $\mathcal{A}$.*

$Expt^{\text{ano-cca}}_{\mathsf{IB\text{-}KEM},\mathcal{A}}(\lambda)$	$Expt^{\text{spr-cca}}_{\mathsf{IB\text{-}KEM},\mathcal{A}}(\lambda)$
$b \xleftarrow{\$} \{0,1\}$, $(P, mk) \leftarrow \mathsf{Setup}(1^\lambda)$	$b \xleftarrow{\$} \{0,1\}$, $(P, mk) \leftarrow \mathsf{Setup}(1^\lambda)$
$(ID_0, ID_1) \leftarrow \mathcal{A}_1^{\textsc{Dec}(\cdot,\cdot),\mathsf{KeyGen}(P,mk,\cdot)}(P)$	$ID^* \leftarrow \mathcal{A}_1^{\textsc{Dec}(\cdot,\cdot),\mathsf{KeyGen}(P,mk,\cdot)}(P)$
$(c^*, K^*) \leftarrow \mathsf{Encaps}(P, ID_b)$	$(c_0^*, K_0^*) \leftarrow \mathsf{Encaps}(P, ID^*)$
$b' \leftarrow \mathcal{A}_2^{\textsc{Dec}(\cdot,\cdot),\mathsf{KeyGen}(P,mk,\cdot)}(c^*, K^*)$	$(c_1^*, K_1^*) \xleftarrow{\$} \mathcal{C} \times \mathcal{K}$
return $[b = b']$	$b' \leftarrow \mathcal{A}_2^{\textsc{Dec}(\cdot,\cdot),\mathsf{KeyGen}(P,mk,\cdot)}(c_b^*, K_b^*)$
	return $[b = b']$
$\textsc{Dec}((ID, c) \neq (ID^*, c^*))$	
$d_{ID} \leftarrow \mathsf{KeyGen}(P, mk, ID)$	
$K := \mathsf{Decaps}(d_{ID}, c)$	
return K	

Fig. 2. Games for IB-KEM.

3 FO Transformations for IBE: from CPA to CCA

In this section, we propose a new FO transformation for IBE. Our transformation is a combination of the T transformation in Sect. 3.2 and the $\mathsf{QU}_{m,ID,c}$ and $\mathsf{U}_{m,ID}$ transformations proposed below. These transformations differ from the transformations for PKE in [6] in that an ID is added to the input of the random function H. If the deterministic IBE scheme, after applying the T transformation, satisfies OW-CPA-secure, then the $\mathsf{QU}_{m,ID,c}$ transformation for the scheme yields an IND-CCA-secure IB-KEM scheme. The theorems and proofs concerning these are omitted due to page constraints. IBE = (Setup, KeyGen, Enc, Dec) is the deterministic IBE scheme. Let $H : \mathcal{M} \times \mathcal{ID} \to \mathcal{K}$ and $H_{prf} : \{0,1\}^l \times \mathcal{C} \to \mathcal{K}$ be hash functions modeled by a (quantum) random oracle. $\mathsf{IB\text{-}KEM} = (\mathsf{Setup}_{\mathsf{IB\text{-}KEM}}, \mathsf{KeyGen}_{\mathsf{IB\text{-}KEM}}, \mathsf{Encaps}, \mathsf{Decaps}) = \mathsf{U}_{m,ID}[\mathsf{IBE}, H, H_{prf}]$ where the $\mathsf{Setup}_{\mathsf{IB\text{-}KEM}}$ algorithm is the same as IBE and the other three algorithms are defined by Fig. 3. Furthermore, in this construction, the $\mathsf{QU}_{m,ID,c}$ transformation is one in which the ciphertext c is also included in the input to the random oracle H.

$\mathsf{KeyGen}_{\mathsf{IB\text{-}KEM}}(P, mk, ID)$	$\mathsf{Encaps}(P, ID)$	$\mathsf{Decaps}(d_{ID}, c)$
$d'_{ID} \leftarrow \mathsf{KeyGen}(P, mk, ID)$	$m \xleftarrow{\$} \mathcal{M}$	Parse $d_{ID} = (d'_{ID}, s)$, $m' := \mathsf{Dec}(d'_{ID}, c)$
$s \xleftarrow{\$} \mathcal{M}$	$c \leftarrow \mathsf{Enc}(P, ID, m)$	**if** $m' = \perp$ or $c \neq \mathsf{Enc}(P, ID, m')$
$d_{ID} := (d'_{ID}, s)$	$K := H(m, ID)$	return $K := H_{prf}(s, c)$
return d_{ID}	return (K, c)	**else** return $K := H(m', ID)$

Fig. 3. $\mathsf{IB\text{-}KEM}{=}\mathsf{U}_{m,ID}[\mathsf{IBE}, H, H_{prf}]$

3.1 New Notions of IBE

We define the new notions of IBE for the proof.

Definition 7 (Valid Ciphertext for IBE). *Let* $\mathsf{IBE} = (\mathsf{Setup}, \mathsf{KeyGen}, \mathsf{Enc}, \mathsf{Dec})$ *be a deterministic IBE scheme. We call a ciphertext* $c \in \mathcal{C}$ *"valid" for a given* ID *if there exists a message* $m \in \mathcal{M}$ *such that* $c = \mathsf{Enc}(P, ID, m)$*, where* $(P, mk) \leftarrow \mathsf{Setup}(1^\lambda)$.

Definition 8 (Finding Failing Ciphertext for IBE). *Let* $\mathsf{IBE} = (\mathsf{Setup}, \mathsf{KeyGen}, \mathsf{Enc}, \mathsf{Dec})$ *be an IBE scheme and* $\mathcal{A}$ *be an adversary executing an attack against the finding failing ciphertext property (FFC), as specified by the following experiment in Fig. 4.*

Definition 9 (Injectivity of an IBE). *Let* $\eta \geq 0$ *be negligible value. A deterministic IBE scheme* $\mathsf{IBE} = (\mathsf{Setup}, \mathsf{KeyGen}, \mathsf{Enc}, \mathsf{Dec})$ *is* η*-injective if*

$\Pr[\mathsf{Enc}(P, ID, \cdot)$ *is not injective*$] \leq \eta$, *where* $(P, mk) \leftarrow \mathsf{Setup}(1^\lambda)$, $ID \xleftarrow{\$} \mathcal{ID}$, $d_{ID} \leftarrow \mathsf{KeyGen}(P, mk, ID)$, *and* $H \xleftarrow{\$} \mathcal{H}$. *We say* IBE *is injective if* $\eta = 0$. *We say that an rIBE is injective if for all pairs* $(ID, m) \neq (ID', m')$ *and all coins* r, r', *we have* $\mathsf{Enc}(ID, m; r) \neq \mathsf{Enc}(ID', m'; r')$.

We define Strong Disjoint Simulatability(SDS) for IBE by extending SDS for ordinary public-key encryption [12].

$Expt^{FFC}_{\mathsf{IBE},\mathcal{A}}(\lambda)$
$H \leftarrow \mathcal{H}$, $(P, mk) \leftarrow \mathsf{Setup}(1^\lambda)$, $L \leftarrow \mathcal{A}^H(P)$
return $[\exists m \in \mathcal{M}; (ID, c) \in L; d_{ID} \leftarrow \mathsf{KeyGen}(P, mk, ID) \mid \mathsf{Enc}(P, ID, m) = c \wedge \mathsf{Dec}(P, d_{ID}, c) \neq m]$

Fig. 4. FFC Games for deterministic IBE schemes.

3.2 T Transformation:from IND-CPA to OW-CPA/FFC

The T transformation [6], which transforms an IBE to a deterministic IBE, is described. The deterministic IBE obtained by applying the T transformation to an IBE satisfying IND-CPA satisfies OW-CPA and FFC. However, due to page constraints, details are omitted.

Definition 10 (T transformation). *Let* IBE_0 *be an IBE scheme. Let* $G : \mathcal{M} \rightarrow \mathcal{R}$ *be a hash function modeled by a (quantum) random oracle. Also, let* $\mathcal{F}$ *be the set of candidates for this hash function* G*. Let* $\mathsf{IBE} = \mathsf{T}[\mathsf{IBE}_0, G]$ *denote the deterministic IBE of this* IBE_0 *by applying the* T *transformation. The* Setup *and* KeyGen *algorithms are similar to those of* IBE_0*, and the* Enc *and* Dec *algorithms are shown in Fig. 5.*

$\mathsf{Enc}(P, ID, m)$	$\mathsf{Dec}(P, d_{ID}, c)$
$c := \mathsf{Enc}_0(P, ID, m; G(m))$	$m' := \mathsf{Dec}_0(d_{ID}, c)$
return c	**if** $m' = \bot$ or $\mathsf{Enc}_0(P, ID, m'; G(m')) \neq c$
	return $\bot$
	else return m'

Fig. 5. IBE=$\mathsf{T}[\mathsf{IBE}_0, G]$

3.3 $\mathsf{QU}_{m,ID,c}$ Transformation : from OW-CPA to IND-CCA

We show that IB-KEM is IND-CCA-secure if the original deterministic IBE is OW-CPA-secure, in the quantum random oracle model. This proof is based on the paper by [10]. Theorem and proof are omitted due to page constraints.

In summary, we obtain the following corollary.

Corollary 1. *Let* G, H *be quantum-accessible random oracles,* H_{prf} *be a PRF, and* IBE_0 *be an IND-CPA secure IBE scheme. Then, an IB-KEM scheme*

$$\mathsf{QIB\text{-}KEM} = \mathsf{QU}_{m,ID,c}[\mathsf{T}[\mathsf{IBE}_0, G], H, H_{prf}]$$

is IND-CCA secure IB-KEM scheme in the QROM.

4 FO Transformations for ANO-CCA Secure IB-KEM

In this section, we show how to obtain an ANO-CCA-secure IB-KEM scheme by applying a $\mathsf{U}_{m,ID}$ transformation in Sect. 3 to an IBE scheme that satisfies an additional property, called Strong Disjoint Simulatability (SDS). We also show that we can obtain a post-quantum IBE satisfying SDS by applying a T transformation in Sect. 3.2 to GPV-IBE [5], a typical post-quantum IBE scheme.

4.1 Strong Disjoint Simulatability for IBE

We define SDS for IBE by extending SDS for PKE [11,12,15] to IBE.

Definition 11 (Strong Disjoint Simulatability for IBE). *Let $\mathcal{D}_{\mathcal{M}}$ denote an efficiently sampleable distribution on a set $\mathcal{M}$. A deterministic IBE scheme* $\mathsf{IBE} = (\mathsf{Setup}, \mathsf{KeyGen}, \mathsf{Enc}, \mathsf{Dec})$ *with message and ciphertext space $\mathcal{M}$ and $\mathcal{C}$ is $\mathcal{D}_{\mathcal{M}}$-strong-disjoint-simulatable if there exists a PPT algorithm* Sim *that satisfies the followings:*

- *(Statistical disjointness:) For all $ID \in \mathcal{ID}$, it holds that*

$$Disj_{\mathsf{IBE},\mathsf{Sim}}(\lambda) := \Pr\left[c \in \mathsf{Enc}(P, ID, \mathcal{M}) \mid \begin{array}{l}(P, mk) \in \mathsf{Setup}(1^{\lambda}) \\ c \leftarrow \mathsf{Sim}(1^{\lambda})\end{array}\right]$$

  is negligible.
- *(Ciphertext-indistinguishability:) For any QPT adversary $\mathcal{A} = (\mathcal{A}_1, \mathcal{A}_2)$, its sds-ind advantage $Adv^{sds\text{-}ind}_{\mathsf{IBE},\mathsf{Sim}}$ is negligible: The advantage is defined as*

$$Adv^{sds\text{-}ind}_{\mathsf{IBE},\mathcal{D}_{\mathcal{M}},\mathsf{Sim},\mathcal{A}} := \left|2\Pr[Expt^{sds\text{-}ind}_{\mathsf{IBE},\mathcal{D}_{\mathcal{M}},\mathsf{Sim},\mathcal{A}}(\lambda) = 1] - 1\right|,$$

  where $Expt^{sds\text{-}ind}_{\mathsf{IBE},\mathcal{D}_{\mathcal{M}},\mathsf{Sim},\mathcal{A}}(\lambda)$ is an experiment described in Fig. 6 and Sim *is a PPT simulator.*

$Expt^{\mathsf{sds\text{-}ind}}_{\mathsf{IBE},\mathcal{D}_{\mathcal{M}},\mathsf{Sim},\mathcal{A}}(\lambda)$
$b \xleftarrow{\$} \{0,1\}$, $(P, mk) \leftarrow \mathsf{Setup}(1^{\lambda})$
$ID \leftarrow \mathcal{A}_1^{\mathsf{KeyGen}(P,mk,\cdot)}(P)$
$\mu^* \xleftarrow{\$} \mathcal{D}_{\mathcal{M}}$, $c_0^* := \mathsf{Enc}(P, ID, \mu^*)$, $c_1^* \xleftarrow{\$} \mathsf{Sim}(1^{\lambda})$
$b' \leftarrow \mathcal{A}_2^{\mathsf{KeyGen}(P,mk,\cdot)}(c_b^*)$
return $[b = b']$

Fig. 6. SDS Games for deterministic IBE schemes.

4.2 $\mathsf{U}_{m,ID}$ Transformation : from SDS to SPR-CCA

In this section, we show that IB-KEM is SPR-CCA-secure if the original deterministic IBE is SDS-secure, in the quantum random oracle model. Regarding the proof of anonymity, we extended the discussion of anonymity in PKE to IBE. That is, rather than directly proving ANO-CCA from ANO-CPA, we referred to the proof in [12] that proves SPR-CCA from SDS-secure and proved it in IBE as well.

Theorem 1 (IBE **SDS** $\overset{QROM}{\Longrightarrow}$ IB-KEM $=$ $\mathsf{U}_{m,ID}[\mathsf{IBE}, H, H_{prf}]$ **SPR-CCA**). *Let* IBE_0 *be an IBE scheme and let* $\mathsf{IBE} = \mathsf{T}[\mathsf{IBE}_0, G]$ *be a deterministic IBE scheme. Suppose that the ciphertext space* $\mathcal{C}$ *of the* IBE *depends only on the public parameters. If* IBE *is SDS-secure and* δ*-correct with negligible* δ*, then* $\mathsf{IB\text{-}KEM} = \mathsf{U}_{m,ID}[\mathsf{IBE}, H, H_{prf}]$ *is SPR-CCA-secure. Formally speaking, for any* $\mathcal{A}$ *against the SPR-CCA-secure of* IB-KEM *issuing at most* q_{Dec} *queries to the decapsulation oracle and* q_G*,* q_H*, and* $q_{H_{prf}}$ *queries to* G*,* H*, and* H_{prf}*, respectively, there exists* $\mathcal{B}$ *against ciphertext indistinguishability of* IBE *such that*

$$Adv^{spr\text{-}cca}_{\mathsf{IB\text{-}KEM},\mathcal{A}}(\lambda) \leq Adv^{sds\text{-}ind}_{\mathsf{IBE},\mathcal{D}_{\mathcal{M}},\mathsf{Sim},\mathcal{B}}(\lambda) + Disj_{\mathsf{IBE},\mathsf{Sim}}(\lambda) + 4(q_{H_{prf}}+q_{\mathrm{DEC}}) \cdot 2^{-\frac{l}{2}}$$
$$+ 4\delta + 16(q_G + q_{\mathrm{DEC}} + 2)^2\delta + 16(q_G + q_H + 2)^2\delta$$

Proof. We use the game-hopping proof. We consider Game_i for $i = \{0, ..., 8\}$. We consider an underlying IBE that is derandomized by T.
<u>Game$_0$:</u> This game is the original game $Expt^{\mathrm{spr\text{-}cca}}_{\mathsf{IB\text{-}KEM},\mathcal{A}}(\lambda)$ with $b = 0$. Thus, we have

$$\Pr[S_0] = 1 - \Pr[Expt^{\mathrm{spr\text{-}cca}}_{\mathsf{IB\text{-}KEM},\mathcal{A}}(\lambda) = 1|b = 0].$$

<u>Game$_1$:</u> This game is the same as Game_0 except that H_{prf} in the decapsulation oracle is replaced by $H_q(c)$ where $H_q : \mathcal{C} \to \mathcal{K}$ is another random oracle. We remark that $\mathcal{A}$ cannot access H_q directly. From Lemma 3, we have the bound

$$|\Pr[S_0] - \Pr[S_1]| \leq 2(q_{H_{prf}} + q_{\mathrm{DEC}}) \cdot 2^{-\frac{l}{2}},$$

where $q_{H_{prf}}$ and q_{Dec} denote the number of queries to H_{prf} and Dec the adversary makes, respectively.
Definition of $\mathcal{F}^{good}_{ID,d}(\mathcal{M}, \mathcal{R})$: We consider a set of good random oracles G, $\mathcal{F}^{good}_{ID,d}(\mathcal{M}, \mathcal{R})$. For $ID \in \mathcal{ID}$ and the corresponding secret key $d_{ID} \leftarrow \mathsf{KeyGen}(P, mk, ID)$, and $m \in \mathcal{M}$, we define a set of good randomness as $\mathcal{R}^{good}_{ID,d,m} := \{r \in \mathcal{R} : \mathsf{Dec}(d_{ID}, \mathsf{Enc}(P, ID, m; r)) = m\}$, which could be empty. Let $\mathcal{F}^{good}_{ID,d}(\mathcal{M}, \mathcal{R})$ be a set of functions $G : \mathcal{M} \to \mathcal{R}$ satisfying $G(m) \in \mathcal{R}^{good}_{ID,d,m}$ for all $m \in \mathcal{M}$. We also define the set of bad randomness as $\mathcal{R}^{bad}_{ID,d,m} = \mathcal{R} \setminus \mathcal{R}^{good}_{ID,d,m}$. Define $\delta_{ID,d,m} := \frac{|\mathcal{R} \setminus \mathcal{R}^{good}_{ID,d,m}|}{|\mathcal{R}|}$, which is the fraction of the bad randomness for m. Define $\delta := \max_{m \in \mathcal{M}, ID \in \mathcal{ID}}[\delta_{ID,d,m}]$.
<u>Game$_{1.1}$:</u> This game is the same as Game_1 except that the random oracle G is chosen from $\mathcal{F}^{good}_{ID,d}(\mathcal{M}, \mathcal{R})$. From Lemma 4, we have the bound

$$|\Pr[S_1] - Pr[S_{1.1}] \leq 8(q_G + q_{\mathrm{DEC}} + 2)^2\delta.$$

Definition of Bad *and* Good: Let us define an event Bad that there exists $(m, ID) \in \mathcal{M} \times \mathcal{ID}$ such that any $r \in \mathcal{R}$ is a bad randomness. Also, define Good $= \neg$Bad. In this case, $\Pr[\neg\text{Good}] = \Pr[\text{Bad}] \leq \delta$. From Lemma 5, for any $p \geq 0$, we also have

$$|\Pr[S_{1.1}] - p| \leq |\Pr[S_{1.1} \wedge \text{Good}] - p| + \delta.$$

Game$_{1.2}$: This game is the same as Game$_{1.1}$ except that the random oracle $H(\cdot,\cdot)$ is simulated by $H'_q(\mathsf{Enc}(P,\cdot,\cdot))$ where $H'_q : \mathcal{C} \to \mathcal{K}$ is yet another random oracle. We remark that the decapsulation oracle and the generation of K^* also use $H'_q(\mathsf{Enc}(P,\cdot,\cdot))$ as $H(\cdot,\cdot)$.
Definition of g :We define the encryption algorithm Enc as $g(m) := \mathsf{Enc}(P, ID, m; G(m))$. If Good occurs, then $\mathsf{IBE} = \mathsf{T}[\mathsf{IBE}_0, G]$ is perfectly correct from the definition of G and g is *injective*. Thus, if Good occurs, then $H'_q \circ g : \mathcal{M} \to \mathcal{C}$ is a random function, and two games Game$_{1.1}$ and Game$_{1.2}$ are equivalent. We have

$$\Pr[S_{1.1} \wedge \text{Good}] = \Pr[S_{1.2} \wedge \text{Good}].$$

Game$_2$: This game is the same as Game$_{1.2}$ except that the random oracle H is simulated by $H_q \circ g$ instead of $H' \circ g$. With this change, the output for a valid ciphertext c in the decryption oracle is H_q. That is, up to Game$_{1.2}$, the attacker cannot obtain the output H_q of the decryption oracle for a valid ciphertext c. If Good occurs, only the output for valid ciphertexts that the attacker did not obtain is changed. Thus, we can show that the two games Game$_{1.2}$ and Game$_2$ are equivalent and we have

$$\Pr[S_{1.2} \wedge \text{Good}] = \Pr[S_2 \wedge \text{Good}].$$

Game$_3$: This game is the same as Game$_2$ except that K^* is set as $H_q(c^*)$ and the decapsulation oracle always returns $H_q(c)$ as long as $c \neq c^*$. If Good occurs, this has already been done in previous game-hopping, so this change is conceptual. Thus we have

$$\Pr[S_2 \wedge \text{Good}] = \Pr[S_3 \wedge \text{Good}].$$

In addition, according to Lemma 5, for any $p \geq 0$, we have

$$|\Pr[S_3 \wedge \text{Good}] - p| \leq |\Pr[S_3] - p| + \delta.$$

Game$_{3.1}$: This game is the same as Game$_3$ except that G is chosen from $\mathcal{F}$. As the difference between Game$_1$ and Game$_{1.1}$, we have

$$|\Pr[S_3] - \Pr[S_{3.1}]| \leq 8(q_G + q_H + 2)\delta,$$

where q_H is the number of queries to H the adversary makes. We note that H queries to G internally.

Game$_4$: This game is the same as Game$_{3.1}$ except that c^* is generated by Sim. The difference between two games Game$_{3.1}$ and Game$_4$ is whether the ciphertext

c is generated by the encryption algorithm Enc or by the simulator Sim, and this difference is bounded by the advantage of ciphertext indistinguishability in SDS. We have

$$|\Pr[S_{3.1}] - \Pr[S_4]| \leq Adv^{\text{sds-ind}}_{\mathsf{IBE},\mathsf{Sim}}(\lambda).$$

Game$_5$: This game is the same as Game$_4$ except that $K^* \leftarrow \mathcal{K}$ instead of $K^* \leftarrow H_q(c^*)$. In Game$_4$, if $c^* \leftarrow \mathsf{Sim}(1^\lambda)$ is not in $\mathsf{Enc}(P, ID^*, \mathcal{M})$, then the adversary has no information about $K^* = H_q(c^*)$ and thus, K^* looks uniformly at random. Hence, the difference between the two games Game$_4$ and Game$_5$ is bounded by the statistical disjointness in SDS. We have

$$|\Pr[S_4] - \Pr[S_5]| \leq Disj_{\mathsf{IBE},\mathsf{Sim}}(\lambda)$$

Game$_{5.1}$: This game is the same as Game$_5$ except that G is chosen from $\mathcal{F}^{good}_{ID,d}(\mathcal{M}, \mathcal{R})$. Similar to the case for Game$_3$ and Game$_{3.1}$, we have

$$|\Pr[S_5] - \Pr[S_{5.1}]| \leq 8(q_G + q_H + 2)^2\delta.$$

In addition, according to Lemma 5, for any $p \geq 0$, we have

$$|\Pr[S_{5.1}] - p| \leq |\Pr[S_{5.1} \wedge \text{Good}] - p| + \delta.$$

Game$_6$: This game is the same as Game$_5$ except that the decapsulation oracle returns $H(m, ID)$ for a valid ciphertext c. Similar to the case for Game$_2$ and Game$_3$, we have

$$\Pr[S_{5.1} \wedge \text{Good}] = \Pr[S_6 \wedge \text{Good}].$$

Game$_{6.1}$: This game is the same as Game$_6$ except that the random oracle H is simulated by $H'_q \circ g$ where $H'_q : \mathcal{C} \to \mathcal{K}$ is yet another random oracle as in Game$_{1.2}$. Similar to the case for Game$_{1.2}$ and Game$_2$, we have

$$\Pr[S_6 \wedge \text{Good}] = \Pr[S_{6.1} \wedge \text{Good}].$$

Game$_{6.2}$: This game is the same as Game$_{6.1}$ except that the random oracle $H(\cdot, \cdot)$ is set as the original. Similar to the case for Game$_{1.1}$ and Game$_{1.2}$, we have $\Pr[S_{6.1} \wedge \text{Good}] = \Pr[S_{6.2} \wedge \text{Good}]$. In addition, according to Lemma 5, we have, for any $p \geq 0$,

$$|\Pr[S_{6.2} \wedge \text{Good}] - p| \leq |\Pr[S_{6.2}] - p| + \delta.$$

Game$_7$: This game is the same as Game$_{6.2}$ except that the random oracle G is chosen from $\mathcal{F}$. Similar to the case for Game$_1$ and Game$_{1.1}$, we have

$$|\Pr[S_{6.2}] - \Pr[S_7]| \leq 8(q_G + q_{\text{DEC}} + 2)^2\delta$$

Game$_8$: This game is the same as Game$_7$ except that H_q in the decapsulation is replaced by H_{prf}. From Lemma 3 we have the bound $|\Pr[S_7] -$

$\Pr[S_8]| \leq 2(q_{H_{prf}} + q_{\mathrm{DEC}}) \cdot 2^{-l/2}$ We note that this game is the original game $Expt^{\text{spr-cca}}_{\text{IB-KEM},\mathcal{A}}(\lambda)$ with $b = 1$. Thus, we have

$$\Pr[S_8] = \Pr[Expt^{\text{spr-cca}}_{\text{IB-KEM},\mathcal{A}}(\lambda) = 1 | b = 1].$$

Summarizing these results yields the theorem formula. □

We obtain the following corollary.

Corollary 2. (SPR-CCA ⇒ ANO-CCA) *If IB-KEM is SPR-CCA-secure, then IB-KEM is ANO-CCA-secure.*

4.3 Instantiation from Lattices

Here, we present an instantiation of a post-quantum IBE scheme that satisfies the SDS. Our instantiation can be obtained by applying the T-transformation to the GPV-IBE scheme [5], which is the first and representative lattice-based IBE scheme. The instantiability of more practical schemes such as [2,8,14] remains a future work.

Premilinaries on Lattices. We briefly recall the preliminaries on lattices.

Definition 12 (Discrete Gaussian Distribution). *We write $D_{\mathbb{Z},\sigma}$ to denote the discrete Gaussian distribution over $\mathbb{Z}$ with parameter $\sigma \in \mathbb{Z}^+$.*

Definition 13 (Learning with Errors). *Let $n, m, q \in \mathbb{N}$ and $\sigma \in \mathbb{Z}$. The learning with errors assumption $LWE_{n,m,q,\sigma}$ states that*

$$(\mathbf{A}, \mathbf{s}^\top \mathbf{A} + \mathbf{e}^\top) \approx_c (\mathbf{A}, \mathbf{u}^\top),$$

where $\mathbf{A} \xleftarrow{\$} \mathbb{Z}_q^{n\times m}$, $\mathbf{s} \xleftarrow{\$} \mathbb{Z}_q^n$, $\mathbf{e} \leftarrow D^m_{\mathbb{Z},\sigma}$, and $\mathbf{u} \xleftarrow{\$} \mathbb{Z}_q^m$.

GPV-IBE. We briefly describe the λ-bit message version of the GPV-IBE [5].

- A system parameter is a matrix $\mathbf{A} \in \mathbb{Z}_q^{n\times m}$ and master key is its trandoor $\mathbf{T_A} \in \mathbb{Z}^{m\times m}$, which enables one to sample a short vector $\mathbf{x} \in \mathbb{Z}_q^m$ from a discrete Gaussian distribution $D^m_{\mathbb{Z},\sigma}$ conditioned on $\mathbf{Ax} = \mathbf{v} \mod q$.
- A private key d_{ID} for an identity $ID \in \mathcal{ID}$ is short vectors $\{\mathbf{e}_{ID,i} \in \mathbb{Z}_q^m\}_{i\in[\lambda]}$ such that $\mathbf{A}\mathbf{e}_{ID,i} = \mathbf{u}_{ID,i}$, where $\mathbf{u}_{ID,i} = H(ID, i)$ for a hash function $H : \mathcal{ID} \to \mathbb{Z}_q^n$, which is modeled as a random oracle.
- A ciphertext for a message $(m_1, \ldots, m_\lambda) \in \{0,1\}^\lambda$ consists of

  $$c_{0,i} = \mathbf{u}_{ID,i}^\top \mathbf{s} + x_i + m_i \lfloor q/2 \rceil \text{ for } i \in [\lambda], \qquad \mathbf{c}_1 = \mathbf{A}^\top \mathbf{s} + \mathbf{x},$$

  where $(\mathbf{s}, \{x_i\}_{i\in[\lambda]}, \mathbf{x}) \xleftarrow{\$} \mathbb{Z}_q^n \times (D_{\mathbb{Z},\alpha' q})^\lambda \times D^m_{\mathbb{Z},\alpha q}$ is an encryption randomness and $\alpha, \alpha' \in \mathbb{Z}$.
- Decryption can be done by computing $w_i = c_{0,i} - \mathbf{c}_1^\top \mathbf{e}_{ID,i} \in \mathbb{Z}_q$ for all $i \in [\lambda]$ and deciding if w_i is closer to 0 or to $\lfloor q/2 \rceil$ modulo q.

Katsumata et al. [9] have shown that the GPV-IBE scheme is both accurate and secure when the parameters are appropriately set.

Lemma 1 (Correctness [9, Lemma 12]). *Suppose the parameters q, σ, and α' are such that*

$$\sigma > ||\mathbf{T_A}||_{\mathrm{GS}} \cdot \sqrt{\log(2m+4)/\pi}, \qquad \alpha' < 1/8\sigma m,$$

where $||\mathbf{T_A}||_{\mathrm{GS}}$ is the longest column of the Gram-Schmidt orthogonalizatio of $\mathbf{T_A}$. Then, the above GPV-IBE scheme is $2^{-\Omega(\lambda)}$-correct.

Lemma 2 (IND-CPA security [9, Theorem 1]). *The above GPV-IBE scheme is tightly IND-CPA-secure in the random oracle model assuming the hardness of $LWE_{n,m,q,\alpha q}$.*

We use the parameter setting proposed in [9] as follows:

$$n = \tilde{\Omega}(\lambda), \qquad m = n^{1+\kappa}, \qquad q = 10n^{3+4\kappa},$$
$$\sigma = n^{0.5+\kappa}, \qquad \alpha' q = n^{1.5+2\kappa}, \qquad \alpha q = 2\sqrt{n},$$

where $\kappa > 0$ is a constant that can be set arbitrarily small. In the above, we round up m to the nearest integer and q to the nearest larger prime.

SDS for the GPV-IBE. We then show that the T-transformed GPV-IBE scheme satisfies SDS. This theorem and its proof are omitted due to space constraints. Using the above parameters, the proof can be demonstrated by showing the two conditions of the SDS definition.

In summary, we obtain the following corollary.

Corollary 3. *Let G, H, H_{prf} be hash functions modeled as random oracles, and GPV be the GPV-IBE scheme. Then, an IB-KEM scheme $\mathsf{U}_{m,ID}[\mathsf{T}[\mathsf{GPV}, G], H, H_{prf}]$ is a (tightly) ANO-CCA secure IB-KEM scheme in the QROM.*

5 Conclusion

The FO (Fujisaki-Okamoto) transformation is a well-known technique to obtain CCA security from CPA security in constructions of PKE and/or KEM in the ROM. In this paper, we have shown that the FO transformation realizes anonymity of IBE in addition to CCA security in QROM, if the underlying CPA secure IBE meets strong disjoint-simulatable (SDS) property. Although the main purpose of the FO transformation is to efficiently realize CCA security, this paper has shown another benefit of the FO transformation, namely how to efficiently obtain anonymity, in addition to CCA security.

Acknowledgements. This work was in part supported by JST K Program Grant Number JPMJKP24U2, Japan. This work was also supported in part by JSPS KAKENHI Grant Numbers JP23K24846, JP25051030.

A Missing Lemmas

The following lemmas are used in our security proofs.

Lemma 3 **([12]).** *Let $l \in \mathbb{N}$ be sufficiently large. $\mathcal{X}$ and $\mathcal{Y}$ be finite sets, and $H : \{0,1\}^l \times \mathcal{X} \to \mathcal{Y}$ and $H' : \mathcal{X} \to \mathcal{Y}$ be two independent random oracles. If an unbounded-time quantum adversary $\mathcal{A}$ makes a query to H at most q_H times, then we have*

$$\left| \Pr[b = 1\, s \leftarrow \{0,1\}^l, b \leftarrow \mathcal{A}^{H,H(s,\cdot)}] - \Pr[b = 1 | b \leftarrow \mathcal{A}^{H,H_q}] \right| \leq 2q_h \cdot 2^{-l/2},$$

where all oracle accesses of $\mathcal{A}$ can be quantum.

Lemma 4 **([7]).** *Let $\mathcal{X}$ be a finite set, let $\delta \in [0,1]$, let $F : \mathcal{X} \to \{0,1\}$ be the following function: for each $x \in \mathcal{X}, F(x) = 1$ with probability $\delta_x \leq \delta$ and $F(x) = 0$ otherwise. Let $Z : \mathcal{X} \to \{0,1\}$ be the zero function, that is, $Z(x) = 0$ for all x. If an unbounded-time quantum adversary $\mathcal{A}$ makes queries to F or Z at most Q times, then we have*

$$|\Pr[b = 1 | b \leftarrow \mathcal{A}^{F(\cdot)}] - \Pr[b = 1 | b \leftarrow \mathcal{A}^{Z(\cdot)}]| \leq 8(Q+1)^2 \delta,$$

where all oracle accesses of $\mathcal{A}$ can be quantum.

Lemma 5 **([15]).** *Let A and B denote events. Suppose that we have* $\Pr[A] \leq \delta$. *For any $p \geq 0$, we have*

$$|\Pr[B] - p| \leq |\Pr[B \wedge \neg A] - p| + \delta \quad \textit{and} \quad |\Pr[B \wedge \neg A] - p| \leq |\Pr[B] - p| + \delta.$$

References

1. Abdalla, M., et al.: Searchable encryption revisited: consistency properties, relation to anonymous IBE, and extensions. J. Cryptol. **21**(3), 350–391 (2008). https://doi.org/10.1007/s00145-007-9006-6
2. Ducas, L., Lyubashevsky, V., Prest, T.: Efficient identity-based encryption over NTRU lattices. In: Sarkar, P., Iwata, T. (eds.) ASIACRYPT 2014, Part II. LNCS, vol. 8874, pp. 22–41. Springer, Heidelberg (2014). https://doi.org/10.1007/978-3-662-45608-8_2
3. Fujisaki, E., Okamoto, T.: Secure integration of asymmetric and symmetric encryption schemes. In: Wiener, M.J. (ed.) CRYPTO 1999. LNCS, vol. 1666, pp. 537–554. Springer, Heidelberg (1999). https://doi.org/10.1007/3-540-48405-1_34
4. Fujisaki, E., Okamoto, T.: Secure integration of asymmetric and symmetric encryption schemes. J. Cryptol. **26**(1), 80–101 (2013). https://doi.org/10.1007/s00145-011-9114-1
5. Gentry, C., Peikert, C., Vaikuntanathan, V.: Trapdoors for hard lattices and new cryptographic constructions. In: Ladner, R.E., Dwork, C. (eds.) 40th ACM STOC, pp. 197–206. ACM Press (2008). https://doi.org/10.1145/1374376.1374407

6. Hofheinz, D., Hövelmanns, K., Kiltz, E.: A modular analysis of the Fujisaki-Okamoto transformation. In: Kalai, Y., Reyzin, L. (eds.) TCC 2017, Part I. LNCS, vol. 10677, pp. 341–371. Springer, Cham (2017). https://doi.org/10.1007/978-3-319-70500-2_12
7. Hövelmanns, K., Kiltz, E., Schäge, S., Unruh, D.: Generic authenticated key exchange in the quantum random oracle model. In: Kiayias, A., Kohlweiss, M., Wallden, P., Zikas, V. (eds.) PKC 2020, Part II. LNCS, vol. 12111, pp. 389–422. Springer, Cham (2020). https://doi.org/10.1007/978-3-030-45388-6_14
8. Jia, H., Hu, Y., Tang, C., Wang, L.: Towards compact identity-based encryption on ideal lattices. In: Oswald, E. (ed.) CT-RSA 2024. LNCS, vol. 14643, pp. 354–378. Springer, Cham (2024). https://doi.org/10.1007/978-3-031-58868-6_14
9. Katsumata, S., Yamada, S., Yamakawa, T.: Tighter security proofs for GPV-IBE in the quantum random oracle model. J. Cryptol. **34**(1), 5 (2021). https://doi.org/10.1007/s00145-020-09371-y
10. Kuchta, V., Sakzad, A., Stehlé, D., Steinfeld, R., Sun, S.: Measure-rewind-measure: tighter quantum random oracle model proofs for one-way to hiding and CCA security. In: Canteaut, A., Ishai, Y. (eds.) EUROCRYPT 2020, Part III. LNCS, vol. 12107, pp. 703–728. Springer, Cham (2020). https://doi.org/10.1007/978-3-030-45727-3_24
11. Liu, X., Wang, M.: QCCA-secure generic key encapsulation mechanism with tighter security in the quantum random oracle model. In: Garay, J. (ed.) PKC 2021, Part I. LNCS, vol. 12710, pp. 3–26. Springer, Cham (2021). https://doi.org/10.1007/978-3-030-75245-3_1
12. Saito, T., Xagawa, K., Yamakawa, T.: Tightly-secure key-encapsulation mechanism in the quantum random oracle model. In: Nielsen, J.B., Rijmen, V. (eds.) EUROCRYPT 2018, Part III. LNCS, vol. 10822, pp. 520–551. Springer, Cham (2018). https://doi.org/10.1007/978-3-319-78372-7_17
13. Targhi, E.E., Unruh, D.: Post-quantum security of the Fujisaki-Okamoto and OAEP transforms. In: Hirt, M., Smith, A.D. (eds.) TCC 2016-B, Part II. LNCS, vol. 9986, pp. 192–216. Springer, Heidelberg (2016). https://doi.org/10.1007/978-3-662-53644-5_8
14. Tomita, T., Shikata, J.: Efficient identity-based encryption with tight adaptive anonymity from RLWE. In: Saarinen, M.J., Smith-Tone, D. (eds.) PQCrypto 2024, Part I, pp. 300–321. Springer, Cham (2024). https://doi.org/10.1007/978-3-031-62743-9_10
15. Xagawa, K.: Anonymity of NIST PQC round 3 KEMs. In: Dunkelman, O., Dziembowski, S. (eds.) EUROCRYPT 2022, Part III. LNCS, vol. 13277, pp. 551–581. Springer, Cham (2022). https://doi.org/10.1007/978-3-031-07082-2_20

Side-Channel and Fault Analysis in PQC

Breaking Masked Kyber: ResNet-Based Masked Kyber Share Recovery Method

Yaoling Ding[1], Haotong Xu[1], Chong Luo[1,2], Annyu Liu[1(✉)], Zheyu Zhang[3(✉)], Jing Yu[1], and An Wang[1]

[1] School of Cyberspace Science and Technology, Beijing Institute of Technology, Beijing 100081, China
{dyl19,haotongxu,annvliu,yujing93,wanganl}@bit.edu.cn
[2] Beijing Institute of Computer Technology and Application, Beijing 100854, China
[3] China Industrial Control Systems Cyber Emergency Response Team (CICS-CERT), Beijing 100040, China
iamzhangzheyu@sina.com

Abstract. As post-quantum cryptography becomes the cornerstone of future security systems, it is crucial to understand its practical resilience under present side-channel analysis. In this paper, we propose an effective side-channel analysis method for the poly_tomsg() function in the decapsulation of the first-order mask implementation of CRYSTALS-Kyber (the NIST-selected post-quantum key encapsulation mechanism). Unlike previous methods that target individual bits, our method targets a masked shared byte. By systematically evaluating multiple neural network architectures (MLP, CNN, ResNet), we find that residual learning has the best robustness under low signal-to-noise ratios. The method achieves up to 98% average accuracy by training a ResNet18 network , and is able to recover m from a single trace with a success rate of over 38%, outperforming classical template attacks without trace alignment. These findings reveal that even well-implemented Boolean masking can be defeated by neural-based profiling attacks, thus emphasizing the need for stronger countermeasures in post-quantum cryptographic implementations.

Keywords: CRYSTALS-Kyber · Masking · Side-channel analysis · Profiling attacks · Neural networks

1 Introduction

Post-quantum cryptography (PQC) has emerged as a critical research frontier [1], with lattice-based key encapsulation mechanisms (KEM) such as CRYSTALS-Kyber selected for standardization by NIST due to their strong security and implementation efficiency [4]. However, physical implementation of these schemes exposes them to side-channel analysis (SCA), where secret-dependent variations in power, electromagnetic radiation, or timing can leak sensitive information [5].

H. Seo (Ed.): ICISC 2025, LNCS 16487, pp. 185–197, 2026.
https://doi.org/10.1007/978-981-95-8034-7_10

To mitigate such leakage, masking is widely adopted. Boolean masking splits sensitive intermediates into random shares, rendering direct observation ineffective [15]. Despite its theoretical guarantees, practical studies reveal that implementation imperfections and low signal-to-noise ratio (SNR) environments, especially on microcontrollers like STM32F4, may still enable leakage exploitation [7,24].

Early profiling-based SCAs relied on template attacks, modeling the leakage distribution via multivariate statistics [5,14,18]. Yet such techniques require precise alignment and suffer from low robustness against noise. Recent advances leverage deep learning to automate feature extraction and improve classification accuracy [3,9,16,25]. Convolutional neural networks (CNN) and multilayer perceptrons (MLP) have demonstrated success on symmetric primitives like AES [10], and have more recently been applied to PQC [2,11].

However, few studies have explored deep learning-based attacks against masked Kyber implementations. Existing work has been mainly on unprotected designs [23], which are difficult to migrate to masked Kyber algorithms. Backlund et al. [2] utilize bit-level leakage for masked Kyber algorithms, but each bit needs to be classified individually, resulting in poor efficiency and scalability is poor. Wang et al. [22] first proposed to attack the poly_frommsg() function with an implementation of an attack method against byte, but they did not realize that the poly_tomsg() function also has exploitable leakage, even though the exploitation of this leakage may be more difficult compared to poly_frommsg() function. For these leaks above, template attacks, while theoretically optimal [7], often fail in high-noise environments due to low SNR, misalignment and masking induced randomness, especially when voting or preprocessing strategies are absent.

In this paper, we establish an efficient and noise-resilient side-channel analysis method against masked Kyber by introducing a deep learning approach. In contrast to prior bit-level or template-based attacks, our method directly targets byte shares in poly_tomsg() function and achieves high single-trace accuracy even under practical noise. Our contributions include:

- We propose a residual neural network (ResNet)-based masked Kyber share recovery method that utilizes the network to efficiently recover sensitive information in the poly_tomsg() function of the Kyber algorithm with masking.
- Our method models each masked byte of the poly_tomsg() function independently, training the model to recover all $share0$ and $share1$ bytes of the message. Unlike previous methods that use individual bits, our method more fully utilizes the leakage of the poly_tomsg() function to enhance recovery.
- We evaluated a variety of neural architectures (including MLP, CNN, and ResNet) and compared their performance.
- We conducted experiments on a real scenario to demonstrate the superiority of the ResNet-based masked Kyber share recovery method and its m recovery accuracy of more than 38% at low SNR, which outperforms equivalent template attacks without relying on preprocessing or aggregate voting.

This work demonstrates that our deep learning approach significantly outperforms both traditional template methods and prior bit-level neural attacks in terms of efficiency, scalability, and resilience to masking noise, which poses a serious threat to masked Kyber implementations.

2 Background

2.1 CRYSTALS-Kyber and Masking

CRYSTALS-Kyber is a lattice-based KEM that relies on Module Learning with Errors problems [19]. Kyber has been selected as part of NIST's PQC standardization process [4].

To resist side-channel analysis, countermeasures such as masking [8] and shuffling [17] have been proposed. One common masking scheme for poly_tomsg() function splits a sensitive variable 32-byte m into two uniformly random shares, $share0$ and $share1$, for each byte $m[i] = share0[i] \oplus share1[i], i \in [0, 31]$.

However, in the masked Kyber implementation adopted by mkm4, the message decoding function as Algorithm 1, reveals a critical vulnerability, the $share0$ and $share1$ are processed serially and bit by bit, leading to deterministic and structured leakage. When the device operates at high clock frequency, this leakage becomes temporally concentrated, reducing the effectiveness of template attacks due to their sensitivity to noise.

Algorithm 1. Masked `poly_tomsg()`: Convert masked polynomial to message

Input: Masked polynomial $a = (a_0, a_1)$
Output: Masked message `msg.share[0]` and `msg.share[1]`

```
1: //Codes Omitted
2: for i = 0 to KYBER_SYMBYTES − 1 do
3:     for j = 0 to 7 do
4:         //Codes Omitted
5:         msg.share[0].u8[i] += ((c[0] >> 15)&1) << j
6:         msg.share[1].u8[i] += ((c[1] >> 15)&1) << j
7:     end for
8: end for
```

In contrast, our deep learning approach remains robust under such conditions. It does not rely on precise alignment or temporal spreading of leakage, allowing it to maintain high classification accuracy even when traditional template attacks fail.

2.2 Side-Channel Analysis and Machine Learning

Template attacks estimate the leakage distribution of sensitive intermediate values using multivariate Gaussian models [5]. Although theoretically optimal under ideal conditions, their practical effectiveness is severely limited by trace misalignment, measurement noise, and the need for large, well-labeled profiling datasets. These limitations are especially pronounced in masked implementations with high-frequency execution, where leakage becomes subtle and difficult to model accurately.

Deep learning has emerged as a powerful alternative, revolutionizing profiling side-channel analysis, which automatically extract local features from raw traces, eliminating the need for manual feature engineering [12,13]. In this work, we propose the residual learning attack on a first-order masked Kyber implementation. Our ResNet-based masked Kyber share recovery method achieves high classification accuracy directly on $share0$ and $share1$ bytes, demonstrating both efficiency and robustness against real-world noise.

3 Methodology

3.1 Threat Model and Assumptions

We consider an adversary operating in the profiling setting, with access to a clone device running the same first-order masked Kyber implementation as the target device. The adversary is assumed to be capable of collecting a large number of side-channel traces using known inputs and is able to observe individual share bytes ($share0$ and $share1$) during the execution of the poly_tomsg() function. While the adversary has full control over the measurement setup, including devices such as oscilloscopes and electromagnetic (EM) probes, they do not have access to the secret key or the internal random source used in the execution.

The target implementation is assumed to follow a correct application of first-order masking. Side-channel leakage is considered to originate from deterministic operations on shared intermediate values, under realistic conditions involving measurement noise and other imperfections typical in embedded environments.

On this basis, unlike template attacks, the adversary does not rely on predefined leakage models (e.g., Hamming weight) and assume well-aligned or denoised traces. This attack strategy is entirely data-driven and operates directly at the trace level without handcrafted assumptions.

3.2 Data Acquisition and Preprocessing

We use a near-field EM probe placed above the power supply to capture the decapsulation process of the masked Kyber algorithm, which includes the poly_tomsg() function. We sample the EM traces at a high frequency to capture fine-grained leakage.

To construct the training dataset, we filtered each trace. Since the single bit positions of $share0$ and $share1$ are difficult to distinguish, we extracted each bit trace location containing both $share0$ and $share1$. We concatenate the 8-bit trace fragments of each shared byte, corresponding to Algorithm 1 (Line 3,5,6), and then normalize each concatenated fragment:

Table 1. ResNet structure in share recovery, $L = 616$ in our case

Layer Type	Input Size	Output Size	Parameters
Input	$1 \times L$	$1 \times L$	-
Convolution (64, kernel=7, stride=2, padding=3)	$1 \times L$	$64 \times \lceil L/2 \rceil$	448
BatchNorm + ReLU	$64 \times \lceil L/2 \rceil$	$64 \times \lceil L/2 \rceil$	128
MaxPooling (kernel=3, stride=2, padding=1)	$64 \times \lceil L/2 \rceil$	$64 \times \lceil L/4 \rceil$	-
Residual Block 1 (2 × BasicBlock)	$64 \times \lceil L/4 \rceil$	$64 \times \lceil L/4 \rceil$	49664
Residual Block 2 (2 × BasicBlock, stride=2)	$64 \times \lceil L/4 \rceil$	$128 \times \lceil L/8 \rceil$	181504
Residual Block 3 (2 × BasicBlock, stride=2)	$128 \times \lceil L/8 \rceil$	$256 \times \lceil L/16 \rceil$	723456
Residual Block 4 (2 × BasicBlock, stride=2)	$256 \times \lceil L/16 \rceil$	$512 \times \lceil L/32 \rceil$	2888704
AdaptiveAvgPool	$512 \times \lceil L/32 \rceil$	512×1	-
Flatten	512×1	512	-
Fully Connected	512	256	131072
Total			**3975232**

1. **Trace Capture:** Collect traces from poly_tomsg() function;
2. **Filter:** Filter the captured trace;
3. **Extract:** Extracts each bit position containing $share0$ and $share1$, for a total of 256 bit positions per trace;
4. **Concatenate:** Concatenate the traces of each byte, every 8 as a dataset, a total of 32 datasets and divide each dataset into two categories based on different $share0$ and $share1$ labels, for a total of 64 datasets;
5. **Normalize:** Each dataset is cropped or zero-padded to a fixed length;
6. **Split:** Each dataset is stratified and split into training, validation, and test sets.

This produces 64 share-specific datasets $\mathcal{D}_{s,b}$, where $s \in \{share0, share1\}$ and $b \in [0, 31]$:

$$\mathcal{D}_{s,b} = \{(\mathbf{x}_i, \text{label}(s_b[i]))\}_{i=1}^{Number\ of\ datasets}$$

3.3 ResNet-Based Masked Kyber Share Method

For each share-byte pair, we train an independent 1D ResNet18 classifier that processes single-channel input traces and outputs 256 logits, using a deep residual architecture composed of an initial convolutional block, four stacked residual layers (channels 64âĂŞ512), global average pooling, and a final fully connected layer. The specific network structure is shown in the Table 1.

Through the ResNet, each $share0[i]$ and $share1[i]$ is predicted by the trained models, and then the information is reconstructed by XOR.

Once we obtain m, we can recover the key by chosen ciphertext attack [6,20,21], i.e., by carefully constructing ciphertext so that the decrypted plaintext information forms a simple one-to-one mapping relationship with the key, thereby inferring the key.

Since our method directly targets each share byte and leverages deep residual networks, it requires neither trace alignment nor pre-computing, unlike traditional template attacks. It can recover full messages from single traces and full keys with only a few observations.

4 Experiments

4.1 Experimental Setup

We implemented the Kyber algorithm with masking at the highest optimization level (-O3) on STM32F407 Discovery at 168 MHZ using the mkm4 library with the arm-none-eabi-gcc compiler. We used a near-field electromagnetic probe to capture the decapsulation process of the masked Kyber algorithm with a total of 100000 traces. By methods such as filtering and splicing, 64 datasets were obtained and divided into training (70000 traces), validation (15000 traces) and test (15000 traces) sets, more details in Table 2.

Table 2. Training setting

Parameter	Value
Input length	616
Batch size	512
Maximum epochs	1000
Optimizer	Adam
Learning rate	1×10^{-4}
Loss function	Cross Entropy
Early stopping patience	50 epochs
Min delta for improvement	0.001
Train/Validation/Test split	70%/15%/15%

We train 64 independent models, one for each share-byte. Each model is optimized using Adam (learning rate 1×10^{-4}), batch size 512, and a maximum of 1000 epochs. Training is monitored via validation accuracy, with early stopping triggered if no improvement is observed for 50 consecutive epochs. Best performing models (in terms of validation accuracy) are saved automatically. All models are trained from scratch using PyTorch on NVIDIA GeForce RTX 3090. Each model completes its training in a few minutes.

4.2 Comparison with Existing Work

To provide a direct comparison against prior classical methods, we implemented the bit-level template attack proposed by Du et al. [7] to recover the single bytes $share0$ and $share1$ of the masked Kyber. For fair comparison, we constructed the templates using the same trace data as our deep learning classifiers. Specifically, we selected 30 byte positions (from byte 1 to byte 30, without byte 0 and byte 31) in each trace and extracted individual bits of $share0$ and $share1$ based on their Hamming weights, resulting in 88 templates in total, referred to as Template Attack Group 1. To mitigate potential noise from inter-byte variation, we also constructed a second template set using only the first byte from 3000 aligned traces, referred to as Template Attack Group 2.

Despite this careful setup, the attack performs poorly in practice. Our experiments reveal that the bit success rates rapidly decline with increasing bit index, dropping from around 50% on bit 0 to below 1% on bit 7 (see Fig. 1). These results reflect the challenges of deploying template attacks in real-world conditions, including trace misalignment, and environmental noise significantly degrade the leakage consistency, especially when no voting or trace alignment is applied.

In contrast, our ResNet18-based classifiers maintain over 96% accuracy across all bytes. With the results in the Table 3, we can see that our method is far more accurate for single byte share experiments than for template attacks. These findings underscore the vulnerability of masked implementations under deep learning attacks, and the limitations of template attacks under practical noise condittions.

Table 3. Comparison of ResNet and template attack of single byte accuracy

Method	Share	Mean
Template Attack Group 1	*share0*	$< 1\%$
Template Attack Group 1	*share1*	$< 1\%$
Template Attack Group 2	*share0*	$< 1\%$
Template Attack Group 2	*share1*	$< 1\%$
ResNet	*share0*	96.89%
ResNet	*share1*	96.78%

4.3 Overall Byte Accuracy and Key Recovery

We evaluate 64 independently trained ResNet18 classifiers, each corresponding to a masked byte (32 for $share0$, 32 for $share1$). Each model is tested on 15000 traces, without trace alignment, averaging, or feature engineering.

The results of the experiment are shown in Fig. 2. Across all 64 classifiers, we observe strong performance despite practical noise summarized in Table 4. Over 97% accuracy is achieved in a majority of byte positions.

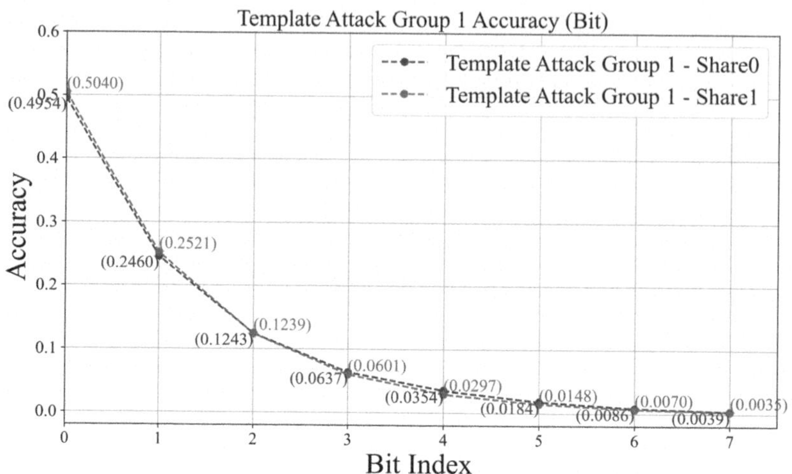

(a) Template Attack Group 1

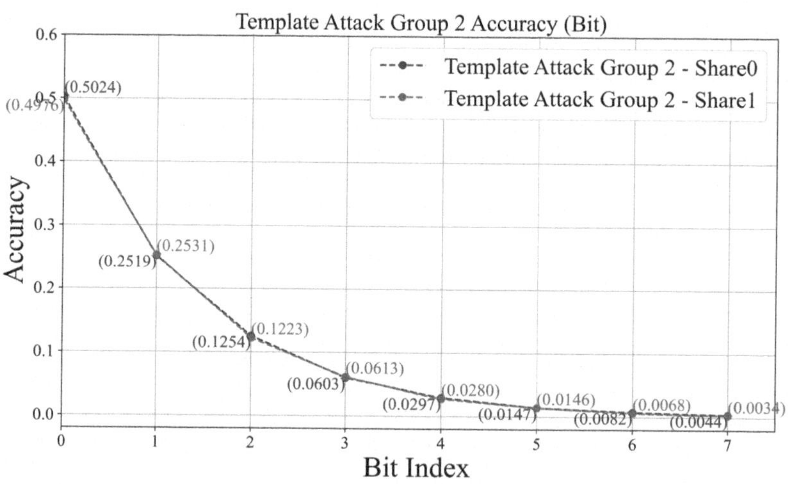

(b) Template Attack Group 2

Fig. 1. Comparison of share0 and share1 template attacks between different groups.

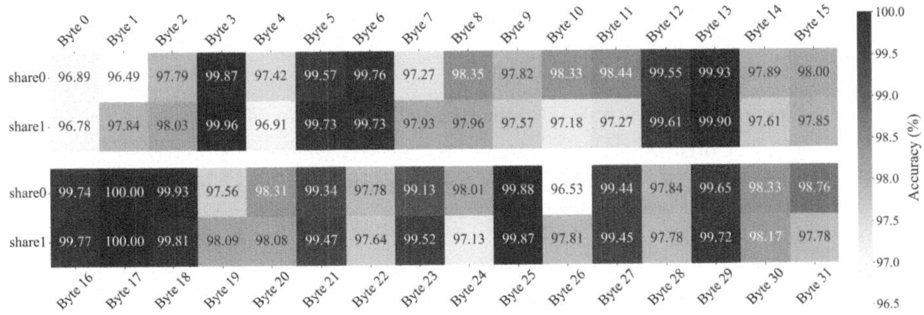

Fig. 2. Distribution of models accuracy. Each bin represents the accuracy of the corresponding share byte.

All 64 classifiers achieve over 96% test accuracy, with 26 exceeding 99%, and some (e.g., $share0[17]$, $share1[17]$) reaching 100%, which demonstrates our stable and robust performance in both sharing and byte location, and proves the effectiveness of our attack on single byte share.

Table 4. Performance summary by share

Share	Min (%)	Max (%)	Mean (%)	Std (%)
share0	96.49	100.00	98.55	0.0106
share1	96.78	100.00	98.50	0.0107

Once both $share0$ and $share1$ byte predictions are obtained from our trained classifiers, the original message bytes are directly reconstructed via XOR.

Our ResNet18 model has a 38.47% success rate in recovering m using a single trace, implying that we only need about three traces to recover the full m. The experiments succeed even under unprocessed, noisy conditions, demonstrating the practical feasibility of attacking first-order masks.

We evaluated the computational cost of training a $share0$ or $share1$ ResNet18 model in terms of time and space complexity. As summarized in Table 5, empirical results from multiple training sessions demonstrate that the adopted Adam optimizer and early stopping strategy significantly enhance training efficiency. The primary advantage of this configuration is a markedly accelerated training cycle. Although this speedup incurs a slight reduction in accuracy, it constitutes a favorable trade-off, as the achieved efficiency gain is substantial and the final model accuracy remains competitive against other benchmarks.

These results indicate that our method weakens the effectiveness of first-order masking in post-quantum cryptography. By reliably recovering information from noisy single traces, we provide a new possibility for analyzing attacks on lattice-based masking schemes.

Table 5. Computational cost of training the ResNet

Computational Resource	Value	
Training Duration	Max:1015.52 s	Mean:572.38 s
RAM Consumption	Max:2297.02 MB	Mean:2218.02 MB
VRAM Usage	Max:2830.00 MB	Mean:1548.79 MB
Number Of Parameters	3,975,232	
Model Size	15.20 MB	

4.4 Comparison of Different Models

The above experiments have demonstrated that our method significantly outperforms template attacks in scenarios with high noise levels. In this section, we will further explore the impact of different models on experimental results. We employed various models to recover single-byte shares $share0$ and $share1$. The training, validation, and test datasets used in the experiments were identical. We compared MLP, CNN, and the ResNet18 model we utilized, with the experimental results summarized in the Table 6 below.

Table 6. Comparison of the accuracy of different models for single-byte share

Model Type	Share	Validation Acc. (%)	Test Acc. (%)
MLP	*share0*	94.87	93.83
MLP	*share1*	94.92	94.18
CNN	*share0*	96.20	95.97
CNN	*share1*	97.05	96.67
ResNet18 (ours)	***share0***	**97.13**	**96.89**
ResNet18 (ours)	***share1***	**97.26**	**96.78**

The experimental results show that the different models have high accuracy when attacking single byte share. And ResNet18 consistently achieves the highest classification accuracy on both shares, outperforming the MLP by over 3%. This gain stems from residual blocks' ability to retain gradient flow across deeper layers, allowing the network to extract more stable features even in the presence of severe trace noise. Without any alignment, our model still learns robust mappings from traces to individual share bytes.

5 Conclusion

In this paper, we propose a ResNet-based masked Kyber share recovery method for the poly_tomsg() function that effectively attacks the first-order masked implementation of CRYSTALS-Kyber. Compared to the previous single bit attack against share, our method targets a single byte, which makes our method more fully utilize the leakage of the poly_tomsg() function and improves the effectiveness of the attack. We also evaluated multiple neural architectures (including MLP, CNN, and ResNet) simultaneously, comparing their performance. By training ResNet18 models (each targeting a single masked byte) we achieved up to 98% single-byte accuracy on realistic high-noise side channel tracking. In this way, we recovered the full m using only about three traces, demonstrating the utility of first-order Boolean masks without the need for alignment.

Compared to traditional template attacks that rely on aligned traces and leakage modeling, our method offers a template-free, architecture-agnostic strategy with strong generalization and minimal assumptions. The use of residual learning proves particularly effective in extracting deep features from low-SNR traces, outperforming both MLP and CNN baselines in classification accuracy and robustness.

Despite its strengths, our approach introduces computational and deployment overheads due to the need for 64 independent models and the size of the ResNet18 architecture. Moreover, current modeling treats each byte and share in isolation, leaving potential performance gains from joint modeling unexplored. These limitations suggest several avenues for future improvement. Compact multi-output architectures could reduce model redundancy and enable joint share prediction. Compression techniques such as pruning, quantization, or knowledge distillation would help reduce model footprint for resource-constrained environments. Additionally, transferability to other PQC schemes and adaptation to higher-order masking scenarios offer promising directions to broaden applicability and resilience.

Overall, our findings indicate that first-order masking alone is no longer sufficient in the presence of advanced profiling techniques. By leveraging modern deep learning architectures, we uncover new capabilities in side-channel analysis, challenging the current assumptions of post-quantum implementation security.

Acknowledgements. This work is supported by National Key R&D Program of China (No. 2022YFB3103800), National Natural Science Foundation of China (Nos. 62272047, 62302036, 62402039), Beijing Natural Science Foundation (Nos. L244044, L251068).

References

1. Alagic, G., et al.: Status report on the third round of the nist post-quantum cryptography standardization process (2022)
2. Backlund, L., Ngo, K., Gärtner, J., Dubrova, E.: Secret key recovery attack on masked and shuffled implementations of crystals-kyber and saber. In: International Conference on Applied Cryptography and Network Security, pp. 159–177. Springer (2023)

3. Batina, L., Bhasin, S., Jap, D., Picek, S.: CSI neural network: Using side-channels to recover your artificial neural network information. arXiv preprint arXiv:1810.09076 (2018)
4. Bos, J., et al.: Crystals-kyber: a CCA-secure module-lattice-based kem. In: 2018 IEEE European symposium on security and privacy (EuroS&P), pp. 353–367. IEEE (2018)
5. Chari, S., Rao, J.R., Rohatgi, P.: Template attacks. In: International workshop on cryptographic hardware and embedded systems, pp. 13–28. Springer (2002)
6. D'Anvers, J., Heinz, D., Pessl, P., Beirendonck, M. V., Verbauwhede, I.: Higher-order masked ciphertext comparison for lattice-based cryptography (2021)
7. Du, J., Wang, J., Yu, A.: Revisiting the masking strategy: a side-channel attack on crystals-kyber. IEEE Transactions on Information Forensics and Security (2025)
8. Heinz, D., Kannwischer, M. J., Land, G., Pöppelmann, T., Schwabe, P., Sprenkels, A.: First-order masked kyber on arm cortex-m4. Cryptology ePrint Archive (2022)
9. Kim, J., Picek, S., Heuser, A., Bhasin, S., Hanjalic, A.: Make some noise. unleashing the power of convolutional neural networks for profiled side-channel analysis. IACR Transactions on Cryptographic Hardware and Embedded Systems, pp. 148–179 (2019)
10. Kubota, T., Yoshida, K., Shiozaki, M., Fujino, T.: Deep learning side-channel attack against hardware implementations of AES. Microprocess. Microsyst. **87**, 103383 (2021)
11. Ma, Y., Yang, X., Wang, A., Wei, C., Chen, T., Xu, T.: Side-channel analysis on lattice-based kem using multi-feature recognition-the case study of kyber. In: International Conference on Information Security and Cryptology, pp. 221–239. Springer (2023)
12. Maghrebi, H.: Deep learning based side channel attacks in practice. Cryptology ePrint Archive (2019)
13. Maghrebi, H., Portigliatt, T., Prouff, E.: Breaking cryptographic implementations using deep learning techniques. In: International Conference on Security, Privacy, and Applied Cryptography Engineering, pp. 3–26. Springer (2016)
14. Mangard, S., Oswald, E.: and Thomas Popp. Revealing the secrets of smart cards. Springer, Power analysis attacks (2007)
15. Mangard, S., Pramstaller, N., Oswald, E.: Successfully attacking masked AES hardware implementations. In: International workshop on cryptographic hardware and embedded systems, pp. 157–171. Springer (2005)
16. Masure, L., Dumas, C., Prouff, E.: A comprehensive study of deep learning for side-channel analysis. IACR Trans. Cryptographic Hardw. Embed. Syst, 348–375 (2020)
17. Ngo, K., Dubrova, E., Johansson, T.: Breaking masked and shuffled CCA secure saber kem by power analysis. In: Proceedings of the 5th Workshop on Attacks and Solutions in Hardware Security, pp. 51–61 (2021)
18. Oswald, E., Mangard, S.: Template attacks on masking—resistance is futile. In: Cryptographers' Track at the RSA Conference, pp. 243–256. Springer (2007)
19. Regev, O.: On lattices, learning with errors, random linear codes, and cryptography. J. ACM (JACM) **56**(6), 1–40 (2009)
20. Sim, B.-Y., Park, A., Han, D.-G.: Chosen-ciphertext clustering attack on crystals-kyber using the side-channel leakage of barrett reduction. IEEE Internet Things J. **9**(21), 21382–21397 (2022)
21. Tanaka, Y., et al.: Multiple-valued plaintext-checking side-channel attacks on post-quantum kems. IACR Trans. Cryptographic Hardw. Embed. Syst. **2023**(3), 473–503 (2023)

22. Wang, J., Cao, W., Chen, H., Li, H.: Practical side-channel attack on message encoding in masked kyber. In: 2022 IEEE International Conference on Trust, Security and Privacy in Computing and Communications (TrustCom), pp. 882–889. IEEE (2022)
23. Wang, R., Dubrova, E.: A side-channel secret key recovery attack on crystals-kyber using k chosen ciphertexts. In: International Conference on Codes, Cryptology, and Information Security, pp. 109–128. Springer (2023)
24. Wang, Z., et al.: SPA-GPT: general pulse tailor for simple power analysis based on reinforcement learning. IACR Trans. Cryptographic Hardw. Embed. Syst. **2024**(4), 40–83 (2024)
25. Zhang, L., Xing, X., Fan, J., Wang, Z., Wang, S.: Multilabel deep learning-based side-channel attack. IEEE Trans. Comput. Aided Des. Integr. Circuits Syst. **40**(6), 1207–1216 (2020)

Side-Channel Leakage Assessment of SMAUG-T: Exploiting Hamming Weight Patterns in Polynomial-to-Message Conversion

Gwang-Sik Kim and Young-Sik Kim(✉)

DGIST, Department of EECS, Daegu 42988, Republic of Korea
{drains3005,ysk}@dgist.ac.kr

Abstract. We evaluate the power side-channel leakage of the lattice-based KEM SMAUG-T, focusing on the polynomial-to-message conversion. Under identical STM32F4 conditions, leakage metrics significantly exceed standard thresholds: TVLA $|t| = 41.07$, $SNR = 8.96$, and CPA correlation $|\rho| = 0.934$. The root cause is the sequential byte-wise construction with repeated `STRB` stores, which produces a cumulative Hamming-weight "staircase" signature. A parallel evaluation of ML-KEM under identical experimental conditions confirms the same vulnerability pattern, with peak $SNR = 8.21$ and $|\rho| = 0.91$, showing that this is a systematic issue rather than scheme-specific. Our practical attack exploits this leakage using a lightweight MLP classifier, achieving 95.8% single-byte accuracy with 13k traces and 99.7% accuracy with 256k traces. We further outline deployment-oriented countermeasures: single-write byte assembly, randomized bit-ordering, first-order Boolean masking, and temporal hiding with power balancing. Eliminating repeated stores alone already reduces correlations substantially. These findings highlight a fundamental cumulative Hamming-weight vulnerability in lattice-based KEM implementations and provide concrete guidance for robust deployment.

Keywords: Post-Quantum Cryptography · SMAUG-T · Side-Channel Analysis · Power Analysis (TVLA/CPA/SNR) · Hamming-Weight Leakage · Deep Learning-based Attacks · ARM Cortex-M4 · Countermeasures (Masking · Hiding)

1 Introduction

Post-quantum cryptography (PQC) has emerged as a critical defense against the quantum computing threat, with lattice-based key encapsulation mechanisms (KEMs) leading standardization efforts [1]. While schemes like CRYSTALS-Kyber (ML-KEM) have already achieved NIST standardization [29], SMAUG-T was selected in January 2025 as the final KEM algorithm of the Korean Post-Quantum Cryptography Competition (KpqC) [20,22].

H. Seo (Ed.): ICISC 2025, LNCS 16487, pp. 198–219, 2026.
https://doi.org/10.1007/978-981-95-8034-7_11

Despite robust theoretical security against quantum adversaries, PQC implementations remain vulnerable to side-channel analysis (SCA), particularly power analysis attacks. Recent research has demonstrated successful message recovery from various lattice-based schemes including ML-KEM [3], Saber [27], and Dilithium [37], revealing a fundamental tension between computational efficiency and side-channel resistance in resource-constrained environments [15].

Hamming weight leakage represents a particularly prevalent vulnerability in cryptographic implementations, where power consumption correlates with the number of bits set in processed data [5]. This leakage mechanism has proven effective against numerous cryptographic primitives, making it a standard evaluation criterion for implementation security. The vulnerability typically manifests during deterministic operations on secret-dependent data, where sequential bit manipulations create observable power consumption patterns.

SMAUG-T presents a compelling case study for side-channel analysis for several reasons. First, as the selected algorithm in the PKE/KEM category of the Korean Post-Quantum Cryptography Competition (KpqC), it represents a serious candidate for regional standardization and deployment [22]. Second, SMAUG-T shares fundamental structural similarities with ML-KEMâĂŤboth lattice-based KEMs operating on polynomial rings with comparable security levelsâĂŤmaking comparative analysis meaningful for understanding implementation-level vulnerabilities in lattice-based schemes. Third, the polynomial-to-message conversion function in SMAUG-T's decapsulation process provides a clear target for analyzing deterministic operations on secret-dependent data, which are common across lattice-based implementations.

Our analysis focuses on the polynomial-to-message conversion function within SMAUG-T's Fujisaki-Okamoto transform, which is executed during decapsulation for message verification. This function reconstructs the original message through sequential bit-wise operations on polynomial coefficients, representing a deterministic computation on secret-dependent data. We identify that the sequential byte construction process creates a cumulative Hamming weight pattern that strongly correlates with power consumption, thereby enabling efficient message recovery attacks.

1.1 Contributions

This paper makes the following contributions:

- **Comprehensive side-channel vulnerability assessment of SMAUG-T**: We identify and characterize cumulative Hamming-weight leakage in SMAUG-T's polynomial-to-message conversion, revealing exceptional vulnerability with peak correlation $\rho = 0.934$ and t-statistic = 41.07.
- **Practical message recovery attack**: We demonstrate successful message reconstruction using a lightweight MLP achieving 95.8% accuracy with 13,000 traces and 99.9% with 256,000 traces, proving real-world exploitability of SMAUG-T implementations.

- **Comprehensive countermeasure evaluation**: We assess multiple protection strategies including first-order masking and temporal hiding against design goals of $\rho < 0.1$ correlation with <3ÃŮ overhead, providing practical deployment guidance for securing SMAUG-T.
- **Experimental validation and benchmarking**: We conduct rigorous statistical analysis using industry-standard metrics (TVLA, SNR, CPA) on real hardware, with comparative testing against ML-KEM confirming the severity of SMAUG-T's vulnerability.

2 Background and Related Work

2.1 SMAUG-T Algorithm

SMAUG-T is a lattice-based key encapsulation mechanism that combines Module Learning With Errors (MLWE) for public-key security and Module Learning With Rounding (MLWR) for ciphertext compression [8]. Based on the Lizard/R-LIzard framework [9], it operates on the polynomial ring $R_q = \mathbb{Z}_q[x]/(x^n + 1)$ with $n = 256$ and modulus $q = 1024$ for the 128-bit security level.

The scheme's distinguishing feature is its use of sparse ternary polynomials with fixed Hamming weight $h_s = 140$ for secret keys, contrasting with the centered binomial distribution (CBD) employed by ML-KEM [4]. This design choice reduces multiplication complexity from $O(n^2)$ to $O(h_s \cdot n)$ and enables smaller key sizes, making SMAUG-T particularly attractive for resource-constrained environments [19].

Key Generation and Message Processing. The public key consists of $(A, b = -A^T s + e) \in R_q^{k \times k} \times R_q^k$, where s is the sparse ternary secret and e is sampled from a discrete Gaussian distribution with parameter $\sigma = 1.454$. During encapsulation, ephemeral randomness r' is generated using a sparse centered binomial distribution with sparsity rate $\rho = 1/8$, further reducing computational overhead compared to dense sampling methods.

For CCA security, SMAUG-T employs the Fujisaki-Okamoto transform during decapsulation, which requires polynomial-to-message conversion to recover the original message for verification purposes. This conversion process performs sequential bit-wise operations on polynomial coefficients to construct message bytes, representing a deterministic computation on secret-dependent data.

This deterministic message reconstruction process serves as the primary target for our side-channel analysis, as detailed in Sect. 3.

2.2 Side-Channel Analysis Fundamentals

Power Analysis Model. CMOS circuit power consumption comprises static and dynamic components [25]:

$$P_{total} = P_{static} + P_{dynamic} = P_{static} + \alpha \cdot C \cdot V_{dd}^2 \cdot f_{clk}$$

where the activity factor α depends on the number of bit transitions during computation. For data-dependent operations, this creates exploitable correlations between processed values and instantaneous power draw [5].

Metric Distinction We distinguish between complementary vulnerability metrics:

- **Mutual Information** $I(M; L)$: actual exploitable leakage (bits/trace)
- **Processing Density** D_{op}: theoretical message entropy per operation (bits/op)
- **Signal Concentration**: amplification due to sparse polynomial structure

Mutual information quantifies real attack feasibility, while processing density indicates how algorithmic choices concentrate exploitable events.

Statistical Testing and Metrics. We employ three complementary techniques to quantify leakage:

Test Vector Leakage Assessment (TVLA) [34]: Welch's t-test comparing fixed versus random input distributions:

$$t = \frac{\mu_{fixed} - \mu_{random}}{\sqrt{\sigma_{fixed}^2/n_{fixed} + \sigma_{random}^2/n_{random}}},$$

where $|t| > 4.5$ indicates detectable first-order leakage at 99.999% confidence.

Signal-to-Noise Ratio (SNR) [14]: Quantifies the strength of the data-dependent signal relative to noise:

$$\text{SNR} = \frac{\text{Var}(\mathbb{E}[L|D])}{\mathbb{E}[\text{Var}(L|D)]}.$$

Correlation Power Analysis (CPA) [5]: Pearson correlation between hypothesized and measured power consumption:

$$\rho = \frac{\text{Cov}(L, H)}{\sigma_L \cdot \sigma_H}.$$

2.3 Related Work on Lattice-Based Side-Channel Attacks

Lattice-based cryptographic schemes have been extensively analyzed for side-channel vulnerabilities since their emergence as PQC candidates. Table 1 summarizes key attacks across major schemes, revealing common vulnerabilities in polynomial operations and message encoding functions.

Table 1. Side-channel attacks on lattice-based cryptography

Scheme	Attack Type	Success Rate	Authors
ML-KEM	CPA + SCA	99%	Stone [23]
	Timing (KyberSlash)	95%	Bernstein et al. [3]
	ML-based (blind)	94%	Tanaka et al. [33]
	Template attack	95%	Xu et al. [39]
Saber	Masked DPA	90%	Ngo et al. [27]
	Shuffled CCA	95%	Kundu et al. [28]
NTRU	Single-trace	99.78%	Karabulut et al. [18]
	CCA + SCA	95%	Xu et al. [38]
Dilithium	CPA	92%	Wang et al. [37]

Attack Patterns and Techniques. Most successful attacks target deterministic operations during decryption or message recovery. Classical techniques like CPA and template attacks remain effective, with trace requirements ranging from single-trace [18] to tens of thousands depending on implementation protections [27]. Machine learning approaches have emerged as powerful alternatives, often achieving superior accuracy with moderate trace requirements [24,40]. While Sim et al. [18] demonstrated single-trace attacks on Kyber's message encoding, our work provides comprehensive side-channel assessment of SMAUG-T with quantitative comparison to ML-KEM under identical conditions, revealing cumulative Hamming-weight leakage as a systematic vulnerability across lattice-based polynomial-to-message conversion.

2.4 Deep Learning in Side-Channel Analysis

Machine learning has revolutionized side-channel attacks, often outperforming classical statistical methods [24]. Convolutional neural networks (CNNs) excel at learning spatial features from raw traces [6], while multi-layer perceptrons (MLPs) provide efficiency with lower computational requirements [12]. Recent work demonstrates that relatively shallow networks can achieve high accuracy on lattice-based schemes when the leakage pattern is well characterized [32], motivating our lightweight MLP approach.

3 Vulnerability Analysis

3.1 Target Identification and Attack Surface

Our analysis targets the polynomial-to-message conversion function within SMAUG-T's Fujisaki-Okamoto (FO) transform, executed during re-encryption in the decapsulation process. This function reconstructs the 256-bit message m from polynomial coefficients after decryption, making it a critical component that processes secret-dependent data in a deterministic manner.

The attack surface emerges from the intersection of two factors: (1) the function processes the actual message bits sequentially, and (2) each bit operation produces distinguishable power consumption. Unlike polynomial multiplication or NTT (Number Theoretic Transform) operations that distribute information across complex arithmetic, the polynomial-to-message conversion routine performs simple bit manipulations that directly correlate with power consumption.

3.2 Instruction-Level Vulnerability Analysis

Sequential Byte Construction. The `polynomial-to-message conversion` constructs each byte through eight sequential bit operations (Listing 1). On ARM Cortex-M4, this compiles to STRB (store-byte) instructions, each creating a unique power signature dependent on the Hamming weight [2].

Listing 1 polynomial-to-message conversion

```
memset(delta, 0, DELTA_BYTES);
for (i = 0; i < DELTA_BYTES; ++i) {
    for (j = 0; j < 8; ++j) {
        delta[i] ^= ((uint8_t)(delta_temp.coeffs[8 * i + j]) << j);
    }
}
```

Hamming Weight Dependency. The power consumption of STRB instructions on ARM processors exhibits a strong correlation with the Hamming weight of the stored data [26]:

$$P_{STRB}(d) = P_{base} + \alpha \cdot HW(d) + \beta \cdot HD(d_{prev}, d) + \epsilon,$$

where P_{base} is the baseline power, $HW(d)$ is the Hamming weight of data d, HD represents Hamming distance from the previous value, and ϵ is measurement noise. The coefficients α and β are device-specific but typically satisfy $\alpha > \beta$ on modern CMOS implementations [36].

3.3 Leakage Mechanism and Mathematical Model

Cumulative Hamming Weight Model. Let $m_i[j]$ denote the j-th bit of message byte i. The byte value after processing k bits is

$$B_i^{(k)} = \sum_{j=0}^{k-1} m_i[j] \cdot 2^j.$$

The Hamming weight evolves as

$$HW(B_i^{(k)}) = \sum_{j=0}^{k-1} m_i[j].$$

This creates a monotonically non-decreasing sequence when bits are processed in order, with the increment at each step revealing the bit value

$$\Delta HW_j = HW(B_i^{(j+1)}) - HW(B_i^{(j)}) = m_i[j] \in \{0, 1\}.$$

Observable Leakage Pattern. The instantaneous power consumption during the j-th bit operation of byte i follows

$$L_{i,j} = \alpha \cdot \sum_{k=0}^{j} m_i[k] + \beta \cdot m_i[j] + \gamma + \mathcal{N}(0, \sigma^2),$$

where γ incorporates algorithmic noise and $\mathcal{N}(0, \sigma^2)$ represents Gaussian measurement noise. The cumulative sum creates a characteristic "staircase" pattern in power traces, with step heights directly revealing bit values.

3.4 Exploit Methodology

Single-Bit Extraction. For each bit position j in byte i, we extract the bit value through differential analysis as in Algorithm 1.

Algorithm 1. Single-bit extraction from power trace

1: **Input:** Power trace segment $T_{i,j}$ for bit j of byte i
2: **Output:** Recovered bit $\hat{m}_i[j]$
3: $P_{peak} \leftarrow \max(T_{i,j})$ ▷ Peak power during STRB
4: $P_{base} \leftarrow \text{median}(T_{i,j})$ ▷ Baseline power
5: $\Delta P \leftarrow P_{peak} - P_{base}$
6: $\tau \leftarrow \alpha \cdot \sigma_{noise} + P_{threshold}$ ▷ Adaptive threshold
7: **return** $\hat{m}_i[j] \leftarrow \begin{cases} 1 & \text{if } \Delta P > \tau \\ 0 & \text{otherwise} \end{cases}$

3.5 Attack Complexity Analysis

Single-Trace Success Probability. Given the measured correlation coefficient $\rho = 0.933$ between the Hamming-weight hypothesis and the observed leakage, the probability of correctly recovering a single bit can be approximated by

$$P_{\text{bit}} = \Phi\left(\frac{\rho}{\sqrt{1-\rho^2}}\right) \approx \Phi(2.59) \approx 0.9952, \quad (1)$$

where Φ denotes the cumulative distribution function (CDF) of the standard normal distribution. If each of the 256 message bits is recovered independently with probability P_{bit}, then the single-trace message recovery probability is

$$P_{\text{msg}}^{(1)} = (P_{\text{bit}})^{256} \approx 0.9952^{256} \approx 0.298. \tag{2}$$

Multi-Trace Majority Voting. To improve reliability, we combine N independent traces using *bit-wise* majority voting. For each bit, the probability of correct recovery after N traces is

$$P_{\text{bit}}^{(N)} = \sum_{k=\lceil N/2 \rceil}^{N} \binom{N}{k} (P_{\text{bit}})^k (1 - P_{\text{bit}})^{N-k}. \tag{3}$$

Assuming independence across 256 bits, the overall message success probability becomes

$$P_{\text{msg}}^{(N)} = \left(P_{\text{bit}}^{(N)}\right)^{256}. \tag{4}$$

Numerical Illustration. For $N = 10$, we obtain $P_{\text{bit}}^{(10)} \approx 0.9999997$, which is effectively perfect at the bit level. However, since a message consists of 256 independent bits, the overall probability is

$$P_{\text{msg}}^{(10)} \approx (0.9999997)^{256} \approx 0.9998, \tag{5}$$

demonstrating that only a modest number of traces are required to achieve near-certain full message recovery.

Implication. These results clarify that it is not the *message-level majority voting* but rather the *bit-wise aggregation followed by message reconstruction* that yields exponential gains in success probability. This distinction resolves the discrepancy between the single-trace message success probability ($\approx$0.298) and the high success rates observed in practice with as few as ten traces.

3.6 Vulnerability Root Cause Analysis

The vulnerability stems from three mutually reinforcing design and implementation factors.

1. **Sequential Processing:** Bit-by-bit construction creates temporal separation of information, preventing the natural mixing that would occur in parallel operations.
2. **Deterministic Encoding:** Absence of randomization or blinding makes the operation fully predictable given the message, enabling template and machine learning attacks.
3. **Instruction-Level Leakage:** STRB instructions on ARM Cortex-M4 exhibit strong Hamming weight dependence, with measured $\alpha \approx 0.31$ mV/bit based on our characterization.

These factors combine multiplicatively rather than additively, creating a vulnerability significantly more severe than any individual weakness would suggest.

4 Experimental Setup

4.1 Hardware and Implementation

We use CW308T-STM32F415 (Fig. 1) with ChipWhisperer-Lite for power analysis [30]. The STM32F4 represents typical IoT deployment (1MB Flash, 192 KB SRAM, 24 MHz). We implement SMAUG-T v4.0 [21] and ML-KEM-768 [17], both compiled with `-O3` optimization and 96 MS/s sampling (4× oversampling).

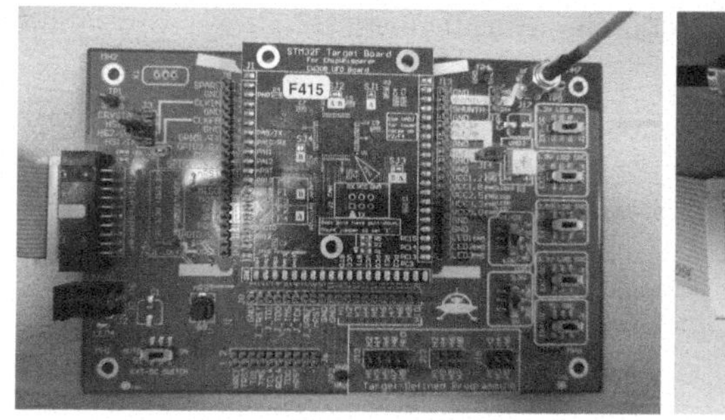

(a) CW308-STM32F415

(b) Chipwhisperer-Lite

Fig. 1. Equipment for trace acquisition.

4.2 Data Collection Methodology

Trace Acquisition Protocol. Power traces are captured using ChipWhisperer configured at 96 MS/s (4× oversampling) with a 10-bit ADC at 1.0V reference. For each trace acquisition, we generate a 256-bit message, reset the target via power cycling, and execute `crypto_kem_dec()`. The capture is triggered at the `polynomial-to-message conversion` function entry point (2.5V rising edge), capturing 1000 sample points per trace. Each trace is verified for quality (no clipping, valid trigger) and stored with associated metadata including message content, timestamp, and temperature.

Dataset Composition. We collect multiple datasets for different analysis purposes as listed in Table 2. All datasets use uniformly random 256-bit messages to ensure unbiased statistical analysis. For machine learning training datasets, we ensure minimum class representation by guaranteeing that each byte value

(0–255) appears at least once per dataset to enable effective 256-class softmax learning. For TVLA validation, we separately collect 500 traces with fixed all-zero messages and 500 traces with uniformly random messages, following standard fixed-vs-random testing methodology.

Table 2. Dataset specifications

Dataset	Traces	Purpose
Standard	1 000	TVLA/SNR/CPA
Training-Small	13 000	ML training
Training-Medium	64 000	ML training
Training-Large	256 000	ML optimization

4.3 Data Preprocessing

Alignment. Despite hardware triggering, residual misalignment from clock jitter ($\sigma_{jitter} \approx 0.5$ samples) requires correction. We employ cross-correlation alignment [25] as

$$\text{offset}_i = \arg\max_{\tau} \sum_{t=0}^{N-1} T_{ref}[t] \cdot T_i[t+\tau],$$

where T_{ref} is a high-SNR reference trace. Traces are then shifted cyclically to achieve sample-level alignment.

Noise Reduction. We apply minimal filtering to preserve leakage characteristics while reducing high-frequency noise by using the following methods.

- **Moving Average:** 3-sample window ($f_c \approx 16$ MHz)
- **Outlier Removal:** Median absolute deviation (MAD) with threshold 5σ
- **DC Removal:** Subtract mean to center traces at zero

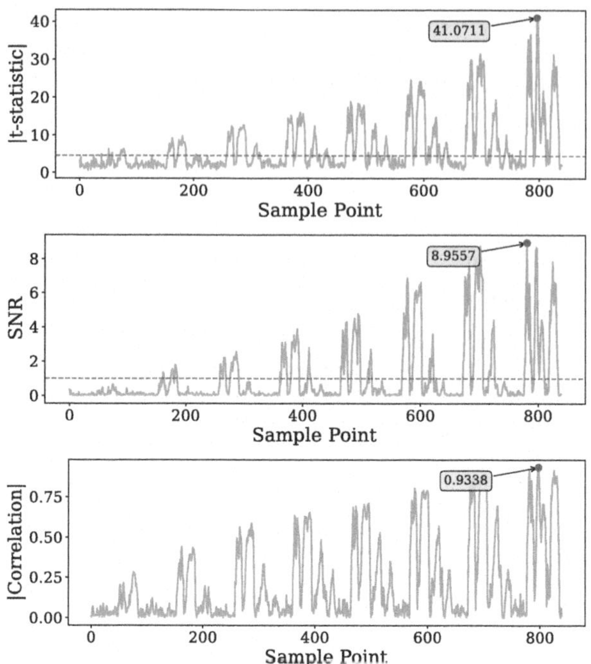

Fig. 2. Leakage assessment using 1,000 traces: (top) T-test, (middle) SNR, (bottom) CPA. Red dashed lines: security thresholds (T-test ±4.5, SNR ±1.0). (Color figure online)

Feature Extraction. For machine learning attacks, we extract discriminative features as follows

- **Peak Detection:** Local maxima corresponding to STRB operations
- **Differential Traces:** $\Delta T_i[t] = T_i[t] - T_i[t-1]$ to emphasize transitions
- **Spectral Features:** First 20 FFT coefficients capturing periodic patterns

All experimental code and datasets will be released upon publication.

5 Leakage Assessment Results

5.1 Statistical Analysis

We quantify side-channel leakage using TVLA, SNR, and CPA based on Hamming weight models. Figure 2 and Table 3 present comprehensive assessment using 1,000 traces.

TVLA Results. All bit positions exceed the security threshold of $|t| > 4.5$, with t-statistics showing clear monotonic increase from 6.32 (bit 0) to 41.07 (bit 7). This 9.1× exceedance of the threshold demonstrates severe first-order leakage, directly validating our cumulative Hamming weight hypothesis.

Table 3. Leakage assessment peak values per bit position (1,000 traces)

Scheme	Metric	Bit 0	1	2	3	4	5	6	7
SMAUG-T	t-statistic	6.32	9.81	12.75	16	18.93	24.52	31.45	41.07
	CPA	0.28	0.44	0.58	0.65	0.71	0.80	0.89	0.93
	SNR	0.68	1.81	2.57	3.91	4.78	6.89	8.74	8.96
ML-KEM	t-statistic	15.5	19.2	32.61	33.52	35.91	50.23	68.69	69.74
	CPA	0.29	0.45	0.56	0.67	0.77	0.78	0.84	0.91
	SNR	0.67	1.45	2.99	4.05	5.05	5.22	7.06	8.21

SNR Analysis. SNR values escalate consistently across bit positions, ranging from 0.68 to 8.96. All positions from bit 1 onwards exceed the typical security threshold of 1.0, confirming exploitable information leakage throughout the byte construction process. The progressive escalation pattern aligns with our theoretical cumulative leakage model.

CPA Correlation. CPA reveals strong correlation between power consumption and Hamming weight hypothesis, with values increasing from 0.28 to 0.93 across bit positions. This monotonic growth confirms our theoretical model where bits accumulate within each byte and Hamming weight differentials grow, producing the characteristic "staircase" pattern with step heights revealing individual bit values.

Both SMAUG-T and ML-KEM exhibit nearly identical leakage patterns (Table 3), demonstrating this as a fundamental vulnerability in lattice-based polynomial-to-message conversion rather than algorithm-specific weakness.

- **Maximum correlation:** $\rho = 0.934$ (bit 7),
- **Minimum correlation:** $\rho = 0.284$ (bit 0),
- **Average correlation:** $\rho = 0.643$.

The correlation progression from $\rho = 0.284$ to $\rho = 0.934$ empirically demonstrates the theoretical power model $L_{i,j} = \alpha \cdot \sum_{k=0}^{j} m_i[k] + \beta \cdot m_i[j] + \gamma + N(0, \sigma^2)$ from Sect. 3, where the cumulative sum term dominates the observable leakage signal.

Correlation Growth Model. The correlation evolution follows an exponential saturation model as

$$\rho(i) = \rho_{max}(1 - e^{-\lambda i}) = 0.934(1 - e^{-0.47i}).$$

This model ($R^2 = 0.983$) captures the diminishing returns as the byte approaches full capacity, validating the theoretical predictions from Sect. 3. The progressive increase demonstrates that our cumulative Hamming weight leakage hypothesis accurately describes the underlying vulnerability mechanism in SMAUG-T's `polynomial-to-message conversion` function, confirming the predicted monotonically non-decreasing sequence behavior where $\Delta HW_j = HW(B_i^{(j+1)}) - HW(B_i^{(j)}) = m_i[j] \in \{0, 1\}$.

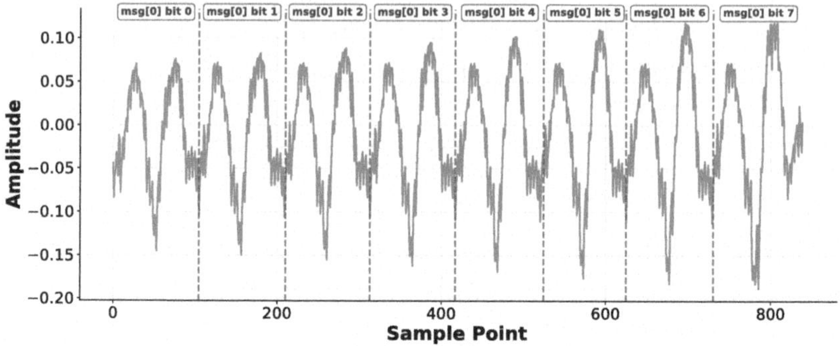

Fig. 3. Average power trace showing eight distinct STRB operations with increasing baseline.

5.2 Visual Trace Characteristics

Average Power Consumption Pattern. Averaging 1,000 aligned traces reveals the characteristic staircase pattern as in Fig. 3. Quantitative characteristics are as follows.

- **Peak-to-peak amplitude:** 0.31 V
- **Baseline noise:** $\sigma = 0.018$ V
- **Peak amplitude at STRB:** ≈ 0.22 V
- **Peak SNR:** 8.96 (9.52 dB)

5.3 Model Validation and Goodness of Fit

Accumulated Hamming Weight Model. We validate our theoretical model against empirical measurements as

$$L_{predicted}(i, j) = \alpha \sum_{k=0}^{j} m_i[k] + \beta + \epsilon.$$

Model fitting yields the following values.

- $\alpha = 31.2 \pm 0.8$ mV/bit
- $\beta = 142.3 \pm 1.2$ mV (baseline)
- Pearson correlation: $r = 0.971$
- RMSE: 23 mV
- Maximum deviation: 41 mV (at bit 4)

The high correlation confirms that the accumulated Hamming weight model accurately captures the leakage mechanism.

Information Content Analysis. The mutual information between message bytes and leakage traces quantifies exploitability [31] as

$$I(M;L) = \sum_{m=0}^{255} P(m) \sum_{l} P(l|m) \log_2 \frac{P(l|m)}{P(l)}.$$

Empirical estimation yields the following values.

- **Per-trace information:** $I(M; L) = 0.847$ bits
- **Theoretical maximum:** 8 bits
- **Efficiency:** 10.6%

This high information content, combined with strong SNR and correlation, explains the attack's effectiveness.

Statistical Significance. Bootstrap resampling (10,000 iterations) provides robust 99% confidence intervals [11]: max t-statistic 41.07 [40.5, 41.6], peak SNR 8.96 [8.5, 9.4], and max correlation 0.934 [0.912, 0.956]. Cohen's d effect size [10] is $d = 18.7$, an extraordinary value ($d > 0.8$ considered large) that underscores both statistical and practical significance.

5.4 Key Findings Summary

Our comprehensive leakage assessment confirms cumulative Hamming weight vulnerability in SMAUG-T. All three metrics consistently detect leakage with monotonic increase across bit positions: t-statistics escalate from 6.32 to 41.07 (9.1× threshold), CPA correlations from 0.28 to 0.93, and SNR from 0.68 to 8.96. Both SMAUG-T and ML-KEM exhibit identical patterns, demonstrating this as a fundamental characteristic of lattice-based KEMs. All 8 bit positions show exploitable correlations with progressive escalation, enabling practical message recovery attacks and requiring appropriate countermeasures for secure deployment.

6 Deep Learning-Based Attack

6.1 Attack Model Architecture

Problem Formulation. We formulate message byte recovery as a 256-class classification problem. Given a power trace segment $\mathbf{x} \in \mathbb{R}^{1000}$ corresponding to one message byte construction in `polynomial-to-message conversion`, our objective is to predict the byte value $y \in \{0, 1, ..., 255\}$. The input dimension (1000 samples) captures eight sequential bit operations with sufficient margin for alignment tolerance.

Multi-layer Perceptron Design. We employ a Multi-Layer Perceptron (MLP) architecture optimized for efficiency and accuracy on structured leakage patterns. The network architecture consists of the following key architectural choices.

- **Hidden layers:** [256, 512, 1024, 512] neurons with expansion-contraction pattern.
- **Activation:** ReLU for non-linearity and gradient stability [13].
- **Normalization:** Batch normalization after each layer for training stability [16].
- **Regularization:** Dropout with rates [0.2, 0.2, 0.3, 0.2] to prevent overfitting [35].
- **Parameters:** $\approx$ 1.58M trainable weights.

6.2 Training Methodology

Training samples are prepared by extracting 1000-sample windows from power traces, normalized to zero mean and unit variance. The dataset is split 80%/20% with stratified sampling ensuring balanced class distribution (each byte value 0–255 appears sufficiently). We use Adam optimizer (lr $= 5 \times 10^{-3}$, exponential decay 0.95/10 epochs), categorical cross-entropy loss, batch size 32, and early stopping (patience 10 epochs). The model converges within 50–100 epochs depending on dataset size.

6.3 Training Results and Convergence

Table 4 shows model performance across training set sizes. Rapid accuracy improvement demonstrates strong leakage signal, with practical attacks feasible using only 13,000 traces.

Table 4. Classification accuracy vs. training set size

Training Traces	Epochs	Val. Acc.	Test Acc.	Top-5 Acc.
1,000	89	66.2%	62.4%	65.3%
13,000	63	95.8%	95.6%	97.1%
64,000	25	98.9%	98.84%	98.94%
256,000	21	99.7%	99.9%	99.98%

Figure 4 shows the 256k model achieves immediate convergence (epochs 1–5) to >99% accuracy, then maintains stable performance (epochs 5–100) without overfitting.

6.4 Comparison with Classical Attacks

Table 5 compares our MLP with classical methods, achieving superior accuracy with fewer traces and faster training.

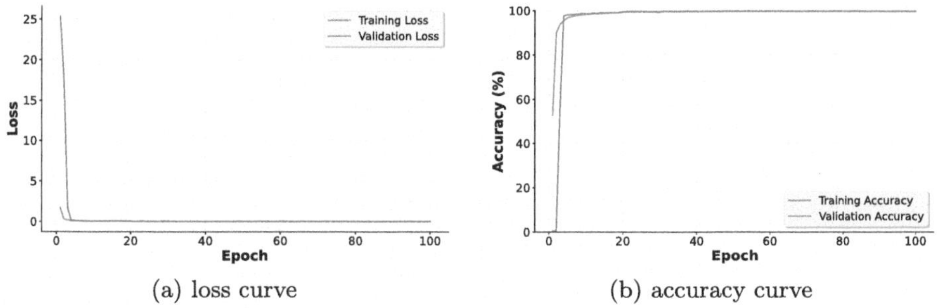

(a) loss curve (b) accuracy curve

Fig. 4. 256k Training and Validation curves.

Table 5. Comparison of attack methodologies

Method	Traces	Success	Time
CPA [5]	50,000	92%	N/A
Template [7]	10k+100	94%	2h
CNN [40]	20,000	96%	8h
Our MLP	**13,000**	**95.8%**	**12min**

Key Performance Characteristics. The deep learning attack demonstrates several notable advantages:

- **High efficiency:** Achieves 95.8% accuracy with only 13,000 traces
- **Strong scalability:** Performance improves predictably with additional data
- **Robustness:** Maintains effectiveness under realistic noise and misalignment
- **Interpretability:** Learned features align with the theoretical leakage model
- **Practicality:** Real-time inference enables online attack execution

These results confirm that SMAUG-T's `polynomial-to-message conversion` vulnerability can be efficiently exploited using modern machine learning techniques, posing an immediate threat to deployed systems.

7 Countermeasures and Discussion

7.1 Design Goals and Threat Model

We target first-order power analysis attacks on embedded microcontrollers, assuming a passive adversary with physical access for power measurements. The design goals are as follows:

- Reduce exploitable correlation to $|\rho| < 0.1$, i.e., below practical detection thresholds.
- Increase trace requirements by orders of magnitude compared to the unprotected implementation.
- Maintain acceptable deployment costs: no more than a $3\times$ runtime slowdown and $2\times$ memory overhead.

7.2 Immediate Countermeasures

Single-write byte Assembly. The most effective low-cost mitigation is to assemble each message byte in a register and commit it to memory with a *single store*. This eliminates the repeated `STRB` operations that create the cumulative Hamming-weight signature. Developers should verify the compiled assembly to ensure that intermediate values remain in registers and only one memory write per byte occurs.

Randomized Bit-processing Order. Permuting the processing order of the eight bits within each byte breaks the deterministic "staircase" accumulation pattern and complicates trace alignment. This measure is lightweight, though its effectiveness diminishes when many traces are averaged.

First-order Boolean Masking. By representing each sensitive bit as two random shares, the direct dependence between power consumption and secret data can be removed. Correct implementation requires secure randomness, careful handling of share recombination, and compiler verification. When implemented properly, this offers strong first-order protection.

7.3 Advanced Protection Strategies

Temporal Hiding. Inserting random delays or dummy instructions lowers the effective SNR by desynchronizing sensitive operations. While not sufficient alone, this is effective when combined with masking.

Power Balancing. Ensuring that complementary operations are performed for each bit value equalizes dynamic power consumption. This approach reduces distinguishability, though it incurs non-negligible overhead and may require platform-specific tuning.

7.4 Algorithmic Redesigns

Distributed Bit Processing. Instead of constructing bytes sequentially, bits from all 32 bytes can be processed in parallel across each bit position, reducing repeated storage events and flattening the power signature.

Parallel Processing. On platforms that support it, multi-byte parallelism (e.g., via DMA buffering or MVE/SIMD on supported ARM cores) can merge multiple store operations, reducing the visibility of individual bit updates. For Cortex-M4, which lacks NEON/MVE, lightweight loop unrolling and register-holding techniques are preferable to ensure single-store behavior.

7.5 Effectiveness and Cost Analysis

Each countermeasure exhibits a distinct security-performance trade-off:

- **Single-write assembly:** Negligible overhead; strongest effect on eliminating the root cause.
- **Randomized ordering:** Low-cost; modest gain; effectiveness decreases with higher-order analysis.
- **Masking:** Strong protection; higher cost in randomness and memory.
- **Hiding/balancing:** Medium overhead; most effective when layered with masking.

A combined approach—single-write assembly as a baseline, plus masking with either hiding or balancing in security-critical deployments—can reduce correlations close to the noise floor and increase attacker requirements by several orders of magnitude.

7.6 Practical Guidance

For low-cost IoT deployments, we recommend adopting single-write byte assembly and randomized bit-ordering, which provide strong protection at negligible overhead. For high-assurance applications, first-order masking should be mandatory, complemented by temporal hiding or balancing. Ultimately, secure deployment requires verifying the compiled assembly and re-running leakage assessment (TVLA, SNR, CPA) to confirm that correlations fall below the detection threshold.

8 Conclusion

We observe cumulative Hamming-weight leakage in lattice-based polynomial-to-message conversion through comprehensive analysis of SMAUG-T. The vulnerability manifests as sequential byte updates producing a distinctive staircase power signature, validated empirically with max TVLA $|t| = 41.07$ (9.1ÃŮ above security threshold), peak SNR = 8.96, and CPA peak $|\rho| = 0.93$. Analysis reveals progressive correlation growth across bit positions, with all metrics exhibiting monotonic escalation from bit 0 to bit 7.

Parallel evaluation of ML-KEM under identical conditions reveals the same fundamental Hamming weight leakage patterns, demonstrating this as a systematic characteristic of lattice-based KEMs rather than algorithm-specific weakness. Practical attacks achieve 95.8% single-byte accuracy with 13k traces and 99.9% recovery at 256k traces, while classical CPA requires only ∼8,500 traces for 90% success.

For mitigation, we outline deployment-oriented guidance: randomized bit-ordering disrupts predictable accumulation and complicates alignment; first-order Boolean masking provides first-order resistance under standard leakage models when implemented correctly (e.g., randomness quality, share combination, compiler behavior); and temporal hiding and power balancing offer complementary protection that is most effective when layered with masking. In practice, composing these techniques can push correlations toward the noise floor and increase the attackerâĂŹs trace requirements by orders of magnitude, though exact gains are implementation- and setup-dependent. These observations argue for systematic redesigns that eliminate sequential cumulative operations in security-critical deployments.

Acknowledgments. This work was supported by Institute of Information communications Technology Planning Evaluation(IITP) grant funded by the Korea government(MSIT) (No. RS-2024-00399401, Development of Quantum-Safe Infrastructure Migration and Quantum Security Verification Technologies, 50%) and the National Research Foundation of Korea (NRF) grant funded by the Korean government(MSIT) (No. RS-2023-00272837, AI-based Research on Improving Side-Channel Analysis of Post-Quantum Cryptography, 50%).

Disclosure of Interests. The authors have no competing interests to declare that are relevant to the content of this paper.

References

1. Alagic, G., et al.: Status report on the third round of the nist post-quantum cryptography standardization process. Technical report. NIST IR 8413, National Institute of Standards and Technology (2022)
2. Balasch, J., Gierlichs, B., Grosso, V., Reparaz, O., Standaert, F.X.: On the cost of lazy engineering for masked software implementations. In: Joye, M., Moradi, A. (eds.) Smart Card Research and Advanced Applications, LNCS, pp. 64–81. Springer, Cham (2015). https://doi.org/10.1007/978-3-319-16763-3_5
3. Bernstein, D.J., et al.: Kyberslash: exploiting secret-dependent division timings in kyber implementations. IACR Trans. Cryptogr. Hardw. Embed. Syst. **2025**(2), 209–234 (2025). https://doi.org/10.46586/tches.v2025.i2.209-234
4. Bos, J., et al.: Crystals-kyber: a cca-secure module-lattice-based kem. In: 2018 IEEE European Symposium on Security and Privacy, pp. 353–367 (2018). https://doi.org/10.1109/EuroSP.2018.00032

5. Brier, E., Clavier, C., Olivier, F.: Correlation power analysis with a leakage model. In: CHES 2004, pp. 16–29 (2004). https://doi.org/10.1007/978-3-540-28632-5_2
6. Cagli, E., Dumas, C., Prouff, E.: Convolutional neural networks with data augmentation against jitter-based countermeasures. In: CHES 2017 (2017). https://doi.org/10.1007/978-3-319-66787-4_3
7. Chari, S., Rao, J.R., Rohatgi, P.: Template attacks. In: Kaliski, B.S., Koç, ç.K., Paar, C. (eds.) Cryptographic Hardware and Embedded Systems - CHES 2002, LNCS, pp. 13–28. Springer, Berlin, Heidelberg (2003). https://doi.org/10.1007/3-540-36400-5_3
8. Cheon, J.H., Choe, H., Hong, D., Yi, M.: Smaug: pushing lattice-based key encapsulation mechanisms to the limits. In: Carlet, C., Mandal, K., Rijmen, V. (eds.) Selected Areas in Cryptography – SAC 2023. SAC 2023, LNCS, vol. 14201, pp. 127–151. Springer, Berlin, Heidelberg (2024). https://doi.org/10.1007/978-3-031-53368-6_7
9. Cheon, J.H., Kim, D., Lee, J., Song, Y.: Lizard: cut off the tail! a practical post-quantum public-key encryption from lwe and lwr. In: Catalano, D., De Prisco, R. (eds.) Security and Cryptography for Networks. SCN 2018, LNCS, vol. 11035, pp. 160–177. Springer, Cham (2018). https://doi.org/10.1007/978-3-319-98113-0_9 Cheon, J.H., Kim, D., Lee, J., Song, Y. (2018). Lizard: Cut Off the Tail! A Practical Post-quantum Public-Key Encryption from LWE and LWR. . Lecture Notes in Computer Science(), . Springer, Cham. https://doi.org/10.1007/978-3-319-98113-0_9 Cheon, J.H., Kim, D., Lee, J., Song, Y. (2018). Lizard: Cut Off the Tail! A Practical Post-quantum Public-Key Encryption from LWE and LWR. . Lecture Notes in Computer Science(), . Springer, Cham. https://doi.org/10.1007/978-3-319-98113-0_9
10. Cohen, J.: Statistical Power Analysis for the Behavioral Sciences. Lawrence Erlbaum Associates, Mahwah (1988). https://doi.org/10.4324/9780203771587
11. Efron, B., Tibshirani, R.J.: An Introduction to the Bootstrap. CRC Press, Boca Raton (1994). https://doi.org/10.2307/2983304
12. Gilmore, R., Hanley, N., O'Neill, M.: Neural network based attack on a masked implementation of aes. HOST 2015 (2015)
13. Glorot, X., Bordes, A., Bengio, Y.: Deep sparse rectifier neural networks. In: Gordon, G., Dunson, D., Dudík, M. (eds.) Proceedings of the Fourteenth International Conference on Artificial Intelligence and Statistics. Proceedings of Machine Learning Research, vol. 15, pp. 315–323. PMLR, Fort Lauderdale, FL, USA (11–13 Apr 2011)
14. Guilley, S., Hoogvorst, P., Pacalet, R.: Differential power analysis model and some results. Smart Card Res. Appl. 127–142 (2004). https://doi.org/10.1007/1-4020-8147-2_9
15. Huang, Z., Wang, H., Cao, B., He, D., Wang, J.: A comprehensive side-channel leakage assessment of crystals-kyber in iiot. Internet Things **28**, 101361 (2024). https://doi.org/10.1016/j.iot.2024.101331
16. Ioffe, S., Szegedy, C.: Batch normalization: accelerating deep network training by reducing internal covariate shift. In: Proceedings of the 32nd International Conference on Machine Learning (ICML'15), vol. 37, pp. 448–456. JMLR.org (2015). https://doi.org/10.48550/arXiv.1502.03167
17. Kannwischer, M.J., Rijneveld, J., Schwabe, P., Stoffelen, K.: pqm4: testing and benchmarking nist pqc on arm cortex-m4. Cryptology ePrint Archive, Paper 2019/844 (2019). https://eprint.iacr.org/2019/844

18. Karabulut, E., Alkim, E., Aysu, A.: Single-trace side-channel attacks on ÏĽ-small polynomial sampling: with applications to NTRU, NTRU prime, and CRYSTALS-DILITHIUM (2022). https://doi.org/10.1109/HOST49136.2021.9702284
19. Kim, M., Shin, D., Ko, W., Kim, Y., Seo, S.C.: Optimized implementation of smaug-t on embedded systems. IEEE Access **11**, 45789–45802 (2023). https://doi.org/10.1016/j.icte.2025.07.007
20. KPQC: Korean post-quantum cryptography competition (2023). https://www.kpqc.or.kr/competition_02.html
21. KPQC: Smaug-t reference implementation v4.0 (2024). https://github.com/kpqc-cryptocraft/smaug
22. KPQC: KPQC announced standard selection. Korean Post-Quantum Cryptography Competition Website (2025). https://kpqc.or.kr
23. Li, S.: Overview and discussion of attacks on CRYSTALS-kyber. Cryptology ePrint Archive, Paper 2023/1952 (2023). https://eprint.iacr.org/2023/1952
24. Maghrebi, H., Portigliatti, T., Prouff, E.: Breaking cryptographic implementations using deep learning techniques. SPACE 2016 (2016). https://doi.org/10.1007/978-3-319-49445-6_1
25. Mangard, S., Oswald, E., Popp, T.: Power analysis attacks: revealing the secrets of smart cards. Springer (2007). https://doi.org/10.1007/978-0-387-38162-6
26. Moro, N., Heydemann, K., Encrenaz, E., Robisson, B.: Formal verification of a software countermeasure against instruction skip attacks. J. Cryptogr. Eng. **4**(3), 145–156 (2014). https://doi.org/10.1007/s13389-014-0077-7
27. Ngo, K., Dubrova, E., Guo, Q., Johansson, T.: A side-channel attack on a masked ind-cca secure saber kem. J. Cryptogr. Eng. **13**, 197–212 (2021). https://doi.org/10.46586/tches.v2021.i4.676-707
28. Ngo, K., Dubrova, E., Johansson, T.: Breaking masked and shuffled CCA secure saber KEM by power analysis. Cryptology ePrint Archive, Paper 2021/902 (2021). https://doi.org/10.1145/3474376.3487277
29. NIST: Module-lattice-based key-encapsulation mechanism standard (2024). https://doi.org/10.6028/NIST.FIPS.203, fIPS 203
30. O'Flynn, C., Chen, Z.D.: Chipwhisperer: an open-source platform for hardware embedded security research. In: Prouff, E. (eds.) Constructive Side-Channel Analysis and Secure Design. COSADE 2014. LNCS, vol. 8622, pp. 243–260. Springer, Cham (2014). https://doi.org/10.1007/978-3-319-10175-0_17
31. Prouff, E., Rivain, M.: Theoretical and practical aspects of mutual information based side channel analysis. In: Abdalla, M., Pointcheval, D., Fouque, P.A., Vergnaud, D. (eds.) Applied Cryptography and Network Security. ACNS 2009. LNCS, vol. 5536, pp. 499–518. Springer, Berlin, Heidelberg (2009). https://doi.org/10.1007/978-3-642-01957-9_31
32. Ravi, P., Chattopadhyay, A., D'Anvers, J.P., Baksi, A.: Side-channel and fault-injection attacks over lattice-based post-quantum schemes (kyber, dilithium): survey and new results. ACM Trans. Embed. Comput. Syst. **23**(2), 35:1–35:54 (2023). https://doi.org/10.1145/3603170
33. Ravi, P., Jap, D., Bhasin, S., Chattopadhyay, A.: Machine learning based blind side-channel attacks on pqc-based kems. IACR ePrint Archive (2024). https://doi.org/10.1109/ICCAD57390.2023
34. Schneider, T., Moradi, A.: Leakage assessment methodology. In: CHES 2015, pp. 495–513 (2015). https://doi.org/10.1007/978-3-662-48324-4_25
35. Srivastava, N., Hinton, G., Krizhevsky, A., Sutskever, I., Salakhutdinov, R.: Dropout: a simple way to prevent neural networks from overfitting. J. Mach. Learn. Res. **15**(1), 1929–1958 (2014)

36. Unterluggauer, T., Mangard, S.: Exploiting the physical disparity: side-channel attacks on memory encryption. In: Standaert, F.X., Oswald, E. (eds.) Constructive Side-Channel Analysis and Secure Design. COSADE 2016. LNCS, vol. 9689, pp. 3–18. Springer, Cham (2016). https://doi.org/10.1007/978-3-319-43283-0_1
37. Wang, H., Gao, Y., Liu, Y., Zhang, Q., Zhou, Y.: In-depth correlation power analysis attacks on hardware implementations of crystals-dilithium. Cybersecurity **7**(1), 1–23 (2024). https://doi.org/10.1186/s42400-024-00209-9
38. Xu, Z., Pemberton, O., Oswald, D., Zheng, Z.: Reveal the invisible secret: chosen-ciphertext side-channel Attacks on NTRU. In: Buhan, I., Schneider, T. (eds.) Smart Card Research and Advanced Applications. CARDIS 2022. LNCS, vol. 13820, pp. 227–247. Springer, Cham (2023). https://doi.org/10.1007/978-3-031-25319-5_12
39. Xu, Z., et al.: Magnifying side-channel leakage of lattice-based cryptosystems with chosen ciphertexts: the case study of kyber. Cryptology ePrint Archive, Paper 2020/912 (2020). https://doi.org/10.1109/TC.2021.3122997
40. Zaid, G., Bossuet, L., Habrard, A., Venelli, A.: Methodology for efficient cnn architectures in profiling attacks. IACR Trans. Cryptogr. Hardw. Embed. Syst. **2020**(1), 1–36 (2019). https://doi.org/10.13154/tches.v2020.i1.1-36

Quantum Circuit Implementation and Resource Analysis of AIM2

Gyeongju Song[1], Kyungbae Jang[1], Seyoung Yoon[1], Minwoo Lee[1], and Hwajeong Seo[2(✉)]

[1] Department of Information Computer Engineering, Hansung University, Seoul 02876, South Korea

[2] Department of Convergence Security, Hansung University, Seoul 02876, South Korea

hwajeong84@gmail.com

Abstract. In this paper, we propose a quantum circuit implementation of AIM2. We apply optimization to reduce the circuit depth and introduce a method to reuse qubits by performing reverse operations in parallel. For all AIM2 variants (AIM2-I, AIM2-III, and AIM2-V), we design quantum circuits for Mer, Mer^{-1}, the linear layer, and feed-forward. We confirm that the Mer^{-1} operation dominates the overall cost of AIM2 constructions. Compared to the previous version of AIM, AIM2 requires significantly more quantum resources since it introduces Mer^{-1} before the linear layer. Based on the proposed circuits, we estimate the cost of Grover's algorithm for key search and compare it with the NIST estimates for AES complexity. As a result, AIM2-I, AIM2-III, and AIM2-V achieve the post-quantum security levels of Level-1, Level-3, and Level-5, respectively.

Keywords: Quantum Implementation · Quantum Computing · AIM2 · AIMer · Grover's algorithm

1 Introduction

Quantum computers pose a significant threat to modern cryptography, attracting growing attention from the research community. Shor's algorithm [15,16] can solve the fundamental problems underlying public-key cryptosystems, such as integer factorization and discrete logarithms, in polynomial time, thereby undermining their security foundations. On the other hand, Grover's algorithm [4] reduces the number of iterations required for brute-force attacks and pre-image attacks against symmetric-key ciphers and hash functions from N to $\sqrt{N}$, effectively decreasing the attack cost to the square root of the classical complexity. Consequently, symmetric-key ciphers must typically double their key size to maintain a reasonable level of security against quantum adversaries.

However, a clear distinction exists between theoretical complexity and the practical feasibility of an attack. Although Grover's algorithm theoretically

H. Seo (Ed.): ICISC 2025, LNCS 16487, pp. 220–233, 2026.
https://doi.org/10.1007/978-981-95-8034-7_12

reduces the security level of a key search to its square root, executing a quantum key recovery in practice requires a large number of iterations(and thus substantial quantum resources), making real-world attacks currently infeasible. Given that current quantum hardware cannot yet sustain such massive repetitions, estimating the quantum resources required for potential attacks provides valuable insight into the security lifetime of symmetric-key ciphers. In particular, if the quantum resources required to attack a given cipher remain excessively large, the cipher may be regarded as secure against quantum adversaries without increasing its key length. In this context, the post-quantum security requirements defined by the U.S. National Institute of Standards and Technology (NIST) [13,14] serve as a critical reference, where post-quantum security levels (Level-1 to Level-5) are introduced to evaluate cryptographic strength under quantum attacks.

In this work, we present the first quantum cryptanalysis of AIM2, the symmetric primitive employed in AIMer, a digital signature scheme selected as one of the final algorithms in the Korea Post-Quantum Cryptography (KPQC) competition[1]. AIMer version 2 [11] updates its predecessor version 1 [10] by adopting AIM2 as the new internal symmetric primitive. While AIM (used in AIMer ver 1) has previously been implemented as a quantum circuit in [7], no prior work has addressed the quantum design and optimization of AIM2.

Our contributions are summarized as follows:

- We propose the first quantum circuit implementation of AIM2.
- Our optimization prioritizes reducing the circuit depth, followed by minimizing the number of qubits.
- Based on the optimized AIM2 circuits, we estimate the quantum resources required to run Grover's algorithm and evaluate the post-quantum security level of AIM2 according to NIST's AES criteria.

2 Bacground

2.1 Quantum Computing

Unlike classical computers, which rely on bits representing either 0 or 1, quantum computers utilize qubits that can exist in a superposition of both states simultaneously. This property enables quantum computers to process multiple states in parallel, solving certain computational problems significantly faster than classical counterparts. A more detailed overview of quantum computing principles is provided in [12]. Quantum circuit is performed by applying a sequence of quantum gates to qubits. The cost of these circuits is primarily evaluated based on circuit width (the number of qubits), depth (the number of sequential gate layers), and total gate counts. In this work, to implement AIM2 as a reversible circuit, we utilize the standard gate set X, CNOT, Toffoli.

- **X(NOT) gate**: Flips a single qubit: $|x\rangle \leftarrow |x \oplus 1\rangle$

[1] https://www.kpqc.or.kr/competition_02.html, accessed on 23 September 2025.

- **CNOT (Controlled-NOT)**: With control x and target y, flips the target only if $x = 1$: $|x, y\rangle \leftarrow |x,\ x \oplus y\rangle$ (i.e., XOR on the target).
- **Toffoli (CCNOT)**: With controls x, y and target z, flips the target only if $x = y = 1$: $|x, y, z\rangle \leftarrow |x, y,\ z \oplus (x \wedge y)\rangle$.

Using only the X, CNOT, and Toffoli gates, we can implement the classical operations NOT, XOR, and AND in a reversible manner. In practice, the Toffoli gate is the most computationally expensive among the standard gate set. We adopt a common decomposition in which one Toffoli $\approx$ 7 T gates + 8 Clifford gates, with T-depth 4 and full depth 8 [1]; other decompositions can be accommodated by adjusting these constants.

2.2 Grover's Algorithm

Grover's algorithm is a quantum search procedure that reduces the cost of brute-force attacks on symmetric ciphers. For a k-bit key, classical search requires $O(2^k)$ operations, while Grover's algorithm achieves the task with $O(\sqrt{2^k})$ evaluations, effectively halving the security level in bits. For example, AES-128, which resists 2^{128} classical operations, can be attacked with about 2^{64} quantum steps.

1. Input preparation. Apply Hadamard gates to k qubits to create an equal superposition of all keys:

$$|\psi\rangle = H^{\otimes k} |0\rangle^{\otimes k} = \frac{1}{2^{k/2}} \sum_{x=0}^{2^k-1} |x\rangle . \tag{1}$$

2. Oracle. The oracle checks whether a candidate key correctly encrypts the known plaintext into the target ciphertext using a quantum circuit and flips the phase if it does:

$$f(x) = \begin{cases} 1 & \text{if } Enc_x(P) = C, \\ 0 & \text{otherwise,} \end{cases} \qquad U_f |x\rangle = (-1)^{f(x)} |x\rangle . \tag{2}$$

3. Diffusion. The diffusion operator amplifies the amplitude through inversion about the mean, thereby increasing the probability of measuring the correct key.

3 NIST Post-quantum Security

To evaluate the security of a cipher against quantum attacks, NIST specifies security bounds for the cipher [13,14]:

- Level 1: Resource requirements for the attack are similar to those for breaking AES-128 ($2^{170} \rightarrow \mathbf{2^{157}}$).
- Level 3: Resource requirements for the attack are similar to those for breaking AES-192 ($2^{233} \rightarrow \mathbf{2^{221}}$).

- Level 5: Resource requirements for the attack are similar to those for breaking AES-256 ($2^{298} \rightarrow \mathbf{2^{285}}$).

According to NIST's estimation, which is based on the quantum cost analysis of Grover's key search for AES variants presented in PQCrypto'16 [3], the quantum attack complexities for security Levels 1, 3 and 5 (corresponding to different key sizes) are approximately 2^{170}, 2^{233} and 2^{298} [13], respectively, where the values represent (the total number of gates) $\times$ (the depth of Grover's search). More recently, following the updated results reported in Eurocrypt'20 [8], NIST revised these estimates, lowering the quantum attack costs for AES-128, AES-192, and AES-256 to 2^{157}, 2^{221}, and 2^{285} [14], respectively. While Grover's algorithm provides a theoretical square-root reduction in brute-force cost, its realization requires quantum circuits of prohibitive depth, far beyond the reach of current technology. To formalize this limitation, NIST introduced the notion of *MAXDEPTH* [13,14].

4 AIM2

AIM2 has been proposed as a tweakable one-way function that provides multi-target one-wayness, making it suitable for signature schemes [11]. Its construction combines non-linear components, a linear layer, and an additional constant injection.

The non-linear part relies on Mersenne-type S-boxes defined by exponentiation of the form x^{2^e-1} together with their inverses. The exponents e are chosen such that $\gcd(e, n) = 1$, ensuring that the inverse exponent is well-defined. This choice further guarantees that the resulting inverse S-box can be expressed by quadratic equations, which strengthens the one-wayness of the primitive.

The linear layer consists of three components: (i) an `AddConst` operation that injects fixed constants $\gamma_1, \ldots, \gamma_\ell$, (ii) an affine transformation based on a random invertible matrix and vector derived from an extendable-output function (XOF) with input iv, and (iii) a feed-forward step where the input is added back to the output, making the overall mapping non-invertible.

The structure of AIM2 used in this work is illustrated in Fig. 1, where the example corresponds to AIM2-V with $\ell = 3$. In this setting, the input pt represents the secret key of the signature scheme, while the pair (iv, ct) can be seen as the corresponding public key.

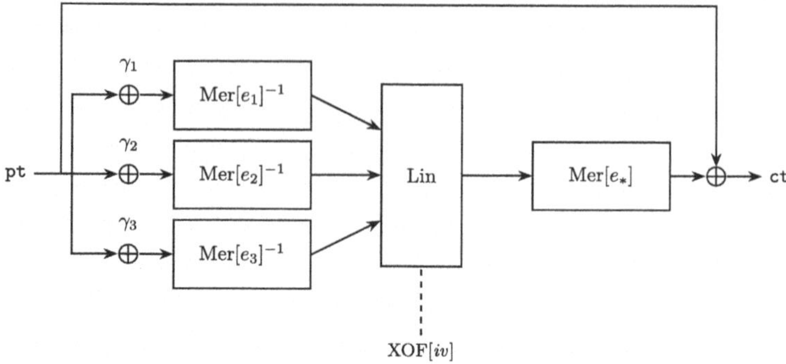

Fig. 1. Structure of the AIM2-V one-way function ($\ell = 3$).

Recommended parameter sets are provided for security levels $\lambda \in \{128, 192, 256\}$. Each variant—AIM2-I, AIM2-III, and AIM2-V—is defined by different input/output sizes n, tuples of exponents $(e_1, \ldots, e_\ell, e_*)$, and irreducible polynomials for the field $\mathbb{F}_{2^n}$. For example, AIM2-V adopts $n = 256$, $\ell = 3$, and exponents $(11, 141, 7; 3)$, with $\mathbb{F}_{2^{256}}$ constructed using the polynomial $X^{256} + X^{10} + X^5 + X^2 + 1$.

5 Quantum Circuit for AIM2

In this paper, we propose a quantum circuit implementation of AIM2. Our first optimization focuses on reducing the circuit depth, and the second aims to minimize the number of qubits. Among the AIM2 components, the one that consumes the largest amount of quantum resources is $\text{Mer}^{-1}(e)$, followed by $\text{Mer}(e)$. Specifically, $\text{Mer}^{-1}(e)$ corresponds to exponentiation by the multiplicative inverse of $(2^e - 1)$ modulo $(2^n - 1)$, which involves a large number of squaring and multiplication operations. In contrast, $\text{Mer}(e)$ is defined as exponentiation by $(2^e - 1)$, and although it is also resource-intensive, its cost is smaller compared to $\text{Mer}^{-1}(e)$.

Before describing the quantum circuit for AIM2, we first outline the multiplication and squaring operations in the binary field $\mathbb{F}_{2^n}$.

For multiplication, we use the Karatsuba algorithm proposed in [6]. This method recursively decomposes the product into smaller blocks until the size becomes 1×1. The main idea is to allocate additional ancilla qubits to prepare all intermediate operands in advance so that the partial multiplications can be performed in parallel. As a result, the overall Toffoli depth of the multiplication is reduced to 1 for any field size, which is lower than other binary multiplication techniques [2,9,17]. The approach in [6] requires many ancilla qubits to achieve low depth. However, in AIM2 the multiplications inside $\text{Mer}^{-1}(e)$ and $\text{Mer}(e)$ are executed sequentially rather than in parallel. This allows the same ancilla qubits to be reused across multiple multiplications, thereby reducing the number of qubits while maintaining a low depth. For squaring, the implementation is simpler and less costly than multiplication. Since no cross products are required, the operation can be realized using only CNOT gates followed by modular reduction. Table 1 provides the estimated quantum resources for multiplication and squaring in $\mathbb{F}_{2^{128}} = (x^{128} + x^7 + x^2 + x + 1)$, $\mathbb{F}_{2^{192}} = (x^{192} + x^7 + x^2 + x + 1)$, and $\mathbb{F}_{2^{256}} = (x^{256} + x^{10} + x^5 + x^2 + 1)$.

Modular reduction is a linear operation, and while an in-place implementation via PLU decomposition is possible, [11] performs the reduction directly for simplicity. In this case, only a small number of additional ancilla qubits (3–5) are required in addition to the input qubits. We also adopt the simplified modular reduction described in [11].

Table 1. Quantum resources required for multiplication and squaring in $\mathbb{F}_{2^{128}}, \mathbb{F}_{2^{192}}$, and $\mathbb{F}_{2^{256}}$.

Field size 2^n	Operation	#CNOT	#1qCliff	#T	T-depth	#Qubit	Full depth
n=128	mul	29867	4374	15309	4	6561	78
	squ	205	–	–	–	131	127
n=192	mul	85577	10206	35721	4	15309	94
	squ	301	–	–	–	195	196
n=256	mul	115558	13122	45927	4	19683	180
	squ	401	–	–	–	261	253

5.1 Mer^{-1}

Before the linear layer, the Mer^{-1} operation is performed as a sequence of squaring and multiplication, which incurs the majority of the computational cost in AIM2. In this paper, we focus on $\mathrm{Mer}^{-1}(49)$ used in AIM2-I. Since this operation involves many multiplications and squarings, the corresponding pseudocode is divided into Algorithm 1 for readability.

$\mathrm{Mer}^{-1}(49)$ consists of 24 multiplications and 24 squarings. Some qubits are reset and reused via inverse operations. Because these inverse operations are executed in parallel with the forward computations, they do not increase the overall circuit depth while restoring qubits to the clean state. In addition, certain sequential steps are parallelized to further improve efficiency.

The pseudocode notation `CNOT`$(a_{[0:127]}, b_{[0:127]})$ indicates bitwise CNOT operations between a and b, which correspond to 128 parallel CNOT gates and therefore contribute depth 1. The `CleanAncilla` operation initializes ancilla qubits used in multiplications (e.g., 4118 qubit) with negligible overhead, as discussed in Sect. 3.3 in [6].

As another optimization, the values $t1$ and $table\_5$ computed in lines 4–10 of Algorithm 1 are no longer required after line 31. Thus, they are reset using an inversion operation in parallel and reused in the subsequent linear layer. Moreover, the multiplications at lines 26 and 29 share the same input *table_b* and would normally be sequential. By applying fan-out to t_1^{copy}, these multiplications can be executed in parallel. After completion, t_1^{copy} is reset and reused at line 32.

These optimization techniques apply not only to $\mathrm{Mer}^{-1}(49)$ but also to $\mathrm{Mer}^{-1}(91)$ and other variants. However, this paper focuses on AIM2-I, and we omit the implementation details of AIM2-III and AIM2-V. Table 2 shows the estimated quantum resources of the Mer^{-1} functions used in AIM2-I, AIM2-III, and AIM2-V.

Table 2. Quantum resources required for the Mer^{-1} of AIM2.

Cipher	Component	#CNOT	$\#T$	#1qCliff	#Qubit	Full depth
AIM2-I	$\mathsf{Mer}^{-1}(49)$	910,893	367,416	104,976	57,627	11,053
	$\mathsf{Mer}^{-1}(91)$	925,597	367,416	104,976	57,372	11,154
AIM2-III	$\mathsf{Mer}^{-1}(17)$	1,718,007	714,420	204,120	113,607	37,970
	$\mathsf{Mer}^{-1}(47)$	2,409,706	1,107,351	316,386	316,386	39,529
AIM2-V	$\mathsf{Mer}^{-1}(11)$	2,600,661	1,010,394	288,684	159,507	67,610
	$\mathsf{Mer}^{-1}(141)$	2,716,910	1,056,321	301,806	166,314	67,555
	$\mathsf{Mer}^{-1}(7)$	2,049,454	872,613	249,318	139,824	67,220

5.2 Mer

The Mer operation consists of multiple multiplications and squarings, as presented in Algorithm 2. For simplicity, we illustrate Mer based on Mer(3) used in AIM2-I and AIM2-V. This function is performed after the linear operation, and Table 3 presents the resource estimation results for Mer.

Table 3. Quantum resources required for the Mer of AIM2.

Cipher	Component	#CNOT	$\#T$	#1qCliff	#Qubit	Full depth
AIM2-I	$\mathsf{Mer}(3)$	68,508	30,618	8,748	8,754	410
AIM2-III	$\mathsf{Mer}(5)$	240,325	107,163	30,618	25,911	1,061
AIM2-V	$\mathsf{Mer}(3)$	206,954	91,854	206,954	26,254	855

Algorithm 1 Quantum circuit implementation of $\mathsf{Mer}^{-1}(49)$.

```
Input: x
Output: out, anc, t1, table_5

    // Allocate ancilla qubits for Mul
 1: anc ← allocate 4118 ancilla qubits

    // Compute Mer^-1(49)
 2: table_d ← allocate new 128 qubits
 3: t1 ← allocate new 128 qubits

    // t1 = x^4
 4: CNOT(x[0:127], table_d[0:127])
 5: table_d ← Squaring(table_d)
 6: CNOT(table_d[0:127], t1[0:127])
 7: t1 ← Squaring(t1)

    // table_5 = x^5
 8: table_5 ← Mul(t1, x, anc)
 9: table_5 ← Reduction(table_5)
10: anc ← CleanAncilla(t1, x, anc)

    // table_6 = x^6
11: table_6 ← Mul(table_5, x, anc)
12: table_6 ← Reduction(table_6)
13: anc ← CleanAncilla(table_5, x, anc)

    // table_a = x^10
14: CNOT(table_5[0:127], table_a[0:127])
15: table_a ← Squaring(table_a)

    // table_b = x^11
16: table_b ← Mul(table_a, x, anc)
17: table_b ← Reduction(table_b)
18: anc ← CleanAncilla(table_a, x, anc)

    // table_d = x^13
19: table_d ← Mul(table_b, table_d, anc)
20: table_d ← Reduction(table_d)
21: anc ← CleanAncilla(table_b, table_d, anc)

    // table_b = x^0xb6, table_5 = x^0xb5
22: for i = 1 to 4 do
23:     table_b ← Squaring(table_b)
24: t1^copy ← allocate new 128 qubits
25: CNOT(table_b, t1^copy)
26: table_b_2 ← Mul(table_b, table_6, anc)
27: table_b_2 ← Reduction(table_b_2)
28: anc ← CleanAncilla(table_b, table_6, anc)
29: table_5_2 ← Mul(t1^copy, table_5, anc)
30: table_5_2 ← Reduction(table_5_2)
31: anc ← CleanAncilla(t1^copy, table_5, anc)

    Inverse operation for lines 4-10 (Parallel)

    // t1 = x^0xb6b6
32: CNOT(table_b_2, t1^copy)
33: for i = 1 to 8 do
34:     t1^copy ← Squaring(t1^copy)
35: t1_2 ← Mul(t1^copy, table_b_2, anc)
36: t1_2 ← Reduction(t1_2)
37: anc ← CleanAncilla(t1^copy, table_b_2, anc)

    // t1 = x^0xb6b6d
38: for i = 1 to 4 do
39:     t1_2 ← Squaring(t1_2)
40: t1_3 ← Mul(t1_2, table_d, anc)
41: t1_3 ← Reduction(t1_3)
42: anc ← CleanAncilla(t1_2, table_d, anc)

    // t1 = x^0xb6b6d6
43: for i = 1 to 4 do
44:     t1_3 ← Squaring(t1_3)
45: t1_4 ← Mul(t1_3, table_6, anc)
46: t1_4 ← Reduction(t1_4)
47: anc ← CleanAncilla(t1_3, table_6, anc)

    // t2 = x^0xb6b6d6d
48: for i = 1 to 4 do
49:     t1_4 ← Squaring(t1_4)
50: t2 ← Mul(t1_4, table_d, anc)
51: t2 ← Reduction(t2)
52: anc ← CleanAncilla(t1_4, table_d, anc)
```

Algorithm 1 Quantum circuit implementation of $\mathsf{Mer}^{-1}(49)$. (continued)

// $t_1 = x^{0xb6b6d6d6}$
53: CNOT(t_2, t_1^{copy})
54: **for** $i = 1$ to 4 **do**
55: $\quad t_2 \leftarrow$ Squaring(t_2)
56: $t_{1\_5} \leftarrow$ Mul(t_2, table_6, anc)
57: $t_{1\_5} \leftarrow$ Reduction(t_{1_5})
58: $anc \leftarrow$ CleanAncilla(t_2, table_6, anc)

// $t_1 = x^{0xb6b6d6d6d}$
59: **for** $i = 1$ to 4 **do**
60: $\quad t_{1\_5} \leftarrow$ Squaring(t_{1_5})
61: $t_{1\_6} \leftarrow$ Mul(t_{1_5}, table_d, anc)
62: $t_{1\_6} \leftarrow$ Reduction(t_{1_6})
63: $anc \leftarrow$ CleanAncilla(t_{1_5}, table_d, anc)

// $t_1 = x^{0xb6b6d6d6da}$
64: **for** $i = 1$ to 4 **do**
65: $\quad t_{1\_6} \leftarrow$ Squaring(t_{1_6})
66: $t_{1\_7} \leftarrow$ Mul(t_{1_6}, table_a, anc)
67: $t_{1\_7} \leftarrow$ Reduction(t_{1_7})
68: $anc \leftarrow$ CleanAncilla(t_{1_6}, table_a, anc)

// $t_1 = x^{0xb6b6d6d6dad}$
69: **for** $i = 1$ to 4 **do**
70: $\quad t_{1\_7} \leftarrow$ Squaring(t_{1_7})
71: $t_{1\_8} \leftarrow$ Mul(t_{1_7}, table_d, anc)
72: $t_{1\_8} \leftarrow$ Reduction(t_{1_8})
73: $anc \leftarrow$ CleanAncilla(t_{1_7}, table_d, anc)

// $t_1 = x^{0xb6b6d6d6dadb5}$
74: **for** $i = 1$ to 8 **do**
75: $\quad t_{1\_8} \leftarrow$ Squaring(t_{1_8})
76: $t_{1\_9} \leftarrow$ Mul(t_{1_8}, table_5_2, anc)
77: $t_{1\_9} \leftarrow$ Reduction(t_{1_9})
78: $anc \leftarrow$ CleanAncilla(t_{1_8}, table_5_2, anc)

// $t_1 = x^{0xb6b6d6d6dadb5b5}$
79: **for** $i = 1$ to 8 **do**
80: $\quad t_{1\_9} \leftarrow$ Squaring(t_{1_9})
81: $t_{1\_10} \leftarrow$ Mul(t_{1_9}, table_5_2, anc)
82: $t_{1\_10} \leftarrow$ Reduction(t_{1_10})
83: $anc \leftarrow$ CleanAncilla(t_{1_9}, table_5_2, anc)

// $t_1 = x^{0xb6b6d6d6dadb5b5b6}$
84: **for** $i = 1$ to 8 **do**
85: $\quad t_{1\_10} \leftarrow$ Squaring(t_{1_10})
86: $t_{1\_11} \leftarrow$ Mul(t_{1_10}, table_b_2, anc)
87: $t_{1\_11} \leftarrow$ Reduction(t_{1_11})
88: $anc \leftarrow$ CleanAncilla(t_{1_10}, table_b_2, anc)

// $t_1 = x^{0xb6b6d6d6dadb5b5b6b6b6d}$
89: **for** $i = 1$ to 28 **do**
90: $\quad t_{1\_11} \leftarrow$ Squaring(t_{1_11})
91: $t_{1\_12} \leftarrow$ Mul(t_{1_11}, t_1^{copy}, anc)
92: $t_{1\_12} \leftarrow$ Reduction(t_{1_12})
93: $anc \leftarrow$ CleanAncilla(t_{1_11}, t_1^{copy}, anc)

// $t_1 = x^{0xb6b6d6d6dadb5b5b6b6b6d6da}$
94: **for** $i = 1$ to 4 **do**
95: $\quad t_{1\_12} \leftarrow$ Squaring(t_{1_12})
96: $t_{1\_13} \leftarrow$ Mul(t_{1_12}, table_a, anc)
97: $t_{1\_13} \leftarrow$ Reduction(t_{1_13})
98: $anc \leftarrow$ CleanAncilla(t_{1_12}, table_a, anc)

// $t_1 = x^{0xb6b6d6d6dadb5b5b6b6b6d6dad}$
99: **for** $i = 1$ to 4 **do**
100: $\quad t_{1\_13} \leftarrow$ Squaring(t_{1_13})
101: $t_{1\_14} \leftarrow$ Mul(t_{1_13}, table_d, anc)
102: $t_{1\_14} \leftarrow$ Reduction(t_{1_14})
103: $anc \leftarrow$ CleanAncilla(t_{1_13}, table_d, anc)

// $t_1 = x^{0xb6b6d6d6dadb5b5b6b6b6d6dada}$
104: **for** $i = 1$ to 4 **do**
105: $\quad t_{1\_14} \leftarrow$ Squaring(t_{1_14})
106: $t_{1\_15} \leftarrow$ Mul(t_{1_14}, table_a, anc)
107: $t_{1\_15} \leftarrow$ Reduction(t_{1_15})
108: $anc \leftarrow$ CleanAncilla(t_{1_14}, table_a, anc)

// $t_1 = x^{0xb6b6d6d6dadb5b5b6b6b6d6dadad}$
109: **for** $i = 1$ to 4 **do**
110: $\quad t_{1\_15} \leftarrow$ Squaring(t_{1_15})
111: $t_{1\_16} \leftarrow$ Mul(t_{1_15}, table_d, anc)
112: $t_{1\_16} \leftarrow$ Reduction(t_{1_16})
113: $anc \leftarrow$ CleanAncilla(t_{1_15}, table_d, anc)

// $t_1 = x^{0xb6b6d6d6dadb5b5b6b6b6d6dadadb5}$
114: **for** $i = 1$ to 8 **do**
115: $\quad t_{1\_16} \leftarrow$ Squaring(t_{1_16})
116: $t_{1\_17} \leftarrow$ Mul(t_{1_16}, table_5_2, anc)
117: $t_{1\_17} \leftarrow$ Reduction(t_{1_17})
118: $anc \leftarrow$ CleanAncilla(t_{1_16}, table_5_2, anc)

// $t_1 = x^{0xb6b6d6d6dadb5b5b6b6b6d6dadadb5b5}$
119: **for** $i = 1$ to 8 **do**
120: $\quad t_{1\_17} \leftarrow$ Squaring(t_{1_17})
121: $out \leftarrow$ Mul(t_{1_17}, table_5_2, anc)
122: $out \leftarrow$ Reduction(out)
123: $anc \leftarrow$ CleanAncilla(t_{1_16}, table_5_2, anc)
124: **return** out, anc, $t1$, $table\_5$

Algorithm 2 Quantum circuit implementation of Mer (3).

Input: *input*
//Compute Mer(3)
1: $t1 \leftarrow$ allocate new 128 qubits
2: CNOT($input_{[0:128]}$, $t1_{0:127}$)

$//t1 = a^{(2^2-1)}$
3: $t1 \leftarrow$ Squaring($t1$)

4: $t_{1\_2} \leftarrow$ Mul($t1$, *input*, *anc*)
5: $t_{1\_2} \leftarrow$ Reduction(t_{1_2})
6: $anc \leftarrow$ CleanAncilla($t1$, *input*, *anc*)

$//out = a^{(2^3-1)}$
7: $t_{1\_2} \leftarrow$ Squaring(t_{1_2})
8: $out \leftarrow$ Mul(t_{1_2}, *input*, *anc*)
9: $out \leftarrow$ Reduction(out)
10: $anc \leftarrow$ CleanAncilla(t_{1_2}, *input*, *anc*)

11: **return** *out*, *anc*

5.3 Linear Layer

The Linear Layer consists of multiplying the input vector by a predefined binary matrix. This matrix is derived from the initial vector (hash input) using SHAKE-128 for AIM-I and SHAKE-256 for AIM-III and AIM-V, and since it is publicly available, it can be treated as a constant. Therefore, the operation is a classical(matrix vector)-quantum rather than a quantum-quantum operation, enabling efficient quantum circuit design based on classically precomputed matrices.

Among various approaches to implement matrix-vector multiplication in quantum circuits, [7] adopted an out-of-place design to optimize the depth. This method allocates new output qubits and performs XOR operations (CNOT gates) between the input and output vectors. Although it requires additional qubits compared to the in-place approach, it offers the advantage of reduced depth. Moreover, since the input vector is public, some operations can be replaced by applying X gates instead of CNOT gates, enabling further optimization.

In this work, we adopt a similar out-of-place Linear Layer design following the approach of [7]. Table 4 presents the estimated quantum resources for the Linear Layer. The CNOT gates depends on the number of ones in the matrix generated by SHAKE-128 or SHAKE-256. As a result, the count of the CNOT gate varies depending on the specific output matrices; thus, the number of CNOT is provided only for reference. The #Qubit denotes the total number of qubits required for the Linear Layer, and the values in parentheses indicate qubits reused from previous operations. In AIM2-I and AIM2-III, both the L-matrix and U-matrix sets consist of two matrices, represented as matrix_L = $[L_0, L_1]$ and matrix_U = $[U_0, U_1]$. In AIM2-V, each matrix set is extended to three, represented as matrix_L = $[L_0, L_1, L_2]$ and matrix_U = $[U_0, U_1, U_2]$. Consequently, AIM2-I and AIM2-III employ a total of four matrix arrays, while AIM2-V uses six. Since the number of ancilla qubits increases proportionally to the number of matrix arrays, AIM2-I and AIM2-III require $2n$ input qubits and $4n$ ancilla qubits, whereas AIM2-V requires $3n$ input qubits and $6n$ ancilla qubits.

Table 4. Quantum resources required for the LinearLayer in AIM2.

LinearLayer	#CNOT	#Qubit	Full depth
AIM2-I ($n = 128$)	16,858	768 (512)	302
AIM2-III ($n = 192$)	37,607	1,152 (768)	457
AIM2-V ($n = 256$)	99,800	2,304 (1,536)	614

Finally, the FeedForward step requires XOR operations between the input and the output, for which CNOT gates are employed. Since the proposed design is based on the Karatsuba multiplication [6], a large number of ancilla qubits are required. However, in exchange for this qubit overhead, the overall circuit is designed to maintain a low full depth (see Table 5).

6 Evaluation

In this section, we discuss the post-quantum security of AIM2 based on its estimated quantum resources.

First, we compare the resource requirements of AIM and AIM2. Table 5 presents this comparison. The AIMer improved the scheme by replacing the internal tweakable one-way function AIM with AIM2. While AIM applies the Mer operation both before and after the linear layer, AIM2 uses Mer^{-1} before the linear layer and Mer afterwards. Since Mer^{-1} is significantly more costly than Mer, AIM2 circuits require more quantum resources than AIM circuits [7].

Next, we estimate the Grover key search cost of AIM2(see Table 6) and compare it with that of AES variants(see Table 7). For AES, we use the NIST estimates [13,14], derived from the analyses of Grassl et al. [3] and Jaques et al. [8].

In our estimation, the diffusion operator is ignored and only the oracle cost is considered [5,8]. The Grover oracle consists of (1) the AIM quantum circuit for encryption, (2) an n-controlled NOT gate to compare the computed ciphertext with a known ciphertext (cost: $(32n - 64)$ T gates, where n is the ciphertext size), and (3) the inverse of the AIM quantum circuit for uncomputation. The total oracle cost is therefore:

$$\left\lfloor \frac{\pi}{4}\sqrt{2^k} \right\rfloor \times \left((32 \cdot n - 64)T \text{ gates} + 2 \times \text{Table 5}\right).$$

Table 5. Estimated quantum resources for the AIM2 quantum circuits.

Cipher	#CNOT	#1qCliff	$\#T$	#Qubit	Full depth	$FD \times M$
AIM-I [7]	358,754	39,430	137,781	25,299	3,499	88,521,201
AIM-III [7]	1,144,536	132,785	464,373	88,395	8,583	758,694,285
AIM-V [7]	1,486,100	157,588	551,124	108,072	16,857	1,821,769,704
AIM2-I (our)	1,921,984	218,768	765,450	119,763	11,861	1,420,508,943
AIM2-III (our)	4,405,986	551,124	1,928,934	300,436	41,045	12,331,354,575
AIM2-V (our)	7,674,035	866,052	3,031,182	479,801	69,072	33,140,814,672

The number of Grover iterations is $\lfloor \pi/4 \cdot \sqrt{2^k} \rfloor$, and the additional decision qubit required for ciphertext verification increases the qubit count by only one, since the iterations are sequential.

Table 6. Costs of the Grover's key search for AIM2

Cipher	Total gates	Total depth	Cost (complexity)	#Qubit	$FD \times M$
AIM2-I	1.09×2^{86}	1.14×2^{78}	1.24×2^{164}	119,764	1.04×2^{95}
AIM2-III	1.29×2^{119}	1.97×2^{111}	1.27×2^{231}	300,435	1.13×2^{130}
AIM2-V	1.08×2^{152}	1.66×2^{144}	1.79×2^{296}	479,801	1.52×2^{163}

We then compare the Grover costs of AES and AIM2 to assess the post-quantum security of AIM2. Table 7 presents the results. A direct comparison with the original NIST estimates [13] suggests that AIM2-I, -III, and -V do not meet the Level-1, -3, and -5 security levels, respectively. This is because AES circuits are extremely costly [3], and the NIST estimates were conservatively set. Later, NIST revised the AES Grover cost estimates [14] based on the work of Jaques et al. [8], and we adopt these updated values in our evaluation. Although some studies have argued that the revised estimates may still be underestimated [5], we conclude that AIM2-I, -III, and -V meet the Level-1, -3, and -5 security levels when compared against the updated AES estimates.

Table 7. Comparison of the Grover's key search costs

Post-quantum	NIST'16 [13]	NIST'22 [14]	AIM2		
Security	(based on [3])	(based on [8])	-I	-III	-V
Level-1 (AES-128)	2^{170}	2^{157}	2^{164}		
Level-3 (AES-192)	2^{233}	2^{221}		2^{231}	
Level-5 (AES-256)	2^{298}	2^{285}			2^{296}

7 Conclusion

In this work, we proposed quantum circuits of AIM2. We performed optimizations to reduce the circuit depth and introduced a qubit-reuse technique. For all AIM2 variants (AIM-I, AIM-III, AIM-V), we designed quantum circuits for the internal operations, including Mer^{-1}, the linear layer, Mer, and feed-forward. Compared to the previous version of AIM, AIM2 requires significantly more quantum resources, mainly because the Mer^{-1} operation is applied before the linear layer. Based on the proposed circuits, we estimate the cost of Grover's algorithm for key search and confirm post-quantum security levels. As a result, AIM2-I, -III, and -V meet Level-1, -3, and -5 security levels, respectively, compared to the updated AES cost estimates by NIST. These results demonstrate that AIM2 provides strong post-quantum security.

Acknowledgment. This work was supported by the Institute of Information & Communications Technology Planning & Evaluation(IITP) grant funded by the Korea government(MSIT) (No. RS-2019-II190033, Study on Quantum Security Evaluation of Cryptography based on Computational Quantum Complexity, 10%) and this work was supported by the National Research Foundation of Korea(NRF) grant funded by the Korea government(MSIT) (No. RS-2025-23523436, 90%).

References

1. Amy, M., Maslov, D., Mosca, M., Roetteler, M.: A meet-in-the-middle algorithm for fast synthesis of depth-optimal quantum circuits. IEEE Trans. Comput. Aided Des. Integr. Circuits Syst. **32**(6), 818–830 (2013)
2. Cheung, D., Maslov, D., Mathew, J., Pradhan, D.K.: On the design and optimization of a quantum polynomial-time attack on elliptic curve cryptography. In: Kawano, Y., Mosca, M. (eds.) Theory of Quantum Computation, Communication, and Cryptography. TQC 2008. LNCS, vol. 5106, pp. 96–104. Springer, Berlin, Heidelberg (2008). https://doi.org/10.1007/978-3-540-89304-2_9
3. Grassl, M., Langenberg, B., Roetteler, M., Steinwandt, R.: Applying Grover's algorithm to AES: quantum resource estimates. In: Takagi, T. (ed.) Post-Quantum Cryptography. PQCrypto 2016. LNCS, vol. 9606, pp. 29–43. Springer, Cham (2016). https://doi.org/10.1007/978-3-319-29360-8_3
4. Grover, L.K.: A fast quantum mechanical algorithm for database search. In: Proceedings of the Twenty-Eighth Annual ACM Symposium on Theory of Computing, pp. 212–219 (1996)
5. Jang, K., Baksi, A., Kim, H., Song, G., Seo, H., Chattopadhyay, A.: Quantum analysis of AES. Cryptology ePrint Archive (2022)
6. Jang, K., Kim, W., Lim, S., Kang, Y., Yang, Y., Seo, H.: Optimized implementation of quantum binary field multiplication with toffoli depth one. In: You, I., Youn, T.Y. (eds.) Information Security Applications. WISA 2022. LNCS, vol. 13720, pp. 251–264. Springer, Cham (2023). https://doi.org/10.1007/978-3-031-25659-2_18
7. Jang, K., Oh, Y., Kim, H., Seo, H.: Quantum implementation of AIM: aiming for low-depth. Appl. Sci. **14**(7), 2824 (2024)

8. Jaques, S., Naehrig, M., Roetteler, M., Virdia, F.: Implementing grover oracles for quantum key search on AES and LowMC. In: Canteaut, A., Ishai, Y. (eds.) Advances in Cryptology – EUROCRYPT 2020. EUROCRYPT 2020. LNCS, vol. 12106, pp. 280–310. Springer, Cham (2020). https://doi.org/10.1007/978-3-030-45724-2_10
9. Kepley, S., Steinwandt, R.: Quantum circuits for $\mathbb{F}_{2^n}$-multiplication with subquadratic gate count. Quantum Inf. Process. **14**(7), 2373–2386 (2015)
10. Kim, S., et al.: The aimer signature scheme. Tech. rep., Technical report. NIST (2023)
11. Lee, J., et al.: The aimer signature scheme
12. Nielsen, M.A., Chuang, I.L.: Quantum Computation and Quantum Information. Cambridge university press, Cambridge (2010)
13. NIST.: Submission requirements and evaluation criteria for the post-quantum cryptography standardization process (2016). https://csrc.nist.gov/CSRC/media/Projects/Post-Quantum-Cryptography/documents/call-for-proposals-final-dec-2016.pdf
14. NIST.: Call for additional digital signature schemes for the post-quantum cryptography standardization process (2022). https://csrc.nist.gov/csrc/media/Projects/pqc-dig-sig/documents/call-for-proposals-dig-sig-sept-2022.pdf
15. Shor, P.W.: Algorithms for quantum computation: discrete logarithms and factoring. In: Proceedings 35th Annual Symposium on Foundations of Computer Science, pp. 124–134. IEEE (1994)
16. Shor, P.W.: Polynomial-time algorithms for prime factorization and discrete logarithms on a quantum computer. SIAM Rev. **41**(2), 303–332 (1999)
17. Van Hoof, I.: Space-efficient quantum multiplication of polynomials for binary finite fields with sub-quadratic Toffoli gate count. arXiv preprint arXiv:1910.02849 (2019)

Network and Application Security

Comprehensive Security Analysis of End-to-End Encryption in LINE

Takehiro Matsumoto[1], Atsushi Tanaka[1], Kyosuke Yamashita[1,2], Ryoma Ito[1,3], and Takanori Isobe[1(✉)]

[1] The University of Osaka, Suita, Japan
{take-matsumoto,a.tanaka,yamashita,takanori.isobe}@ist.osaka-u.ac.jp
[2] AIST, Tokyo, Japan
[3] NICT, Koganei, Japan
itorym@nict.go.jp

Abstract. LINE is the most widely used messaging application worldwide, with 196 million monthly active users as of March 2025. Given its broad adoption, ensuring the security of its communication protocol is of significant importance. However, its end-to-end encryption protocol, Letter Sealing, has not undergone comprehensive formal verification. Although Letter Sealing Version 2—introduced after vulnerabilities were identified in Version 1—is now widely deployed, its security guarantees remain insufficiently scrutinized. In this work, we formally model the one-to-one communication protocol in both Letter Sealing versions using the symbolic verification tool Tamarin-Prover and analyze key security properties, including confidentiality, authentication, and integrity. For Letter Sealing Version 1, we reproduce previously reported vulnerabilities, such as impersonation and replay attacks, and additionally conduct an exhaustive verification of a broad range of security properties. For Letter Sealing Version 2, we represent the first comprehensive formal analysis. We confirm that several vulnerabilities have been mitigated through changes in cryptographic algorithms; however, our analysis also reveals several previously unidentified weaknesses that persist in the protocol. This work provides a foundational step toward a rigorous evaluation of the security guarantees offered by LINE's encryption mechanisms and underscores the ongoing need for formal verification in widely deployed communication systems.

Keywords: End-to-End Encryption · LINE · Cryptographic Protocol · Security Analysis · Formal Verification

1 Introduction

In recent years, messaging applications have become widely used in both private and business contexts, making communication confidentiality and security critical issues tied directly to social infrastructure. To address these concerns, major messaging services have adopted End-to-End Encryption (E2EE) to

H. Seo (Ed.): ICISC 2025, LNCS 16487, pp. 237–256, 2026.
https://doi.org/10.1007/978-981-95-8034-7_13

ensure strong privacy protection. E2EE refers to an encryption scheme in which only the communicating parties can send and receive messages; no one else—including even the service provider—can eavesdrop on or forge the messages. This mechanism is essential for achieving advanced security properties such as confidentiality, integrity, authentication, forward secrecy. However, due to the complexity of cryptographic protocol design, many cases have been reported where vulnerabilities still remain [1,5,8].

LINE is the most widely used messaging application, boasting 196 million monthly active users worldwide as of March 2025 [3]. Its secure communication is supported by the E2EE protocol called Letter Sealing. The specifications of this protocol are described in the white paper published in 2016 [6].

In 2018, Isobe and Minematsu conducted a security evaluation of Letter Sealing Version 1 (v1), demonstrating that impersonation and forgery attacks were feasible [4]. In response to these results, LINE Corporation released a revised protocol in 2019, updating Letter Sealing to Version 2 (v2), and published a corresponding white paper. Their study was conducted through manual analysis of the protocol. While such analyses are effective in identifying vulnerabilities, they do not provide a guarantee of the overall security of the protocol.

Formal verification has become an important methodology for evaluating the security of cryptographic protocols, as it enables security requirements to be mathematically modeled and automatically checked against desired properties. Building on this approach, Shi and Yoneyama [9] applied ProVerif to the Letter Sealing protocol, and successfully verified a set of fundamental properties for Version 1, including confidentiality, replay attack resistance, and spoofing resistance. Their work provided valuable insights into the security of Letter Sealing; however, the scope of the analysis was necessarily limited to partial verification of Version 1 and did not encompass the full range of properties expected in end-to-end encrypted (E2EE) messaging. In addition, a comprehensive formal security evaluation of the currently deployed Letter Sealing Version 2 has not yet been reported in the literature.

In this study, we conduct a comprehensive verification of the one-to-one communication protocols of both Letter Sealing versions using the formal verification tool Tamarin Prover, focusing on various security properties required in messaging applications, such as confidentiality, authentication, forward secrecy, replay attack resistance, and more [10]. The reason for adopting Tamarin Prover lies in its flexibility to describe the intended security properties in detail as lemmas and its support for a powerful adversary model. This allows rigorous verification not only of standard properties such as confidentiality and authentication, but also of messaging-specific properties such as forward secrecy and backward secrecy. The protocol behavior is modeled step by step as rules, formally describing the processes of key exchange and message transmission between the sender and the receiver. On the other hand, the target security properties are defined as lemmas, for example, in the form of statements such as "if the sender transmits a message, only the legitimate receiver can decrypt its contents" or "even if an adversary obtains past key material, future communication contents cannot be decrypted."

Table 1. Comparison between our and existing formal verification results for LINE Letter Sealing Versions 1 and 2 (v1 and v2). Our verification targets the security properties defined by Unger et al. [10].

Security Property	[9]	This Paper	
	v1	v1	v2
Confidentiality	✓	✓	✓
Authentication	×	×	✓
Integrity	×	×	✓
Forward secrecy	×	×	×
Backward secrecy	–	×	×
Replay attack resistance	×	×	✓
Metadata tampering detection	–	×	✓
Recipient verification	–	×	✓
Resistance to global adversary	×	×	×
Ciphertext tampering detection	–	✓	✓
Sender/receiver anonymity	–	×	×

✓ denotes that the security property holds, × denotes that the security property does not hold, and "–" denotes that the security property was unverified.

Table 1 summarizes the evaluation results for Letter Sealing Versions 1 and 2. The contributions of this paper are as follows:

- For Letter Sealing v1, we reproduce several vulnerabilities identified by Isobe and Minematsu [4], and conduct the first systematic verification of several security properties that had not been verified in the prior ProVerif-based study by Shi and Yoneyama [9].
- We perform the first comprehensive formal verification of Leater Sealing v2, which is currently deployed in practice. As a result, we confirm that some vulnerabilities were mitigated by improvements in cryptographic algorithms; however, we also revealed that multiple security properties remain insufficiently satisfied.

This study presents the first comprehensive formal verification of the currently deployed version of Letter Sealing, clarifying both the extent of its security guarantees and the challenges that remain.

Ethical Considerations. This study does not identify previously unknown vulnerabilities that would require responsible disclosure to the vendor. Rather, our analysis reveals residual weaknesses that continue to exist in both versions of the Letter Sealing protocol. These weaknesses should not be regarded as entirely new exploits, but as underexplored aspects that remain despite the introduction of

Version 2. Our findings aim to clarify the security guarantees and limitations of Letter Sealing, thereby contributing to a more comprehensive understanding of its practical security.

2 Preliminaries

2.1 End-to-End Encryption

End-to-End Encryption (E2EE) is an encryption method designed so that only legitimate users at both ends of the communication can decrypt the message contents. Internet providers, communication carriers, and even the service provider of the communication system itself cannot access the encryption keys. With such a design, E2EE is highly resistant to interception and tampering by third parties.

2.2 Adversary Model and Security Requirements

In this study, the adversary is defined as an *active E2E adversary*. This adversary has the capability to intercept, tamper with, and generate arbitrary messages on the communication path. In particular, it is assumed that the adversary has access to all information transmitted to the server. This model assumes a realistic and powerful threat in an E2EE environment.

In this study, we examine the following security properties: confidentiality, authentication, integrity, forward secrecy, backward secrecy, replay attack resistance, metadata tampering detection, recipient verification, resistance to global adversary, ciphertext tampering detection, and sender/receiver anonymity. These properties are those defined in a study that systematically organized secure messaging protocols [10], and they are widely referenced in the design and evaluation of protocols. It should be noted here that communication protocols do not necessarily satisfy all security properties simultaneously. Each protocol is often designed by prioritizing the properties emphasized by the designer based on the usage environment and threat model, sometimes at the expense of other properties.

2.3 Basic Concepts of Tamarin Prover

Tamarin Prover [7] is a tool for modeling security protocols and automatically verifying their security properties. Protocols are described using *multiset rewriting rules*, which formally represent state transitions, including the behavior of attackers and the exchange of messages over the network. This allows verification of whether the specified security properties hold, even when considering numerous parallel executions and attacker interventions.

In Tamarin Prover, the behavior of the protocol and the sending/receiving of messages are described using **rules**. On the other hand, the security properties that cryptographic protocols should satisfy are defined as **lemmas**, which are verified in the form of trace properties or equivalence properties. If the properties hold, automated exploration outputs a proof of it; if not, an attack scenario is presented as a counterexample.

Furthermore, **restrictions** are used to express constraints on protocol execution. They exclude unnatural scenarios regarding attacker behavior or protocol operations, thereby enabling verification in more realistic communication environments.

A central modeling element in Tamarin Prover is the use of *facts*. Facts represent pieces of knowledge or state at a specific point in the protocol. If a fact is written without the prefix "!", it is treated as a **linear fact**, which disappears once it is consumed by a rule. This models transient data such as a message that exists only while it is being transmitted. In contrast, **persistent facts** (denoted with a leading "!") remain in the state indefinitely and are never removed. They are used to represent long-term information such as secret keys or registered public keys.

In this way, **rules** describe the behavior of the protocol, **lemmas** specify the security requirements to be verified, **restrictions** define the underlying assumptions, and **facts** model the evolving state of the system. Together, they constitute the foundation for modeling and verification in this study.

In addition, Tamarin Prover offers several practical features that are crucial when modeling real-world protocols such as LINE's Letter Sealing. For instance, the `Fr()` fact enables the generation of fresh values, which is essential for representing nonces, salts, and secret keys as independent random numbers across different executions. Moreover, function symbols (e.g., `enc`, `kdf`, `mac`, `senc/sdec`) allow cryptographic primitives to be abstractly expressed while preserving their fundamental properties, such as invertibility or verifiability. Finally, the Dolev–Yao attacker model embedded in Tamarin Prover provides a powerful abstraction of adversarial behavior, allowing us to analyze threats such as eavesdropping, message tampering, replay, and even key leakage within a unified framework.

3 Description of LINE's E2EE Protocol

In this section, we describe the protocol flow of one-to-one communication in LINE's E2EE protocol, known as Letter Sealing. Throughout this paper, we refer to Letter Sealing Version 1 and Version 2 as v1 and v2, respectively.

3.1 Key Generation and Sharing

Each client generates a key pair (sk, pk) based on Curve25519 and registers the public key on the server. When sending a message, *SharedSecret* is computed using the sender's private key and the recipient's public key, serving as the foundation for cryptographic operations:

$$\begin{aligned} \mathit{SharedSecret} &= \mathit{ECDH}_{\text{Curve25519}}(sk_A, pk_B) \\ &= \mathit{ECDH}_{\text{Curve25519}}(sk_B, pk_A). \end{aligned}$$

3.2 One-to-One Communication of Letter Sealing v1

Encryption Process

The sender derives the encryption key K_{enc} and initialization vector IV_{enc} from the shared secret *SharedSecret* and a random value *salt*. These are used as inputs to AES-256-CBC to encrypt the message M:

$$C = AES\text{-}CBC(K_{enc}, IV_{enc}, M).$$

The generated ciphertext C is then input into SHA-256, and the output is used as input to AES-ECB to produce the MAC value:

$$\begin{aligned} MAC_{plain} &= SHA256(C), \\ MAC_{enc} &= AES\text{-}ECB(K_{enc},\ MAC_{plain}[0:15] \oplus MAC_{plain}[16:31]). \end{aligned}$$

Sending Data Structure and Decryption

The transmitted data has the following structure, which bundles the ciphertext with associated metadata:

$$\left\{ \begin{array}{l} \texttt{version}, \texttt{content\_type}, \texttt{salt}, \texttt{C}, \texttt{MAC\_enc}, \\ \texttt{sender\_key\_ID}, \texttt{recipient\_key\_ID} \end{array} \right\}$$

The recipient performs the same key derivation, decrypts C, and compares the transmitted MAC_{enc} with the locally computed MAC. Only if they match is the message considered valid and displayed to the user.

3.3 One-to-One Communication of Letter Sealing v2

Letter Sealing v2 is an improved protocol introduced to overcome the vulnerabilities in integrity verification and tamper detection identified in Letter Sealing v1. The most significant change is the transition from AES-CBC plus MAC to the authenticated encryption scheme AES-GCM. This enables integrated realization of both encryption and integrity verification. Furthermore, explicit inclusion of header information in the packet structure and the introduction of Additional Authenticated Data (AAD) strengthen message uniqueness and sender/recipient authenticity verification.

Key exchange is still performed using Curve25519-based ECDH, but in the subsequent key derivation process, a 16-byte random *salt* is used so that a different encryption key is generated for each message. The nonce N required for AES-GCM is generated for each message transmission and ensures uniqueness in encryption and authentication processes:

$$(C, tag) = AES\text{-}GCM(K_{enc}, N, M, AAD).$$

The recipient performs the same key derivation and nonce generation, and verifies the tag to detect tampering. If the tag does not match, the message is discarded. Through this design, integrity and authenticity are significantly improved compared to Letter Sealing v1.

Sending Data Structure and Decryption

The transmitted data in Letter Sealing v2 has the following structure, which includes the ciphertext, GCM tag, and additional metadata:

$$\left\{\begin{array}{l}\texttt{version}, \texttt{content\_type}, \texttt{salt}, \texttt{C} \,||\, \texttt{tag}, \texttt{nonce}, \\ \texttt{sender\_key\_ID}, \texttt{recipient\_key\_ID}\end{array}\right\}$$

The recipient derives the same encryption key using the shared secret and the transmitted *salt*, reconstructs the *nonce*, and verifies the integrity of the message by checking the GCM tag. If the verification succeeds, C is decrypted to recover the original message M; otherwise, the message is discarded as invalid.

Compared to Letter Sealing v1, Letter Sealing v2 introduces two key differences:

- The ciphertext and GCM tag are concatenated into a single field ($C||tag$).
- The *nonce* is explicitly included as a separate field in the transmitted structure.

3.4 Limitations of Existing Work

In 2018, Isobe and Minematsu evaluated Letter Sealing v1, demonstrating that impersonation and forgery attacks were feasible [4]. In response, LINE released Letter Sealing v2 in 2019 along with a white paper. Their study relied on manual analysis, which is effective for uncovering vulnerabilities but cannot ensure the overall security of the protocol.

Formal verification provides a rigorous methodology for analyzing cryptographic protocols by mathematically modeling security requirements and automatically checking whether a protocol satisfies them. Building on this approach, Shi and Yoneyama applied ProVerif to Letter Sealing v1, and their study verified important properties such as confidentiality and resistance to replay and impersonation attacks [9]. This work offered valuable insights into the security of Letter Sealing; however, its scope was necessarily limited to partial verification of Letter Sealing v1 and did not encompass the full range of requirements for end-to-end encryption (E2EE). Moreover, to the best of our knowledge, a comprehensive formal verification of the currently deployed Letter Sealing v2 has not yet been conducted

In summary, existing research on Letter Sealing v1 remains partial, and sufficient verification of Letter Sealing v2 has not yet been conducted.

4 Automated Verification Using Tamarin Prover

In this section, we realize the automated comprehensive verification of LINE's Letter Sealing v1 and Letter Sealing v2. While previous studies have been limited to partial analyses of Letter Sealing v1 and have not examined Letter Sealing v2 at all, this work formally models both versions and comprehensively verifies their key security properties. In particular, we focus on the difference in cryptographic constructions—Letter Sealing v1 adopting AES-CBC with MAC and Letter Sealing v2 employing AES-GCM as AEAD—and clarify how these design choices affect security.

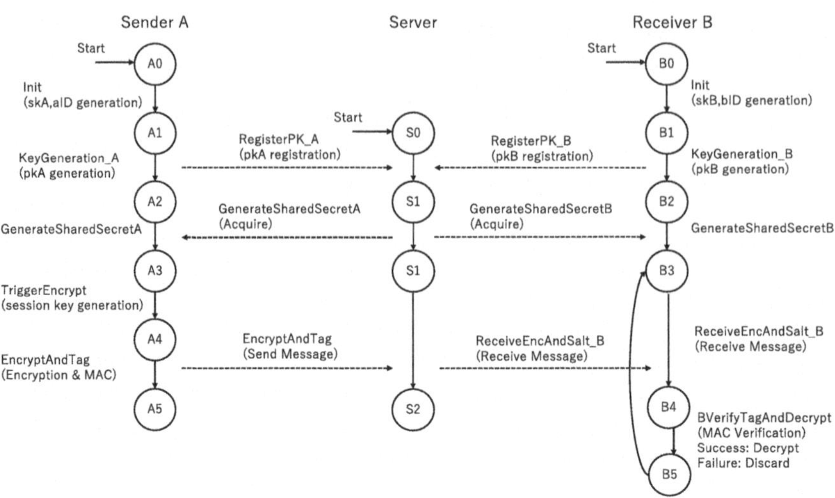

Fig. 1. State transition diagram of one-to-one communication in Letter Sealing v1.

4.1 Our Approach

We employ the Tamarin Prover to comprehensively verify both Letter Sealing v1 and Letter Sealing v2 against a wide range of security properties. While existing studies only analyzed Letter Sealing v1 partially and did not address Letter Sealing v2, our modeling enables a systematic comparison between the two versions.

Figure 1 presents the state transition diagram of one-to-one communication in Letter Sealing v1, illustrating the interactions between the sender (`A`) and the receiver (`B`), along with the server. The diagram includes the generation and registration of long-term keys, the derivation of the shared secret, and the subsequent encryption and verification processes. This visual representation provides an overview of the protocol flow, which will be formally described in Tamarin Prover using multiset rewriting rules in the following subsections.

All source code used in this study is available on GitHub [2].

4.2 Modeling of Key Exchange

The key exchange in one-to-one communication is modeled as Tamarin Prover rules. At the initial stage, each party generates a random identifier and a long-term secret key, which are kept local and never revealed to the attacker.

Generation and Registration of Long-Term Secret Keys
The `Init` rule formalizes this process: both participants generate fresh identifiers and long-term secret keys, and these values are stored as persistent facts for later use in key generation and exchange.

```
1  rule Init:
2    [ Fr(~aID), Fr(~skA), Fr(~bID), Fr(~skB) ]
3    --[ InitPhase(~aID, ~skA, ~bID, ~skB) ]->
4    [ !InitA(~aID, ~skA), !InitB(~bID, ~skB) ]
```

Here, `InitPhase` records the initialization in the trace, while `!InitA` and `!InitB` represent the long-term keys that remain available throughout the execution.

Public Key Generation and Registration

Each client derives its public key from the long-term secret key using exponentiation g^{sk}, which forms the basis of Diffie–Hellman key exchange. This corresponds to LINE's implementation with Curve25519 in ECDH.

```
1  rule KeyGeneration_A:
2    let pkA = 'g' ^ ~skA in
3    [ !InitA(~aID, ~skA) ]
4    --[ GenKeyA(~aID, ~skA) ]->
5    [ !LongTermKey(~aID, ~skA), !PublicKey(~aID, pkA) ]
6
7  rule KeyGeneration_B:
8    let pkB = 'g' ^ ~skB in
9    [ !InitB(~bID, ~skB) ]
10   --[ GenKeyB(~bID, ~skB) ]->
11   [ !LongTermKey(~bID, ~skB), !PublicKey(~bID, pkB) ]
```

Here, the `let` expression assigns the result of g^{sk} to the public key variable. The generated keys are stored as persistent facts, ensuring availability for later rules. While the public key is assumed to be distributed via the server, the secret key remains local to the client and never exposed. This design matches LINE's specification: secret keys are securely stored on devices, and only public keys are registered for key exchange.

Registration of Public Keys to the Server

Each client registers its generated public key with the server. This corresponds to the mechanism in LINE where the client uploads its public key to the messaging server, which then manages it by associating it with the user's account.

```
1  rule RegisterPK_A:
2    [ !PublicKey(~aID, pkA) ]
3    --[ PKRegisteredA(~aID, pkA) ]->
4    [ !KeyServer(~aID, pkA) ]
5
6  rule RegisterPK_B:
7    [ !PublicKey(~bID, pkB) ]
8    --[ PKRegisteredB(~bID, pkB) ]->
9    [ !KeyServer(~bID, pkB) ]
```

Here, `!PublicKey` ensures that key generation has been completed. The actions `PKRegisteredA` and `PKRegisteredB` explicitly record the registration event in the trace, while the conclusion `!KeyServer` represents the server's internal state, meaning that the registered public key remains stored and available for reference by other clients.

This model faithfully reflects LINE's security design: the server relays and stores public keys but never accesses private keys. Even under the assumption that the attacker fully controls the server, the correctness of key exchange is preserved. Thus, this rule provides the foundation for verifying whether clients can securely share keys in an untrusted server environment.

Computing the Shared Secret

We model the process by which `A` and `B` derive a shared secret (`SharedSecret`) using their own secret key and the other parth's public key. This value, represented as `ss` in our model, is directly used in subsequent encryption and decryption and forms the foundation of protocol security.

```
1  rule GenerateSharedSecretA:
2    let ss = pkB ^ ~skA in
3    [ !LongTermKey(~aID, ~skA), !PublicKey(~bID, pkB), In(pkB) ]
4    --[ A_SharedSecretGen(~aID, ~bID, pkB), SessionInit(), SessionSecret(~
         aID, ~bID, ss) ]->
5    [ !SharedSecret_A(ss, ~aID, ~bID) ]
6
7  rule GenerateSharedSecretB:
8    let ss = pkA ^ ~skB in
9    [ !LongTermKey(~bID, ~skB), !PublicKey(~aID, pkA), In(pkA) ]
10   --[ B_SharedSecretGen(~bID, ~aID, pkA), SessionInit(), SessionSecret(~
         bID, ~aID, ss) ]->
11   [ !SharedSecret_B(ss, ~bID, ~aID) ]
```

Here, the `let` syntax executes the Diffie–Hellman operation. For example, on `A`'s side, the shared secret is computed as `ss = pkB ^ ~skA`; on `B`'s side, as `ss = pkA ^ ~skB`, ensuring both parties derive the same value. This corresponds to the ECDH mechanism with Curve25519 used in LINE.

The premises ensure that each participant retains its own secret key (`!LongTermKey`), and that the other's public key has been registered (`!PublicKey`) and received over the network (`In`). This models the realistic risk of public key tampering by an attacker.

The actions `A_SharedSecretGen`, `B_SharedSecretGen`, `SessionInit`, and `SessionSecret` record session establishment events, which are later referenced in lemmas. Finally, the persistent facts `!SharedSecret_A` and `!SharedSecret_B` provide the basis for subsequent encryption and decryption rules. If the attacker manipulates public keys during transmission, inconsistent shared values are generated, which can be detected during verification.

Thus, the rules formally capture ECDH-based key exchange, serving as the core of security in LINE's one-to-one communication.

4.3 Modeling of Letter Sealing v1 and v2

After completing key exchange, we model the encryption, decryption, and attacker operations for both versions of Letter Sealing.

4.3.1 Modeling of Letter Sealing v1

Message Encryption and MAC

In Letter Sealing v1, the shared secret obtained from ECDH is combined with a random salt, and a key derivation function (KDF) is applied to generate the session key. Encryption and integrity protection are modeled abstractly using function symbols such as **enc**, **kdf**, and **mac**, and the necessary properties (e.g., decryption as the inverse operation of encryption, verifiability of MACs) are expressed as equations. The process is represented in two rules: preparation of encryption and the actual encryption with MAC computation.

```
1  rule TriggerEncrypt:
2    [ !SharedSecret_A(ss, ~aID, ~bID), Fr(~m), Fr(~salt)]
3    --[ TriggerEncryptMessage(ss, ~aID, ~bID) ]->
4    [ !TriggerEncryptData(~m, ~salt, ss, ~aID, ~bID) ]
5
6  rule EncryptAndTag:
7    [ !TriggerEncryptData(~m, ~salt, ss, ~aID, ~bID) ]
8    --[ Sent(~aID, ~bID, ~m) ]->
9    [ Out(< <~aID, ~bID>,
10         < pair(enc(~m, kdf(ss, ~salt)), ~salt),
11           mac(enc(~m, kdf(ss, ~salt)), kdf(ss, ~salt))>>)
12   ]
```

In the first rule `TriggerEncrypt`, sender `A` generates a fresh message and salt using `Fr`, ensuring session independence. The resulting `!TriggerEncryptData` stores the necessary information for encryption. In the subsequent rule `EncryptAndTag`, the ciphertext and MAC are computed using the derived session key and then output together with the salt and sender/receiver IDs.

Verification and Decryption of Received Messages
On the receiver side `B`, the goal is to ensure that only legitimate ciphertexts are accepted and decrypted.

```
1  rule ReceiveEncAndSalt_B:
2    [ !SharedSecret_B(ss, ~bID, ~aID), In(< <sender, ~bID>, <payload,
         mac_val> >) ]
3    --[ ReceivedByB(sender, payload) ]->
4    [ !ReceivedDataB(ss, ~bID, sender, payload, mac_val) ]
5
6  rule BVerifyTagAndDecrypt:
7    let
8      ct = fst(payload)
9      salt = snd(payload)
10     expected_mac = mac(payload, kdf(ss, salt))
11     m = dec(ct, kdf(ss, salt))
12   in
13   [ !ReceivedDataB(ss, ~bID, sender, payload, mac_val) ]
14   --[ Eq(mac_val, expected_mac), BVerifiedTag(m, sender, ~bID) ]->
15   [ !BDecryptedMessage(m) ]
```

The first rule `ReceiveEncAndSalt_B` records the arrival of ciphertext along with its salt and MAC, storing them as persistent data. The second rule `BVerifyTagAndDecrypt` regenerates the session key using the same KDF as the sender, recomputes the MAC, and compares it with the received value. If they match, the message is decrypted and stored as `!BDecryptedMessage`. The action `BVerifiedTag` confirms in the trace that the message has been authenticated, which can later be referenced in lemmas to prove authenticity and integrity.

4.3.2 Modeling of Letter Sealing v2

Figure 2 presents the state transition diagram of Letter Sealing v2, covering the entire process from encryption to decryption. The diagram shows how the sender generates a nonce, encrypts both the message body and associated metadata

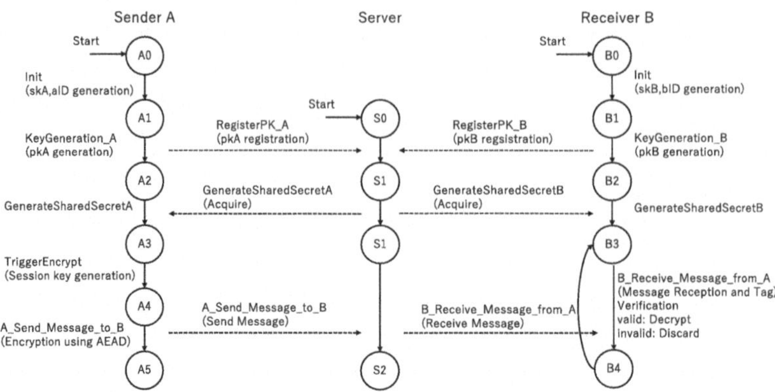

Fig. 2. State transition diagram of encryption and decryption in Letter Sealing v2.

using AES-GCM, and produces the ciphertext together with an authentication tag. On the receiver side, the tag is verified: if the verification succeeds, the ciphertext is decrypted to recover the message; if it fails, the message is discarded. This figure provides an overview of the complete behavior of Letter Sealing v2 and serves as a foundation for the subsequent rule-based modeling.

Message Encryption with AEAD and Tag Output

In Letter Sealing v2, encryption and integrity are integrated using the AEAD scheme AES-GCM, replacing the separate AES-CBC and MAC used in Letter Sealing v1. This design allows not only the message body but also metadata such as sender ID, receiver ID, and key IDs to be protected as Additional Authenticated Data (AAD), enabling detection of tampering during decryption.

The equation below ensures that ciphertext is uniquely defined by these parameters and that valid decryption always recovers the original plaintext:

```
1 functions: aead_enc/4, AEAD_Cipher/5
```

Based on this, the sender A encrypts and transmits a message as follows:

```
1  rule EncryptAndTag_B:
2    let
3      ad = <~bID, ~aID>
4      k  = kdf(ss, ~salt)
5      ct = aead_enc(~m, k, ~salt, ad)
6    in
7    [  TriggerEncryptData_B(~m, ~salt, ss, ~bID, ~aID) ]
8    --[ Sent(~bID, ~aID, ~m) ]->
9    [ Out( < ad, < ct, ~salt > > ),
10     !AEAD_Cipher(ss, ad, ~salt, ct, ~m) ]
```

Here, A uses the shared secret ss, generates a fresh message m, a random salt, and a fresh nonce. The nonce is critical for the security of AES-GCM; in LINEvs implementation, it is derived from a counter combined with randomness, abstracted here as Fr(~nonce).

The trace actions Sent and Sent_with_key record that a message was encrypted under a specific key, enabling later verification. The conclusion Out

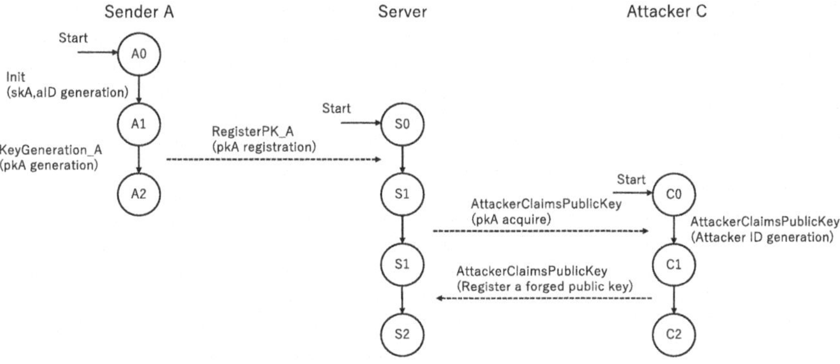

Fig. 3. State transition diagram of the `AttackerClaimsPublicKey` rule.

outputs the ciphertext-tag pair, which the receiver will use to perform both decryption and integrity verification. The tag is modeled as `get_tag`, representing the authentication tag of AES-GCM.

In this way, Tamarin Prover modeling for Letter Sealing v2 faithfully reflects the AEAD design, integrating encryption and authentication as a unified process rather than separate steps.

Explicit Attacker Conditions

We explicitly model the attacker's behaviors assumed for this protocol. In Tamarin Prover, the attacker is based on the strong Dolev-Yao model, which allows interception, modification, and retransmission of all messages exchanged over the public network. Furthermore, by appropriately adding rules, specific threats such as public key impersonation and key leakage can be injected into the system. Below, we define three typical attacker behaviors related to the security of Letter Sealing and explicitly describe them as rules.

`AttackerClaimsPublicKey`: Figure 3 illustrates the state transition diagram of this rule. The attacker forges another user's public key as their own. This reproduces an impersonation attack in a public key infrastructure, modeling a situation where the attacker can register a fake public key for an arbitrary ID.

`ServerManipulatesHeader`: Figure 4 illustrates the state transition diagram of this rule. The attacker tampers with the header of a sent message (the sender ID). This represents an attack in which the server or intermediary, if untrusted, inserts a different ID to impersonate the legitimate sender.

`Reveal_LTK`: Figure 5 illustrates the state transition diagram of this rule. The attacker obtains the client's long-term secret key (Long-Term Key). This corresponds to device compromise or insider threats and is necessary to verify security properties such as forward secrecy and impersonation detection in the presence of key leakage.

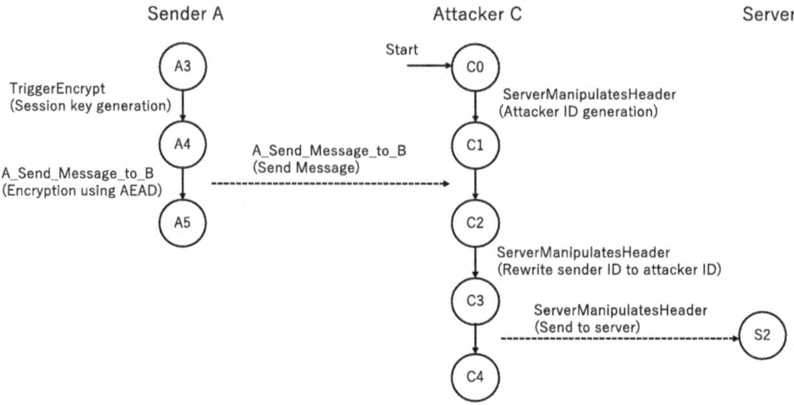

Fig. 4. State transition diagram of the `ServerManipulatesHeader` rule.

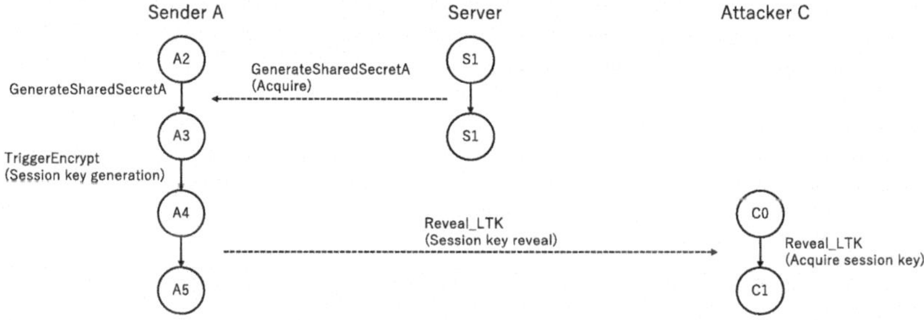

Fig. 5. State transition diagram of the `Reveal_LTK` rule.

These behaviors are described in Tamarin Prover as the following rules:

```
1  rule AttackerClaimsPublicKey:
2    [ Fr(~attackerID), In(pk) ]
3    -->
4    [ !PublicKey(attackerID, pk) ]
5
6  rule ServerManipulatesHeader:
7    [ Fr(~attackerID),
8      In(< <aID, bID>, payload >)
9    ]
10   -->
11   [ Out(< <~attackerID, bID>, payload >) ]
12
13 rule Reveal_LTK:
14   [ !LongTermKey(id, sk) ]
15   --[ Corrupted(id) ]->
16   [ Out(sk) ]
```

The first rule `AttackerClaimsPublicKey` creates a situation where the attacker generates a new ID and binds an arbitrary public key to it. This allows verification of the possibility that the receiver mistakenly believes the attacker's public key belongs to a legitimate user and performs key exchange with it.

The next rule `ServerManipulatesHeader` represents an attacker tampering with a sent message by rewriting the sender ID and retransmitting it. By explicitly modeling such attacks, it is possible to verify whether properties such as metadata tamper detection and sender authentication hold correctly.

The final rule `Reveal_LTK` models the impact of long-term key leakage. By recording the action `Corrupted(id)` in the trace, it becomes possible to track when key leakage occurred during verification and analyze its effects on subsequent communications (e.g., whether forward secrecy is maintained).

In this way, explicitly modeling attacker behaviors as rules enables Tamarin Prover to comprehensively reproduce realistic threat scenarios and make protocol security verification more rigorous.

4.4 Restrictions and Security Verification

This section describes the restrictions applied to our modeling and the lemmas used to verify protocol security.

Restriction for Verifying Session Uniqueness
As the most basic restriction, this study introduces `single_session`. This requires that only one session occurs, eliminating complex cases where multiple key exchanges or encrypted communications between `A` and `B` run simultaneously. By imposing this restriction, the verification target is limited to a single communication, making it easier to focus on attacker behavior. In practice, LINE's 1-to-1 communication establishes sessions sequentially for each user, and thus, this simplification does not contradict the real usage model.

```
1 restriction single_session:
2   "All #i #j. SessionInit() @ i & SessionInit() @ j ==> #i = #j"
```

This restriction means that "for any two points in time `#i`, `#j`, if `SessionInit` is observed at both, then they must be the same point." In other words, multiple session initialization events are not allowed during a protocol execution. As a result, security verification can focus on whether sending, receiving, and verification are correctly associated with one session.

Lemma for Verifying Message Secrecy
As the most fundamental security requirement, we verify that the message body `m` sent by the sender does not leak to the attacker. This is the central purpose of an E2EE protocol, guaranteeing that even if the attacker can intercept all communications on the network, the plaintext can never be reconstructed.

In Tamarin Prover, the attacker's knowledge is represented as a special fact `K(m)`. That is, if the attacker can reconstruct the message `m`, then `K(m)` holds at that point in time. Conversely, if `K(m)` never holds at any time, it means that the attacker cannot obtain the message.

```
1 lemma message_secrecy:
2   "All aID bID m #i.
3       Sent(aID, bID, m) @ i
4       ==> not(Ex #j. K(m) @ j)"
```

Lemma for Verifying Authenticity
We verify authenticity, which guarantees that the message received by the recipient was indeed sent by the legitimate sender. If this property holds, it prevents the recipient from accepting forged messages or those sent by an impersonator.

```
1 lemma auth_A_believes_B_sent:
2   "All m aID bID #i.
3      AVerifiedTag(m, bID, aID) @ i
4      ==> Ex #j. (Sent(bID, aID, m) @ j & j < i)"
```

Lemma for Verifying Resilience against Replay Attacks
We verify resilience against replay attacks. A replay attack occurs when the attacker saves ciphertext previously sent by the legitimate sender and resends it later to deceive the recipient. If the recipient accepts the same ciphertext multiple times as a legitimate message, it could lead to incorrect processing or duplicate execution, causing serious security problems.

The property that the same message is never authenticated multiple times on the recipient's side is expressed in the following lemma:

```
1 lemma no_replay_to_A:
2   "All m sender recipient #i #j.
3      AVerifiedTag(m, sender, recipient) @ i
4      & AVerifiedTag(m, sender, recipient) @ j
5      ==> #i = #j"
```

Lemma for Verifying Metadata Tampering Detection
As a property specific to Letter Sealing v2, we verify that metadata tampering detection is correctly reflected. Letter Sealing v2 adopts AEAD encryption using AES-GCM, in which not only the plaintext but also identifiers such as the sender ID and recipient ID are included as AAD. As a result, even if the attacker does not tamper with the ciphertext itself but rewrites only the metadata (e.g., sender ID or recipient ID), verification at decryption will always fail.

To reflect this behavior in our model, we define the following lemma:

```
1 lemma metadata_tampering_detection:
2   "All m ss ct salt sender recipient #i #j.
3      (BVerifiedTag(m, sender, recipient) @ #i
4       & AEAD_Cipher(ss, <sender, recipient>, salt, ct, m) @ #j)
5      ==> (Ex #k. Sent(sender, recipient, m) @ #k)"
```

To summarize, in Letter Sealing v1, the integrity of ciphertext was guaranteed by the MAC, but the integrity of metadata was not ensured. In contrast, Letter Sealing v2 adopts AEAD, making it clear that both the message body and accompanying metadata can be protected as a single unit.

5 Verification Results

In this section, we present the results of the formal verification using the Tamarin Prover's model constructed in Sect. 4, in response to the unresolved issues identified in Sect. 3.4. In particular, we organize which security properties are satisfied by Letter Sealing v1 and v2, and clarify to what extent the vulnerabilities pointed out in Sect. 3.4 have been resolved.

Table 1 compares the results reported in existing studies with the verification results obtained in this study. This made it possible to comprehensively evaluate the security of both versions, including properties that had not been examined in previous studies.

5.1 Considerations on Letter Sealing v1

This verification revealed that the one-to-one communication protocol in LINE's Letter Sealing v1 does not satisfy several basic and advanced security properties, including metadata protection, destination validation, and anonymity (of sender, receiver, and all participants). The absence of these properties leads to the following concrete risks and potential attacks.

Lack of Metadata Tampering Detection: In the message structure of Letter Sealing v1, metadata such as sender ID, receiver ID, version, and encryption scheme are all transmitted in plaintext as headers without encryption. As a result, an attacker can easily monitor network traffic and identify communication patterns, such as who is messaging whom and when. Such leakage of metadata results in loss of anonymity and severe privacy violations, including the visualization of social relationships.

Lack of Destination Validation: In the message structure of Letter Sealing v1, the receiver ID is included in plaintext, and there is no mechanism to verify its validity. Due to this design flaw, an attacker can tamper with the receiver ID of an encrypted message and redirect it to any third party. The absence of destination validation poses a significant security risk in terms of both information leakage and loss of reliability.

Lack of Anonymity (Sender, Receiver, and All Participants): In Letter Sealing v1, since the sender and receiver IDs are explicitly included in the message, an external attacker can identify the communicators and their relationships. Furthermore, it is possible to identify all participants involved in the communication, meaning that participant anonymity is also not achieved. This represents a critical flaw for applications that prioritize privacy, such as anonymous bulletin boards and secure chat services.

5.2 Considerations on Letter Sealing v2

In the considerations on Letter Sealing v1 (Sect. 5.1), the focus was mainly on the fact that important security requirements such as authentication and integrity were not sufficiently satisfied. In contrast, this section focuses on the newly implemented security functions and improvements in Letter Sealing v2, and organizes how the existing vulnerabilities have been resolved. In particular, we evaluate the specific aspects of security enhancement achieved through design improvements such as the use of AAD and the change of encryption mode.

Authentication: By including the sender ID and receiver ID in the AAD, the receiver can verify whether the origin of the message is legitimate. Furthermore, with tamper detection in place, resistance against impersonation and spoofed transmissions has been strengthened.

Integrity: AES-GCM generates an authentication tag along with the ciphertext, enabling the receiver to detect any tampering at the same time as decryption. This resolves the problem of lack of message integrity that existed in Letter Sealing v1.

Replay Attack Resistance: By attaching different salt and version values to each message, the receiver can detect retransmission (replay) of the same message, thereby ensuring the session's uniqueness.

Metadata Tampering Detection: Tampering with or tracking of metadata included in the communication (such as sender ID, receiver ID, and key ID) has become difficult, thereby improving communication privacy.

Destination Validation: By including tamper detection on the receiver ID within the AAD, the risk of misdelivery to unintended third parties or tampering-based forwarding has been mitigated.

5.3 Summary

With these improvements, the overall security of one-to-one communication in LINE has been significantly enhanced. Users' risks of message eavesdropping, tampering, and unauthorized sending and receiving have been reduced, establishing a foundation for safer communication.

While several properties, such as authentication and integrity, have been improved in Letter Sealing v2, several vulnerabilities remain in important security requirements such as anonymity, forward secrecy, and backward secrecy. Thus, although Letter Sealing v2 shows significant progress in protocol security, fundamental design issues related to user privacy and the confidentiality of long-term communications still persist. In future improvements, enhancing anonymity and introducing a key update mechanism will be indispensable.

6 Conclusion

In this paper, we used Tamarin Prover to conduct a formal and comprehensive security verification of Letter Sealing v1 and v2, used in LINE's E2EE one-to-one communication protocol. Previous studies have not comprehensively verified the security properties of these protocols, and Letter Sealing v2 had not been verified at all.

We explicitly defined multiple security properties as described in [10] and constructed verification code accordingly. As a result, we revealed that Letter

Sealing v1 lacks several important properties, including authenticity, integrity, forward secrecy, replay attack resistance, metadata protection, destination validation, and sender/receiver anonymity.

On the other hand, in Letter Sealing v2, the protocol design was significantly revised, and the introduction of AEAD and the use of AAD led to substantial improvements in authenticity, integrity, and replay attack resistance. However, forward secrecy and sender/receiver anonymity are still not guaranteed, leaving vulnerabilities against long-term key leakage and traffic analysis attacks.

These results indicate that while LINE's E2EE communication has achieved a certain level of security improvement through version updates, it does not fully satisfy the ideal requirements of E2EE, highlighting the need for further enhancements in the future.

Acknowledgments. This work has been supported by JST AIP Acceleration Research JPMJCR24U1, Japan, JSPS KAKENHI Grant Number JP24H00696, and JST START Project Promotion Type (Supporting Small Business Innovation Research (SBIR) Phase 1), Japan Grant Number JPMJST2552.

References

1. Albrecht, M.R., Dowling, B., Jones, D.: Formal analysis of multi-device group messaging in whatsapp. In: Fehr, S., Fouque, P. (eds.) EUROCRYPT 2025, Part VIII. LNCS, vol. 15608, pp. 242–271. Springer, Cham (2025). https://doi.org/10.1007/978-3-031-91101-9_9
2. AnonymousGithub: tamarin_line: A library for working with tamarin-prover (2025). https://anonymous.4open.science/r/tamarin_line_ICISC2025-8C44. Accessed 24 Sept 2025
3. Forming LY Corporation: LY Communications Factbook. Technical report (2024). https://lycomm.co.jp/hubfs/LYCommCorprateSite_Renewal2025/pdf/2024_lycomm_FACTBOOK_EN.pdf
4. Isobe, T., Minematsu, K.: Breaking message integrity of an end-to-end encryption scheme of LINE. In: López, J., Zhou, J., Soriano, M. (eds.) ESORICS 2018, Part II. LNCS, vol. 11099, pp. 249–268. Springer, Cham (2018). https://doi.org/10.1007/978-3-319-98989-1_13
5. Kimura, H., Ito, R., Minematsu, K., Shiraki, S., Isobe, T.: Not in the prophecies: practical attacks on nostr. In: 10th IEEE European Symposium on Security and Privacy, EuroS&P 2025, Venice, Italy, 30 June–4 July 2025. IEEE (2025)
6. LINE Corporation: LINE Encryption Overview. Technical report, LINE Corporation (2021). https://scdn.line-apps.com/stf/linecorp/en/csr/line-encryption-whitepaper-ver2.1.pdf. Accessed 22 Aug 2025
7. Meier, S., Schmidt, B., Cremers, C., Basin, D.A.: The TAMARIN prover for the symbolic analysis of security protocols. In: Sharygina, N., Veith, H. (eds.) CAV 2013. LNCS, vol. 8044, pp. 696–701. Springer, Cham (2013). https://doi.org/10.1007/978-3-642-39799-8_48
8. Paterson, K.G., Scarlata, M., Truong, K.T.: Three lessons from threema: analysis of a secure messenger. In: Calandrino, J.A., Troncoso, C. (eds.) 32nd USENIX Security Symposium, USENIX Security 2023, Anaheim, CA, USA, 9–11 August 2023,

pp. 1289–1306. USENIX Association (2023). https://www.usenix.org/conference/usenixsecurity23/presentation/paterson
9. Shi, C., Yoneyama, K.: Verification of line encryption version 1.0 using proverif. IEICE Trans. Inf. Syst. **102**(8), 1439–1448 (2019)
10. Unger, N., et al.: SoK: secure messaging. In: 2015 IEEE Symposium on Security and Privacy, SP 2015, San Jose, CA, USA, 17–21 May 2015, pp. 232–249. IEEE Computer Society (2015). https://doi.org/10.1109/SP.2015.22, https://doi.org/10.1109/SP.2015.22

Revealing the Chain with pytm-Seq: Approach for Multi-step Threat Detection

Geunwoo Baek, Jiwon Kwak, and Seungjoo Kim(✉)

School of Cybersecurity, Korea University, Seoul 02841, South Korea
{sinse100,jwkwak4031,skim71}@korea.ac.kr

Abstract. As software complexity increases and cyberattacks grow more sophisticated, the need for tools that can automatically identify threats within systems has become increasingly evident. However, prior research has primarily focused on detecting attacks or vulnerabilities at individual points within a system, limiting its ability to identify multi-step threats that arise when adversaries exploit the order in which data is transferred among system components. To address this limitation, this paper extends the Data Flow Diagram (DFD) metamodel of the OWASP-ODTM project by incorporating additional information such as data-transfer sequence. Using this extended metamodel, we developed a methodology capable of automatically identifying multi-step threats within a system. We further implemented this methodology in pytm, an existing threat-modelling automation tool, and proposed an enhanced version named pytm-Seq. To demonstrate that pytm-Seq can identify multi-step threats exploited in real-world attacks, we analyzed 52 incidents and derived 7 multi-step threat patterns. We then verify whether these patterns can be detected within DFDs using pytm-Seq. Finally, we quantitatively evaluate the tool's detection accuracy for the patterns and observe an accuracy of 86%. These findings confirm that the proposed methodology and tool can support multi-step threat analysis by accounting for interactions among multiple components and the sequence of data transfers. (All of the case study results and our tool is open to the public through the following url https://github.com/sinse100/pytm-Seq).

Keywords: Threat modeling · Threat modeling automation · Multi-Step threat

1 Introduction

Threat modelling has gained attention as a methodology that identifies and mitigates potential threats early in the system-development process, thereby reducing unnecessary development costs and improving overall security levels [17]. Reports such as those by IBM Systems show that threat modelling enhances security in practice, and fixing vulnerabilities at the design stage is 10 to 100 times less costly than patching them later through code modification [5,31].

H. Seo (Ed.): ICISC 2025, LNCS 16487, pp. 257–277, 2026.
https://doi.org/10.1007/978-981-95-8034-7_14

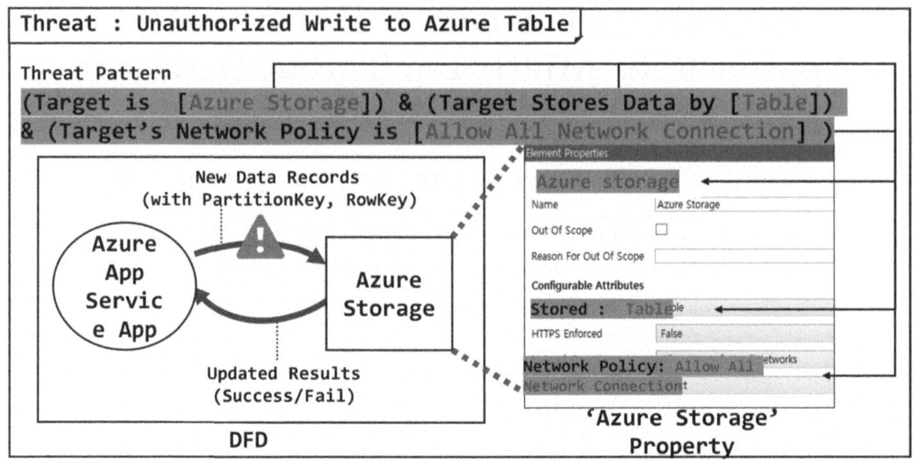

Fig. 1. Threat identification in MS-TMT

However, due to the comprehensive nature of threat modelling—which aims to identify all potential threats related to system components—manual execution can be extremely time-consuming. According to a report by Security Compass, threat modelling for small- to medium-sized organizations takes an average of 18 h [6]. Consequently, many organizations have adopted automated tools such as Microsoft Threat Modelling Tool (MS-TMT) to reduce the costs [14,20,23,24].

Nevertheless, widely used tools primarily focus on identifying threats at the level of individual system components, limiting their ability to capture multi-step threats based on data-flow order or functional interaction [12–14,20,23,24]. For example, TOCTOU (Time-of Check-to-Time-of-Use), a multi-step threat, occurs when a system reads a value and then performs an operation (e.g., write/execute) based on that value. If the value changes between the read and write stages, unintended behavior can occur. An attacker can exploit a sequence such as read → write → state change → read to trigger unauthorized operations [19]. Existing automated tools such as MS-TMT fail to account for such ordered sequences between functions (e.g., read/write) or consider threats only from the perspective of a single component such as a database. This limitation is also evident in the operation of MS-TMT. For instance, when identifying the threat "Unauthorized write to Azure Table", MS-TMT performs the following steps (Fig. 1):

1. MS-TMT selects one of the data flows in the modelled DFD.
2. It checks whether the destination of the data flow is an Azure Storage component, whether the component stores data in Table form, and whether the network access policy allows arbitrary access.
3. If all conditions are met, it marks the result as Matched and reports the threat; otherwise, it repeats steps (2)–(3) for the next flow

Contribution. To overcome the limitations, this study proposes a method for identifying multi-step threats within a single system that may occur when data is transmitted or processed in a specific order. The approach utilizes a DFD metamodel enriched with additional attributes, such as the order of data flows and the functional types of processes. Specifically, we extended the DFD metamodel provided by OWASP's ODTM project by adding two attributes—data flow order and process function type—and defined multi-step threat patterns that leverage these properties. The defined patterns were then converted into a format recognizable by the existing threat-modelling tool pytm Seq, enabling the automated identification of attack paths corresponding to multi-step threat patterns within a DFD. To demonstrate the applicability of the proposed method in detecting real-world multi-step threats, we analyzed 52 previously reported attack cases and derived 7 patterns, which were subsequently applied to pytm-Seq to identify the patterns. Finally, a quantitative evaluation was conducted to assess how accurately the tool could identify the defined patterns within a DFD, achieving an accuracy rate of 86%. These results demonstrate that the proposed approach and tool can be effectively utilized for the automated detection of multi-step threats within a system.

Paper Organization. The remainder of this paper is organized as follows: Sect. 2 introduces the background of related research. Section 3 reviews existing studies. Section 4 presents the proposed methodology for deriving and identifying multi-step threats, along with its tool-level implementation results. Section 5 applies the proposed methodology to the smart-contract domain and presents a case study demonstrating its effectiveness in detecting multi-step threats. Section 6 evaluates the detection accuracy of the proposed method and tool. Section 7 discusses limitations and future research directions. Finally, Sect. 8 summarizes the key findings and concludes the paper.

2 Background

2.1 Threat Modeling Methodologies

Threat modeling is a methodology to identify all known threats to a system early in system development [4,10,27,28]. As threat modeling has spread across organizations, a variety of methodologies have been developed. Below we summarize three threat modeling methodologies—TARA, LINDDUN and STRIDE—that have been most widely used in research over the past five years [16].

STRIDE. STRIDE is a methodology proposed by Microsoft for identifying 6 types of threats: Spoofing, Tampering, Repudiation, Information Disclosure, Denial of Service, and Elevation of Privilege. The STRIDE procedure consists of (1) creating a DFD in sufficient detail from an analyst's perspective, (2) defining the analysis units(elements or interactions) and deriving STRIDE threats, (3) identifying the overall attack scenarios, and (4) performing risk assessment and selecting mitigations for identified scenarios [35].

LINDDUN. LINDDUN is a privacy-centred threat modeling methodology proposed by Deng et al. in 2011, motivated by the shortage at that time of privacy-focused threat modeling approaches. LINDDUN classifies privacy threats into Linkability (the ability to link different data/actions to the same subject), Identifiability (identification of an individual from combinations of identifiers), Non-repudiation (actions can be traced), Detectability (the mere existence of data/actions is observable and sensitive context is ex-posed), Information Disclosure (unintended disclosure during storage/transmission/processing), Unawareness (lack of awareness of collection purposes/rights), and Non-compliance (design/operation inconsistent with regulations). The LINDDUN procedure is as follows: (1) model the analysis target using a DFD, (2) apply the LINDDUN categories to each DFD element to derive potential threats, (3) construct Threat Trees representing privacy violation scenarios per category, and (4) perform risk assessment, select and apply mitigations for identified scenarios [32].

TARA. TARA quantifies and links threats, vulnerabilities and impacts to support risk based decision making and optimization of mitigations, focusing on mission-critical domains such as defense. Its primary objective is to proactively identify weak points and the attack surface before attacks occur, and to produce risk and mitigation effectiveness metrics. The procedure comprises three stages—KM (Knowledge Management), CTSA(Cyber Threat Susceptibility Analysis), and CRRA(Cyber Risk Remediation Assessment). In KM, information about threats and mitigations is collected and organized into a database; in CTSA, the system attack surface is identified and risk is estimated; and in CRRA, optimal mitigations are selected based on the CTSA risk estimates [37].

2.2 Threat Modeling Automation Techniques

This section provides background on five threat modeling tools [14,20,23,24,29]. The tools selected here include four that are widely used in practice and mainly focus on security threat analysis (Microsoft-TMT, pytm, IriusRisk, OWASP-TD) and one that addresses both privacy and security threats with substantial related research (SPARTA). Background for each tool is as follows:

MS-TMT (Microsoft Threat Modeling Tool). MS-TMT is a threat modeling automation tool developed by Microsoft [20]. An analyst constructs a DFD using drag-and drop; MS-TMT then automatically identifies STRIDE threats based on that DFD and generates reports. Although not open source, MS-TMT provides templates for analysts to de-fine domain-specific threats and assets. Analysts can define stencils that concretize DFD elements for their domain, and they can define domain-specific threats within templates [12].

pytm. pytm is an open-source threat modeling automation tool developed by OWASP [23]. Analysts declare system elements and attributes in Python code to generate a system model in DFD or Sequence Diagram form; pytm's threat-identification engine compares the input model against threat patterns defined as JSON and presents identified threats in an HTML report. Analysts can freely add threat patterns. However, since it uses a programming style, pytm has a steeper entry barrier for non-developer analysts [12].

IriusRisk. IriusRisk is a commercial, web-based threat modeling tool that offers drag and-drop DFD modelling, many threat libraries (CAPEC/ATT&CK, etc.), regulation (e.g. GDPR) mapping, reporting, and integration with vulnerability scanning tools [14]. By providing risk assessment functionality, IriusRisk allows analysts to construct qualitative and quantitative metrics aligned with organizational policies and provides trace ability matrices between requirements, mitigations and test cases to facilitate analysis. It also supports role-based access control (RBAC) and project governance. However, analysts cannot define domain-specialized threat detection or domain-specific assets.

OWASP-TD(OWASP Threat Dragon). OWASP-TD is an open-source tool supporting both desktop and web, offering drag-and-drop DFD construction and threat/mitigation management [24]. The related Dragon-GPT project provides AI-based analysis using model file inputs. OWASP-TD project files are typically in human-readable formats such as JSON, making version control and review easy; outputs include diagram images and summary reports of identified issues. At present, automatic threat identification is at the testing stage, so OWASP-TD's automatic identification capabilities are substantially more limited than pytm(for example, it ships with fewer built-in patterns).

SPARTA. SPARTA, developed at KU Leuven, distinguishes itself by jointly considering security and privacy threats [29]. SPARTA supports drag-and-drop DFD modelling and assigns asset values to DFD elements. It applies Monte Carlo simulation to each component of risk in the FAIR (Factor Analysis of Information Risk) model to numerically reflect uncertainties in threat occurrence probability rather than a binary safe/vulnerable judgement. Based on this, it computes and ranks threat risks to enable more realistic risk management. However, SPARTA does not provide detailed explanations or concrete remediation steps for individual threats and is not open source, limiting modification.

3 Related Works

This section summarizes research trends in threat modeling methodologies and related automation tools and techniques discussed in Sect. 2. In particular, for prior studies directly related to threat modeling automation, we present their limitations and then indicate how our work differs.

3.1 Threat Modeling Methodologies

This section presents recent research trends related to the threat-modelling methodologies introduced in Sect. 2, namely TARA, LINDDUN, and STRIDE. The details are as follows.

Extension of the STRIDE Methodology. The STRIDE methodology has been continuously expanded in response to changes in analytical domains and evolving environments. These extensions have primarily aimed to address the limitation that the original STRIDE, being security-centric, could not adequately capture privacy, physical, or APT-related threats. First, Monteuuis et al. (2018) pointed out that in autonomous vehicle environments, STRIDE fails to account for threats such as Confusion, where even data from trusted sources may be mishandled due to malfunction, and Linkability, where an attacker can infer the identity of a data owner by analyzing correlations among data (equivalent to Linkability in Sect. 2.2) [21]. To address this, they proposed STRIDELC (STRIDE + Linkability + Confusion), which enhances the original security-oriented model with aspects of privacy protection and data accuracy. Later, Hollerer et al. (2021) observed that attacks are no longer limited to single intrusions but often involve persistent behaviors such as privilege escalation and lateral movement, characteristic of Advanced Persistent Threats (APTs) [11]. Accordingly, they proposed STRIDELM, which extends STRIDE by adding a Lateral Movement category, and further applied it to Industrial Control System(ICS) and Operational Technology (OT) environments, incorporating safety properties. STRIDELM represents an evolution from STRIDELC, which supplemented information reliability and privacy, towards addressing the persistence and propagation of attacks. Finally, Srikumar et al. (2022) argued that STRIDE still primarily focuses on cyber threats and fails to reflect physical aspects such as device tampering, sensor spoofing, and unauthorized physical access in IoT environments. To overcome this, they proposed the STRIPED methodology, which adds Physical(P) as a new threat category. STRIPED enables systematic identification of physically based threats and reflects the security requirements of IoT and Cyber-Physical Systems(CPS) domains [30]. In summary, as shown in these studies, STRIDE has evolved through successive extensions—from security-centric → privacy-centric → APT-centric → physical-security-centric approaches.

Extension of the LINDDUN Methodology. The LINDDUN methodology has long been criticized for its complexity and length, which make it difficult for non-experts or industry practitioners to apply due to its intricate threat-tree structures used for threat identification and refinement. Recognizing this issue, subsequent studies have extended LINDDUN in directions such as lightweight adaptation, domain specialization, and granular unit analysis. First, Sion et al. (2020) highlighted that traditional LINDDUN has a steep learning curve and requires excessive time to perform. They proposed LINDDUN GO, which introduces structured question sets and threat cards [36]. This simplified the complex threat trees into 35 core cards, reducing the typical analysis time from over 40 h to about 1–2 h. Next, Antonio et al. (2021) argued that LINDDUN does not reflect phase-specific threat characteristics during identification and authentication processes. They proposed a phase-based threat-derivation structure that considers the privacy characteristics of each step [26], thereby addressing the granularity issue unresolved by both LINDDUN and LINDDUN GO. Subsequently, Raciti et al. (2023) pointed out that LINDDUN still does not adequately account for domain specificity, and proposed 56 privacy threat types tailored to the automotive domain including 8 new threats not represented in existing LINDDUN categories [25]. This study is recognized as a representative attempt to evolve LINDDUN into a domain specific privacy-threat modelling framework. In summary, research on LINDDUN has progressed along the trajectory of procedure simplification → phase specific structural enhancement → industrial-domain expansion.

Extension of the TARA Methodology. The original TARA methodology has also faced ongoing criticism for its insufficient reflection of domain-specific characteristics and its low procedural efficiency due to operational complexity. Consequently, subsequent research has evolved towards domain specialization, procedural clarity, and efficiency enhancement. Zainab et al. (2019) noted that conventional TARA struggles to ensure alignment with cybersecurity regulations and standards(e.g., UN R155, ISO/SAE 21434) and lacks linkage among threat catalogues [3]. Specifically, traditional TARA shows inconsistency in threat-path analysis because it cannot comprehensively reference multiple threat databases. To address this, they proposed a TARA Threat Catalogue that integrates the MITRE ATT&CK framework, VicOne's Automotive Attack Matrix, and UN R155 Annex 5 threat lists. This work expanded TARA beyond a project-level risk-identification tool into a systematic threat-reference model aligned with international standards and practical frameworks. Later, Rusydi et al. (2021) observed that TARA requires excessive time and resources, and suffers from unclear task allocation and poor consistency between phases, reducing reliability [18]. They empirically confirmed that, in real-world practice, collaborative analyses are of ten delayed due to ambiguous role boundaries. To mitigate this, they proposed the TAARA(Trigger–Acquire–Analysis–Report–Action) methodology, which subdivides and clearly defines each phase of TARA. TAARA specifies inputs, outputs, and roles for each stage, thereby ensuring traceability and consistency in analysis, while allowing certain steps to be executed in parallel to reduce total analysis time. Additionally, it formalized inter-team communication to alleviate the subjectivity issues in TARA.

3.2 Threat Modeling Automation Techniques

This section summarizes recent research trends and limitations in automated threat modeling techniques and tools that are closely related to this study, and highlights how the proposed work differs from them. The details are as follows.

Threat Identification Techniques Based on Single Elements. Although numerous studies have attempted to improve existing automated threat modeling tools widely used in organizations—such as MS-TMT, IriusRisk, OWASP Threat Dragon, and pytm—most have focused on developing tools specialized for specific domains. For example, Flå et al.(2021) developed a domain-specific TMT template for smart grid environments [8]. Leveraging TMT's customizable template feature, they proposed a smart-grid DFD stencil and a STRIDE-based threat library that reflect communication interfaces and control processes of power networks. This enabled automatic identification of

OT(Operational Technology) threats—such as GPS spoofing and remote circuit-breaker manipulation—that were not addressed by traditional IT-centric tools. Similarly, Jansson (2021) applied MS-TMT to perform threat modeling for Software as a Medical Device (SaMD) and linked it to ISO 14971 risk management processes and EU-MDR(European Union Medical Device Regulation) requirements. By using TMT's template feature, he defined domain-specific stencils(e.g., medical sensors, analysis servers, hospital networks) and designed a STRIDE+DREAD-based risk assessment template [15]. This approach enabled modeling of domain-specific threats such as data integrity loss, manipulation of diagnostic algorithms, and misuse of patient data. However, these studies inherited MS-TMT's fundamental limitation: they could not model causal relationships among threats or identify attacks involving multiple interacting system elements.

Threat Identification Techniques Based on Multiple Elements. Shamal et al. proposed a methodology that combines DFDs with Use-Case Diagrams (including task and functional usage scenarios) to more accurately determine the possibility of abnormal or incorrect data flows by analyzing the flow of information from external entities to sensitive processes [7]. In particular, by integrating information provided by Use-Case Diagrams—such as personas, roles, tasks, and attacker motivations and capabilities with the details of multiple system assets, their method enables a more contextual judgement of potential data flow anomalies. However, this approach has the limitation of requiring additional models beyond the DFD to analyze exploitable assets and their interdependencies. Meanwhile, Hanaa et al. (2022) proposed a method that enables the analysis of incorrect data flows using only a single DFD model. Their approach explicitly specifies how input data is transformed during output (e.g., whether one data item is replicated into multiple outputs or multiple inputs are merged into one) and assigns priorities to output data flows within the same process [2]. However, this method requires the analyst to manually specify the data flows to be verified within the tool, as well as to define the start and end points of the information flow, resulting in significant reliance on human intervention. Sara et al. (2024) proposed the STRIDEThreatAttack.py tool, which represents threat patterns within a DFD using source nodes, destination nodes, and the data flows between them. The tool identifies threats based on these relationships and connects the destination of one threat pattern to the source of another to construct an attack graph [1]. However, this linkage does not consider constraints such as data flow or functional execution order. Consequently, as attacks are identified without incorporating order or temporal dependencies, the generated attack graph may contain infeasible attack paths. Similarly, Fu et al. (2025) proposed the AGGTA framework, which leverages the Meta Attack Language(MAL) to integrate CAPEC and ATT&CK information, automatically generating and visualizing attack graphs. MAL defines logical dependencies(OR, AND) and transition logic based on network connectivity between attack stages, enabling representation of the logical flow of attacks. However, it does not specify the temporal or sequential order of data transfers necessary for attack success.

As a result, AGGTA fails to account for execution-order constraints in multi-step attacks, and its attack path and success probability analysis rely mainly on the existence of network connections and individual component vulnerabilities, limiting its ability to accurately capture threat propagation dependent on data flow order [9]. Additionally, Anh et al. (2025) proposed a cloud-domain-specific approach that augments DFD elements with additional attributes(e.g., cloud VMs) and compares them with predefined threat patterns representing specific data movements between elements [34]. In defining cloud-domain threat patterns, they explicitly incorporated whether the data flow crosses a trust boundary—an important distinction in cloud architectures. However, their method did not include sequence information for data flows, thereby limiting its ability to identify multi-step threats that depend on execution order.

4 pytm-Seq: a Pytm-Based Tool for Multi-step Threat Detection Using Data-Transfer Order

This section presents a methodology that detects multi-step threats by leveraging data transfer order and function-type information in DFDs, and describes the implementation of that methodology in the tool pytm-Seq. The method consists of four stages: (1) adding attribute information to the DFD metamodel to support multi-step threat pattern identification; (2) defining multi-step threat patterns based on real attack cases and publicly available vulnerability information; (3) analyzing whether the defined multi-step threat patterns exist in a given DFD; and (4) generating multi-step threat findings and an analysis report from the analysis results. We implemented this methodology by extending the open-source threat modeling tool pytm, thereby automating the proposed process. The resulting tool, pytm-Seq, accepts as input DFDs and multi-step threat patterns encoded in JSON. It then uses a data-transfer-order-aware search algorithm to determine whether the patterns appear in the DFD and outputs the analysis results in HTML. The pytm-Seq implementation is available in the associated GitHub repository (Fig. 2).

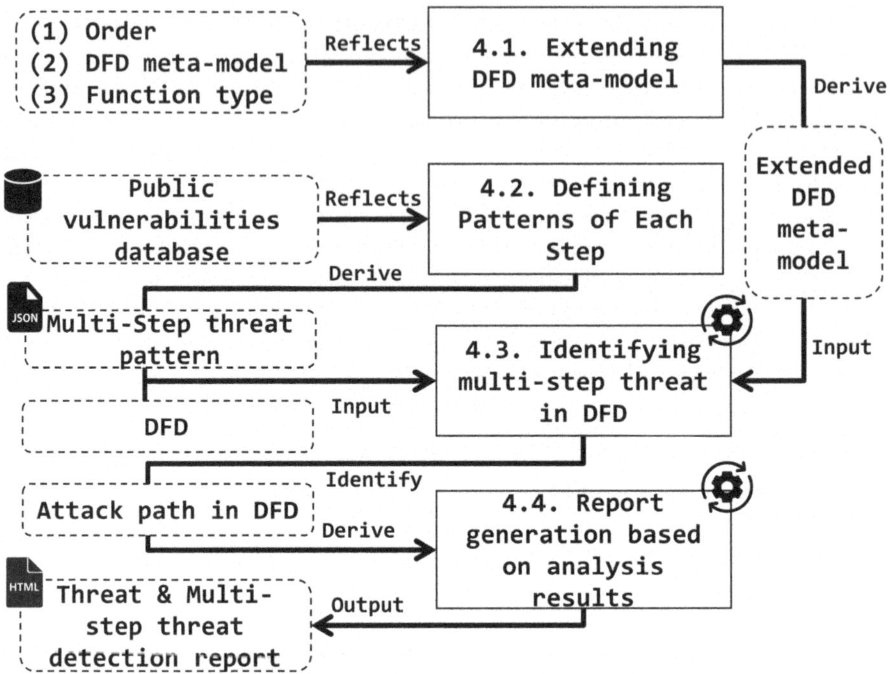

Fig. 2. Overview of our approach

4.1 DFD Metamodel Extension

This section describes the step of adding data-transfer order and function-type information to the DFD metamodel. Prior to extending the metamodel, we selected the DFD metamodel provided by the OWASP-ODTM (Ontology-Driven Threat Modeling) project as the baseline [22]. We then extended that metamodel by adding a 'FunctionType' attribute to processes (to represent the type of function the process provides) and an Order attribute to data flows (to represent transfer order). Figure 3 below shows the DFD metamodel after these extensions.

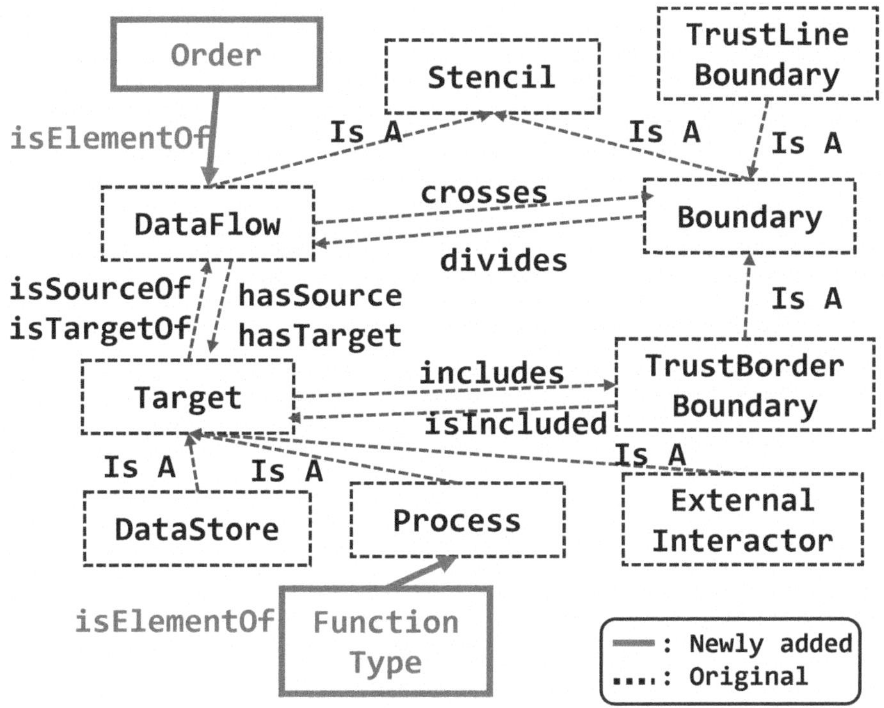

Fig. 3. Extended DFD metamodel

4.2 Definition of Multi-step Threat Patterns

This section demonstrates how we define a multi-step threat pattern—specifically the TOCTOU threat—using publicly disclosed vulnerability information, and how we convert that pattern into a JSON format that pytm-Seq can recognize. Based on descriptions in public vulnerability databases (e.g., CAPEC, CWE), TOCTOU can be defined as a multi-step threat that may occur when multiple programs can read from and write to a shared resource. The threat arises when one program reads a shared resource while another program performs a write, resulting in a mismatch between the value observed at the time of the check (read) and the value present at the time of use. We decompose the TOCTOU threat into the following sub steps: (1) some program first issues a read request to the shared resource; (2) while the read request is being processed, another program issues a write to the shared resource; and (3) the program that issued the read receives and uses shared data whose value differs from the value observed at the read request in (1). When converted to DFD data-transfer patterns, the first sub-step is represented by a data flow in which a process of read FunctionType sends a read request to the data store holding the shared resource (first data flow). The second sub step is represented by a second data flow in which a process of write FunctionType sends a write request to the same data store, and a third data flow in which the data store returns the write result to that process. The third sub step is represented by a data flow in which the data store delivers the updated shared data to the read-type process. The code below shows the TOCTOU multi-step threat pattern constructed from these 4 data-transfer patterns, encoded in the JSON format recognized by pytm-Seq. In the JSON, the keys id and name denote the pattern identifier and name; phases lists the data-transfer patterns; and each data-transfer pattern contains src(the source node) and dst(the destination node). An asterisk (*) indicates an arbitrary FunctionType or that the field is not applicable.

```
{ "id" : "TOCTOU1", "name":"Time-Of-Check-to Time-Of-Use",
  "phases": [
        {"order‘‘:1,"src":["Read","Process"], "dst": ["*","DataStore"]},
        {"order" : 2, "src": ["*", "DataStore"], "dst": ["Read", "Process"]},
        {"order":3, "src": ["Read", "Process"], "dst": ["*", "DataStore"]},
        {"order" : 4, "src": ["*","DataStore"], "dst": ["Read","Process"]},
]}
```

4.3 DFD-Based Threat-Pattern Analysis

This section describes how we analyze a DFD to determine whether defined multi-step threat patterns exist. The analysis proceeds in two stages: (1) identifying candidate start nodes for the multi-step threat pattern, and (2) performing a graph search to detect the pattern within the DFD. The stages are detailed below. The first stage aims to exclude infeasible threat patterns in order to reduce unnecessary effort. pytm-Seq checks whether any DFD element exists whose FunctionType matches the first node of the multi-step threat pattern. If no such starting node is present in the DFD, the scenario is considered unlikely and is excluded from further search. The second stage performs graph exploration from the start nodes identified in (1) to determine whether a subgraph matching the multi-step threat pattern exists in the DFD. For the graph search, pytm-Seq selects one of the identified start nodes and follows outgoing data flows from that node. If multiple outgoing flows exist, it compares their Order values and follows the flow with the smallest order value. pytm-Seq then attempts to match the data-transfer patterns defined in the multi-step threat pattern to the current path in the DFD; when a data-transfer pattern matches, the corresponding DFD path segment is recorded as part of an attack path. pytm-Seq continues until either all data-transfer patterns in the defined multi-step pattern are matched(yielding a full at tack path from the initial node to the terminal node) or no continuation is possible. If no complete attack path is found, the tool changes the initial node (from the set identified in step (1)) and repeats the procedure. The code below shows an example output in JSON produced by applying this process to the DFD for the attack pattern in Sect. 4.2.

```
{ "id" : "TOCTOU1","name": "Time-of-check-to-Time-Of-Use",
    "steps" : {
        "step_1" : { "src":{"src_name":"DB Reader","src_type":["Read",Process]},
            "dst":{"dst_name":"User DB","dst_type":["DataStore","-"]}},
        "step_2" : { "src":{"src_name":"User DB","src_type":["DataStore",-]},
            "dst":{"dst_name":"User DB","dst_type":["DataStore","-"]}}
        ...}
}
```

4.4 Report Generation from Analysis Results

This section explains the step that takes the attack paths output by Sect. 4.3 and produces an analysis report describing the identified attack paths. Concretely, the tool first generates a threat/multi-step threat analysis report based on the DFD attack paths that match a multi-step threat pattern; the steps element records the identified data-transfer patterns. Next, pytm-Seq generates an HTML detection report. As shown in the text below, the detection report contains summary information for each detected multi-step threat, including the DFD attack path corresponding to the pattern.

```
Potential Threats
- Name: Time-Of-check to Time-Of-Use-Example
  Multi-Step: Database Reader→User Database→Database Writter→User Database→Database Reader
```

5 Case-Study: Price Oracle Manipulation and Flash Loan Attack

This section demonstrates whether pytm-Seq can identify multi-step threats in the smart-contract domain. To that end, we selected and analyzed 52 incidents related to the major multi-step attack classes against smart contracts—Oracle Manipulation and Flash Loan Attacks—and derived a total of 7 multi-step threat patterns. In this section we focus on one of the largest incidents by loss at the time of writing, the MBUToken contract hack, and describe the pattern-definition process and the results showing that the pattern was detected in the actual system [38]. The patterns and detection results for the remaining incidents can be found in the pytm-Seq GitHub repository.

5.1 Creating a Smart-Contract DFD Based on the Extended DFD Metamodel

In this section, based on the analysis of the 2025 MBUToken contract hacking incident, we identify the functional types used during the data transmission processes throughout the attack, and describe the procedure and results of modeling the system involved in the incident as a Data Flow Diagram (DFD) [33]. According to the analysis report on this attack case, the attacker first borrowed a large amount of CHEESE tokens without collateral from a flash-loan contract, then exchanged them for vETH tokens via an asset-exchange contract, thereby causing a sharp increase in the vETH price. Subsequently, by inducing the portfolio management contract to reference this inflated price through the oracle contract, the attacker manipulated the system so that fund rewards were issued excessively, based on the overvalued vETH price.

Through this procedure, the research team identified 5 smart contracts and components used in the attack and mapped each of them to a corresponding functional category defined by a smart contract statistics service. As a result, 5 functional types were derived: Peer Node(blockchain nodes), Flash Loan(uncollateralized lending), Exchange(token swapping), Price Oracle(price-feed services), and Yield Aggregator(automated portfolio management). Next, the research team assigned these service types to the function_type attribute of each process, as illustrated in the code below. For example, the function_type of the Sushiswap contract—which receives CHEESE tokens from the user, exchanges them for vETH, and forwards price information to the oracle—was assigned Asset Exchange to represent its exchange service. In addition, to specify the order of data flows between the elements, the order attribute of the data flow(oracle_to_defi_pro1) was set accordingly.

```
pro1 = Process("Asset Exchange Contract")  # Process - Asset Exchange Smart Contract
pro1.function_type = "Asset Exchange"...
oracle_to_pro1 = Dataflow(oracle,pro1, "Liquidity Read") # DataFlow - token price value
oracle_to_pro1.order = 4 ...
```

5.2 Defining Smart-Contract Multi-Step Threat Patterns and Encoding Them for Pytm-Seq

This section presents how we identified the data-transfer sequence among the FunctionTypes derived in Sect. 5.1 for the MBUToken hack and converted that sequence into the JSON format recognizable by pytm-Seq. Blockchain transaction explorer data show that the attacker used a sequence of transfers in the order: Peer Node → Flash Loan → Peer Node → Exchange → Price Oracle → Yield Aggregator → Peer Node. In this case, 6 consecutive data-transfer patterns were identified. Based on those data transfer patterns, we defined the multi-step threat pattern in JSON form—the result is shown in the code below

```
{ "id": "FL_OCPOM_4","name": "2025 MBUToken Hack",
    "phases":[ {‘‘order’’:1, "src":["Peer Node","Process"], "dst":["Flash Loan","Process‘‘]},
       {‘‘order’’:2,"src":["Flash Loan","Process‘‘], "dst":["Peer Node", "Process"]},
       {‘‘order’’:3, "src":["Peer Node","Process"], "dst":["Asset Exchange", "Process"]},
       {‘‘order’’:4, "src":["Asset Exchange","Process"], "dst":["Price Oracle","Process"]},
       {‘‘order’’:5, "src":["Price Oracle","Process"], "dst":["Yield Aggregator","Process"]}
       {‘‘order’’:6, "src":["Yield Aggregator","Process"], "dst":["Peer Node","Process"]}]
}
```

5.3 DFD-Based Analysis of Smart-Contract Multi-step Threat Patterns Using Pytm-Seq

In this section we describe the process and results of using pytm-Seq to detect the pattern defined in Sect. 5.2 within actual system. First, using the DFD constructed in Sect. 5.1, we identified the node corresponding to the start of the pattern defined in Sect. 5.2. In this process, Peer Node 3, which initiates an unsecured loan request to the flash-loan contract, was confirmed as the initial node of the pattern. Next, to locate a subgraph in the DFD matching the multi-step pattern, we started graph from Peer Node 3 and followed the procedure described in Sect. 4.3. As a result, an attack path was identified that starts at the initial node Peer Node 3, passes through flash-loan providers such as dYdX, and returns to the terminal node Peer Node 3. The path identified is shown in Fig. 4, and pytm-Seq's JSON output for that path is shown in the code below.

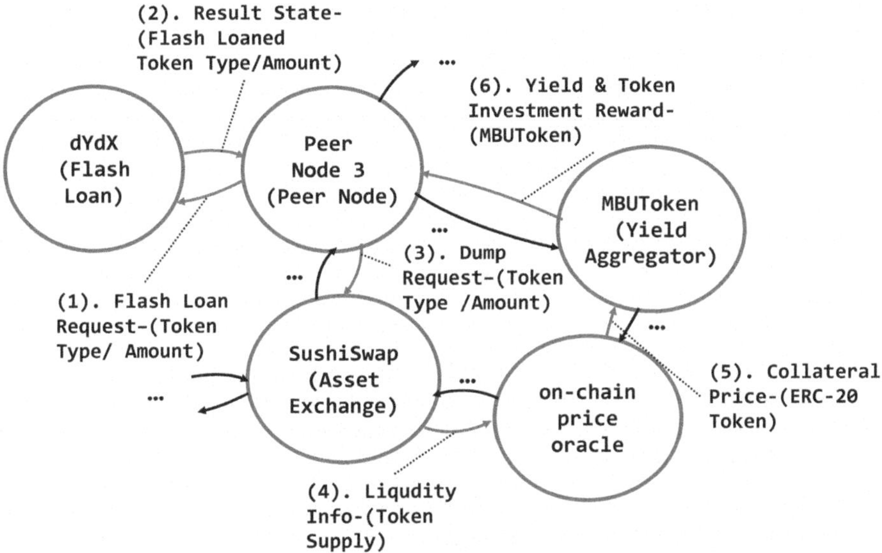

Fig. 4. Identified attack path in DFD

```
{ "id": "FL_OCPOM_4", "name": "2025 MBUToken Hack",
    "steps" : {
        "step_1" :{
            "src":{"src_name" : "Peer Node 3", "src_type": ["Peer Node","Process"]},
            "dst" :{ "dst_name":"dYdX", "dst_type":["Flash Loan","Process"]}},
        "step_2" :{
            "src":{ "src_name":"dYdX", "src_type":["Flash Loan","Process"]},
            "dst" :{"dst_name":"Peer Node 3","dst_type : ["Peer Node","Process"]}},...
}
```

5.4 Generating Reports from Smart-Contract Multi-Step Threat Analysis Results

This section explains how the identified attack path in Sect. 5.3 is transformed into an HTML-format analysis report describing the detected multi-step threat. pytm-Seq takes the attack path output (the code in Sect. 5.3) and generates the HTML detection report shown in the text below. As the report illustrates, the attack-path identified in the DFD is included under the Multi-Step item of the analysis report.

```
Potential Threats
- Name: 2025 MBUToken Contract Hacking
  Multi-Step: Peer Node 3→dYdX→Peer Node 3→SushiSwap→Price Oracle→MBUToken→Peer Node 3
```

6 Performance Evaluation

This section describes the evaluation process and results used to determine whether pytm-Seq can be used to accurately detect multi-step threats. The details are as follows.

6.1 Process of Performance Evaluation

This section explains the process we established to evaluate how accurately pytm-Seq can identify multi-step threats. The research team aimed to verify whether the multi-step threats defined in Sect. 5 could be correctly detected within the corresponding DFDs. For this purpose, excluding the 52 cases used to derive the 7 patterns derived from Sect. 5.2, a total of 28 smart-contract attack cases reported over the past five years were selected. These 28 cases consist of attacks that either conform to the defined multi step threat patterns or do not. These cases were selected so that cases matching the defined threat patterns could be used to examine potential false negatives, while non matching cases could be used to verify potential false positives.

6.2 Results of Performance Evaluation

This section explains the results that how accurately pytm-Seq identified multi-step threats, following the process described in Sect. 6.1. We analyzed 28 attack cases, created DFDs representing the systems where the attacks occurred, and then identified the corresponding multi-step threats. The results obtained by applying pytm-Seq for threat identification are summarized in Table 1. As shown in Table 1, except for 4 cases, the multi-step threats were successfully identified in all DFDs created from the attack cases. For the total of 28 attack cases, the detection results showed a precision of 0.81, recall of 0.92, and accuracy of 0.86. During the evaluation, however, 3 false positives and 1 false negative were observed. As an example of a false negative, the multi-step threat associated with the PizzaX contract in Case 5 was not detected. This occurred because the functional type of PizzaX was classified as Ponzi, which represents a very small portion of all smart contracts, and no attack cases involving this functional type were included among those used for pattern derivation in Sect. 5. This issue can be mitigated by analyzing a larger and more diverse set of attack cases to derive a broader range of complex patterns. Conversely, Case 8 was misclassified (false positive). In that incident the attacker exploited an integer overflow vulnerability in a contract and no price manipulation activity occurred, yet the presence of

Table 1. Detection results for attack scenarios (**TP**: True Positive, **FN**: False Negative, **TN**: True Negative, **FP**: False Positive)

Attack scenarios	Detection result			
	TP	FN	TN	FP
Case 1 – Balancer Hack	✓	-	-	-
Case 2 – NovaCron Hack	-	-	✓	-
Case 3 – 1inch Hack	✓	-	-	-
Case 4 – BTNFT Hack	-	-	✓	-
Case 5 – PizzaX Hack	-	✓	-	-
Case 6 – Tradeonion Hack	-	-	✓	-
Case 7 – Excommunity Hack	✓	-	-	-
Case 8 – NORMIE Hack	-	-	-	✓
Case 9 – Sonne Finance Hack	✓	-	-	-
Case 10 – TGC Hack	-	-	-	✓
Case 11 – OSN Hack	✓	-	-	-
Case 12 – Yield Hack	-	-	-	✓
Case 13 – LW2 Hack	✓	-	-	-
Case 14 – SBT Hack	-	-	✓	-
Case 15 – LifiProtocol Hack	✓	-	-	-
Case 16 – Spectra_finance Hack	-	-	✓	-
Case 17 – Convergence Hack	✓	-	-	-
Case 18 – iVest Hack	-	-	✓	-
Case 19 – VOW Hack	✓	-	-	-
Case 20 – 0MPX Hack	-	-	✓	-
Case 21 – Predy Finance Hack	✓	-	-	-
Case 22 – Woofi Hack	-	-	✓	-
Case 23 – UnizenIO Hack	✓	-	-	-
Case 24 – LavaLending Hack	-	-	✓	-
Case 25 – PrismaFi Hack	✓	-	-	-
Case 26 – BigBangSwap Hack	-	-	✓	-
Case 27 – ChaingeFinance Hack	✓	-	-	-
Case 28 – HedgeyFinance Hack	-	-	✓	-

the data-transfer patterns defined in Sect. 5.2 caused the case to be incorrectly matched to the related multi-step threat. To reduce such false positives, the DFD metadata should be extended to include additional information such as parameters and data types transmitted between contracts.

7 Discussion

This section summarizes the limitations of the proposed methodology and pytm-Seq, and outlines future works to address these issues. The details are as follows.

In the version of pytm-Seq proposed in this paper, multi-step threat patterns must be manually defined, which introduces the possibility of errors during the pattern-generation process. This limitation becomes more evident when compared with the attack graph auto-generation tools discussed in Sect. 2, which support automatic derivation of threat patterns. Therefore, to overcome the limitations highlighted through comparison with related research, future work may focus on automating the process of deriving threat patterns. First, one possible approach is to collect diverse Cyber Threat Intelligence (CTI) sources in real time, extract abused functions and targeted assets, and then link these pairs sequentially to construct multi-step threat patterns. However, CTI sources differ in how they represent vulnerability and threat information, and thus a standardized interface is required to integrate and utilize them. STIX (Structured Threat Information Expression) is a standardized format for expressing CTI, and Attack Flow objects represented in STIX provide information about the functions exploited in an attack and the targeted assets, along with a series of attack activities conducted during a specific period. Accordingly, future work may develop a system capable of automatically updating and generating attack patterns in real time using CTI expressed in STIX. In addition to automating attack-pattern definition, further validation should be conducted by applying a broader range of attack patterns and test cases to the accuracy evaluation. This study implemented and validated only seven representative patterns for domain-specific attacks in smart-contract systems; therefore, accuracy assessments for more diverse domains and more complex patterns are required. To this end, future work should: (1) derive new attack patterns not only in the smart-contract domain but also in other areas such as blockchain, web, embedded systems, and ICS; (2) increase the number of patterns per domain; and (3) expand the number of test cases, enabling broader and more rigorous accuracy evaluation.

8 Conclusion

This study proposed a methodology to define and detect multi-step threats by adding execution-order (Order) and function-type (Function Type) information to DFDs, thereby addressing the limitation of existing automated threat-modelling tools that fo cus on single-component threat identification and do not consider multiple functions and data-transfer ordering. The proposed methodology comprises: (1) extending the OWASP ODTM-based DFD metamodel, (2) defining multi-step threat patterns based on public vulnerabilities and real attack cases, (3) determining pattern existence via graph-search algorithms, and (4) outputting the results as a final report. Based on this methodology, we implemented pytm-Seq, which compares input DFDs with JSON encoded threat patterns to automatically analyze execution-order-based data-transfer structures and identify attack paths that match the patterns. In a case study targeting DeFi smart contracts, we analyzed 52 real-world attack incidents and derived seven multi-step threat patterns encompassing Price Oracle Manipulation and Flash Loan Attacks. We then evaluated the methodology and tool for accuracy; pytm-Seq achieved an overall detection accuracy of 86%, demonstrating practical applicability for detecting real multi-step attacks. Future work should include: (1) automatic derivation of multi-step threat patterns from CTI, (2) expanding pattern definitions, evaluation scope and test-case scale across other domains, and (3) improving usability—for example by integrating with MS-TMT and supporting GUI-based drag-and-drop modelling.

Acknowledgments. This work was supported by the Institute of Information and Communications Technology Planning and Evaluation (IITP) Grant funded by Korean Government [Ministry of Science and ICT (MSIT)], (RS-2018-II180532, Development of High-Assurance (EAL6) Secure Microkernel).

Disclosure of Interests. This work was supported by the Institute of Information and Communications Technology Planning and Evaluation (IITP) Grant funded by Korean Government [Ministry of Science and ICT (MSIT)], (RS-2018-II180532, Development of High-Assurance (EAL6) Secure Microkernel).

References

1. Abbaspour Asadollah, S., Imtiaz, S., Dehlaghi-Ghadim, A., Sjödin, M., Sirjani, M.: Enhancing cybersecurity through comprehensive investigation of data flow-based attack scenarios. J. Cybersecur. Priv. **4**(4), 823–852 (2024)
2. Alshareef, H.: Precise analysis of purpose limitation in data flow diagrams. In: Proceedings of the 17th International Conference on Availability, Reliability and Security, pp. 1–11. Springer, Cham (2022)
3. Anifowose, Z.: Aligning Mitre attack framework with threat analysis and risk assesment (TARA) to support R155 compliance. https://www.diva-portal.org/smash/get/diva2:1775733/FULLTEXT01.pdff. Accessed 19 Sept 2025
4. Cho, H., Kim, S.: Threat modeling for the defense industry: past, present, and future. IEEE Access (2025)
5. Compass, S.: Security compass: measuring threat modeling ROI. https://www.securitycompass.com/blog/measuring-threat-modeling-roi/. Accessed 19 Sept 2025
6. Compass, S.: Security compass: understanding the developer-centric threat modeling process. https://www.securitycompass.com/whitepapers/understanding-the-developer-centric-threat-modeling-process/. Accessed 19 Sept 2025
7. Faily, S., Scandariato, R., Shostack, A., Sion, L., Ki-Aries, D.: Contextualisation of data flow diagrams for security analysis. In: International Workshop on Graphical Models for Security, pp. 186–197. Springer, Cham (2020)
8. Flå, L.H., Borgaonkar, R., Tøndel, I.A., Jaatun, M.G.: Tool-assisted threat modeling for smart grid cyber security. In: 2021 International Conference on Cyber Situational Awareness, Data Analytics and Assessment (CyberSA), pp. 1–8. IEEE (2021)

9. Fu, C., Zhang, H., Zhou, Y.: An approach to generating attack graphs and analyzing threats based on CAPEC and ATT&CK matrix. Softw. Syst. Model. (2025)
10. Hasan, Ragib, R.: Towards a threat model and security analysis of spacecraft computing systems. In: 2022 IEEE International Conference on Wireless for Space and Extreme Environments (WiSEE), pp. 87–92. IEEE (2022)
11. Hollerer, S., Chabrová, M., Sauter, T., Kastner, W.: Combined modeling techniques for safety and security in industrial automation: a case study. In: 2022 15th International Conference on Security of Information and Networks (SIN), pp. 1–4. IEEE (2022)
12. Hwang, I., Cho, H., Kim, S.: Deriving usability evaluation criteria for threat modeling tools. IEEE Access (2025)
13. IriusRisk: 2024–2025 State of Threat Modeling Report. https://www.threatmodelingconnect.com/state-of-threat-modeling-2024-25. Accessed 19 Sept 2025
14. IriusRisk: IriusRisk: Automated Threat Modeling Platform. https://www.iriusrisk.com/. Accessed 19 Sept 2025
15. Jansson, K.: Cybersecurity threat modeling on medical devices (2021)
16. Gim, J., Jiwon Kwak, K.C., Kim, S.: Analysis of the problems of domestic studies on threat modeling. J. Korea Inst. Inf. Secur. Cryptol. 397–413 (2025)
17. Kelly, J.: Red Hat: a collaborative approach to threat modeling. https://www.redhat.com/ko/blog/collaborative-approach-threat-modeling. Accessed 19 Sept 2025
18. Kusuma, R.S., Umar, R., Riadi, I.: Network forensics against ryuk ransomware using trigger, acquire, analysis, report, and action (taara) method. Kinetik: Game Technology, Information System, Computer Network, Computing, Electronics, and Control (2021)
19. Lilienthal, D., Hong, S.: Mind the gap: Time-of-check to time-of-use vulnerabilities in llm-enabled agents. arXiv preprint arXiv:2508.17155 (2025)
20. Microsoft: Microsoft Threat Modeling Tool Releases. https://learn.microsoft.com/ko-kr/azure/security/develop/threat-modeling-tool-releases-73002061. Accessed 19 Sept 2025
21. Monteuuis, J.P., Boudguiga, A., Zhang, J., Labiod, H., Servel, A., Urien, P.: Sara: security automotive risk analysis method. In: Proceedings of the 4th ACM Workshop on Cyber-Physical System Security, pp. 3–14 (2018)
22. OWASP: OWASP: OdTM — OWASP Ontology-driven Threat Modelling framework. https://github.com/OWASP/OdTM/. Accessed 19 Sept 2025
23. OWASP: OWASP Pytm. https://github.com/OWASP/pytm. Accessed 19 Sept 2025
24. OWASP: OWASP Threat Dragon. https://owasp.org/www-project-threat-dragon/. Accessed 19 Sept 2025
25. Raciti, M., Bella, G.: How to model privacy threats in the automotive domain. arXiv preprint arXiv:2303.10370 (2023)
26. Robles-González, A., Parra-Arnau, J., Forné, J.: A linddun-based framework for privacy threat analysis on identification and authentication processes. Comput. Secur. **94**, 101755 (2020)
27. Seo, J., Kwak, J., Kim, S.: Formally verified software update management system in automotive. In: Symposium on Vehicles Security and Privacy (VehicleSec) (2023)
28. Shostack, A.: Threat Modeling: Designing for Security. Wiley, Hoboken (2014)
29. Sion, L.: Automated threat analysis for security and privacy (2020)

30. Srikumar, K., et al.: Striped: a threat analysis method for IoT systems. In: Proceedings of the 17th International Conference on Availability, Reliability and Security, pp. 1–6 (2022)
31. Stevens, R., Votipka, D., Redmiles, E.M., Ahern, C., Sweeney, P., Mazurek, M.L.: The battle for new york: a case study of applied digital threat modeling at the enterprise level. In: 27th USENIX Security Symposium (USENIX Security 18), pp. 621–637 (2018)
32. Stingelová, B., Thrakl, C.T., Wrońska, L., Jedrej-Szymankiewicz, S., Khan, S., Svetinovic, D.: User-centric security and privacy threats in connected vehicles: a threat modeling analysis using stride and linddun. In: 2023 IEEE International Conference on Dependable, Autonomic and Secure Computing, International Conference on Pervasive Intelligence and Computing, International Conference on Cloud and Big Data Computing, International Conference on Cyber Science and Technology Congress (DASC/PiCom/CBDCom/CyberSciTech), pp. 0690–0697. IEEE (2023)
33. SunWeb3Sec: DeFiHackLabs GitHub Repository. https://github.com/SunWeb3Sec/DeFiHackLabs/blob/main/src/test/2025-05/MBUToken_exp.sol. Accessed 19 Sept 2025
34. Tran, A.D., Sion, L., Yskout, K., Joosen, W.: Terrara: automated security threat modeling for infrastructure as code. In: Proceedings of the Fifteenth ACM Conference on Data and Application Security and Privacy (CODASPY 2025), pp. 1–12. ACM (2025)
35. Van Landuyt, D., Joosen, W.: A descriptive study of assumptions in stride security threat modeling. Softw. Syst. Model. **21**(6), 2311–2328 (2022)
36. Wuyts, K., Sion, L., Joosen, W.: Linddun go: a lightweight approach to privacy threat modeling. In: 2020 IEEE European Symposium on Security and Privacy Workshops (EuroS&PW), pp. 302–309. IEEE (2020)
37. Wynn, J.: Threat Assessment and Remediation Analysis (TARA). https://apps.dtic.mil/sti/tr/pdf/AD1016629.pdf. Accessed 19 Sept 2025
38. Zhou, L., et al.: Sok: decentralized finance (DeFI) attacks. In: Proceedings of the 2023 IEEE Symposium on Security and Privacy (SP), pp. 2444–2461. IEEE (2023)

Vector-Input Hashing Modes for Collision-Resistant Pseudorandom Function

Shoichi Hirose[1](✉), Tetsu Iwata[2], and Hidenori Kuwakado[3]

[1] University of Fukui, Fukui, Japan
hrs_shch@u-fukui.ac.jp
[2] Nagoya University, Nagoya, Japan
tetsu.iwata@nagoya-u.jp
[3] Kansai University, Takatsuki, Japan
kuwakado@kansai-u.ac.jp

Abstract. This paper presents vector-input keyed hashing modes that construct collision-resistant pseudorandom functions (CR PRFs) using a keyed hash function, where a vector refers to a sequence of variable-length strings. The proposed vector-input keyed hashing modes, VIM1 and VIM2, originate from the intuition that a string-input keyed hashing mode using a compression function results in a vector-input keyed hashing mode by replacing the compression function with a hash function. Combined with the recently proposed string-input keyed hashing modes KHC1 or KHC2, VIM1 and VIM2 are shown to yield CR PRFs from a compression function satisfying extended collision resistance and being a secure PRF under related-key attacks. Extended collision resistance means that it is intractable to find a distinct input pair whose output difference falls within a small set. This paper also introduces a keyed hashing mode, PVIM, which allows parallel processing of strings in a vector. However, it requires more calls to the underlying keyed hash function than VIM1 and VIM2 do. To the best of our knowledge, this is the first proposal of dedicated vector-input CR PRFs.

Keywords: Keyed hashing mode · Vector input · Collision resistance · Pseudorandom function · Compression function

1 Introduction

Background. Cryptographic hash functions are useful for various applications such as message digest, message authentication, and pseudorandom generation. It is well known that a keyed hash function H that satisfies both collision-resistance and pseudorandomness instantiates computationally hiding and computationally binding string commitment. For message M, one chooses key K uniformly at random and computes commitment $\sigma \leftarrow H_K(M)$. Recently, some interesting cryptographic schemes were constructed with such collision-resistant pseudorandom functions (CR PRFs): compactly committing authenticated encryption with associated data (ccAEAD) [11,16] and hash-based post-quantum EPID signatures [9].

H. Seo (Ed.): ICISC 2025, LNCS 16487, pp. 278–292, 2026.
https://doi.org/10.1007/978-981-95-8034-7_15

Conventional CR PRFs such as HMAC [3,12] and KMAC [22] are defined over strings. However, data to be processed have specific formats or structures in many practical situations. A recognized method to process such data is to encode a given datum into a string and feed it to a conventional string-input CR PRF. An example of such encoding is included in the specification of TupleHash [22] for a sequence of variable-length strings, which is often called a vector. Although this method always works, the encoding process introduces an efficiency loss.

Our Contribution. Our goal is to construct a vector-input CR PRF using a compression function. Our idea is to nest compression-function-based keyed hashing modes constructing string-input CR PRFs, that is, to replace the compression function of a keyed hashing mode with a string-input CR PRF using a compression function. To the best of our knowledge, this is the first proposal of dedicated vector-input CR PRFs.

For the proposed construction, we adopt two string-input keyed hashing modes KHC1 and KHC2 [19], which are cascades of a compression function. Precisely, simple nesting is incomplete since it cannot handle the 0-dimensional vector (the vector with no string). Thus, we first present two vector-input keyed hashing modes VIM1 and VIM2 based on KHC1 and KHC2, respectively. They construct vector-input keyed hash functions using a string-input keyed hash function. VIM1 and VIM2 using a keyed hash function $H : \{0,1\}^n \times \{0,1\}^* \rightarrow \{0,1\}^n$ are depicted in Figs. 1 and 2, respectively. In these figures, $K \in \{0,1\}^n$ is a secret key, d_0, d_1, d_2, d_3 are constants in $\{0,1\}^n$, and ε is the empty string.

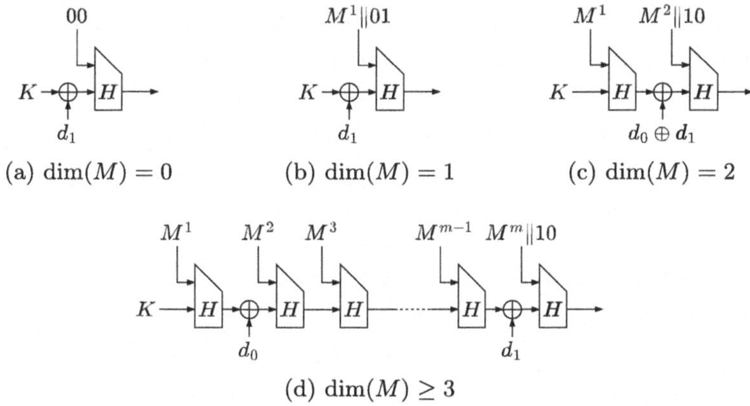

Fig. 1. Proposed vector-input keyed hashing mode VIM1

VIM1 and VIM2 are shown to be collision-resistant if the underlying keyed hash function satisfies extended collision resistance, that is, it is intractable to find a pair of distinct inputs to the underlying keyed hash function such that the difference of their corresponding outputs is in a small set defined by the constants specifying VIM1 and VIM2. VIM1 and VIM2 are also shown to be a

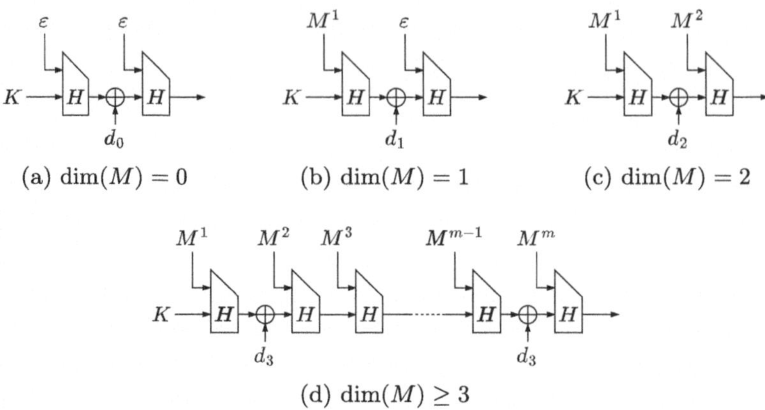

Fig. 2. Proposed vector-input keyed hashing mode VIM2

secure PRF, using the hybrid argument for cascade construction of a string-input PRF [4], if the underlying keyed hash function is a secure PRF under related-key attacks [5]. Their key derivation functions are defined by the constants specifying VIM1 and VIM2.

KHC1 and KHC2 were shown to construct string-input CR PRFs [19]. However, it is not sufficient for constructing vector-input CR PRFs by using them as a building block of VIM1 and VIM2. Thus, in this paper, KHC1 and KHC2 are shown to satisfy extended collision resistance if the underlying compression function satisfies it. KHC1 and KHC2 are also shown to be a secure PRF under related-key attacks if the underlying compression function is a secure PRF under related-key attacks.

Finally, we present a parallelizable vector-input keyed hashing mode, which constructs CR PRFs by using KHC1 or KHC2. While it enables parallel processing when the strings in a vector are simultaneously available, it requires more calls to the underlying compression function than VIM1 and VIM2 with KHC1 or KHC2.

All the proofs are omitted due to the page limit.

Related Work. An iterated hash function consisting of a compression function is called a Merkle-Damgård hash function [10,25]. Pseudorandom functions were first introduced by Goldreich, Goldwasser, and Micali [15].

KHC1 and KHC2 [19] are inspired by the suffix-free-prefix-free (SFPF) hash function construction [1] and KMDP^+ [17]. KMDP^+, which improves Keyed-MDP [21], is the most efficient string-input keyed hashing mode of a compression function to construct a CR PRF. KMDP^+ cannot be utilized for VIM1 and VIM2 since it only accepts secret keys shorter than the outputs. Both KHC1 and KHC2 are competitive with KMDP^+ in terms of the number of calls to the underlying compression function.

There are many proposals of string-input keyed hashing constructions based on the Merkle-Damgård construction and satisfying collision resistance and pseudorandomness. They are classified by their underlying primitives: HMAC [3], Sandwich construction [28], H^2-MAC [29], and AMAC [2] use a cryptographic hash function, while NMAC [3], EMD [6], Keyed MDP [21], Prefix MDP [21], and KMDP$^+$ [17] use a compression function.

There are several proposals of constructions for a vector-input PRF, which do not address collision resistance. Rogaway and Shrimpton [27] presented the first vector-input PRF called S2V as a component of their SIV construction for deterministic authenticated encryption. Minematsu [26] proposed a universal hash function based on bit rotation and used it to construct a vector-input PRF. Hirose, Kuwakado, and Yoshida [20] constructed a vector-input PRF based on the lightweight hash function Lesamnta-LW [18] and MDP [21], employing the protected counter sum construction [7]. Furuya et al. [13] adopted PMAC2x [24] using a tweakable block cipher [23] as the baseline scheme and constructed the vector-input PRF called PMACrx that achieved the beyond-the-birthday-bound security. Furuya and Minematsu [14] presented a vector-input PRF based on PMAC [8], which attains optimal efficiency with respect to the number of calls to the underlying block cipher.

Organization. Section 2 gives notations and definitions. It also introduces KHC1 and KHC2. Section 3 proposes vector-input keyed hashing modes VIM1 and VIM2. Section 4 shows that both KHC1 and KHC2 construct keyed hash functions satisfying extended collision resistance and being a secure PRF under related-key attacks. Section 5 confirms that both VIM1 and VIM2 construct CR PRFs by using KHC1 or KHC2. Section 6 presents a parallelizable vector-input keyed hashing mode for CR PRFs. Section 7 gives a concluding remark.

2 Preliminaries

2.1 Notations

For set $\mathcal{S}$, let $\mathcal{S}^* := \bigcup_{i=0}^{\infty} \mathcal{S}^i$ and $\mathcal{S}^+ := \bigcup_{i=1}^{\infty} \mathcal{S}^i$. Let $s \twoheadleftarrow \mathcal{S}$ denote that s is assigned an element chosen uniformly at random from set $\mathcal{S}$.

Let $\Sigma := \{0,1\}$. $\Sigma^0 = \{\varepsilon\}$, where ε is the empty sequence.

For binary sequence $u \in \Sigma^*$, let $|u|$ be the length of u in bits. For binary sequences $z_i, z_{i+1}, \ldots, z_{i+j} \in \Sigma^*$, let $z_i \| z_{i+1} \| \cdots \| z_{i+j}$ be their concatenation, which is also denoted by $z_{[i,i+j]}$ for simplicity.

For integer κ, the identity permutation over Σ^κ is denoted by id, and the permutation $x \mapsto x \oplus c$ over Σ^κ is denoted by x_c, where $c \in \Sigma^\kappa$. For $\Delta \subseteq \Sigma^\kappa$ and $c \in \Sigma^\kappa$, let $\Delta \oplus c := \{\delta \oplus c \mid \delta \in \Delta\}$.

Let $\Sigma^{**} := (\Sigma^*)^*$ be the set of vectors. For $V \in \Sigma^{**}$, let $\dim(V)$ be the dimension of V. $(\Sigma^*)^0 = \{\lambda\}$, where $\lambda := ()$ is the zero-dimensional vector.

For integers a, b, and d, $a \equiv b \pmod{d}$ is denoted by $a \equiv_d b$.

A random function $\rho : \mathcal{D} \to \mathcal{R}$ is called a random oracle if for any $x \in \mathcal{D}$, $\rho(x)$ is assigned an element chosen uniformly at random from $\mathcal{R}$.

2.2 Collision Resistance and Its Extension

Let $H^F : \mathcal{X} \to \Sigma^n$ be a hash function that uses compression function F. An input pair X and X' for H^F is called colliding if $X \neq X'$ and $H^F(X) = H^F(X')$. H^F is called collision-resistant if it is intractable to find a colliding input pair for H^F.

We extend the notion of collision resistance as follows. For $\Delta \subset \Sigma^n$, an input pair X and X' for H^F is called Δ-colliding if $X \neq X'$ and $H^F(X) \oplus H^F(X') \in \Delta$. H^F is called Δ-collision-resistant if it is intractable to find a Δ-colliding input pair for H^F. $\{0^n\}$-collision resistance refers to collision resistance.

2.3 Pseudorandom Function

Let $f : \mathcal{K} \times \mathcal{X} \to \mathcal{Y}$ be a keyed function with key space $\mathcal{K}$ and $f_K(\cdot) := f(K, \cdot)$. Let $\mathbf{A}$ be an adversary against f. The goal of $\mathbf{A}$ is to distinguish between f_K and a random oracle $\rho : \mathcal{X} \to \mathcal{Y}$, where $K \twoheadleftarrow \mathcal{K}$. $\mathbf{A}$ is given either f_K or ρ as an oracle and makes adaptive queries in $\mathcal{X}$. $\mathbf{A}$ outputs 0 or 1. The prf advantage of $\mathbf{A}$ against f is defined as

$$\mathrm{Adv}_f^{\mathrm{prf}}(\mathbf{A}) := \left|\Pr\left[\mathbf{A}^{f_K} = 1\right] - \Pr\left[\mathbf{A}^{\rho} = 1\right]\right|,$$

where $\mathbf{A}$ is regarded as a random variable that takes values in $\{0, 1\}$. f is called a secure pseudorandom function (PRF) if no efficient adversary $\mathbf{A}$ has any significant prf advantage.

2.4 PRF Under Related-Key Attack

Let $\mathbf{A}$ be an adversary against $f : \mathcal{K} \times \mathcal{X} \to \mathcal{Y}$. Let Φ be a set of functions from $\mathcal{K}$ to $\mathcal{K}$. $\mathbf{A}$ makes a Φ-related-key attack (Φ-RKA) [5]: $\mathbf{A}$ is given $g\langle K \rangle : \Phi \times \mathcal{X} \to \mathcal{Y}$ such that $g\langle K \rangle(\varphi, X) := g(\varphi(K), X)$ as an oracle, where g is either f or a random oracle $\rho : \mathcal{K} \times \mathcal{X} \to \mathcal{Y}$ and $K \twoheadleftarrow \mathcal{K}$. $\varphi \in \Phi$ is called a related-key-derivation function. $\mathbf{A}$ makes adaptive queries to the oracle and outputs 0 or 1. The prf-rka advantage of $\mathbf{A}$ making a Φ-RKA on f is given by

$$\mathrm{Adv}_{f,\Phi}^{\mathrm{prf\text{-}rka}}(\mathbf{A}) := \left|\Pr[\mathbf{A}^{f\langle K \rangle} = 1] - \Pr[\mathbf{A}^{\rho\langle K \rangle} = 1]\right|.$$

f is called a secure PRF under Φ-RKAs if no efficient adversary $\mathbf{A}$ has any significant prf-rka advantage.

The prf-rka advantage of $\mathbf{A}$ with access to p oracles is defined as

$$\mathrm{Adv}_{f,\Phi}^{p\text{-}\mathrm{prf\text{-}rka}}(\mathbf{A}) := \left|\Pr[\mathbf{A}^{f\langle K_1 \rangle, \ldots, f\langle K_p \rangle} = 1] - \Pr[\mathbf{A}^{\rho_1\langle K_1 \rangle, \ldots, \rho_p\langle K_p \rangle} = 1]\right|,$$

where $(K_1, \ldots, K_p) \twoheadleftarrow \mathcal{K}^p$ and $\rho_1, \ldots, \rho_p$ are independent random oracles.

In the subsequent sections, $\mathcal{K} := \Sigma^\kappa$ for some integer κ, and we are only interested in bitwise XOR for related-key-derivation functions. For $\Delta \subset \Sigma^\kappa$, $\{x \oplus \delta \mid \delta \in \Delta\}$-RKA is called Δ-XOR related-key attack (Δ-XRKA), and $\mathrm{Adv}_{f,\{x \oplus \delta \mid \delta \in \Delta\}}^{\mathrm{prf\text{-}rka}}$ is simply denoted by $\mathrm{Adv}_{f,\Delta}^{\mathrm{prf\text{-}rka}}$.

2.5 Keyed Hashing Modes: KHC1 and KHC2

KHC1 and KHC2 [19] are keyed hashing modes using a compression function $F : \Sigma^n \times \Sigma^w \to \Sigma^n$, where $n \geq 1$ and $w \geq 2$ are integers. F is treated as a keyed function with key space Σ^n.

KHC1 constructs a keyed hash function $\mathsf{KHC1}^F : \Sigma^n \times \Sigma^* \to \Sigma^n$. It is specified in Algorithm 1 and depicted in Fig. 3. It uses two distinct non-zero constants $c_0, c_1 \in \Sigma^n$. It uses a padding function $\mathtt{pad1} : \Sigma^* \to (\Sigma^w)^+$ such that

$$\mathtt{pad1}(M) := \begin{cases} M \| 10^d \| 0 & \text{if } |M| \leq w-2, \\ M \| 10^d \| 1 & \text{otherwise,} \end{cases}$$

where d is the smallest non-negative integer that satisfies $|M| + 2 + d \equiv_w 0$.

Algorithm 1: $\mathsf{KHC1}^F : \Sigma^n \times \Sigma^* \to \Sigma^n$

input : (K, M)
output: $\mathsf{KHC1}^F(K, M)$
$M_1 \| M_2 \| \cdots \| M_m \leftarrow \mathtt{pad1}(M)$; /* $|M_i| = w$ for $1 \leq i \leq m$ */
if $m = 1$ **then** $V_1 \leftarrow F(K \oplus c_1, M_1)$;
else
  $V_1 \leftarrow F(K, M_1) \oplus c_0$;
  for $i = 2$ **to** $m - 1$ **do** $V_i \leftarrow F(V_{i-1}, M_i)$;
  $V_m \leftarrow F(V_{m-1} \oplus c_1, M_m)$;
return V_m;

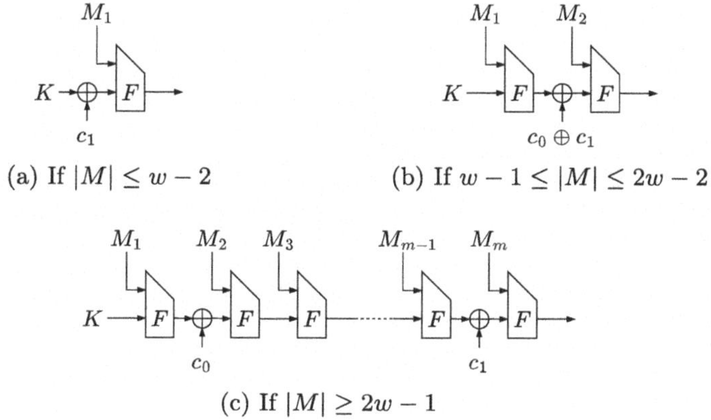

(a) If $|M| \leq w - 2$ (b) If $w - 1 \leq |M| \leq 2w - 2$

(c) If $|M| \geq 2w - 1$

Fig. 3. Keyed hashing mode $\mathsf{KHC1}$

KHC2 constructs a keyed hash function $\mathsf{KHC2}^F : \Sigma^n \times \Sigma^* \to \Sigma^n$. It is specified in Algorithm 2 and depicted in Fig. 4. It uses three distinct non-zero constants $c_0, c_{1,0}, c_{1,1} \in \Sigma^n$, satisfying $c_0 \oplus c_{1,0} \oplus c_{1,1} \neq 0^n$. It uses a padding function $\mathsf{pad2} : \Sigma^* \to (\Sigma^w)^+$ such that

$$\mathsf{pad2}(M) := \begin{cases} M & \text{if } |M| \geq 2w \text{ and } |M| \equiv_w 0, \\ M\|10^d & \text{otherwise,} \end{cases}$$

where d is the smallest non-negative integer that satisfies $|\mathsf{pad2}(M)| \geq 2w$ and $|\mathsf{pad2}(M)| \equiv_w 0$. Notice that, for any M such that $0 \leq |M| \leq 2w-1$, $\mathsf{pad2}(M) = M\|10^{2w-1-|M|}$.

Algorithm 2: $\mathsf{KHC2}^F : \Sigma^n \times \Sigma^* \to \Sigma^n$

input : (K, M)
output: $\mathsf{KHC2}^F(K, M)$
$M_1\|M_2\|\cdots\|M_m \leftarrow \mathsf{pad2}(M)$; /* $|M_i| = w$ for $1 \leq i \leq m$ */
$V_1 \leftarrow F(K, M_1) \oplus c_0$;
for $i = 2$ **to** $m-1$ **do** $V_i \leftarrow F(V_{i-1}, M_i)$;
if $|M| \geq 2w \wedge |M| \equiv_w 0$ **then** $V_m \leftarrow F(V_{m-1} \oplus c_{1,0}, M_m)$;
else $V_m \leftarrow F(V_{m-1} \oplus c_{1,1}, M_m)$;
return V_m;

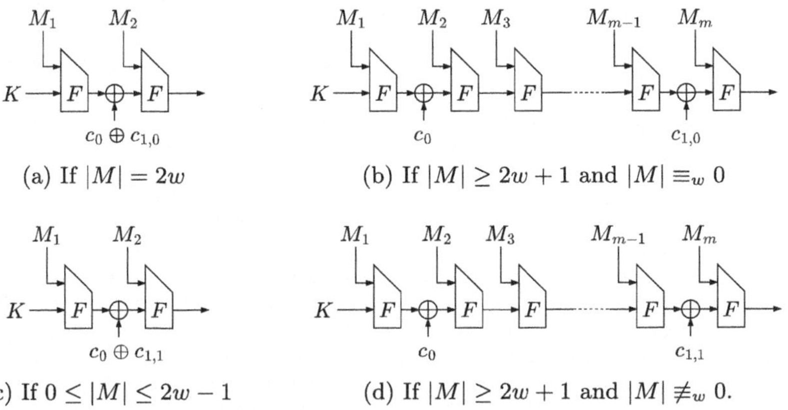

Fig. 4. Keyed hashing mode KHC2

The following theorems are obtained for collision resistance and pseudorandomness of $\mathsf{KHC1}^F$ and $\mathsf{KHC2}^F$ [19]:

Theorem 1 (Collision resistance of KHC1). *If a colliding input pair is found for* $\mathsf{KHC1}^F$*, then a* $\{0^n, c_0\}$*-colliding input pair is found for* F.

Theorem 2 (Collision resistance of KHC2). *If a colliding input pair is found for* $\mathsf{KHC2}^F$*, then a* $\{0^n, c_0, c_{1,0} \oplus c_{1,1}, c_0 \oplus c_{1,0} \oplus c_{1,1}\}$*-colliding input pair is found for* F*.*

Theorem 3 (Pseudorandomness of KHC1). *For any adversary* $\mathbf{A}$ *taking at most* t *time and making at most* q *queries each of which has at most* ℓ_{m} *blocks after padding, there exist some adversaries* $\dot{\mathbf{A}}$ *and* $\ddot{\mathbf{A}}$ *such that*

$$\mathrm{Adv}^{\mathrm{prf}}_{\mathsf{KHC1}^F}(\mathbf{A}) \le \mathrm{Adv}^{\mathrm{prf\text{-}rka}}_{F,\{0^n,c_1\}}(\dot{\mathbf{A}}) + (\ell_{\mathrm{m}} - 1) \cdot \mathrm{Adv}^{q\text{-}\mathrm{prf\text{-}rka}}_{F,\{0^n,c_1\}}(\ddot{\mathbf{A}}).$$

$\dot{\mathbf{A}}$ *and* $\ddot{\mathbf{A}}$ *take at most about* $t + O(q\ell_{\mathrm{m}}\tau_F)$ *time and make at most* q *queries, where* τ_F *is time required to compute* F*.*

Theorem 4 (Pseudorandomness of KHC2). *For any adversary* $\mathbf{A}$ *taking at most* t *time and making at most* q *queries each of which has at most* ℓ_{m} *blocks after padding, there exist some adversaries* $\dot{\mathbf{A}}$ *and* $\ddot{\mathbf{A}}$ *such that*

$$\mathrm{Adv}^{\mathrm{prf}}_{\mathsf{KHC2}^F}(\mathbf{A}) \le \mathrm{Adv}^{\mathrm{prf}}_{F}(\dot{\mathbf{A}}) + (\ell_{\mathrm{m}} - 1) \cdot \mathrm{Adv}^{q\text{-}\mathrm{prf\text{-}rka}}_{F,\{0^n,c_{1,0},c_{1,1}\}}(\ddot{\mathbf{A}}).$$

$\dot{\mathbf{A}}$ *and* $\ddot{\mathbf{A}}$ *take at most about* $t + O(q\ell_{\mathrm{m}}\tau_F)$ *time and make at most* q *queries, where* τ_F *is time required to compute* F*.*

3 Vector-Input Keyed Hashing Modes

We propose two vector-input keyed hashing modes VIM1 and VIM2 using a hash function $H : \Sigma^n \times \Sigma^* \to \Sigma^n$, where $n \ge 1$ is an integer. H is treated as a keyed hash function with key space Σ^n. VIM1 and VIM2 are based on KHC1 and KHC2, respectively.

3.1 Description

VIM1 constructs a vector-input keyed hash function $\mathsf{VIM1}^H : \Sigma^n \times \Sigma^{**} \to \Sigma^n$. It is specified in Algorithm 3 and depicted in Fig. 1. It uses two distinct non-zero constants $d_0, d_1 \in \Sigma^n$.

VIM2 constructs a vector-input keyed hash function $\mathsf{VIM2}^H : \Sigma^n \times \Sigma^{**} \to \Sigma^n$. It is specified in Algorithm 4 and depicted in Fig. 2. It uses four distinct non-zero constants $d_0, d_1, d_2, d_3 \in \Sigma^n$.

3.2 Collision Resistance

Collision resistance of $\mathsf{VIM1}^H$ is implied by extended collision resistance of H:

Theorem 5. *If a colliding input pair is found for* $\mathsf{VIM1}^H$*, then a* $\{0^n, d_0\}$*-colliding input pair is found for* H*.*

Collision resistance of $\mathsf{VIM2}^H$ is also implied by extended collision resistance of H:

Theorem 6. *If a colliding input pair is found for* $\mathsf{VIM2}^H$*, then a* $(\{0^n, d_3\} \cup \{d_i \oplus d_j\}_{0 \le i < j \le 3})$*-colliding input pair is found for* H*.*

Algorithm 3: $\mathsf{VIM1}^H : \Sigma^n \times \Sigma^{**} \to \Sigma^n$

input : (K, M)
output: $\mathsf{VIM1}^H(K, M)$
$m \leftarrow \dim(M)$; /* $M := (M^1, \ldots, M^m)$ for $m \geq 1$ */
if $m = 0$ **then** $V_0 \leftarrow H(K \oplus d_1, 00)$;
else if $m = 1$ **then** $V_1 \leftarrow H(K \oplus d_1, M^1 \| 01)$;
else
  $V_1 \leftarrow H(K, M^1) \oplus d_0$;
  for $i = 2$ **to** $m - 1$ **do** $V_i \leftarrow H(V_{i-1}, M^i)$;
  $V_m \leftarrow H(V_{m-1} \oplus d_1, M^m \| 10)$;
return V_m;

Algorithm 4: $\mathsf{VIM2}^H : \Sigma^n \times \Sigma^{**} \to \Sigma^n$

input : (K, M)
output: $\mathsf{VIM2}^H(K, M)$
$m \leftarrow \dim(M)$; /* $M := (M^1, \ldots, M^m)$ for $m \geq 1$ */
if $m = 0$ **then** $V_0 \leftarrow H(H(K, \varepsilon) \oplus d_0, \varepsilon)$;
else if $m = 1$ **then** $V_1 \leftarrow H(H(K, M^1) \oplus d_1, \varepsilon)$;
else if $m = 2$ **then** $V_2 \leftarrow H(H(K, M^1) \oplus d_2, M^2)$;
else
  $V_1 \leftarrow H(K, M^1) \oplus d_3$;
  for $i = 2$ **to** $m - 1$ **do** $V_i \leftarrow H(V_{i-1}, M^i)$;
  $V_m \leftarrow H(V_{m-1} \oplus d_3, M^m)$;
return V_m;

3.3 Pseudorandomness

The following theorem states that $\mathsf{VIM1}^H$ is a secure vector-input PRF if H is a secure PRF under $\{0^n, d_1\}$-XRKAs:

Theorem 7. *For any adversary* $\mathbf{A}$ *taking at most* t *time and making at most* q *queries each of which is at most* ℓ_{v}*-dimensional, there exist some adversaries* $\dot{\mathbf{A}}$ *and* $\ddot{\mathbf{A}}$ *such that*

$$\mathrm{Adv}^{\mathrm{prf}}_{\mathsf{VIM1}^H}(\mathbf{A}) \leq \mathrm{Adv}^{\mathrm{prf\text{-}rka}}_{H,\{0^n,d_1\}}(\dot{\mathbf{A}}) + (\ell_{\mathrm{v}} - 1) \cdot \mathrm{Adv}^{q\text{-}\mathrm{prf\text{-}rka}}_{H,\{0^n,d_1\}}(\ddot{\mathbf{A}}).$$

$\dot{\mathbf{A}}$ *and* $\ddot{\mathbf{A}}$ *take at most about* $t + O(q\ell_{\mathrm{v}}\tau_H)$ *time and make at most* q *queries, where* τ_H *is the time required to compute* H.

The following theorem states that $\mathsf{VIM2}^H$ is a secure vector-input PRF if H is a secure PRF under $\{0^n, d_0, d_1, d_2, d_3\}$-XRKAs:

Theorem 8. *For any adversary* $\mathbf{A}$ *taking at most* t *time and making at most* q *queries each of which is at most* ℓ_{v}*-dimensional, there exist adversaries* $\dot{\mathbf{A}}$, $\ddot{\mathbf{A}}$, *and* $\dddot{\mathbf{A}}$ *such that*

$$\mathrm{Adv}^{\mathrm{prf}}_{\mathsf{VIM2}^H}(\mathbf{A}) \leq \mathrm{Adv}^{\mathrm{prf}}_{H}(\dot{\mathbf{A}}) + \mathrm{Adv}^{q\text{-}\mathrm{prf\text{-}rka}}_{H,\{0^n,d_0,d_1,d_2,d_3\}}(\ddot{\mathbf{A}}) + (\ell_{\mathrm{v}} - 2) \cdot \mathrm{Adv}^{q\text{-}\mathrm{prf\text{-}rka}}_{H,\{0^n,d_3\}}(\dddot{\mathbf{A}}).$$

$\dot{\mathbf{A}}$, $\ddot{\mathbf{A}}$, and $\dddot{\mathbf{A}}$ take at most about $t + O(q\,\ell_{\mathrm{v}}\,\tau_H)$ time and make at most q queries, where τ_H is time required to compute H.

4 Further Security Analyses of KHC1 and KHC2

Our goal is to construct vector-input CR PRFs by using $\mathsf{KHC1}^F$ or $\mathsf{KHC2}^F$ for keyed hash function H of $\mathsf{VIM1}^H$ or $\mathsf{VIM2}^H$. Thus, in this section, we will see that the security requirements of $\mathsf{VIM1}^H$ and $\mathsf{VIM2}^H$ for H, that is, extended collision resistance and PRF under related-key attacks, can be satisfied by $\mathsf{KHC1}^F$ and $\mathsf{KHC2}^F$.

4.1 Extended Collision Resistance

The following theorems are obtained from Theorems 1 and 2 and from the fact that, for any $\delta \in \Sigma^n \setminus \{0^n\}$, a $\{\delta\}$-colliding input pair for $\mathsf{KHC1}^F$ or $\mathsf{KHC2}^F$ yields a $\{\delta\}$-colliding input pair for F:

Theorem 9. *For any $\Delta \subseteq \Sigma^n$ such that $0^n \in \Delta$, a Δ-colliding input pair for $\mathsf{KHC1}^F$ yields a $(\Delta \cup \{c_0\})$-colliding input pair for F.*

Theorem 10. *For any $\Delta \subseteq \Sigma^n$ such that $0^n \in \Delta$, a Δ-colliding input pair for $\mathsf{KHC2}^F$ yields a $(\Delta \cup \{c_0, c_{1,0} \oplus c_{1,1}, c_0 \oplus c_{1,0} \oplus c_{1,1}\})$-colliding input pair for F.*

4.2 PRF Under Related-Key Attacks

The following theorem states that $\mathsf{KHC1}^F$ is a secure PRF under Δ-XRKAs if Δ and $\Delta \oplus c_1$ are mutually disjoint, and F is a secure PRF under $(\Delta \cup (\Delta \oplus c_1))$-XRKAs:

Theorem 11. *Let $\Delta \subseteq \Sigma^n$ be any set such that $0^n \in \Delta$. Suppose that $\Delta \cap (\Delta \oplus c_1) = \emptyset$. Then, for any adversary $\mathbf{A}$ taking at most t time and making at most q queries each of which has at most ℓ_{m} blocks after padding, there exist some adversaries $\dot{\mathbf{A}}$ and $\ddot{\mathbf{A}}$ such that*

$$\mathrm{Adv}^{p\text{-prf-rka}}_{\mathsf{KHC1}^F,\Delta}(\mathbf{A}) \le \mathrm{Adv}^{p\text{-prf-rka}}_{F,\Delta \cup (\Delta \oplus c_1)}(\dot{\mathbf{A}}) + (\ell_{\mathrm{m}} - 1) \cdot \mathrm{Adv}^{q\text{-prf-rka}}_{F,\{0^n, c_1\}}(\ddot{\mathbf{A}}).$$

$\dot{\mathbf{A}}$ and $\ddot{\mathbf{A}}$ take at most about $t + O(q\,\ell_{\mathrm{m}}\,\tau_F)$ time and make at most q queries, where τ_F is time required to compute F.

The following theorem states that $\mathsf{KHC2}^F$ is a secure PRF under Δ-XRKAs if F is a secure PRF under Δ-XRKAs and $\{0^n, c_{1,0}, c_{1,1}\}$-XRKAs:

Theorem 12. *Let $\Delta \subseteq \Sigma^n$ be any set such that $0^n \in \Delta$. Then, for any adversary $\mathbf{A}$ taking at most t time and making at most q queries each of which has at most ℓ_{m} blocks after padding, there exist adversaries $\dot{\mathbf{A}}$ and $\ddot{\mathbf{A}}$ such that*

$$\mathrm{Adv}^{p\text{-prf-rka}}_{\mathsf{KHC2}^F,\Delta}(\mathbf{A}) \le \mathrm{Adv}^{p\text{-prf-rka}}_{F,\Delta}(\dot{\mathbf{A}}) + (\ell_{\mathrm{m}} - 1) \cdot \mathrm{Adv}^{q\text{-prf-rka}}_{F,\{0^n, c_{1,0}, c_{1,1}\}}(\ddot{\mathbf{A}}).$$

$\dot{\mathbf{A}}$ and $\ddot{\mathbf{A}}$ take at most about $t + O(\ell_{\mathrm{m}} \cdot q \cdot \tau_F)$ time and make at most q queries, where τ_F is time required to compute F.

5 Vector-Input CR PRF

This section summarizes the results on reduction of security of vector-input keyed hash functions $\mathsf{VIM1}^{\mathsf{KHC1}^F}$, $\mathsf{VIM1}^{\mathsf{KHC2}^F}$, $\mathsf{VIM2}^{\mathsf{KHC1}^F}$, and $\mathsf{VIM2}^{\mathsf{KHC2}^F}$ to that of the underlying compression function F.

5.1 Collision Resistance

Collision resistance of $\mathsf{VIM1}^{\mathsf{KHC1}^F}$, $\mathsf{VIM1}^{\mathsf{KHC2}^F}$, $\mathsf{VIM2}^{\mathsf{KHC1}^F}$, and $\mathsf{VIM2}^{\mathsf{KHC2}^F}$ is reduced to extended collision resistance of F:

Corollary 1. *A colliding input pair for* $\mathsf{VIM1}^{\mathsf{KHC1}^F}$ *yields a* $\{0^n, c_0, d_0\}$*-colliding input pair for* F.

Corollary 2. *A colliding input pair for* $\mathsf{VIM1}^{\mathsf{KHC2}^F}$ *yields a* $\{0^n, c_0, c_{1,0} \oplus c_{1,1}, c_0 \oplus c_{1,0} \oplus c_{1,1}, d_0\}$*-colliding input pair for* F.

Corollary 3. *A colliding input pair for* $\mathsf{VIM2}^{\mathsf{KHC1}^F}$ *yields a* $(\{0^n, c_0, d_3\} \cup \{d_i \oplus d_j\}_{0 \le i < j \le 3})$*-colliding input pair for* F.

Corollary 4. *A colliding input pair for* $\mathsf{VIM2}^{\mathsf{KHC2}^F}$ *yields a* $(\{0^n, c_0, c_{1,0} \oplus c_{1,1}, c_0 \oplus c_{1,0} \oplus c_{1,1}, d_3\} \cup \{d_i \oplus d_j\}_{0 \le i < j \le 3})$*-colliding input pair for* F.

The corollaries above suggest that any adversary treating F as a black box needs $\Omega(2^{n/2})$ queries to find a colliding input pair for $\mathsf{VIM1}^{\mathsf{KHC1}^F}$, $\mathsf{VIM1}^{\mathsf{KHC2}^F}$, $\mathsf{VIM2}^{\mathsf{KHC1}^F}$, or $\mathsf{VIM2}^{\mathsf{KHC2}^F}$.

5.2 PRF Property

Pseudorandomness of $\mathsf{VIM1}^{\mathsf{KHC1}^F}$, $\mathsf{VIM1}^{\mathsf{KHC2}^F}$, $\mathsf{VIM2}^{\mathsf{KHC1}^F}$, and $\mathsf{VIM2}^{\mathsf{KHC2}^F}$ is reduced to pseudorandomness of F under XOR related-key attacks:

Corollary 5. *Suppose that* $c_1 \ne d_1$. *Let* $\mathbf{A}$ *be any adversary against* $\mathsf{VIM1}^{\mathsf{KHC1}^F}$ *taking at most* t *time and making at most* q *queries. Suppose that for each query* $M = (M^1, \ldots, M^m)$ *made by* $\mathbf{A}$, $m \le \ell_{\mathrm{v}}$ *and padded* M^i *results in at most* ℓ_{m} *blocks for* $1 \le i \le m$. *Then, there exist adversaries* $\dot{\mathbf{A}}$ *and* $\ddot{\mathbf{A}}$ *such that*

$$\mathrm{Adv}^{\mathrm{prf}}_{\mathsf{VIM1}^{\mathsf{KHC1}^F}}(\mathbf{A}) \le \ell_{\mathrm{v}} \cdot \mathrm{Adv}^{q\text{-prf-rka}}_{F,\{0^n, c_1, d_1, c_1 \oplus d_1\}}(\dot{\mathbf{A}}) + \ell_{\mathrm{v}} \cdot \ell_{\mathrm{m}} \cdot \mathrm{Adv}^{q\text{-prf-rka}}_{F,\{0^n, c_1\}}(\ddot{\mathbf{A}}).$$

$\dot{\mathbf{A}}$ *and* $\ddot{\mathbf{A}}$ *take at most about* $t + O(q \ell_{\mathrm{v}} \ell_{\mathrm{m}} \tau_F)$ *time and make at most* q *queries, where* τ_F *is the time required to compute* F.

Corollary 6. *Let* $\mathbf{A}$ *be any adversary against* $\mathsf{VIM1}^{\mathsf{KHC2}^F}$ *taking at most* t *time and making at most* q *queries. Suppose that for each query* $M = (M^1, \ldots, M^m)$ *made by* $\mathbf{A}$, $m \le \ell_{\mathrm{v}}$ *and padded* M^i *results in at most* ℓ_{m} *blocks for* $1 \le i \le m$. *Then, there exist adversaries* $\dot{\mathbf{A}}$ *and* $\ddot{\mathbf{A}}$ *such that*

$$\mathrm{Adv}^{\mathrm{prf}}_{\mathsf{VIM1}^{\mathsf{KHC2}^F}}(\mathbf{A}) \le \ell_{\mathrm{v}} \cdot \mathrm{Adv}^{q\text{-prf-rka}}_{F,\{0^n, d_1\}}(\dot{\mathbf{A}}) + \ell_{\mathrm{v}} \cdot \ell_{\mathrm{m}} \cdot \mathrm{Adv}^{q\text{-prf-rka}}_{F,\{0^n, c_{1,0}, c_{1,1}\}}(\ddot{\mathbf{A}}).$$

$\dot{\mathbf{A}}$ *and* $\ddot{\mathbf{A}}$ *take at most about* $t + O(q \ell_{\mathrm{v}} \ell_{\mathrm{m}} \tau_F)$ *time and make at most* q *queries, where* τ_F *is the time required to compute* F.

Corollary 7. *Suppose that* $c_1 \notin \{d_0, d_1, d_2, d_3\} \cup \{d_i \oplus d_j\}_{0 \le i < j \le 3}$. *Let* $\mathbf{A}$ *be any adversary against* $\mathsf{VIM2}^{\mathsf{KHC1}^F}$ *taking at most* t *time and making at most* q *queries. Suppose that for each query* $M = (M^1, \ldots, M^m)$ *made by* $\mathbf{A}$, $m \le \ell_\mathrm{v}$ *and padded* M^i *results in at most* ℓ_m *blocks for* $1 \le i \le m$. *Then, there exist adversaries* $\dot{\mathbf{A}}$, $\ddot{\mathbf{A}}$, *and* $\dddot{\mathbf{A}}$ *such that*

$$\mathrm{Adv}^{\mathrm{prf}}_{\mathsf{VIM2}^{\mathsf{KHC1}^F}}(\mathbf{A}) \le \mathrm{Adv}^{q\text{-prf-rka}}_{F,\{0^n,c_1\}\cup\{d_i,c_1\oplus d_i\}_{0\le i\le 3}}(\dot{\mathbf{A}}) + \ell_\mathrm{v} \cdot \mathrm{Adv}^{q\text{-prf-rka}}_{F,\{0^n,c_1,d_3,c_1\oplus d_3\}}(\ddot{\mathbf{A}}) + \ell_\mathrm{v} \cdot \ell_\mathrm{m} \cdot \mathrm{Adv}^{q\text{-prf-rka}}_{F,\{0^n,c_1\}}(\dddot{\mathbf{A}}).$$

$\dot{\mathbf{A}}$, $\ddot{\mathbf{A}}$, *and* $\dddot{\mathbf{A}}$ *take at most about* $t + O(q\ell_\mathrm{v}\ell_\mathrm{m}\tau_F)$ *time and make at most* q *queries, where* τ_F *is time required to compute* F.

Corollary 8. *Let* $\mathbf{A}$ *be any adversary against* $\mathsf{VIM2}^{\mathsf{KHC2}^F}$ *taking at most* t *time and making at most* q *queries. Suppose that for each query* $M = (M^1, \ldots, M^m)$ *made by* $\mathbf{A}$, $m \le \ell_\mathrm{v}$ *and padded* M^i *results in at most* ℓ_m *blocks for* $1 \le i \le m$. *Then, there exist adversaries* $\dot{\mathbf{A}}$, $\ddot{\mathbf{A}}$, *and* $\dddot{\mathbf{A}}$ *such that*

$$\mathrm{Adv}^{\mathrm{prf}}_{\mathsf{VIM2}^{\mathsf{KHC2}^F}}(\mathbf{A}) \le \mathrm{Adv}^{q\text{-prf-rka}}_{F,\{0^n,d_0,d_1,d_2,d_3\}}(\dot{\mathbf{A}}) + \ell_\mathrm{v} \cdot \mathrm{Adv}^{q\text{-prf-rka}}_{F,\{0^n,d_3\}}(\ddot{\mathbf{A}}) + \ell_\mathrm{v} \cdot \ell_\mathrm{m} \cdot \mathrm{Adv}^{q\text{-prf-rka}}_{F,\{0^n,c_{1,0},c_{1,1}\}}(\dddot{\mathbf{A}}).$$

$\dot{\mathbf{A}}$, $\ddot{\mathbf{A}}$, *and* $\dddot{\mathbf{A}}$ *take at most about* $t + O(q\ell_\mathrm{v}\ell_\mathrm{m}\tau_F)$ *time and make at most* q *queries, where* τ_F *is time required to compute* F.

In Corollaries 5, 6, 7, and 8, the number of message blocks in each query is at most $\ell_\mathrm{v}\ell_\mathrm{m}$. Thus, their upper bounds are as tight as the upper bound shown by Bellare et al. [4] for the cascade construction of a string-input PRF using a compression function.

6 Parallelizable Vector-Input Keyed Hashing Mode

We present a parallelizable vector-input keyed hashing mode PVIM. It constructs a vector-input keyed hash function $\mathsf{PVIM}^H : \Sigma^n \times \Sigma^{**} \to \Sigma^n$, where $H : \Sigma^n \times \Sigma^* \to \Sigma^n$ is a keyed hash function. It is specified in Algorithm 5 and depicted in Fig. 5, where $d \in \Sigma^n$ is a non-zero constant.

Algorithm 5: $\mathsf{PVIM}^H : \Sigma^n \times \Sigma^{**} \to \Sigma^n$

input : (K, M)
output: $\mathsf{PVIM}^H(K, M)$
$m \leftarrow \dim(M)$; /* $M := (M^1, \ldots, M^m)$ for $m \ge 1$ */
if $m = 0$ **then** $V \leftarrow H(K \oplus d, \varepsilon)$;
else $V \leftarrow H(K \oplus d, H(K, M^1) \| H(K, M^2) \| \cdots \| H(K, M^m))$;
return V;

Collision resistance of PVIM^H is implied by collision resistance of H:

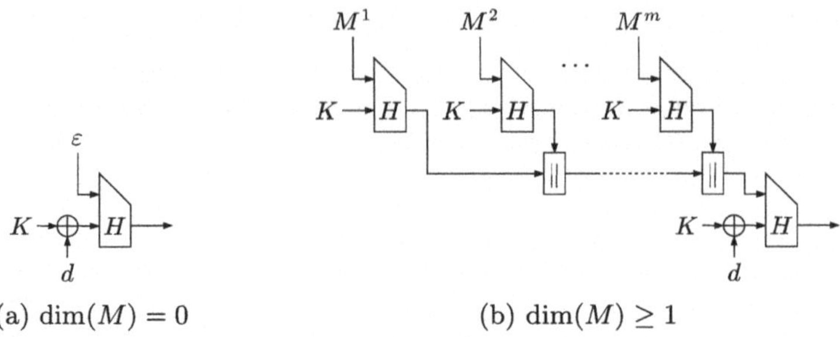

(a) $\dim(M) = 0$ (b) $\dim(M) \geq 1$

Fig. 5. Proposed parallelizable vector-input keyed hashing mode PVIM

Theorem 13. *If a colliding pair of inputs is found for* PVIM^H*, then a colliding pair of inputs is found for* H*.*

PVIM^H is a secure PRF if H is a secure PRF under $\{0^n, d\}$-XRKAs:

Theorem 14. *Let* $\mathbf{A}$ *be any adversary against* PVIM^H *taking at most* t *time and making at most* q *queries. Suppose that the total number of strings in the queries (the sum of dimensions of the queries) made by* $\mathbf{A}$ *is at most* σ*. Then, there exists an adversary* $\dot{\mathbf{A}}$ *such that*

$$\mathrm{Adv}^{\mathrm{prf}}_{\mathsf{PVIM}^H}(\mathbf{A}) \leq \mathrm{Adv}^{\mathrm{prf\text{-}rka}}_{H,\{0^n,d\}}(\dot{\mathbf{A}}) + \frac{\sigma^2}{2^{n+1}}.$$

$\dot{\mathbf{A}}$ *takes at most about* t *time and makes at most* $(q + \sigma)$ *queries.*

When $\mathsf{KHC1}^F$ or $\mathsf{KHC2}^F$ is used for H, PVIM^H generally needs more calls to F than $\mathsf{VIM1}^H$ and $\mathsf{VIM2}^H$ though it is parallelizable.

7 Conclusion

We have proposed vector-input keyed hashing modes, VIM1, VIM2, and PVIM using a string-input keyed hash function. The sequential modes VIM1 and VIM2 extend conventional string-input keyed hashing modes KHC1 and KHC2 using a compression function. We have combined VIM1, VIM2, or PVIM with KHC1 or KHC2 and constructed vector-input CR PRFs by using a compression function satisfying extended collision resistance and pseudorandomness under related-key attacks. Though PVIM allows parallel processing, it requires more calls to the underlying compression function than VIM1 and VIM2.

Acknowledgments. The first and third authors were supported by JSPS KAKENHI Grant Number 24K14944.

References

1. Bagheri, N., Gauravaram, P., Knudsen, L.R., Zenner, E.: The suffix-free-prefix-free hash function construction and its indifferentiability security analysis. Int. J. Inf. Secur. **11**(6), 419–434 (2012). https://doi.org/10.1007/s10207-012-0175-4
2. Bellare, M., Bernstein, D.J., Tessaro, S.: Hash-function based PRFs: AMAC and its multi-user security. In: Fischlin, M., Coron, J. (eds.) EUROCRYPT 2016, Proceedings, Part I, LNCS, vol. 9665, pp. 566–595. Springer (2016). https://doi.org/10.1007/978-3-662-49890-3_22
3. Bellare, M., Canetti, R., Krawczyk, H.: Keying hash functions for message authentication. In: Koblitz, N. (ed.) CRYPTO '96, LNCS, vol. 1109, pp. 1–15. Springer (1996). https://doi.org/10.1007/3-540-68697-5_1
4. Bellare, M., Canetti, R., Krawczyk, H.: Pseudorandom functions revisited: the cascade construction and its concrete security. In: Proceedings of the 37th IEEE Symposium on Foundations of Computer Science, pp. 514–523 (1996). https://doi.org/10.1109/SFCS.1996.548510
5. Bellare, M., Kohno, T.: A theoretical treatment of related-key attacks: RKA-PRPs, RKA-PRFs, and applications. In: Biham, E. (ed.) EUROCRYPT 2003, LNCS, vol. 2656, pp. 491–506. Springer (2003). https://doi.org/10.1007/3-540-39200-9_31
6. Bellare, M., Ristenpart, T.: Multi-property-preserving hash domain extension and the EMD transform. In: Lai, X., Chen, K. (eds.) ASIACRYPT 2006, LNCS, vol. 4284, pp. 299–314. Springer (2006). https://doi.org/10.1007/11935230_20
7. Bernstein, D.J.: How to stretch random functions: the security of protected counter sums. J. Cryptol. **12**(3), 185–192 (1999). https://doi.org/10.1007/s001459900051
8. Black, J., Rogaway, P.: A block-cipher mode of operation for parallelizable message authentication. In: Knudsen, L.R. (ed.) EUROCRYPT 2002, LNCS, vol. 2332, pp. 384–397. Springer (2002). https://doi.org/10.1007/3-540-46035-7_25
9. Boneh, D., Eskandarian, S., Fisch, B.: Post-quantum EPID signatures from symmetric primitives. In: Matsui, M. (ed.) CT-RSA 2019, LNCS, vol. 11405, pp. 251–271. Springer (2019). https://doi.org/10.1007/978-3-030-12612-4_13
10. Damgård, I.: A design principle for hash functions. In: Brassard, G. (ed.) CRYPTO '89, LNCS, vol. 435, pp. 416–427. Springer (1989). https://doi.org/10.1007/0-387-34805-0_39
11. Dodis, Y., Grubbs, P., Ristenpart, T., Woodage, J.: Fast message franking: from invisible salamanders to encryptment. In: Shacham, H., Boldyreva, A. (eds.) CRYPTO 2018, Proceedings, Part I, LNCS, vol. 10991, pp. 155–186. Springer (2018). https://doi.org/10.1007/978-3-319-96884-1_6
12. FIPS PUB 198–1: The keyed-hash message authentication code (HMAC) (2008). https://doi.org/10.6028/NIST.FIPS.198-1
13. Furuya, I., Kasahara, H., Inoue, A., Minematsu, K., Iwata, T.: PMAC*rx*: a vector-input MAC for high-dimensional vectors with BBB security. In: Shikata, J., Kuzuno, H. (eds.) IWSEC 2023, LNCS, vol. 14128, pp. 77–97. Springer (2023). https://doi.org/10.1007/978-3-031-41326-1_5
14. Furuya, I., Minematsu, K.: Revisiting vector-input MACs. IACR Trans. Symmetric Cryptol. **2025**(3), 261–288 (2025). https://doi.org/10.46586/tosc.v2025.i3.261-288
15. Goldreich, O., Goldwasser, S., Micali, S.: How to construct random functions. J. ACM **33**(4), 792–807 (1986). https://doi.org/10.1145/6490.6503
16. Grubbs, P., Lu, J., Ristenpart, T.: Message franking via committing authenticated encryption. In: Katz, J., Shacham, H. (eds.) CRYPTO 2017, Proceedings, Part III, LNCS, vol. 10403, pp. 66–97. Springer (2017). https://doi.org/10.1007/978-3-319-63697-9_3

17. Hirose, S.: Collision-resistant and pseudorandom function based on Merkle-Damgård hash function. In: Park, J.H., Seo, S. (eds.) ICISC 2021, LNCS, vol. 13218, pp. 325–338. Springer (2021). https://doi.org/10.1007/978-3-031-08896-4_17
18. Hirose, S., Ideguchi, K., Kuwakado, H., Owada, T., Preneel, B., Yoshida, H.: A lightweight 256-bit hash function for hardware and low-end devices: Lesamnta-LW. In: Rhee, K.H., Nyang, D. (eds.) ICISC 2010, LNCS, vol. 6829, pp. 151–168. Springer (2010). https://doi.org/10.1007/978-3-642-24209-0_10
19. Hirose, S., Kuwakado, H.: Collision-resistant and pseudorandom hashing modes of compression functions. IEICE Trans. Fundam. **E109-A**(3), 185–193 (2026). https://doi.org/10.1587/transfun.2025CIP0005
20. Hirose, S., Kuwakado, H., Yoshida, H.: A pseudorandom-function mode based on Lesamnta-LW and the MDP domain extension and its applications. IEICE Trans. Fundam. **101-A**(1), 110–118 (2018). https://doi.org/10.1587/transfun.E101.A.110
21. Hirose, S., Park, J.H., Yun, A.: A simple variant of the Merkle-Damgård scheme with a permutation. In: Kurosawa, K. (ed.) ASIACRYPT 2007, LNCS, vol. 4833, pp. 113–129. Springer (2007). https://doi.org/10.1007/978-3-540-76900-2_7
22. Kelsey, J., Chang, S., Perlner, R.: SHA-3 derived functions: cSHAKE, KMAC, TupleHash and ParallelHash. NIST Spec. Publ., 800–135 (2016). https://doi.org/10.6028/NIST.SP.800-185
23. Liskov, M.D., Rivest, R.L., Wagner, D.A.: Tweakable block ciphers. In: Yung, M. (ed.) CRYPTO 2002, LNCS, vol. 2442, pp. 31–46. Springer (2002). https://doi.org/10.1007/3-540-45708-9_3
24. List, E., Nandi, M.: Revisiting full-PRF-secure PMAC and using it for beyond-birthday authenticated encryption. In: Handschuh, H. (ed.) CT-RSA 2017, LNCS, vol. 10159, pp. 258–274. Springer (2017). https://doi.org/10.1007/978-3-319-52153-4_15
25. Merkle, R.C.: One way hash functions and DES. In: Brassard, G. (ed.) CRYPTO '89, LNCS, vol. 435, pp. 428–446. Springer (1989). https://doi.org/10.1007/0-387-34805-0_40
26. Minematsu, K.: A short universal hash function from bit rotation, and applications to Blockcipher modes. In: Susilo, W., Reyhanitabar, R. (eds.) ProvSec 2013, LNCS, vol. 8209, pp. 221–238. Springer (2013). https://doi.org/10.1007/978-3-642-41227-1_13
27. Rogaway, P., Shrimpton, T.: A provable-security treatment of the key-wrap problem. In: Vaudenay, S. (ed.) EUROCRYPT 2006, LNCS, vol. 4004, pp. 373–390. Springer (2006). https://doi.org/10.1007/11761679_23
28. Yasuda, K.: "Sandwich" is indeed secure: How to authenticate a message with just one hashing. In: Pieprzyk, J., Ghodosi, H., Dawson, E. (eds.) ACISP 2007, LNCS, vol. 4586, pp. 355–369. Springer (2007). https://doi.org/10.1007/978-3-540-73458-1_26
29. Yasuda, K.: HMAC without the "second" key. In: Samarati, P., Yung, M., Martinelli, F., Ardagna, C.A. (eds.) ISC 2009, LNCS, vol. 5735, pp. 443–458. Springer (2009). https://doi.org/10.1007/978-3-642-04474-8_35

Quantum Cryptanalysis & Theoretical Limits

Can Quantum Break ZUC? Only with a Million Qubits and a Billion Years to Spare

Anik Basu Bhaumik[1(✉)], Suman Dutta[2], Kyungbae Jang[3], Anubhab Baksi[4], Siyi Wang[1], Amit Saha[5,6], Hwajeong Seo[3], and Anupam Chattopadhyay[1]

[1] College of Computing and Data Science, Nanyang Technological University, Singapore, Singapore
anikbasu001@e.ntu.edu.sg
[2] Applied Statistics Unit, Indian Statistical Institute, Kolkata, India
[3] Division of IT Convergence Engineering, Hansung University, Seoul, South Korea
[4] Elektro- och informationsteknik, Lunds Universitets, Lund, Sweden
[5] Institut National de Recherche en Informatique et en Automatique (Inria), Paris, France
[6] École Normale Supérieure (ENS), PSL University, Paris, France

Abstract. The ZUC stream cipher is integral to modern mobile communication standards, including 4G and 5G, providing secure data transmission across global networks. Recently, Dutta et al. (Indocrypt, 2024) presented the first quantum resource estimation of ZUC under Grover's search, although preliminary, this work marks the beginning of quantum security analysis for ZUC. In this paper, we present an improved quantum resource estimation for ZUC, offering tighter bounds for Grover-based exhaustive key search. Beyond traditional quantum resource estimations, we also provide a concrete timescale required to execute such attacks using the specified quantum resources. Our findings show that a full-round, low depth implementation of ZUC-128 can be realized with a maximum of 375 ancilla qubits, a T-count of 106536, and a T-depth of 15816. Furthermore, the Grover-based key search can be performed most efficiently using 1201 logical qubits, 170681 T gates, and a T-depth of 78189, resulting in a runtime of 1.78×10^{11} years, an improvement of 93.43% over the estimated 2.71×10^{12} years by the implementation given by Dutta et al., we also provide akin analysis for ZUC-256 with an 99.23% decrease in time. These estimations are done assuming state-of-the-art superconducting qubit error-correcting technology.

Keywords: Fault-tolerant quantum computing · Grover's algorithm · Quantum circuit optimisation · Resource estimation · Surface code · Space-depth trade-offs · ZUC stream cipher

1 Introduction

With the advent of quantum computing, cryptographic standards face an imminent threat from quantum-based attacks, making ZUC an integral cipher in mod-

H. Seo (Ed.): ICISC 2025, LNCS 16487, pp. 295–324, 2026.
https://doi.org/10.1007/978-981-95-8034-7_16

ern mobile communication standards—a critical subject of study. The ZUC cipher is currently deployed heavily for communication of 5G and 4G communications as a part of its contribution in the 3GPP security standards (128-EEA3 and 128-EIA3). Every modern mobile device or smaller IoT devices connected via LTE relies on this encryption algorithm. Since its conception in 2010, various classical cryptanalytic techniques have been applied to ZUC [29,44,46], with a comprehensive overview provided in [33]. However, with the development of quantum computing, there has been a fundamental change in the landscape of cryptanalysis. While public-key schemes are most vulnerable due to Shor's efficient factorisation [39] algorithm, several quantum attacks have also been theoretically demonstrated against symmetric-key ciphers using Grover's and Simon's algorithms or their combinations. Hence a quantum cryptanalysis on ZUC is imminent due to its immediate implications to global security. Very recently, a preliminary study on the quantum cryptanalysis of ZUC has been conducted by Dutta et al. [13], which is extensively used in this work as a groundwork study.

To the best of our knowledge, the importance of such estimations was first emphasized by Grassl et al. [21] in their resource analysis for Grover-based attacks on AES. This work was subsequently followed-up by a series of studies on the quantum security analysis of symmetric-key cryptography and the associated resource optimisation, [3,6,22–25,28,30,38,48] to name a few. These analyses typically focus on resource metrics such as qubit count, gate count, and circuit depth to gauge scalability on real-world quantum hardware.

Continuing on this trend, in this work, we focus on another commonly used cipher. We improve upon the earlier work [13] by leveraging logic synthesis tools that help us optimise for the resource metrics mentioned before, thereby enabling a proper execution of a full round of the cipher.

Execution on actual quantum hardware requires a significant level of optimisations on the logical circuit designed into a circuit using only a few specific gate sets, known as universal gate sets—analogous to netlists in classical HDL workflows, implying logical gates as the Toffoli gate to be decomposed into compatible gate sets. One of the most popular universal gate-set is the Clifford + T gate set, discussed in Sect. 2. We further explore the trade-offs between space and depth using the techniques proposed by Dutta et al. [14]. When estimating circuit depth (including T-depth), we assume that gates acting on disjoint qubit sets can be executed in parallel, contributing to depth of 1.

Once these circuits are decomposed to the said gate-sets, we are able to measure on the actual metrics that matter for execution in the quantum hardware, like T-depth and T-count. Quantum depth reflects the execution time, while the number of qubits corresponds to memory requirements. In execution of large circuits such as that of a full round of ZUC in real-quantum hardware, there is a requirement of a continuous error correcting mechanism, an example of which is the surface code [18]. This error correcting flow introduces significant overhead in both the number of physical qubits required and the overall runtime. Therefore to estimate for a practical and feasible attack on ZUC it is also necesarry to analyse the runtime of the entire cipher and the total resources required for the flow.

Organisation and Contributions

We discuss about the prerequisites in Sect. 2. The main contributions of this paper are summarised as follows:

- Sect. 3 is our first contributory section which provides an improved quantum resource estimation for the core components of the ZUC cipher. This includes a brief overview of the synthesis tools employed, along with key heuristics used to optimize intermediate Boolean circuit representations.
- The next section (Sect. 4) details the quantum resource requirements in terms of qubit count, T-count, and T-depth, based on advanced Clifford+T decompositions of both standard (2-controlled) and multi-controlled Toffoli gates. These gates are used in constructing the non-linear components of ZUC and Grover's oracle. Additionally, we present a comparative analysis of different synthesis strategies (shallow, compact, and optimal) to highlight trade-offs among various resource metrics.
- Sect. 5 combines the estimated quantum resources (qubits, T-count, T-depth, and total depth) with quantum error-correcting codes to derive practical hardware requirements and attack times. Benchmarking against current superconducting qubit platforms shows substantial runtime reductions: 93.43% for ZUC-128 and 99.52% for ZUC-256 compared to prior estimates.

Finally, in Sect. 6, we conclude the paper with a brief summary of our results and future research directions. We also evaluate the updated MAXDEPTH criterion from NIST [34] for both the T-decomposed logical circuit (A.6) and the fault-tolerant circuit.

2 Preliminaries

We begin with a preliminary discussion of key quantum computing, logic synthesis, and quantum error correction concepts that will be used throughout this paper. We move from basic quantum computing to decomposition and reduction techniques for complex quantum gates and the role synthesis plays in these decompositions, to finally understanding how logical circuits are mapped to physical circuits and the role of error correcting codes in the scenario.

2.1 Quantum Computing Basics: Qubits and Quantum Gates

A qubit is the fundamental unit of quantum information represented as $|\psi\rangle = \alpha|0\rangle + \beta|1\rangle$, where $\alpha, \beta \in \mathbb{C}$ satisfying $|\alpha|^2 + |\beta|^2 = 1$.

Quantum gates are represented by unitary matrices U, with inverses indicated by $U^\dagger$. Like the classical NAND and NOR gates, there are quantum gate sets that can approximate any unitary transformation on a quantum computer to an arbitrary degree of precision, known as universal gate sets. The Clifford+T gate set, rotation gates combined with the CNOT gate set, are common examples of universal gate sets.

The Clifford group is generated by three gates: Hadamard (H) $= \frac{1}{\sqrt{2}}\left(\begin{smallmatrix} 1 & 1 \\ 1 & -1 \end{smallmatrix}\right)$, phase (S) $= \left(\begin{smallmatrix} 1 & 0 \\ 0 & i \end{smallmatrix}\right)$, and CNOT $= \left(\begin{smallmatrix} \mathrm{I} & 0 \\ 0 & \mathrm{X} \end{smallmatrix}\right)$, where I $= \left(\begin{smallmatrix} 1 & 0 \\ 0 & 1 \end{smallmatrix}\right)$ and X $= \left(\begin{smallmatrix} 0 & 1 \\ 1 & 0 \end{smallmatrix}\right)$. The set is minimal, as the removal of any single gate would make it incapable of implementing certain Clifford operations. However, the Clifford gates alone do not constitute a universal gate set, as the T gate, defined as $\mathrm{T} = \sqrt{\mathrm{S}}$, cannot be generated solely using the Clifford operations. Consequently, the Clifford group, when augmented with the T-gate, forms a universal quantum gate set, enabling arbitrary quantum computations.

The Toffoli gate is a three-qubit gate in which the first two qubits act as control qubits, while the third (target) qubit is flipped if and only if both control qubits are in the $|1\rangle$ state. Mathematically, Toffoli $: |a, b, c\rangle \rightarrow |a, b, c \oplus ab\rangle$. Consequently, the Toffoli gate is also denoted as CCNOT (or CCX) gate.

The (2-controlled) Toffoli gate can be further extended to multi-controlled Toffoli (MCT) gates. Despite its utility, the implementation of MCT gates using the Clifford+T gate set requires careful decomposition to minimise the T-count, T-depth, and the required number of qubits. These optimisations are essential for practical quantum computation, where resource efficiency is critical. A comprehensive summary of the existing benchmarks for Clifford+T decompositions of single and multi-controlled Toffoli gates is provided in [14, Tables I, II]. For more details, one may refer to sources as [36, Chapter 3].

2.2 Design of ZUC-128/256

ZUC is a word-oriented stream cipher. ZUC-128 takes a 128-bit key, 128-bit IV, and a 240-bit constant; whereas ZUC-256 utilizes a 256-bit key, 128-bit IV, and a 112-bit constant. ZUC operates on three interconnected layers: (a) Linear Feedback Shift Register (LFSR) layer, (b) Bit-Reorganization (BR) layer, (c) Non-Linear Function (NLF) layer.

The key, IV, and constants (496 bits in total for both variants of ZUC) are loaded into the LFSR, as described in [13, Sections 2.1 and 2.2]. After the key/IV loading, both variants follow an almost identical process, allowing for a unified description of the cipher's operation.

There are two phases in the operation of ZUC: The initialisation phase and the key-stream generation phase. The schematic diagrams for the initialisation and key-stream generation are omitted from here for brevity but can be found in [42, Figures 1, 2]. The initialisation phase runs for 32 rounds (without generating the key-stream bits). The key-stream generation happens thereafter. The operational descriptions for each components are described in [42]. A small description of the operational semantics of the components can be found in the Appendices A.2

2.3 Grover's Search on Stream Ciphers

Given $f : \{0,1\}^n \rightarrow \{0,1\}$ with the promise that $f(x_0) = 1$ for a fixed $x_0 \in \{0,1\}^n$, and $f(x) = 0$ if $x \neq x_0$, Grover's algorithm can find $x_0 \in \{0,1\}^n$ using $\mathcal{O}(\sqrt{2^n})$ oracle queries, whereas the classical search may require up to $\mathcal{O}(2^n)$ queries in the worst case.

The algorithm relies on amplitude amplification, a technique that increases the amplitude of the target state while suppressing the amplitudes of non-solution states, thereby enhancing search efficiency.

Given any key, $K \in \{0,1\}^k$ and an $IV \in \{0,1\}^m$, let $\texttt{ZUC}_{K,IV} = ks$ denote the key-stream generated from ZUC. For any given key stream ks of length ρ, we employ Grover's search for key recovery as follows.

Algorithm 1. Grover Search for Key K_0 via ZUC Oracle

1: Construct oracle U_f s.t. $f(K, IV) = 1$ if $\texttt{ZUC}_{K,IV} = ks$, else 0.
2: Init k qubits: $|0\rangle^{\otimes k} \xrightarrow{H^{\otimes k}} |\mathcal{K}\rangle = \frac{1}{\sqrt{2^k}} \sum_j |K_j\rangle$.
3: Apply U_f: $\frac{1}{\sqrt{2^k}} \sum_j (-1)^{f(K_j)} |K_j\rangle$.
4: Apply diffusion $D = 2|\mathcal{K}\rangle\langle\mathcal{K}| - I$.
5: Repeat Steps 3–4 for $\mathcal{O}(\sqrt{2^k})$ iterations.
6: Measure qubits; output observed key K_0.

Since IV is typically public information, the first step can be modified such that f takes only K as input and satisfies $f(K) = 1$ if $\texttt{ZUC}_K$ generates the key-stream ks. Considering the scenario where two different keys, K_i and K_j, generate the same key-stream of length ρ, the collision probability, $\Pr\left(C_\rho(K_i) = C_\rho(K_j)\right) \approx \frac{2^k - 1}{2^\rho}$, can be reduced to $\mathcal{O}\left(2^{-c}\right)$ by setting the key-stream length to $\rho = k + c$. We refer to the oracle used for marking as $\mathcal{ENC}$, this oracle contains the ZUC cipher implemented as a quantum circuit. The schematic diagram of the corresponding Grover's oracle is shown in [3, Fig. 1].

2.4 Logic Synthesis and its Applications

In the logic synthesis phase, Register Transfer Level (RTL) descriptions are translated into gate-level netlists supported by specific technology libraries. The primary optimization metrics in this process are the per-gate cost and the total number of gates, which together determine the area of the resulting circuit. In the quantum domain, a similar optimization problem arises, aimed at minimizing the logical depth and the number of qubits, which correspond to execution time and hardware area, respectively. Notably, reducing circuit depth often incurs an exponential increase in the number of required qubits. Therefore, a critical trade-off must be achieved between circuit depth and the ancilla qubits used. In Sect. 3, we explore a range of tools like the EPFL Logic synthesis libraries [41] and ABC [9] designed to effectively manage this trade-off between depth and ancilla.

2.5 Reduction of Multi-Controlled Toffoli into Toffoli Gates

Efficient decomposition of **M**ulti-**C**ontrolled **T**offoli (MCT) gates into the Clifford+T gate set, via Toffoli-based constructions, has seen significant advancements in recent years. The techniques used have been described below.

Optimal Toffoli-Depth. As demonstrated in [14], an n-controlled Toffoli gate can be decomposed into $n-1$ basic Toffoli gates using $n-2$ additional ancilla qubits, achieving an optimal Toffoli-depth of $\lceil \log_2 n \rceil$. For example, [14, Figure 12] presents a 7-MCT circuit decomposition with a Toffoli depth of $\lceil \log_2 7 \rceil = 3$, using 5 ancilla qubits, and 6 Toffoli gates.

Conditionally Clean Ancilla. In the conditionally clean ancilla technique (Khattar et al. [27]), the construction begins with at least one clean ancilla qubit. Initially, a basic Toffoli gate is applied with the clean ancilla as the target. If the ancilla is flipped, this indicates that both control qubits were in the $|1\rangle$ state. Applying Pauli-X gates to these control qubits then transforms them to the $|0\rangle$ state, making them available to be reused as ancilla qubits in subsequent rounds.

The process continues iteratively until all control qubits are exhausted. Once the relevant information from all control qubits is accumulated into a smaller set, a final (smaller) MCT gate is applied. This gate uses the accumulated qubits and the original ancilla qubits as controls and the original target qubit as the final target. Note that, if the initial clean ancilla remains unmodified in the first step, the target qubit remains unaffected.

Using this method, an n-controlled Toffoli (MCT) gate can be decomposed into a circuit with $2n-3$ Toffoli gates where the Toffoli-depth id bounded by $4 \log_2 n$. In Fig. 1a, we illustrate an 8-controlled Toffoli decomposition using two ancilla qubits, achieving a Toffoli-depth of 6.

Trade-Offs Between Clean Ancilla and Toffoli Depth. In a recent work [14], the conditionally clean ancilla technique has been extended to scenarios where additional clean ancilla qubits are available at the outset, resulting in a precise trade-off formulation between the number of clean ancilla used and the Toffoli-depth of the resulting circuit decomposition. Under constraints on available ancilla, this method yields the minimum Toffoli-depth achievable using conditionally clean ancilla. An example of the decomposition of a 10-controlled Toffoli (10-MCT) gate using additional clean ancilla is illustrated in Fig. 1b.

2.6 Reduction of Toffoli into T Gates

Toffoli gates are further reduced to T-Gates, such that the entire circuit can be modelled on the Clifford + T gate set. To do so, we employ two decomposition techniques, Amy et al. [1] proposed a decomposition with T-depth of 4 but one less Clifford gate, with overall circuit depth 8, they also propose a decomposition with T-Depth of 3 and overall depth of 9 as shown in Fig. 2a which is employed

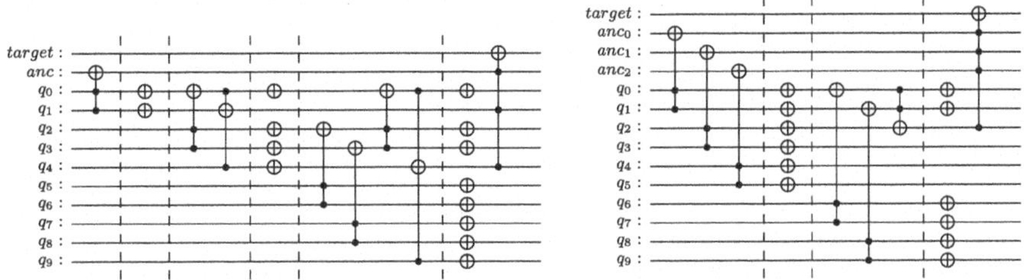

(a) Conditionally clean ancilla technique (based on [27]). (b) Conditionally clean ancilla with space-depth trade-offs (based on [14]).

Fig. 1. 10-MCT circuit decompositions following implementation strategies.

in our decompositon techniques. Gidney et al. [19] gives a measurement-based uncomputation strategy for T decomposition with a T-depth of 1 + 1 and overall depth of 8, the fanout gates provided by Gidney in this construction in [19] is decomposed into 2 CNOT gates in Fig 2b, they also mention that the third qubit starts with $|T\rangle = \frac{1}{\sqrt{2}}\left(|0\rangle + e^{i\pi/4}|1\rangle\right)$, which we derive from $TH|0\rangle = \frac{1}{\sqrt{2}}T\left(|0\rangle + |1\rangle\right) = |T\rangle$.

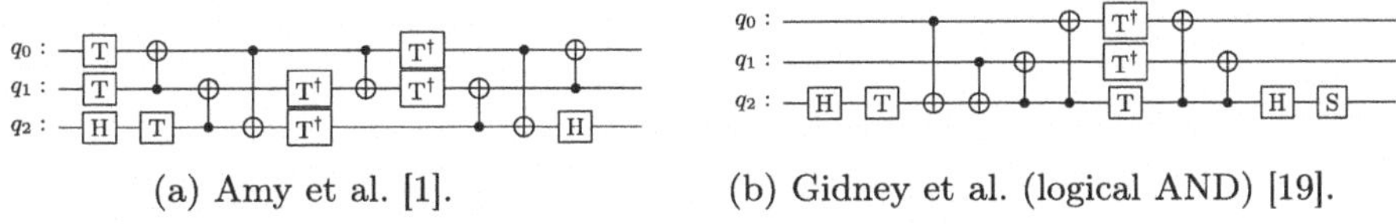

(a) Amy et al. [1]. (b) Gidney et al. (logical AND) [19].

Fig. 2. Toffoli → Clifford+T decomposition methods.

2.7 Quantum Error Correction

Physical qubits are noisy and short-lived unlike logical qubits, building dependable representations of logical qubits with given physical qubits requires Quantum Error Correction (QEC), fixing errors made during idle storage and gate operations. A stronger QEC scheme is required for longer and larger algorithms like Grover's search in ZUC, increasing requirement in time and resources. The surface code [18] is considered to be the most promising model in application to real quantum hardware for error correction models. A 2D array of nearest-neighbor physical qubits is used by the surface code to detect and correct errors. One logical qubit in an $n \times n$ array of physical qubits ($n = 2d - 1$) is encoded by a distance-d surface code. Each cycle 1–2-qubit gates, qubit measurements, and standard error correction mechanisms (required to monitor errors to prevent logical failures). The technique in [16] assumes a mesh of classical computing units and an $L \times L$ grid of logical qubits to accomplish constant-time error detection rounds. Hence, the physical qubits and quantum gates estimated for a surface-code-based quantum computer give a good approximation of the resources needed for running large-scale circuits like those for ZUC.

The surface code cannot directly realize non-Clifford gates such as the T gate, which are essential for universal quantum computation. These gates are implemented using magic state distillation [8], this protocol repeatedly prepares and purifies noisy ancilla states to achieve the high fidelity needed for fault-tolerant execution. Magic state distillation is resource-intensive, demanding dedicated factories and many qubits per state, and becomes a key bottleneck for T-gate–heavy algorithms like Grover's search.

3 Efficient Quantum Synthesis of ZUC

As outlined in Sect. 2, ZUC comprises three primary layers: the Linear Feedback Shift Register (LFSR) layer, the Bit Reorganization layer, and the Non-Linear Function (NLF) layer. The NLF layer includes both a linear component and S-box operations. To enable an efficient quantum implementation of the NLF layer, we employ reversible circuit synthesis techniques, as detailed below.

3.1 Synthesis of Linear Layers

There are two linear layers L_1 and L_2 in the ZUC cipher, each can be represented by a 32×32 binary matrix, they are related by $L_1 = L_2^T$. To optimally synthesise these matrices we use various tools and convert them into lists of XOR expressions. These are subsequently translated into quantum representations by mapping each XOR operation to a corresponding CNOT gate. The methodologies and outcomes of these tools are as follows.

Summary of Algorithms in Linear Layer Synthesis. Dutta et al. [13] present a two-step CNOT-based synthesis using the technique from [35], achieving depth 46 and 202 CNOT gates for $m = 10$ (see [13, Table 3]) by triangularizing, transposing, and grouping matrices to minimize depth beyond Gauss–Jordan elimination. Xiang et al. [45] propose an s-XOR approach for efficient 32×32 matrix decomposition, outperforming Boyar–Peralta and Paar algorithms for AES and ZUC (Table 1). Baksi et al. [5] extend the Boyar–Peralta tool to higher fan-in XOR gates for efficient XOR3 implementations and further enhance Xiang's in-place synthesis for larger matrices [4]. Yuan et al. [47] generalize this framework to optimize XOR count or depth, achieving state-of-the-art AES results and the lowest-depth ZUC synthesis with minimal qubit overhead. A comprehensive summary of various synthesis tools with the corresponding resource requirements generated for the ZUC linear layers L_1 and L_2 are presented in Table 1.

Table 1. Synthesis results of ZUC linear layers.

Method	L_1			L_2		
	Depth	#CNOT	#Qubits	Depth	#CNOT	#Qubits
Patel et al. [35]	46	202	32	46	202	32
Baksi et al. [5]	13	150	87	13	150	87
Xiang et al. [45]	25	84	32	19	84	32
Baksi et al. [4]	19	182	32	19	182	32
Yuan et al. [47]	10	89	32	10	88	32

3.2 Synthesis of S-boxes

Various classical optimisation techniques for S-boxes exist in the literature. In our work, we leverage classical algorithms to optimise S-box logic and apply appropriate mapping strategies to synthesise efficient quantum circuit representations. During our optimization process of the S-box, we followed certain synthesis flows, described as follows.

The **EPFL logic synthesis** toolkit provides a suite of tools for classical logic optimization and quantum circuit synthesis. The process begins with *Lorina*, which parses classical logic representations (e.g., given in PLA, Verilog formats) into internal formats such as **X**OR-**A**ND **G**raphs (XAGs) or k-input **L**ook **U**p **T**able graphs or (k-LUT graphs). These graphs are then processed using *Mockturtle*, a logic network manipulation library. Subsequently, *Caterpillar* maps the optimized logic networks into quantum logic using various strategy algorithms [41] (see Fig. 3), The mapped logic is converted into executable Python code using the *Tweedledum* library, facilitating simulation and integration into larger quantum algorithms.

ABC is a classical logic synthesis and optimization tool [9] that operates on various representations, such as **A**ND-**I**nverter **G**raphs (AIG). In our experiments, we use ABC to simplify both raw logic (e.g., truth tables) and pre-optimized representations (e.g., from [26]) encoded in bench format. The resulting logic is mapped to k-LUTs, which are subsequently synthesized into a quantum circuit using the EPFL flow as shown in Fig. 4.

DORCIS [4,10] and **LIGHTER-R** [12], which are in-place synthesis algorithms particularly suitable for small permutation functions (typically up to 4-bit S-boxes). We also utilize **Tweedledum** which supports implementation of certain synthesis algorithms [32] for Boolean functions and permutations, including those relevant to S-box design.

S_0 as Feistel Structure. The S-box S_0 can be represented as a composition of three distinct 4-bit mappings (which can be interpreted as S-boxes), as described in [15, Chapter 10.3.1], namely P_1: 9F0EFF2A040C7539, P_2: 8D6570C4B1EAF392 and P_3: 26A60DAF33D509CD. Among these, P_2 is a bijective mapping, for which we employed in-place synthesis techniques. For the non-bijective mappings P_1

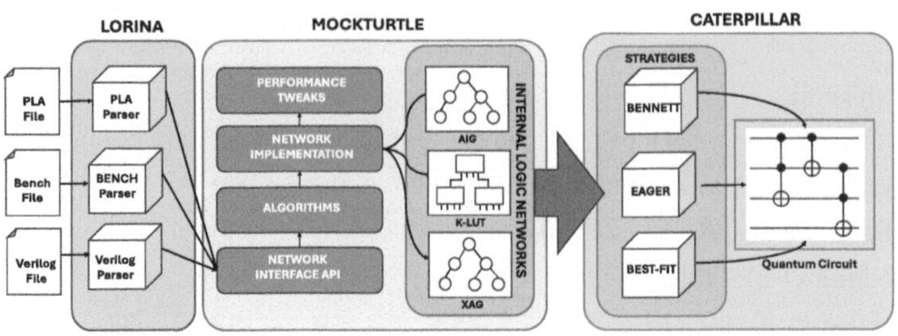

Fig. 3. EPFL logic synthesis schematic.

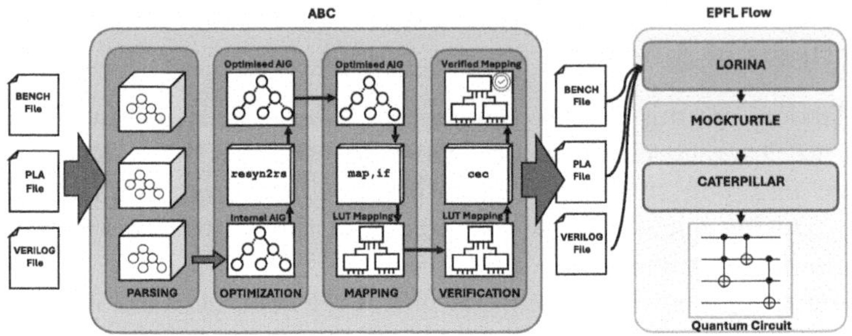

Fig. 4. Synthesis schematic of quantum circuits with ABC.

and P_3, we utilised mapping-based synthesis tools. The overall structure is illustrated in [15, Fig 10.1]. A similar diagram has also been added in the appendices for reference A.3

Synthesis of P_1 and P_3: As observed, both P_1 and P_3 are non-bijective. In-place synthesis tools such as DORCIS, LIGHTER-R, and the TBS algorithm from the Tweedledum library are not capable of handling non-bijective mappings. Consequently, we resorted to out-of-place synthesis methods. In particular, we employed synthesis flows based on the ABC frontend and the EPFL logic synthesis toolkit for these mappings.

Synthesis of P_2: Given that P_2 is bijective, both in-place and out-of-place synthesis techniques are applicable. In-place synthesis methods are usually preferred because of their lower ancillary requirements.We provide two quantum circuit implementations across these configurations:

(i) An 8-qubit implementation with P_2 in-place (Fig. 5a).
(ii) A 16-qubit implementation with P_2 in-place (Fig. 5b).

Table 2. Comparison of metrics for various flows for ZUC S_0 mappings.

#Qubits	P_1 flow	P_2 flow	P_3 flow	NCT-depth	#3-MCT	#Toffoli	#CNOT	#NOT
8	EPFL	DORCIS	EPFL	65	2	26	30	15
8	EPFL	LIGHTER-R	EPFL	63	2	26	30	15
8	EPFL	TBS	EPFL	81	14	34	34	15
16	EPFL	DORCIS	EPFL	49	1	21	27	14
16	EPFL	LIGHTER-R	EPFL	48	1	21	27	14
16	EPFL	TBS	EPFL	58	7	25	29	14
16	ABC	DORCIS	ABC	47	1	21	27	4
16	ABC	LIGHTER-R	ABC	46	1	21	27	4
16	ABC	TBS	ABC	56	7	25	29	4

Table 2 shows that implementing P_2 using LIGHTER-R provides better depth compared to DORCIS or Tweedledum. In Table 2 NCT-depth refers to the depth of the circuit when it is at a level containing only **N**OT-**C**NOT-**T**offoli gates. For EPFL, the best-fit mapping strategy was employed, as it provides a compact 8-qubit representation suitable for our quantum implementation. ABC was used as the frontend, and we observed an overall reduction in circuit depth. Across all mappings, the pre-optimized versions generated using ABC demonstrated improvements in both gate count and depth. The ABC commands used were: "`if -K 4 -a; resyn2rs; if -K 4`". Additionally, in the EPFL back-end of the ABC flow, we also applied the best-fit strategy.

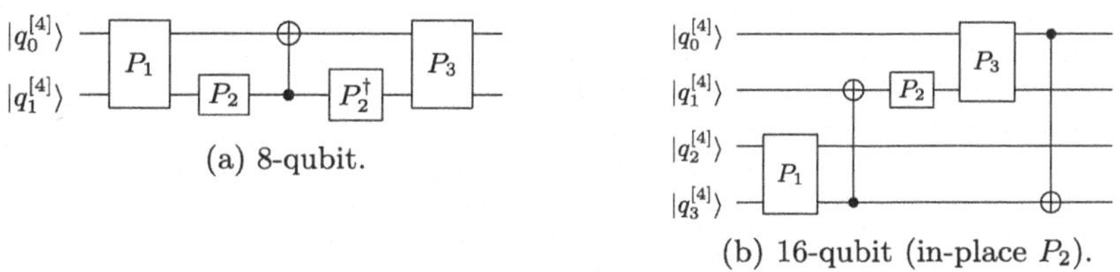

Fig. 5. Quantum Implementations for S_0.

Various Quantum Realisations of S_1. The S_1 S-box has highly non-linear properties, as is evident from our results in Table 3, synthesising S_1, yields a lot of and operation implying large number of Toffoli gates. We employ classical logic synthesis techniques, for generating the quantum versions of this S-box. We apply classical optimization algorithms to various logic representations, exclusively for the S-box S_1. Among the classical representations, we employ the XOR-AND expression lists proposed by Zou et al. [26] for different components of S_1 (available online)[1].

[1] https://github.com/xsm222/classical-circuit-implementation-of-ZUC-S1-box/tree/master.

Result Summary. Our results clearly demonstrate the space–depth trade-off described in [14]: reducing qubit count generally increases circuit depth, and vice versa. For example, synthesising for Zou et al.'s [26] implementation generally we require 160 qubits, but applying ABC ("`resyn2rs; if -K 6 -a;`") three to four times reduces qubits at the cost of depth (Zou-ABC (6-LUT)), We also observe increasing LUT size in ABC decreases qubits but increases depth (Fig. 4), See Table 3. showing the space-depth trade-off.

Using EPFL-based synthesis strategies (Sect. 2), we see that free-qubit allocation strategies like Bennett and Eager reduce depth, whereas the best-fit strategy, which minimises qubits, causes substantial depth growth. These results highlight the inherent spatial–temporal trade-off in quantum circuit design. Resource details for implementing S_1 are shown in Table 3.

Table 3. Quantum resource estimation of S_1 following multiple synthesis flows.

Flow	#Qubits	NCT-Depth	#X	#CX	#CCX	#n-MCT				
						3	4	5	6	7
Tweedledum (TBS) [32]	8	939	4	37	125	226	250	206	79	15
Tweedledum (TBS-Bi)	8	755	4	30	97	155	241	163	56	13
Tweedledum (TBS-Multi) [40]	8	654	3	18	80	144	206	132	70	9
EPFL (Best-fit) [31]	16	1037	12	32	116	225	292	216	118	32
EPFL (Bennett) [7]	1220	154	20	3604	2400	0	0	0	0	0
EPFL (Eager)	472	414	16	3600	2394	0	0	0	0	0
ABC-EPFL (Best-fit)	16	1036	4	32	116	225	292	216	118	32
ABC-EPFL (Bennett)	963	1386	714	2304	1902	0	0	0	0	0
ABC-EPFL (Eager)	262	1445	714	2304	1902	0	0	0	0	0
Zou et al. [26]	160	103	14	218	34	0	0	0	0	0
Zou-ABC (4-LUT)	81	205	60	294	137	22	4	0	0	0
Zou-ABC (5-LUT)	68	209	50	245	169	22	4	0	0	0
Zou-ABC (6-LUT)	62	252	42	226	222	12	0	0	0	0

4 Improved Quantum Resource Estimation for ZUC

In this section, we present the improved quantum resource estimations for ZUC-128 and ZUC-256. As discussed earlier, S-box construction can involve multi-controlled Toffoli gates. However, such gates are not must be decomposed into a universal gate-set (See Sect. 2.1). To accurately estimate the required resources, we first decompose the multi-controlled Toffoli gates into standard Toffoli and Clifford gates using the strategies outlined in Sect. 2.5. Subsequently, we apply the Toffoli → T gate decomposition techniques (see Sect. 2.6) to obtain the final resource metrics in terms of Clifford + T gates.

For MCT decomposition, we use the strategy of Khattar et al. [27], which employs conditionally clean ancilla qubits. Specifically, for the S_0, we consider the in-place 8-bit result labeled EPFL – DORCIS – EPFL from Table 2, and for S_1, we use the Zou – ABC (6-LUT) synthesis result from Table 3. The linear layer implementation follows Baksi et al. [5], as stated in Table 1.

4.1 Quantum Resource Estimation for LFSR

We propose a parallelization strategy that enables the LFSR operations from consecutive rounds to be executed concurrently, improving from the ripple carry adder implementation [11] as implemented in [13]. In particular, the LFSR computation for a given round can be initiated in parallel with that of the preceding round, thereby improving circuit-level efficiency. Consider the LFSR computation at any given round, which performs five modular additions: $s_{16} = 2^{15}s_{15} + 2^{17}s_{13} + 2^{21}s_{10} + 2^{20}s_4 + (1 + 2^8)s_0$.

The input to the next round is a right-shifted version of the current state, i.e., $(s_1, s_2, \ldots, s_{15}, s_{16})$. Hence, most of the additions for the next LFSR round can be executed in parallel with the current round, with the exception of the term involving s_{16}, which depends on the current computation: $s_{17} = 2^{15}s_{16} + 2^{17}s_{14} + 2^{21}s_{11} + 2^{20}s_5 + (1 + 2^8)s_1$. As a result of this parallelization, only the remaining addition involving $2^{15}s_{16}$ needs to be performed in the next round[2]

Table 4. Comparison of the quantum resources for ZUC LFSR.

Source/Reference	Round	#Qubits	#X	#CX	#CCX	NCT-Depth
Dutta et al. [13]	Each	31 + 2	348	893	364	337
This Work	Initial	31 + 6	348	893	364	337
	Subsequent					134

To enable this level of parallelism, we assign six ancilla qubits to allow for three parallel quantum adders. Empirically, we observe that three such instances are sufficient, as each quantum adder can be reused after three rounds. For example, the adder used in round i is reused in round $(i + 3)$. Table 4 presents a comparison of the quantum resources required for the LFSR between our implementation and that of Dutta et al. [13]. In our design (See Fig 8), except for the initial round $(i = 1)$, the depth in each round i accounts only for the final addition of $2^{15}s_{14+i}$, which contributes to the quantum circuit depth by 134.

4.2 Quantum Resource Estimation for NLF Layer

The NLF layer comprises two main components: the linear layers(L_1 and L_2) and the S-box (S_0 and S_1). Structurally, each linear layer is connected to four S-boxes. This motivates the need to estimate the resource requirements for both S-box and linear layer implementations, as detailed in Sect. 3.

[2] More precisely, a final modulo-2^{31} addition is performed to incorporate any carry.

We consider two distinct implementations for S_0 and S_1 with minimal ancilla requirements: an out-of-place implementation of S_1 (Zou – ABC(5-LUT)), and an in-place implementation of S_0 (EPFL – DORCIS - EPFL), chosen for its significantly lower circuit depth and zero ancilla usage. As evident from Table 5, the maximum size of the MCT gate in the S-box construction is $n = 4$. Applying the conditionally clean ancilla method [27], each 3-MCT and 4-MCT gate requires one additional ancilla qubit. Specifically, each 4-MCT is implemented using 5 Toffoli gates and 4 NOT (X) gates, whereas each 3-MCT uses 3 Toffoli gates and does not require any additional X gates. Each MCT decomposition incurs an additional depth of $(2n - 3)$. The total Toffoli-count for implementing S_0 is given by: $26 + 0 \times 5 + 2 \times 3 = 32$, and that of S_1 is $169 + 4 \times 5 + 22 \times 3 = 255$. The corresponding Toffoli depth after decomposition (using [27]) for S_0 is $65 + (2 \times 3 - 3) \times 2 = 71$, and that of S_1 is $209 + (2 \times 4 - 3) \times 4 + (2 \times 3 - 3) \times 22 = 295$. The total NOT gate count for S_1 is $4 \times 4 + 50 = 66$. NCT-Depth in all tables henceforth signifies the depth of NOT, CNOT, and Toffoli gates together in the circuit.

Table 5. Quantum resource estimation for ZUC S-boxes.

S-box	Ancilla	NCT-depth	#X	#CX	#CCX
S_0	$0 + 1$	71	15	30	32
S_1	$60 + 1$	295	66	245	255
S	122	295	162	550	574

From [13, Sec. 4.4], implementing in-place operations $W_1 = R_1 \boxplus X_1$ requires $2\times(31-2) = 58$ NOT gates, $5\times(31+1)-7 = 153$ CNOT gates, $2\times(31+1)-3 = 61$ Toffoli gates, and a depth of $2\times(31+1)+2 = 66$, and implementing $W_2 = R_2 \oplus X_2$ requires 32 CNOT gates to map the 16 least significant bits of s_7 and the 16 most significant bits of s_5.

Therefore, total quantum resource required for the NLF layer, assuming the linear layer design from [4] (182 CNOT gates, circuit depth 19), updating R_1 and R_2 require a total of $(58+162) = 220$ NOT gate, $(153+32+2\times182+550) = 1099$ CNOT gate, and $(61 + 574) = 635$ Toffoli gates, with a circuit depth of $(66 + 1 + 19 + 295) = 381$.

4.3 Quantum Resource Estimation at Various Stages

Here, we provide a detailed estimation of quantum resource requirement at different stages of ZUC, depending on its internal architecture and execution sequence.

Key/IV Loading. The LFSR comprises 16 registers, each of 31 bits. Assuming that one qubit is allocated per bit, the total qubit requirement is $31 \times 16 = 496$ qubits. The Key, Initialization Vector (IV), and the constant d_i are embedded within this register space. For ZUC-128, loading the key requires 128 CNOT gates, while the IV requires a maximum of 128 NOT gates. Similarly, the constant d_i requires up to 240 NOT gates. For ZUC-256, loading the key requires 256 CNOT gates, and loading the IV and the constants requires 240 NOT gates.

ZUC Initialisation. Prior to key-stream generation, the ZUC circuit must undergo 32 rounds of initialisation. After updating R_1 and R_2, one needs to compute $W = (X_0 \oplus R_1) \boxplus R_2$. Storing W requires 32 working qubits, where we copy X_0 using 32 CNOT gates. The XOR operation $(X_0 \oplus R_1)$ involves another 32 CNOT gates. For the in-place modular addition with R_2, the operation requires one ancilla qubit, $2(31-2) = 58$ NOT gates, $5(32-7) = 153$ CNOT gates, and $2 \times 31 - 1 = 61$ Toffoli gates, having a circuit depth of $2 \times 32 + 2 = 66$, as per the design in [11, Table 1]. Subsequently, the rightmost bit of W is discarded, and the remaining bits are added to the LFSR module using two ancilla qubits. This process requires: $2(31-2) = 58$ NOT gates, $5(31+1) = 156$ CNOT gates, and $2 \times 31 - 3 = 61$ Toffoli gates, with a circuit depth of $2 \times 31 + 6 = 68$ (following [11, Table 1.]). Hence, the total resources required: $(58 + 58) = 116$ NOT gates $(32 + 32 + 153 + 156) = 373$ CNOT gates $(61 + 61) = 122$ Toffoli gates and a depth of $(1 + 1 + 66 + 68) = 136$.

ZUC Key-stream Generation. In Key-stream generation, after computing $W = (X_0 \oplus R_1) \boxplus R_2$, instead of discarding the last qubit and adding it to the LFSR, X_3 is XOR-ed with W using 32 CNOT gates, and produces the key-stream $Z = X_3 \oplus W$. Therefore, total the resource required: 58 NOT gates, $32 + 32 + 153 + 32 = 249$ CNOT gates, 61 Toffoli gates, and a circuit depth of $1 + 1 + 66 + 1 = 69$.

Consequently, the resource requirements for one complete round of ZUC initialization can be determined by adding the resources needed for the key/IV loading, LFSR update, NLF layer, and the generation of W in the post-NLF layer. One complete round of ZUC-128/256 initialisation requires $(496 + 31 + 64 + 120 + 32) = 743$ working qubits, $(368/240 + 348 + 220 + 116) = 1052/924$ NOT gates, $(128/256 + 893 + 1099 + 373) = 2493/2621$ CNOT gates, and $(364 + 635 + 122) = 1121$ Toffoli gates, with the maximum circuit depth of $(1 + 337 + 381 + 136) = 855$ for the first round and $(1 + 134 + 381 + 136) = 652$ for the subsequent rounds.

Similarly, one complete round of ZUC-128/256 key-stream generation requires $(348 + 220 + 58) = 626$ NOT gates, $(893 + 1099 + 249) = 2241$ CNOT gates, and $(364 + 635 + 61) = 1060$ Toffoli gates, with the maximum circuit depth of $(134 + 381 + 69) = 584$.

4.4 Total Quantum Resources for $\mathcal{ENC}$

Let us now estimate the total quantum resources required to implement the ZUC cipher ($\mathcal{ENC}$), as illustrated in Fig. 6, with the circuit decomposed into Toffoli gates. It is essential to consider that ZUC undergoes 32 rounds of initialization prior to the key stream (key-stream) generation. From Sect. 4.3, the initialization of ZUC-128/256 requires 29568/33664 NOT gates, 79776/83872 CNOT gates, and a total of 35872 Toffoli gates.

Once the key-stream generation begins, each round produces a 32-bit key. To prevent collision in the exhaustive search, we assume that at least 5 and 9 rounds are necessary for ZUC-128 and ZUC-256, respectively; we denote this as $k = 5/9$. The number of NOT gates required during key stream generation is 3130/5634; the number of CNOT gates is 11205/20169; and the number of Toffoli gates is 5300/9540. The overall circuit depth is computed as $(855 + 652 \times 31 + k \times 584) = 23987/26323$, corresponding to ZUC-128 and ZUC-256, respectively. A summary of the total resources required is provided in Table 6.

Table 6. Gate counts and circuit depth for ZUC-128 and ZUC-256.

Variant	#X	#CX	#CCX	NCT-depth
ZUC-128	36794	90981	41172	23987
ZUC-256	35202	104041	45412	26323

4.5 Comparison of ZUC $\mathcal{ENC}$ Variants Based on Resource Metrics

In this section, we compare different versions of the ZUC cipher based on the selection of synthesized variants of its components, as outlined in Table 10. We adopt a straightforward strategy to guide our selection: Identify one variant optimized for depth and another for space (i.e., qubit count). For the depth-optimized (shallow) architecture, we select two linear layer implementations with the lowest depth, along with two implementations of each S-box namely $S_0 \rightarrow S_{00}, S_{01}$ and $S_1 \rightarrow S_{10}, S_{11}$. We select three configurations, Shallow, Compact and Optimal. **Shallow** focuses on minimizing the circuit depth, hence uses Baksi et al. (13 depth, 87q) for L_1/L_2 (See Table 1), EPFL–LIGHTER-R–EPFL and ABC–LIGHTER-R–ABC for S_0 (See Table 2), and Zou et al. with EPFL (Bennett) for S_1 (See Table 3). **Compact** focuses on a minimum size circuit hence uses Yuan et al. (10 depth) for L_1/L_2 (See Table 1), EPFL–LIGHTER-R–EPFL (63q) and EPFL–TBS–EPFL (81q) for S_0 (See Table 2), and TBS-Multi and TBS-Bi for S_1 (See Table 3). **Optimal** versions aim for a balanced implementation hence it reuses Yuan et al. (10 depth) (See Table 1) and the Compact S_0 choices, with Zou–ABC (5-LUT) and Zou–ABC (6-LUT) for S_1 (See Table: 3).

4.6 Resource Estimation of Grover Circuit for ZUC

The total resource requirements for single iteration of the Grover circuit are estimated using the formula: $2 \times \mathcal{ENC}_{res} + \mathcal{MCT}_{res}$, where $\mathcal{MCT}_{\text{res}}$ denotes the resource cost of the n-MCT used in amplitude amplification. The resources for $\mathcal{ENC}$ is summed twice for the state marking phase, namely for $\mathcal{ENC}$ and $\mathcal{ENC}^\dagger$ We utilize the decomposition strategy from Dutta et al. [14], which leverages at least six reusable ancilla qubits from the parallel LFSR structure (Sect. 3).

It requires only five ancillas ($m_1 = 3$, $m_2 = 2$) and reduces depth without additional qubit overhead.

From the configurations in Sub-sect. 4.5, the total resource requirements for a complete Grover iteration is calculated. Given that parallel Toffoli gates contribute only once to the circuit depth, we assume that the Toffoli depth scales linearly with circuit depth. Thus, to obtain the quantum depth, we multiply the circuit depth in Toffoli level to the total depth, as given by Amy et al. [1] and Gidney et al. [19], which is 9. The data for comparison with different parameters and techniques for each of these versions is available in Appendices A.5.

Resources for n-MCT in Grover's Search. In Grover's search algorithm, the MCT gate plays a crucial role, responsible for flipping the phase of the target state. The key-stream length for ZUC-128/256 is 160 and 288 bits, respectively. Therefore, we consider n-MCT constructions for $n = 160$ and $n = 288$.

From Sect. 2.5, there are several decomposition strategies for converting n-MCT gates into standard (2-controlled) Toffoli gates. These are subsequently decomposed into T gates following Sect. 2.6. The total number of Toffoli gates required for implementing an n-MCT is $2n - 3$, resulting in Toffoli counts of 317 and 573 for ZUC-128 and ZUC-256, respectively. The Dutta et al. (optimal) [14] decomposition yields Toffoli depths of $\lceil \log_2(160) \rceil = 8$ and $\lceil \log_2(288) \rceil = 9$. In contrast, the conditionally clean ancilla method by Khattar et al. [27] results in depths of 317 and 573, respectively. Additionally, we apply the depth-reduction method proposed in [14], where the ancilla configuration is chosen as $m_1 = 2$ and $m_2 = 3$. A detailed estimation for all the combinations can be found in Appendices A.4

Resources for ZUC $\mathcal{ENC}$ Variants. *Shallow version* results in the lowest circuit depth (18082), lowest qubit count (881), and the most efficient gate count among the variants for **ZUC-256**. The corresponding Toffoli count obtained is 26634, implying the T-count is $26634 \times 7 = 186438$ (from Amy et al. [1]), or the T-count is $26634 \times 4 = 106536$ using Gidney et al. [19]. Similarly, the corresponding resource requirement for **ZUC-128** are: 32132 NOT gates, 81879 CNOT gates, 24226 Toffoli gates, which implies, a T count of $24226 \times 7 = 169582$ (from Amy et al. [1]) and a T count of $24226 \times 4 = 96904$ (from Gidney et al. [19]). Further, the circuit depth becomes 16890 with a qubit count of 881. Since the S-box S_1 requires an additional 8 ancilla, we include 320 extra ancilla qubits, bringing the total qubit count to $881 + 320 = 1201$.

Compact version achieves the lowest circuit depth (168,388) using only 563 qubits, and contains an overall minimal gate count, we adopt the n-MCT reduction strategy by [27], to recieve a Toffoli-count of 286492, implying a T count of $286492 \times 7 = 2005444$ (from [1]) and a T count of $286492 \times 4 = 1145968$ (from [19]) for **ZUC-256**. In a similar setup, **ZUC-128** requires 202332 NOT gates, 67301 CNOT gates, 258732 Toffoli gates, which implies a T count of $258732 \times 7 = 1811124$ (Amy et al. [1]) and a T count of $258732 \times 4 = 1034928$ (Gidney et al. [19]). Furthermore, the circuit depth becomes 152532 with a qubit count of 563. No additional ancilla is required, as all NLF components are implemented in-place.

Optimal version adopts the optimal decomposition from [14]. The resource profile for ZUC-**256** is as follows. full depth: 24560, qubit count: 685, Toffoli count: 45412, which implies T-count: 317884 (Amy et al. [1]), or 181648 (Gidney et al. [19]). For ZUC-**128** with the same configuration requires 35610 NOT gates, 84099 CNOT gates, 41172 Toffoli gates, which implies 288204 (Amy et al.), or 164688 (Gidney et al.) T gates, with a circuit depth of 22736 using 685 qubits. Here, we have an additional 120 ancilla qubits required for the S block, the final qubit count becomes: $685 + 120 = 805$.

Estimation of T-Depth. The T gates in this circuit are primarily generated through the decomposition of Toffoli gates. The main sources of Toffoli gates in ZUC arise from the LFSR, the NLF, and the n-MCT gates used in the amplification stage. We compute the T-depth of the LFSR based on its structure: six sequential quantum additions in the initial round, followed by two additions in each subsequent round. According to Toffoli decompositions provided by Amy et al. [1] and Gidney et al. [19]

Each quantum addition (for LFSR) contributes a T-depth of 244 and 32, respectively for the decomposition by Amy et al. [1] and Gidney et al. [19]. The total T-depth for the LFSR is $6 \times 244 = 1464$ for the initial round, and $2 \times 244 = 488$ for subsequent rounds. Similarly, using the decomposition by Gidney et al. [19], the total T-depth for the LFSR is: 192 for the initial round, and 64 for subsequent rounds.

For the NLF, we use the Toffoli-depth of the selected configurations, as previously discussed. The cipher requires $k = 5/9$ rounds of key-stream generation, along with 32 rounds of initialization. The total T-depth of ZUC, therefore, can be expressed as: $\text{T-depth}_{\texttt{ZUC}} = \text{T-depth}_{\text{LFSR(init.)}} + (31 + k)\,\text{T-depth}_{\text{LFSR(sub.)}} + (32 + k)\,\text{T-depth}_{\text{NLF}}$. For the **shallow version**, with Toffoli $\text{depth}_{\text{NLF}} = 180$, the $\text{T-depth}_{\texttt{ZUC}} = 39012/43124$ (Amy et al. [1]) and $\text{T-depth}_{\texttt{ZUC}} = 15816/17512$ (Gidney et al. [19]) for $k = 5/9$. In the **compact version**, where $\text{Toffoli-depth}_{\text{NLF}} = 3846$, $\text{T-depth}_{\texttt{ZUC}} = 445938/494042$ and $\text{T-depth}_{\texttt{ZUC}} = 287100/318124$ under the respective decompositions. Finally, the **optimal version** with $\text{Toffoli-depth}_{\text{NLF}} = 338$ yields $\text{T-depth}_{\texttt{ZUC}} = 56550/62558$ and $\text{T-depth}_{\texttt{ZUC}} = 27508/30468$. The final T-depth values, including contributions from the amplification stage as per the decomposition from [14], are summarized in Table 7.

5 Runtime Estimation on Fault-Tolerant Architectures

The most resource-intensive task of fault-tolerant surface codes is implementing the T gate, which relies on a faulty magic state that must be purified via magic state distillation. The circuits responsible for state purification demand significant logical qubit resources. In this section, we estimate the additional overhead required for executing ZUC under this paradigm.

Let T_U^c denote the T-count of a circuit U, and T_U^d its T-depth. The T-width is defined as $T^w U = T_U^c / T_U^d$, representing the average number of T gates that can

Table 7. Resource comparison of various versions for one iteration of ZUC.

Version	Variant	Toffoli decomposition	#Qubits	#T	T-depth	Full-depth
Shallow	ZUC-128	Amy et al. [1]	1201	170681	78189	304515
	ZUC-128	Gidney et al. [19]	1201	97532	31742	304515
	ZUC-256	Amy et al. [1]	1201	188433	86467	326133
	ZUC-256	Gidney et al. [19]	1201	107676	35170	326133
Compact	ZUC-128	Amy et al. [1]	563	1812223	892041	2746071
	ZUC-128	Gidney et al. [19]	563	1035556	574310	2746071
	ZUC-256	Amy et al. [1]	563	2007439	988303	3031641
	ZUC-256	Gidney et al. [19]	563	1147108	636394	3031641
Optimal	ZUC-128	Amy et al. [1]	805	289303	113265	409743
	ZUC-128	Gidney et al. [19]	805	165316	55126	409743
	ZUC-256	Amy et al. [1]	805	319879	125335	442737
	ZUC-256	Gidney et al. [19]	805	182788	61082	442737

be executed in parallel per depth layer. Each T gate requires a logical magic state $|A_L\rangle := \frac{|0_L\rangle + e^{i\pi/4}|1_L\rangle}{\sqrt{2}}$. For a successful execution of U, these states must have an error rate no greater than $p_{\text{out}} = 1/T_U^c$.

We adopt the Bravyi-Kitaev 15-to-1 distillation scheme [8] and follow the modified methodology proposed by Amy et al. [2], which begins with a magic state of error rate p_{in}, injects it into an error-correcting code, and distils it to a lower error rate. If the resulting error still exceeds p_{out}, additional rounds of distillation are applied, exponentially decreasing the error. Assuming negligible logical errors during distillation (valid for sufficiently high code distances), the ideal output error after one round is $p_{\text{dist}} = 35p_{\text{in}}^3$. Following [18], we assume that the error rate of surface code gate p_g is approximately one-tenth of p_{in}, i.e., $p_g = p_{\text{in}}/10$, since about 10 gates must function correctly before error protection becomes effective.

To account for logical errors introduced during distillation, we introduce a parameter ε such that $\varepsilon p_{\text{dist}}$ quantifies this contribution, giving $p_{\text{out}} = (1 + \varepsilon)p_{\text{dist}}$. In a balanced scenario where $\varepsilon = 1$, the logical circuit introduces as much error as is eliminated by distillation. Fowler et al. [17] provides a framework for estimating the number of distillation rounds required to achieve a target output error rate, along with the minimum code distances necessary at each stage. This process is summarized in Algorithm 2; where d_1 denotes the code distance for the top distillation layer, d_2 for the next, and so on.

We consider the shallow version of ZUC-128 (with the Toffoli decomposition by Gidney et al. [19]) as a representative example for quantum resource estimation. The T-count of our ZUC-128 circuit is denoted as $T_{\text{ZUC-128}}^c$ (see Table 7) for this shallow implementation. The T-count for the complete Grover-based exhaustive key search algorithm (hereafter referred to as GA) is given by $T_{GA}^c = \lfloor \pi/4 \times 2^{64} \rfloor \times T_{\text{ZUC-128}}^c$. The corresponding target output error rate for

Algorithm 2. Estimating number of rounds of magic state distillation and corresponding distances of concatenated codes (based on [2]).

```
1: Input: ε, p_in, p_out, p_g(= p_in/10)
2: d ← empty list []
3: p ← p_out
4: i ← 0
5: repeat
6:     i ← i + 1
7:     p_i ← p
8:     Find minimum d_i such that 192 d_i (100 p_g)^((d_i+1)/2) < ε p_i/(1+ε)
9:     p ← ∛(p_i/(35(1+ε)))
10:    d.append(d_i)
11: until p > p_in
12: Output: d = [d_1, ..., d_i]
```

magic state distillation is $p_{\text{out}} = 1/T^c_{GA}$. Assuming a magic state injection error rate of $p_{\text{in}} = 0.02$, a per-gate error rate of $p_g = 10^{-3}$, and setting $\varepsilon = 1$, Algorithm 2 recommends a three-layer magic state distillation scheme with code distances $d_1 = 21$, $d_2 = 10$, and $d_3 = 7$.

The bottom distillation layer generates a single $|A_L\rangle$ magic state through three distillation layers requires $N_{\text{dist}} = 16 \times 15 \times 15 = 3600$ input states. These are encoded using a distance-d_3 surface code, which requires approximately $2.5 \times 1.25 \times d_3^2$ physical qubits per logical qubit, each round of distillation requires $10d_3 = 70$ surface code cycles. The middle layer uses a surface code with distance $d_2 = 10$, requiring approximately $2.5 \times 1.25 \times d_2^2$ physical qubits per logical qubit. The total number of physical qubits required in this layer is approximately $16 \times 15 \times 2.5 \times 1.25 \times d_2^2$, and the distillation round completes in $10d_2 = 100$ surface code cycles. The top distillation layer employs a distance-$d_1 = 21$ surface code, with each logical qubit occupying about $2.5 \times 1.25 \times d_1^2$ physical qubits. The total qubit requirement at this layer is $16 \times 2.5 \times 1.25 \times d_1^2$, and the distillation takes $10d_1 = 210$ surface code cycles to complete.

It is important to note that the physical qubits in the bottom distillation layer can be reused in the subsequent layers. Thus, the maximum physical qubits required to successfully distill a single purified state $|A_L\rangle$ is approximately equal to that required by the bottom layer. The full concatenated distillation process spans a total of $\sigma_{dist} = 70 + 100 + 210 = 380$ surface code cycles.

The T-depth and total depth of the full Grover's algorithm the total number of surface code cycles (σ_{GA}) is calculated in Table 8. T-gates dominate most of the computational runtime, as the qubits involved in Clifford operations remain idle for most of the computation. Hence, the overall runtime is primarily dictated by the time-consuming generation of magic states.

Table 8 focuses on the `ZUC` variants decomposed by Gidney et al. [19], which demonstrate lower T-depth and T-count relative to other known constructions. Among these, the shallow variant stands out for requiring the least total number of surface code cycles to execute the entire algorithm.

Table 8. Resource analysis of various versions of $\mathcal{ENC}$ using Grover's search with surface code.

Version	Variant	Code distances	#Physical qubits	Total cycles
Shallow	ZUC-128	[21, 10, 7]	$2^{22.9}$	$\mathbf{2^{82}}$
	ZUC-256	[34, 15, 9]	$2^{24.18}$	$\mathbf{2^{146.3}}$
Compact	ZUC-128	[22, 11, 8]	$2^{22.3}$	$2^{85.3}$
	ZUC-256	[34, 15, 9]	$2^{23.8}$	$2^{149.5}$
Optimal	ZUC-128	[21, 10, 7]	$2^{22.51}$	$2^{82.6}$
	ZUC-256	[34, 15, 9]	$2^{24.07}$	$2^{146.7}$

The space–depth trade-off costs for various ZUC quantum circuit designs from Table 8 using NIST's MAXDEPTH [34] model are shown in Table 9. It demonstrates that while compact circuits suffer significantly from large depth even though they use fewer qubits, shallow circuits achieve the lowest costs because their smaller depth keeps the squared-depth cost manageable. Under the depth-dominated cost metric, optimal designs are in the middle but still trail Shallow.

Table 9. Trade-off metrics for decomposed ZUC quantum circuits for fault tolerance analysis considering NIST's MAXDEPTH [34].

Version	Variant	$Td-M$	Td^2-M
Shallow	ZUC-128	$\mathbf{1.87 \times 2^{104}}$	$\mathbf{1.87 \times 2^{186}}$
	ZUC-256	$\mathbf{1.39 \times 2^{170}}$	$\mathbf{1.72 \times 2^{316}}$
Compact	ZUC-128	1.52×2^{107}	1.87×2^{192}
	ZUC-256	1.23×2^{173}	1.74×2^{322}
Optimal	ZUC-128	1.08×2^{105}	1.64×2^{187}
	ZUC-256	1.71×2^{170}	1.39×2^{317}

The duration of a surface code cycle varies across quantum hardware platforms. For superconducting qubits, such as those employed by IBM and Google, it typically ranges from 200 ns to 1 μs, depending on factors like code distance and control precision [19]. In contrast, trapped-ion systems operate more slowly, with cycle times generally between 10 μs and 1 ms, owing to longer gate and measurement durations [43]. In Table 10, we estimate the total runtime of our algorithm assuming a superconducting qubit platform. Furthermore, we compare our results with the current state-of-the-art implementation of ZUC [13], highlighting the improved runtime achieved through a more efficient circuit design.

Table 10. Run-time estimation of Grover's search on ZUC as per latest (in 2025) superconducting qubit technology.

Variant	#Physical qubits	Time (years)*	Time (years)‡
ZUC-128 [13]	$2^{23.5}$	5.41×10^{11}	2.71×10^{12}
ZUC-128 [This work]	$2^{22.9}$	$\mathbf{3.56 \times 10^{10}}$	$\mathbf{1.78 \times 10^{11}}$
ZUC-256 [13]	$2^{24.9}$	1.46×10^{32}	7.29×10^{32}
ZUC-256 [This work]	$2^{24.18}$	$\mathbf{7.04 \times 10^{29}}$	$\mathbf{3.52 \times 10^{30}}$

⋆ : 200ns for 1-surface code cycle, ‡ : 1μs for 1-surface code cycle.

6 Conclusion

In this paper, we demonstrated that synthesis and optimization flows enable practical quantum circuit design for the ZUC stream cipher. The implementation for synthesis[3] and the runtime estimation is available online. Our techniques achieve a significant trade-off between qubit count and circuit depth, reducing execution cycles by $2^{2.7}$ times and the physical qubit requirement by over 1.85 million in the ZUC-128 implementation. Compared to the currently best-known results, our approach yields a 93.43% and 99.52% reduction in runtime for ZUC-128 and ZUC-256, respectively. Additionally, the lowest T-depth and the circuit depth have been reduced to 1.03×2^{26} and 1.00×2^{28}, respectively; with the optimal designs maintaining low depth while outperforming compact versions. As an idea for future works, we aim to refine these estimates even further using the advanced distillation methods such as Litinski's protocol, magic state cultivation and use other error correcting methods such as the yoke surface code as provided in [20].

Acknowledgement. We gratefully acknowledge the support of MoE AcRF Tier 1 award RT10/23 for supporting this work.

A More Details on Synthesis and Time Estimation of ZUC

A.1 Grover Oracle for ZUC

A schematic diagram of the Grover's oracle for an exhaustive key search of a stream cipher, is provided in Fig. 6 derived from [3].

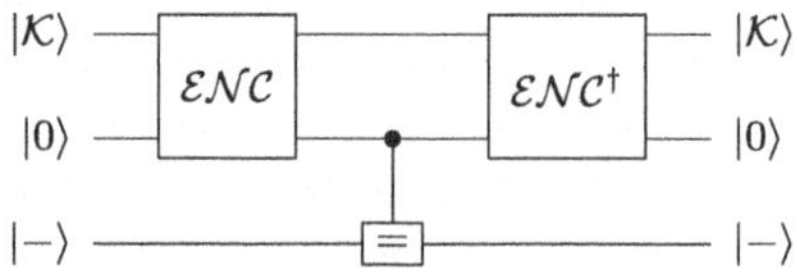

Fig. 6. Grover's oracle for comparing all possible key-stream bits from $|\mathcal{K}\rangle$ with the input key-stream and ks.

[3] https://github.com/anik314159/ZUC_caterpillar/tree/zuc_version2.

A.2 Design of ZUC 128/256

We now provide a brief operational description of the individual layers. ZUC is based on a single LFSR in the Fibonacci configuration, i.e., the feedback occurs only at the highest-indexed state. The LFSR contains sixteen states, each a 31-bit register, with the taps defined by the primitive polynomial $f(x) = x^{16} - (2^{15}x^{15} + 2^{17}x^{13} + 2^{21}x^{10} + 2^{20}x^4 + (1+2^8))$ over the field $\mathbb{F}_p$, where $p = 2^{31} - 1$. Consequently, the LFSR update function is given by $\mathsf{feedback}_f(s_0, \ldots, s_{15}) = 2^{15}s_{15} + 2^{17}s_{13} + 2^{21}s_{10} + 2^{20}s_4 + (1+2^8)s_0$.

In the bit-reorganization (BR) layer, specific registers from the LFSR are selected and reorganized as: $X_0 = s_{15H} \| s_{14L}$; $X_1 = s_{11L} \| s_{9H}$; $X_2 = s_{7L} \| s_{5H}$; $X_3 = s_{2L} \| s_{0H}$, where s_{iH} denotes the 16 most significant bits (MSB) of s_i, and s_{iL} represents the 16 least significant bits (LSB) of s_i.

The non-linear feedback (NLF) layer takes (X_0, X_1, X_2) as input and, based on the registers R_1, R_2 (32-bit, each), generates the output $W = (X_0 \oplus R_1) \boxplus R_2$ through the intermediate computations $W_1 = R_1 \boxplus X_1$ and $W_2 = R_2 \oplus X_2$. The registers R_1 and R_2 are then updated as $R_1 = S(L_1(W_{1L} \| W_{2H}))$ and $R_2 = S(L_2(W_{2L} \| W_{1H}))$, respectively. The substitution box (S-box) S utilized within the non-linear function is defined using two components S-boxes, S_0 and S_1, as specified in [33, Tables 3.1 and 3.2]. Note that, $S_0, S_1 : \{0,1\}^8 \rightarrow \{0,1\}^8$, while $S : \{0,1\}^{32} \rightarrow \{0,1\}^{32}$. For a 32-bit tuple (x_1, x_2, x_3, x_4) with $x_i \in \{0,1\}^8$, S is applied as follows: $S(x_1 \| x_2 \| x_3 \| x_4) := S_0(x_1) \| S_1(x_2) \| S_0(x_3) \| S_1(x_4)$. The linear maps L_1 and L_2 used in the non-linear function are defined as: $L_1(X) = X \oplus (X \lll 2) \oplus (X \lll 10) \oplus (X \lll 18) \oplus (X \lll 24)$, $L_2(X) = X \oplus (X \lll 8) \oplus (X \lll 14) \oplus (X \lll 22) \oplus (X \lll 30)$. The only difference between the initialisation phase and the key-stream generation phase lies in the handling of W. During initialisation, the rightmost bit of W is discarded, and the remaining 31-bit value is added to the LFSR feedback. In contrast, during key-stream generation, W is XOR-ed with X_3 to produce the key-stream.

A.3 Synthesis of ZUC S-box S_0

The Feistel-like structure of the ZUC S-box S_0, consisting of P_1, P_2 and P_3 is shown in Fig. 7.

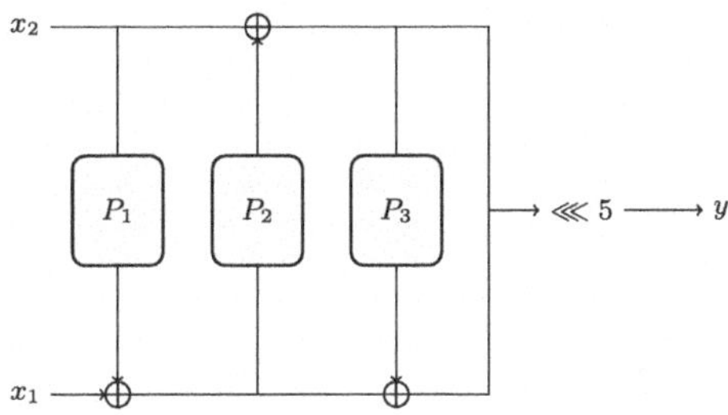

Fig. 7. Feistel structure of ZUC S-box S_0. [15]

A.4 Resource Estimation for n-MCT in Grover's Amplification

Table 11 shows a comparison of resources required for decomposing the an n-MCT with $n = 160, 288$ for amplification in Grover's (see Sect. 4.6) with different Toffoli reduction techniques as described in Sect. 2.5

Table 11. Comparison of resources for n-MCT decompositions of ZUC.

(a) ZUC-128

n-MCT → Toffoli	Toffoli → T	#CCX	#Clifford	#T	Toffoli depth	T-depth	Full depth
Khattar et al. [27]	Amy et al. [1]	317	2853	2219	317	951	2853
Khattar et al. [27]	Gidney et al. [19]	317	3170	1268	317	634	2853
Dutta et al. (optimal) [14]	Amy et al. [1]	317	2853	2219	8	24	72
Dutta et al. (optimal) [14]	Gidney et al. [19]	317	3170	1268	8	16	72
Dutta et al. [14]	Amy et al. [1]	157	1727	1099	55	165	495
Dutta et al. [14]	Gidney et al. [19]	157	1727	628	55	110	495

(b) ZUC-256

n-MCT → Toffoli	Toffoli → T	#CCX	#Clifford	#T	Toffoli depth	T-depth	Full depth
Khattar et al. [27]	Amy et al. [1]	573	5157	4011	573	1719	5157
Khattar et al. [27]	Gidney et al. [19]	573	5730	2292	573	1074	5157
Dutta et al. (optimal) [14]	Amy et al. [1]	573	5157	4011	9	27	81
Dutta et al. (optimal) [14]	Gidney et al. [19]	573	5730	2292	9	18	81
Dutta et al. [14]	Amy et al. [1]	285	3135	1995	73	219	657
Dutta et al. [14]	Gidney et al. [19]	285	3135	1140	73	146	657

A.5 Resource Estimation of ZUC $\mathcal{ENC}$ till Toffoli Level

In this section we describe the resources required for different combinations of the models we have selected for our $\mathcal{ENC}$ considering the shallow, compact and optimal versions. This decomposition is till the Toffoli level (Table 12).

Table 12. Resource comparison on NLF variants in the ZUC-256 circuit decomposed to Toffoli-level.

(a) Shallow versions.

Linear layer	S_0 depth	S_1 depth	#X	#CX	#CCX	NCT-depth	#Qubits
Yuan et al. [47]	46	103	30036	93955	26880	18082	881
Yuan et al. [47]	46	154	30528	371607	220892	20173	3001
Yuan et al. [47]	48	103	30856	93955	26880	18082	881
Yuan et al. [47]	48	154	31348	371607	220892	20173	3001
Baksi et al. [5]	46	103	30036	98957	26880	18205	991
Baksi et al. [5]	46	154	30528	376609	220892	20296	3111
Baksi et al. [5]	48	103	30856	98957	26880	18205	991
Baksi et al. [5]	48	154	31348	376609	220892	20296	3111

(b) Compact versions.

Linear layer	S_0	S_1	Toffoli reduction	#X	#CX	#CCX	NCT-depth	#Qubits
Yuan et al. [47]	S_{00}	S_{10}	Khattar et al. [27]	230526	79359	316012	186592	563
Yuan et al. [47]	S_{00}	S_{11}	Khattar et al. [27]	218636	77801	286492	168388	563
Yuan et al. [47]	S_{01}	S_{10}	Khattar et al. [27]	230526	79687	319620	186592	563
Yuan et al. [47]	S_{01}	S_{11}	Khattar et al. [27]	218636	78129	290100	168388	563
Baksi et al. [4]	S_{00}	S_{10}	Khattar et al. [27]	230526	86985	316012	186961	563
Baksi et al. [4]	S_{00}	S_{11}	Khattar et al. [27]	218636	85427	286492	168757	563
Baksi et al. [4]	S_{01}	S_{10}	Khattar et al. [27]	230526	87313	319620	186961	563
Baksi et al. [4]	S_{01}	S_{11}	Khattar et al. [27]	218636	85755	290100	168757	563
Yuan et al. [47]	S_{00}	S_{10}	Dutta et al. [14]	258406	79359	316012	142148	571
Yuan et al. [47]	S_{00}	S_{11}	Dutta et al. [14]	237660	77801	286492	127716	571
Yuan et al. [47]	S_{01}	S_{10}	Dutta et al. [14]	258406	79687	319620	142148	571
Yuan et al. [47]	S_{01}	S_{11}	Dutta et al. [14]	237660	78129	290100	127716	571
Baksi et al. [4]	S_{00}	S_{10}	Dutta et al. [14]	258406	86985	316012	142517	571
Baksi et al. [4]	S_{00}	S_{11}	Dutta et al. [14]	237660	85427	286492	128085	571
Baksi et al. [4]	S_{01}	S_{10}	Dutta et al. [14]	258406	87313	319620	142517	571
Baksi et al. [4]	S_{01}	S_{11}	Dutta et al. [14]	237660	85755	290100	128085	571
Yuan et al. [47]	S_{00}	S_{10}	Dutta et al. (optimal) [49]	30118	79359	316012	105822	571
Yuan et al. [47]	S_{00}	S_{11}	Dutta et al. (optimal) [49]	30036	77801	286492	95326	571
Yuan et al. [47]	S_{01}	S_{10}	Dutta et al. (optimal) [49]	30118	79687	319620	105822	571
Yuan et al. [47]	S_{01}	S_{11}	Dutta et al. (optimal) [49]	30036	78129	290100	95326	571
Baksi et al. [4]	S_{00}	S_{10}	Dutta et al. (optimal) [49]	30118	86985	316012	106191	571
Baksi et al. [4]	S_{00}	S_{11}	Dutta et al. (optimal) [49]	30036	85427	286492	95695	571
Baksi et al. [4]	S_{01}	S_{10}	Dutta et al. (optimal) [49]	30118	87313	319620	106191	571
Baksi et al. [4]	S_{01}	S_{11}	Dutta et al. (optimal) [49]	30036	85755	290100	95695	571

(c) Optimal versions.

Linear layer	S_0	S_1	Toffoli reduction	#X	#CX	#CCX	NCT-depth	#Qubits
Yuan et al. [47]	S_{00}	S_{10}	Khattar et al. [27]	35202	96415	45412	25954	681
Yuan et al. [47]	S_{00}	S_{11}	Khattar et al. [27]	33234	94857	45658	25667	667
Yuan et al. [47]	S_{01}	S_{10}	Khattar et al. [27]	35202	96743	49020	25954	681
Yuan et al. [47]	S_{01}	S_{11}	Khattar et al. [27]	33234	95185	49266	25667	667
Yuan et al. [47]	S_{00}	S_{10}	Dutta et al. [14]	33890	96415	45412	25626	691
Yuan et al. [47]	S_{00}	S_{11}	Dutta et al. [14]	33234	94857	45658	25667	679
Yuan et al. [47]	S_{01}	S_{10}	Dutta et al. [14]	33890	96743	49020	25626	691
Yuan et al. [47]	S_{01}	S_{11}	Dutta et al. [14]	33234	95185	49266	25667	679
Yuan et al. [47]	S_{00}	S_{10}	Dutta et al. (optimal) [49]	33890	96415	45412	24560	685
Yuan et al. [47]	S_{00}	S_{11}	Dutta et al. (optimal) [49]	33234	94857	45658	25175	671
Yuan et al. [47]	S_{01}	S_{10}	Dutta et al. (optimal) [49]	33890	96743	49020	24560	685
Yuan et al. [47]	S_{01}	S_{11}	Dutta et al. (optimal) [49]	33234	95185	49266	25175	671

A.6 Impact of MAXDEPTH Criterion

We assume that the adversary is constrained by a limit on the allowable circuit depth for executing Grover's search. Given the substantial circuit depth required when applying Grover's algorithm to cryptography in general, NIST introduced a constraint known as MAXDEPTH, which ranges from 2^{40} to 2^{96}. If the total circuit depth exceeds the threshold, the algorithm must be parallelised. However, as discussed in [25,37], Grover's algorithm exhibits poor scalability under parallelisation.

Specifically, reducing the circuit depth by a factor S requires launching S^2 parallel instances of Grover's algorithm. This results in a suboptimal trade-off between depth and resource usage. To enforce the MAXDEPTH constraint, a parallelisation strategy must be applied such that the depth is reduced to MAXDEPTH, i.e., $D/S = \text{MAXDEPTH}$, implying $S = D/\text{MAXDEPTH}$.

Under this setting, the gate count per Grover instance is reduced by a factor of S, but the number of parallel instances increases by S^2, resulting in a total gate complexity of $G \times D/\text{MAXDEPTH}$, derived from $G/S \times S^2$. This formulation illustrates how NIST integrates gate count, circuit depth, and the MAXDEPTH constraint when evaluating the cost of quantum attacks.

For space-depth trade-off metrics such as D-M, where M denotes the number of qubits, the parallelization increases the qubit requirement by a factor of S^2. Consequently, the adjusted cost becomes $\frac{D^2 \times M}{\text{MAXDEPTH}^2}$. Since the actual depth is capped at MAXDEPTH, the effective cost is expressed as $\frac{D^2 \times M}{\text{MAXDEPTH}^2}$, where D is effectively replaced by MAXDEPTH.

In summary, the D-M trade-off metric under the MAXDEPTH constraint is reformulated to minimize $D^2 \times M$, indicating that optimizing circuit depth has a greater impact on resource efficiency than reducing the number of qubits. Let Td and Fd represent the T-depth and full circuit depth, respectively. Table 13 presents the comparative trade-off metrics for various quantum circuit realizations of `ZUC`, including Grover-parallelized settings (i.e., Td^2–M and Fd^2–M). The shallow version of the `ZUC` quantum circuit exhibits the best trade-off performance in terms of Td-M and Fd-M, and also outperforms others under Grover's parallelisation in terms of Td^2-M and Fd^2-M.

Table 13. Comparison of trade-off metrics for ZUC quantum circuits with respect to Grover's parallelisation.

Version	Variant	Toffoli decomposition	*Td-M*	*Fd-M*	*Td²-M*	*Fd²-M*
Shallow	ZUC-128	Amy et al. [1]	1.03×2^{26}	1.00×2^{28}	1.22×2^{42}	1.16×2^{46}
	ZUC-128	Gidney et al. [19]	1.67×2^{24}	1.00×2^{28}	1.61×2^{39}	1.16×2^{46}
	ZUC-256	Amy et al. [1]	1.14×2^{26}	1.07×2^{28}	1.50×2^{42}	1.33×2^{46}
	ZUC-256	Gidney et al. [19]	1.85×2^{24}	1.07×2^{28}	1.98×2^{39}	1.33×2^{46}
Compact	ZUC-128	Amy et al. [1]	1.87×2^{28}	1.44×2^{30}	1.59×2^{48}	1.89×2^{51}
	ZUC-128	Gidney et al. [19]	1.20×2^{28}	1.44×2^{30}	1.32×2^{47}	1.89×2^{51}
	ZUC-256	Amy et al. [1]	1.14×2^{29}	1.59×2^{30}	1.95×2^{48}	1.15×2^{52}
	ZUC-256	Gidney et al. [19]	1.33×2^{28}	1.59×2^{30}	1.62×2^{47}	1.15×2^{52}
Optimal	ZUC-128	Amy et al. [1]	1.16×2^{26}	1.05×2^{28}	1.00×2^{43}	1.63×2^{46}
	ZUC-128	Gidney et al. [19]	1.13×2^{25}	1.05×2^{28}	1.89×2^{40}	1.63×2^{46}
	ZUC-256	Amy et al. [1]	1.28×2^{26}	1.13×2^{28}	1.22×2^{43}	1.91×2^{46}
	ZUC-256	Gidney et al. [19]	1.25×2^{25}	1.13×2^{28}	1.16×2^{41}	1.91×2^{46}

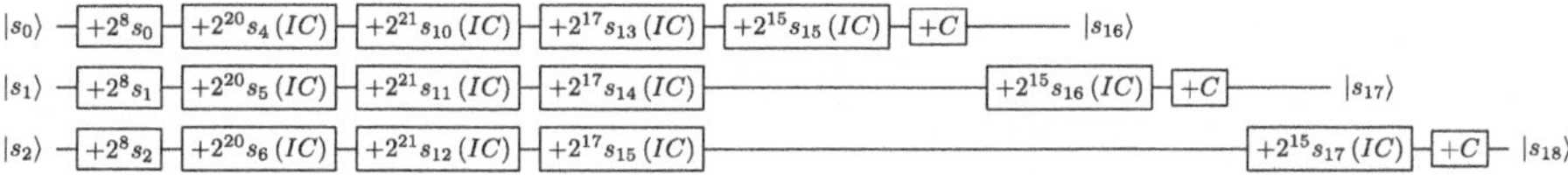

Fig. 8. Circuit diagram of the LFSR (for the first three rounds).

References

1. Amy, M., Maslov, D., Mosca, M., Roetteler, M.: A meet-in-the-middle algorithm for fast synthesis of depth-optimal quantum circuits. Trans. Comp.-Aided Des. Integ. Cir. Sys. **32**(6), 818–830 (2013). https://doi.org/10.1109/TCAD.2013.2244643
2. Amy, M., Matteo, O.D., Gheorghiu, V., Mosca, M., Parent, A., Schanck, J.: Estimating the cost of generic quantum pre-image attacks on SHA-2 and SHA-3 (2017). https://doi.org/10.1007/978-3-319-69453-5_18
3. Anand, R., Maitra, A., Maitra, S., Mukherjee, C.S., Mukhopadhyay, S.: Quantum resource estimation for FSR based symmetric ciphers and related Grover's attacks. In: Progress in Cryptology - INDOCRYPT 2021, pp. 179–198. Springer, Cham (2021). https://doi.org/10.1007/978-3-030-92518-5_9
4. Baksi, A., et al.: Quantum implementation of linear and non-linear layers. In: IEEE 37th International System-on-Chip Conference (SOCC), pp. 1–6 (2024). https://doi.org/10.1109/SOCC62300.2024.10737862
5. Baksi, A., Dasu, V.A., Karmakar, B., Chattopadhyay, A., Isobe, T.: Three input Exclusive-OR gate support for Boyar-Peralta's algorithm (2021). https://doi.org/10.1007/978-3-030-92518-5_7
6. Bathe, B., Anand, R., Dutta, S.: Evaluation of Grover's algorithm toward quantum cryptanalysis on ChaCha. Quant. Inf. Process **20** (2021). https://doi.org/10.1007/s11128-021-03322-7

7. Bennett, C.H.: Time/space trade-offs for reversible computation. SIAM J. Comput. **18**(4), 766–776 (1989). https://doi.org/10.1137/0218053
8. Bravyi, S., Kitaev, A.: Universal quantum computation with ideal Clifford gates and noisy ancillas. Phys. Rev. A **71**, 022316 (2005). https://doi.org/10.1103/PhysRevA.71.022316
9. Brayton, R., Mishchenko, A.: ABC: an academic industrial-strength verification tool. In: Computer Aided Verification, vol. 6174, pp. 24–40. Springer, Heidelberg (2010). https://doi.org/10.1007/978-3-642-14295-6_5
10. Chun, M., A., B., Chattopadhyay, A.: DORCIS: depth optimized quantum implementation of substitution boxes. Cryptology ePrint Archive (2023). https://eprint.iacr.org/2023/286
11. Cuccaro, S.A., Draper, T.G., Kutin, S.A., Moulton, D.P.: A new quantum ripple-carry addition circuit. arXiv (2004). https://arxiv.org/abs/quant-ph/0410184
12. Dasu, V.A., Baksi, A., Sarkar, S., Chattopadhyay, A.: LIGHTER-R: Optimized reversible circuit implementation for SBoxes. In: 32nd IEEE International System-on-Chip Conference (SOCC), pp. 260–265 (2019). https://doi.org/10.1109/SOCC46988.2019.1570548320
13. Dutta, S., Ghatak, A., Chattopadhyay, A., Maitra, S.: Quantum cryptanalysis of ZUC and related resource estimation. In: Progress in Cryptology - INDOCRYPT 2024, pp. 329–355. Springer, Heidelberg (2024). https://doi.org/10.1007/978-3-031-80308-6_15
14. Dutta, S., Wang, S., Baksi, A., Chattopadhyay, A., Maitra, S.: Exact space-depth trade-offs in multicontrolled toffoli decomposition (2025). https://doi.org/10.1103/PhysRevA.111.052611
15. ETSI/SAGE Technical report, V.: Specification of the 3gpp confidentiality and integrity algorithms 128-EEA3 and 128-EIA3 - document 4: Design and evaluation report (2011). https://www.gsma.com/about-us/wp-content/uploads/2014/12/EEA3_EIA3_Design_Evaluation_v2_0.pdf
16. Fowler, A.G.: Minimum weight perfect matching of fault-tolerant topological quantum error correction in average $o(1)$ parallel time (2014). https://arxiv.org/abs/1307.1740
17. Fowler, A.G., Devitt, S.J., Jones, C.: Surface code implementation of block code state distillation. Sci. Rep. **3**(1) (2013). https://doi.org/10.1038/srep01939
18. Fowler, A.G., Mariantoni, M., Martinis, J.M., Cleland, A.N.: Surface codes: towards practical large-scale quantum computation. Phys. Rev. A **86**(3) (2012). https://doi.org/10.1103/physreva.86.032324
19. Gidney, C.: Halving the cost of quantum addition. Quantum **2**, 74 (2018). https://doi.org/10.22331/q-2018-06-18-74
20. Gidney, C.: How to factor 2048 bit RSA integers with less than a million noisy qubits (2025). https://arxiv.org/abs/2505.15917
21. Grassl, M., Langenberg, B., Roetteler, M., Steinwandt, R.: Applying Grover's algorithm to AES: quantum resource estimates. In: Post-Quantum Cryptography, pp. 29–43. Springer, Cham (2016). https://doi.org/10.1007/978-3-319-29360-8_3
22. Huang, Z., Sun, S.: Synthesizing quantum circuits of AES with lower T-depth and less qubits. In: Agrawal, S., Lin, D. (eds.) Advances in Cryptology - ASIACRYPT 2022, pp. 614–644. Springer, Cham (2022). https://doi.org/10.1007/978-3-031-22969-5_21
23. Jang, K., Baksi, A., Kim, H., Song, G., Seo, H., Chattopadhyay, A.: Quantum analysis of AES. IACR Commun. Cryptol. **2**(1) (2025). https://doi.org/10.62056/ay11zo-3y

24. Jang, K., et al.: Quantum implementation and analysis of SHA-2 and SHA-3. IEEE Trans. Emerg. Topics Comput. 1–15 (2025). https://doi.org/10.1109/TETC.2025.3546648
25. Jaques, S., Naehrig, M., Roetteler, M., Virdia, F.: Implementing grover oracles for quantum key search on AES and LowMC (2020). https://doi.org/10.1007/978-3-030-45724-2_10
26. Jian, Z., SiMing, X., ChangZhong, Z., WenLing, W.: An efficient quantum circuit implementation of ZUC-128 cipher with low T-depth. SCIENTIA SINICA Physica, Mechanica Astronomica **54**(12), 120311 (2024). https://doi.org/10.1360/SSPMA-2024-0147
27. Khattar, T., Gidney, C.: Rise of conditionally clean ancillae for optimizing quantum circuits. Quantum **9**, 1752 (2025). https://doi.org/10.22331/q-2025-05-21-1752
28. Leander, G., May, A.: Grover meets Simon - Quantumly attacking the FX-construction. In: Takagi, T., Peyrin, T. (eds.) Advances in Cryptology - ASIACRYPT 2017, pp. 161–178. Springer, Cham (2017). https://doi.org/10.1007/978-3-319-70697-9_6
29. Liu, F., Meier, W., Sarkar, S., Wang, G., Ito, R., Isobe, T.: New cryptanalysis of ZUC-256 initialization using modular differences. IACR Trans. Symmetric Cryptol. **2022**, 152–190 (2022). https://doi.org/10.46586/tosc.v2022.i3.152-190
30. Liu, Q., Preneel, B., Zhao, Z., Wang, M.: Improved quantum circuits for AES: reducing the depth and the number of qubits. In: Guo, J., Steinfeld, R. (eds.) Advances in Cryptology - ASIACRYPT 2023, pp. 67–98. Springer, Singapore (2023). https://doi.org/10.1007/978-981-99-8727-6_3
31. Meuli, G., Soeken, M., Rötteler, M., Wiebe, N., Micheli, G.D.: A best-fit mapping algorithm to facilitate ESOP-decomposition in Clifford+T quantum network synthesis. In: 23rd Asia and South Pacific Design Automation Conference (ASP-DAC), pp. 664–669 (2018). https://doi.org/10.1109/ASPDAC.2018.8297398
32. Miller, D.M., Maslov, D., Dueck, G.W.: A transformation based algorithm for reversible logic synthesis. In: DAC '03: Proceedings of the 40th annual Design Automation Conference, pp. 318–323 (2003). https://doi.org/10.1145/775832.775915
33. Mukherjee, C.S., Roy, D., Maitra, S.: Design and Cryptanalysis of ZUC - A Stream Cipher in Mobile Telephony. Springer, Singapore (2021). https://doi.org/10.1007/978-981-33-4882-0
34. NIST.: Call for additional digital signature schemes for the post-quantum cryptography standardization process (2022). https://csrc.nist.gov/csrc/media/Projects/pqc-dig-sig/documents/call-for-proposals-dig-sig-sept-2022.pdf
35. Patel, K.N., Markov, I.L., Hayes, J.P.: Optimal synthesis of linear reversible circuits. Quant. Info. Comput. **8**(3), 282–294 (2008). https://doi.org/10.26421/QIC8.3-4-4
36. Perriello, S.: Quantum circuits for information set decoding quantum cryptanalysis of code-based cryptosystems. Ph.D. thesis, Politecnico di Milano (2024). https://www.politesi.polimi.it/retrieve/ef311c33-5427-4869-865f-94dc5ee733ed/Thesis.pdf
37. Sarah, D., Peter, C.: On the practical cost of grover for AES key recovery. NIST Standardization Conference (Fifth) (2024). https://csrc.nist.gov/csrc/media/Events/2024/fifth-pqc-standardization-conference/documents/papers/on-practical-cost-of-grover.pdf
38. Shi, H., Feng, X.: Quantum circuits of AES with a low-depth linear layer and a new structure. In: Chung, K.M., Sasaki, Y. (eds.) Advances in Cryptology -

ASIACRYPT 2024, pp. 358–395. Springer, Singapore (2025). https://doi.org/10.1007/978-981-96-0944-4_12

39. Shor, P.W.: Polynomial-time algorithms for prime factorization and discrete logarithms on a quantum computer. SIAM J. Comput. **26**(5), 1484–1509 (1997). https://doi.org/10.1137/S0097539795293172
40. Soeken, M., Dueck, G.W., Rahman, M.M., Miller, D.M.: An extension of transformation-based reversible and quantum circuit synthesis. In: 2016 IEEE International Symposium on Circuits and Systems (ISCAS), pp. 2290–2293 (2016). https://doi.org/10.1109/ISCAS.2016.7539041
41. Soeken, M., et al.: The EPFL logic synthesis libraries (2022). https://arxiv.org/abs/1805.05121
42. Design team: The ZUC-256 stream cipher (2018). http://www.is.cas.cn/ztzl2016/zouchongzhi/201801/W020180416526664982687.pdf
43. Todaro, S.L., et al.: State readout of a trapped ion qubit using a trap-integrated superconducting photon detector. Phys. Rev. Lett. **126**, 010501 (2021). https://doi.org/10.1103/PhysRevLett.126.010501
44. Wu, H., Huang, T., Nguyen, P.H., Wang, H., Ling, S.: Differential attacks against stream cipher ZUC. In: Advances in Cryptology - ASIACRYPT 2012, vol. 7658, pp. 262–277. Springer, Heidelberg (2012). https://doi.org/10.1007/978-3-642-34961-4_17
45. Xiang, Z., Zeng, X., Lin, D., Bao, Z., Zhang, S.: Optimizing implementations of linear layers. IACR Trans. Symmetric Cryptol. **2020**(2), 120–145 (2020). https://doi.org/10.13154/tosc.v2020.i2.120-145
46. Yang, J., Johansson, T., Maximov, A.: Spectral analysis of ZUC-256. IACR Trans. Symmetric Cryptol. **2020**, 266–288 (2020). https://doi.org/10.13154/tosc.v2020.i1.266-288
47. Yuan, Y., Wu, W., Shi, T., Zhang, L., Zhang, Y.: A framework to improve the implementations of linear layers. IACR Trans. Symmetric Cryptol. **2024**(2), 322–347 (2024). https://doi.org/10.46586/tosc.v2024.i2.322-347
48. Zou, J., Wei, Z., Sun, S., Liu, X., Wu, W.: Quantum circuit implementations of AES with fewer qubits. In: Moriai, S., Wang, H. (eds.) Advances in Cryptology - ASIACRYPT 2020, pp. 697–726. Springer, Cham (2020). https://doi.org/10.1007/978-3-030-64834-3_24
49. Dutta, S., Bhaumik, A.B., Chattopadhyay, A., Maitra, S.: Optimal T depth quantum circuits for implementing arbitrary Boolean functions. arXiv preprint, arXiv:2506.01542 (2025)

Homomorphic Transciphering for Secure Migration from LEA-128 to LEA-256

Jaeyeon Lee[1], Seunghyun Cho[1], Saehoon Jung[2], and Young-Sik Kim[1](✉)

[1] Department of EECS, DGIST, Daegu, Republic of Korea
{ljy8733,seunghyuncho,ysk}@dgist.ac.kr
[2] Department of School of Undergraduate Studies, DGIST, Daegu, Republic of Korea
shoon723@dgist.ac.kr

Abstract. We present a CKKS native homomorphic transciphering framework that converts existing LEA-128 ciphertexts into LEA-256 ciphertexts without exposing plaintext. Motivated by the post-quantum reduction in symmetric key security, our design shows that, by using homomorphic encryption, especially CKKS, it is possible to transition to post-quantum cryptography without revealing sensitive information. Furthermore, we propose a method that optimizes ARX operations by leveraging the SIMD structure of CKKS.

Our approach combines: (*i*) bitwise packing that maps LEA's ARX to CKKS primitive operations; (*ii*) a CKKS adapted Kogge–Stone adder that implements modular addition with logarithmic carry depth using masked rotations; and (*iii*) a low degree noise attenuation polynomial that preserves binary fixed points and suppresses near binary perturbations at a modest depth overhead.

With 2^{15} CKKS slots and 32 CPU threads, the pipeline that converts LEA-128 to LEA-256 completes with an amortized time of 6.61 s, and the results decrypt correctly under our parameters. Compared with TFHE style Boolean gate baselines, our circuit formulation and 1-bit encoding deliver over 3× speedups for bootstrapped modular addition and subtraction, while XOR and rotation are substantially faster due to SIMD packing. These results indicate that CKKS based transciphering is practical for ARX ciphers like LEA and provides a confidential migration path from 128-bit to 256-bit keys without plaintext exposure in the post-quantum era.

Keywords: Homomorphic Encryption · CKKS · Transciphering · ARX · Lightweight Encryption Algorithm · LEA-128 to LEA-256 Migration · Ciphertext-to-Ciphertext Conversion

1 Introduction

The advent of quantum computing poses a fundamental threat to the security of cryptographic systems currently in widespread use. Shor's algorithm [15] enables

H. Seo (Ed.): ICISC 2025, LNCS 16487, pp. 325–344, 2026.
https://doi.org/10.1007/978-981-95-8034-7_17

a quantum computer to efficiently factor large integers and solve discrete logarithm problems, thereby directly compromising the security of RSA and elliptic curve cryptography. While Shor's algorithm primarily targets public-key cryptosystems, Grover's algorithm [10] provides a quadratic speedup for brute-force key search, effectively reducing the security of an n-bit symmetric key from $O(2^n)$ to $O(2^{n/2})$. Consequently, a 128-bit symmetric cipher that offers 2^{128} classical security provides only 2^{64} security against a quantum adversary. This reduction urges a transition to at least 256-bit keys for long-term resilience in the post-quantum era.

The Lightweight Encryption Algorithm (LEA), developed in Korea and standardized as *KS X 3246*, is a widely deployed lightweight block cipher supporting a 128-bit block size and key sizes of 128, 192, and 256 bits [11]. LEA is used across national security infrastructures and diverse computing environments from IoT devices to high-performance servers. With the prospective realization of large-scale quantum computing, the commonly deployed LEA-128 variant no longer provides an adequate security margin. Migrating existing LEA-128 to LEA-256 is therefore not merely a technical upgrade but a critical security task with a significant operational impact.

A naive migration would decrypt LEA-128 ciphertexts to plaintext and then re-encrypt them under LEA-256. This approach violates confidentiality by exposing plaintext during conversion. An alternative is cascade encryption, which directly encrypts LEA-128 ciphertexts with LEA-256. While confidentiality can be preserved, this doubles key management complexity and enlarges the attack surface by requiring secure handling of two independent keys during the transition.

Transciphering addresses these challenges by enabling ciphertext-to-ciphertext conversion without revealing the underlying plaintext. In our setting, transciphering leverages homomorphic encryption (HE) to evaluate cryptographic transformations entirely within the encrypted domain [16]. Concretely, the original ciphertext is *homomorphically* decrypted into an encrypted plaintext and then *homomorphically* re-encrypted under the target cipher, never exposing intermediate plaintext to any party.

HE schemes can be broadly grouped by their plaintext encoding and supported operations: (i) BGV [3] and BFV [9] offer exact modular arithmetic over integers; (ii) FHEW [5] and TFHE [6] target Boolean circuits via functional bootstrapping; and (iii) CKKS [4] supports approximate arithmetic over complex numbers (additions, multiplications, and rotations) and is widely adopted in privacy-preserving machine learning [12,13]. Unlike FHEW/TFHE, CKKS provides powerful Single Instruction Multiple Data (SIMD) parallelism, applying the same operation across many slots in a single ciphertext. This high-throughput capability makes CKKS attractive for large-scale transciphering workloads, provided that approximation error is carefully controlled.

Our Contributions. We present a CKKS-based transciphering framework that securely converts LEA-128 ciphertexts to LEA-256 ciphertexts using ARX operations without exposing plaintext at any stage. Our specific contributions are:

- **End-to-end HE pipeline.** We design a transciphering pipeline that evaluates LEA-128 decryption followed by LEA-256 encryption entirely under CKKS, ensuring that neither plaintext nor key material is revealed during conversion.
- **Bitwise packing for ARX.** We introduce a bitwise encoding strategy that maps LEA's 32-bit ARX operations to CKKS primitives: XOR is evaluated by a depth-1 polynomial ($x + y - 2xy$), and word rotations are realized as native slot rotations; 32-bit modular addition is implemented with a Kogge–Stone adder adapted to CKKS to achieve logarithmic carry depth.
- **Feasibility at scale.** We provide an ARX operation-level analysis and end-to-end measurements under a high-throughput SIMD setting. On our setup (32,768 slots), the full LEA-128→LEA-256 transciphering workflow completes in approximately 6.61 seconds *per 128-bit block, amortized per instance.* We also report speedups over comparable schemes on ARX operations, and these results validate the effectiveness and scalability of our approach.

To the best of our knowledge, this is the first work to demonstrate a practical, CKKS-native transciphering pipeline for an ARX-based lightweight block cipher. By keeping all operations within the HE domain and exploiting SIMD parallelism, our approach offers a confidential and operationally tractable path for large-scale migration from LEA-128 to LEA-256.

1.1 Related Work

Transciphering with Homomorphic Encryption. Transciphering is a hybrid approach that combines the efficiency of symmetric-key cryptography with the privacy-preserving computation capability of HE. Instead of encrypting the entire dataset under HE, which inflates communication and client-side computation during encryption, the client encrypts data with a lightweight symmetric cipher and sends only the symmetric key encrypted under the HE public key. The server then evaluates the symmetric decryption circuit inside HE to convert the symmetric ciphertext into an HE ciphertext and proceeds with the desired computation. This design substantially reduces client memory and bandwidth burden while retaining end-to-end privacy, and it is compatible with existing symmetric-encrypted data pipelines. In the CKKS setting, prior work largely follows two lines: (*i*) hybrid frameworks that combine CKKS with exact-integer schemes, and (*ii*) CKKS-native methods that optimize nonlinear and binary operations while managing approximation error.

Hybrid Framework Approaches. The Real-to-Finite-field (RtF) framework of Cho *et al.* [7] combines CKKS with an BFV style exact integer scheme to avoid approximation error in critical integer computations. In RtF, the client encrypts data with an HE friendly stream cipher, the server homomorphically decrypts it in the BFV domain, and then converts the resulting ciphertext to CKKS for high-throughput processing. A low-depth cipher such as HERA is particularly well-suited to this pipeline. Under their reported parameters and hardware, RtF attains 1.6μs client-side latency and 21.7 MB/s throughput, substantially improving over pure-CKKS baselines. The main trade-offs are the complexity of scheme switching, additional evaluation keys, and cipher-specific tailoring, which may complicate direct application to generic ARX-based lightweight ciphers.

CKKS-Native Nonlinear Optimization. The other method keeps everything in CKKS while explicitly managing approximation error, scale, and depth. CKKS bootstrapping restores the consumed level and, when coupled with functional bootstrapping, can also evaluate target functions during the bootstrapping via the *EvalMod* stage [1]. Recent results show that bit-level encodings can be refreshed and even combined with Boolean gate evaluation inside the CKKS bootstrapping, enabling binary computation previously thought to be the domain of TFHE/FHEW, while avoiding additional multiplicative depth for these gates [2]. Amortized Look-Up Table (LUT) evaluation via multivariate polynomial interpolation also provides an efficient way to realize nonlinear mappings by encoding small input domains and evaluating bijective lookups in a batched manner [8]. These CKKS-native techniques are well-suited to table-based nonlinear layers like AES SubBytes, but offer limited direct benefit for ARX primitives whose core operations are modular addition and rotation.

Binary Operation Acceleration in CKKS. XBOOT [14] introduces a lazy-reduction strategy that accumulates XORs additively between bootstrappings and extracts the final parity with modular overflow property, making the inter-bootstrapping XORs multiplication-free. Unlike functional bootstrapping that evaluates an arbitrary function in EvalMod, XBOOT alters the SlotToCoeff transform matrix so that the LSB is mapped to the MSB. The bootstrapping then extracts that MSB to recover the XOR result. Beyond XOR, the paper also uses a monomial-LUT construction to evaluate AES's nonlinear components. Under their setup, they report 1KB/s throughput for AES and 2KB/s for Rasta transciphering, about 2.5$\times$ and 10$\times$ speedups over prior art, respectively. These techniques are particularly effective for S-box-heavy pipelines; however, direct gains for ARX workloads are limited.

Position of Our Work. Existing transciphering systems either rely on hybrid designs with scheme-conversion overhead or focus on S-box-oriented ciphers. In contrast, we propose ciphertext-to-ciphertext migration for an ARX lightweight cipher entirely within CKKS. Our design keeps everything CKKS-native while working with 1-bit encoding for intermediate states, which are stabilized via low-degree noise-management functions. Instead of table lookups, we use circuit-based methods and CKKS primitive operations leveraging SIMD structure.

Table 1. Notations used in the LEA algorithm [11]

Symbol	Meaning
P	128-bit plaintext, $P = P[0] \parallel P[1] \parallel P[2] \parallel P[3]$, where each $P[n]$ is a 32-bit word
C	128-bit ciphertext, $C = C[0] \parallel C[1] \parallel C[2] \parallel C[3]$, where each $C[n]$ is a 32-bit word
K	Master key; for LEA-128, $K = (K[0], K[1], K[2], K[3])$ with 32-bit words
N_r	Number of encryption/decryption rounds
RK_i^{enc}	192-bit round key for encryption round i: $RK_i^{enc} = RK_i^{enc}[0] \parallel \ldots \parallel RK_i^{enc}[5]$ (six 32-bit words)
RK_i^{dec}	192-bit round key for decryption round i: $RK_i^{dec} = RK_i^{dec}[0] \parallel \ldots \parallel RK_i^{dec}[5]$
$\text{KeySchedule}_i^{enc}$	Function generating RK_i^{enc} for $0 \le i \le N_r - 1$
$\text{KeySchedule}_i^{dec}$	Function generating RK_i^{dec} for $0 \le i \le N_r - 1$
$\wedge, \vee, \neg, \oplus$	Bitwise AND, OR, NOT, and XOR
$\boxplus, \boxminus$	Addition and subtraction in modulo 2^{32}
$ROL_i(x), ROR_i(x)$	Rotate x left and right by i bits

These choices avoid scheme switching, eliminate LUT overhead, and enable faster end-to-end ARX migration with lower depth while preserving privacy.

2 Preliminaries

2.1 Lightweight Encryption Algorithm (LEA)

LEA is a software-friendly ARX (Addition, Rotation, XOR) block cipher operating on 128-bit blocks and supporting 128-bit, 192-bit, and 256-bit keys [11]. Its 32-bit word design aligns well with modern processor architectures and enables high-throughput implementations across a wide range of platforms. Across diverse software settings, LEA is reported to be about 1.5× faster than AES for encryption.

Notation. We adopt the notation in Table 1 to describe LEA's structure.

Key Schedule. LEA derives per-round keys from the master key using fixed 32-bit constants specified in the standard. In our setting, once the client provides the encrypted master key, the server precomputes all round keys homomorphically and caches them, thereby eliminating on-the-fly key scheduling during encryption. For a 128-bit master key $K = (K[0], K[1], K[2], K[3])$ in LEA-128, the encryption round keys for $0 \le i < 24$ are generated as:

$$
\begin{aligned}
T[0] &\leftarrow ROL_1(T[0] \oplus ROL_i(\delta[i \bmod 4]))\,, \\
T[1] &\leftarrow ROL_3(T[1] \oplus ROL_{i+1}(\delta[i \bmod 4]))\,, \\
T[2] &\leftarrow ROL_6(T[2] \oplus ROL_{i+2}(\delta[i \bmod 4]))\,, \\
T[3] &\leftarrow ROL_{11}(T[3] \oplus ROL_{i+3}(\delta[i \bmod 4]))\,, \\
RK_i &\leftarrow (T[0], T[1], T[2], T[1], T[3], T[1]).
\end{aligned}
$$

where $\delta[\cdot]$ are the round constants defined by the LEA specification [11].

Encrypt and Decrypt Procedures. LEA performs N_r rounds of ARX transformations. LEA uses 24, 28, 32 rounds for 128, 192, 256-bit keys, respectively. Let $X_0 = P$ and $X_{N_r} = C$. Each encryption round updates the 32-bit words as

$$
\begin{aligned}
X_{i+1}[0] &\leftarrow ROL_9\Big((X_i[0] \oplus RK_i[0]) \boxplus (X_i[1] \oplus RK_i[1])\Big), \\
X_{i+1}[1] &\leftarrow ROL_5\Big((X_i[1] \oplus RK_i[2]) \boxplus (X_i[2] \oplus RK_i[3])\Big), \\
X_{i+1}[2] &\leftarrow ROR_3\Big((X_i[2] \oplus RK_i[4]) \boxplus (X_i[3] \oplus RK_i[5])\Big), \\
X_{i+1}[3] &\leftarrow X_i[0].
\end{aligned}
$$

Decryption applies the inverse operations in reverse round order. Writing $X_0 = C$ and $X_{N_r} = P$, the decryption procedure is

$$
\begin{aligned}
X_{i+1}[0] &\leftarrow X_i[3], \\
X_{i+1}[1] &\leftarrow ROL_9(X_i[0]) \boxminus (X_{i+1}[0] \oplus RK_i^{dec}[0]) \oplus RK_i^{dec}[1], \\
X_{i+1}[2] &\leftarrow ROL_5(X_i[1]) \boxminus (X_{i+1}[1] \oplus RK_i^{dec}[2]) \oplus RK_i^{dec}[3], \\
X_{i+1}[3] &\leftarrow ROL_3(X_i[2]) \boxminus (X_{i+1}[2] \oplus RK_i^{dec}[4]) \oplus RK_i^{dec}[5].
\end{aligned}
$$

2.2 CKKS Scheme

Homomorphic encryption (HE) enables arithmetic on ciphertexts such that decrypting the result matches the outcome of the corresponding plaintext computation. Among HE schemes, CKKS [4] supports *approximate* arithmetic over complex numbers.

CKKS is instantiated over the $2N$-th cyclotomic polynomial $\Phi_{2N}(X) = X^N + 1$, working in the ring $R = \mathbb{Z}[X]/(X^N + 1)$ and its residue $R_q = R/qR$ for an integer modulus q. A plaintext vector in $\mathbb{C}^{N/2}$ is encoded into R with a scaling factor Δ, typically a power of two, producing a fixed-point representation. Noise is part of the message representation and grows with homomorphic operations, but remains bounded under correct parameterization and scale management. CKKS natively offers SIMD with $N/2$ complex slots per ciphertext, enabling the same operation to be applied in parallel to many data items.

Parameters and Level/Scale Management. We use a modulus chain $Q = \prod_{j=0}^{L} q_j$ that supports L effective multiplication levels. A ciphertext carries a scale and a level. After a ciphertext–ciphertext multiplication, we perform relinearization to reduce degree and rescaling to divide out q_j and keep the scale near Δ, which consumes one level. Additions require aligned scales and levels. When misaligned, we rescale or adjust by plaintext constants. We employ bootstrapping only when the level drops below a preset threshold, refreshing level while incurring the usual bootstrapping latency.

Core CKKS Primitives. We rely on the following operations:

- **Add/Sub:** componentwise addition/subtraction of ciphertexts at matched scale/level.
- **Mul (ct-ct):** ciphertext–ciphertext multiplication, followed by relinearization and rescaling. This multiplication consumes one level.
- **Mul (ct-pt):** ciphertext–plaintext multiplication. This multiplication does not require relinearization, but requires rescaling if needed.
- **Rot:** rotation of slots by k positions via a Galois automorphism and key switching. Rot requires the corresponding Galois key. Throughout this paper, Rot denotes a right rotation.

Why CKKS for Transciphering. Compared to BFV/BGV (exact modular arithmetic) and TFHE (Boolean/functional bootstrapping), CKKS offers higher throughput for large batched workloads via SIMD and efficient rotations. This advantage aligns well with our goal of converting large volumes of LEA-128 ciphertexts to LEA-256. Although CKKS is approximate, we stabilize the near-binary semantics of ARX through two main techniques: (i) depth efficient circuits (depth-1 XOR, logarithmic-depth addition) and (ii) a low-degree noise-attenuation polynomial that preserves $\{0, 1\}$ fixed points and attenuates small perturbations at a modest depth overhead. Under the concrete parameters reported in our experiments, these measures keep error growth under control for full-round evaluation.

2.3 Kogge-Stone Adder

In our CKKS-based transciphering framework, the 32-bit modular addition ($\boxplus$) in each LEA round is implemented using a Kogge-Stone adder. This choice is motivated by the adder's carry look-ahead structure and parallel prefix computation, which generate carries in logarithmic stages. Such logarithmic depth circuits are particularly well-suited to the CKKS setting, where minimizing multiplicative depth and the number of costly rotation operations is critical for speedup and maintaining bit-level correctness across many rounds.

The Kogge-Stone adder consists of three stages, as illustrated in Fig. 1.

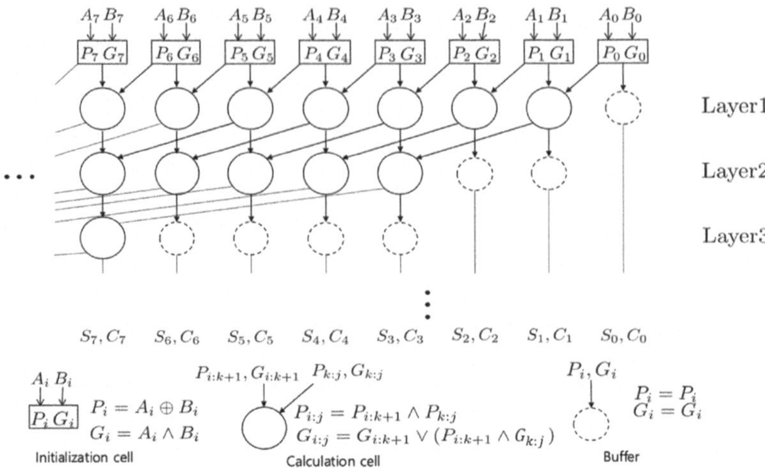

Fig. 1. Kogge–Stone adder adapted to CKKS: 5-stage parallel-prefix network with masked rotations, enabling logarithmic-depth 32-bit modular addition in the LEA transciphering pipeline.

1. Pre-processing: For each bit position i, the *propagate* bit P_i and the *generate* bit G_i are computed from the two input words A and B:

$$P_i = A_i \oplus B_i$$
$$G_i = A_i \wedge B_i.$$

In our CKKS mapping, $\oplus$ is implemented via homomorphic XOR, and $\wedge$ is realized via ciphertext-ciphertext multiplication.

2. Carry Look-Ahead Network: Group propagate and group generate signals are computed recursively to determine carries for all bit positions:

$$P_{i:j} = P_{i:k+1} \wedge P_{k:j}$$
$$G_{i:j} = G_{i:k+1} \vee (P_{i:k+1} \wedge G_{k:j}).$$

3. Post-processing: The sum bits S_i are then obtained as:

$$C_i = G_{i:0}$$
$$S_i = P_i \oplus C_{i-1}$$

where C_{i-1} is the carry into position i.

Subtraction. We do not implement subtraction as adding two's complement $(\neg B) + 1$ to A. Instead, we use a Kogge–Stone subtractor that computes per-bit borrow (C): $C_{i+1} = G_i \vee (P_i \wedge C_i)$ with $P_i = \neg(A_i \oplus B_i)$ (borrow-propagate) and $G_i = (\neg A_i) \wedge B_i$ (borrow-generate), and output is $(A_i \oplus B_i) \oplus C_i$. The parallel-prefix topology is identical to the Kogge–Stone adder.

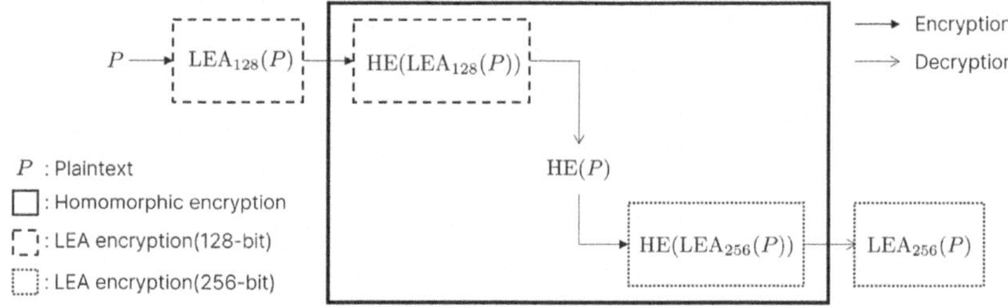

Fig. 2. Homomorphic transciphering framework: LEA-128 ciphertexts are converted to LEA-256 ciphertexts fully within CKKS, with keys pre-encrypted and no plaintext exposure at any stage.

Complexity and HE Costs. For 32-bit words, KS requires 5 stages. Each stage entails a constant number of rotations and ct-ct multiplications, followed by relinearization and rescaling. Masks are pre-encrypted plaintexts and incur no heavy computation. This structure minimizes both multiplicative depth and rotation count, which is essential for preserving the noise budget across full-round LEA-256 evaluation.

3 CKKS-Native Transciphering Framework for LEA

3.1 Overall Structure

As illustrated in Fig. 2, the transciphering pipeline is executed entirely in the CKKS domain. The client sends the LEA-128 ciphertext together with CKKS encrypted LEA-128 master key and required CKKS keys to the server. The server homomorphically derives the per-round keys inside the encrypted domain. The server precomputes and caches the derived round keys to reduce overhead during the pipeline.

The server then encrypts given LEA-128 ciphertext under the CKKS public key and evaluates two circuits in sequence: (i) LEA-128 decryption under CKKS, yielding an encrypted plaintext and (ii) LEA-256 encryption under CKKS, yielding the target LEA-256 ciphertext, while the intermediate state remains encrypted at all times. We employ depth-aware ARX circuits together with a low degree noise-attenuation functions to control error growth and recover the correct LEA outputs in transciphering pipeline. Throughout, all sensitive material stays encrypted end-to-end, mitigating privacy concerns.

3.2 LEA State Encoding Using SIMD

Bitwise Encoding. In LEA, both key generation and round operations are performed on 32-bit words using ARX operations. While the number of operations in the key scheduling stage varies depending on the key size, the underlying operations remain the same. CKKS supports only addition, multiplication, and slot rotations in its SIMD structure, which restricts direct evaluation of ARX

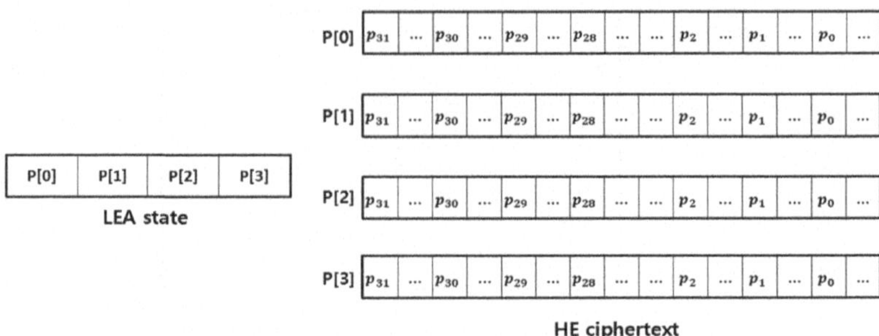

Fig. 3. Bitwise encoding strategy that maps each 32-bit LEA state word into CKKS ciphertext slots to enable efficient parallel evaluation of ARX operations.

operations. Thus, ARX operations must be reformulated into expressions that are compatible with the CKKS environment.

A common approach is to construct LUT polynomials using interpolation. Given a set of input–output pairs, one can find a bijective polynomial f that passes through all pairs and then evaluate it under CKKS. Prior work has shown that bit values can be encoded as roots on the complex unit circle, and multivariate interpolation can then be applied. For example, AES-128's SubBytes operation has been approximated in this way using 8-bit-to-8-bit or 8-bit-to-4-bit LUT polynomials [8].

Applying the same idea to ARX operations, each 32-bit word can be divided into smaller chunks (e.g., 4 bits) and encoded into ciphertexts. XOR, which takes two 4-bit inputs and produces a 4-bit output, requires an 8-bit-to-4-bit LUT polynomial. Similarly, rotations also require an 8-bit-to-4-bit LUT. In practice, these LUT-based evaluations incurred substantial computation overhead. XOR required depth 5 and about 12.5 s, while rotation required depth 6 and about 5.4 s in our experimental settings.

However, XOR and rotation can be evaluated far more efficiently when encoded at the 1-bit level. XOR can be directly expressed as $x + y - 2xy$, eliminating the need for approximation, while rotation can be directly realized using CKKS slot rotations. Since each round of LEA requires 8 XOR and 3 rotation operations, LEA-256 (32 rounds) demands 352 such operations in total. By using bitwise encoding, the depth and runtime of these operations are significantly reduced. Therefore, we adopt the strategy of partitioning each state word into individual bits and embedding them into CKKS ciphertexts.

Full-State Representation. CKKS provides $N/2 = N'$ complex slots that can be processed in parallel. We align packing with LEA's 32-bit word structure. Each 32-bit word is represented in *one* CKKS ciphertext. The four words of the LEA state therefore occupy *four* ciphertexts. Within a ciphertext, the 32 bits of

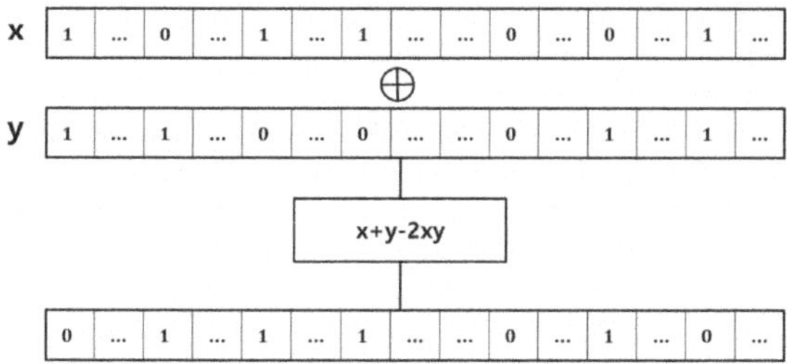

Fig. 4. Homomorphic XOR in CKKS: bitwise exclusive-or evaluated slotwise in parallel.

a word are mapped to slots with a fixed spacing (*gap* Δ)

$$\Delta = \frac{N'}{32}.$$

Let p_ℓ be the bit at position $\ell \in \{0, \ldots, 31\}$ of a word, and let $t \in \{0, \ldots, \Delta - 1\}$ index the parallel instance within the batch. We assign

$$\text{slot}(p_\ell, t) = \ell \cdot \Delta + t.$$

As described in Fig. 3, bits $p_0, \ldots, p_{31}$ of each word occupy slots separated by Δ, while different parallelizable instances interleave across the gaps. We adopt a consistent bit order so that rotation by i bits corresponds to a slot rotation by $i \cdot \Delta$ *within each 32-slot group.*

With this layout, a single ciphertext holds up to $\Delta = N'/32$ independent 32-bit words in parallel. The full LEA state uses four ciphertexts and processes Δ states concurrently. For typical parameters, Δ is large, enabling high-throughput evaluation without LUTs or table lookups.

3.3 ARX Operations

Exclusive OR. XOR is used both at the word level in LEA rounds and inside the 32-bit modular addition implemented by the Kogge-Stone adder. With bitwise encoding, XOR can be expressed as the depth-1 polynomial

$$\text{XOR}(x, y) = x + y - 2xy,$$

requiring only a single ciphertext–ciphertext multiplication. With CKKS's SIMD structure, this operation is applied slotwise in parallel (Fig. 4). This avoids LUT-based approximations. The OR used in Kogge-Stone adder is realized as

$$\text{OR}(x, y) = x + y - xy.$$

Algorithm 1. BUILDMASK

Require: usable slot count N'

Ensure: STAGE_MASK[d], STAGE_KEEP[d], CARRY_MASK, MSB_MASK for $d \in \{1, 2, 3, 4, 5\}$

```
1  gap ← N'/32
2  for d ∈ {1,2,3,4,5} do
3      m ← zeros(N');  m_keep ← ones(N')
4      s ← (32 − 2^d) · gap
5      m[: s] ← 1
6      m_keep[: s] ← 0
7      STAGE_MASK[d] ← Encode(m)
8      STAGE_KEEP[d] ← Encode(m_keep)
9  end for
10 m_c ← ones(N');  m_c[31 · gap :] ← 0
11 CARRY_MASK ← Encode(m_c)
12 m_msb ← zeros(N');  m_msb[: gap] ← 1
13 MSB_MASK ← Encode(m_msb)
14 return STAGE_MASK, STAGE_KEEP, CARRY_MASK, MSB_MASK
```

32-Bit Modular Addition. The BUILDMASK (Algorithm 1) procedure constructs the hierarchical structure of the Kogge–Stone adder circuit and generates masks that facilitate carry propagation and extraction. The STAGE MASK selects only the bit positions corresponding to calculation cells within the ciphertext while excluding the buffer bits from computation. Conversely, the STAGE KEEP identifies the buffer elements so that they can be directly forwarded to the next layer without modification. Through the loop in lines 2 to 9, masks for all layers from layer 1 to layer 5 are generated.

The CARRY MASK is initialized to isolate only the carry bits required during carry computation, ensuring that irrelevant bits are excluded from processing. Finally, the MSB MASK enables the extraction of the 33rd bit, which represents the final carry after the addition result has been computed.

The 32-bit Kogge–Stone Adder (Algorithm 2) takes two ciphertexts as input and performs 32-bit modular addition. Lines 1 and 2 constitute the preprocessing stage, where the initial values of P and G are computed. These correspond to the initialization cells of the Kogge–Stone adder. In line 3, the initialized value of P is also copied into P_{orig}, as it will be required again during the post-processing stage.

From line 4 to 12, the carry look-ahead network is constructed, where each iteration of the loop adds one layer to the network. In line 6, $P^{\leftarrow}$ is prepared to represent $P_{k:j}$. In line 7, the calculation $P_{i:k+1} \wedge P_{k:j}$ is performed, and the result, $P_{i:j}$ is stored in $P_{\wedge}$. Line 8 computes $PG = P_{i:k+1} \wedge G_{k:j}$. In line 9, the expression $G_{i:k+1} \vee (P_{i:k+1} \wedge G_{k:j})$ is evaluated, producing $G_{i:j}$, which is stored in $G_{\vee}$. Lines 10 and 11 then use STAGE_MASK and STAGE_KEEP to combine

Algorithm 2. 32-bit Kogge-Stone Adder

Require: ciphertexts $\mathrm{CT}_X, \mathrm{CT}_Y$ (bitwise-packed words)
Ensure: $\mathrm{CT}_{\mathrm{SUM}}, \mathrm{CT}_{\mathrm{COUT}}$

1 $G \leftarrow \mathsf{CMult}(\mathrm{CT}_X, \mathrm{CT}_Y)$ ▷ $G_i = X_i \wedge Y_i$
2 $P \leftarrow \mathsf{Sub}(\mathsf{Add}(\mathrm{CT}_X, \mathrm{CT}_Y), \mathsf{SMult}(G, 2))$ ▷ $P_i = X_i \oplus Y_i$
3 $P_{\mathrm{orig}} \leftarrow P$
4 **for** $d \in \{1, 2, 3, 4, 5\}$ **do**
5 $\quad \mathrm{sh} \leftarrow -2^{d-1} \cdot \mathrm{gap}$
6 $\quad P^{\leftarrow} \leftarrow \mathsf{Rot}(P, \mathrm{sh});\ G^{\leftarrow} \leftarrow \mathsf{Rot}(G, \mathrm{sh})$
7 $\quad P_{\wedge} \leftarrow \mathsf{CMult}(P, P^{\leftarrow})$ ▷ $P_{i:j} = P_{i:k+1} \wedge P_{k:j}$
8 $\quad PG \leftarrow \mathsf{CMult}(P, G^{\leftarrow})$ ▷ $P_{i:k+1} \wedge G_{k:j}$
9 $\quad G_{\vee} \leftarrow \mathsf{Sub}(\mathsf{Add}(G, PG), \mathsf{CMult}(G, PG))$ ▷ $G_{i:j} = G_{i:k+1} \vee (P_{i:k+1} \wedge G_{k:j})$
10 $\quad G \leftarrow \mathsf{Add}(\mathsf{SMult}(G_{\vee}, \mathrm{STAGE\_MASK}[d]), \mathsf{SMult}(G, \mathrm{STAGE\_KEEP}[d]))$
11 $\quad P \leftarrow \mathsf{Add}(\mathsf{SMult}(P_{\wedge}, \mathrm{STAGE\_MASK}[d]), \mathsf{SMult}(P, \mathrm{STAGE\_KEEP}[d]))$
12 **end for**
13 $C \leftarrow \mathsf{SMult}(\mathsf{Rot}(G, -\mathrm{gap}), \mathrm{CARRY\_MASK})$ ▷ carry-in C_{i-1}
14 $PC \leftarrow \mathsf{CMult}(P_{\mathrm{orig}}, C)$
15 $\mathrm{CT}_{\mathrm{SUM}} \leftarrow \mathsf{Sub}(\mathsf{Add}(P_{\mathrm{orig}}, C), \mathsf{SMult}(PC, 2))$ ▷ $S_i = P_i \oplus C_{i-1}$
16 $\mathrm{CT}_{\mathrm{COUT}} \leftarrow \mathsf{SMult}(G, \mathrm{MSB\_MASK})$ ▷ outgoing carry
17 **return** $\mathrm{CT}_{\mathrm{SUM}}, \mathrm{CT}_{\mathrm{COUT}}$

the results of calculation cells with the preserved buffer values and pass them to the next layer.

Beginning with line 13, the post-processing stage is executed. Here, rotation is applied to correctly align the carry value C_{i-1} for use in the final sum computation, while CARRY_MASK is applied to filter out irrelevant bits. In line 14, the product of P_i and C_{i-1} is stored in PC. Line 15 then performs an XOR operation between P_i and C_{i-1}, which is stored in CT_{SUM}.

32-Bit Modular Subtraction. The 32-bit Kogge–Stone Subtractor (Algorithm 3) takes two ciphertexts as input and performs 32-bit modular subtraction. In lines 1 and 2, an XOR operation is applied to the input ciphertexts, and the result is stored in $XY_{\oplus}$. In line 3, the bits are inverted to produce P, which serves as the borrow-propagate signal. Specifically, $P = \neg(X \oplus Y)$. In line 4, the borrow-generate signal G is initialized as $G = Y - (X \wedge Y) = (\neg X) \wedge Y$.

As in the case of addition, the loop from lines 5 to 13 constructs the layers of the borrow look-ahead network. Although the conditions for borrow-propagate and borrow-generate differ from those in addition, the iterative operations applied to P and G are structurally identical. After completing the loop, the borrow look-ahead network is fully established.

Similar to the carry signal C_{i-1} of addition, line 14 uses rotation to correctly align the borrow signal B_{i-1} for computing the final result. To perform the XOR between $XY_{\oplus}$ and B, line 15 computes $(X \oplus Y) \wedge B$ and stores the result in PB. Finally, line 16 computes the XOR as $(X \oplus Y) \oplus B$, which corresponds exactly to the subtraction bit $X \boxminus Y$.

Algorithm 3. 32-bit Kogge-Stone Subtractor

Require: ciphertexts $\mathrm{CT}_X, \mathrm{CT}_Y$

Ensure: $\mathrm{CT}_{\mathrm{DIFF}}$

1 $XY \leftarrow \mathsf{CMult}(\mathrm{CT}_X, \mathrm{CT}_Y)$

2 $XY_{\oplus} \leftarrow \mathsf{Sub}(\mathsf{Add}(\mathrm{CT}_X, \mathrm{CT}_Y), \mathsf{SMult}(XY, 2))$

3 $P \leftarrow \mathsf{Sub}(1,\ XY_{\oplus})$ ▷ $P_i = \neg(X_i \oplus Y_i)$: borrow-propagate

4 $G \leftarrow \mathsf{Sub}(\mathrm{CT}_Y, XY)$ ▷ $G_i = (\neg X_i) \wedge Y_i$: borrow-generate

5 **for** $d \in \{1, 2, 3, 4, 5\}$ **do**

6 $\quad \mathrm{sh} \leftarrow -2^{d-1} \cdot \mathrm{gap}$

7 $\quad P^{\leftarrow} \leftarrow \mathsf{Rot}(P, \mathrm{sh});\quad G^{\leftarrow} \leftarrow \mathsf{Rot}(G, \mathrm{sh})$

8 $\quad P_{\wedge} \leftarrow \mathsf{CMult}(P, P^{\leftarrow})$

9 $\quad PG \leftarrow \mathsf{CMult}(P, G^{\leftarrow})$

10 $\quad G_{\vee} \leftarrow \mathsf{Sub}(\mathsf{Add}(G, PG), \mathsf{CMult}(G, PG))$

11 $\quad G \leftarrow \mathsf{Add}(\mathsf{SMult}(G_{\vee}, \mathrm{STAGE\_MASK}[d]), \mathsf{SMult}(G, \mathrm{STAGE\_KEEP}[d]))$

12 $\quad P \leftarrow \mathsf{Add}(\mathsf{SMult}(P_{\wedge}, \mathrm{STAGE\_MASK}[d]), \mathsf{SMult}(P, \mathrm{STAGE\_KEEP}[d]))$

13 **end for**

14 $B \leftarrow \mathsf{SMult}(\mathsf{Rot}(G, -\mathrm{gap}), \mathrm{CARRY\_MASK})$ ▷ borrow-in B_{i-1}

15 $PB \leftarrow \mathsf{CMult}(XY_{\oplus}, B)$

16 $\mathrm{CT}_{\mathrm{DIFF}} \leftarrow \mathsf{Sub}(\mathsf{Add}(XY_{\oplus}, B), \mathsf{SMult}(PB, 2))$ ▷ $(X \oplus Y) \oplus B$

17 **return** $\mathrm{CT}_{\mathrm{DIFF}}$

Rotation. LEA's rotation operations ROL_i and ROR_i map directly to CKKS slot rotations followed by key switching (Fig. 5). With the packing in Sect. 3.2, if N' denotes the number of usable slots and $\mathrm{gap} = N'/32$, rotating a 32-bit word by i bits corresponds to a slot rotation by $i \cdot \mathrm{gap}$ *within the word's 32-slot group*:

$$\mathsf{Rot}(\mathrm{ct},\ \pm i \cdot \mathrm{gap}).$$

3.4 Noise Reduction Function

Noise management is a critical factor in determining both performance and accuracy in HE. In the CKKS scheme, each homomorphic operation inevitably increases the noise level of a ciphertext, with multiplications in particular causing exponential noise growth. Since each round of LEA involves multiple XOR and modular addition operations, accumulated noise can exceed the permissible threshold after several rounds. In practice, we observed that decryption results began to diverge from the correct values after more than 12 rounds of accumulated operations.

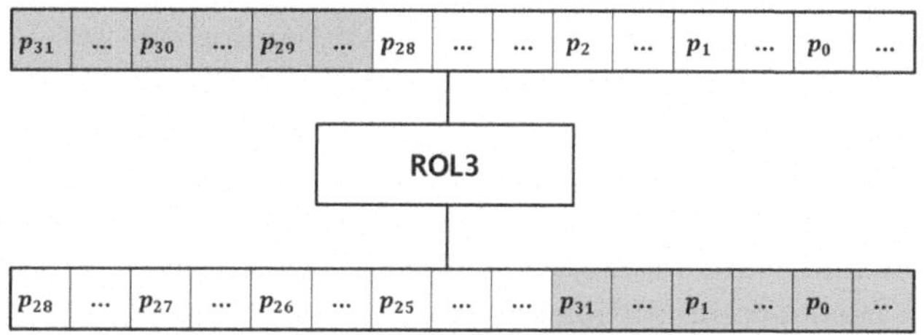

Fig. 5. Homomorphic word rotation in CKKS: LEA's ROL_i/ROR_i as slot rotations by $i \cdot \text{gap}$.

Cubic Noise Attenuation. We insert a low-degree *noise-attenuation* polynomial at the end of a round (or every few rounds) to attenuate perturbations around the binary fixed points:

$$f(x) = 3x^2 - 2x^3.$$

This is the standard smoothstep cubic with fixed points $f(0) = 0$ and $f(1) = 1$. Its derivative

$$f'(x) = 6x - 6x^2$$

vanishes at $x \in \{0, 1\}$, so f is flat at the binary endpoints and attenuates small deviations. Writing a bit as $b \in \{0, 1\}$ perturbed by $x = b + \varepsilon$ with $|\varepsilon| \ll 1$, the Taylor expansion gives

$$f(b + \varepsilon) = f(b) + f'(b)\varepsilon + \tfrac{1}{2} f''(b)\varepsilon^2 + \tfrac{1}{6} f'''(b)\varepsilon^3 + O(\varepsilon^4),$$

and, since $f'(0) = f'(1) = 0$,

$$f(0 + \varepsilon) = 3\varepsilon^2 - 2\varepsilon^3, \qquad f(1 + \varepsilon) = 1 - 3\varepsilon^2 - 2\varepsilon^3.$$

Thus the leading perturbation scales quadratically ($\propto \varepsilon^2$) near $\{0, 1\}$, which damps accumulated error between rounds.[1]

Depth and Evaluation Cost. $f(x) = x^2(3-2x)$ uses two ciphertext-ciphertext multiplications (depth 2), plus inexpensive ciphertext-plaintext multiplications by small constants (3 and -2). After each ct-ct multiplication, we relinearize and rescale to keep scales aligned. This modest depth overhead proves sufficient to stabilize the full-round transciphering pipeline, and its shallow depth does not materially affect the overall round budget.

4 Experimental Results

Hardware and Library. All experiments were run on an AMD Ryzen Threadripper PRO 3995WX using `DesiloFHE` v1.3.0 in Parallel engine mode with 32 threads.

[1] CKKS error is not assumed Gaussian in our analysis; we only require small-magnitude perturbations around $\{0, 1\}$.

CKKS Parameters and Policy. The CKKS parameters were configured to support 2^{15} slots, enabling SIMD parallelism across 32,768 slots within a single ciphertext. Bootstrapping was enabled during engine initialization, restoring ciphertexts to level 10 after each invocation. Bootstrapping was selectively applied once the ciphertext level fell below a predefined threshold, particularly during addition and subtraction operations where depth consumption is relatively high. We used a computation modulus with total bit-length $\log_2 Q \approx 1600$. The modulus chain was formed from base primes of size approximately 2^{60}. The initial scaling factor was set to $\Delta = 2^{54}$.

Reporting Modes. We report *amortized per-element latency*, i.e., the total latency divided by the number of independent elements packed and evaluated in parallel with SIMD. With 32-bit word packing, one ciphertext carries $\Delta = N'/32$ independent 32-bit words in parallel, so dividing total time by Δ gives the amortized cost per element. Tables 2, 3 and 4 present single operator results measured on one ciphertext and normalized by the number of independent elements in that ciphertext; these values reflect the efficiency of the core ARX operations. Table 5 reports the time for a full 128-bit LEA block, which is split across four CKKS ciphertexts (one 32-bit word per ciphertext); this figure is the measured per block latency of the end-to-end pipeline.

ARX Primitive Analysis

Table 2 summarizes *amortized* latencies and multiplicative depths of 32-bit modular ARX operations measured at initial level 26 without bootstrapping. Bitwise encoding allows XOR and rotation to be evaluated with negligible depth consumption. XOR is executed in 0.15 s and requires only one multiplication (depth 1), while rotation is executed in 0.08 s and realized as a slot permutation (depth 0). Modular addition and subtraction requires repeated carry propagation using propagation (P) and generation (G) signals. Consequently, addition and subtraction, which share the same carry-lookahead structure (parallel-prefix), both achieve a multiplicative depth of 18. Their amortized latencies are 2.88 ms and 3.09 ms, respectively. A naive ripple-carry design would make the depth grow linearly with the word size due to per-bit carry propagation, whereas our carry-lookahead with logarithmic stages bounds the propagation and reduces the effective depth by roughly 1.5× in practice.

Table 2. Amortized latency (ms) of 32-bit modular ARX operations, starting from initial level 26 and without bootstrapping.

	Addition	Subtraction	XOR	Rotation
time(ms)	2.88	3.09	0.14	0.08
depth	18	18	1	0

The proposed modular addition design is not restricted to 32-bit words. It extends to general n-bit modular arithmetic by appropriately scaling the masking patterns and the number of prefix propagation stages. Table 3 reports the amortized per-element latency (ms) for 8-bit, 16-bit, 32-bit, and 64-bit modular addition, measured at initial level 26 and without bootstrapping during the operation. As the word size increases, the multiplicative depth grows by 3 per stage. Notably, for 64-bit addition a naive ripple-carry adder requires 64 levels of carry propagation. Our Kogge-Stone adder reduces this to 21 stages representing more than a 3× reduction in multiplicative depth. This depth reduction lowers the frequency of bootstrapping and yields substantial performance gains. This adder is well-suited to large-word modular operations. The observed amortized latencies increase smoothly with word size: 1.06 ms, 1.77 ms, 2.88 ms, and 7.01 ms for 8-bit, 16-bit, 32-bit, and 64-bit, respectively. Beyond LEA, the structure applies broadly to ARX-based primitives like SHA and ChaCha, where efficient addition and rotation dominate the workload.

Table 3. Amortized per-element latency (ms) for 8-bit, 16-bit, 32-bit, and 64-bit modular addition, measured at initial level 26 and without bootstrapping.

	8-bit Addition	16-bit Addition	32-bit Addition	64bit-Addition
time(ms)	1.06	1.77	2.88	7.01
depth	12	15	18	21

To compare against Boolean-FHE baselines, Table 4 reports amortized per-element latencies. "Proposed*" begins at level 10 and therefore includes bootstrapping during evaluation, whereas the other CKKS rows begin at level 26 and complete without bootstrapping. TFHE-rs denotes Zama's modular operation results. Evaluations run using TFHE-rs v1.4.2 on an identical CPU configuration with 32 threads. Relative to TFHE's gate-bootstrapped Boolean evaluation, our CKKS design achieves about 3× lower latency for Addition* and Subtraction*, and even larger gains for XOR and Rotation due to SIMD packing. In Addition* and Subtraction*, three bootstraps are invoked, which results in an additional 20 ms of latency compared to evaluations without bootstrapping.

Table 4. Amortized per-element latency (ms) of 32-bit ARX operations: comparison of CKKS (this work) and TFHE. "Proposed*" and the other configurations differ in their initial level and whether bootstrapping is invoked.

	Addition	Addition*	Subtraction	Subtraction*	XOR	Rotation
Proposed(ms)	2.88	26.82	3.09	27.12	0.14	0.08
TFHE-rs(ms)	109	109	114	114	29	85

End-to-End LEA and Transciphering

Table 5 summarizes amortized round and total times for LEA-128 and LEA-256 encryption and decryption, and for the full transciphering pipeline. The round cost remains essentially constant across rounds (0.11–0.12 s), while the total time scales approximately linearly with the number of rounds. Our target pipeline, migrating LEA-128 decryption to LEA-256 encryption, completes in 6.61 s, after which the final ciphertext decrypts correctly. This indicates that the noise reduction function inserted at each round (or at appropriate inter-round intervals) effectively preserves near-binary $\{0, 1\}$ semantics by preventing noise from corrupting the bit values. We perform 15–18 bootstraps per round. Depth accumulates across three Addition* or Subtraction* operations and the noise reduction function. We bootstrap the G and P signals as well as the 32-bit modular ciphertexts. The count can be reduced by tuning the timing of G and P bootstraps and the frequency of noise-reduction step. In our setup, we trigger bootstrapping whenever the noise falls below a safety threshold and apply the noise-reduction function every round.

Table 5. Amortized per-element latency (s) for LEA-128 and LEA-256 encryption and decryption pipelines. Round cost is approximately constant across key sizes; totals reflect the number of rounds.

Workload	Round(s)	Total(s)	Notes
LEA-128 Encrypt	0.11	2.64	24 rounds
LEA-128 Decrypt	0.11	2.68	24 rounds
LEA-256 Encrypt	0.12	3.93	32 rounds
LEA-256 Decrypt	0.12	3.95	32 rounds
Transcipher (LEA-128 → LEA-256)	—	6.61	Decrypt + Encrypt

5 Conclusion

We present a CKKS-native transciphering framework that converts LEA-128 ciphertexts to LEA-256 ciphertexts without exposing plaintext at any stage. The design hinges on three key components: (i) *bitwise packing* that maps LEA's ARX to CKKS primitives, (ii) a CKKS-adapted *Kogge–Stone* adder that achieves logarithmic carry depth with masked slot operations, and (iii) a low-degree *noise-attenuation* polynomial that stabilizes near-binary values.

Under our experimental setup, the end-to-end transciphering pipeline completes with 6.61 s of amortized time per block, demonstrating its large-scale feasibility. Moreover, for ARX primitives measured per element, our implementation achieves significantly faster throughput than TFHE-style Boolean gate frameworks, validating the proposed CKKS SIMD packing and circuit-based design.

By keeping all computation within the HE domain and exploiting CKKS's characteristics, our approach provides a practical route for large-scale ciphertext-to-ciphertext migration from LEA-128 to LEA-256 without plaintext exposure. Moreover, the proposed Kogge-Stone adder is not specific to LEA. It is parameterizable and extends naturally to general ARX workloads and larger word sizes, offering significant depth reductions and improved performance across diverse word-size configurations.

Future work will focus on (i) extending the pipeline to other ARX ciphers, and (ii) exploring alternative adder circuits under tight level budgets, leveraging circuit-level optimizations to further reduce depth and latency.

Acknowledgments. This work was supported by Institute of Information & communications Technology Planning & Evaluation (IITP) grant funded by the Korea government(MSIT) (No. RS-2024-00399401, Development of Quantum-Safe Infrastructure Migration and Quantum Security Verification Technologies, 50%)(No. RS-2024-00442085, Development of V2X Infra Security Core Technologies for Autonomous Vehicle Services, 50%).

Disclosure of Interests. The authors have no competing interests to declare that are relevant to the content of this article.

References

1. Alexandru, A., Kim, A., Polyakov, Y.: General functional bootstrapping using CKKS. Cryptology ePrint Archive, Paper 2024/1623 (2024). https://eprint.iacr.org/2024/1623
2. Bae, Y., Cheon, J.H., Kim, J., Stehlé, D.: Bootstrapping bits with CKKS. In: Joye, M., Leander, G. (eds.) EUROCRYPT 2024. LNCS, vol. 14652, pp. 94–123. Springer, Cham (2024). https://doi.org/10.1007/978-3-031-58723-8_4
3. Brakerski, Z., Gentry, C., Vaikuntanathan, V.: Fully homomorphic encryption without bootstrapping. Cryptology ePrint Archive, Paper 2011/277 (2011). https://eprint.iacr.org/2011/277
4. Cheon, J.H., Kim, A., Kim, M., Song, Y.: Homomorphic encryption for arithmetic of approximate numbers. In: Takagi, T., Peyrin, T. (eds.) ASIACRYPT 2017. LNCS, vol. 10624, pp. 409–437. Springer, Cham (2017). https://doi.org/10.1007/978-3-319-70694-8_15
5. Chillotti, I., Gama, N., Georgieva, M., Izabachène, M.: Faster fully homomorphic encryption: bootstrapping in less than 0.1 seconds. In: Cheon, J.H., Takagi, T. (eds.) ASIACRYPT 2016. LNCS, vol. 10031, pp. 3–33. Springer, Heidelberg (2016). https://doi.org/10.1007/978-3-662-53887-6_1
6. Chillotti, I., Gama, N., Georgieva, M., Izabachène, M.: TFHE: fast fully homomorphic encryption over the torus. J. Cryptol. **33**, 34–91 (2020). https://doi.org/10.1007/s00145-019-09319-x
7. Cho, J., Ha, J., Kim, S., Lee, B., Lee, J., Lee, J., Moon, D., Yoon, H.: Transciphering framework for approximate homomorphic encryption. In: Tibouchi, M., Wang, H. (eds.) ASIACRYPT 2021. LNCS, pp. 640–669. Springer, Cham (2021). https://doi.org/10.1007/978-3-030-92078-4_22

8. Chung, H., Kim, H., Kim, Y.S., Lee, Y.: Amortized large look-up table evaluation with multivariate polynomials for homomorphic encryption. Cryptology ePrint Archive, Paper 2024/274 (2024). https://eprint.iacr.org/2024/274
9. Fan, J., Vercauteren, F.: Somewhat practical fully homomorphic encryption. Cryptology ePrint Archive, Paper 2012/144 (2012). https://eprint.iacr.org/2012/144
10. Grover, L.K.: A fast quantum mechanical algorithm for database search. In: Proceedings of the Twenty-Eighth Annual ACM Symposium on Theory of Computing, STOC 1996, pp. 212–219. Association for Computing Machinery, New York (1996). https://doi.org/10.1145/237814.237866
11. Hong, D., Lee, J.K., Kim, D.C., Kwon, D., Ryu, K.H., Lee, D.G.: LEA: a 128-bit block cipher for fast encryption on common processors. In: Kim, Y., Lee, H., Perrig, A. (eds.) WISA 2013. LNCS, vol. 8267, pp. 3–27. Springer, Cham (2014). https://doi.org/10.1007/978-3-319-05149-9_1
12. Lee, E., et al.: Low-complexity deep convolutional neural networks on fully homomorphic encryption using multiplexed convolutions. In: Proceedings of the 39th International Conference on Machine Learning (ICML 2022). Proceedings of Machine Learning Research, vol. 162, pp. 12403–12422. PMLR (2022). https://eprint.iacr.org/2021/1688. Cryptology ePrint Archive, Report 2021/1688
13. Lee, J.W., et al.: Privacy-preserving machine learning with fully homomorphic encryption for deep neural network. IEEE Access **10**, 30039–30054 (2022). https://doi.org/10.1109/ACCESS.2022.3158732, https://eprint.iacr.org/2021/783. Cryptology ePrint Archive, Report 2021/783
14. Niu, C., et al.: XBOOT: free-XOR gates for CKKS with applications to transciphering. Cryptology ePrint Archive, Paper 2025/074 (2025). https://eprint.iacr.org/2025/074
15. Shor, P.W.: Polynomial-time algorithms for prime factorization and discrete logarithms on a quantum computer. SIAM J. Comput. **26**(5), 1484–1509 (1997). https://doi.org/10.1137/S0097539795293172
16. Thakur, I., Karmakar, A., Li, C., Preneel, B.: A survey on transciphering and symmetric ciphers for homomorphic encryption. Cryptology ePrint Archive, Paper 2025/093 (2025). https://eprint.iacr.org/2025/093

Reconsidering Naito Feed-Forward-Free Double-Block-Length Hash Function

Zhuoxi Lin[1,2,3] and Chun Guo[1,2,3,4](✉)

[1] School of Cyber Science and Technology, Shandong University, Qingdao, China
202417033@mail.sdu.edu.cn, chun.guo@sdu.edu.cn

[2] State Key Laboratory of Cryptography and Digital Economy Security, Shandong University, Qingdao 266237, China

[3] Key Laboratory of Cryptologic Technology and Information Security of Ministry of Education, Shandong University, Qingdao 266237, Shandong, China

[4] Shandong Research Institute of Industrial Technology, Jinan 250102, Shandong, China

Abstract. At ACISP 2017, Naito proposed a double-block-length (DBL) hash function NHash with the following features: (i) without the costly feed-forward operations; (ii) of rate 1/2, and every pair of blockcipher-calls is parallelizable; (iii) achieving n-bit indifferentiability security using a blockcipher with n-bit blocks and κ-bit keys. This is one of the state-of-the-art DBL hash constructions. The only shortage is the use of a finalization function by two blockcipher-calls, which is unfriendly to short messages.

We consider MDPN, which is obtained by injecting Naito's feed-forward-free compression function into the Merkle-Damgård with permutation construction (JoC 2008), and prove $n - \log_2 n$ indifferentiability for it. To our knowledge, this is the first time to achieve the three aforementioned properties of NHash plus finalization-freeness simultaneously.

We also investigate the (second) preimage security of NHash and MDPN. When $\kappa \geq 2n + 1$ and a strengthened Merkle-Damgård message padding is used, for any challenge message with at least $n + 2$ blocks, we show an attack finding a second preimage on NHash with the same number of blocks, using $O(n2^n)$ time and $O(2^n)$ memory. Our idea also yields a preimage attack against MDPN with the same complexities.

Keywords: Double-block-length hash · Indifferentiability · Preimage attack

1 Introduction

Hash functions are central primitives in cryptography. Conventional security notions for a hash function include collision resistance, preimage resistance and second preimage resistance, and a complete discussion was first given in [25]. Besides, strong cryptographic hash functions are frequently used as pseudorandom oracles in protocols. To formalize this idea, using the notion of indifferentiability of Maurer et al. [14], Coron et al. [3] put forward *indifferentiability*

H. Seo (Ed.): ICISC 2025, LNCS 16487, pp. 345–367, 2026.
https://doi.org/10.1007/978-981-95-8034-7_18

from a random oracle as a new security goal for hash functions. Indifferentiability implies all single-stage security notions [6,24], including those that have not been clearly identified. Consequently, indifferentiability has been widely adopted by hash function designers.

Hash functions can be constructed from blockciphers (e.g., SHA-2 [5]) or permutations (e.g., SHA-3 [26] and Ascon-Hash [27]). This paper focuses on the former approach. Using a blockcipher with n-bit blocks, the PGV constructions [1,22] yield n-bit hash functions; to have hash functions with beyond $n/2$-bit security, Double-Block-Length (DBL) constructions with $2n$-bit outputs are developed [2,11,21]. Ideally, a DBL hash shall achieve (nearly) n-bit indifferentiability, so that its security w.r.t. most single-stage definitions is also of (nearly) n-bit. This is a non-trivial goal, and Mennink [15] actually showed that popular DBL *compression functions* either admit attacks or only deliver poor concrete security. Fortunately, later in [17], Naito showed that (nearly) n-bit indifferentiability can be achieved *in the iteration.* Concretely:

1. The first construction of Naito [17] employs a finalization function but gets rid of the memory-inefficient feed-forward operations, as depicted in Fig. 1 (Top). We call this construction NHash (Naito DBL hash with finalization). Naito proved n-bit indifferentiability for NHash.
2. The second construction of Naito [19] was named MDPH (Merkle-Damgård with permutation [12] and Hirose function [11]), which, as depicted in Fig. 1 (Bottom), avoids the finalization by adding feed-forward back. Naito [19] proved $n - \log_2 n$-bit indifferentiability for MDPH, and Guo et al. [9] subsequently identified a flaw in Naito's proof and proposed a fix to retain the $n - \log_2 n$-bit indifferentiability claim. MDPH has been adopted as the hashing mode of $\mathsf{Romulus}$ [8,13], one of the finalists of the NIST Lightweight Cryptography for lightweight authenticated encryption (AE).
3. Finally, at ASIACRYPT 2022, Naito, Sasaki and Sugawara [20] proposed the construction $\mathsf{EXEX\text{-}NI}$, which *serializes* its blockcipher-calls to minimize memory cost. Naito [19] proved $n - \log_2 n$-bit indifferentiability for $\mathsf{EXEX\text{-}NI}$.

We refer to Table 1 for a detailed comparison between these constructions. The three constructions represent state-of-the-art indifferentiable DBL hash functions. We stress that the significant advantage of $\mathsf{EXEX\text{-}NI}$ is a lower memory cost, while that of NHash and MDPH is to allow parallel (and potentially more efficient) implementations of the underlying compression function. On the other hand, the use of a finalization function makes NHash less friendly to short messages, while the use of feed-forward increases the memory cost of MDPH. For clarity, we refer to Fig. 1 for a comparison between NHash and MDPH.

1.1 Our Results

We reconsider the NHash construction, and deliver new results along two axes: first, we show that the compression function in NHash can be used in the Merkle-Damgård with permutation construction [12] to yield an indifferentiable

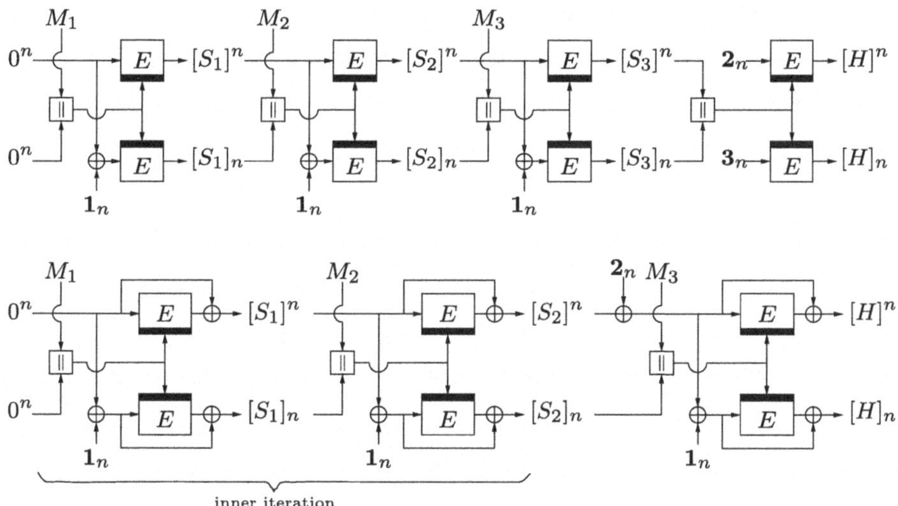

Fig. 1. (Top) NHash: Naito's DBL hash function with finalization, upon three message blocks; (Bottom) MDPH: Merkle-Damgård with permutation and Hirose function, upon three message blocks.

finalization-free construction MDPN; second, we show that the (second) preimage security bounds of NHash and MDPN are capped at $3n/2$ or $n + \log_2 n$ bits, depending on the blockcipher key-length.

MDPN: Indifferentiability Without Finalization. As discussed before, neither NHash nor MDPH is strictly better: the former uses a finalization, while the latter uses feed-forward. It is tempting to combine their core components, i.e., the feed-forward-free compression function of NHash and the finalization-free overall structure Merkle-Damgård with permutation [12] of MDPH, to gather their advantages. Denote by MDPN the obtained construction, as shown in Fig. 2. We prove that MDPN is indifferentiable up to $2^n/n$ adversarial queries, which is comparable with MDPH. Therefore, the idea is sound. To our knowledge, MDPN is the first construction that simultaneously achieves: (i) feed-forward-freeness; (ii) finalization-freeness; (iii) parallelizable compression function; and (iv) $n - \log_2 n$-bit indifferentiability security. We refer to Table 1 for a comparison among indifferentiable DBL modes.

A Glimpse of the Proof. Despite being feed-forward-free (and thus allowing inverse, to some extent), our proof for MDPN is surprisingly similar to Guo et al.'s proof [9] for MDPH (which crucially relied on feed-forward). The reason is that MDPH and MDPN share the same crucial feature in the indifferentiability setting: with high probability, a sequence of adversarial query records capturing a hash evaluation is fully constituted by forward ideal cipher queries (except for the last pair of ideal cipher queries, which are defined to be consistent with the random oracle). By this, Guo et al.'s proof [9] for MDPH was centered around

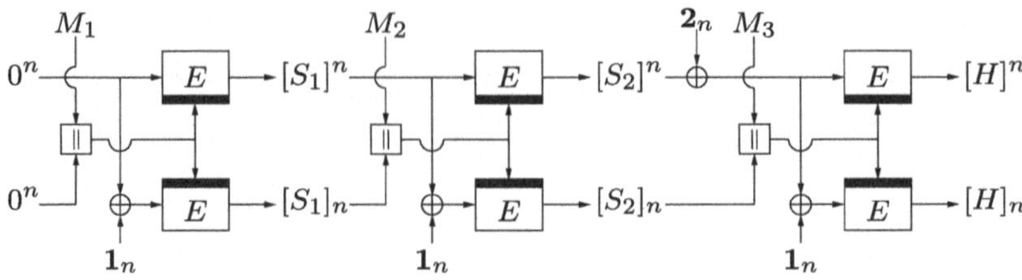

Fig. 2. MDPN: Merkle-Damgård with permutation construction using NCF compression function.

Table 1. Comparison of indifferentiable DBL modes. k is the key-length of the underlying blockcipher. Modes in this table are all of rate 1/2.

Scheme	Memory	Security	#BC calls	message length	key length	Parallel	Reference
NHash	$2n+k$	n	$2\ell+2$	$k-n$	$k \geq 2n$	Yes	[17]
MDPH	$3n+k$	$n-\log_2 n$	2ℓ	$k-n$	$k > n$	Yes	[9,18]
EXEX-NI	$n+k$	$n-\log_2 n$	$2\ell+2$	$k-n$	$k \geq 2n$	No	[7,10]
MDPN	$2n+k$	$n-\log_2 n$	2ℓ	$k-n$	$k > n$	Yes	Ours

such pairs of forward ideal cipher queries $E(K,X) \to Y_1, E(K,X \oplus \mathbf{1}_n) \to Y_2$: they yield $2n$-bit random output $Y_1 \| Y_2$ and simplify Guo et al.'s arguments. Since MDPN shares this feature, a significant part of Guo et al.'s arguments also hold. We only need to:

1. Adapt the simulator of Guo et al. (so that its simulated answers are consistent with the computations of MDPN);
2. Modify the definition and analysis of some events. Some of them did bring in added complexity. For example, an event called PathLock was defined in [9] to capture the unexpected interference between adaptations of different hash computations. In our context, the analysis of its analogue has to rely on a sort of multi-collision-freeness of the random oracle responses, which is formalized as a new event HMCol. Though, we are eventually able to manage all these adaptations. We refer to Sect. 3.2 for details.

(Second) Preimage Attacks Against NHash and MDPN. The indifferentiability bounds of NHash and MDPN imply respectively n-bit and $n-\log_2 n$-bit security w.r.t. many single-stage security notions. But for (second) preimage, we may expect (nearly) $2n$-bit security. Regarding such feed-forward-free constructions, in [20, page 380] Naito et al. commented that

- *(NHash etc.) uses a vulnerable CF (compression function), which actually allows an attacker to easily find a preimage of the CF. This implies that there exists a preimage attack on hash function by using the meet-in-the-middle approach with $O(2^n)$ computational cost...*

Such a $O(2^n)$ preimage attack indeed exists in $\mathsf{EXEX\text{-}NI}$ of [20], but it does *not* apply to NHash: finding a preimage of NCF actually consumes $O(2^n)$ inverse blockcipher queries. In fact, it is straightforward to prove $2n$-bit preimage security for NHash, whereas its exact second preimage security remains open. Regarding the new construction MDPN, both preimage and second preimage exact security remain open.

We bridge this gap by exhibiting a second preimage attack against NHash using a strengthened Merkle-Damgård message padding. Concretely, for any integer t and any challenge message M of $\ell \geq t+2$ blocks, when $\kappa \geq \frac{(2t+1)n}{t}$, we show an attack finding a second preimage M^* (i.e., $\mathsf{NHash}^E(M^*) = \mathsf{NHash}^E(M)$) with $O(t2^{\frac{(t+1)n}{t}})$ time and $O(2^{\frac{(t-1)n}{t}})$ memory, and $|M^*| = |M|$. Setting $t = n$ yields an attack running in $O(n2^n)$ time, using $O(2^n)$ memory and outputting a second preimage for any challenge message of more than $n+2$ blocks, and it works as long as $\kappa \geq 2n+1$. Therefore, the second preimage security of NHash is capped at $n + \log_2 n$ bits in general.

The attack is easily adapted to yield a preimage attack against MDPN with the same complexities. We stress that these attacks have higher than 2^n complexities and thus do not violate their n or $n - \log_2 n$ bits indifferentiability bounds of [17] and this paper. These just indicate that the feed-forward-free construction NHash (resp. MDPN) should not be used in protocols that require $2n$-bit second preimage security (e.g., certain hash-based signatures [4]).

Open Questions. We leave two open questions: (i) Whether $\mathsf{EXEX\text{-}NI}$ can be made finalization-free using similar ideas; (ii) Our second preimage attack is not applicable to $\kappa = 2n$ (which is of particular interest due to matching the parameters of important blockciphers such as the AES-256), and whether it is possible to prove beyond n-bit (second) preimage security for NHash and MDPN for the case of $\kappa = 2n$.

Organization. We serve necessary notations and definitions (of our new construction MDPN) in Sect. 2. We then prove indifferentiability for MDPN in Sect. 3 and exhibit our (second) preimage attacks in Sect. 4.

2 Preliminaries

Notations. Let $\{0,1\}^*$ be the set of all bit strings, and λ be the empty string. For an integer $n \geq 0$, let $\{0,1\}^n$ be the set of all n-bit strings, and $(\{0,1\}^n)^*$ be the set of all bit strings whose lengths in bits are a multiple of n. For a non-negative integer i, let $[i] = \{0, 1, \ldots, i\}$, the set of non-negative integers at most i. For positive integers ℓ, ν and an $\ell\nu$-bit string M, we write its partition into ν-bit strings as $M_1, M_2, \ldots, M_\ell \xleftarrow{\nu} M$. For positive integers r, s with $s \leq r$ and an r-bit string X, $[X]^s$ (resp. $[X]_s$) denotes the most (resp. least) significant s bits of X. Denote by $X \| Y$ the concatenation of bit strings X and Y. For a bit string Y, $X \leftarrow Y$ means that Y is assigned to X. For a finite set $\mathcal{X}$,

$X \xleftarrow{\$} \mathcal{X}$ means that an element is sampled uniformly at random from $\mathcal{X}$ and is assigned to X. $\mathcal{Y} \leftarrow \mathcal{X}$ means that a finite set $\mathcal{X}$ is assigned to $\mathcal{Y}$, and $\mathcal{Y} \xleftarrow{\cup} \mathcal{X}$ means that $\mathcal{Y} \leftarrow \mathcal{X} \cup \mathcal{Y}$. For a positive integer a, $\mathsf{Func}(*, a)$ denotes the set of all functions from $\{0,1\}^*$ to $\{0,1\}^a$. For positive integers k and n, $\mathsf{BC}(k, n)$ denotes the set of all blockciphers with k-bit keys and n-bit blocks. Hence, for each $E \in \mathsf{BC}(k, n)$, $E : \{0,1\}^k \times \{0,1\}^n \to \{0,1\}^n$ is a set of permutations over $\{0,1\}^n$ indexed by a key in $\{0,1\}^k$. The decryption function of E is denoted by $E^{-1} : \{0,1\}^k \times \{0,1\}^n \to \{0,1\}^n$. For a positive integer i, let $\boldsymbol{i}_n$ be the n-bit representation of i, e.g., $\mathbf{1}_n = 0^{n-1}1$, $\mathbf{2}_n = 0^{n-2}10$, and $\mathbf{3}_n = 0^{n-2}11$.

Naito DBL Construction NCF and Its Variant MDPN. Naito's DBL hash is defined upon a compression function obtained by removing the feeding forward operations from the Hirose compression function, as shown in Fig. 1 (Top). We will call this *Naito compression function (*NCF*)*. Formally, for $E \in \mathsf{BC}(k, n)$, let $\nu = k - n$. The NCF compression function $\mathsf{NCF}^E : \{0,1\}^{2n} \times \{0,1\}^\nu \to \{0,1\}^{2n}$ is defined as $\mathsf{NCF}^E(S_{i-1}, M_i) = S_i$ for a ν-bit message M_i and a $2n$-bit state S_{i-1}, where

$$[S_i]^n = E(M_i \,\|\, [S_{i-1}]_n, [S_{i-1}]^n) \quad \text{(Top Part)},$$
$$[S_i]_n = E(M_i \,\|\, [S_{i-1}]_n, [S_{i-1}]^n \oplus \mathbf{1}_n) \quad \text{(Bottom Part)}.$$

We inject NCF into the Merkle-Damgård*with a permutation* construction and obtain MDPN, as depicted in Fig. 2. Concretely, MDPN uses 0^{2n} as the initial state, and XORs another constant $\mathbf{2}_n$ into the intermediate value before the last invocation of NCF. A formal description is given in Algorithm 1. To simplify the proof, we let the input message M be a multiple of ν.

Algorithm 1. $\mathsf{MDPN}^E(M)$

```
1: S_0 ← 0^{2n}
2: M_1, M_2, ..., M_ℓ ←^ν pad(M)
3: for i = 1, ..., ℓ − 1 do
4:     S_i ← NCF^E(S_{i−1}, M_i)
5: end for
6: [S_{ℓ−1}]^n ← [S_{ℓ−1}]^n ⊕ 2_n
7: H ← NCF^E(S_{ℓ−1}, M_ℓ)
8: return H
```

Indifferentiability of Hash. Let $\mathsf{H}^E : \{0,1\}^* \to \{0,1\}^\omega$ be a hash function using a blockcipher $E \in \mathsf{BC}(k, n)$ as an oracle. Indifferentiability of H^E from a random oracle $\mathcal{RO} \xleftarrow{\$} \mathsf{Func}(*, \omega)$ is the indistinguishability between the real and ideal worlds described as follows. In the real world, a distinguisher (an adversary) D interacts with H^E and a pair of encryption and decryption functions (E, E^{-1}) of E. Here, E is the ideal-cipher, that is, we let $E \xleftarrow{\$} \mathsf{BC}(k, n)$. In the ideal world, for a simulator S that has oracle access to a random oracle $\mathcal{RO}$, a distinguisher

D interacts with $\mathcal{RO}$ and S. After the interaction, D outputs a bit to indicate the decision. For a simulator S, the advantage function of a distinguisher D is defined as

$$\mathbf{Adv}^{\mathsf{indiff}}_{\mathsf{H},\mathcal{RO},\mathsf{S}}(D) = \left| \Pr\left[E \xleftarrow{\$} \mathsf{BC}(k,n); D^{\mathsf{H}^E, E, E^{-1}} \Rightarrow 1\right] - \Pr\left[\mathcal{RO} \xleftarrow{\$} \mathsf{Func}(*,\omega); D^{\mathcal{RO}, \mathsf{S}^{\mathcal{RO}}} \Rightarrow 1\right] \right|.$$

In the above definition, the probabilities are taken over D, E, $\mathcal{RO}$, and S. We say that our target hash function H is indifferentiable from the random oracle if for any D, there exists a simulator S such that: (i) $\mathsf{Adv}^{\mathsf{indiff}}_{\mathsf{H},\mathcal{RO},\mathsf{S}}(D)$ is negligibly small, and (ii) the simulator S runs in polynomial time. Hereafter, H^E and $\mathcal{RO}$ are called hash oracles, queries to a hash oracle are called hash queries, (E, E^{-1}) and S are called primitive oracles, and queries to $(E, E^{-1})/\mathsf{S}$ are called primitive queries.

3 Indifferentiability of MDPN

For MDPN, we present the following bound.

Theorem 1. *Let D be a distinguisher that makes q hash queries of σ message blocks in total and p primitive queries, and runs in time t, which we call a (p,q,σ)-indifferentiability distinguisher. Let $Q = \sigma + p$, and assume $3Q + np \le 2^n/4$ and $n \ge 4$. Then, there exists a simulator S such that*

$$\mathbf{Adv}^{\mathsf{indiff}}_{\mathsf{MDPN},\mathcal{RO}_{2n},\mathsf{S}}(D) \le \frac{11Q + 20nQ + 2np}{2^n} + \frac{64Q^2 + 12(3Q+np)^2}{2^{2n}}.$$

The simulator makes no more than np queries to $\mathcal{RO}$ in total and runs in time $t + O(np)$.

To prove Theorem 1, we first describe a simulator and bound its complexities in Sect. 3.1. Then, in Sect. 3.2 we then prove indistinguishability of the real and ideal worlds using this simulator.

3.1 Simulator

Formally, the simulator $\mathsf{S}^{\mathcal{RO}} = (\mathsf{S}^{\mathcal{RO}}_E, \mathsf{S}^{\mathcal{RO}}_{E^{-1}})$ is defined in Algorithm 2, where $\mathsf{S}_E : \{0,1\}^k \times \{0,1\}^n \to \{0,1\}^n$ simulates an encryption oracle E, and $\mathsf{S}_{E^{-1}} : \{0,1\}^k \times \{0,1\}^n \to \{0,1\}^n$ simulates a decryption oracle E^{-1}. For clarity, statements in red deviate from the simulator in [9]. In order to work properly, the simulator S keeps multiple data structures: first, it keeps query-response triples in table ET and ET^{-1} whose entries are the special symbol $\perp$ indicating "undefined". If a query-response triple (K, X, Y) where $\mathsf{S}_E(K,X) = Y$ or $\mathsf{S}_{E^{-1}}(K,Y) = X$ is defined, then the tables are defined such that $\mathsf{ET}[K](X) = Y$ and $\mathsf{ET}^{-1}[K](Y) = X$. The simulator S also keeps paths in PathT that are constructed from ET and

Algorithm 2. Simulator $\mathsf{S}^{\mathcal{RO}} = (\mathsf{S}_E^{\mathcal{RO}}, \mathsf{S}_{E^{-1}}^{\mathcal{RO}})$

Initialization

1: $\mathsf{S}^{\mathcal{RO}}$ maintains a table PathT to keep track of encountered paths, indexed by their $2n$-bit endpoints. Initially, $\mathsf{PathT}[0^{2n}] = \left(0^{2n} \xrightarrow{\lambda} 0^{2n}\right)$ for the empty string λ, while $\mathsf{PathT}[S] = \bot$ for any other $S \in \{0,1\}^{2n} \backslash \{0^{2n}\}$.

2: $\mathsf{S}^{\mathcal{RO}}$ maintains another index structure Index on PathT, such that $\mathsf{Index}[R]$ returns the set $\left\{\left(0^{2n} \xrightarrow{M} S\right) : [S]_n = R\right\}$.

3: $\mathsf{S}^{\mathcal{RO}}$ maintains two tables ET and ET^{-1}, with entries initialized to $\bot$.

4: $\mathsf{S}^{\mathcal{RO}}$ maintains a set $\mathcal{L}_{\mathsf{block}}(\mathsf{ET})$ for the already defined blocks. Elements in $\mathcal{L}_{\mathsf{block}}(\mathsf{ET})$ are of the form $\left(S_1 \xrightarrow{M} S_2, d\right)$, $S_1, S_2 \in \{0,1\}^{2n}$, $M \in \{0,1\}^{\nu}$, $d \in \{\rightarrow, \leftarrow, \bot\}$. Initially, $\mathcal{L}_{\mathsf{block}}(\mathsf{ET}) = \left\{\left(0^{2n} \xrightarrow{\lambda} 0^{2n}, \rightarrow\right)\right\}$.

Simulator $\mathsf{S}_E^{\mathcal{RO}}(K, X)$

1: **if** $\mathsf{ET}[K](X) \neq \bot$ **then return** $\mathsf{ET}[K](X)$
2: **if** $\mathsf{PathT}[(X \| [K]_n) \oplus (\mathbf{2}_n \| 0^n)] \neq \bot \wedge \mathsf{PathT}[(X \| [K]_n) \oplus (\mathbf{3}_n \| 0^n)] \neq \bot$ **then**
3:     **abort**
4: **end if**
5: $S \leftarrow X \| [K]_n$
6: **if** $\mathsf{PathT}[S \oplus (\mathbf{2}_n \| 0^n)] \neq \bot$ **then**
7:     $\left(0^{2n} \xrightarrow{M} S \oplus (\mathbf{2}_n \| 0^n)\right) \leftarrow \mathsf{PathT}\left[S \oplus (\mathbf{2}_n \| 0^n)\right]$
8:     $H \leftarrow \mathcal{RO}(M \| [K]^{\nu})$
9:     $Y_1 \leftarrow [H]^n$; $Y_2 \leftarrow [H]_n$
10:     $\mathsf{CreateBlock}\big((K, X, Y_1), (K, X \oplus \mathbf{1}_n, Y_2), \bot\big)$
11: **end if**

12: **if** $\mathsf{PathT}[S \oplus (\mathbf{3}_n \| 0^n)] \neq \bot$ **then**
13:     $\left(0^{2n} \xrightarrow{M} S \oplus (\mathbf{3}_n \| 0^n)\right) \leftarrow \mathsf{PathT}\left[S \oplus (\mathbf{3}_n \| 0^n)\right]$
14:     $H \leftarrow \mathcal{RO}(M \| [K]^{\nu})$
15:     $Y_1 \leftarrow [H]^n$; $Y_2 \leftarrow [H]_n$
16:     $\mathsf{CreateBlock}\big((K, X \oplus \mathbf{1}_n, Y_1), (K, X, Y_2), \bot\big)$
17: **end if**
18: **if** The conditions of lines 6 and 12 are not satisfied **then**
19:     $Y_1 \xleftarrow{\$} \{0,1\}^n \backslash \mathsf{Rng}[K]$; $Y_2 \xleftarrow{\$} \{0,1\}^n \backslash (\mathsf{Rng}[K] \cup \{Y_1\})$
20:     $\mathsf{CreateBlock}\big((K, X, Y_1), (K, X \oplus \mathbf{1}_n, Y_2), \rightarrow\big)$
21: **end if**
22: **return** $\mathsf{ET}[K](X)$

ET^{-1}. We write $X \in \mathsf{ET}[K]$ if $\mathsf{ET}[K](X) \neq \bot$, $Y \in \mathsf{ET}^{-1}[K]$ if $\mathsf{ET}^{-1}[K](Y) \neq \bot$, and vice versa. We also write $\mathsf{Dom}[K] = \{X \in \{0,1\}^n : X \in \mathsf{ET}[K]\}$ and $\mathsf{Rng}[K] = \{Y \in \{0,1\}^n : Y \in \mathsf{ET}^{-1}[K]\}$.

A *block* is a triple (S_{i-1}, M_i, S_i) which is obtained from $(\mathsf{ET}, \mathsf{ET}^{-1})$ and satisfies the relation $S_i = \mathsf{NCF}^{R_E}(S_{i-1}, M_i)$. The block is denoted by $\left(S_{i-1} \xrightarrow{M_i} S_i, d\right)$, where d indicates how it was defined: the block is called *leftward* if $d = \leftarrow$;

Algorithm 2. Simulator $\mathsf{S}^{\mathcal{RO}} = (\mathsf{S}_E^{\mathcal{RO}}, \mathsf{S}_{E^{-1}}^{\mathcal{RO}})$ (Cont'd)

Simulator $\mathsf{S}_{E^{-1}}^{\mathcal{RO}}(K, Y)$

1: **if** $\mathsf{ET}^{-1}[K](Y) \neq \bot$ **then return** $\mathsf{ET}^{-1}[K](Y)$
2: **if** $\left|\mathsf{Index}\left[[K]_n\right]\right| \geq n$ **then abort**
3: **for all** $\left(0^{2n} \xrightarrow{M} S\right) \in \mathsf{Index}\left[[K]_n\right]$ **do**
4: $\quad H \leftarrow \mathcal{RO}(M \| [K]^{\nu})$
5: $\quad$ // If $\mathsf{ET}^{-1}[K](Y)$ acts as the top part: check the chaining condition
6: $\quad$ **if** $[H]^n = Y$ **then**
7: $\quad\quad X \leftarrow [S]^n \oplus \mathbf{2}_n$
8: $\quad\quad Y' \leftarrow [H]_n$
9: $\quad\quad \mathsf{CreateBlock}\left((K, X, Y), (K, X \oplus \mathbf{1}_n, Y'), \bot\right)$
10: $\quad$ **end if**
11: $\quad$ // If $\mathsf{ET}^{-1}[K](Y)$ acts as the bottom part: check the chaining condition
12: $\quad$ **if** $[H]_n = Y$ **then**
13: $\quad\quad X \leftarrow [S]^n \oplus \mathbf{3}_n$
14: $\quad\quad Y' \leftarrow [H]^n$
15: $\quad\quad \mathsf{CreateBlock}\left((K, X \oplus \mathbf{1}_n, Y'), (K, X, Y), \bot\right)$
16: $\quad$ **end if**
17: **end for**
18: **if** $\mathsf{ET}^{-1}[K](Y) = \bot$ **then**
19: $\quad X \xleftarrow{\$} \{0,1\}^n \backslash \mathsf{Dom}[K]$; $Y' \xleftarrow{\$} \{0,1\}^n \backslash (\mathsf{Rng}[K] \cup \{Y\})$
20: $\quad \mathsf{CreateBlock}\left((K, X, Y), (K, X \oplus \mathbf{1}_n, Y'), \leftarrow\right)$
21: **end if**
22: **return** $\mathsf{ET}^{-1}[K](Y)$

rightward if $d = \rightarrow$; and *adapted* if $d = \bot$. We refer to $\left(0^{2n} \xrightarrow{\lambda} 0^{2n}, \rightarrow\right)$ as the *initial block*, which is also viewed as rightward.

A *path* is a block or a concatenation of blocks which starts from the initial value 0^{2n}. For a sequence of blocks $0^{2n} \xrightarrow{M_1} S_1, S_1 \xrightarrow{M_2} S_2, \ldots, S_{\ell-2} \xrightarrow{M_{\ell-1}} S_{\ell-1}$, we denote the concatenation by $0^{2n} \xrightarrow{M_1 \| M_2 \| \cdots \| M_{\ell-1}} S_{\ell-1}$. Hence, the path represents the inner iteration of MDPN^{R_E} (See Fig. 1). $\mathcal{L}_{\mathsf{path}}(\mathsf{ET})$ is a set of all paths obtained from $\mathcal{L}_{\mathsf{block}}(\mathsf{ET})$. To ease access, $\mathsf{S}^{\mathcal{RO}}$ maintains a table PathT to keep track of encountered paths. In PathT, paths are indexed by their $2n$-bit end value, so that the time complexity for random access is constant.

In the pseudocodes, $P \leftarrow \mathsf{PathT}[L]$ means a read of path P from $\mathsf{PathT}[L]$ for a label (an endpoint) $L \in \{0,1\}^{2n}$, and $\mathsf{PathT}[L] \leftarrow P$ means a write of path P to $\mathsf{PathT}[L]$. In principle, $\mathsf{PathT}[L]$ for any L may contain multiple paths, and if so, a path read picks the arbitrary one and a path write adds one to the existing ones. However, the game is defined so that it aborts whenever such the read/write operation is going to happen.

Algorithm 2. Simulator $\mathsf{S}^{\mathcal{RO}} = (\mathsf{S}_E^{\mathcal{RO}}, \mathsf{S}_{E^{-1}}^{\mathcal{RO}})$(Cont'd)

Subroutine $\mathsf{CreateBlock}((K, X, Y_1), (K, X \oplus \mathbf{1}_n, Y_2), dir)$

1: // Update the ideal-cipher tables
2: **if** $dir = \perp$ **then** // Inconsistency only possible for adapted blocks
3: **if** $X \in \mathsf{ET}[K]$ or $X \oplus \mathbf{1}_n \in \mathsf{ET}[K]$ **then abort**
4: **if** $Y_1 \in \mathsf{ET}^{-1}[K]$ or $Y_2 \in \mathsf{ET}^{-1}[K]$ or $Y_1 = Y_2$ **then abort**
5: **end if**
6: $\mathsf{ET}[K](X) \leftarrow Y_1$; $\mathsf{ET}[K](X \oplus \mathbf{1}_n) \leftarrow Y_2$; $\mathsf{ET}^{-1}[K](Y_1) \leftarrow X$; $\mathsf{ET}^{-1}[K](Y_2) \leftarrow X \oplus \mathbf{1}_n$
7:
8: $S^{(1)} \leftarrow X \| [K]_n$, $S^{(2)} \leftarrow (Y_1 \| Y_2)$, $m \leftarrow [K]^{\nu}$
9: $S^{(3)} \leftarrow (X \oplus \mathbf{1}_n) \| [K]_n$, $S^{(4)} \leftarrow (Y_2 \| Y_1)$
10: Add $\left(S^{(1)} \xrightarrow{m} S^{(2)}, dir\right)$ and $\left(S^{(3)} \xrightarrow{m} S^{(4)}, dir\right)$ to $\mathcal{L}_{\mathsf{block}}(\mathsf{ET})$
11: // Update the table PathT and check abort conditions
12: **if** $\mathsf{PathT}[S^{(1)}] \neq \perp$ **then**
13: $\left(0^{2n} \xrightarrow{M'} S^{(1)}\right) \leftarrow \mathsf{PathT}[S^{(1)}]$
14: **if** $\mathsf{PathT}[S^{(2)}] \neq \perp$ **then abort**
15: $\mathsf{PathT}[S^{(2)}] \leftarrow \left(0^{2n} \xrightarrow{M' \| M} S^{(2)}\right)$
16: **end if**
17: **if** $\mathsf{PathT}[S^{(3)}] \neq \perp$ **then**
18: $\left(0^{2n} \xrightarrow{M''} S^{(3)}\right) \leftarrow \mathsf{PathT}[S^{(3)}]$
19: **if** $\mathsf{PathT}[S^{(4)}] \neq \perp$ **then abort**
20: $\mathsf{PathT}[S^{(4)}] \leftarrow \left(0^{2n} \xrightarrow{M'' \| M} S^{(2)}\right)$
21: **end if**
22: Update the index Index

In the real world, for a hash query $\mathsf{MDPN}^E(M' \| M^*) \rightarrow H$, the response is defined by using E via the MDPN structure, and thus the following is satisfied:

$$\exists\left(0^{2n} \xrightarrow{M'} S'\right) \in \mathcal{L}_{\mathsf{path}}(\mathsf{ET}), \left(S^* \xrightarrow{M^*} H\right) \in \mathcal{L}_{\mathsf{block}}(\mathsf{ET}) \text{ s.t. } S^* = S' \oplus (\mathbf{2}_n \| 0^n) : \mathsf{MDPN}^E(M' \| M^*) = H. \quad (1)$$

On the other hand, in the ideal world, for a hash query, the hash value is defined by a monolithic function $\mathcal{RO}$. Hence, the goal of simulator is to simulate an ideal-cipher so that the query-responses of $\mathcal{RO}$ and of S satisfy the relation given in Eq. (1).

In order to ensure the relation in Eq. (1) in the ideal world, for an encryption query (K, X), if there exists a path $\left(0^{2n} \xrightarrow{M'} S'\right)$ in $\mathcal{T}_{path}$ to which the query connects, i.e., $S' = (X \oplus \mathbf{2}_n) \| [K]_n$ or $S' = (X \oplus \mathbf{1}_n \oplus \mathbf{2}_n) \| [K]_n$, then the response is defined by using $\mathcal{RO}$ (otherwise, the response is defined by lazy sampling). For NCF's compression function, when a top (resp., bottom) part is defined, the bottom (resp., top) part can immediately be defined. In addition, switching top and bottom parts, the result also has NCF's structure. Hence, for each (encryption or decryption) query, two outputs corresponding to the top and bottom parts are defined, and two blocks are defined. The initialization procedure is performed before the first query by D.

As explained earlier, S aborts in certain bad situations. In particular, this includes the case where S fails to simulate an ideal-cipher. In addition, S also aborts if it encounters certain bad situations, e.g., obtaining distinct paths $\left(0^{2n} \xrightarrow{M} S\right)$ and $\left(0^{2n} \xrightarrow{M'} S\right)$ with the identical endpoint (see lines 14 and 19 of $\mathsf{CreateBlock}$).

Complexities of the Simulator. Since the overall simulation process is the same as [9], the complexity and size of tables are the same as [9], i.e., when D makes q hash queries of σ message blocks and p primitive queries and running in time t, it holds: (i) the simulator makes no more than np queries to $\mathcal{RO}$ in total and runs in time $t + O(np)$; (ii) $|\mathsf{HQueries}| \leq 3Q + np$, $|\mathsf{ET}| \leq 2Q$ and $|\mathcal{L}_{\mathsf{block}}(\mathsf{ET})| \leq 2Q + 1$. We refer to the full version for a complete analysis.

3.2 Indistinguishability of the Real and Ideal Worlds

The analysis is further divided into three subsections: first, we introduce some additional terminology and conventions; second, we identify several bad events that could potentially render the simulation failed in the interaction between D and the random oracle; finally, assuming absence of the aforementioned bad events, we show that the simulated oracle responses are indeed consistent with the random oracle responses, and the simulated responses are indeed indistinguishable from the real world oracles.

Additional Terminology and Conventions. We assume that D makes no repeated queries, and ignore the padding, that is, the length of hash queries made by D is always a multiple of ν.

We define two cryptographic games. In each game, a distinguisher D interacts with three oracles $(L, R_E, R_{E^{-1}})$, where L is a hash oracle, and $(R_E, R_{E^{-1}})$ are primitive oracles. Game 1 or G_1 captures the interaction between the distinguisher and the ideal world oracles $(L, R_E, R_{E^{-1}}) = (\mathcal{RO}, \mathsf{S}_E^{\mathcal{RO}}, \mathsf{S}_{E^{-1}}^{\mathcal{RO}})$, where $\mathsf{S}^{\mathcal{RO}} = (\mathsf{S}_E^{\mathcal{RO}}, \mathsf{S}_{E^{-1}}^{\mathcal{RO}})$ is the simulator defined in Sect. 3.1. Game 2 or G_2 has $(L, R_E, R_{E^{-1}}) = (\mathsf{MDPN}^E, E, E^{-1})$, i.e., it captures the interaction with the real world oracles.

In the subsequent analyses, D is permitted to make additional encryption queries after finishing the "normal" q hash and p primitive queries but before outputting a decision bit. There are two types of additional queries.

- The first type is that D can make queries to R_E according to the procedure of $\mathsf{MDPN}^{R_E}(M)$ for all hash queries $L(M)$, i.e., D can obtain all input-output triples of R_E to calculate $\mathsf{MDPN}^{R_E}(M)$.

- The second type is that D can make queries to R_E whose partner, according to NCF's structure, has been defined by a primitive query. More precisely, if D obtains a triple (K, X, Y) by a primitive query but does not obtain the partner $(K, X \oplus \mathbf{1}_n, Y')$, then D can make the additional encryption query $(K, X \oplus \mathbf{1}_n)$ and obtain the response Y'.

With this added power, D makes at most $2Q$ primitive queries in total. Note that the additional queries do not reduce the advantage of D. Moreover, $|\mathcal{L}_{\mathsf{block}}(\mathsf{ET})| \leq 2Q$, i.e., these queries create at most $2Q$ blocks in total.

As additional notations:

- We imagine that the game G_1 maintains a set HQueries that records *all* random oracle queries appearing during the execution. Namely, every time the distinguisher D or the simulator $\mathsf{S}^{\mathcal{RO}}$ makes a random oracle query $\mathcal{RO}(M) \to H$, the pair (M, H) is added to the set HQueries. Note that pairs added to HQueries due to simulator queries may be unknown to D.
- A *simulator cycle* consists of the execution period starting from when an adversary makes a query to when the adversary receives an answer. During a simulator cycle, if the simulator makes at least one call to $\mathsf{CreateBlock}(\star, \star, \perp)$, then it is an *adapted (simulator) cycle*. Otherwise,
  - it is a *rightward (simulator) cycle* if the simulator cycle was due to D querying $\mathsf{S}_E^{\mathcal{RO}}$;
  - it is a *leftward (simulator) cycle* if it was due to D querying $\mathsf{S}_{E^{-1}}^{\mathcal{RO}}$.

Bad Events in G_1 Executions. A table entry $\mathsf{ET}[K_1](X_1)$ is *rightward*, if it is defined via lazy sampling (i.e., by line 19 in $\mathsf{S}_E^{\mathcal{RO}}$). We first put forward collision and multi-collision events on such rightward ideal-cipher queries and random oracle queries.

$$\begin{aligned}
\mathsf{Hit0} &\Leftrightarrow \exists \text{ a rightward table entry } \mathsf{ET}[K](X) \text{ s.t. } \mathsf{ET}[K](X) = 0^n, \\
\mathsf{MCol} &\Leftrightarrow \exists n \text{ distinct rightward table entries } \mathsf{ET}[K_1](X_1), \ldots, \mathsf{ET}[K_n](X_n) \\
&\qquad \text{s.t. } \mathsf{ET}[K_1](X_1) = \cdots = \mathsf{ET}[K_n](X_n), \\
\mathsf{HMCol} &\Leftrightarrow \exists n \text{ distinct RO query records } (M_1, H_1), ..., (M_n, H_n) \in \mathsf{HQueries} \\
&\qquad \text{s.t. } \big([H_1]^n = ... = [H_n]^n\big) \vee \big([H_1]_n = ... = [H_n]_n\big), \\
\mathsf{HCol} &\Leftrightarrow \exists (M, H) \in \mathsf{HQueries} \text{ s.t. } [H]^n = [H]_n.
\end{aligned}$$

It is easy to show (see the full version for a full proof):

$$\Pr\big[\mathsf{Hit0} \vee \mathsf{MCol} \vee \mathsf{HMCol} \vee \mathsf{HCol}\big] \leq \frac{11Q + 2np}{2^n}. \tag{2}$$

We then define three events over the simulated blocks $\mathcal{L}_{\mathsf{block}}(\mathsf{ET})$.

$$\begin{aligned}\mathsf{Hit} \Leftrightarrow \exists\Big(S^{(1)} \xrightarrow{M'} S^{(2)}, \rightarrow\Big), \Big(S^{(3)} \xrightarrow{M^*} S^{(4)}, d_2\Big) \in \mathcal{L}_{\mathsf{block}}(\mathsf{ET}) \text{ s.t.}\\ \Big(S^{(2)} = S^{(3)} \vee S^{(2)} = S^{(3)} \oplus (\mathbf{2}_n \| 0^n)\Big) \wedge\\ \Big((S^{(3)} \xrightarrow{M^*} S^{(4)}) \text{ is defined before } (S^{(1)} \xrightarrow{M'} S^{(2)}) \text{ is defined}\\ \vee\, (S^{(1)} \xrightarrow{M'} S^{(2)}) \text{ and } (S^{(3)} \xrightarrow{M^*} S^{(4)}) \text{ are defined}\\ \text{in the same } \mathsf{CreateBlock} \text{ call}\Big)\end{aligned}$$

$$\begin{aligned}\mathsf{DHit} \Leftrightarrow \exists\Big(S^{(1)} \xrightarrow{M'} S^{(2)}, \rightarrow\Big), \Big(S^{(3)} \xrightarrow{M^*} S^{(4)}, \leftarrow\Big) \in \mathcal{L}_{\mathsf{block}}(\mathsf{ET}) \text{ s.t.}\\ \Big(S^{(2)} = S^{(3)} \vee S^{(2)} = S^{(3)} \oplus (\mathbf{2}_n \| 0^n)\Big)\\ \wedge \Big((S^{(1)} \xrightarrow{M'} S^{(2)}) \text{ is defined before } (S^{(3)} \xrightarrow{M^*} S^{(4)}) \text{ is defined}\Big)\\ \mathsf{BCol} \Leftrightarrow \exists \text{ distinct } \Big(S^{(1)} \xrightarrow{M'} S^{(2)}, \rightarrow\Big), \Big(S^{(3)} \xrightarrow{M^*} S^{(4)}, \rightarrow\Big) \in \mathcal{L}_{\mathsf{block}}(\mathsf{ET}) \text{ s.t.}\\ \Big(S^{(2)} = S^{(4)} \vee S^{(2)} = S^{(4)} \oplus (\mathbf{1}_n \| 0^n)\\ \vee\, S^{(2)} = S^{(4)} \oplus (\mathbf{2}_n \| 0^n) \vee S^{(2)} = S^{(4)} \oplus (\mathbf{3}_n \| 0^n)\Big).\end{aligned}$$

Following the ideas of [9], it can be shown that

$$\Pr\big[\mathsf{Hit} \vee \mathsf{DHit} \vee \mathsf{BCol}\big] \leq \frac{64Q^2}{2^{2n}} + \frac{8nQ}{2^n}. \tag{3}$$

Note that in DHit, the first involved block $\big(S^{(1)} \xrightarrow{M'} S^{(2)}, \rightarrow\big)$ is restricted to be rightward, which ensures the randomness of its right endpoint and is crucial for its $O(nQ/2^n)$ probability. We refer to the full version for a full proof. For convenience, define $\mathsf{BadBlock} := \mathsf{Hit0} \vee \mathsf{MCol} \vee \mathsf{HMCol} \vee \mathsf{HCol} \vee \mathsf{Hit} \vee \mathsf{DHit} \vee \mathsf{BCol}$.

Finally, we identify a subset $\mathcal{L}^{\rightarrow}_{\mathsf{path}}(\mathsf{ET})$ of $\mathcal{L}_{\mathsf{path}}(\mathsf{ET})$, which consists of all the paths that are fully constituted by rightward blocks. We define four additional events on $\mathcal{L}^{\rightarrow}_{\mathsf{path}}(\mathsf{ET})$.

$$\begin{aligned}\mathsf{PathCol} \Leftrightarrow \exists \text{ distinct } \Big(0^{2n} \xrightarrow{M} S\Big), \Big(0^{2n} \xrightarrow{M'} S'\Big) \in \mathcal{L}^{\rightarrow}_{\mathsf{path}}(\mathsf{ET}) \text{ s.t.}\\ \Big(S = S' \vee S = S' \oplus (\mathbf{1}_n \| 0^n) \vee S = S' \oplus (\mathbf{2}_n \| 0^n) \vee S = S' \oplus (\mathbf{3}_n \| 0^n)\Big),\\ \mathsf{PathMCol} \Leftrightarrow \exists n \text{ distinct paths } \Big(0^{2n} \xrightarrow{M_1} S_1\Big), \ldots, \Big(0^{2n} \xrightarrow{M_n} S_n\Big) \in \mathcal{L}^{\rightarrow}_{\mathsf{path}}(\mathsf{ET}) \text{ s.t.}\\ [S_1]_n = [S_2]_n = \cdots = [S_n]_n,\\ \mathsf{HBCol} \Leftrightarrow \exists (M \| m, H) \in \mathsf{HQueries}, \Big(0^{2n} \xrightarrow{M} S\Big) \in \mathcal{L}^{\rightarrow}_{\mathsf{path}}(\mathsf{ET}), m \in \{0,1\}^{\nu} \text{ s.t.}\\ \Big([H]^n \in \mathsf{ET}^{-1}\big[m \| [S]_n\big] \bigvee [H]_n \in \mathsf{ET}^{-1}\big[m \| [S]_n\big]\Big),\\ \mathsf{PathLock} \Leftrightarrow \exists \text{ distinct } \Big(0^{2n} \xrightarrow{M} S\Big), \Big(0^{2n} \xrightarrow{M'} S'\Big) \in \mathcal{L}^{\rightarrow}_{\mathsf{path}}(\mathsf{ET}),\end{aligned}$$

$$m \in \{0,1\}^\nu, (M\|m, H), (M'\|m, H') \in \mathsf{HQueries} \text{ s.t.}$$
$$\Big([S]_n = [S']_n\Big) \bigwedge \Big([H]_n = [H']^n \bigvee [H]_n = [H']_n \bigvee [H]^n = [H']^n\Big).$$

Similarly to [9], conditioned on $\neg\mathsf{BadBlock}$, neither $\mathsf{PathCol}$ nor $\mathsf{PathMCol}$ is ever possible. For completeness, we include a proof in the full version. The remaining two events HBCol and $\mathsf{PathLock}$ are analyzed below.

Analyzing HBCol. The event HBCol is divided into two sub-events as follows.

- ROHit: upon a random oracle query $\mathcal{RO}(M\|m) \to H$ (by either D or the simulator), there exists a path $\left(0^{2n} \xrightarrow{M} S\right) \in \mathcal{L}^{\rightarrow}_{\mathsf{path}}(\mathsf{ET})$ such that $[H]^n \in \mathsf{ET}^{-1}[m\|[S]_n]$ or $[H]_n \in \mathsf{ET}^{-1}[m\|[S]_n]$;
- $\mathsf{BlockHit}$: After the simulator created a rightward block $\left(S' \xrightarrow{m} S, \rightarrow\right)$, there exists a path $\left(0^{2n} \xrightarrow{M} S'\right) \in \mathcal{L}^{\rightarrow}_{\mathsf{path}}(\mathsf{ET})$ and a random oracle query $(M\|m\|m', H) \in \mathsf{HQueries}$ with $[H]^n \in \mathsf{ET}^{-1}[m\|[S]_n]$ or $[H]_n \in \mathsf{ET}^{-1}[m\|[S]_n]$.

According to [9], it holds

$$\Pr[\mathsf{ROHit} \mid \neg\mathsf{BadBlock} \wedge \neg\mathsf{PathMCol}] \le \frac{4nQ}{2^n}. \tag{4}$$

We include a proof in the full version for completeness. Below we focus on $\mathsf{BlockHit}$. For this, define

$$\mathsf{HQueries}[M] := \{(M\|m, H) \in \mathsf{HQueries} \text{ for some } m \in \{0,1\}^\nu, H \in \{0,1\}^{2n}\}. \tag{5}$$

Furthermore, for $Y \in \{0,1\}^n$, define

$$\mathsf{KeyHalfET}[Y] := \{R : Y \in \mathsf{ET}^{-1}[m\|R] \text{ for some } m \in \{0,1\}^\nu\}$$

as the set of key-halves that can be "indexed" by the ciphertext Y. Clearly, $\sum_{Y\in\{0,1\}^n} |\mathsf{KeyHalfET}[Y]| \le |\mathsf{ET}^{-1}| \le 2Q$.

Then, consider any rightward block $\left(S' \xrightarrow{m} S, \rightarrow\right)$, where the underlying pair of ideal-cipher queries is $\mathsf{ET}[m\|[S']_n]([S']^n) = [S]^n$ and $\mathsf{ET}[m\|[S']_n]([S']^n \oplus \mathbf{1}_n) = [S]_n$. Conditioned on $\neg\mathsf{PathCol}$, there exists at most one path of the form $\left(0^{2n} \xrightarrow{M} S'\right)$. The number of random oracle queries of the form $(M\|m\|m', H)$, $m' \in \{0,1\}^\nu$, is $\big|\mathsf{HQueries}[M\|m]\big|$ (see Eq. (5)). Since $[S]^n$ and $[S]_n$ are lazily sampled and are uniform in at least $2^n - 2Q$ possibilities, for any random oracle query $(M\|m\|m', H) \in \mathsf{HQueries}[M\|m]$, the probability to have $[H]^n \in \mathsf{ET}^{-1}[m\|[S]_n]$ or $[S]_n \in \mathsf{KeyHalfET}\big[[H]^n\big]$ is at most

$$\frac{\big|\mathsf{KeyHalfET}\big[[H]^n\big]\big|}{2^n - 2Q}.$$

Similarly, the probability to have $[H]_n \in \mathsf{ET}^{-1}[m\|[S]_n]$ is at most

$$\frac{\left|\mathsf{KeyHalfET}\left[[H]_n\right]\right|}{2^n - 2Q}.$$

Summing over all the rightward blocks $\left(S' \xrightarrow{m} S, \rightarrow\right) \in \mathcal{L}_{\mathsf{block}}(\mathsf{ET})$ and all relevant RO-queries $(M\|m\|m', H) \in \mathsf{HQueries}$, we have

$$\begin{aligned}
&\Pr[\mathsf{BlockHit} \mid \neg\mathsf{BadBlock} \wedge \neg\mathsf{PathMCol}] \\
&\leq \sum_{\left(S' \xrightarrow{m} S, \rightarrow\right) \in \mathcal{L}_{\mathsf{block}}(\mathsf{ET})} \\
&\quad \sum_{\substack{\left(0^{2n} \xrightarrow{M} S'\right) \in \mathcal{L}_{\overrightarrow{\mathsf{path}}}(\mathsf{ET}), \\ (M\|m\|m', H) \in \mathsf{HQueries}}} \frac{\left|\mathsf{KeyHalfET}\left[[H]^n\right]\right| + \left|\mathsf{KeyHalfET}\left[[H]_n\right]\right|}{2^n - 2Q}. \qquad (6)
\end{aligned}$$

For distinct blocks $\left(S_1 \xrightarrow{m_1} S_2, \rightarrow\right), \left(S_3 \xrightarrow{m_2} S_4, \rightarrow\right)$, the induced prefixes $M_1\|m_1$ and $M_2\|m_2$ are distinct: either $m_1 \neq m_2$ which immediately indicates the distinctness, or $S_1 \neq S_3$ indicating distinct corresponding paths $\left(0^{2n} \xrightarrow{M_1} S_1\right)$ and $\left(0^{2n} \xrightarrow{M_2} S_3\right)$ with $M_1 \neq M_2$. By this, every RO query $(M\|m\|m', H) \in \mathsf{HQueries}$ appears at most once in the sum in Eq. (6). This means

$$\begin{aligned}
&\Pr[\mathsf{BlockHit} \mid \neg\mathsf{BadBlock} \wedge \neg\mathsf{PathMCol}] \\
&\leq \sum_{(M\|m\|m', H) \in \mathsf{HQueries}} \frac{\left|\mathsf{KeyHalfET}\left[[H]^n\right]\right| + \left|\mathsf{KeyHalfET}\left[[H]_n\right]\right|}{2^n - 2Q} \\
&\leq \frac{\sum_{Y \in \{0,1\}^n} \sum_{(M\|m\|m', H) \in \mathsf{HQueries}: [H]^n = Y} \left|\mathsf{KeyHalfET}\left[Y\right]\right|}{2^n - 2Q} \\
&\quad + \frac{\sum_{Y \in \{0,1\}^n} \sum_{(M\|m\|m', H) \in \mathsf{HQueries}: [H]_n = Y} \left|\mathsf{KeyHalfET}\left[Y\right]\right|}{2^n - 2Q} \\
&\leq \frac{\sum_{Y \in \{0,1\}^n} n\left|\mathsf{KeyHalfET}\left[Y\right]\right|}{2^n - 2Q} + \frac{\sum_{Y \in \{0,1\}^n} n\left|\mathsf{KeyHalfET}\left[Y\right]\right|}{2^n - 2Q} \\
&\leq \frac{4nQ}{2^n - 2Q} \leq \frac{8nQ}{2^n}. \qquad (7)
\end{aligned}$$

The above used that conditioned on $\neg\mathsf{HMCol}$, for each $Y \in \{0,1\}^n$, the number of $(M\|m\|m', H) \in \mathsf{HQueries}$ with $[H]^n = Y$ (or $[H]_n = Y$) is at most n.

Taking a union bound over ROHit and $\mathsf{BlockHit}$ yields

$$\Pr[\mathsf{HBCol} \mid \neg\mathsf{BadBlock} \wedge \neg\mathsf{PathMCol}] \leq \frac{12nQ}{2^n}. \qquad (8)$$

Analyzing PathLock. Consider any pair of distinct paths $\left(0^{2n} \xrightarrow{M} S\right), \left(0^{2n} \xrightarrow{M'} S'\right) \in \mathcal{L}_{\mathsf{path}}^{\rightarrow}(\mathsf{ET})$ and any $m \in \{0,1\}^{\nu}$ such that the two random oracle queries $(M\|m, H)$ and $(M'\|m, H')$ indeed appeared during the interaction. To address the probabilities of the conditions, we distinguish several cases as follows.

CASE 1: $M = \lambda$ OR $M' = \lambda$ Note that they cannot both be λ since the two paths are distinct. Wlog consider the case of $M' = \lambda$ and $S' = 0^{2n}$. Let $\left(T \xrightarrow{m} S, d\right)$ be the last block of $\left(0^{2n} \xrightarrow{M} S\right)$. Since $\left(0^{2n} \xrightarrow{M} S\right) \in \mathcal{L}_{\mathsf{path}}^{\rightarrow}(\mathsf{ET})$, it holds $d = \rightarrow$, and there exist $K = m\|[T]_n, X = [T]^n$ such that $\mathsf{ET}[K](X) = [S]^n$ and $\mathsf{ET}[K](X \oplus \mathbf{1}_n) = [S]_n$, and that $\mathsf{ET}[K](X)$ and $\mathsf{ET}[K](X \oplus \mathbf{1}_n)$ are both lazily sampled. Then:

- The condition $[S]_n = [S']_n$ translates into $\mathsf{ET}[K](X \oplus \mathbf{1}_n) = 0^n$, the probability of which is at most $1/(2^n - 2Q)$;
- The condition $[H]_n = [H']^n$ holds with probability $1/2^n$, regardless of the order of sampling $[H]_n$ and $[H']^n$ during the execution;
- Similarly, the probability to have $[H]_n = [H']_n$ is $1/2^n$; the probability to have $[H]^n = [H']^n$ is $1/2^n$.

In all, in this case, the probability that the condition $([S]_n = [S']_n) \wedge ([H]_n = [H']^n \vee [H]_n = [H']_n \vee [H]^n = [H']^n)$ holds is $\leq 3/(2^n - 2Q)2^n \leq 3/(2^n - 2Q)^2$.

CASE 2: $M, M' \neq \lambda$ Similarly to Case 1, there exist K, X, K', X' such that

$$\mathsf{ET}[K](X) = [S]^n, \quad \mathsf{ET}[K](X \oplus \mathbf{1}_n) = [S]_n,$$
$$\mathsf{ET}[K'](X') = [S']^n, \quad \mathsf{ET}[K'](X' \oplus \mathbf{1}_n) = [S']_n,$$

and that $\mathsf{ET}[K](X)$, $\mathsf{ET}[K](X \oplus \mathbf{1}_n)$, $\mathsf{ET}[K'](X')$, and $\mathsf{ET}[K'](X' \oplus \mathbf{1}_n)$ are all lazily sampled. Conditioned on $\neg$PathCol, we have $S \neq S'$, which means $(K, X \oplus \mathbf{1}_n) \neq (K', X' \oplus \mathbf{1}_n)$: otherwise, $(K, X \oplus \mathbf{1}_n) = (K', X' \oplus \mathbf{1}_n)$ implies $(K, X) = (K', X')$ and further $[S]^n = [S']^n$ and $[S]_n = [S']_n$, contradicting $S \neq S'$. By these, we have:

- The probability to have $[S]_n = [S']_n$ or $\mathsf{ET}[K](X \oplus \mathbf{1}_n) = \mathsf{ET}[K'](X' \oplus \mathbf{1}_n)$ is always at most $1/(2^n - 2Q)$ regardless of the order of sampling $\mathsf{ET}[K](X \oplus \mathbf{1}_n)$ and $\mathsf{ET}[K'](X' \oplus \mathbf{1}_n)$ during the execution;
- The probability to have $[H]_n = [H']^n$ is $1/2^n$ regardless of the order of sampling $[H]_n$ and $[H']_n$. Similarly, the probability to have $[H]_n = [H']_n$ is $1/2^n$; the probability to have $[H]^n = [H']^n$ is $1/2^n$.

In all, in this case, the probability that the condition $([S]_n = [S']_n) \wedge ([H]_n = [H']^n \vee [H]_n = [H']_n \vee [H]^n = [H']^n)$ holds is $\leq 3/(2^n - 2Q)2^n \leq 3/(2^n - 2Q)^2$.

SUMMARY. We conclude by counting the number of choices as above. For any $\left(0^{2n} \xrightarrow{M} S\right), \left(0^{2n} \xrightarrow{M'} S'\right) \in \mathcal{L}_{\mathsf{path}}^{\rightarrow}(\mathsf{ET})$, the number of random oracle queries of the form $(M\|m, H)$ appeared during the execution is $|\mathsf{HQueries}[M]|$, and the number of queries $(M'\|m, H')$ is at most $|\mathsf{HQueries}[M']|$. For every such four queries, the probability that the whole event occurs is at most $3/(2^n-2Q)^2$ as argued. Therefore, using $3Q+np \le 2^n/4$, we have

$$\begin{aligned}
&\Pr[\mathsf{PathLock}|\neg\mathsf{BadBlock}\wedge\neg\mathsf{PathCol}] \\
\le &\sum_{\left(0^{2n}\xrightarrow{M}S\right)\in\mathcal{L}^{\rightarrow}_{\mathsf{path}}(\mathsf{ET})}\ \sum_{\left(0^{2n}\xrightarrow{M'}S'\right)\in\mathcal{L}^{\rightarrow}_{\mathsf{path}}(\mathsf{ET})} \frac{3|\mathsf{HQueries}[M]|\cdot|\mathsf{HQueries}[M']|}{(2^n-2Q)^2} \\
= &\sum_{\left(0^{2n}\xrightarrow{M}S\right)\in\mathcal{L}^{\rightarrow}_{\mathsf{path}}(\mathsf{ET})} |\mathsf{HQueries}[M]| \sum_{\left(0^{2n}\xrightarrow{M'}S'\right)\in\mathcal{L}^{\rightarrow}_{\mathsf{path}}(\mathsf{ET})} |\mathsf{HQueries}[M']|\cdot\frac{3}{(2^n-2Q)^2} \\
\le &\frac{3(3Q+np)^2}{(2^n-2Q)^2} \le \frac{12(3Q+np)^2}{2^{2n}}. \qquad (9)
\end{aligned}$$

A G_1 execution is *good*, if none of the bad events occurred. Summing over the above concludes the probability of observing good G_1 executions.

Lemma 1. *The probability to have a bad* G_1 *execution is at most*

$$\frac{11Q+20nQ+2np}{2^n}+\frac{64Q^2+12(3Q+np)^2}{2^{2n}}.$$

Proof. Gathering Eqs. (2), (3), (8) and (9) yields

$$\begin{aligned}
&\frac{11Q+2np}{2^n}+\frac{64Q^2}{2^{2n}}+\frac{8nQ}{2^n}+\frac{12nQ}{2^n}+\frac{12(3Q+np)^2}{2^{2n}} \\
\le &\frac{11Q+20nQ+2np}{2^n}+\frac{64Q^2+12(3Q+np)^2}{2^{2n}},
\end{aligned}$$

as claimed. □

Simulation Consistency in Good G_1 Executions. We next establish consistency of the simulation, namely, in G_1, for any hash query M, the response $\mathcal{RO}(M)$ is equal to $\mathsf{MDPN}^{\mathsf{S}_E^{\mathcal{RO}}}$, and the simulator never aborts due to adaptations. Lemmas in this section and their proofs are the *same* as [9, Sect. 5.5 and 5.6]. For completeness, we include the proofs in the full version.

Lemma 2. *In a good* G_1 *execution, it holds that* $\mathcal{L}_{\mathsf{path}}(\mathsf{ET}) = \mathcal{L}^{\rightarrow}_{\mathsf{path}}(\mathsf{ET})$, *i.e., all paths are fully constituted by rightward blocks.*

The detailed proof is given in the full version. Briefly speaking: (i) $\mathcal{L}_{\mathsf{path}}(\mathsf{ET}) = \mathcal{L}^{\rightarrow}_{\mathsf{path}}(\mathsf{ET})$ holds before the first simulator cycle, since there was only one path $\left(0^{2n}\xrightarrow{\lambda}0^{2n}\right)$; (ii) $\neg\mathsf{Hit}$ prevents newly extended paths from "hitting" existing backward/adapted blocks and causing $\mathcal{L}_{\mathsf{path}}(\mathsf{ET}) \neq \mathcal{L}^{\rightarrow}_{\mathsf{path}}(\mathsf{ET})$; (iii) $\neg\mathsf{DHit}$ prevents backward blocks from "joining in" paths in $\mathcal{L}_{\mathsf{path}}(\mathsf{ET})$ and causing $\mathcal{L}_{\mathsf{path}}(\mathsf{ET}) \neq \mathcal{L}^{\rightarrow}_{\mathsf{path}}(\mathsf{ET})$; (iv) $\neg\mathsf{PathCol}$, or the fact that no two paths of the form $\left(0^{2n} \xrightarrow{\star} S \oplus (\mathbf{2}_n \| 0^n)\right)$ and $\left(0^{2n} \xrightarrow{\star} S \oplus (\mathbf{2}_n \| 0^n)\right)$ exist, prevents adapted blocks from "joining in" paths in $\mathcal{L}_{\mathsf{path}}(\mathsf{ET})$ and causing $\mathcal{L}_{\mathsf{path}}(\mathsf{ET}) \neq \mathcal{L}^{\rightarrow}_{\mathsf{path}}(\mathsf{ET})$.

Thanks to $\mathcal{L}_{\mathsf{path}}(\mathsf{ET}) = \mathcal{L}^{\rightarrow}_{\mathsf{path}}(\mathsf{ET})$ by Lemma 2 and to $\neg\mathsf{PathCol}$, we are able to show the abort due to maintaining the table PathT cannot occur.

Lemma 3. *In a good* G_1 *execution, the simulator never aborts due to lines 14 and 19 in* $\mathsf{CreateBlock}$ *(i.e., maintaining the table* PathT*).*

The detailed proof is given in the full version.

We then address the abort due to adaptations.

Lemma 4. *In a good* G_1 *execution, the simulator never aborts in adapted simulator cycles.*

The detailed proof is given in the full version.

By Lemma 4, the probability of observing inconsistency in the simulation does not exceed the probability that G_1 is bad (Lemma 1). With this conclusion, the indistinguishability of G_1 and G_2 can be proved via a randomness mapping argument that is virtually the same as [9]. The conclusion is stated below.

Lemma 5. *For any distinguisher D making q hash queries of σ message blocks in total and p primitive queries, when $3Q + np \leq 2^n/4$, it holds*

$$\left|\Pr[D^{\mathsf{G}_1} \Rightarrow 1] - \Pr[D^{\mathsf{G}_2} \Rightarrow 1]\right| \leq \frac{11Q + 20nQ + 2np}{2^n} + \frac{64Q^2 + 12(3Q + np)^2}{2^{2n}}.$$

For completeness, we include its full proof in the full version.

4 (Second) Preimage Attacks Against NHash and MDPN

Recall from the Introduction that we are given a challenge message M such that $\mathsf{pad}(M)$ is of $\ell \geq t + 2$ blocks $M_1, ..., M_\ell \in \{0,1\}^\nu$, and our goal is to find another message M^* such that $\mathsf{NHash}^E(M^*) = \mathsf{NHash}^E(M)$. Also recall that we consider NHash^E using a strengthened Merkle-Damgård message padding pad, which means: (i) the bit length $|M|$ is "embedded" in the last block M_ℓ; (ii) the block $M_{\ell-1}$ may also contain padded bits. E.g., if $|M|$ is encoded with $\alpha < \nu$ bits and the last block of the original message M has more than $\nu - \alpha$ bits but less than ν bits, existing padding schemes [16,23] typically yield $M_\ell = 0^* \| |M|$ and $M_{\ell-1} = \star \| 0^*$ or $M_{\ell-1} = \star \| 10^*$. These should be considered by the attack.

Following the notations in Fig. 1 (Top), let $S_0, ..., S_\ell$ be the $2n$-bit chain values in the inner iteration of $\mathsf{NHash}^E(M)$, i.e., $S_0 = 0^{2n}$, $S_i = \mathsf{NCF}^E(S_{i-1}, M_i)$ for $i = 1, ..., \ell$. By construction, this means $\mathsf{NHash}^E(M) = E(S_\ell, \mathbf{2}_n) \| E(S_\ell, \mathbf{3}_n)$.

We will use $O(t2^{\frac{(t+1)n}{t}})$ time and $O(2^{\frac{(t-1)n}{t}})$ memory to find another sequence of t message blocks $M_1^*, ..., M_t^*$ that yields $S_t^* = S_t$, where $S_i^* = \mathsf{NCF}^E(S_{i-1}^*, M_i^*)$ for $i = 1, ..., t$ and $S_0^* = 0^{2n}$. By this, $M^* = \mathsf{pad}^{-1}(M_1^* \| ... \| M_t^* \| M_{t+1} \| ... M_\ell)$ yields a valid second preimage for M: note that we "recycled" the last $\ell - t$ blocks, including $M_{\ell-1}$ and M_ℓ, to obtain a valid padded message. Below we first describe our general ideas, and then the detailed steps of our attack.

Ideas. We first present a basic observation. Given any chain value $(L_0, R_0) \in \{0,1\}^{2n}$ and another half chain value $R_1 \in \{0,1\}^n$, one can use q inverse blockcipher computations

$$E^{-1}(R_0\|m_{1,i}, R_1) \to \overline{X}_{1,i},\ E(R_0\|m_{1,i}, \overline{X}_{1,i} \oplus \mathbf{1}_n) \to L_{1,i},\ i = 1, ..., q$$

to "append" blocks to (L_0, R_0). For each i, the block is successfully appended if $\overline{X}_{1,i} \oplus \mathbf{1}_n = L_0$, the probability of which is approximately $1/2^n$. Therefore, the number of blocks that can be "appended" to (L_0, R_0) is $\approx q/2^n$ on average (assume that the key-length is large enough, i.e., $2^{k-n} \geq q$).

Let $(L_0\|R_0 \xrightarrow{m_{i_1}} L_{1,i_1}\|R_1), ..., (L_0\|R_0 \xrightarrow{m_{i_\lambda}} L_{1,i_\lambda}\|R_1)$ be the λ blocks "appended" to (L_0, R_0) by the previous q computations. One can then fix another half $R_2 \in \{0,1\}^n$ and use q more inverse blockcipher computations

$$E^{-1}(R_1\|m_{2,i}, R_2) \to \overline{X}_{2,j},\ E(R_1\|m_{2,j}, \overline{X}_{2,j} \oplus \mathbf{1}_n) \to L_{2,j},\ j = 1, ..., q$$

to "append" blocks to $(L_{1,i_1}, R_1), ..., (L_{1,i_\lambda}, R_1)$: this is possible because these λ chain values share the same second half R_1. For each j, the block is successfully appended to one of $(L_{1,i_1}, R_1), ..., (L_{1,i_\lambda}, R_1)$ as long as $\overline{X}_{2,j} \oplus \mathbf{1}_n \in \{L_{1,i_1}, ..., L_{1,i_\lambda}\}$, the probability of which is $\approx \lambda/2^n \approx q/2^{2n}$. Therefore, the number of blocks that can be "appended", or the number of paths of 2 blocks that can be obtained in this step, is $\approx q^2/2^{2n}$ on average.

By repeating the above $t-1$ times, we obtain $O(q^{t-1}/2^{(t-1)n})$ paths of $t-1$ blocks that start from (L_0, R_0) and end with $(L_{t-1,i_1}, R_{t-1}), (L_{t-1,i_2}, R_{t-1}), ...$ for some chosen value R_{t-1}. We finally consider the target hash chain value S_t (as mentioned) and make q inverse blockcipher computations

$$E^{-1}(R_{t-1}\|m_{t,j}, [S_t]^n) \to X_{t-1,j},\ E(R_{t-1}\|m_{t,j}, X_{t-1,j} \oplus \mathbf{1}_n) \to R_{t,j},\ j = 1, ..., q.$$

As long as there exists j such that both $X_{t-1,j} \in \{L_{t-1,i_1}, L_{t-1,i_2}, ...\}$ and $R_{t,j} = [S_t]_n$, the length-$(t-1)$ path ending at (L_{t-1,i_1}, R_{t-1}) is "linked" with the target S_t, and a second preimage is found. The probability to have such a collision is $\approx \frac{q^{t-1}}{2^{(t-1)n}} \times \frac{q}{2^{2n}} \approx q^t/2^{(t+1)n}$, which becomes a constant as long as $q \approx 2^{\frac{(t+1)n}{t}}$.

The next subsection gives a formal description of these ideas.

Formal Attack. Consider a challenge message M such that $\mathsf{pad}(M)$ is of $\ell \geq t+2$ blocks $M_1, ..., M_\ell$, let $H = \mathsf{NHash}^E(M)$, $S_0 = 0^{2n}$, and let $S_i = \mathsf{NCF}^E(S_{i-1}, M_i)$ for $i = 1, ..., \ell$. The attack constructs a message M^* with $|M^*| = |M|$ and $\mathsf{NHash}^E(M^*) = \mathsf{NHash}^E(M)$, by proceeding as follows:

1. Set $R_0 \leftarrow 0^n$, $S_0 \leftarrow 0^n$, and let $(0^{2n} \xrightarrow{\lambda} S_0\|R_0)$ be the initial path (of 0 blocks);
2. For $i = 1, ..., t-1$, repeat the following actions:
   (a) Pick R_i such that $R_i \notin \{R_0, ..., R_{i-1}\}$, and pick q distinct message blocks $m_{i,1}, ..., m_{i,q} \in \{0,1\}^\nu$ in arbitrary;

(b) For $j = 1, ..., q$, compute $\overline{X}_{i,j} \leftarrow E^{-1}(R_{i-1} \| m_{i,j}, R_i)$, $X_{i,j} \leftarrow \overline{X}_{i,j} \oplus \mathbf{1}_n$ and $L_{i,j} \leftarrow E(R_{i-1} \| m_{i,j}, X_{i,j})$. If $X_{i,j} = L_{i-1,j'}$ for some $(i-1)$-block path $\left(0^{2n} \xrightarrow{m^*} L_{i-1,j'} \| R_{i-1}\right)$, then store the i-block path $\left(0^{2n} \xrightarrow{m^* \| m_{i,j}} L_{i,j} \| R_i\right)$;

3. Pick q distinct message blocks $m_{t,1}, ..., m_{t,q} \in \{0,1\}^{\nu}$;
4. For $j = 1, ..., q$, compute the values $X_{t,j} \leftarrow E^{-1}(R_{t-1} \| m_{t,j}, [S_t]^n)$ and $R_{t,j} \leftarrow E(R_{t-1} \| m_{t,j}, X_{t,j} \oplus \mathbf{1}_n)$. If:
   - $R_{t,j} = [S_t]_n$, and
   - $X_{t,j} = L_{t-1,j'}$ for some $(t-1)$-block path $\left(0^{2n} \xrightarrow{m^*} L_{t-1,j'} \| R_{t-1}\right)$,

   then output $M^* = \mathsf{pad}^{-1}(m^* \| m_{t,j} \| M_{t+1} \| ... \| M_\ell)$ as the second preimage.

Once succeeded, the attack outputs a second preimage M^* with $|M^*| = |M|$. Considering randomness of the first t blocks in M^*, it's negligible to have $m^* \| m_{t,j} = M_1 \| ... \| M_t$. As analyzed in the previous subsection, the success probability is $\approx q^t / 2^{(t+1)n}$ on average, which is close to 1 as long as $q \approx 2^{\frac{(t+1)n}{t}}$. By making q computations t times, the total computation complexity becomes $O(t2^{\frac{(t+1)n}{t}})$, and the memory cost due to storing the length-$(t-1)$ chains is $O(\frac{q^{t-1}}{2^{(t-1)n}}) = O(2^{\frac{(t-1)n}{t}})$. Step 2 (b) and 4 require $2^{k-n} \geq q = 2^{\frac{(t+1)n}{t}}$, meaning that $k \geq \frac{(2t+1)n}{t}$.

Setting $t = n$ yields an attack running in $O(n2^n)$ time, using $O(2^n)$ memory and outputting a second preimage for challenge messages of at least $n+2$ blocks, and it works as long as $k \geq 2n+1$. In practice, one usually has $n \leq 1024$, and the second preimage is not too long.

Preimage Attack Against MDPN. With a little more efforts, the above idea yields a preimage attack against MDPN^E using a strengthened Merkle-Damgård message padding. Concretely, given a challenge image $H \in \{0,1\}^{2n}$, we construct a message M of $t\nu$ bits, so that $\mathsf{pad}(M)$ has $t+1$ blocks and the last block of $\mathsf{pad}(M)$ is $M_{t+1} = f(t\nu)$ for a function defined by pad.[1] Pick q distinct values $R_1, ..., R_q \in \{0,1\}^n$. For each $i = 1, ..., q$, we make a pair of queries $E^{-1}(R_i \| f(t\nu), [H]^n) \rightarrow L_i$ and $E(R_i \| f(t\nu), L_i \oplus \mathbf{1}_n) \rightarrow H'_i$, and store $L_i \| R_i$ as a "valid chain value" if $H'_i = [H]_n$. When $q = 2^n$, such a "valid chain value" $L_i \| R_i$ with $E(R_i \| f(t\nu), L_i \oplus \mathbf{1}_n) = [H]_n$ is expected to be found. We then use our NHash attack ideas to find a sequence of t message blocks $M_1, ..., M_t$ that yields $S_t = (L_i \oplus \mathbf{2}_n) \| R_i$, where $S_i = \mathsf{NCF}^E(S_{i-1}, M_i)$ for $i = 1, ..., t$ and $S_0 = 0^{2n}$. By this, $\mathsf{pad}^{-1}(M_1 \| ... \| M_t \| f(t\nu))$ yields a valid $t\nu$-bit preimage for H.

[1] E.g., using Merkle's padding scheme [16], it has $M_{t+1} = 0^* \| [t\nu]_a$ for some $a < \nu$; using SHA256 padding scheme [5], it has $M_{t+1} = 10^* \| [t\nu]_a$ for some $a < \nu$.

Acknowledgments. The authors were supported by the National Key Research and Development Program of China (grant 2023YFA1011200), the National Natural Science Foundation of China (grant 62372274), and the Taishan Scholars Program (for Young Scientists) of Shandong.

References

1. Black, J., Rogaway, P., Shrimpton, T., Stam, M.: An analysis of the blockcipher-based hash functions from PGV. J. Cryptol. **23**(4), 519–545 (2010). https://doi.org/10.1007/s00145-010-9071-0
2. Brachtl, B.O., et al.: Data Authentication Using Modification Detection Codes Based on a Public One Way Encryption Function, US Patent 4,908,861 (1990)
3. Coron, J.S., Dodis, Y., Malinaud, C., Puniya, P.: Merkle-Damgård revisited: how to construct a hash function. In: Shoup, V. (ed.) Advances in Cryptology – CRYPTO 2005. Lecture Notes in Computer Science, vol. 3621, pp. 430–448. Santa Barbara, CA, USA (2005). https://doi.org/10.1007/11535218_26
4. Dahmen, E., Okeya, K., Takagi, T., Vuillaume, C.: Digital signatures out of second-preimage resistant hash functions. In: Buchmann, J., Ding, J. (eds.) Post-Quantum Cryptography, Second International Workshop, PQCRYPTO 2008, pp. 109–123. Cincinnati, Ohio, United States (2008). https://doi.org/10.1007/978-3-540-88403-3_8
5. Dang, Q., et al.: Secure hash standard (2015)
6. Demay, G., Gaži, P., Hirt, M., Maurer, U.: Resource-restricted indifferentiability. In: Johansson, T., Nguyen, P.Q. (eds.) Advances in Cryptology – EUROCRYPT 2013. Lecture Notes in Computer Science, vol. 7881, pp. 664–683. Athens, Greece (2013). https://doi.org/10.1007/978-3-642-38348-9_39
7. Dobraunig, C., Mennink, B.: Leakage resilience of the duplex construction. In: Galbraith, S.D., Moriai, S. (eds.) Advances in Cryptology – ASIACRYPT 2019, Part III. Lecture Notes in Computer Science, vol. 11923, pp. 225–255. Kobe, Japan (2019). https://doi.org/10.1007/978-3-030-34618-8_8
8. Guo, C., Iwata, T., Khairallah, M., Minematsu, K., Peyrin, T.: Romulus v1.3. Submission to NIST Lightweight Cryptography Project (2021). https://csrc.nist.gov/Projects/lightweight-cryptography/
9. Guo, C., Iwata, T., Minematsu, K.: New indifferentiability security proof of MDPH hash function. IET Inf. Secur. **16**(4), 262–281 (2022)
10. Guo, C., Pereira, O., Peters, T., Standaert, F.X.: Towards low-energy leakage-resistant AE from the duplex sponge. IACR Trans. Symmetric Cryptol. **2020**(1), 6–42 (2020). https://doi.org/10.13154/tosc.v2020.i1.6-42
11. Hirose, S.: Some plausible constructions of double-block-length hash functions. In: Robshaw, M.J.B. (ed.) Fast Software Encryption – FSE 2006. Lecture Notes in Computer Science, vol. 4047, pp. 210–225. Springer, Heidelberg (2006). https://doi.org/10.1007/11799313_14
12. Hirose, S., Park, J.H., Yun, A.: A simple variant of the Merkle-Damgård scheme with a permutation. J. Cryptol. **25**(2), 271–309 (2012). https://doi.org/10.1007/s00145-010-9095-5
13. Iwata, T., Khairallah, M., Minematsu, K., Peyrin, T.: Duel of the titans: The Romulus and Remus families of lightweight AEAD algorithms. IACR Trans. Symmetric Cryptol. **2020**(1), 43–120 (2020). https://doi.org/10.13154/tosc.v2020.i1.43-120

14. Maurer, U.M., Renner, R., Holenstein, C.: Indifferentiability, impossibility results on reductions, and applications to the random oracle methodology. In: Naor, M. (ed.) TCC 2004: 1st Theory of Cryptography Conference. Lecture Notes in Computer Science, vol. 2951, pp. 21–39. Cambridge, MA, USA (2004). https://doi.org/10.1007/978-3-540-24638-1_2
15. Mennink, B.: Indifferentiability of double length compression functions. In: Stam, M. (ed.) 14th IMA International Conference on Cryptography and Coding. Lecture Notes in Computer Science, vol. 8308, pp. 232–251. Oxford, UK (2013). https://doi.org/10.1007/978-3-642-45239-0_14
16. Merkle, R.C.: One way hash functions and DES. In: Brassard, G. (ed.) Advances in Cryptology – CRYPTO'89. Lecture Notes in Computer Science, vol. 435, pp. 428–446. Santa Barbara, CA, USA (1990). https://doi.org/10.1007/0-387-34805-0_40
17. Naito, Y.: Indifferentiability of double-block-length hash function without feedforward operations. In: Pieprzyk, J., Suriadi, S. (eds.) ACISP 17: 22nd Australasian Conference on Information Security and Privacy, Part II. Lecture Notes in Computer Science, vol. 10343, pp. 38–57. Auckland, New Zealand (2017)
18. Naito, Y.: Keyed sponge with prefix-free padding: independence between capacity and online queries without the suffix key. In: Susilo, W., Yang, G. (eds.) ACISP 18: 23rd Australasian Conference on Information Security and Privacy. Lecture Notes in Computer Science, vol. 10946, pp. 225–242. Wollongong, NSW, Australia (2018). https://doi.org/10.1007/978-3-319-93638-3_14
19. Naito, Y.: Optimally indifferentiable double-block-length hashing without postprocessing and with support for longer key than single block. In: Schwabe, P., Thériault, N. (eds.) Progress in Cryptology - LATINCRYPT 2019 - 6th International Conference on Cryptology and Information Security in Latin America, Santiago de Chile, Chile, 2–4 October 2019, Proceedings. Lecture Notes in Computer Science, vol. 11774, pp. 65–85. Springer (2019). https://doi.org/10.1007/978-3-030-30530-7_4
20. Naito, Y., Sasaki, Y., Sugawara, T.: Double-block-length hash function for minimum memory size. In: Tibouchi, M., Wang, H. (eds.) Advances in Cryptology – ASIACRYPT 2021, Part III. Lecture Notes in Computer Science, vol. 13092, pp. 376–406. Singapore (2021). https://doi.org/10.1007/978-3-030-92078-4_13
21. Nandi, M.: Towards optimal double-length hash functions. In: Maitra, S., Madhavan, C.E.V., Venkatesan, R. (eds.) Progress in Cryptology - INDOCRYPT 2005: 6th International Conference in Cryptology in India. Lecture Notes in Computer Science, vol. 3797, pp. 77–89. Bangalore, India (2005)
22. Preneel, B., Govaerts, R., Vandewalle, J.: Hash functions based on block ciphers: a synthetic approach. In: Stinson, D.R. (ed.) Advances in Cryptology – CRYPTO'93. Lecture Notes in Computer Science, vol. 773, pp. 368–378. Santa Barbara, CA, USA (1994). https://doi.org/10.1007/3-540-48329-2_31
23. Pub, F.: Secure hash standard (SHS). Fips Pub **180**(4), 2012 (2012)
24. Ristenpart, T., Shacham, H., Shrimpton, T.: Careful with composition: limitations of the indifferentiability framework. In: Paterson, K.G. (ed.) Advances in Cryptology – EUROCRYPT 2011. Lecture Notes in Computer Science, vol. 6632, pp. 487–506. Tallinn, Estonia (2011). https://doi.org/10.1007/978-3-642-20465-4_27
25. Rogaway, P., Shrimpton, T.: Cryptographic hash-function basics: definitions, implications, and separations for preimage resistance, second-preimage resistance, and collision resistance. In: Roy, B.K., Meier, W. (eds.) Fast Software Encryption – FSE 2004. Lecture Notes in Computer Science, vol. 3017, pp. 371–388. Springer, Heidelberg (2004). https://doi.org/10.1007/978-3-540-25937-4_24

26. Sha, N., Draft, N.: Permutation-based hash and extendable-output functions. FIPS PUB **202**, 2015 (3)
27. Turan, M.S., McKay, K.A., Chang, D., Kang, J., Kelsey, J.: Ascon-Based Lightweight Cryptography Standards for Constrained Devices: Authenticated Encryption, Hash, and Extendable Output Functions (2024)

Impossibility Results of Card-Based Protocols via Mathematical Optimization

Shunnosuke Ikeda[1] and Kazumasa Shinagawa[1,2,3](✉)

[1] University of Tsukuba, Tsukuba, Ibaraki, Japan
shinagawa@cs.tsukuba.ac.jp
[2] Kyushu University, Fukuoka, Fukuoka, Japan
[3] National Institute of Advanced Industrial Science and Technology, Koto-ku, Tokyo, Japan

Abstract. This paper introduces mathematical optimization as a new method for proving impossibility results in the field of card-based cryptography. While previous impossibility proofs were often limited to cases involving a small number of cards, this new approach establishes results that hold for a large number of cards. The research focuses on single-cut full-open (SCFO) protocols, which consist of performing one random cut and then revealing all cards. The main contribution is that for any three-variable Boolean function, no new SCFO protocols exist beyond those already known, under the condition that all additional cards have the same color. The significance of this work is that it provides a new framework for proving impossibility results and delivers a proof that is valid for any number of cards, as long as all additional cards have the same color.

Keywords: Card-based cryptography · Combinatorics on words · Mathematical optimization

1 Introduction

It is known that cryptographic techniques such as secure multiparty computation and zero-knowledge proof can be physically represented using cards, and such a research area is called card-based cryptography [1,3,15]. Unlike ordinary cryptographic techniques, it is performed physically and visually, which makes the protocol intuitive and provides a high degree of confidence in its security. Due to this feature, its application to security education has been considered, and it has been used in lectures for cryptography [2,13,14,17].

An important research problem in this field is to determine which functions can be securely computed under specific conditions. To achieve this, it is necessary to provide proofs that the function cannot be securely computed under specific conditions. A representative method for proving impossibility results is the technique by Koch–Walzer–Hätel [8–10,12]. In this technique, a protocol is represented by a directed graph, and it is shown that there is no transition from

H. Seo (Ed.): ICISC 2025, LNCS 16487, pp. 368–382, 2026.
https://doi.org/10.1007/978-981-95-8034-7_19

a starting vertex to a terminal vertex. Using this method, impossibility proofs for AND protocols with five or fewer cards [8,9,12] and for COPY protocols of k copies with $2k + 1$ or fewer cards [8] have been obtained. However, both of these results are in a setting where at most one additional card is used besides those required for the input and output. In general, when the number of cards is large, a combinatorial explosion occurs. Therefore, to obtain further impossibility results, the development of new proof techniques seems to be necessary.

1.1 Single-Cut Full-Open Protocols

A *random cut* is a shuffling operation that cyclically and randomly shifts a sequence of cards. For a sequence of k face-down cards $(c_0, c_1, \ldots, c_{k-1})$, a random cut is a probabilistic operation that chooses a uniformly random number $r \in \{0, 1, \ldots, k-1\}$ and outputs a new sequence $(c_r, c_{r+1}, \ldots, c_{r+k-1})$, where the subscript is taken modulo k. Here, r is hidden from all players. The following is an example for applying a random cut to a sequence of four cards:

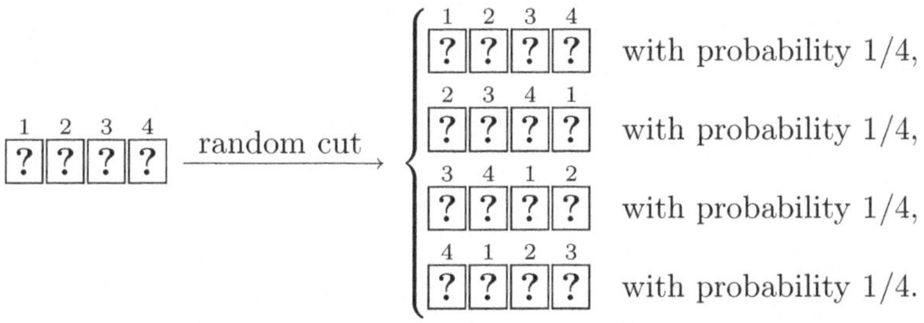

$$\overset{1}{\boxed{?}}\overset{2}{\boxed{?}}\overset{3}{\boxed{?}}\overset{4}{\boxed{?}} \xrightarrow{\text{random cut}} \begin{cases} \overset{1}{\boxed{?}}\overset{2}{\boxed{?}}\overset{3}{\boxed{?}}\overset{4}{\boxed{?}} & \text{with probability } 1/4, \\ \overset{2}{\boxed{?}}\overset{3}{\boxed{?}}\overset{4}{\boxed{?}}\overset{1}{\boxed{?}} & \text{with probability } 1/4, \\ \overset{3}{\boxed{?}}\overset{4}{\boxed{?}}\overset{1}{\boxed{?}}\overset{2}{\boxed{?}} & \text{with probability } 1/4, \\ \overset{4}{\boxed{?}}\overset{1}{\boxed{?}}\overset{2}{\boxed{?}}\overset{3}{\boxed{?}} & \text{with probability } 1/4. \end{cases}$$

A *single-cut full-open (SCFO) protocol* is a protocol of the following form:

1. Place a sequence of cards encoding an input.
2. Turn over all face-up cards face-down, and then rearrange the sequence.
3. Apply a random cut to the sequence of face-down cards.
4. Open all cards and determine an output value from the revealed symbols.

An SCFO protocol is *standard* if the sequence in Step 1 is of the following form:

$$\underset{x_1}{\boxed{?}}\underset{\overline{x_1}}{\boxed{?}}\underset{x_2}{\boxed{?}}\underset{\overline{x_2}}{\boxed{?}}\cdots\underset{x_n}{\boxed{?}}\underset{\overline{x_n}}{\boxed{?}}\underbrace{\boxed{\clubsuit}\boxed{\clubsuit}\cdots\boxed{\clubsuit}}_{k_0 \text{ cards}}\underbrace{\boxed{\heartsuit}\boxed{\heartsuit}\cdots\boxed{\heartsuit}}_{k_1 \text{ cards}},$$

where a card with x_i (resp. $\overline{x_i}$) represents a face-down card whose front side is $\boxed{\clubsuit}$ if $x_i = 0$ (resp. $\overline{x_i} = 0$) and $\boxed{\heartsuit}$ otherwise. A standard SCFO protocol using k_0 $\boxed{\clubsuit}$s and k_1 $\boxed{\heartsuit}$s as additional cards is called a *standard* (k_0, k_1)*-SCFO protocol*, and hereafter we simply call it a (k_0, k_1)*-SCFO protocol*. When the value of k_0 is not specified, we refer to it as a $(*, k_1)$-SCFO protocol. That is, a $(*, k_1)$-SCFO protocol uses k_1 $\boxed{\heartsuit}$s and any number of $\boxed{\clubsuit}$s as additional cards. Similarly, when the value of k_1 is not specified, we call it a $(k_0, *)$-SCFO protocol.

Table 1 shows a summary of existing SCFO protocols for Boolean functions. Except for the protocol for $x_1 \oplus x_2 \oplus x_3$, all protocols are standard. For 2-variable Boolean functions, we can observe that any function (i.e., AND and XOR functions) can be computed by a standard SCFO protocol [1,19]. However, for functions with 3 or more variables, only a few can be computed by a standard SCFO protocol. Whether there are other functions computable by standard SCFO protocols is an open problem[1].

Table 1. Summary of Existing SCFO Protocols for Boolean Functions

Category	Authors	Function	#Cards	Standard	(k_0, k_1)
2-variable	Shinagawa–Mizuki [19]	$x_1 \oplus x_2$	4	✓	$(0, 0)$
	den Boer [1]	$x_1 \wedge x_2$	5	✓	$(0, 1)$
3-variable	Heather et al. [7]	$(x_1 = x_2 = x_3)?$	6	✓	$(0, 0)$
	Shinagawa–Nuida [22]	$(x_1 \wedge x_2) \vee (\overline{x_1} \wedge x_3)$	8	✓	$(1, 1)$
	Shinagawa–Nuida [22]	$x_1 \oplus x_2 \oplus x_3$	8		–
4-variable	Shinagawa–Nuida [22]	$\overline{x_1} x_2 \overline{x_4} \vee \overline{x_2} x_3 \overline{x_4} \vee$ $x_1 \overline{x_2} x_4 \vee x_2 \overline{x_3} x_4$	8	✓	$(0, 0)$

1.2 Our Contribution

We propose a new technique for proving impossibility results in card-based cryptography, based on mathematical optimization. This is the first work to apply mathematical optimization to card-based cryptography, and an important contribution of our work is demonstrating the effectiveness of mathematical optimization in this field. Our concrete contributions are as follows:

- We formulated the search for a $(*, 0)$-SCFO protocol as an integer optimization problem and developed an algorithm that takes a function as input and determines whether a protocol exists and, if so, outputs a protocol with the minimum number of additional cards.
- We implemented this algorithm and conducted experiments for all 3-variable Boolean functions (see Sect. 2.1). As a result, we obtained an impossibility proof for a $(*, 0)$-SCFO protocol for all 3-variable functions except for the 3-variable equality function (see Table 2).

[1] Recently, Eriguchi–Shinagawa [4] showed that any function can be securely computed by (non-standard) SCFO protocols. In this paper, on the other hand, we study the (im)possibility of standard SCFO protocols.

Table 2. Summary of Our Results for $(*, 0)$-SCFO Protocols

Category	Function	Existence of Protocol	Protocol
2-variable	$x_1 \wedge x_2$	✓	$(1, 0)$-SCFO protocol [1]
	$x_1 \oplus x_2$	✓	$(0, 0)$-SCFO protocol [19]
3-variable	$x_1 \wedge x_2 \wedge x_3$	×	—
	$x_1 \oplus x_2 \oplus x_3$	×	—
	$(x_1 = x_2 = x_3)?$	✓	$(0, 0)$-SCFO protocol [7]
	$(x_1 + x_2 + x_3 \geq 2)?$	×	—
	$(x_1 + x_2 + x_3 = 1)?$	×	—
	$x_1 \oplus (x_2 \wedge x_3)$	×	—
	$(x_1 \wedge x_2) \vee (\overline{x_1} \wedge x_3)$	×	—
	$x_1 \wedge (x_2 \oplus x_3)$	×	—
	$(x_1 \vee x_2) \wedge (x_1 \oplus x_3)$	×	—
	$x_1 \wedge (x_2 \vee x_3)$	×	—

1.3 Existing Methods for Proving Impossibility Results

This section introduces existing methods for proving impossibility results in the field of card-based cryptography. The technique proposed in this paper is a new proof method that does not belong to any of these classifications.

- **Information-theoretic proofs:** Mizuki–Shizuya [15] proved that no perfect COPY protocol exists for single-card encoding. Intuitively, this means that in a protocol with single-card encoding, it is necessary to reveal the input card to satisfy correctness, but doing so leaks information, making correctness and security mutually exclusive.
- **Proofs based on KWH diagrams:** Koch–Walzer–Härtel [12] proposed a diagram to visually represent protocols and, based on it, proved the impossibility of a (committed-format) 4-card AND protocol with finite-runtime. Although many results have been proven in follow-up studies [8,10], this method is difficult to apply when the number of cards is large, and all previous results are for cases with zero or one additional cards.
- **Proofs based on formal verification:** Koch–Schrempp–Kirsten [10,11] and its subsequent work [5] proved impossibility results using formal verification. This method is also difficult to apply when the number of cards is large, and its impossibility results are for cases with four or fewer cards.
- **Proofs based on the ABC conjecture:** Hashimoto et al. [6] proved that $\Omega(n \log n)$ cards are required for the uniform random generation of a derangement of order n. The proof is based on the integer factorization of the number of derangements and uses the ABC conjecture.
- **Proofs based on PSM protocols:** Shinagawa–Nuida [20] proposed a general method for converting card-based protocols into PSM protocols. In particular, a single-shuffle full-open (SSFO) protocol with n inputs and k cards

can be converted into a PSM protocol with communication complexity nk. This shows that a lower bound on the number of cards for an SSFO protocol can be derived from a lower bound on communication complexity of the PSM protocol.

2 Preliminaries

In Sect. 2.1, we introduce 3-variable Boolean functions. In Sect. 2.2, we define *cyclically equal* [21] from combinatorics on words. Sections 2.3 to 2.5 provide the basic definitions from card-based cryptography.

For a finite set A, we denote the set of finite-length sequences of A by A^*. For example, $\{0\}^* = \{\epsilon, 0, 00, 000, 0000, \ldots\}$ and $\{0,1\}^* = \{\epsilon, 0, 1, 00, 01, 10, 11, \ldots\}$, where ϵ is an empty sequence.

2.1 NPN-Equivalence of 3-Variable Boolean Functions

For an n-variable Boolean function, the equivalence class obtained by a combination of the following three operations is called an NPN-equivalence class.

- Negation of some or all of the input variables
- Permutation of the n input variables
- Negation of the output

When functions $f, g : \{0,1\}^n \to \{0,1\}$ belong to the same NPN-equivalence class, if a protocol for f exists, then a protocol for g also exists. Therefore, to perform secure computation for any n-variable Boolean function, it is sufficient to construct protocols for representatives of the NPN-equivalence classes.

There are 14 representatives for the NPN-equivalence classes of 3-variable Boolean functions as follows.

1. 0 (constant function)
2. x_1
3. $x_1 \wedge x_2$
4. $x_1 \oplus x_2$
5. $x_1 \wedge x_2 \wedge x_3$
6. $x_1 \oplus x_2 \oplus x_3$
7. $(x_1 = x_2 = x_3)?$
8. $(x_1 + x_2 + x_3 \geq 2)?$
9. $(x_1 + x_2 + x_3 = 1)?$
10. $x_1 \oplus (x_2 \wedge x_3)$
11. $(x_1 \wedge x_2) \vee (\overline{x_1} \wedge x_3)$
12. $x_1 \wedge (x_2 \oplus x_3)$
13. $(x_1 \vee x_2) \wedge (x_1 \oplus x_3)$
14. $x_1 \wedge (x_2 \vee x_3)$

2.2 Cyclically Equal

Two words $w, w' \in \{0,1\}^n$ are cyclically equal if there exist $u, v \in \{0,1\}^*$ such that $w = uv$ and $w' = vu$, where uv and vu represent the concatenation of words. We write $w \sim w'$ if w and w' are cyclically equal, and $w \not\sim w'$ otherwise. For example, for $w = 10110$ and $w' = 11010$, we can take $u = 10$ and $v = 110$, thus $w \sim w'$. A set of words $\boldsymbol{w} \subseteq \{0,1\}^n$ is said to be cyclically equal if $w \sim w'$ holds for any $w, w' \in \boldsymbol{w}$.

For a set of words $\boldsymbol{w} \subseteq \{0,1\}^n$, an insertion is defined as an operation that transforms each word $w = w_1 w_2 \cdots w_n \in \boldsymbol{w}$ into a word $w' = w_1 u_1 w_2 u_2 \cdots w_n u_n$ for some common words $u_1, \ldots, u_n \in \{0,1\}^*$, where each u_i may be the empty word. We denote an insertion by $\boldsymbol{u} = (u_1, \ldots, u_n)$, and we write $w \xrightarrow{\boldsymbol{u}} w'$ to denote that the word w is transformed into the word w' by the simultaneous insertion $\boldsymbol{u}$. In particular, a 0-insertion is defined as an insertion such that $u_1, \ldots, u_n \in \{0\}^*$, i.e., they are repetitions of 0. Similarly, a 1-insertion is defined as an insertion such that $u_1, \ldots, u_n \in \{1\}^*$.

2.3 Cards and Encoding

We use a set of cards with two types of faces $\boxed{\clubsuit}$ and $\boxed{\heartsuit}$, and identical backs $\boxed{?}$. In the Mizuki–Shizuya model [15], face-up cards are denoted by $\clubsuit/?$ or $\heartsuit/?$, and face-down cards are denoted by $?/\clubsuit$ or $?/\heartsuit$. For example, the following sequence

$$\underset{\clubsuit}{\boxed{?}}\,\underset{\heartsuit}{\boxed{?}}\,\boxed{\clubsuit}\,\boxed{\heartsuit}\,\underset{\heartsuit}{\boxed{?}}$$

is represented as $(?/\clubsuit, ?/\heartsuit, \clubsuit/?, \heartsuit/?, ?/\heartsuit)$. In this paper, we represent a sequence of cards such as $\clubsuit\heartsuit\clubsuit\heartsuit\heartsuit$ since we only deal with face-up or face-down sequences, so the context determines whether a sequence is face-up or face-down without ambiguity. We also denote the set of all sequences of n cards by $\{\clubsuit, \heartsuit\}^n$.

We let $\clubsuit = 0$ and $\heartsuit = 1$. That is, we identify the set of all sequences of n cards $\{\clubsuit, \heartsuit\}^n$ with the set of all n-bit words $\{0,1\}^n$; for example, $\clubsuit\clubsuit\heartsuit\heartsuit\heartsuit = 00111$.

For a bit value $x \in \{0,1\}$, a pair of face-down cards $(x, \overline{x})$ is called a commitment to x. That is, it is $(\clubsuit, \heartsuit)$ when $x = 0$, and $(\heartsuit, \clubsuit)$ when $x = 1$. A commitment to x is represented as follows:

In card-based cryptography, we typically consider situations where a sequence of commitments is given as input; thus, at least $2n$ cards are used for an n-bit input. It is known that perfect security cannot be achieved if the single-card encoding [16,18] representing each bit with a single card is used [15]. Therefore, single-card encoding is not typically used.

2.4 Random Cut

A random cut is a shuffling operation that performs a cyclic shift on a sequence of cards a random number of times (see also Sect. 1.1). When a random cut is applied to a sequence of n cards $w = w_1 w_2 \cdots w_n \in \{\clubsuit, \heartsuit\}^n$, a word is chosen uniformly at random from the set of all words that are cyclically equal to w. Therefore, if $w_0 \sim w_1$ holds, the probability distribution of the resulting sequence of cards when a random cut is applied to w_0 is identical to the probability distribution of the resulting sequence when a random cut is applied to w_1.

For example, if a random cut is applied to a face-down sequence of five cards ♣♣♡♡♡, the five possible sequences of cards (♣♣♡♡♡, ♣♡♡♡♣, ♡♡♡♣♣, ♡♡♣♣♡, and ♡♣♣♡♡) will each occur with probability 1/5, and no one can guess which sequence was actually chosen.

It is known that a random cut can be easily implemented by human hand. Furthermore, a method of implementing a random cut by placing cards on a spinning top and performing a rotation operation is also known.

2.5 Single-Cut Full-Open Protocols

In this section, we introduce the notation used in SCFO protocols for subsequent sections. See Sect. 1.1 for the definition of SCFO protocols. Let $\mathfrak{S}_n$ denote the symmetric group of degree n.

A (k_0, k_1)-SCFO protocol proceeds as follows:

1. Arrange the input sequence as $x_1\overline{x_1} \cdots x_n\overline{x_n} \in \{\clubsuit, \heartsuit\}^{2n}$.
2. Permute the sequence with a permutation $\pi \in \mathfrak{S}_{2n}$.
3. Insert k_0 $\boxed{\clubsuit}$s and k_1 $\boxed{\heartsuit}$s at arbitrary positions in the sequence.
4. Apply a random cut to the sequence.
5. Open all cards.

Let $f : \{0,1\}^n \to \{0,1\}$ be a function. For each $b \in \{0,1\}$, let $\boldsymbol{v}^{(b)}$ be the set of input sequences at Step 1 corresponding to the output value b defined as:

$$\boldsymbol{v}^{(b)} := \{\pi(x_1\overline{x_1}x_2\overline{x_2} \cdots x_n\overline{x_n}) \mid x_i \in \{0,1\}, f(x_1, \ldots, x_n) = b\}. \tag{1}$$

Let $\boldsymbol{w}^{(b)}$ be the set of sequences at Step 2 corresponding to b defined as:

$$\boldsymbol{w}^{(b)} := \{\pi(v) \mid v \in \boldsymbol{v}^{(b)}\}. \tag{2}$$

Let $\boldsymbol{w}'^{(b)}$ be the set of sequences at Step 3 corresponding to b defined as:

$$\boldsymbol{w}'^{(b)} := \{w' \mid w \in \boldsymbol{w}^{(b)}, w \xrightarrow{\boldsymbol{u}} w'\}, \tag{3}$$

where $\boldsymbol{u} \in (\{0,1\}^*)^{2n}$ denotes the insertion at Step 3. The above protocol correctly and securely computes f if it satisfies the following two conditions:

Correctness. For any $w_0 \in \boldsymbol{w}'^{(0)}$ and $w_1 \in \boldsymbol{w}'^{(1)}$, we have $w_0 \not\sim w_1$.
Security. For each $b \in \{0,1\}$ and any $w_b, w_b' \in \boldsymbol{w}'^{(b)}$, we have $w_b \sim w_b'$.

3 Searching for $(*, 0)$-SCFO Protocols

In this section, we propose a method to search for $(*, 0)$-SCFO protocols based on mathematical optimization. To search for $(*, 0)$-SCFO protocols, we need to find a permutation $\pi \in \mathfrak{S}_{2n}$ and a 0-insertion $\boldsymbol{u} \in (\{0\}^*)^{2n}$ that yield $\boldsymbol{w}'^{(b)}$ satisfying the correctness and security conditions in Sect. 2.5.

Our search method is based on an integer optimization formulation for finding a 0-insertion $\boldsymbol{u}$. The overall search procedure consists of the following two steps:

Step 1. For each permutation $\pi \in \mathfrak{S}_{2n}$, we compute $\boldsymbol{w}^{(b)}$ of Eq. (2), and then solve an integer optimization problem to find a 0-insertion $\boldsymbol{u}$ such that $\boldsymbol{w}'^{(b)}$ of Eq. (3) is cyclically equal, which corresponds to the security condition. The objective is to minimize the bit length of $\boldsymbol{u}$. This step returns a minimal-length insertion if a solution exists.

Step 2. If we find a feasible pair $(\pi, \boldsymbol{u})$ in the above step, it is then verified that $w_0 \in \boldsymbol{w}'^{(0)}$ and $w_1 \in \boldsymbol{w}'^{(1)}$ are not cyclically equal, which corresponds to the correctness. If the correctness is satisfied, the pair is output as a valid solution.

The problem formulation used in Step 1 is detailed in Sects. 3.1 and 3.2. Note that the optimization problem in Step 1 requires not only a permutation π but also shift amounts as input, which are described later. We address Step 2 in Sect. 3.3. Using this algorithm, we demonstrate the impossibility of a $(*, 0)$-SCFO protocol for three-variable Boolean functions. Furthermore, due to the symmetry between $\boxed{\clubsuit}$ and $\boxed{\heartsuit}$, our result also implies the impossibility of a $(0, *)$-SCFO protocol for three-variable Boolean functions.

3.1 Notation

Suppose that $\boldsymbol{w}^{(b)}$ of Eq. (2) is given for each $b \in \{0, 1\}$. In this subsection and the next subsection, we search for the insertion $\boldsymbol{u} = (u_1, u_2, \ldots, u_{2n}) \in (\{0\}^*)^{2n}$ that yields $\boldsymbol{w}'^{(b)}$ of Eq. (3) satisfying the correctness and security in Sect. 2.5.

We denote the set of positive integers from 1 to n by $[n] := \{1, 2, \ldots, n\}$. Let $K^{(b)}$ denote the number of elements of $\boldsymbol{w}^{(b)}$. Since the number of elements of $\boldsymbol{w}^{(0)} \sqcup \boldsymbol{w}^{(1)}$, the disjoint union of $\boldsymbol{w}^{(0)}$ and $\boldsymbol{w}^{(1)}$, is equal to the number of all inputs, we have $K^{(0)} + K^{(1)} = 2^n$. Define $I := 2n$ and $J := n$. Here, I represents the bit length of sequences, and J represents the number of 1 s in each sequence.

Let $w_k^{(b)}$ be the k-th sequence of $\boldsymbol{w}^{(b)}$, i.e., $\boldsymbol{w}^{(b)} = \{w_1^{(b)}, \ldots, w_{K^{(b)}}^{(b)}\}$. Let $t_{j,k}^{(b)} \in [I]$ for $j \in [J]$ be the position of the j-th 1 from the left. If we treat the 1 s as "separators", the sequence can be regarded as consisting of J segments by considering the leftmost and the rightmost segments are connected. For example, an 8-bit sequence 01100110 consists of four segments as follows:

$$\underbrace{0}_{\text{1st}}\ 1 \underbrace{}_{\text{2nd}} 1\ \underbrace{0\ 0}_{\text{3rd}}\ 1 \underbrace{}_{\text{4th}} 1\ \underbrace{0}_{\text{1st}}.$$

Then the number of 0 s in the j-th segment ($j \in [J]$) is given by

$$x_{j,k}^{(b)} = \begin{cases} (t_{j,k}^{(b)} - 1) + (I - t_{J,k}^{(b)}) & (j = 1), \\ t_{j,k}^{(b)} - t_{j-1,k}^{(b)} - 1 & (1 < j \leq J). \end{cases}$$

We now consider the insertion. For an I-bit sequence, there are I possible insertion positions. For example, 01100110 has 8 possible insertion positions as follows.

$$\begin{array}{cccccccc} 1 & 2 & 3 & 4 & 5 & 6 & 7 & 8 \\ \downarrow & \downarrow & \downarrow & \downarrow & \downarrow & \downarrow & \downarrow & \downarrow \\ 0 & 1 & 1 & 0 & 0 & 1 & 1 & 0 \end{array}$$

For a sequence $w_k^{(b)} \in \{0,1\}^I$, define a constant $a_{i,j,k}^{(b)} \in \{0,1\}$ to indicate whether an insertion position i belongs to a segment j:

$$a_{i,j,k}^{(b)} = \begin{cases} 1 & \text{if position } i \text{ belongs to segment } j, \\ 0 & \text{otherwise,} \end{cases}$$

for all $i \in [I]$, $j \in [J]$, $k \in [K^{(b)}]$, and $b \in \{0,1\}$. Let $y_i \in \mathbb{Z}_{\geq 0}$ ($i \in [I]$) be the number of 0 s inserted at position i. After the insertion, the number of 0 s for the j-th segment in $w_k^{(b)}$ is given by:

$$x'^{(b)}_{j,k} = x_{j,k}^{(b)} + \sum_{i \in [I]} a_{i,j,k}^{(b)} y_i .$$

Then, two sequences $w_k^{(b)}$ and $w_{k+1}^{(b)}$ will become cyclically equal by the insertion if the vector of integers $(x'^{(b)}_{1,k}, \ldots, x'^{(b)}_{J,k})$ is equal to a cyclic shift of the vector of integers $(x'^{(b)}_{1,k+1}, \ldots, x'^{(b)}_{J,k+1})$. In other words, if the shift amount is $s_{k+1}^{(b)} \in \{0, 1, \ldots, J-1\}$, the following equation holds for all $j \in [J]$:

$$x'^{(b)}_{j,k} = x'^{(b)}_{\left((j+s_{k+1}^{(b)}-1) \bmod J\right)+1,k+1}. \tag{4}$$

3.2 Problem Formulation

Given a set of input sequences $\boldsymbol{w} := \boldsymbol{w}^{(0)} \sqcup \boldsymbol{w}^{(1)}$, the search for a $(*, 0)$-SCFO protocol consists of finding the following two vectors:

- 0-insertion vector: $\boldsymbol{y} := (y_i)_{i \in [I]} \in \mathbb{Z}_{\geq 0}^I$.
- Shift amount vector: $\boldsymbol{s} := (s_k^{(b)})_{b \in \{0,1\}, k \in \{2,3,\ldots,K^{(b)}\}} \in \mathbb{Z}_{\geq 0}^{K^{(0)}+K^{(1)}-2}$.

Here, the index k of the shift amount vector starts from 2 because the shift amount $s_k^{(b)}$ represents the shift amount of $w_k^{(b)}$ relative to $w_1^{(b)}$ for $2 \leq k \leq K^{(b)}$. These vectors must be determined such that all sequences corresponding to the same output value become cyclically equal after the 0-insertion.

To achieve this, we formulate the search as an optimization problem. We consider the shift amount vector $\boldsymbol{s}$ to be a fixed parameter, and seek an insertion vector $\boldsymbol{y}$ that achieves cyclic equality with the minimum number of inserted 0 s. This leads to the following integer optimization problem, denoted $\mathrm{P}(\boldsymbol{s}, \boldsymbol{w})$.

$\mathrm{P}(\boldsymbol{s}, \boldsymbol{w})$:

$$\underset{\boldsymbol{x}', \boldsymbol{y}}{\text{minimize}} \quad \sum_{i \in [I]} y_i \tag{5}$$

$$\text{subject to} \quad {x'}_{j,k}^{(b)} = x_{j,k}^{(b)} + \sum_{i \in [I]} a_{i,j,k}^{(b)} y_i \quad (b \in \{0,1\},\ j \in [J],\ k \in [K^{(b)}]), \tag{6}$$

$${x'}_{j,1}^{(b)} = {x'}^{(b)}_{\left((j+s_{k+1}^{(b)}-1) \bmod J\right)+1,k+1} \quad (b \in \{0,1\},\ j \in [J],\ k \in [K^{(b)}-1]), \tag{7}$$

$${x'}_{j,k}^{(b)} \in \mathbb{Z}_{\geq 0} \quad (b \in \{0,1\},\ j \in [J],\ k \in [K^{(b)}]), \tag{8}$$

$$y_i \in \mathbb{Z}_{\geq 0} \quad (i \in [I]), \tag{9}$$

where $\boldsymbol{x}' := ({x'}_{j,k}^{(b)})_{b \in \{0,1\}, (j,k) \in [J] \times [K^{(b)}]} \in \mathbb{Z}_{\geq 0}^{J(K^{(0)}+K^{(1)})}$. The objective function in Eq. (5) represents the total number of inserted 0s to be minimized. Equation (6) gives the number of 0 s for each segment after the 0-insertion, and Eq. (7) ensures that sequences with the same output value become cyclically equal after the 0-insertion. Equations (8)–(9) restrict the decision variables to non-negative integers. The set of optimal solutions is denoted by $\mathcal{Z}^*(\boldsymbol{s}, \boldsymbol{w})$.

While the above formulation guarantees the security condition, a valid $(*, 0)$-SCFO protocol must satisfy the correctness condition as described in Sect. 2.5. Therefore, for any optimal solution $\boldsymbol{z}^* := (\boldsymbol{x}'^*,\ \boldsymbol{y}^*)$ to the optimization problem $\mathrm{P}(\boldsymbol{s}, \boldsymbol{w})$, the following condition must hold:

$${w'}_1^{(0)} \not\sim {w'}_1^{(1)}, \tag{10}$$

where $w_1^{(b)} \xrightarrow{\boldsymbol{u}^*} {w'}_1^{(b)}$ for $b \in \{0,1\}$ and $\boldsymbol{u}^* = (0^{y_1^*}, 0^{y_2^*}, \ldots, 0^{y_I^*})$. This condition means that a sequence with output value 0 and a sequence with output value 1 are not cyclically equal after the 0-insertion. Note that since sequences ${w'}_k^{(b)}$ with the same output value are cyclically equal, it is sufficient to verify this condition for a single pair $({w'}_1^{(0)}, {w'}_1^{(1)})$.

3.3 Search Algorithm

In Sect. 3.2, we formulated the search for a $(*, 0)$-SCFO protocol as the optimization problem $\mathrm{P}(\boldsymbol{s}, \boldsymbol{w})$ given the set of sequences $\boldsymbol{w}$ and shift amounts $\boldsymbol{s}$.

To verify the existence of a $(*, 0)$-SCFO protocol, we present an exhaustive search algorithm that attempts to solve the optimization problem (5)–(9) for all permutations of the input sequence bits and all combinations of the shift amounts. Our algorithm is shown in Algorithm 1. If our algorithm outputs $\mathcal{F} = \varnothing$, there are no $(*, 0)$-SCFO protocols computing f.

4 Experimental Results

In this section, we apply Algorithm 1 to the 10 representative 3-variable Boolean functions (Nos. 5–14 in the list in Sect. 2.1) and demonstrate the impossibility of $(*, 0)$-SCFO protocols for these functions. The existence of a protocol can be confirmed by finding at least one solution.

Algorithm 1 Search Algorithm for $(*, 0)$-SCFO Protocols

Input: A function $f : \{0,1\}^n \rightarrow \{0,1\}$

1: Compute the set of input sequences $\boldsymbol{v} = \boldsymbol{v}^{(0)} \sqcup \boldsymbol{v}^{(1)}$ of Eq. (1).
2: Initialize the set of optimal solutions $\mathcal{F} \leftarrow \varnothing$.
3: **for** $\pi \in \mathfrak{S}_I$ **do**
4: $\quad \boldsymbol{w} \leftarrow \pi(\boldsymbol{v})$
5: $\quad$ **for** $\boldsymbol{s} \in \{0, 1, \ldots, J-1\}^{K^{(0)}+K^{(1)}-2}$ **do**
6: $\quad\quad$ **if** the optimization problem $\mathrm{P}(\boldsymbol{s}, \boldsymbol{w})$ is feasible **then**
7: $\quad\quad\quad$ **for** $\boldsymbol{z}^* \in \mathcal{Z}^*(\boldsymbol{s}, \boldsymbol{w})$ **do**
8: $\quad\quad\quad\quad$ **if** $\boldsymbol{z}^*$ satisfies Eq. (10) **then**
9: $\quad\quad\quad\quad\quad$ $\mathcal{F} \leftarrow \mathcal{F} \cup \{(\boldsymbol{s}, \boldsymbol{w}, \boldsymbol{z}^*)\}$
10: $\quad\quad\quad\quad$ **end if**
11: $\quad\quad\quad$ **end for**
12: $\quad\quad$ **end if**
13: $\quad$ **end for**
14: **end for**

Output: The set of optimal solutions $\mathcal{F}$

To solve the optimization problem defined by Eqs. (5)–(9), we used the HiGHS 1.8.0 solver, which is integrated into the SciPy library in Python. All experiments were conducted on a MacBook Air equipped with an Apple M3 processor (8 threads, 4.05 GHz) and 16 GB of RAM.

The exhaustive search found no feasible solution for any of the representative functions, except for the 3-variable equality function (No. 7 in the list in Sect. 2.1). This result establishes that it is impossible to construct a $(*, 0)$-SCFO protocol for the other nine functions. The computation time for each function ranged from approximately 3 to 60 min.

5 Conclusion

In this paper, we proposed a new method for proving impossibility results in card-based cryptography based on mathematical optimization. Specifically, we formulated the constructability of $(*, 0)$-SCFO and $(0, *)$-SCFO protocols as an integer optimization problem and proposed a search algorithm. As a result of applying the proposed method to all 3-variable Boolean functions, we demonstrated through computer experiments that no $(*, 0)$-SCFO protocol exists, except for known protocols (e.g., the equality protocol).

This research has shown the usefulness of mathematical optimization in card-based cryptography. On the other hand, research on card-based cryptography based on mathematical optimization is still in its early stages, and many open problems remain. For example, the following problems are open:

- The constructability of $(*, 0)$-SCFO protocols for Boolean functions with four or more variables is an open problem. Since the computational complexity of the proposed method is at least exponential with respect to the number of variables n, applying it directly to 4-variable functions is difficult from a computational complexity standpoint.
- While the constructability in this study is for $(*, 0)$-SCFO and $(0, *)$-SCFO protocols, the impossibility of general SCFO protocols that use any number of both ♣ and ♡ as additional cards remains an open problem.
- Modeling protocols other than SCFO protocols as integer optimization problems to investigate their constructability is an open problem.

Acknowledgments. This work was supported by JSPS KAKENHI Grant Numbers JP21K17702 and JP23H00479, JST CREST Grant Number JPMJCR22M1, and JST K Program Grant Number JPMJKP24U2.

A Protocol for $x_1 \oplus x_2$

This protocol is a $(0, 0)$-SCFO protocol for the 2-variable XOR function $x_1 \oplus x_2$. It was proposed by Shinagawa–Mizuki [19].

1. The input sequence is given as follows:

$$\underset{x_1}{?}\ \underset{\overline{x_1}}{?}\ \underset{x_2}{?}\ \underset{\overline{x_2}}{?}\,.$$

2. Apply a random cut to the sequence.
3. Open all cards. Output 0 if it is a cyclic shift of ♡ ♣ ♡ ♣, and 1 if it is a cyclic shift of ♡ ♡ ♣ ♣.

B Protocol for $x_1 \wedge x_2$

This protocol is a $(0, 1)$-SCFO protocol for the 2-variable AND function $x_1 \wedge x_2$. It was proposed by den Boer [1].

1. The input sequence is given as follows:

$$\underset{\overline{x_1}}{?}\ \underset{x_1}{?}\ \underset{\heartsuit}{?}\ \underset{x_2}{?}\ \underset{\overline{x_2}}{?}\,.$$

2. Apply a random cut to the sequence.
3. Open all cards. Output 0 if it is a cyclic shift of ♡ ♣ ♡ ♣ ♡, and 1 if it is a cyclic shift of ♡ ♡ ♡ ♣ ♣.

C Protocol for $(x_1 = x_2 = x_3)$?

This protocol is a $(0, 0)$-SCFO protocol for the 3-variable equality function $(x_1 = x_2 = x_3)$? that outputs 1 if and only if $x_1 = x_2 = x_3$. It was proposed by Heather–Schneider–Teague [7] and independently rediscovered by Shinagawa–Mizuki [19].

1. The input sequence is given as follows:

$$\underset{x_1}{\boxed{?}}\,\underset{\overline{x_2}}{\boxed{?}}\,\underset{x_3}{\boxed{?}}\,\underset{\overline{x_1}}{\boxed{?}}\,\underset{x_2}{\boxed{?}}\,\underset{\overline{x_3}}{\boxed{?}}.$$

2. Apply a random cut to the sequence.
3. Open all cards. Output 0 if it is a cyclic shift of $\boxed{\heartsuit}\boxed{\clubsuit}\boxed{\heartsuit}\boxed{\clubsuit}\boxed{\heartsuit}\boxed{\clubsuit}$, and 1 if it is a cyclic shift of $\boxed{\heartsuit}\boxed{\heartsuit}\boxed{\heartsuit}\boxed{\clubsuit}\boxed{\clubsuit}\boxed{\clubsuit}$.

D Protocol for $(x_1 \wedge x_2) \vee (\overline{x_1} \wedge x_3)$

This protocol is a $(1, 1)$-SCFO protocol for a 3-variable function $(x_1 \wedge x_2) \vee (\overline{x_1} \wedge x_3)$. It was proposed by Shinagawa–Nuida [22].

1. The input sequence is given as follows:

$$\underset{x_2}{\boxed{?}}\,\underset{\overline{x_1}}{\boxed{?}}\,\underset{\overline{x_3}}{\boxed{?}}\,\underset{1}{\boxed{?}}\,\underset{\overline{x_2}}{\boxed{?}}\,\underset{x_1}{\boxed{?}}\,\underset{x_3}{\boxed{?}}\,\underset{0}{\boxed{?}}.$$

2. Apply a random cut to the sequence.
3. Open all cards. Output 0 if it is a cyclic shift of $\boxed{\heartsuit}\boxed{\heartsuit}\boxed{\heartsuit}\boxed{\heartsuit}\boxed{\clubsuit}\boxed{\clubsuit}\boxed{\clubsuit}\boxed{\clubsuit}$, and 1 if it is a cyclic shift of $\boxed{\clubsuit}\boxed{\clubsuit}\boxed{\heartsuit}\boxed{\clubsuit}\boxed{\heartsuit}\boxed{\heartsuit}\boxed{\clubsuit}\boxed{\heartsuit}$.

E Protocol for $x_1 \oplus x_2 \oplus x_3$

This protocol is an SCFO protocol for the 3-variable XOR function $x_1 \oplus x_2 \oplus x_3$. It is not standard since the input sequence contains two pairs of $(x_1, \overline{x_1})$. It was proposed by Shinagawa–Nuida [22].

1. The input sequence is given as follows:

$$\underset{x_1}{\boxed{?}}\,\underset{x_2}{\boxed{?}}\,\underset{\overline{x_1}}{\boxed{?}}\,\underset{x_3}{\boxed{?}}\,\underset{x_1}{\boxed{?}}\,\underset{\overline{x_2}}{\boxed{?}}\,\underset{\overline{x_1}}{\boxed{?}}\,\underset{\overline{x_3}}{\boxed{?}}.$$

2. Apply a random cut to the sequence.
3. Open all cards. Output 0 if it is a cyclic shift of $\boxed{\clubsuit}\boxed{\clubsuit}\boxed{\heartsuit}\boxed{\clubsuit}\boxed{\clubsuit}\boxed{\heartsuit}\boxed{\heartsuit}\boxed{\heartsuit}$, and 1 if it is a cyclic shift of $\boxed{\heartsuit}\boxed{\heartsuit}\boxed{\clubsuit}\boxed{\heartsuit}\boxed{\heartsuit}\boxed{\clubsuit}\boxed{\clubsuit}\boxed{\clubsuit}$.

F Protocol for $\overline{x_1}x_2\overline{x_4} \vee \overline{x_2}x_3\overline{x_4} \vee x_1\overline{x_2}x_4 \vee x_2\overline{x_3}x_4$

This protocol is a (0, 0)-SCFO protocol for a 4-variable function $\overline{x_1}x_2\overline{x_4} \vee \overline{x_2}x_3\overline{x_4} \vee x_1\overline{x_2}x_4 \vee x_2\overline{x_3}x_4$. This protocol was proposed by Shinagawa–Nuida [22].

1. The input sequence is given as follows:

$$\underset{x_1}{\boxed{?}}\underset{x_2}{\boxed{?}}\underset{x_3}{\boxed{?}}\underset{x_4}{\boxed{?}}\underset{\overline{x_1}}{\boxed{?}}\underset{\overline{x_2}}{\boxed{?}}\underset{\overline{x_3}}{\boxed{?}}\underset{\overline{x_4}}{\boxed{?}}.$$

2. Apply a random cut to the sequence.
3. Open all cards. Output 0 if it is a cyclic shift of $\boxed{\heartsuit}\boxed{\heartsuit}\boxed{\heartsuit}\boxed{\heartsuit}\boxed{\clubsuit}\boxed{\clubsuit}\boxed{\clubsuit}\boxed{\clubsuit}$, and 1 if it is a cyclic shift of $\boxed{\clubsuit}\boxed{\clubsuit}\boxed{\heartsuit}\boxed{\clubsuit}\boxed{\heartsuit}\boxed{\heartsuit}\boxed{\clubsuit}\boxed{\heartsuit}$.

References

1. Boer, B.D.: More efficient match-making and satisfiability the five card trick. In: Quisquater, J.-J., Vandewalle, J. (eds.) Advances in Cryptology - EUROCRYPT' 89. LNCS, vol. 434, pp. 208–217. Springer, Heidelberg (1990)
2. Cheung, E., Hawthorne, C., Lee, P.: CS 758 project: secure computation with playing cards (2013)
3. Crépeau, C., Kilian, J.: Discreet solitary games. In: Stinson, D.R. (ed.) Advances in Cryptology–CRYPTO' 93. LNCS, vol. 773, pp. 319–330. Springer, Heidelberg (1994)
4. Eriguchi, R., Shinagawa, K.: Single-shuffle full-open card-based protocols for any function. arXiv:2510.17308 (2025)
5. Fujita, K., Ikeda, S., Shinagawa, K., Yoneyama, K.: Formal verification and proof of impossibility for four-card XOR protocols using only random cuts. In: Emura, K., Morita, H. (eds.) ACM ASIA Public-Key Cryptography Workshop, New York. ACM (2025)
6. Hashimoto, Y., Nuida, K., Shinagawa, K., Inamura, M., Hanaoka, G.: Toward finite-runtime card-based protocol for generating a hidden random permutation without fixed points. IEICE Trans. Fundam. **E101.A**(9), 1503–1511 (2018)
7. Heather, J., Schneider, S., Teague, V.: Cryptographic protocols with everyday objects. Formal Aspects Comput. **26**(1), 37–62 (2014)
8. Kastner, J., et al.: The minimum number of cards in practical card-based protocols. In: Takagi, T., Peyrin, T. (eds.) Advances in Cryptology–ASIACRYPT 2017. LNCS, vol. 10626, pp. 126–155. Springer, Cham (2017)
9. Koch, A.: The landscape of optimal card-based protocols. Math. Cryptol. **1**(2), 115–131 (2022)
10. Koch, A., Schrempp, M., Kirsten, M.: Card-based cryptography meets formal verification. In: Galbraith, S.D., Moriai, S. (eds.) Advances in Cryptology-ASIACRYPT 2019. LNCS, vol. 11921, pp. 488–517. Springer, Cham (2019)
11. Koch, A., Schrempp, M., Kirsten, M.: Card-based cryptography meets formal verification. New Gener. Comput. **39**(1), 115–158 (2021)
12. Koch, A., Walzer, S., Härtel, K.: Card-based cryptographic protocols using a minimal number of cards. In: Iwata, T., Cheon, J.H. (eds.) Advances in Cryptology–ASIACRYPT 2015. LNCS, vol. 9452, pp. 783–807. Springer, Heidelberg (2015)

13. Marcedone, A., Wen, Z., Shi, E.: Secure dating with four or fewer cards. Cryptology ePrint Archive, Report 2015/1031 (2015)
14. Mizuki, T.: Applications of card-based cryptography to education. In: Information Security Workshop (ISEC) (2016). (in Japanese)
15. Mizuki, T., Shizuya, H.: A formalization of card-based cryptographic protocols via abstract machine. Int. J. Inf. Secur. **13**(1), 15–23 (2014)
16. Niemi, V., Renvall, A.: Secure multiparty computations without computers. Theor. Comput. Sci. **191**(1–2), 173–183 (1998)
17. Shinagawa, K.: A report on a lecture for elementary and junior high school using card-based cryptography. In: 2022 Symposium on Cryptography and Information Security (SCIS 2022) (2022). (in Japanese)
18. Shinagawa, K.: Card-based protocols with single-card encoding. In: Anutariya, C., Bonsangue, M.M. (eds.) Theoretical Aspects of Computing. LNCS, vol. 15373, pp. 182–194. Springer, Cham (2025)
19. Shinagawa, K., Mizuki, T.: The six-card trick: secure computation of three-input equality. In: Lee, K. (ed.) Information Security and Cryptology. LNCS, vol. 11396, pp. 123–131. Springer, Cham (2018)
20. Shinagawa, K., Nuida, K.: Card-based protocols imply PSM protocols. In: Beyersdorff, O., Pilipczuk, M., Pimentel, E., Thàng, N.K. (eds.) Theoretical Aspects of Computer Science. LIPIcs, vol. 327, pp. 72:1–72:18, Dagstuhl. Schloss Dagstuhl (2025)
21. Shinagawa, K., Nuida, K.: Cyclic equalizability of words and its application to card-based cryptography. In: Fundamentals of Computation Theory. LNCS. Springer, Cham (2025)
22. Shinagawa, K., Nuida, K.: A note on single-cut full-open protocols. arXiv:2507.03323 (2025)

Implementation & Hardware Acceleration

High-Speed 16-Radix Polynomial Multiplication on ARM Cortex-M4 with Recursive Karatsuba Layers

Minjoo Sim, Hyunjun Kim, Minwoo Lee, and Siwoo Eum(✉)

Department of Information Computer Engineering, Hansung University, Seoul 02876, South Korea
shuraatum@gmail.com

Abstract. Polynomial multiplication over $\mathbb{F}_2[x]$ is a fundamental building block in code-based and lattice-based cryptography, particularly on lightweight embedded devices where dedicated carry-less multiply instructions are unavailable. This paper presents a high-speed, constant-time implementation of radix-16 polynomial multiplication on the ARM Cortex-M4, combining zero-padding with recursive Karatsuba layers. Building on the radix-16 decomposition proposed by Chen et al. in TCHES'21, we replace the conventional schoolbook inner multiplier with a multi-level Karatsuba scheme. This optimization reduces cycle counts on the ARM Cortex-M4 while preserving constant-time execution. To further optimize efficiency, the design minimizes packing and unpacking overhead by operating at 128-bit granularity and employs a five-stage pipeline—Decomposition, Padding, Multiplication, Unpadding, and Reassembly—implemented entirely with data-independent shifts, XORs, and masks. Experimental results on the Cortex-M4 show that our optimized `ct_poly32_mul_64_bit` implementation achieves up to 31% improvement over the best existing constant-time baseline, demonstrating the efficiency and scalability of recursive Karatsuba for resource-constrained cryptographic applications.

Keywords: Polynomial Multiplication · Software Implementation · Recursive Karatsuba · Cortex-M4

1 Introduction

Polynomial multiplication in $\mathbb{F}_2[x]$ is a core operation in many cryptographic primitives, including code-based and lattice-based post-quantum schemes. Its efficiency directly influences the practicality of encryption, decryption, key generation, and signature verification in resource-constrained environments. On high-performance CPUs, dedicated carry-less multiply instructions (e.g., Intel CLMUL) allow efficient realization of this task, often achieving single-cycle throughput for small field multiplications [1]. However, embedded devices such as the ARM Cortex-M4 lack such instructions, requiring alternative approaches

H. Seo (Ed.): ICISC 2025, LNCS 16487, pp. 385–399, 2026.
https://doi.org/10.1007/978-981-95-8034-7_20

to achieve competitive performance without compromising security. This limitation poses a significant challenge since microcontrollers remain a dominant platform for secure IoT devices, medical sensors, and industrial control systems, where post-quantum cryptographic primitives are expected to be deployed in the near future [2–4].

The schoolbook method, also known as long multiplication, provides a simple and direct implementation by computing all pairwise coefficient products [5]. While conceptually straightforward, its quadratic complexity $O(n^2)$ leads to rapidly increasing cycle counts as operand sizes grow, which is prohibitive for many cryptographic applications. In contrast, Karatsuba's divide-and-conquer approach reduces the complexity to $O(n^{\log_2 3}) \approx O(n^{1.585})$, offering tangible cycle savings for moderate operand sizes that frequently appear in code-based cryptosystems and structured lattice schemes [6,7].

On the ARM Cortex-M4 in particular, several works have investigated optimized polynomial multipliers. Erdem [8] explored comb and Karatsuba techniques for efficient software multiplication over $\mathbb{F}_2[x]$ on embedded platforms, while Kannwischer [9] evaluated multiplication strategies including Karatsuba and Toom–Cook in the context of NIST PQC candidates. Chen et al. [10] introduced a radix-16 packing scheme for Classic McEliece, demonstrating the benefits of bit-sliced convolution. More recent studies have further optimized lattice- and code-based schemes on this platform, such as ESPM-D for Dilithium [11] and HQC implementations leveraging Karatsuba multipliers [12].

These results highlight that packing and bit-sliced representations are effective in exploiting the native word size of 32-bit processors. By representing polynomials in packed formats, carry-less multiplication can be emulated with ordinary integer multiplication followed by masking and shifting. Nevertheless, most prior work continues to rely on schoolbook multiplication at the core, which leaves room for more efficient constant-time engines.

To address this gap, we explore recursive Karatsuba layers as a promising alternative. By reducing the number of base multiplications without introducing data-dependent control flow, and by combining them with constant-time masking, shifting, and packing routines, our approach provides both security and performance advantages. Building on these insights, this paper proposes a new design that integrates radix-16 zero-padding with recursive Karatsuba multipliers, tailored for the ARM Cortex-M4 platform.

The remainder of this paper is structured as follows. Section 2 reviews the Schoolbook and Karatsuba algorithms together with related work on polynomial multiplication. Section 3 presents our proposed method, Sect. 4 reports the performance evaluation, and Sect. 5 concludes with a discussion of future work.

Contributions

This paper makes the following contributions:

- **Recursive Karatsuba optimization**: We propose a constant-time multiplier that extends the radix-16 zero-padding framework of Chen et al. [10] by introducing recursive multi-level Karatsuba layers in place of the traditional schoolbook multiplier.

- **Pipeline refinement**: We design a five-stage multiplication pipeline (Decomposition, Padding, Multiplication, Unpadding, Reassembly) that is implemented entirely with data-independent shifts, XORs, and masks. By operating at 128-bit granularity, the design minimizes packing and unpacking overhead on 32-bit processors.
- **Scalable implementations (64- and 128-bit variants)**: Our implementation includes two constant-time designs: `ct_poly32_mul_64_bit` for efficiency and `ct_poly32_mul_128_bit` for scalability to larger operands. The 64-bit variant offers the best efficiency (up to 31% cycle-count reduction over the constant-time baseline [13]), while the 128-bit variant demonstrates the scalability of our approach to wider operands and larger field sizes. We further benchmark multiple recursion depths (L2, L3, L4) on the Cortex-M4, confirming the practical efficiency of recursive Karatsuba on resource-constrained devices.

2 Background

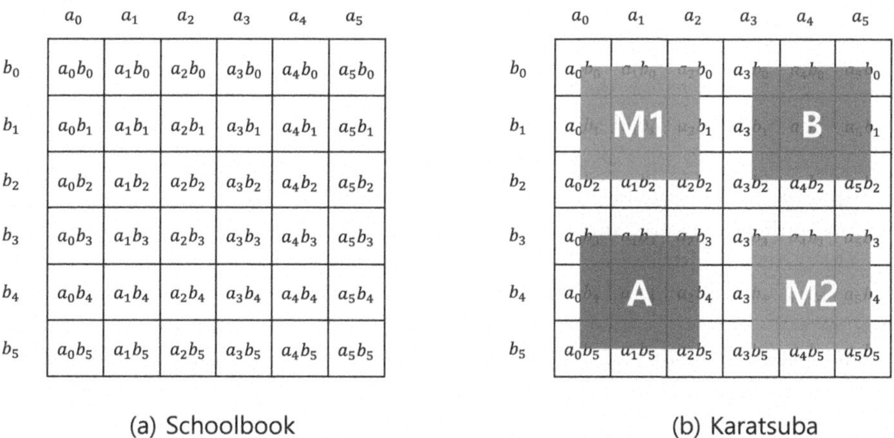

Fig. 1. (a) Schoolbook (direct) polynomial multiplication: each cell is a partial product a_ib_j; each output coefficient c_k is the sum along the diagonal $i + j = k$. (b) Karatsuba partition of the same operand: split inputs into lower/upper halves X_0, X_1 and compute A, B, M (highlighted). Recompose via Karatsuba to reduce base multiplications.

2.1 Schoolbook Multiplication

The *Schoolbook multiplication*, also called *long multiplication* or the *grade-school method*, follows the direct application of the distributive law. Given two n-digit numbers (or degree-$(n-1)$ polynomials)

$$x = \sum_{i=0}^{n-1} a_i B^i, \qquad y = \sum_{j=0}^{n-1} b_j B^j,$$

Here, B denotes the radix used for representing polynomial coefficients (typically $B = 2$). the product expands as

$$x \cdot y = \sum_{i=0}^{n-1} \sum_{j=0}^{n-1} a_i b_j B^{i+j}.$$

This requires computing all n^2 pairwise products, leading to quadratic time complexity $O(n^2)$ [5]. Its strength lies in simplicity and straightforward implementation, as it essentially mirrors the manual multiplication process taught in elementary arithmetic.

Figure 1(a) illustrates this method: each cell corresponds to a partial product $a_i b_j$, and an output coefficient c_k is obtained by summing (XOR-ing in $\mathbb{F}_2$) all partial products on the diagonal $i + j = k$,

$$c_k = \sum_{i=0}^{k} a_i \, b_{k-i} \qquad \text{(addition is XOR in } \mathbb{F}_2\text{)}.$$

This representation maps naturally to word-oriented implementations: operands are split into fixed-size limbs (words or nibbles), partial products are formed by word multiplications, and the diagonal contributions are combined by shifts and XORs. On platforms without a dedicated carry-less multiply instruction (e.g., ARM Cortex-M4), the schoolbook approach can be realized by packing limbs into bit-spaced (radix) words and using native integer multiply operations together with shifts and XORs to emulate carry-less polynomial multiplication.

2.2 Karatsuba Multiplication

The *Karatsuba algorithm*, introduced by Karatsuba and Ofman in 1963 [6], improves upon the Schoolbook method using a divide-and-conquer strategy. This process is visualized in Fig. 1(b).

First, the inputs are split into lower and upper halves:

$$x = x_1 K^m + x_0, \qquad y = y_1 K^m + y_0.$$

In this context, K represents the splitting base (e.g., $K = 2^m$), which determines the partitioning width in the recursive formulation.

While a naive expansion of this form requires four sub-multiplications, Karatsuba's key insight is that the result can be computed with only three:

$$z_2 = x_1 y_1$$
$$z_0 = x_0 y_0$$
$$z_1 = (x_1 + x_0)(y_1 + y_0) - z_2 - z_0.$$

The final product is then reconstructed by shifting and adding these partial products:

$$x \cdot y = z_2 K^{2m} + z_1 K^m + z_0.$$

This recursive approach reduces the time complexity to $O(n^{\log_2 3}) \approx O(n^{1.585})$ [14], making it the first widely known multiplication algorithm with sub-quadratic complexity.

2.3 32-Bit Cortex-M4

The ARM Cortex-M4 is a widely deployed 32-bit microcontroller core that combines energy efficiency with moderate computational capability, making it a representative platform for cryptographic benchmarking [15,16]. It implements the ARMv7E-M instruction set, including Thumb-2 instructions, DSP extensions, and a hardware floating-point unit (FPU). With features such as a three-stage pipeline and dedicated multiplication-accumulation instructions (e.g., UMAAL), the Cortex-M4 provides efficient support for arithmetic-intensive applications while remaining suitable for resource-constrained embedded devices.

Due to these characteristics, the Cortex-M4 has become a standard platform for benchmarking lightweight and post-quantum cryptography. For instance, the `pqm4` framework provides a unified benchmarking environment for NIST PQC candidates on Cortex-M4 [17], and numerous studies have reported implementations of ECC, DSA, and lattice-based schemes on this architecture [11,18–20]. These works demonstrate that the Cortex-M4 is an appropriate and widely recognized target for evaluating high-performance cryptographic primitives in constrained environments.

2.4 Related Work on Polynomial Multiplication

LD Multiplication [21] Lookup-table (LUT) based approaches such as the Lopez–Dahab (LD) method trade bitwise operations for table lookups and XORs, yielding fast word-oriented polynomial multiplication but exposing potential timing side channels unless implemented in constant time.

D. J. Bernstein's 64-Bit Bit-Sliced Multiplier [13] D. J. Bernstein's 64-bit bit-sliced carry-less multiplier removes data-dependent table lookups, but because it is implemented around 64-bit slices it incurs packing/unpacking overhead when executed on 32-bit targets (e.g., ARM Cortex-M4), which can reduce its practical benefit on such platforms.

Classic McEliece on the ARM Cortex-M4 (TCHES'21) [10] Chen *et al.* adopt a radix-16 (4-bit digit) bit-sliced packing to map small carry-less polynomial multiplications onto integer multiplications on 32-bit processors. A polynomial

$$a(x) = a_0 + a_1 x + a_2 x^2 + \cdots + a_7 x^7 \in \mathbb{F}_2[x]$$

is represented as the 32-bit integer

$$A = a_0 \cdot 2^0 + a_1 \cdot 2^4 + a_2 \cdot 2^8 + \cdots + a_7 \cdot 2^{28},$$

and similarly for B. The integer product

$$A \cdot B = \sum_{i=0}^{7} \sum_{j=0}^{7} a_i b_j \, 2^{4(i+j)}$$

places the contribution $a_i b_j$ at bit position $4(i+j)$; consequently, the bit at index $4k$ of the integer product equals the carry-less coefficient c_k of the polynomial product. Thus, small carry-less convolutions can be realized by a sequence of 32-bit integer multiply-accumulate instructions (e.g. `UMLAL`) together with masking and shifts to extract and rearrange the relevant bits.

Because the Cortex-M4 lacks a dedicated CLMUL instruction, the authors implement the core multiplication loop in assembly using a few `UMLAL` (and when needed `MLA`) instructions for the polynomial phase and similarly for the reduction phase. By carefully designing the packing, masks/shifts and the assembly inner loop, the radix-16 scheme attains low cycle counts on 32-bit ARM cores at the cost of increased packing/unpacking and assembly complexity. The approach is therefore particularly effective when many small parallel multiplications are executed or when hand-tuned assembly is acceptable to amortize the packing overhead.

3 Proposed Method

Building on Chen et al.'s 16-radix decomposition, data layout, and zero-padding scheme [10], we retain their high-level structure and platform optimizations but replace the schoolbook inner multiplier with a recursive multiple Karatsuba engine. Packing/unpacking is performed once at 128-bit granularity rather than repeatedly at smaller widths, substantially reducing packing overhead on 32-bit targets and improving throughput and scalability for larger field sizes.

3.1 Zero-Padding Method

For a binary polynomial represented as

$$a = \sum_{i \geq 0} a_i \, 2^i \quad (a_i \in \{0, 1\}),$$

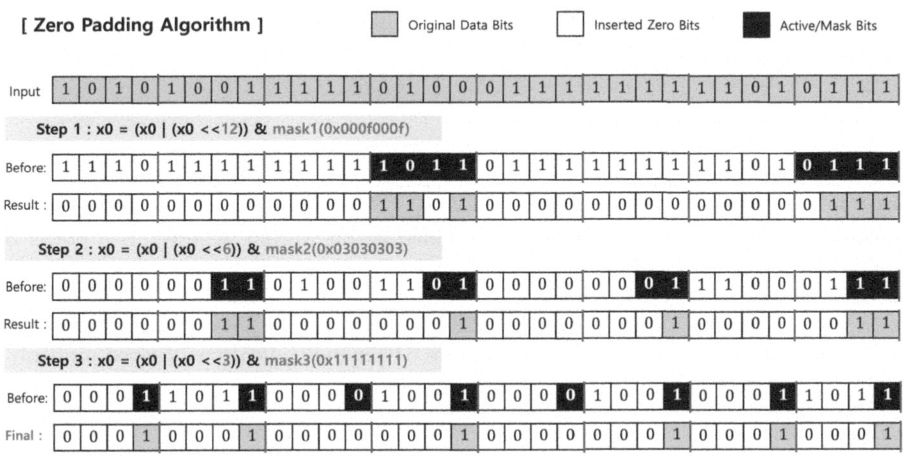

Fig. 2. Step-by-step execution of the zero-padding transformation on the 16-bit input $x_0 = \text{0xB4D2}$. The process applies OR–shift–mask operations with three masks (`mask1`, `mask2`, and `mask3`) to insert zero bits between every original coefficient, yielding the 32-bit output $x_0 = \text{0x01000010}$. Gray boxes indicate original bits, white boxes show inserted zeros, and black boxes mark active mask bits.

the zero-padding transformation is defined as

$$\mathrm{Pad}(a) := \sum_{i \geq 0} a_i \, 2^{4i},$$

which inserts three zero bits between consecutive coefficients to prevent carry propagation during native integer multiplication. On 32-bit processors, this mapping is efficiently realized through a sequence of *shift–OR–mask* operations (e.g., shifts by 12, 6, and 3 positions).

The inverse transformation is defined as

$$\mathrm{InvPad}(b) := \sum_{i \geq 0} \left(\left\lfloor \frac{b}{2^{4i}} \right\rfloor \bmod 2 \right) 2^i,$$

where $b = \mathrm{Pad}(a)$. In other words, every fourth bit of b is extracted to recover the original word a, and $\mathrm{InvPad}(\mathrm{Pad}(a)) = a$ holds.

As illustrated in Fig. 2, the `zero_padding` and `inv_zero_padding` macros implement these Pad and InvPad transformations. In Algorithm 2, Lines 3–6 correspond to the Padding stage, while Lines 10–11 correspond to the Unpadding stage.

3.2 Recursive Karatsuba Layers

Although Algorithm 1 presents the recursive structure in an abstract form, the base-case MUL requires an efficient, constant-time instantiation. Rather than relying on a traditional schoolbook multiplication, our design realizes this base case through a recursive combination of Karatsuba multiplications, as shown in Fig. 3.

Algorithm 1 Recursive Karatsuba on Zero-Padded Blocks

Require: Arrays X, Y of length n (zero-padded 32-bit words), where n is a power of two

Ensure: Array C of length $2n$, where each entry is either a padded 64-bit word (for `ct_poly32_mul_64_bit`) or a padded 128-bit block (for `ct_poly32_mul_128_bit`)

1: **if** $n = 1$ **then** ▷ Base case: one 64-bit multiplication (2-word multiply)
2: $\quad C \leftarrow \textsc{Mul}(X_0, Y_0)$
3: $\quad$ **return** C
4: **else**
5: $\quad X_L \leftarrow (X_0, \ldots, X_{n/2-1}), \quad X_H \leftarrow (X_{n/2}, \ldots, X_{n-1})$
6: $\quad Y_L \leftarrow (Y_0, \ldots, Y_{n/2-1}), \quad Y_H \leftarrow (Y_{n/2}, \ldots, Y_{n-1})$
7: $\quad C_L \leftarrow \textsc{Karatsuba}(X_L, Y_L, n/2)$
8: $\quad C_H \leftarrow \textsc{Karatsuba}(X_H, Y_H, n/2)$
9: $\quad C_M \leftarrow \textsc{Karatsuba}(X_L \oplus X_H, Y_L \oplus Y_H, n/2)$
10: $\quad T \leftarrow C_M \oplus C_L \oplus C_H$
11: $\quad$ **return** $C \leftarrow (C_H \ll n) \oplus (T \ll (n/2)) \oplus C_L$
12: **end if**

For comparison, the conventional schoolbook expansion for two 32-bit words is

$$XY = x_0y_0 \; + \; (x_0y_1 \oplus x_1y_0)\, 2^{32} \; + \; x_1y_1\, 2^{64},$$

where $\oplus$ denotes addition over $\mathbb{F}_2$, which corresponds to the bitwise XOR operation between two 32-bit words in the implementation. This contrasts with our recursive Karatsuba-based instantiation, motivating the use of multiple Karatsuba multiplications in the constant-time implementation. The bitsliced Karatsuba multiplier further achieves high cycle efficiency per multiplication, making it well suited for resource-constrained embedded platforms.

The recursive Karatsuba structure of Algorithm 1 provides the multiplication core invoked in Algorithm 2 (Line 7), which is explicitly marked as the Multiplication stage in the overall pipeline of Fig. 4.

3.3 Top-Level Multiplication Pipeline

The overall multiplication procedure is organized as an *algorithmic* five-stage pipeline (Decomposition, Padding, Multiplication, Unpadding, and Reassembly), as illustrated in Algorithm 2 and Fig. 4. The term *pipeline* refers to the logical dataflow within our algorithm, distinct from the hardware instruction pipeline of the Cortex-M4 processor. This structured decomposition improves modularity and ensures that each stage can be implemented with data-independent operations.

```
1  // Constant-time 2-word Karatsuba multiplier (base case)
2  void ct_poly_karatsuba_mul_2word(uint64_t *c_out,
3                                   uint32_t *x_in,
4                                   uint32_t *y_in) {
5      uint32_t *x_part = x_in, *y_part = y_in;
6      uint32_t x_mid, y_mid;
7      uint64_t a_part, b_part, c_part;
8
9  #ifdef KARATSUBA_L4
10     // Karatsuba (L4)
11     a_part = ((uint64_t)x_part[0] * (uint64_t)y_part[0]) &
           mask3_64; // x0*y0
12     b_part = ((uint64_t)x_part[1] * (uint64_t)y_part[1]) &
           mask3_64; // x1*y1
13     x_mid = x_part[0] ^ x_part[1];
14     y_mid = y_part[0] ^ y_part[1];
15     c_part = ((uint64_t)x_mid * (uint64_t)y_mid) & mask3_64;
                  // (x0^x1)*(y0^y1)
16     c_part ^= a_part ^ b_part;
                                                    // middle term
17     a_part ^= (c_part << 32);
18     b_part ^= (c_part >> 32);
19 #else
20     // Schoolbook fallback (carry-less)
21     a_part = ((uint64_t)x_part[0] * (uint64_t)y_part[0]) &
           mask3_64; // x0*y0
22     b_part = (((uint64_t)x_part[0] * (uint64_t)y_part[1]) &
           mask3_64) ^
23               (((uint64_t)x_part[1] * (uint64_t)y_part[0]) &
                     mask3_64)); // x0*y1 ^ x1*y0
24     a_part ^= (b_part << 32);
                                                      // add middle
           at 2^32
25     b_part  = (b_part >> 32) ^
26               (((uint64_t)x_part[1] * (uint64_t)y_part[1]) &
                     mask3_64);  // add x1*y1 at 2^64
27 #endif
28
29     // Result (padded 128-bit)
30     c_out[0] = a_part;
31     c_out[1] = b_part;
32 }
```

Fig. 3. Base constant-time two-word Karatsuba multiplier used at the lowest recursion layer.

In Algorithm 2, Lines 1–2 normalize the input length and allocate arrays to hold the zero-padded chunks. Lines 3–6 decompose the 32- or 128-bit input into 8-bit slices, each representing eight $\mathbb{F}_2$ coefficients in 16-radix bit-sliced form. These slices are then expanded via the Pad operation (Line 5), which inserts zeros between coefficient bits to yield zero-padded 32-bit words. On these padded inputs, recursive Karatsuba multiplication is applied (Line 7, Algorithm 1), producing arrays of padded 64-bit partial products. The results are subsequently compressed by Unpad (Line 10), which extracts every fourth bit to obtain compact 16-bit words, and are stored in array Z (Line 11). Finally, in Lines 13–16, pairs of 16-bit words are reassembled into 32-bit outputs using `c_out[i] = low | (high << 16)`, and in Line 17 the output words are placed at byte-aligned offsets to form the final product.

As summarized in Fig. 4, the five stages—Decomposition → Padding → Multiplication → Unpadding → Reassembly—are implemented with data-independent shifts, XORs, and masks to ensure constant-time execution on the Cortex-M4. Algorithm 2 explicitly reflects this pipeline: Lines 3–6 correspond to Decomposition and Padding (Pad is applied at Line 5); Line 7 invokes Algorithm 1 as the Multiplication core; Lines 10–11 implement Unpadding; Lines 13–16 perform the 16-to-32-bit Reassembly; and Line 17 assembles the final output at byte-aligned offsets.

Algorithm 2 Top-level constant-time multiplication pipeline, illustrated for the 64-bit base multiplier; the 128-bit variant applies the similar structure with wider Unpad and Reassembly stages.

Require: Bitstrings A, B of length N (multiple of 8)
Ensure: Product bitstring P (length $\leq 2N$)
1: $k \leftarrow N/8$ ▷ number of 8-bit chunks
2: Allocate arrays $X[0..k-1], Y[0..k-1]$ ▷ zero-padded 32-bit words
3: **for** $i \leftarrow 0$ to $k-1$ **do**
4: $a_i \leftarrow i$-th 8-bit chunk of A; $b_i \leftarrow i$-th 8-bit chunk of B
5: $X[i] \leftarrow \text{Pad}(a_i)$; $Y[i] \leftarrow \text{Pad}(b_i)$
6: **end for**
7: $C \leftarrow \text{KARATSUBA}(X, Y, k)$ ▷ Algorithm 1
8: Allocate array $Z[0..(4k-1)]$ ▷ packed 16-bit words
9: **for** $j \leftarrow 0$ to $2k-1$ **do**
10: $(\ell, h) \leftarrow \text{Unpad}(C[j])$
11: $Z[2j] \leftarrow \ell$; $Z[2j+1] \leftarrow h$
12: **end for**
13: Allocate array $P_w[0..(2k-1)]$ ▷ final 32-bit words
14: **for** $t \leftarrow 0$ to $2k-1$ **do**
15: $P_w[t] \leftarrow Z[2t] \,|\, (Z[2t+1] \ll 16)$
16: **end for**
17: Assemble P from P_w at byte-aligned offsets
18: **return** P

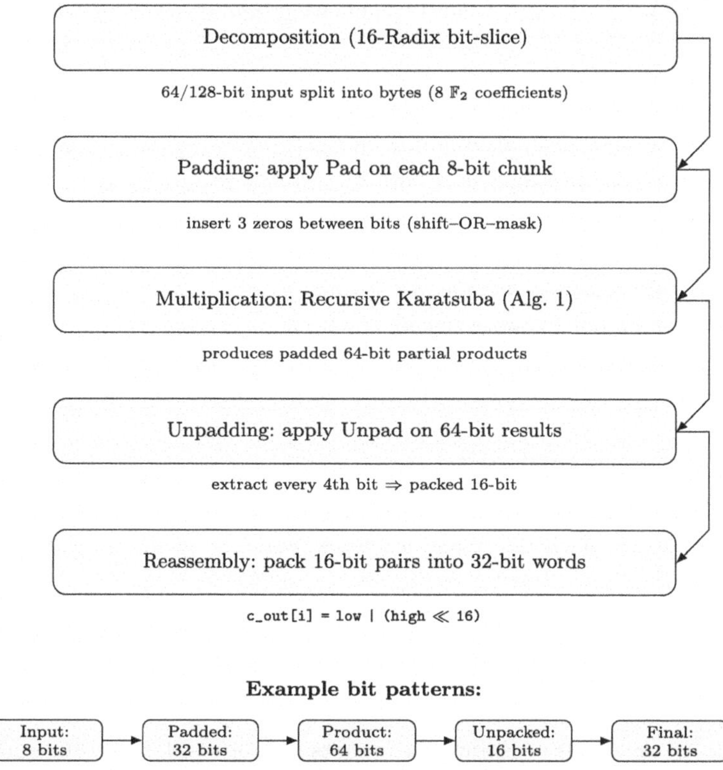

Fig. 4. Five-stage dataflow of the proposed multiplier, shown for the 64-bit variant; the 128-bit case follows the similar structure with adjusted block widths.

4 Evaluation

In this section, we implemented two constant-time base multipliers: `ct_poly32_mul_64_bit`, which returns padded 64-bit words, and `ct_poly32_mul_128_bit`, which extends the recursion to produce 128-bit outputs. Both variants were benchmarked on the STM32F407 Cortex-M4 under aggressive compiler optimization (`OPT=-O3`). The exact combinations of Karatsuba levels and their operation modes are summarized separately in Table 1.

4.1 Experimental Platform

All experiments were conducted on the STM32F407G-DISC1 evaluation board, equipped with an STMicroelectronics STM32F407G microcontroller. The device integrates a 32-bit ARM Cortex-M4 core with a hardware floating-point unit (FPU) and operates at a maximum clock frequency of 168 MHz. It provides 1 MB of on-chip Flash memory and 192 KB of SRAM, which provide sufficient resources for cryptographic implementations. The STM32F407G-DISC1 thus represents a typical resource-constrained embedded platform for evaluating lightweight cryptographic algorithms.

Table 1. Karatsuba level combinations and operation modes

Combination	Operation mode
Baseline	Pure schoolbook multiplication
L3 only	Karatsuba applied at 4-word level; 2-word blocks remain schoolbook
L3+L4	Karatsuba applied at both 4-word and 2-word levels
L4 only	Karatsuba applied at 2-word level only
L2 only	Karatsuba applied at 8-word level
L2+L3	Recursive Karatsuba: 8→4-word
L2+L3+L4	Full multi-level recursion: 8→4→2
L2+L4	Top-level 8-word is schoolbook; only 2-word uses Karatsuba

4.2 Performance Evaluation

Table 2 summarizes the measured cycle counts across different Karatsuba variants in comparison with reference baselines. For reference, we include the original `poly64_mul0` [21] and constant-time `ct_poly64_mul1` [13]. Our proposed implementations (`ct_poly32_mul_64_bit` and `ct_poly32_mul_128_bit`) achieve competitive performance across multiple recursion levels (L2, L3, and L4), confirming the efficiency of the recursive design on 32-bit targets.

Table 2. Cycle counts of Karatsuba variants on Cortex-M4 (`OPT=-O3`)(unit : cc)

`Variant`	`poly64_mul0` [21]	`ct_poly64_mul1` [13]	`ct_poly32_mul_64_bit`	`ct_poly32_mul_128_bit`
Baseline	421	1,643	1,135	3,400
L3 only	421	1,641	1,171	3,392
L3+L4	421	1,641	1,207	3,407
L4 only	421	1,641	1,128	3,422
L2+L3	421	1,643	1,175	3,383
L2+L3+L4	421	1,643	1,231	3,510
L2+L4	421	1,643	1,124	3,407

Table 3 complements Table 2 by presenting the same results in relative terms. It reports the percentage differences in cycle counts with respect to the constant-time baseline (`ct_poly64_mul1` [13]) and the non-constant-time reference (`poly64_mul0` [21]).

As shown, the proposed `ct_poly32_mul_64_bit` achieves up to 31.6% improvement over the constant-time baseline (L2+L4 configuration), while deeper recursion (L2+L3+L4) slightly increases overhead due to additional subroutine calls.

Among our proposed designs, `ct_poly32_mul_64_bit` consistently outperformed `ct_poly32_mul_128_bit`. For the 64-bit variant, the L2+L4 configuration

Table 3. Relative performance (% difference) of Karatsuba variants on Cortex-M4

Variant	vs. ct_poly64_mul1 [13]	vs. poly64_mul0 [21]
Baseline	+30.92%	−169.60%
L3 only	+28.64%	−178.15%
L3+L4	+26.45%	−186.70%
L4 only	+31.26%	−167.93%
L2+L3	+28.48%	−179.10%
L2+L3+L4	+25.08%	−192.40%
L2+L4	+31.59%	−166.98%

achieved the best result with 1,124 cycles, making it the most efficient option on Cortex-M4. In the 128-bit variant, the L2+L3 configuration was the fastest, requiring 3,383 cycles, though still about three times slower than the 64-bit design.

Across recursion levels, our implementations achieved a 25–31% improvement over the constant-time reference [13]. This gain is attributable not only to the recursive Karatsuba structure but also to reduced packing and unpacking overhead, as these operations are performed only once at the 128-bit granularity rather than repeatedly at smaller widths. Although the absolute fastest multiplier remains `poly64_mul0` [21] at 421 cycles, it is not constant-time and therefore unsuitable for secure applications.

Overall, the results demonstrate that our proposed `ct_poly32_mul_64_bit` with selective recursion (notably L2+L4) offers the best balance between efficiency and constant-time security, whereas `ct_poly32_mul_128_bit` provides scalability at the cost of higher cycle overhead.

5 Conclusion

In this paper, we presented a high-speed, constant-time implementation of radix-16 polynomial multiplication on the ARM Cortex-M4. By integrating recursive Karatsuba layers into the radix-16 zero-padding framework, we replaced the conventional schoolbook multiplier with a more efficient design while preserving constant-time execution. Our five-stage pipeline—Decomposition, Padding, Multiplication, Unpadding, and Reassembly—was carefully optimized to minimize packing overhead at the 128-bit granularity.

Experimental results on the STM32F407 Cortex-M4 demonstrated that the proposed `ct_poly32_mul_64_bit` implementation achieves up to 31% improvement over the best existing constant-time baseline, confirming the effectiveness of recursive Karatsuba on resource-constrained devices. These results highlight the practicality of our approach for accelerating polynomial arithmetic in code-based and lattice-based post-quantum cryptography on embedded microcontrollers.

Future work will primarily focus on integrating the proposed multiplier into post-quantum cryptographic schemes such as HQC and AIMer on the Cortex-M4, aiming to enhance their performance on resource-constrained embedded platforms. In addition, while our main target remains public-key primitives, the proposed multiplier could also be applied to symmetric-key settings—for example, accelerating the GHASH component of Galois/Counter Mode (GCM)—as a secondary possibility.

Acknowledgment. This work was supported by Institute for Information & communications Technology Promotion(IITP) grant funded by the Korea government(MSIT) (No.2018-0-00264, Research on Blockchain Security Technology for IoT Services, 10%) and this work was supported by Institute of Information & communications Technology Planning & Evaluation (IITP) grant funded by the Korea government(MSIT) (No. RS-2025-02306395, Development and Demonstration of PQC-Based Joint Certificate PKI Technology, 45%) and this work was supported by the Institute of Information & Communications Technology Planning & Evaluation(IITP) grant funded by the Korea government(MSIT) (No. RS-2025-25394739, Development of Security Enhancement Technology for Industrial Control Systems Based on S/HBOM Supply Chain Protection, 45%).

References

1. Lemire, D., Kaser, O.: Faster 64-bit universal hashing using carry-less multiplications. J. Cryptogr. Eng. **6**(3), 171–185 (2016)
2. Lopez, J., Cadena, V., Rahman, M.S.: Evaluating post-quantum cryptographic algorithms on resource-constrained devices, arXiv preprint arXiv:2507.08312 (2025)
3. Atkins, D.: Requirements for post-quantum cryptography on embedded devices in the IoT. In: Third PQC Standardization Conference (2021)
4. Nielsen, M.V., Kjeldsen, M.R., Turnip, T., Andersen, B.: Post-quantum digital signature algorithms on IoT: evaluating performance on lora ESP32 microcontroller. In: 22nd International Conference on Security and Cryptography (2025)
5. Knuth, D.E.: The Art of Computer Programming, Volume 2: Seminumerical Algorithms, 3rd edn. Addison-Wesley (1997)
6. Karatsuba, A., Ofman, Y.: Multiplication of multidigit numbers on automata. Soviet Phys. Doklady **7**(7), 595–596 (1963)
7. Seo, H., Liu, Z., Choi, J., Kim, H.: Karatsuba-block-comb technique for elliptic curve cryptography over binary fields. Secur. Commun. Netw. **8**(17), 3121–3130 (2015)
8. Erdem, S.S.: Fast software multiplication in $\mathbb{F}_2[x]$ for embedded processors. Turk. J. Electr. Eng. Comput. Sci. **20**(4), 593–605 (2012)
9. Kannwischer, M.J.: Polynomial multiplication for post-quantum cryptography. Ph.D. thesis, Sl: sn (2022)
10. Chen, M.-S., Chou, T.: Classic mceliece on the arm cortex-m4. IACR Transactions on Cryptographic Hardware and Embedded Systems, pp. 125–148 (2021)
11. Zheng, J., et al.: ESPM-D: efficient sparse polynomial multiplication for dilithium on arm Cortex-M4 and Apple M2, arXiv preprint arXiv:2404.12675 (2024)

12. Kim, D., Choi, J., Yoon, S., Seo, S.C.: Optimized implementation of HQC on cortex-M4. ICT Exp. (2025)
13. Bernstein, D.J.: KPQC Google Group post, 2023. Code snippet: ct_poly64_mul1 (KPQC post)
14. Brent, R.P., Zimmermann, P.: Modern Computer Arithmetic. Cambridge University Press (2010)
15. STMicroelectronics: STM32F407xx datasheet. Datasheet (device-specific; e.g. STM32F407VG), 2014. Device datasheet and electrical characteristics; see ST product page for exact part and revision
16. STMicroelectronics: STM32F405/407 and related devices — Reference Manual (RM0090), 2012. Reference manual for STM32F405xx/STM32F407xx advanced ARM-based 32-bit MCUs; check ST site for revision number
17. Kannwischer, M.J., Rijneveld, J., Schwabe, P., Stoffelen, K.: PQM4: testing and benchmarking NIST PQC on arm Cortex-M4 (2019)
18. Owens, D., El Khatib, R., Bisheh-Niasar, M., Azarderakhsh, R., Kermani, M.M.: Efficient and side-channel resistant ED25519 on arm Cortex-M4. IEEE Trans. Circuits Syst. I Regul. Pap. **71**(6), 2674–2686 (2024)
19. Anastasova, M., Bisheh-Niasar, M., Seo, H., Azarderakhsh, R., Kermani, M.M.: Efficient and side-channel resistant design of high-security ED448 on arm Cortex-M4. In: 2022 IEEE International Symposium on Hardware Oriented Security and Trust (HOST), pp. 93–96. IEEE (2022)
20. Fujii, H., Aranha, D.F.: Curve25519 for the Cortex-M4 and beyond. In: International Conference on Cryptology and Information Security in Latin America, pp. 109–127. Springer (2017)
21. López, J., Dahab, R.: Fast multiplication on elliptic curves over GF (2M) without precomputation. In: International Workshop on Cryptographic Hardware and Embedded Systems, pp. 316–327. Springer (1999)

Maximizing ARIA-CTR Performance Through Kernel-Level Memory Optimization on the Apple M1 GPU

Siwoo Eum, Minho Song, and Minjoo Sim(✉)

Department of Information Computer Engineering, Hansung University, Seoul 02876, South Korea
minjoos9797@gmail.com

Abstract. The emergence of CPU-GPU integrated System-on-Chip architectures like Apple's M1 has made Unified Memory Architecture mainstream in computing. While UMA eliminated the CPU-GPU data copy overhead that was a major bottleneck in traditional dGPU systems, it shifted the optimization focus to kernel-internal memory access patterns. This paper analyzes how memory optimization strategies based on data access patterns affect cryptographic algorithm performance in SoC environments. We implemented the block cipher ARIA in Counter (CTR) mode on Apple M1 GPU using the Metal framework, designing six implementation configurations that systematically vary the storage locations of ARIA's primary data structures—S-boxes and round keys—across device, threadgroup, and constant memory spaces. Experimental results confirmed that memory strategies optimized for data access patterns have a decisive impact on performance. A hybrid strategy placing S-boxes with irregular access patterns in threadgroup memory and round keys with uniform broadcast access patterns in constant memory achieved 451.93 MB/s throughput, representing 47.07% improvement over the baseline configuration. These findings demonstrate that precisely analyzing data access patterns and utilizing appropriate memory hierarchies remains key for maximizing GPU kernel performance even in UMA environments.

Keywords: ARIA · GPU Computing · Apple M1 · Unified Memory Architecture · Memory Optimization · Metal

1 Introduction

The exponential growth of digital data has highlighted the critical importance of data protection across modern society. As sensitive information is increasingly stored and transmitted digitally, cryptographic technologies ensuring data confidentiality, integrity, and availability have become fundamental cybersecurity elements. The need to protect vast amounts of real-time data in cloud computing, big data analytics, and IoT environments has driven the development of high-performance cryptography beyond simple encryption implementations.

H. Seo (Ed.): ICISC 2025, LNCS 16487, pp. 400–414, 2026.
https://doi.org/10.1007/978-981-95-8034-7_21

Graphics Processing Units(GPUs), specialized for large-scale parallel processing, have attracted attention as platforms for accelerating cryptographic operations [6,12]. Recent computing architectures are experiencing a paradigm shift with CPU-GPU integrated System-on-a-Chip(SoC) like Apple's M-series chips becoming mainstream in mobile, desktop, and laptop markets. These SoCs adopt fundamentally different memory models from traditional PC architectures, requiring reconsideration of existing optimization methodologies [7].

Apple's M1 chip adopts Unified Memory Architecture(UMA), where CPU and GPU share the same physical memory pool. This eliminates the explicit data copy overhead between CPU and GPU memory, which was a major bottleneck in discrete GPU systems [5]. However, UMA does not make all memory access costs uniform. Complex memory hierarchies still exist within the GPU, consisting of registers, threadgroup memory, constant memory cache, L1/L2 caches, and system RAM [12,16]. This raises important questions: how dependent is GPU kernel performance on internal memory hierarchy when host-device transfer costs are eliminated? Are traditional GPU optimization techniques still valid in new architectures like M1?

The core paradox is that while UMA freed programmers from explicit memory copying burdens, kernel-internal memory access latency has emerged as the decisive performance factor. The optimization battlefield has shifted from PCIe buses to subtle GPU core-memory interactions. Some research showing performance degradation compared to dGPUs despite UMA demonstrates potential pitfalls when UMA is regarded as 'one giant memory pool' while ignoring internal hierarchical characteristics [8].

Based on these issues, this paper explores the impact of memory strategies on performance when implementing and optimizing the ARIA block cipher in Apple M1 GPU environment. Section 2 describes ARIA algorithm, CTR mode, and M1 GPU architecture. Section 3 explains six ARIA-CTR implementation strategies. Section 4 presents experimental methodology, results, and analysis. Section 5 summarizes conclusions and future directions.

2 Related Work

2.1 ARIA Block Cipher [10]

ARIA is a 128-bit block cipher algorithm jointly developed in 2003 by cryptographic experts from academia, research institutions, and industry under the leadership of the National Security Research Institute(NSRI) of South Korea. It was established as a Korean standard (KS X 1213) in 2004 and was subsequently published as RFC 5794 [9] by the IETF(Internet Engineering Task Force), securing international recognition [13].

ARIA is based on a Substitution-Permutation Network(SPN) structure similar to AES algorithm, which is currently an international standard. The SPN structure is a method that makes the relationship between input and output nonlinearly complex by repeatedly applying substitution and permutation operations to data blocks. ARIA has a fixed block size of 128 bits and supports three key lengths: 128, 192, and 256 bits. Depending on the key length used, it performs 12, 14, or 16 rounds of encryption processes respectively, with a unique 128-bit round key used for each round.

Each round of ARIA consists of three core operation layers:

- **Round Key Addition:** This is the process of performing bitwise XOR ($\oplus$) operation between the 128-bit (16-byte) intermediate data state and the 128-bit round key assigned to that round. This is the most fundamental operation that makes the security of the cipher dependent on the key.
- **Substitution Layer:** This is a core operation that provides non-linearity to the cipher and satisfies the confusion property. It substitutes the 16-byte state on a byte-by-byte basis using S-boxes (Substitution-boxes), which are 8-bit input/output lookup tables. ARIA uses a total of four different S-boxes ($S_1, S_2, S_1^{-1}, S_2^{-1}$), applying them in different combinations for odd and even rounds to break symmetry and enhance cryptographic strength.
- **Diffusion Layer:** This is a linear operation layer that provides the diffusion property of the cipher. It ensures that a single bit change in the state affects multiple bits in the next round, making statistical analysis difficult. ARIA performs diffusion by multiplying the state vector with a fixed 16×16 binary matrix, and this matrix multiplication is actually implemented efficiently as a combination of simple XOR operations [15].

Memory Access Pattern Analysis. The performance of GPU kernels is largely determined by how well the algorithm's memory access patterns align with the characteristics of the GPU's memory subsystem. The core data requiring memory access in ARIA—S-boxes and round keys—exhibit very contrasting access patterns.

- **S-box:** Access to S-box tables in the substitution layer is determined by the data being encrypted, i.e., the byte values of the state. This is data-dependent access. When hundreds of threads within a GPU threadgroup simultaneously process different data blocks, each thread's state values are likely to be different. Therefore, simultaneous access to S-box tables exhibits an **irregular scatter/gather** pattern distributed across the entire memory address space. Moreover, this S-box lookup operation occurs very **frequently**, hundreds of times per block (e.g., for 128-bit keys: 12 rounds $\times$ 16 bytes $=$ 192 times).
- **Round Key:** In round key addition operations, all threads processing a specific round (e.g., round 3) read and use the **identical** round 3 key value. While the access location moves sequentially to the next round key as rounds progress, within a single round, all threads' memory accesses concentrate on a single address, showing a very **uniform** pattern. This corresponds to a typical broadcast access pattern.

The fundamentally different access patterns of S-boxes and round keys strongly suggest that storing them in the same type of memory may be inefficient. Irregular and frequent access is suited for low-latency memory close to the cores, while uniform broadcast access benefits from utilizing specialized hardware caching and delivery mechanisms. Therefore, optimal performance requires understanding the access patterns of operations that require memory access in algorithm design and placing them in specialized memory spaces that match those patterns.‘

2.2 Counter Mode

Block Cipher Mode of Operation defines methods for encrypting arbitrary-length data using block ciphers that process fixed-size blocks. CTR (Counter) mode is one such mode, characterized by its ability to use a block cipher like a stream cipher.

The operating principle of CTR mode is as follows. For each plaintext block to be encrypted, an input block is created by combining a nonce (a random value that is not reused) with a sequentially incrementing counter value. This input block is encrypted with the encryption key to generate a keystream block. Finally, this generated keystream is XORed bitwise with the corresponding plaintext block to obtain the final ciphertext block [1]. Decryption follows exactly the same process as encryption: XORing the ciphertext with the same keystream restores the original plaintext.

$$C_i = P_i \oplus E_K(\text{Nonce}\|\text{Counter}_i) \quad (1)$$

$$P_i = C_i \oplus E_K(\text{Nonce}\|\text{Counter}_i) \quad (2)$$

The most important and powerful characteristic of CTR mode is **parallelizability**. The process of computing the i-th keystream block has no correlation whatsoever with the computation of any other j-th keystream block. That is, the encryption process (more precisely, keystream generation) for all blocks can be performed completely independently of each other. This characteristic stands in stark contrast to CBC (Cipher Block Chaining) mode, which has sequential dependencies (e.g., the previous ciphertext block is used as input for the next plaintext block). The perfect parallelism of CTR mode ideally matches the GPU's SIMT (Single Instruction, Multiple Threads) execution model, where thousands of threads can be assigned different counter values to simultaneously generate keystreams, thereby maximizing encryption throughput.

2.3 Apple M1 GPU Architecture and Metal Memory Model

Unified Memory Architecture (UMA). Apple's M1 chip is a SoC with CPU cores, GPU cores, Neural Engine, and other I/O controllers highly integrated on a single silicon die. One of the defining features of this chip is its Unified Memory Architecture (UMA). In traditional dGPU systems, the CPU and GPU each had separate physical memory (system DRAM and GPU VRAM) and communicated through the PCIe bus. This required explicit data copying using APIs like ‘cudaMemcpy‘before and after GPU work, causing significant latency and bandwidth bottlenecks in GPU-accelerated data processing.

In contrast, M1's UMA allows all processing units to directly share LPDDR4X system RAM [7]. Since the CPU and GPU access the same physical address space, the concept of data copying itself disappears. Data written to memory by the CPU can be immediately read by the GPU without any transfer process, and vice versa. This provides many benefits including dramatically reduced data transfer latency, simplified programming models, and improved energy efficiency [5].

Memory of Metal Shading Language. Metal is a low-level graphics and computing API provided for GPU programming on Apple platforms. MSL, Metal's shader programming language, provides several address space qualifiers to specify the location and characteristics of memory where data is stored within GPU kernel code. Using the correct address space according to data access patterns is key to optimizing performance on the M1 GPU.

- **device**: Points to the main memory space accessible by GPU kernels. In a UMA environment, this corresponds to system RAM. It has the largest capacity and serves as the foundation for data sharing between CPU and GPU, but has the longest access latency as it is physically furthest from GPU cores. Buffers declared without special optimization are located in this space by default.
- **threadgroup**: Very fast on-chip memory shared by all threads within a single threadgroup (equivalent to CUDA blocks or OpenCL workgroups) [11]. This operates like scratchpad memory that programmers must explicitly load, store, and manage. Access latency is tens to hundreds of times shorter than `device` memory, making it ideal for caching frequently reused data within a threadgroup to minimize `device` memory access.
- **constant**: A memory space specially designed for read-only data that does not change during kernel execution. Data in this space is accessed through a separate read-only data cache, the constant cache. The most important feature of this memory space is hardware-level broadcast optimization. When all threads within a warp (typically a bundle of 32 threads) simultaneously attempt to read the same address in `constant` memory, the hardware processes this request with a single memory read and efficiently delivers the result to all threads. This greatly reduces memory bandwidth usage and provides significant performance improvements for uniform read access patterns [2,17].
- **thread**: The fastest and smallest private memory space belonging to each individual thread. The MSL compiler primarily attempts to allocate variables declared in this space to the GPU's physical registers.

3 Comparison of SoC GPU and dGPU

3.1 SoC GPU: Unified Memory Architecture (UMA)

SoC GPUs feature various processor cores including CPU, GPU, and Neural Engine integrated within a single chip or package. Apple's UMA is a prime example that maximizes the advantages of this structure. UMA is an architecture where physically unified memory is shared by all processors in the system. Unlike traditional approaches where CPU and GPU have separate memory spaces, this eliminates the need for separate copy processes for data transfer. Consequently, data access latency is dramatically reduced and overall system power efficiency is improved. This can be understood as a concept of data 'sharing' rather than 'movement'.

3.2 dGPU: Discrete and Software-Level Unified Memory

dGPUs are mounted on independent processor boards together with VRAM. They connect to the system's main memory(System RAM) through PCIe(Peripheral Component Interconnect Express) buses to exchange data. While this structure allows GPUs to secure large amounts of dedicated memory for extreme parallel computation, explicit or implicit data copying through the PCIe bus is essential during data exchange between CPU and GPU. NVIDIA's CUDA Unified Memory is a software-level abstraction designed to address the programming inconvenience of this discrete structure. Memory allocated through APIs like *cudaMallocManaged* appears as a single address space to both CPU and GPU, but internally the data moves to the physical memory of the processor that needs it. While this improves programmer convenience, latency from data movement still exists due to hardware constraints (Fig. 1).

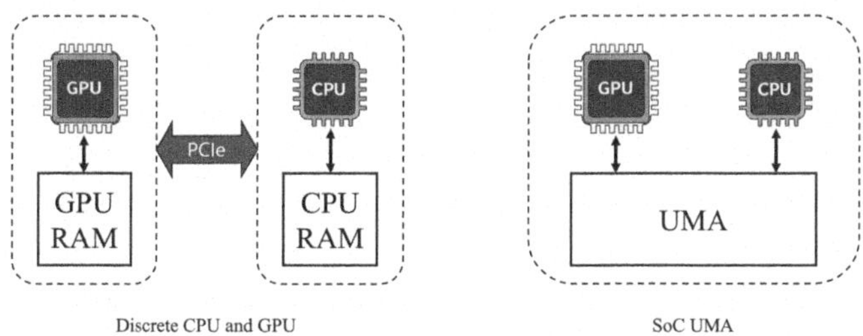

Fig. 1. Schematic diagram of the memory architecture of dGPU and SoC GPU. The left side shows a separated structure where the CPU and GPU each use independent memory (System RAM, VRAM), and the right side shows a unified memory structure where they share a single physical memory.

SoC GPUs and dGPUs are architectures that have evolved based on different design philosophies. SoC GPUs focus on overall system efficiency and responsiveness. Through unified memory structures, they demonstrate excellent performance in complex workflows like video editing and graphic design where CPU and GPU must work organically together. Their advantages are particularly maximized in mobile and laptop environments where power consumption is limited. In contrast, dGPUs target maximum peak throughput. They provide overwhelming performance in tasks such as large-scale AI model training or scientific simulations that require housing vast amounts of data within the GPU and performing extreme parallel computations independently.

4 Implementation Strategy of ARIA-CTR on M1 GPU

The core hypothesis of this study is that "memory space selection optimized for data access patterns remains an important factor for performance optimization even in UMA environments". To experimentally verify this, we design and implement six specific implementation models that systematically vary the memory storage locations of the two key data structures in the ARIA encryption algorithm: S-box tables and round keys.

Previous research in dGPU environments has extensively analyzed the impact of memory hierarchy utilization on performance. In particular, it has been proven that simply moving frequently accessed lookup tables like S-box tables from global memory to shared memory can achieve significant performance improvements [3,4,14].

This study aims to empirically verify whether such memory optimization strategies remain equally effective in integrated GPUs in SoC environments. In UMA environments, since CPU and GPU share the same physical memory, they may exhibit different characteristics from traditional dGPU memory hierarchies. Therefore, the core of this research is to confirm whether memory access pattern optimization still has a decisive impact on performance in such environments.

All models are written using Metal Shading Language(MSL) and are based on ARIA-128-CTR (Table 1).

Table 1. ARIA Kernels: Memory Usage Comparison

Type	Kernel Name	S-box	Round Keys
1	`device_kernel`	`device`	`device`
2	`threadgroup_kernel`	`threadgroup`	`device`
3	`constant_kernel`	`constant`	`device`
4	`threadgroup_kernel_threadgroup_rk`	`threadgroup`	`threadgroup`
5	`threadgroup_kernel_constant_rk`	`threadgroup`	`constant`
6	`device_kernel_constant_rk`	`device`	`constant`

4.1 Type 1: S-Box in Device, Round Keys in Device

This implementation represents the most straightforward and intuitive approach. All data required for ARIA encryption is placed in the default memory space, 'device' memory. Specifically, both the S-box tables and the array of 13 128-bit round keys generated from the 128-bit key are passed to the kernel as 'MTL-Buffer' residing in 'device' memory. The GPU encryption kernel directly queries S-boxes in 'device' memory for every round and every byte substitution operation, and also directly reads round keys from 'device' memory for round key addition.

The goal is to measure performance when no additional optimizations are performed on the GPU's sophisticated internal memory hierarchy. The performance measurements of this model serve as a clear baseline for comparing and evaluating the performance improvements of other optimization models. This enables quantitative isolation and analysis of the pure effects of each optimization technique applied in subsequent models.

4.2 Type 2: S-Box in Threadgroup Memory, Round Keys in Device

This implementation applies the most classic and effective technique for optimizing lookup table-based algorithms in dGPU environments to the M1 environment [14]. It aims to improve performance by moving the S-box tables, which have the highest access frequency and most irregular access patterns during encryption operations, to high-speed on-chip 'threadgroup' memory. When the kernel begins execution, each threadgroup copies the original S-box table from 'device' memory to its 'threadgroup' memory space only once. After this initial copying operation is completed, all S-box lookup operations throughout the 12 rounds of encryption are performed through 'threadgroup' memory with extremely low access latency, rather than 'device' memory. Round keys remain in 'device' memory as in the baseline model.

The objective is to measure how effectively 'threadgroup' memory can resolve the performance bottleneck caused by the relatively high latency of 'device' memory due to frequent and irregular access patterns of S-boxes. Through performance comparison with Implementation 1, we can confirm whether 'threadgroup' memory utilization remains a core optimization strategy even in the M1 UMA environment.

4.3 Type 3: S-Box in Constant Memory, Round Keys in Device

This implementation attempts to improve S-box lookup performance by utilizing constant memory specialized for read-only data access. Based on the characteristic that S-box tables never change during the encryption process, they are placed in the constant memory region. Round keys are maintained in device memory as in the baseline model (Implementation 1). The GPU kernel queries S-boxes located in constant memory for every round and every byte substitution operation, benefiting from caches optimized for constant memory. Round keys are read directly from device memory as before.

The goal of this implementation is to evaluate how efficiently S-box access patterns can be processed through constant memory's caching mechanisms. While S-box lookups are read-only, access locations vary depending on the content of data blocks being encrypted, potentially causing divergent access patterns between threads. The purpose is to confirm how much performance improvement constant memory cache provides for such irregular read access compared to direct ‘device‘ memory access(Type 1), and what performance differences exist compared to explicitly managed ‘threadgroup‘ memory(Type 2).

4.4 Type 4: S-Box in Threadgroup Memory, Round Keys in Constant Memory

This implementation uses a hybrid optimization strategy that assigns the most suitable memory type for each data's access pattern characteristics. S-boxes with irregular and frequent access patterns are placed in threadgroup memory as in Implementation 2 to minimize access latency. Simultaneously, round keys, which are read-only and commonly used by all threads, are placed in constant memory. When the kernel executes, threadgroups copy S-boxes to threadgroup memory and access round keys through constant memory to perform round key addition operations.

The goal of this implementation is to verify how effective customized memory hierarchy utilization based on data access patterns can be. It aims to confirm whether synergy can be created by combining the advantages of threadgroup memory, which is strong against irregular access, and constant memory optimized for read-only uniform access. In particular, the purpose is to explore the optimal combination that most effectively utilizes the characteristics of each memory layer in GPU architecture by comparing and analyzing performance changes when round keys are placed in constant memory instead of device memory(Type 2) or threadgroup memory(Type 5).

4.5 Type 5: S-Box in Threadgroup Memory, Round Keys in Threadgroup Memory

This implementation represents the most aggressive optimization approach that places both core data required for encryption operations—S-boxes and round keys—in threadgroup memory to maximize performance. When the kernel starts, each threadgroup copies both the original S-box tables and all 13 round keys from device memory to its threadgroup memory space. Subsequently, byte substitution and round key addition operations in all rounds are performed exclusively within ultra-fast threadgroup memory, with no device memory access occurring except during the initial copying phase.

The purpose of this implementation is to measure the maximum performance improvement achievable when all frequently accessed data is moved to the fastest programmer-managed memory. In particular, it aims to confirm whether moving not only S-boxes with irregular access patterns but also round keys with relatively regular access patterns to threadgroup memory provides additional performance benefits. Through performance comparison with Type 2(using threadgroup memory only for S-boxe), it quantitatively evaluates whether the initial copying overhead and increased memory usage of moving round keys to threadgroup memory is worthwhile.

4.6 Type 6: S-Box in Device Memory, Round Keys in Constant Memory

This implementation employs a selective optimization strategy to isolate and measure the effect of optimizing round key access. Of the algorithm's core data, the S-box tables remain in default device memory, identical to Type 1, while only the round keys, which are read-only and accessed uniformly, are moved to constant memory. When the kernel executes, S-box lookups for byte substitution operations are performed by directly accessing device memory, whereas round key addition operations are performed via the caching mechanism of constant memory.

The primary objective of this implementation is to quantitatively isolate and evaluate the impact of round key access pattern optimization on overall performance. By intentionally leaving S-box access unoptimized(using device memory), this model measures the performance improvement gained solely from optimizing round key access.

A performance comparison with Type 1(Device/Device) directly shows how much performance gain can be achieved by only changing round key access from device to constant memory. Furthermore, a comparison with Type 3(Constant/Device) provides a basis for analyzing whether the constant memory cache is more effective for the irregular access of S-boxes(Type 3) or the uniform access of round keys(Type 6).

5 Experimental Results and Analysis

5.1 Experimental Environment and Performance Measurement Method

Table 2. Experimental Environment for Performance Measurement

Category	Specification
Model	MacBook Pro (MacBookPro17,1)
Chip	Apple M1
CPU	8-core (4 performance + 4 efficiency)
GPU	Apple M1 8-core integrated GPU
Memory	8 GB Unified Memory (UMA)
Operating System	macOS 15.5 Sequoia (Build 24F74, ARM64)
Development Language	Swift 6.1.2
GPU Framework	Metal (Version 32023.620)

This chapter quantitatively measures and comparatively analyzes the performance of the five GPU implementation models of the ARIA encryption algorithm designed in Sect. 3. The objective is to confirm the actual degree of performance improvement that memory optimization techniques applied to each implementation model bring in Apple M1's Unified Memory Architecture(UMA) environment and to evaluate the effectiveness of each technique.

The detailed performance measurement environment is shown in Table 2.

The encryption processing performance of each implementation model was measured by distributing computations to the GPU through the Metal framework. The ultimate goal of this experiment is to perform a total of $\mathbf{2^{35}}$ ARIA-CTR-128 encryption operations. To efficiently handle this massive workload, the GPU kernel was executed with the following configuration:

- **Threads Per Threadgroup:** `MTLSize(width: 512, height: 1, depth: 1)` One threadgroup consists of 512 threads.
- **Threadgroups Per Grid:** `MTLSize(width: 1024, height: 1, depth: 1)` The entire grid consists of 1024 threadgroups.
- **Total Threads:** $512 \times 1024 =$ **524,288 threads**

This means that a total of 524,288 threads execute simultaneously in a single kernel call. The entire workload of 2^{35} block encryptions is evenly distributed among these 524,288 threads. All threads encrypt different data blocks without duplication, effectively utilizing the parallelization characteristics of counter mode. Each thread was implemented to repeatedly perform encryption operations within a loop until completing its assigned workload.

The core performance metric was set as the **Total Execution Time** required for each implementation model to encrypt the entire workload (2^{35} blocks), using **seconds(s)** as the unit. Throughput(MB/s) was calculated from the measured units for performance comparison and analysis.

5.2 Performance Analysis

(see Table 3).

Table 3. Performance comparison of different memory configurations for ARIA-CTR

Type	S-box	Round Keys	Time (s)	MB/s
Type 1	Device	Device	106.64	307.32
Type 2	Threadgroup	Device	96.75	338.70
Type 3	Constant	Device	115.08	284.73
Type 4	Threadgroup	Threadgroup	73.58	445.12
Type 5	**Threadgroup**	**Constant**	**72.52**	**451.93**
Type 6	Device	Constant	80.52	406.90

The experimental results demonstrate significant performance variations based on memory placement strategies (Fig. 2):

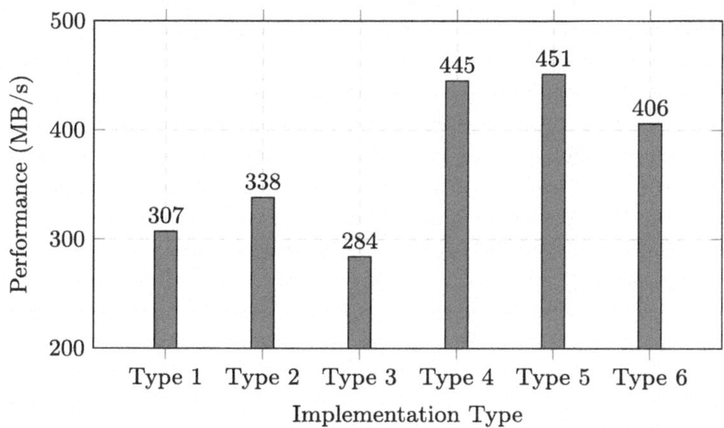

Fig. 2. Performance comparison of different memory configurations for ARIA-CTR

Best Performance Configuration(Type 5): The optimal configuration achieved 451.93 MB/s throughput with S-boxes in shared memory and round keys in constant memory. This configuration completed the workload in 72.52 s, representing a 47.07% improvement over the baseline Type 1 configuration.

Impact of S-Box Memory Placement: Comparing Types 1, 2, and 3 (all with round keys in device memory), we observe:

- Device memory S-boxes (Type 1): 307.32 MB/s
- Threadgroup memory S-boxes (Type 2): 338.70 MB/s
- Constant memory S-boxes (Type 3): 284.73 MB/s

Interestingly, threadgroup memory configuration outperformed both device and constant memory when round keys remained in device memory, showing a 10.2% improvement over the baseline device memory configuration.

Impact of Round Key Memory Placement:

When S-boxes are in threadgroup memory (Types 2, 4, 5):

- Round keys in constant memory (Type 5): 451.93 MB/s
- Round keys in threadgroup memory (Type 4): 445.12 MB/s
- Round keys in device memory (Type 2): 338.70 MB/s

When S-boxes are in device memory (Types 1, 6):

- Round keys in constant memory (Type 6): 406.90 MB/s
- Round keys in device memory (Type 1): 307.32 MB/s

This clearly demonstrates that constant memory is the optimal location for round keys, providing consistent performance improvements of 33.4% (threadgroup S-box) and 32.4% (device S-box) over device memory placement.

The experimental results clearly demonstrate that memory utilization strategies optimized for data access patterns have a decisive impact on performance in modern SoC environments, just as in discrete GPU (dGPU) environments. In particular, for operations with irregular memory access patterns such as S-box substitution, where each thread references different locations in the table, we confirmed that using threadgroup memory with short access latency and fast intra-threadgroup data sharing is most effective. Conversely, round keys exhibit uniform access patterns where all threads within a warp simultaneously reference the same values. Storing pre-computed round key values in constant memory enables aggressive utilization of the constant cache's broadcast functionality, serving as a key factor in maximizing memory access efficiency and increasing overall throughput.

6 Conclusion

This study aimed to experimentally verify the impact of memory utilization strategies optimized for data access patterns on high-performance cryptographic kernel implementation in Unified Memory Architecture (UMA) environments such as Apple's M1. By implementing six configurations with different storage locations for S-boxes and round keys using the ARIA-128-CTR algorithm and measuring their performance, we clearly confirmed our core hypothesis that selecting memory spaces according to data access characteristics has a decisive impact on performance.

In particular, the hybrid strategy (Type 5) that places S-boxes with irregular and frequent references in `threadgroup` memory for high-speed data sharing within threadgroups, and round keys accessed simultaneously by all threads in `constant` memory to maximize hardware broadcast functionality benefits, achieved the highest throughput of 451.93 MB/s. This represents a 47.07% improvement over the baseline model (Type 1) with no memory optimization, suggesting that traditional GPU memory optimization principles remain valid and even more important amid the structural changes brought by UMA.

The most significant contribution of this study lies in empirically demonstrating that while UMA eliminated the macroscopic bottleneck of CPU-GPU data transfer, kernel-internal memory access latency has emerged as the key factor determining overall performance. This research shows that developers should not simply regard UMA as "one giant single memory pool", but rather must develop a deeper understanding of the subtle interactions between GPU cores and memory hierarchies, precisely analyze data access patterns, and make essential efforts to place data in optimal memory spaces.

Future research could verify generalizability by applying the same optimization methodology to other symmetric or public key cryptographic algorithms besides ARIA, or track performance changes in subsequent chip architectures such as M2 and M3 released after M1. Additionally, analyzing the interactions between memory strategies and other optimization variables such as threadgroup size or data placement would constitute meaningful follow-up research.

Acknowledgment. This work was supported by Institute for Information & communications Technology Promotion(IITP) grant funded by the Korea government(MSIT) (No. 2018-0-00264, Research on Blockchain Security Technology for IoT Services, 10%) and this work was supported by Institute of Information & communications Technology Planning & Evaluation (IITP) grant funded by the Korea government(MSIT) (No. RS-2025-02306395, Development and Demonstration of PQC-Based Joint Certificate PKI Technology, 45%) and this work was supported by the Institute of Information & Communications Technology Planning & Evaluation(IITP) grant funded by the Korea government(MSIT) (No. RS-2025-25394739, Development of Security Enhancement Technology for Industrial Control Systems Based on S/HBOM Supply Chain Protection, 45%).

References

1. An, S., Kim, Y., Kwon, H., Seo, H., Seo, S.C.: Parallel implementations of ARX-based block ciphers on graphic processing units. Mathematics **8**(11), 1894 (2020)
2. Apple Inc.: Advanced metal shader optimization. WWDC 2016, Session 606 (2016). https://developer.apple.com/videos/play/wwdc2016/606/. Accessed 16 Mar 2026
3. Eum, S., Kim, H., Kwon, H., Sim, M., Song, G., Seo, H.: Parallel implementations of aria on arm processors and graphics processing unit. Appl. Sci. **12**(23), 12246 (2022)
4. Eum, S., Song, M., Kim, S., Seo, H.: Efficient GPU parallel implementation and optimization of aria for counter and exhaustive key-search modes. Electronics **14**(10), 2021 (2025)
5. Gebraad, L., Fichtner, A.: Seamless GPU acceleration for C++-based physics with the metal shading language on apple's m series unified chips. Seismol. Soc. Am. **94**(3), 1670–1675 (2023)
6. Go, Y., Jamshed, M.A., Moon, Y., Hwang, C., Park, K.: {APUNet}: revitalizing {GPU} as packet processing accelerator. In: 14th USENIX Symposium on Networked Systems Design and Implementation (NSDI 2017), pp. 83–96 (2017)
7. Hübner, P., Hu, A., Peng, I., Markidis, S.: Apple vs. oranges: evaluating the apple silicon m-series socs for HPC performance and efficiency. arXiv preprint arXiv:2502.05317 (2025)
8. Jarząbek, Ł, Czarnul, P.: Performance evaluation of unified memory and dynamic parallelism for selected parallel CUDA applications. J. Supercomput. **73**, 5378–5401 (2017)
9. Kim, J., Lee, J., Kim, C., Lee, J., Kwon, D.: A Description of the ARIA Encryption Algorithm. RFC 5794 (2010). https://doi.org/10.17487/RFC5794. https://www.rfc-editor.org/info/rfc5794
10. Kwon, D., et al.: New block cipher: aria. In: International Conference on Information Security and Cryptology, pp. 432–445. Springer, Cham (2003)
11. Lee, W.K., Goi, B.M., Phan, R.C.W., Poh, G.S.: High speed implementation of symmetric block cipher on GPU. In: 2014 International Symposium on Intelligent Signal Processing and Communication Systems (ISPACS), pp. 102–107. IEEE (2014)
12. Li, Q., Zhong, C., Zhao, K., Mei, X., Chu, X.: Implementation and analysis of AES encryption on GPU. In: 2012 IEEE 14th International Conference on High Performance Computing and Communication & 2012 IEEE 9th International Conference on Embedded Software and Systems, pp. 843–848. IEEE (2012)

13. Seo, H., Kwon, H., Kim, H., Park, J.: ACE: aria-ctr encryption for low-end embedded processors. Sensors **20**(13), 3788 (2020)
14. Tezcan, C.: Optimization of advanced encryption standard on graphics processing units. IEEE Access **9**, 67315–67326 (2021)
15. Wu, W., Zhang, W., Feng, D.: Impossible differential cryptanalysis of aria and camellia. Cryptology ePrint Archive (2006)
16. Yi, X.: A study of performance programming of CPU, GPU accelerated computers and simd architecture. arXiv preprint arXiv:2409.10661 (2024)
17. Yuan, S., Awad, A., Yudha, A.W.B., Solihin, Y., Zhou, H.: Adaptive security support for heterogeneous memory on GPUs. In: 2022 IEEE International Symposium on High-Performance Computer Architecture (HPCA), pp. 213–228. IEEE (2022)

Optimized Frobenius and Cyclotomic Cubing for Enhanced Pairing Computation

Leila Ben Abdelghani[1], Nadia El Mrabet[2(✉)], Loubna Ghammam[3], and Lina Mortajine[3]

[1] Laboratory of Analysis, Probability and Fractals, University of Monastir, Boulevard de l'environnement, 5019 Monastir, Tunisia
leila.benabdelghani@fsm.rnu.tn

[2] Mines Saint-Etienne, Institut Mines-Télécom, CMP - SAS - Campus Aix Marseille Provence, Gardanne, France
nadia.el-mrabet@emse.fr

[3] ITK Engineering GmbH, Im Speyerer Tal 6, 76761 Rülzheim, Germany
{loubna.ghammam,lina.mortajine}@itk-engineering.de

Abstract. Efficient implementation of pairing-based cryptosystems relies on high-performance arithmetic in finite fields $\mathbb{F}_p$ and their extensions $\mathbb{F}_{p^k}$, where k denotes the embedding degree. A small embedding degree is crucial since a part of the arithmetic for pairing computation occurs in $\mathbb{F}_{p^k}$, including squaring, multiplication, and Frobenius operations. In this paper, we present a fast and efficient method for computing the Frobenius endomorphism in the finite field $\mathbb{F}_{p^k}$, along with an analysis of its computational complexity. Furthermore, we introduce an optimization for cyclotomic cubing operations tailored to several pairing-friendly elliptic curves, which are essential for the calculation of Tate pairing and its derivatives.

Keywords: Optimal Ate Pairing · Frobenius maps · Kronecker products · Finite fields · Cyclotomic cubing

1 Introduction

Bilinear pairing is a mathematical operation that maps a pair of points on an elliptic curve to an element of a finite field. Pairings on elliptic curves enable a wide range of advanced cryptographic constructions, including identity-based encryption [5], short signatures [6], and key exchange [10]. Their efficiency, however, depends heavily on the speed of pairing computation. Consequently, modern optimizations focus on pairing-friendly elliptic curves [9], efficient variants of the Tate pairing [14], and improvements to the two main components of pairing evaluation: Miller's algorithm and the final exponentiation [8].

To delve into the specifics of Miller's algorithm and final exponentiation, we consider E as an ordinary elliptic curve over the finite field $\mathbb{F}_p$, and let r be a large prime number that divides the order of the group of points $E(\mathbb{F}_p)$. The

H. Seo (Ed.): ICISC 2025, LNCS 16487, pp. 415–430, 2026.
https://doi.org/10.1007/978-981-95-8034-7_22

embedding degree k of E with respect to r and the prime number p is defined as the smallest integer k such that r divides $p^k - 1$. Miller's algorithm is used to compute an intermediate result, a function $f_{s,Q}(P)$ where P and Q are two points on the elliptic curve E, and s an integer related to the order of the points. This intermediate value, which is an element in the finite field $\mathbb{F}_{p^k}$, is raised to the power $\frac{p^k-1}{r}$ in order to ensure the unicity of the pairing. This final exponentiation is computationally demanding, as it involves arithmetic in the extension field $\mathbb{F}_{p^k}$, including multiplications, squarings, Frobenius evaluations, and operations in the cyclotomic subgroup. Its efficiency depends on the sizes of $\mathbb{F}_p$ and $\mathbb{F}_{p^k}$, the embedding degree k, and the cost of arithmetic in $\mathbb{F}_{p^k}$. Several studies have already been conducted on optimizing arithmetic operations in $\mathbb{F}_{p^k}$, and the search for suitable embedding degrees k. In [3], the authors identify families of elliptic curves with embedding degrees $k = 9$ and $k = 15$ that offer competitive security–performance trade-offs compared to BN and BLS curves with $k = 12$. A drawback of these odd embedding degrees is the absence of fast cyclotomic squaring. To mitigate this, in [13], Nanjo et al. introduce the first explicit formulas for fast cyclotomic cubing, particularly useful when k is a multiple of three. These formulas exploit the cyclotomic structure to reduce the cost of cubing in the final exponentiation, but they remain less efficient than simple square-and-multiply and require further optimization. Moreover, accurately assessing the cost of the final exponentiation also requires understanding the complexity of the Frobenius morphism. However, the Frobenius morphism depends strongly on the structure of the underlying field, leading to different algebraic operations and varying operation counts. This variability makes it difficult to estimate the overall cost of the final exponentiation, highlighting the need for methods that precisely determine the complexity of the Frobenius evaluation.

Our Contribution. In this paper, we introduce new methods to improve arithmetic in $\mathbb{F}_{p^k}$, simplifying the complexity analysis of the Frobenius evaluation and reducing the operation count in the final exponentiation. These results apply in particular to BLS curves with suitable embedding degrees. Our main contributions are:

- Frobenius computation: a new approach based on the Kronecker product of matrices, enabling a more efficient Frobenius evaluation and a clearer complexity assessment.
- Cyclotomic cubing: optimized cubing formulas for embedding degrees divisible by 3, improving the operation counts over the method of [13].

Organization of the Paper. In Sect. 2, we provide an overview of the necessary background information to comprehend this work. In Sect. 3, we introduce a novel approach based on the Kronecker product to compute the Frobenius map. In Sect. 4, we focus on optimizing the cubing computation, which could be used in pairing-based cryptography.

Notations. In this paper, we use the following notations to define the operations in the finite field $\mathbb{F}_{p^k}$: M_k, S_k, A_k, F_k, and $m_{k,c}$ denote multiplication, squaring, addition, Frobenius, and multiplication by an element c in $\mathbb{F}_{p^k}$, respectively. To simplify the notations, we denote by M, S, A, and m_c multiplication, squaring, addition, and multiplication by an element c in $\mathbb{F}_p$, respectively.

In addition, we refer to C_{cyc_k} as the cyclotomic cubing and to I_{cyc_k} as an inversion in the cyclotomic subgroup of the finite field $\mathbb{F}_{p^k}$.

2 Background

In this paper, we aim to optimize operations essential for the computation of the final exponentiation, specifically Frobenius operation and cyclotomic cubing.

Let us first recall the definition of the Frobenius endomorphism that is used at different steps of the final exponentiation.

2.1 Frobenius Endomorphism

Definition 1. *Let p be a prime number and $k \in \mathbb{N}^*$.*

For a field extension $\mathbb{F}_{p^k}/\mathbb{F}_p$, the p-Frobenius mapping is the $\mathbb{F}_p$-linear mapping

$$\begin{array}{rccc} \pi_p : & \mathbb{F}_{p^k}/\mathbb{F}_p & \longrightarrow & \mathbb{F}_{p^k}/\mathbb{F}_p \\ & x & \longmapsto & x^p. \end{array}$$

Observe that π_p is in fact an $\mathbb{F}_p$-algebra automorphism of $\mathbb{F}_{p^k}$. In particular,

$$(x+y)^p = x^p + y^p,$$

for all $x, y \in \mathbb{F}_{p^k}$.

For $i \in \mathbb{N}^*$, the ith iterate of the Frobenius map, $\pi^i := \underbrace{\pi_p \circ \ldots \circ \pi_p}_{i \text{ times}}$, is the automorphism

$$\begin{array}{rccc} \pi^i : & \mathbb{F}_{p^k}/\mathbb{F}_p & \longrightarrow & \mathbb{F}_{p^k}/\mathbb{F}_p \\ & x & \longmapsto & x^{p^i}. \end{array}$$

Note that we have $\pi^k = Id_{\mathbb{F}_{p^k}}$.

In this paper, the new method proposed to improve the Frobenius endomorphism calculation is based on the use of the Kronecker product of matrices. In the following, we provide some general details on the Kronecker product.

2.2 Kronecker Product

The Kronecker product is defined for two matrices of arbitrary size over any ring. However, in this work, we focus on matrices over finite fields $\mathbb{F}$.

Definition 2. *Let $p, q, r, s \in \mathbb{N}^*$, the Kronecker product, also known as tensor product, of matrix $A \in \mathcal{M}_{p,q}(\mathbb{F})$ and matrix $B \in \mathcal{M}_{r,s}(\mathbb{F})$ is defined as*

$$A \otimes B = \begin{pmatrix} a_{11}B \dots a_{1q}B \\ \vdots \qquad \vdots \\ a_{p1}B \dots a_{pq}B \end{pmatrix} \in \mathcal{M}_{pr,qs}(\mathbb{F}) \, .$$

The Kronecker product has interesting properties; many of them are stated and proven in the basic literature about matrix analysis. We provide the following properties which are needed in the sequel.

Basic Properties

1. The product of two Kronecker products yields another Kronecker product:

$$(A \otimes B)(C \otimes D) = AC \otimes BD \quad \forall\, A \in \mathcal{M}_{p,q}, B \in \mathcal{M}_{r,s}, C \in \mathcal{M}_{q,k}, D \in \mathcal{M}_{s,l}.$$

In particular,

$$(A \otimes B)^s = A^s \otimes B^s \quad \forall s \in \mathbb{N},\ \forall\, A \in \mathcal{M}_p,\ B \in \mathcal{M}_r.$$

2. If A and B are diagonal matrices, then $A \otimes B$ is a diagonal matrix.
3. $I_m \otimes I_n = I_{nm}$, where I_r is the $(r \times r)$ identity matrix.

3 Efficient Frobenius Operation in a Tower of Subfields

The Frobenius operation is an integral part of several steps in the final exponentiation process in pairing-based cryptography. Therefore, analyzing the number of operations required for the Frobenius morphism in various finite fields is essential for optimal performance. In this section, we introduce a method to simplify the complexity analysis of the Frobenius operation using the matrix representation and the Kronecker product of matrices. This approach offers a structured and efficient means of determining the operation counts required for the Frobenius morphism. We also provide examples of this method applied to different pairing-friendly fields.

3.1 Frobenius Operation in a Simple Field Extension

We first explain how the Frobenius morphism can be computed in a simple field extension using a matrix representation, and then provide the operation counts needed to perform the Frobenius operation.

Lemma 1. *Let p be a prime number and $k \geq 2$ an integer. Let $\beta \in \mathbb{F}_p$ be an element such that $k \mid p-1$ and such that the polynomial $X^k - \beta$ is irreducible over $\mathbb{F}_p$.*

We denote $\mathbb{F}_{p^k} = \mathbb{F}_p(\lambda)$ and $B = (1, \lambda, \lambda^2, \dots, \lambda^{k-1})$ the standard basis of $\mathbb{F}_{p^k}/\mathbb{F}_p$.

Consider the p-Frobenius mapping

$$\begin{array}{rcl}\pi_p : \mathbb{F}_{p^k}/\mathbb{F}_p & \longrightarrow & \mathbb{F}_{p^k}/\mathbb{F}_p \\ x & \longmapsto & x^p.\end{array}$$

Then,

$$Mat_B(\pi_p) = \text{diag}(1, \theta, \cdots, \theta^{k-1}),$$

where $\theta := \beta^{(p-1)/k} \in \mathbb{F}_p$.

Moreover, for all $1 \leq i \leq k$, *we have*

$$Mat_B(\pi^i) = (Mat_B(\pi_p))^i = \text{diag}(1, \theta^i, \cdots, \theta^{i(k-1)})$$

Proof. We note that

$$\pi_p(\lambda) = \lambda^p = \lambda\lambda^{p-1} = \lambda(\lambda^k)^{(p-1)/k} = \lambda\beta^{(p-1)/k} = \theta\lambda.$$

Consequently, $\pi_p(\lambda^j) = \theta^j\lambda^j$ for all $0 \leq j \leq k-1$.

In particular, for $A = \sum_{j=0}^{k-1} a_j\lambda^j \in \mathbb{F}_{p^k}$ with $a_j \in \mathbb{F}_p$, we have

$$A^p = \pi_p(A) = \text{diag}(1, \theta, \cdots, \theta^{k-1})(a_0, a_1, \cdots, a_{k-1})^T = \sum_{j=0}^{k-1} a_j\theta^j\lambda^j.$$

This formula is essential for determining the cost of a p^i-Frobenius map. Its complexity depends on the number of multiplications by coefficients $\theta^j \neq \pm 2^l$, since multiplications by $\pm 2^l$ reduce to inexpensive bit shifts (and a possible negation). Thus, rather than evaluating the Frobenius on a general $A \in \mathbb{F}_{p^k}$, it suffices to count the occurrences of such coefficients in its matrix representation. This observation leads directly to Proposition 31.

Proposition 31. *Using the same notations as in Lemma 1, we have the following*

1. *Let* $s_1 := Card\{0 \leq j \leq k-1 \mid \theta^j = \pm 2^l;\ l \in \mathbb{N}\}$; *then the number of multiplications to compute the p-Frobenius map is*

$$(k - s_1)M.$$

2. *More generally, for* $1 \leq i \leq k-1$, *let* $s_i := Card\{0 \leq j \leq k-1 \mid \theta^{ji} = \pm 2^l;\ l \in \mathbb{N}\}$. *Then, for all* $1 \leq i \leq k-1$, *the number of multiplications to compute the* p^i*-Frobenius map is*

$$(k - s_i)M.$$

3.2 Frobenius Operation in a Tower Field Extension

Similar to the approach used for a simple field extension, in this section, a matrix representation of the Frobenius map is used to calculate the number of operations needed to compute the Frobenius morphism. Specifically, for a Frobenius map on a tower field extension, we write a representative matrix of the Frobenius map as a Kronecker product of smaller matrices, according to the decomposition of the finite field extension.

Let p be a prime number and let $k_1, k_2 \in \mathbb{N}^*$ be two integers such that $k_1, k_2 \mid p-1$.

Suppose that $\beta_1 \in \mathbb{F}_p$ and $\beta_2 \in \mathbb{F}_{p^{k_1}}$ are two elements such that we have the following tower of finite fields:

$$\mathbb{F}_{p^{k_1}} = \mathbb{F}_p(\lambda_1);\ \lambda_1^{k_1} = \beta_1 \in \mathbb{F}_p$$

$$\mathbb{F}_{p^{k_2 k_1}} = \mathbb{F}_{p^{k_1}}(\lambda_2);\ \lambda_2^{k_2} = \beta_2 \in \mathbb{F}_{p^{k_1}}.$$

Let $B_1 := (1, \lambda_1, \lambda_1^2, \ldots, \lambda_1^{k_1-1})$ and $B_2 := (1, \lambda_2, \lambda_2^2, \ldots, \lambda_2^{k_2-1})$ be the respective standard basis of the vector spaces $\mathbb{F}_{p^{k_1}}/\mathbb{F}_p$ and $\mathbb{F}_{p^{k_2 k_1}}/\mathbb{F}_{p^{k_1}}$.

Let $B := B_2 \otimes B_1 = (\lambda_2^j, \lambda_2^j \lambda_1, \ldots, \lambda_2^j \lambda_1^{k_1-1})_{0 \le j \le k_2-1}$. Then it is straightforward to see that B is a basis of the vector space $\mathbb{F}_{p^{k_2 k_1}}/\mathbb{F}_p$, leading to the result stated in Proposition 32.

Proposition 32. *The representative matrix of the Frobenius map*

$$\begin{array}{rccc} \pi_p : & \mathbb{F}_{p^{k_2 k_1}}/\mathbb{F}_p & \longrightarrow & \mathbb{F}_{p^{k_2 k_1}}/\mathbb{F}_p \\ & x & \longmapsto & x^p \end{array}$$

with respect to the basis $B := B_2 \otimes B_1$ *is given by*

$$Mat_B(\pi_p) = \mathrm{diag}(M_{\theta_1}, \cdots, \theta_2^j M_{\theta_1}, \cdots, \theta_2^{k_2-1} M_{\theta_1}) = M_{\theta_2} \otimes M_{\theta_1}$$

where $\theta_1 := \beta_1^{(p-1)/k_1} \in \mathbb{F}_p$, $\theta_2 := \beta_2^{(p-1)/k_2} \in \mathbb{F}_{p^{k_1}}$ *and*

$$M_{\theta_l} := \mathrm{diag}(1, \theta_l, \cdots, \theta_l^{k_l-1});\ l = 1, 2.$$

Proof. As π_p is a $\mathbb{F}_p$-linear map, to determine the representative matrix of the Frobenius map, it suffices to compute the images of the basis elements

$$B := B_2 \otimes B_1 = (\lambda_2^j, \lambda_2^j \lambda_1, \ldots, \lambda_2^j \lambda_1^{k_1-1})_{0 \le j \le k_2-1}$$

of the vector space $\mathbb{F}_{p^{k_2 k_1}}/\mathbb{F}_p$.

We have

$$\lambda_1^p = \lambda_1 \lambda_1^{p-1} = \lambda_1 (\lambda_1^{k_1})^{(p-1)/k_1} = \lambda_1 \beta_1^{(p-1)/k_1} = \theta_1 \lambda_1,$$

and

$$\lambda_2^p = \lambda_2 \lambda_2^{p-1} = \lambda_2 (\lambda_2^{k_2})^{(p-1)/k_2} = \lambda_2 \beta_2^{(p-1)/k_2} = \theta_2 \lambda_2.$$

Thus,

$$\pi_p(\lambda_2^j \lambda_1^i) = (\lambda_2^j)^p (\lambda_1^i)^p = \theta_2^j \theta_1^i \lambda_2^j \lambda_1^i.$$

This completes the proof and provides us with the desired representative matrix of the Frobenius map π_p.

From the representative matrix, we derive the Theorem 33 which provides the formula to determine the operation counts of the Frobenius map π_p.

Theorem 33. *Using the same notations as in Proposition 32, the number of operations to compute the p-Frobenius map is*

$$(k_1 - s_1)M + k_1(k_2 - 1)m_{k_1,\theta_2},$$

where $s_1 = Card\{0 \leq i \leq k_1 - 1 \mid \theta_1^i = \pm 2^l;\ l \in \mathbb{N}\}$. *More precisely, we can distinguish two cases:*

- *If* $\theta_2 \in \mathbb{F}_{p^{k_1}} \setminus \mathbb{F}_p$, *then* $m_{k_1,\theta_2} = k_1 M$, *and the number of multiplications to compute the p-Frobenius map is*

$$(k_1 - s_1)M + k_1^2(k_2 - 1)M.$$

- *If* $\theta_2 \in \mathbb{F}_p$, *then* $m_{\theta_2} = M$, *and the number of multiplications to compute the p-Frobenius map is*

$$(k_1 - s_1)M + k_1(k_2 - 1)M.$$

Proof. To determine the operation counts of the Frobenius map π_p, we need to compute the number of multiplications required when performing the power x^p for $x \in \mathbb{F}_{p^{k_2 k_1}}/\mathbb{F}_p$.

Let $x \in \mathbb{F}_{p^{k_2 k_1}}/\mathbb{F}_p$, then $x = \sum_{j=0}^{k_2-1} x_j \lambda_2^j$ with $x_j \in \mathbb{F}_{p^{k_1}}$ for $0 \leq j \leq k_2 - 1$.

For all $0 \leq j \leq k_2 - 1$, $x_j = \sum_{i=0}^{k_1-1} x_{j,i} \lambda_1^i$ with $x_{j,i} \in \mathbb{F}_p$ for $0 \leq i \leq k_1 - 1$, then

$$x = \sum_{j=0}^{k_2-1} \sum_{i=0}^{k_1-1} x_{j,i} \lambda_2^j \lambda_1^i$$

with $x_{j,i} \in \mathbb{F}_p$ for all $0 \leq i \leq k_1 - 1$, $0 \leq j \leq k_2 - 1$.

By Fermat's Theorem, $x_{j,i}^p = x_{j,i}$ for all $0 \leq i \leq k_1 - 1$, $0 \leq j \leq k_2 - 1$, thus

$$\pi_p(x) = x^p = \sum_{j=0}^{k_2-1} \sum_{i=0}^{k_1-1} x_{j,i} (\lambda_2^p)^j (\lambda_1^p)^i = \sum_{j=0}^{k_2-1} \sum_{i=0}^{k_1-1} x_{j,i} (\theta_2 \lambda_2)^j (\theta_1 \lambda_1)^i$$
$$= \sum_{j=0}^{k_2-1} \sum_{i=0}^{k_1-1} x_{j,i} \theta_2^j \theta_1^i \lambda_2^j \lambda_1^i.$$

This demonstrates that raising x to the power of p requires multiplications involving $\theta_2^j \theta_1^i$ in the finite field $\mathbb{F}_p$. Consequently, the number of operations needed to compute the Frobenius map π_p is determined by the number of the multiplication by $\theta_2^j \theta_1^i$ in the finite field $\mathbb{F}_p$.

More precisely, for a simple computation of this complexity, we consider the matrix representation of π_p as the Kronecker product:

$$Mat_B(\pi_p) = M_{\theta_2} \otimes M_{\theta_1}.$$

Thus,

$$Mat_B(\pi_p(x)) = (M_{\theta_2} \otimes M_{\theta_1})x = \left(\theta_2^j x_j^p\right)_{0 \le j < k_2} = \left(\theta_2^j \sum_{i=0}^{k_1-1} x_{j,i}\theta_1^i \lambda_1^i\right)_{0 \le j < k_2}.$$

This implies that the count of the operations of π_p is as follows: we count the number of multiplications by θ_1^i such that $\theta_1^i \neq \pm 2^l$; $l \in \mathbb{N}$. This corresponds to $(k_1 - s_1)M$. Then, we need to perform $(k_2 - 1) \times k_1$ multiplications by θ_2^j; $1 \le j \le k_2 - 1$. This completes the proof.

The preceding result can be readily extended to a finite tower of finite fields, as presented in Proposition 34.

Proposition 34. *Let $k = k_1 \dots k_s$ be a composite number such that $k_i \mid p - 1$, for all $1 \le i \le s$, and suppose that*

$$\mathbb{F}_{p^{k_1}} = \mathbb{F}_p(\lambda_1);\ \lambda_1^{k_1} = \beta_1 \in \mathbb{F}_p;$$

$$\vdots$$

$$\mathbb{F}_{p^{k_s \dots k_1}} = \mathbb{F}_{p^{k_{s-1} \dots k_1}}(\lambda_s);\ \lambda_s^{k_s} = \beta_s \in \mathbb{F}_{p^{k_{s-1} \dots k_1}}$$

forms a finite tower of finite fields. For $1 \le j \le s$, let B_j denote a standard basis of $\mathbb{F}_{p^{k_j}} / \mathbb{F}_{p^{k_{j-1}}}$, and π_p the p-Frobenius mapping,

$$\begin{aligned} \pi_p : \mathbb{F}_{p^{k_s \cdots k_1}}/\mathbb{F}_p &\longrightarrow \mathbb{F}_{p^{k_s \cdots k_1}}/\mathbb{F}_p \\ x &\longmapsto x^p. \end{aligned}$$

Then,

$$Mat_B(\pi_p) = M_{\theta_s} \otimes \cdots \otimes M_{\theta_1}$$

where $B = B_s \otimes \cdots \otimes B_1$, and for $1 \le l \le s$; $\theta_l := \beta_l^{(p-1)/k_l}$, and

$$M_{\theta_l} := \operatorname{diag}(1, \theta_l, \cdots, \theta_l^{k_l - 1});\ l = 1, 2.$$

Remark 35. *We note that:*

1. *In the case of a finite tower of finite fields with more than two levels, the operation count of the p-Frobenius mapping can be computed using a recursive approach.*
2. *To determine the number of operations needed to compute an iterate of the Frobenius mapping, we use the fact that $Mat_B(\pi^i) = (Mat_B(\pi_p))^i$ for all $i \in \mathbb{N}$.*
3. *In order to have an optimized cost for the Frobenius map and its iterates, one should choose the path in the construction of the tower of subfields for which the cardinality of $\{0 \le i \le k_j - 1 \mid \theta_j^i = \pm 2^l;\ l \in \mathbb{N}\}$ is maximum. (See the following examples).*

3.3 Examples of Frobenius Computations in Pairing Friendly Fields

In [12], Koblitz and Menezes highlight the importance of certain finite fields for efficient pairing computation. A field $\mathbb{F}_{p^k}$ is considered pairing-friendly when $p \equiv 1 \bmod 12$ and $k = 2^i 3^j$ with $i, j \in \mathbb{N}$. Under these conditions, the polynomial $X^k - \beta$ is irreducible over $\mathbb{F}_p$ whenever β is neither a square nor a cube in $\mathbb{F}_p$, allowing the extension to be built by successively adjoining square and cube roots of a small element β. If $j = 0$, it suffices that $p \equiv 1 \bmod 4$ and that β be a quadratic non-residue. This provides a simple method for constructing towers: choose $\beta \in \mathbb{F}_p$ that is a quadratic (and, if needed, cubic) non-residue, and iteratively adjoin its roots. Selecting β small makes multiplications by β reduced to a few additions, making their cost negligible.

Frobenius Computation in $\mathbb{F}_{p^{12}}$. Let p a prime number such that $p \equiv 1$ [12]. One can construct the finite field $\mathbb{F}_{p^{12}}$ using different paths leading to different complexities of the Frobenius map and its iterates.

Path 1. We have the following tower of extension, as given in [2]:

$$\mathbb{F}_{p^2} = \mathbb{F}_p[u]; \quad \text{where } u^2 = 2$$

$$\mathbb{F}_{p^6} = \mathbb{F}_{p^2}[v]; \quad \text{where } v^3 = 2^{1/2}$$

$$\mathbb{F}_{p^{12}} = \mathbb{F}_{p^6}[w]; \quad \text{where } w^2 = 2^{1/6}.$$

Let $\theta_1 = 2^{(p-1)/2}$, $\theta_2 = 2^{(p-1)/6}$ and $\theta_3 = 2^{(p-1)/12}$. We note that $\theta_1 = -1$ as 2 is quadratic nonresidue in $\mathbb{F}_p$ and that θ_2, $\theta_3 \in \mathbb{F}_p$ as $p \equiv 1$ [12]. Thus, we obtain

$$Mat_B(\pi_p) = \text{diag}(1, \theta_3) \otimes \text{diag}(1, \theta_2, \theta_2^2) \otimes \text{diag}(1, -1).$$

Lemma 2. *In the finite field $\mathbb{F}_{p^{12}}$, and supposing that $12 \mid (p-1)$,*

1. *The computation of the p, p^2, p^4, p^5-Frobenius maps costs $10M$.*
2. *The computation of the p^3-Frobenius maps costs $6M$.*
3. *The computation of the p^6-Frobenius map is free.*

Proof. The result is a consequence of Theorem 33 and the fact that $\theta_1^2 = 1$, $\theta_2^3 = -1$, $\theta_3^6 = -1$. Thus, we obtain

$$Mat_B(\pi^3) = \text{diag}(1, theta_3^3) \otimes \text{diag}(1, -1, 1) \otimes \text{diag}(1, -1), \text{ and}$$
$$Mat_B(\pi^6) = diag(1, -1) \otimes I_3 \otimes I_2.$$

Path 2. We can also use the following tower of extension:

$$\mathbb{F}_{p^2} = \mathbb{F}_p[u]; \quad \text{where } u^2 = 2$$

$$\mathbb{F}_{p^{12}} = \mathbb{F}_{p^2}[\sigma]; \quad \text{where } \sigma^6 = 2^{1/2}.$$

Let $\theta_1 = 2^{(p-1)/2}$ and $\tilde{\theta}_2 = 2^{(p-1)/12}$. Then $\theta_1 = -1$, $\tilde{\theta}_2 \in \mathbb{F}_p$ and $\tilde{\theta}_2^6 = -1$. Thus, we obtain

$$Mat_B(\pi_p) = \text{diag}(1, \tilde{\theta}_2, \tilde{\theta}_2^2, \tilde{\theta}_2^3, \tilde{\theta}_2^4, \tilde{\theta}_2^5) \otimes \text{diag}(1, -1)$$

Lemma 3. *In the finite field $\mathbb{F}_{p^{12}}$, and supposing that $12 \mid (p-1)$,*

1. *The computation of the p, p^4, p^5-Frobenius maps costs $10M$.*
2. *The computation of the p^2-Frobenius maps costs $8M$.*
3. *The computation of the p^3-Frobenius maps costs $6M$.*
4. *The computation of the p^6-Frobenius map is free.*

Proof. The result is a consequence of the fact that $\theta_1 = -1$ and $\tilde{\theta}_2^6 = -1$. Thus, we obtain

$$Mat_B(\pi^2) = \text{diag}(1, \tilde{\theta}_2^2, \tilde{\theta}_2^4, -1, -\tilde{\theta}_2^2, -\tilde{\theta}_2^4) \otimes \text{diag}(1, -1), \text{ and}$$
$$Mat_B(\pi^3) = \text{diag}(1, \tilde{\theta}_2^3, -1, -\tilde{\theta}_2^3, 1, \tilde{\theta}_2^3) \otimes \text{diag}(1, -1)$$

Frobenius Computation in $\mathbb{F}_{p^{15}}$. Let p a prime number such that $\{3,\ 5\} \mid p-1$. Suppose that we have a tower extension for $\mathbb{F}_{p^{15}}$ as follows:

$$\mathbb{F}_{p^5} = \mathbb{F}_p[u]; \quad \text{with } u^5 = \beta_1 = 7$$

$$\mathbb{F}_{p^{15}} = \mathbb{F}_{p^5}[v]; \quad \text{with } v^3 = \beta_2 = u \in \mathbb{F}_{p^5}.$$

Let $\theta_1 = 7^{(p-1)/5}$ and $\theta_2 = 7^{(p-1)/15}$. Then $\theta_1 \neq 1$, $\theta_1 \in \mathbb{F}_p$ and, as $15 \mid p-1$, $\theta_2 \in \mathbb{F}_p$. Moreover, $\theta_2 \neq 1$, $(\theta_2)^3 = 7^{(p-1)/5} = \theta_1 \neq 1$ and $(\theta_2)^{15} = 1$. Thus,

$$Mat_B(\pi_p) = \text{diag}(1, \theta_2, \theta_2^2) \otimes \text{diag}(1, \theta_1, \theta_1^2, \theta_1^3, \theta_1^4)$$

Lemma 4. *In the finite field $\mathbb{F}_{p^{15}}$, and supposing that $15 \mid (p-1)$,*

1. *For $1 \leq i \leq 14$ and $i \neq 5$ or $i \neq 10$, the computation of the p^i-Frobenius maps costs $14M$.*
2. *The computation of the p^5 or p^{10}-Frobenius map costs $10M$.*

Proof. The result is a consequence of Theorem 33 and the fact that $\theta_1^5 = \theta_1^{10} = 1$. Thus, we obtain

$$Mat_B(\pi^5) = diag(1, \theta_2^5, \theta_2^{10}) \otimes I_5.$$

Remark 36. *In this study, we distinguish between the different exponents of p in Frobenius evaluations, achieving more efficient Frobenius computations. For instance,in $\mathbb{F}_{p^{12}}$, Frobenius evaluation can be reduced to 6 multiplications in specific cases and in $\mathbb{F}_{p^{15}}$, Frobenius evaluation can be reduced to 10 multiplications in specific cases.*

4 Cubing Computation

Efficient cubing also contributes significantly to the performance of pairing-based cryptosystems. Nanjo et al. [13] note that elliptic curves with odd embedding degrees such as $k = 9$ and 15 lack fast cyclotomic squaring, motivating alternative techniques. They introduce fast cyclotomic cubing for curves with k divisible by 3. In this section, we present improved methods for both typical cubing and cyclotomic cubing, achieving better complexity.

In the following, let p be a prime number and let $k \in \mathbb{N}^*$, divisible by 3, be such that $k \mid (p-1)$, we denote $q = p^{k/3}$. The cubic extension field of $\mathbb{F}_q$, $\mathbb{F}_{q^3}$ is defined as $\mathbb{F}_q[x]/(x^3 - \xi)$, where ξ is an element of $\mathbb{F}_q^*$ that does not have a cube root in $\mathbb{F}_q$.

4.1 Typical Cubing

Building upon the method proposed by Nanjo et al. [13], we introduce an alternative approach in this section that combines the Chung–Hasan technique for squaring with the Karatsuba algorithm for multiplication in $\mathbb{F}_q$, aiming to improve the efficiency of typical cubing operations in $\mathbb{F}_q$.

Let a be an element in $\mathbb{F}_{q^3}$ represented as $a = a_0 + a_1x + a_2x^2$, with coefficients $a_0,\ a_1,\ a_2 \in \mathbb{F}_q$. Then,

$$a^3 = (a_0 + a_1x + a_2x^2)^3 = (a_0 + a_1x + a_2x^2)^2 \cdot (a_0 + a_1x + a_2x^2).$$

For the first part, which involves squaring the polynomial $(a_0 + a_1x + a_2x^2)$, we employ the Chung-Hasan method as detailed in [7]. According to this method, the computational complexity of performing a squaring in $\mathbb{F}_q$ is given by

$$2M_{k/3} + 3S_{k/3} + 8A_{k/3} + 2m_{k/3,\xi}.$$

After computing the first part (i.e., the squaring), we need to perform a multiplication. For the multiplication involving the result of the squaring and the second term $(a_0 + a_1x + a_2x^2)$, we use the Karatsuba method as described in [11]. The computational complexity of this multiplication in $\mathbb{F}_q$ is given by

$$6M_{k/3} + 15A_{k/3} + 2m_{k/3,\xi}.$$

By combining the Chung-Hasan method [7] for squaring calculations, and the Karatsuba method [11] for multiplication computations, we find that the complexity of computing a typical cubing in $\mathbb{F}_q$ is given by

$$8M_{k/3} + 3S_{k/3} + 23A_{k/3} + 4m_{k/3,\xi}.$$

Thus, as shown in Table 1, using the Chung-Hasan method combined with the Karatsuba method reduces the complexity for performing a typical cubing in $\mathbb{F}_q$ compared to the method explained in [13].

Table 1. Comparaison of operations counts for typical cubing in $\mathbb{F}_q$

Method	Complexity
This work	$\mathbf{8M_{k/3} + 3S_{k/3} + 23A_{k/3} + 4m_{k/3,\xi}}$
Nanjo et *al.* [13]	$7M_{k/3} + 5S_{k/3} + 18A_{k/3} + 4m_{k/3,\xi}$

4.2 Cyclotomic Cubing

In their use of fast cubing for the final exponentiation calculation in the Tate pairing on BLS curves, Nanjo et *al.* [13] demonstrate that the cyclotomic cubing calculation is more efficient than typical cubing but remains less efficient than the squaring even though it is performed in the cyclotomic subgroup.

In this section, we introduce a new method for computing cyclotomic cubing, which enhances the complexity measure obtained in [13], thus improving the efficiency of the final exponentiation in the Tate pairing and its derivatives in specific cases.

Our proposal presents a new approach for decomposing the cube a^3, where a belongs to the cyclotomic subgroup of $\mathbb{F}_q$, denoted as $G_{\phi_3(q)}$. The element $a \in G_{\phi_3(q)}$ can be represented as $a_0 + a_1 x + a_2 x^2$, with coefficients $a_0, a_1, a_2 \in \mathbb{F}_q$.

In [13], the authors provide an explicit formula for the cube of a, as detailed in Lemma 5. This formula is derived from the typical cubing equation, by utilizing the specific order of the element a and the following relation:

$$a^{\phi_3(q)} = a_0^3 + (-3a_0a_1a_2 + a_1^3)\xi + a_2^3\xi^2 = 1.$$

Lemma 5. *Let a an element of $G_{\phi_3(q)}$. The cyclotomic cubing a^3 is calculated as follows:*

$$\begin{aligned} a^3 = (a_0 + a_1 x + a_2 x^2)^3 &= 1 + 9a_0a_1a_2\xi + 3\left(\underbrace{a_0^2 a_1 + a_2(a_0a_2 + a_1^2)\xi}_{(1)}\right) x \\ &\quad + 3\left(\underbrace{a_0(a_0a_2 + a_1^2) + a_1a_2^2\xi}_{(2)}\right) x^2. \end{aligned}$$

By developing the terms in the brackets (1) and (2), we can establish a relation between them as given in Lemma 6.

Lemma 6. *Let $B_1 = a_0^2 a_1 + a_2(a_0a_2 + a_1^2)\xi$ and $B_2 = a_0(a_0a_2 + a_1^2) + a_1a_2^2\xi$. We obtain the following equations:*

$$\begin{cases} B_1 + B_2 = (a_1 + a_0)(a_1 + a_2)(\xi a_2 + a_0) - (\xi + 1)a_0a_1a_2 \\ B_1 - B_2 = (a_1 - a_0)(a_1 - a_2)(\xi a_2 - a_0) + (\xi - 1)a_0a_1a_2 \end{cases}$$

Proof. The expressions for B_1+B_2 and B_1-B_2 are obtained by direct expansion and regrouping of terms.

With this presentation of $B_1 + B_2$ and $B_1 - B_2$, we can deduce that:

$$\begin{cases} B_1 = \frac{1}{2}\Big((B_1 + B_2) + (B_1 - B_2)\Big) \\ B_2 = \frac{1}{2}\Big((B_1 + B_2) - (B_1 - B_2)\Big) \end{cases} \tag{1}$$

By expanding Eq. 1, we obtain the following formulas.
Let ξ be an odd positive integer, then B_1 and B_2 are given by:

$$\begin{cases} B_1 = \frac{1}{2}(a_1 + a_0)(a_1 + a_2)(\xi a_2 + a_0) + \frac{1}{2}(a_1 - a_0)(a_1 - a_2)(\xi a_2 - a_0) - a_0 a_1 a_2 \\ B_2 = \frac{1}{2}(a_1 + a_0)(a_1 + a_2)(\xi a_2 + a_0) - \frac{1}{2}(a_1 - a_0)(a_1 - a_2)(\xi a_2 - a_0) - \xi a_0 a_1 a_2 \end{cases}$$

In particular, the multiplication by $\frac{1}{2}$ consists in the multiplication of an element of $\mathbb{F}_p$ by an element of $\mathbb{F}_{p^{k/3}}$. This multiplication costs $k/3$ multiplications in $\mathbb{F}_p$.

From the above formulas, we can count the operations needed to calculate B_1 and B_2, and thus, the cyclotomic cubing in $G_{\phi_3(q)}$.

Complexity Measure. To determine the complexity of the cyclotomic cubing of an element $a \in G_{\phi_3(q)}$, we first need to calculate the number of operations needed to compute B_1 and B_2.

1: $t_0 = a_1 + a_0$	9: $t_0 = a_1 - a_0$
2: $t_1 = a_1 + a_2$	10: $t_1 = a_1 - a_2$
3: $t_2 = \xi a_2$	
4: $t_3 = t_2 + a_0$	11: $t_3 = t_2 - a_0$
5: $t_4 = a_0 a_1 a_2$	
6: $t_5 = \xi t_4$	13: $t_7 = \frac{1}{2} t_0 t_1 t_3$
8: $t_6 = \frac{1}{2} t_0 t_1 t_3$	
14: $\mathbf{B1} = \frac{1}{2}(\mathbf{t_6} + \mathbf{t_7} - \mathbf{t_4})$	15: $\mathbf{B_2} = \frac{1}{2}(\mathbf{t_6} - \mathbf{t_7} - \mathbf{t_5})$

In total, the calculation of B_1 and B_2 takes $6M_{k/3} + 10A_{k/3} + 2m_{k/3,\xi} + (2 \times k/3)M$.

Moreover, to compute the cube of a (see Lemma 5), we have:

$$1 + 9a_0a_1a_2\xi = 1 + (2^3 + 1)t_5 = 1 + 2^3 t_5 + t_5,$$

$$3B_1 = 2B_1 + B_1 \quad \text{and} \quad 3B_2 = 2B_2 + B_2.$$

A multiplication by 2 is equivalent to a bitwise shift, and thus it is not considered in the complexity calculation. Then, the above calculations takes $3A_{k/3}$.

In conclusion, we find that the complexity of a cyclotomic cube is $6M_{k/3} + 13A_{k/3} + 2m_{k/3,\xi} + (2 \times k/3)M$.

A comparison of the complexity measures between this work and the results presented in [13] is given in Table 2.

Table 2. Comparaison operation counts for cyclotomic cubing

Method	Complexity
This work	$\mathbf{6M_{k/3} + 13A_{k/3} + 2m_{k/3,\xi} + (2 \times k/3)M}$
Nanjo et *al.* [13]	$5M_{k/3} + 4S_{k/3} + 9A_{k/3} + 3m_{k/3,\xi}$

From the results presented in Table 2, we can conclude that the cyclotomic cubing calculation proposed in this work is slightly more efficient than the method calculation presented in [13]. Please note that, for the remainder of this paper, we will not consider the additions in our complexity calculations (see Table 3).

Example 41 *Based on the results presented below, we can calculate the number of multiplications needed to perform a cyclotomic cubing within the cyclotomic subgroups of* $\mathbb{F}_{p^{15}}$ *and* $\mathbb{F}_{p^{27}}$.

Indeed, using the results presented in [13], *and considering the costs of multiplications and squarings in* $\mathbb{F}_{p^k}$ *as detailed in* [1], *we obtain:*

- $C_{cyc_{15}} = 5M_5 + 4S_5 + 3m_{5,\xi} = 5 \times 13M + 4 \times 13S + 3m_{5,\xi} \simeq 132\text{M}.$
- $C_{cyc_{27}} = 5M_9 + 4S_9 + 3m_{9,\xi} = 5 \times 36M + 4 \times (18M + 9S) + 3m_{9,\xi} \simeq 315\text{M}$

However, using our results, we obtain the following:

- $C_{cyc_{15}} = 6M_5 + 2m_{5,\xi} = 6 \times 13M + 2m_{5,\xi} + 10M \simeq \mathbf{98M}.$
- $C_{cyc_{27}} = 6M_9 + 2m_{9,\xi} = 6 \times 36M + 2m_{9,\xi} + 18M \simeq \mathbf{252M}.$

Table 3. Examples of cyclotomic cubing complexity (in terms of multiplications)

Operation	Nanjo et al. [13]	**This work**	**Gain**
$C_{cyc_{15}}$	132 M	**98** M	**25.7 %**
$C_{cyc_{27}}$	315 M	**252** M	**20 %**

4.3 Application to Pairing

Cyclotomic cubing is useful in the final exponentiation of pairings, particularly on Barreto–Lynn–Scott (BLS) curves [4]. In particular, BLS15 and BLS27 benefit from this technique since their embedding degrees are divisible by 3, allowing the use of cyclotomic subgroups. Nanjo et al. [13] showed that cyclotomic cubing improves the execution time of the Optimal Ate pairing on BLS15. Our method further reduces the number of operations required for cyclotomic cubing, and although we do not provide direct benchmarks, this reduction should translate into improved efficiency in the hard part of the final exponentiation for both BLS15 and BLS27.

5 Conclusion

In this paper, we presented two methods to optimize pairing computations, focusing on the costly operations of the final exponentiation: the Frobenius map and cyclotomic cubing. The first method uses the Kronecker product to perform the Frobenius operation efficiently and to simplify its complexity analysis over $\mathbb{F}_{p^k}$. The second provides improved formulas for cyclotomic cubing, relevant for curves with odd embedding degrees divisible by 3. Finally, we outlined how these improvements apply to the Optimal Ate pairing on BLS15 and BLS27, whose full performance evaluation will be addressed in future work.

References

1. Aranha, D.F., Fotiadis, G., Guillevic, A.: A short-list of pairing-friendly curves resistant to the special TNFS algorithm at the 192-bit security level. IACR Commun. Cryptol. **1**(3), 3 (2024)
2. Assoujaa, I., Ezzouak, S., Mouanis, H.: Tower building technique on elliptic curve with embedding degree 72. WSEAS Trans. Comput. Res. **10**, 126–138 (2022)
3. Barbulescu, R., El Mrabet, N., Ghammam, L.: A taxonomy of pairings, their security, their complexity. IACR Cryptol. ePrint Arch., 485 (2019)
4. Barreto, P.S.L.M., Lynn, B., Scott, M.: Constructing elliptic curves with prescribed embedding degrees. Secur. Commun. Netw. (2002)
5. Boneh, D., Franklin, M.K.: Identity-based encryption from the Weil pairing. In: Advances in Cryptology – CRYPTO 2001, volume 2139 of LNCS (2001)
6. Boneh, D., Lynn, B., Shacham, H.: Short signatures from the Weil pairing. J. Cryptol. **17**(4) (2004)
7. Chung, J., Hasan, M.A.: Asymmetric squaring formulae. In: 18th IEEE Symposium on Computer Arithmetic (ARITH '07), pp. 113–122 (2007)
8. Costello, C., Hisil, H., Boyd, C., Gonzalez Nieto, J., Wong, K.K.H.: Faster pairings on special Weierstrass curves. In: Shacham, H., Waters, B. (eds.) Pairing-Based Cryptography - Pairing 2009, Third International Conference, Palo Alto, CA, USA, 12–14 August 2009, Proceedings, volume 5671 of Lecture Notes in Computer Science, pp. 89–101. Springer (2009)
9. Freeman, D., Scott, M., Teske, E.: A taxonomy of pairing-friendly elliptic curves. J. Cryptol. **23**(2), 224–280 (2010)
10. Joux, A.: A one round protocol for tripartite Diffie-Hellman. In: Algorithmic Number Theory (ANTS-IV), volume 1838 of Lecture Notes in Computer Science (2000)
11. Karatsuba, A.A., Yu, O.: Multiplication of multidigit numbers on automata. In: Soviet Physics Doklady, vol. 7, pp. 595–596 (1963)

12. Koblitz, N., Menezes, A.: Pairing-based cryptography at high security levels. In: Smart, N.P. (ed.) Cryptography and Coding, pp. 13–36,. Springer, Berlin (2005)
13. Nanjo, Y., Shirase, M., Kusaka, T., Nogami, Y.: An explicit formula of cyclotomic cubing available for pairings on elliptic curves with embedding degrees of multiple of three. In: 2020 35th International Technical Conference on Circuits/Systems, Computers and Communications (ITC-CSCC), pp. 288–292 (2020)
14. Vercauteren, F.: Optimal pairings. IEEE Trans. Inf. Theory **56**(1), 455–461 (2010)

Symmetric Cryptanalysis & New Constructions

On the Resistance of Rijndael-256 Against Related-Key Boomerang and Rectangle Attacks

Namil Kim[1], Wonwoo Song[1], Seungjun Baek[3], Yongjin Jeon[3], Jongsung Kim[1,2(✉)], and Kihyo Nam[4]

[1] Department of Cyber Security, Kookmin University, Seoul 02707, Republic of Korea
{handisu,sww1129,jskim}@kookmin.ac.kr

[2] Department of Information Security, Cryptology, and Mathematics, Kookmin University, Seoul 02707, Republic of Korea

[3] Department of Financial Information Security, Kookmin University, Seoul 02707, Republic of Korea
{hellosj3,idealtop18}@kookmin.ac.kr

[4] Eunicesoft Co., Ltd., Daejeon 34365, Republic of Korea
nkh@eunicesoft.co.kr

Abstract. This paper examines the resistance of Rijndael-256 to related-key attacks by presenting robust boomerang and rectangle distinguishers. We first revisit the local collision construction method used by Biryukov et al. to find related-key differential trails for AES-192 and AES-256. Leveraging that approach, we show that local collisions cannot be constructed by separating disturbance and correction in Rijndael-256 by analyzing how differences propagate through its key schedule and their implications for related-key trails. In particular, the internal state and the key state are updated simultaneously, which makes it impossible to construct a related-key differential distinguisher based on local collisions. Our in-depth analysis yields 7-round related-key boomerang and rectangle distinguishers for Rijndael-256 without relying on local collisions. With data complexities of $2^{108.83}$ and $2^{167.92}$ 256-bit blocks, respectively, these distinguishers enable us to distinguish Rijndael-256 from a random oracle in the related-key setting. To the best of our knowledge, this is the first analysis of related-key boomerang and rectangle attacks on Rijndael-256 in the literature.

Keywords: Rijndael-256 · Related-Key Attack · Boomerang Distinguisher · Rectangle Distinguisher

1 Introduction

Rijndael [8] is a block cipher that supports block and key sizes of 128, 160, 192, 224, and 256-bit. It was submitted to the National Institute of Standards and

H. Seo (Ed.): ICISC 2025, LNCS 16487, pp. 433–455, 2026.
https://doi.org/10.1007/978-981-95-8034-7_23

Technology (NIST) in response to its 1997 call for a new block cipher standard [16]. The versions with a 128-bit block size and key sizes of 128, 192, and 256-bit were selected as the standard and are collectively referred to as the Advanced Encryption Standard (AES).

AES is commonly used in conjunction with operation modes such as Galois/Counter Mode (GCM). AES-GCM has been widely adopted in internet protocols (TLS, IPsec) as well as in cloud services (AWS KMS, Google Cloud Platform, and Microsoft Azure). However, a NIST report [14] highlighted several security concerns with the AES-GCM mode, including a lack of key commitment, vulnerability to nonce misuse, and performance limitations. Accordingly, the report emphasized the need for new operation modes and block ciphers with block sizes larger than 128-bit. NIST organized a workshop on Accordion Mode [20] to discuss requirements for new operation modes, where some proposals suggested using 256-bit block ciphers such as TurboSHAKE256 [1] and Threefish [10] as internal primitives. Subsequently, NIST issued a notice regarding Accordion Mode [17], announcing its plan to standardize Rijndael-256, a block cipher with a 256-bit block size, for use in Accordion Mode, and called for comprehensive analyses of Rijndael-256.

Contrary to the extensive research on AES, studies on Rijndael-256 have been limited to implementation [9] and analyses of some known attacks [5, 6] leaving its overall analysis insufficient for adoption in new operation modes. In particular, studies on the resistance of Rijndael-256 under the related-key model are scarce, especially with respect to boomerang and rectangle attacks. On the related-key model, attacks are conducted based on the relation among keys used in different encryption and decryption oracles, with the goal of recovering the actual secret key of each oracle. Although this model may appear to rely on strong assumptions, it presents a realistic threat scenario because in block-cipher-based hash functions message or chaining values are used as the encryption keys of the block cipher (e.g., Davies–Meyer, Miyaguchi–Preneel, Matyas–Meyer–Oseas constructions) [13, 15, 19]. Therefore, related-key attacks on block ciphers can represent a practical threat model. For AES-192 and AES-256, full-round related-key boomerang attacks [4] have been proposed, along with countermeasures involving key schedule modifications to improve resistance [18]. However, no security analysis from the perspective of related-key boomerang and rectangle attacks has been conducted for Rijndael-256.

Contributions. This paper presents the first related-key analysis of Rijndael-256, where both the internal and key states are 256-bit, and provides valuable insights into the security of Rijndael-256. Our contributions are mainly twofold. First, we show that generic related-key boomerang and rectangle attacks against the full-round Rijndael-256 are infeasible. While AES-192 and AES-256 are conducted to full-round related-key attacks [4], Rijndael-256 simultaneously updates both the internal and key states, preventing the construction of local collisions; thus, the existing analysis techniques for AES cannot be directly applied. Due to these structural challenges, related-key boomerang and rectangle attacks have not been reported for Rijndael-256 to date. Motivated by this gap, we focus on how differences evolve through the key schedule and derive conditions that determine the extent to which related-key trails can be constructed. This allows us to characterize the maximal feasible trails under the related-key model.

Second, based on the preceding analysis, we propose the first related-key boomerang and rectangle distinguishers for Rijndael-256. Both boomerang and rectangle distinguishers exist up to 7-round trails. Specifically, boomerang distinguisher has a trail probability of $2^{-170.83}$ and can distinguish with a data complexity of approximately $2^{108.83}$ blocks for encryption only. The rectangle distinguisher has a trail probability of $2^{-365.83}$ and can distinguish from a random oracle with a data complexity of about $2^{167.92}$ blocks for encryption and decryption both. These results indicate that Rijndael-256 provides sufficient security margin against related-key boomerang and rectangle attacks, offering strong assurance of security for future applications in block cipher modes or hash function designs requiring larger block sizes.

2 Preliminaries

In this section, we describe the structure of Rijndael-256, its key schedule, and the notation used throughout this paper.

2.1 Rijndael-256

Rijndael-256 refers to the variant with both block and key sizes of 256-bit (32-byte), arranged as a state matrix of 4 rows $\times$ 8 columns, and it is defined with 14 rounds. As in AES, the round function comprises four transformations, each transformation is described below:

- **SubBytes (SB):** A nonlinear byte substitution in which each state byte is replaced by an S-box value defined over $GF(2^8)$.
- **ShiftRows (SR):** Each state row is cyclically shifted to the left by a fixed offset.
- **MixColumns (MC):** A linear mixing operation where each column of the state is interpreted as a polynomial over $GF(2^8)$ and multiplied by a fixed polynomial.
- **AddRoundKey (ARK):** A bitwise XOR between the state and the round key to inject key material into each round.

Rijndael-256 consists of an initial ARK, 14 rounds of the round function, and a final round without MC. Its transformations are identical to AES except for the wider state and the SR offsets: AES shifts by $0, 1, 2, 3$ bytes, while Rijndael-256 shifts by $0, 1, 3, 4$.

2.2 Rijndael-256 Key Schedule

The key schedule of Rijndael-256 is defined in Algorithm 1. $\text{RotWord}(a_0a_1a_2a_3) = (a_1a_2a_3a_0)$ denotes one byte left rotation of a 32-bit word. The function $\text{SubWord}(w)$ applies the S-box to each byte of the word w. Furthermore, $\text{Rcon}[j]$ is predefined constant and $\text{Word}(K[4i, \ldots, 4i+3])$ represents the 32-bit word obtained by concatenating the bytes $K[4i], \ldots, K[4i+3]$ in big-endian order.

Algorithm 1 Key Schedule for Rijndael-256

```
1: Input: K                                          ▷ 256-bit key, bytes K[0...31]
2: Output: K^{0,...,14}                              ▷ all 15 round keys, each 256-bit
3: N_b ← 8, N_k ← 8, N_r ← 14                        ▷ words are 32-bit
4: for i ← 0 to N_k − 1 do
5:     W[i] ← Word(K[4i...4i + 3])                   ▷ split key into 32-bit words
6: end for
7: for i ← N_k to N_b · (N_r + 1) − 1 do             ▷ here: i = 8...119
8:     temp ← W[i − 1]
9:     if i mod 8 = 0 then
10:        temp ← SubWord(RotWord(temp)) ⊕ Rcon(i/8)
11:    else if i mod 8 = 4 then
12:        temp ← SubWord(temp)
13:    end if
14:    W[i] ← W[i − 8] ⊕ temp
15: end for
16: for r ← 0 to N_r do
17:     K^r ← W[r · N_b] || W[r · N_b + 1] || ··· || W[r · N_b + N_b − 1]
18: end for
```

2.3 Notation

Table 1 presents the notation adopted herein.

Table 1. Notation

Symbol	Meaning
P_i	Plaintexts
C_i	Ciphertexts
$A(i,j)$	Byte at row i column j of a state A
$A(i,*_L)$	All four bytes in the left half of row i, i.e., $\{A(i,0), A(i,1), A(i,2), A(i,3)\}$
$A(i,*_R)$	All four bytes in the right half of row i, i.e., $\{A(i,4), A(i,5), A(i,6), A(i,7)\}$
$A(*,j)$	All four bytes in column j of a state A, i.e., $\{A(0,j), A(1,j), A(2,j), A(3,j)\}$
K_x	Secret key of oracle x
K_x^r	Secret subkey of oracle x in round r
ΔK_{xy}^r	Difference in the related-keys of oracles x and y in round r
E_0	Forward differential trail (input $\alpha \mapsto$ intermediate β)
E_1	Backward differential trail (output $\gamma \mapsto$ intermediate δ)
$S(\cdot)$	S-box operation

3 Related-Key Boomerang and Rectangle Attacks

In this section, we define the related-key model and discuss boomerang and rectangle attacks based on it. The related-key attack model [2] refers to a class of cryptographic attacks in which the adversary is assumed to know the relation among the keys used by the encryption and decryption oracles. In our setting, we assume that the adversary can query four encryption and decryption oracles as follows:

$$\mathcal{O}_{K_\ell}^{\text{enc}}(X) = E_{K_\ell}(X), \quad \mathcal{O}_{K_\ell}^{\text{dec}}(Y) = E_{K_\ell}^{-1}(Y), \qquad \ell \in \{A, B, C, D\}.$$

The adversary is also assumed to know the relation of the keys K_A, K_B, K_C, and K_D of these oracles. In general, the relation among K_A, K_B, K_C, and K_D is expressed in terms of the differences in the master keys or in specific round keys. We assume the scenario where the adversary knows the differences in the round keys of a particular round, where Fig. 1 depicts the key relations among the oracles and the overall structure of the related-key model ($\Delta K_{AB} = \Delta K_{CD}$ and $\Delta K_{AC} = \Delta K_{BD}$).

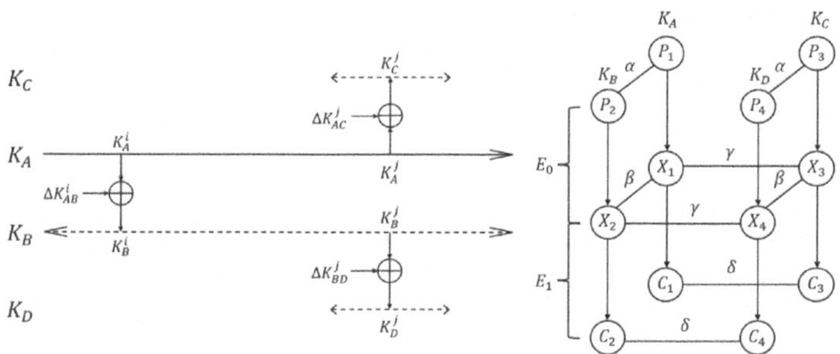

Fig. 1. Key relation(left) and a related-key model(right)

3.1 Related-Key Boomerang Attacks

The related-key boomerang attack [11] is a variant of the boomerang attack originally proposed by Wagner [21], extended to the related-key model. In this model, the encryption function E is considered as two subciphers E_0 and E_1, i.e., $E = E_1 \circ E_0$. The attack relies on two related-key differentials with a random key K, which are defined as follows.

$$\alpha \xrightarrow[\Delta K_{AB}]{E_0} \beta \text{ with prob. } p, \qquad \text{i.e., } p = \Pr_{X,K}\big[E_0(X,K) \oplus E_0(X \oplus \alpha,\, K \oplus \Delta K_{AB}) = \beta\big],$$

$$\gamma \xrightarrow[\Delta K_{AC}]{E_1} \delta \text{ with prob. } q, \qquad \text{i.e., } q = \Pr_{X,K}\big[E_1(X,K) \oplus E_1(X \oplus \gamma,\, K \oplus \Delta K_{AC}) = \delta\big].$$

A related-key boomerang distinguisher can be constructed by combining these two related-key differentials ($\alpha \rightarrow \beta$) and ($\gamma \rightarrow \delta$). The following are the steps for carrying out a related-key boomerang distinguishing attack, which utilizes the differentials above.

1. Choose N random plaintexts P_1, and set $P_2 = P_1 \oplus \alpha$.
2. Encrypt P_1 and P_2 under K_A and K_B, respectively, obtaining $C_1 = E_{K_A}(P_1)$ and $C_2 = E_{K_B}(P_2)$, where $K_B = K_A \oplus \Delta K_{AB}$.
3. For the generated C_1 and C_2, compute $C_3 = C_1 \oplus \delta$ and $C_4 = C_2 \oplus \delta$.
4. Decrypt C_3 and C_4 under K_C and K_D to obtain $P_3 = E^{-1}_{K_C}(C_3)$ and $P_4 = E^{-1}_{K_D}(C_4)$, where K_C and K_D are derived by applying the related-key difference ΔK_{AC}, i.e., $K_C = K_A \oplus \Delta K_{AC}$ and $K_D = K_B \oplus \Delta K_{AC}$.
5. For the resulting quartets (P_1, P_2, P_3, P_4), those satisfying $P_3 \oplus P_4 = \alpha$ are considered right quartets and are used in the attack.

Because $\alpha \rightarrow \beta$ and $\gamma \rightarrow \delta$ exist in two ways, the probability of constructing a right quartet for the overall boomerang distinguisher is $(pq)^2$.

To obtain a tighter probability bound, all possible values of β and γ (with $\beta \neq \gamma$) are considered. Accordingly, the probabilities of the two related-key differentials $\alpha \rightarrow \beta$ and $\gamma \rightarrow \delta$ are given by

$$\hat{p} = \sqrt{\sum_{\beta} \Pr[\alpha \xrightarrow[\Delta K_{AB}]{E_0} \beta]^2}, \qquad \hat{q} = \sqrt{\sum_{\gamma} \Pr[\gamma \xrightarrow[\Delta K_{AC}]{E_1} \delta]^2}.$$

Therefore, $N \cdot (\hat{p}\hat{q})^2$ right quartets are expected in the attack.

3.2 Related-Key Rectangle Attacks

The related-key rectangle attack [3,11,12] is closely related to the boomerang attack: both rely on two related-key differentials ($\alpha \rightarrow \beta$) and ($\gamma \rightarrow \delta$) defined under the same model. However, whereas the boomerang attack requires both the encryption and decryption oracles, the rectangle attack does only the encryption oracle. The rectangle attack considers all possible intermediate values β and γ (with $\beta \neq \gamma$), leading to the use of RMS probabilities in its analysis. The following outlines the procedure of a related-key rectangle distinguishing attack.

1. Given the input difference α specified by the trail, choose N random plaintexts P_1 and generate P_2 such that $P_2 = P_1 \oplus \alpha$.
2. Encrypt P_1 and P_2 under K_A and K_B, respectively, obtaining $C_1 = E_{K_A}(P_1)$ and $C_2 = E_{K_B}(P_2)$, where $K_B = K_A \oplus \Delta K_{AB}$.
3. Similarly, choose another N random plaintexts P_3 and define $P_4 = P_3 \oplus \alpha$. Encrypt them under K_C and K_D to obtain $C_3 = E_{K_C}(P_3)$ and $C_4 = E_{K_D}(P_4)$, where $K_C = K_A \oplus \Delta K_{AC}$ and $K_D = K_A \oplus \Delta K_{AB} \oplus \Delta K_{AC}$.
4. For the generated quartet (P_1, P_2, P_3, P_4) and the corresponding ciphertexts (C_1, C_2, C_3, C_4), we consider it a right quartet if it satisfies the conditions $C_1 \oplus C_3 = \delta$ and $C_2 \oplus C_4 = \delta$, and use such quartets in the attack.

Accordingly, when the block length is n-bit, the probability of constructing a right quartet is $2^{-n}\,(\hat{p}\,\hat{q})^2$. Therefore, $N \cdot 2^{-n}\,(\hat{p}\,\hat{q})^2$ right quartets are expected in the attack.

3.3 Boomerang Connectivity Table

Conventionally, the probabilities of the boomerang and rectangle distinguishers are approximated by the product of the differential probabilities of E_0 and E_1 ($E = E_1 \circ E_0$). However, this approximation ignores the dependency between E_0 and E_1. To estimate the probability of a boomerang and rectangle distinguisher more accurately, the Boomerang Connectivity Table (BCT) [7] was introduced. When the encryption function E is represented as $E = E_1 \circ E_m \circ E_0$, the BCT at the switching point E_m captures the probability that, when the output difference Δ_i of E_0 and the input difference Δ_o of E_1 meet at the switch, the difference after the switch returns to the same output difference Δ_i of E_0 (Fig. 2).

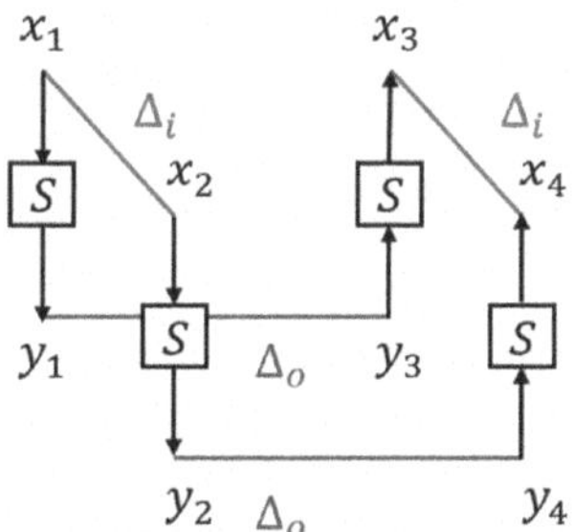

Fig. 2. Computing r for a single S-box in E_m

For a single n-bit S-box S, the BCT can be expressed as follows:

$$\mathrm{BCT}[\Delta_i, \Delta_o] = \#\{x \in \{0,1\}^n \mid S^{-1}(S(x) \oplus \Delta_o) \,\oplus\, S^{-1}(S(x \oplus \Delta_i) \oplus \Delta_o) = \Delta_i\}.$$

If m S-boxes are active in parallel with differences $(\Delta_i^{(j)}, \Delta_o^{(j)})$ for $j = 1, \ldots, m$, where n is the S-box input/output size (in bits), the per-S-box and overall switching probabilities are

$$r_S(\Delta_i^{(j)}, \Delta_o^{(j)}) = \frac{\mathrm{BCT}[\Delta_i^{(j)}, \Delta_o^{(j)}]}{2^n}, \qquad r = \prod_{j=1}^{m} r_S(\Delta_i^{(j)}, \Delta_o^{(j)}).$$

Therefore, the probabilities of the boomerang and rectangle distinguishers can be expressed more precisely as

$$\begin{aligned} \Pr[\text{boomerang distinguisher}] &\approx (p\,q)^2 \cdot r, \\ \Pr[\text{rectangle distinguisher}] &\approx 2^{-n}\,(\hat{p}\,\hat{q})^2 \cdot r. \end{aligned}$$

4 Obstacles in Applying Related-Key Boomerang and Rectangle Attacks to Rijndael-256

In this section, we describe the differences between AES-256 and Rijndael-256 in the construction of collision trails for related-key boomerang-style attacks. Furthermore, through an analysis of the key schedule, we present an optimal trail search strategy for Rijndael-256.

Given an input difference through a nonlinear transformation, we obtain the corresponding output difference, which we classify as follows:

- If the input difference is zero, or if both the input value x and the difference Δx are known so that the output difference is uniquely determined, then the output difference is called a *fixed difference*, denoted by Δ_{fix}.
- If the input difference is nonzero and the input value x is unknown, so that the output difference can take multiple values, then the output difference is called an *unfixed difference*, denoted by Δ_{unf}.

4.1 Feasibility of Local Collisions in AES-256 and Rijndael-256

Here, we examine the feasibility of local collision in AES-256 and Rijndael-256.

Local Collision of AES-256. A local collision is a differential that starts and ends with a zero difference in the internal state but exhibits a nonzero difference in intermediate rounds. A key difference injected at a specific round is called a *disturbance*, and an additional key difference inserted to cancel part or all of the resulting internal state difference is called a *correction*.

In AES-256, the block state (128-bit) and key state (256-bit) differ in size, causing the disturbance and correction appear in different round keys. Thus, by propagating the disturbance injected into the internal state through SB, SR, and MC and then treating the result as the correction, a local collision can be constructed. The AES-256 key schedule exhibits a two-round periodicity of local collisions, which can be exploited to construct related-key attacks based on local collisions [4].

Local Collision of Rijndael-256. Rijndael-256 exhibits structural properties different from those of AES-256.

Property 1. *In Rijndael-256, the disturbance and correction occur simultaneously within the same round key. Therefore, unlike AES-256, local collision cannot be constructed by separating these components.*

An all-zero difference refers to a state in which every byte is zero. In Rijndael-256, when a disturbance is injected, the corresponding key state into which the correction is applied does not exhibit an all-zero difference. Therefore, the correction cannot make the internal state an all-zero difference, and a local collision analogous to that in AES-256 cannot be constructed. Figure 3 illustrates the collision trails of AES-256 and Rijndael-256. When the disturbance is given as a single byte at position $(0, 0)$, a valid correction exists in AES-256 that produces a local collision. By contrast, no such correction can be found in Rijndael-256 under the same conditions.

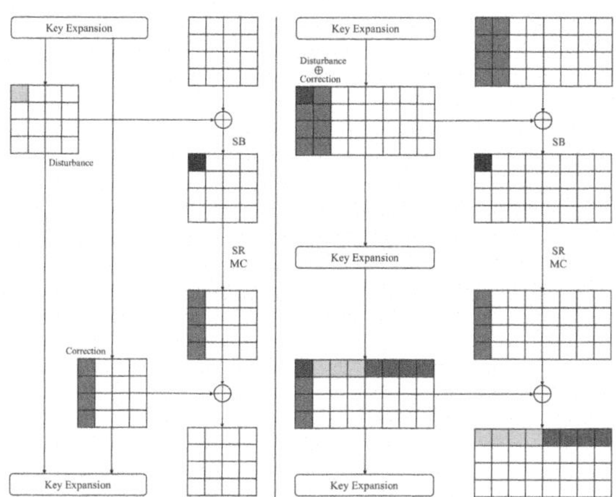

Fig. 3. Comparison of collision trails in AES-256 and Rijndael-256

4.2 Analysis of Differential Propagation in the Rijndael-256 Key Schedule

In this section, we analyze differential propagation in the Rijndael-256 key schedule and propose an efficient method for exploring partial differential trails, thereby reducing the number of candidates to be considered when constructing boomerang-style trails.

In our attack model, the adversary has no control over the key; therefore, we make the following assumption.

Assumption 1. *In constructing a key differential trail, an unfixed output difference that passes through an S-box of the key schedule is treated as an indeterminate variable.*

In our related-key model, the adversary has no control over the key. However, when passing through an SB transformation of the round function, the adversary can adjust the plaintexts so that the resulting output difference matches the intended value with a probability determined by the difference distribution table (DDT).

By contrast, for the S-box in the key schedule (i.e., SubWord), the input is determined entirely by key bytes, which remain beyond the adversary's control.

Although the corresponding output difference is uniquely determined for each key, it is unknown to the adversary. Therefore, all possible outputs must be taken into account in trail construction, and the resulting difference is treated as a key-dependent indeterminate value.

For a key state K, let U_i $(i = 0, 1, \ldots, 7)$ represent the 4-byte words obtained by splitting each row into left and right halves. In particular, $U_{2i} = K(i, *_L)$ and $U_{2i+1} = K(i, *_R)$ for $i = 0, 1, 2, 3$. The partitioned form is shown in Fig. 4. Under this partitioning, the key state exhibits the following properties with respect to the key schedule function.

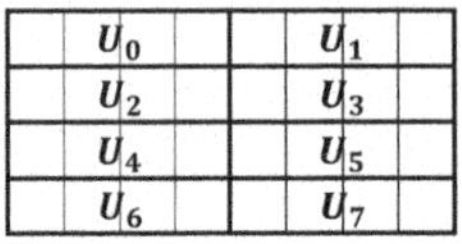

U_0	U_1
U_2	U_3
U_4	U_5
U_6	U_7

Fig. 4. Key state division

Property 2. *If the active bytes are located in different words, the differences generated during the key schedule process do not cancel each other out.*

Suppose multiple distinct words are activated simultaneously. For the active difference in U_i to cancel that in U_j, its difference would need to propagate through the key schedule into the bytes of U_j. However, any difference propagated into a different word becomes a key-dependent indeterminate value, regardless of whether a difference already exists at that position. Therefore, differences across distinct words do not cancel each other out.

This property can be applied to reduce the range of possible disturbance choices, as disturbances are propagated according to the key schedule.

Property 3. *Any trail generated by an arbitrary disturbance can be decomposed into trails generated by single-word disturbances.*

According to Property 2, the propagation of disturbance can be regarded as the superposition of disturbances activated in each single word independently, prior to the emergence of indeterminate differences when multiple words are activated simultaneously. The length of this fixed-only segment is determined by occurrence of an indeterminate difference among the individual trails, and the number of active bytes during this segment equals the sum of active bytes in each trail.

Since the key schedule consists mostly of linear operations, we make the following expectation.

Expectation 1. *If a disturbance is confined to a single word, the pattern for achieving minimal-weight disturbance propagation is expected when all disturbance bytes take the same value.*

Suppose a disturbance is confined to a single word U_i, denoted by $U_i = (w_0, w_1, w_2, w_3)$. Here, each w_j denotes the difference value at the corresponding position. This also includes partially activated cases such as $(w_0, w_1, w_2, w_3) = (a, b, 0, 0)$. Because the key schedule involves linear operations between adjacent columns, linear relations among the w_js (e.g., $w_0 \oplus w_1 = 0$) may cause some bytes to cancel out during the propagation of disturbance. Consequently, partial cancellations occur in certain combinations. From a long-term diffusion perspective, cancellation is expected to be most significant if all nonzero bytes take the same value.

In addition to this expectation-based reduction, the candidate disturbances can be further compressed by structural equivalences, as stated in the following property.

Property 4. *With respect to the propagation of disturbance, the set of candidate disturbances includes 16 representative cases.*

According to Property 3 and Expectation 1, the disturbance is assumed to be confined to a single word U_i, with all active bytes taking the same value. When the active byte value is fixed to α, there are 15 possible disturbance patterns.

For instance, consider a disturbance α in the first column byte of U_i, represented as $(\alpha, 0, 0, 0)$. Backward propagation yields $(\alpha, \alpha, 0, 0)$ in the previous round, which can be regarded as an equivalent disturbance: propagating $(\alpha, \alpha, 0, 0)$ forward produces the original $(\alpha, 0, 0, 0)$. Taking all such equivalence relations into account, only eight distinct trails remain within a single word U_i. Furthermore, although α can take any value from `0x00` to `0xff`, this only changes the difference value and does not affect the trail structure. Therefore, there are eight trails within a single word U_i, yielding 64 representative trails for $i = 0, \ldots, 7$. Figure 8 in the Appendix A illustrates the disturbance groups within a single word.

In cases where a key state resulting from a disturbance propagation contains an indeterminate difference, it is injected into the internal state and propagates through the rounds without cancellation, which makes the construction of longer trails disadvantageous. Therefore, we target disturbance propagation in which the state consisting solely of Δ_{fix} is preserved for at least three rounds. Consequently, only the cases with a single active byte in column 0 or column 1 of a word U_i are relevant, giving two cases per word and thus 16 representative trails in total.

However, to retain the benefit described above, the key differential trail must also remain fixed for at least 3 rounds; consequently, we restrict our attention to such trails.

Observation 1. *Only seven differential trails exist in which the key differential trail is maintained entirely in fixed differences for at least 3-round.*

The key state in a key differential trail should also consist solely of Δ_{fix} for at least 3-round. Otherwise, an indeterminate difference is injected into the internal state and does not cancel out. If the key differential state contains an indeterminate difference, it is likewise injected into the internal state, and the expected benefit described in Property 4 is lost. To construct long trails, it is therefore desirable to target key differential trails that remain composed solely of Δ_{fix} for at least 3-round.

Among the 16 candidate disturbances identified in Property 4, only seven trails satisfy this criterion. These correspond to single-byte disturbances located at positions (0,0), (0,4), (1,1), (1,5), (2,4), (3,4), and (3,5). The concrete forms of these trails are illustrated in Fig. 9 of the Appendix B.

To construct the longest possible trails with favorable probabilities, one should therefore build the overall boomerang-style trail by combining only these seven cases.

4.3 Key Differences Conditions for Valid Related-Key Boomerang and Rectangle of Rijndael-256

In a related-key boomerang-style attack, a single differential trail is applied in both directions. Therefore, for a given key relation, the key differential trail must be identical in both directions. In particular, in the case of a fixed difference, the values in both directions must match, and in the case of an indeterminate difference, both directions must remain indeterminate. If the key differential trail is consistent only for specific key values, this implicitly reduces the key space. However, as the attacker cannot control the keys of the given oracles, such key relations are excluded from consideration in our attack model. Suppose the adversary is given a key relation as shown in Fig. 5, where the key conditions are $K_A^j \oplus \Delta\gamma = K_C^j$ and $K_B^j \oplus \Delta\gamma = K_D^j$. From this, it follows that the relation below always holds:

$$\Delta\delta = K_A^j \oplus K_B^j = (K_A^j \oplus \Delta\gamma) \oplus (K_B^j \oplus \Delta\gamma) = K_C^j \oplus K_D^j = \Delta\delta'. \quad (1)$$

As shown in Fig. 5, $\Delta\alpha = K_A^{j-1} \oplus K_B^{j-1}$ and $\Delta\alpha' = K_C^{j-1} \oplus K_D^{j-1}$. If the key schedule function F consists only of linear operations, the following relation holds:

$$\begin{aligned}
\Delta\alpha &= K_A^{j-1} \oplus K_B^{j-1} \\
&= F^{-1}(K_A^j) \oplus F^{-1}(K_B^j) \\
&= F^{-1}(K_C^j \oplus \Delta\gamma) \oplus F^{-1}(K_D^j \oplus \Delta\gamma) \quad \text{(by the given key relation)} \\
&= F^{-1}(K_C^j) \oplus F^{-1}(K_D^j) \oplus F^{-1}(\Delta\gamma) \oplus F^{-1}(\Delta\gamma) \quad (\text{linearity of} F^{-1}) \\
&= F^{-1}(K_C^j) \oplus F^{-1}(K_D^j) \\
&= K_C^{j-1} \oplus K_D^{j-1} \\
&= \Delta\alpha'.
\end{aligned}$$

When the key schedule function involves nonlinear operations, the equality $\Delta\alpha = \Delta\alpha'$ generally does not hold. If $\Delta\gamma = 0$, then $\Delta\beta{=}\Delta\beta'{=}0$, which directly yields $K_A^{j-1} = K_C^{j-1}$ and $K_B^{j-1} = K_D^{j-1}$. Therefore, we obtain

$$\Delta\alpha = K_A^{j-1} \oplus K_B^{j-1} = K_C^{j-1} \oplus K_D^{j-1} = \Delta\alpha'.$$

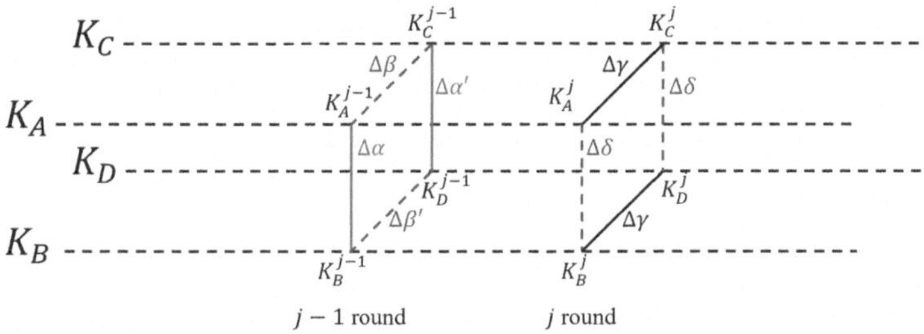

Fig. 5. Key relation at round j

Alternatively, if $\Delta\alpha = 0$, then we have $\Delta\delta = 0$, and by Eq. (1) it follows that $\Delta\delta = \Delta\delta'$, which implies that $\Delta\delta'$ also takes the all zero value. Hence, we obtain $\Delta\alpha = \Delta\alpha' = 0$. The same conclusion holds when the condition $\Delta\delta = 0$ is given.

In Rijndael-256, the key schedule applies nonlinear operations only to specific bytes of the key state. Thus, to ensure that the key relations are independent of the key values, it is enough to impose conditions on certain bytes of the differences. According to the key schedule, the differential propagation can be expressed column-wise in cases:

$$\Delta K^{r-1}(*,j) = \begin{cases} \text{SubWord}(\text{RotWord}(\Delta K^{r-1}(*,7))) \oplus \Delta K^r(*,0), & j=0, \\ \text{SubWord}(\Delta K^r(*,3)) \oplus \Delta K^r(*,4), & j=4, \\ \Delta K^r(*,j-1) \oplus \Delta K^r(*,j), & j \in \{1,2,3,5,6,7\}. \end{cases} \tag{2}$$

According to the key schedule, we have

$$\begin{aligned} \Delta\gamma(*,3) = {} & \text{SubWord}(\text{RotWord}(\Delta\beta(*,7))) \\ & \oplus \Delta\beta(*,0) \oplus \Delta\beta(*,1) \oplus \Delta\beta(*,2) \oplus \Delta\beta(*,3). \end{aligned}$$

If $\Delta\gamma(*,3) = 0$, then both $\Delta\beta(*,7) = 0$ and $\Delta\beta(*,0) \oplus \Delta\beta(*,1) \oplus \Delta\beta(*,2) \oplus \Delta\beta(*,3) = 0$ must hold. The same relations apply symmetrically to $\Delta\beta'$. Consequently, when $\Delta\gamma(*,3) = 0$ and $\Delta\beta(*,7) = 0$, the input difference to the nonlinear part of Eq. (2) is zero, so that the relation can be equivalently expressed as the linear form in Eq. (3).

$$\Delta\beta(*,j) = \begin{cases} \Delta\gamma(*,j), & j=0,4, \\ \Delta\gamma(*,j-1) \oplus \Delta\gamma(*,j), & j \in \{1,2,3,5,6,7\}. \end{cases} \tag{3}$$

The same condition also applies to $\Delta\beta'$, and since $\Delta\gamma$ is fixed, we have $\Delta\beta = \Delta\beta'$ regardless of the key values. Hence, it follows that $\Delta\alpha = \Delta\alpha'$. In addition to the condition $\Delta\gamma(*,3) = 0$, one can similarly show that $\Delta\alpha = \Delta\alpha'$ also holds when $\Delta\delta(*,3) = 0$, $\Delta\alpha(*,7) = 0$, or $\Delta\beta(*,7) = 0$ is given.

However, when $\Delta\alpha(*,0)$ or $\Delta\alpha(*,4)$ contains Δ_{unf}, then the difference values at those positions need not be equal; accordingly, the above conditions are not required. However, if the byte values constituting Δ_{unf} differ, the form of key differences changes in subsequent rounds. It is therefore reasonable to conclude that no key relation can enforce identical key difference forms in both directions across all key values when the values constituting Δ_{unf} differ.

4.4 Procedure for Trail Construction

For any of the seven trails identified after Observation 1, the differential trail is constructed in detail through the following procedure.

1. Select one of the seven representative disturbances identified in Observation 1, and suppose it is injected in round r. We denote by $\Delta D^r \in (\mathbb{F}_2^8)^{4\times 8}$ the key state with all-zero difference except at the injected position.
2. Obtain ΔD^{r-1} by applying one step of the inverse key schedule to ΔD^r.
3. Apply the round transformations SB, SR, and MC to ΔD^{r-1} to obtain the correction ΔC^r that cancels the disturbance in round r.
4. Compute the round-r key state as $\Delta K^r = \Delta D^r \oplus \Delta C^r$. This key state is then propagated through the key schedule to construct the key differential trail.

The disturbance correction combinations derived through this procedure constitute partial differential trails. As a boomerang-style trail can only be realized when the associated key states satisfy the conditions specified in Sect. 4.3, the partial trails are truncated so as to enforce these constraints. Among the resulting candidates, those yielding the most favorable balance between trail probability and data complexity are selected in order to construct the longest feasible boomerang-style trails.

5 Boomerang and Rectangle Distinguishers for 7-Round Rijndael-256

In this section, we present optimal boomerang and rectangle distinguishers for 7-round Rijndael-256, derived using the trail construction method described in Sect. 4. We show that an adversary, using these distinguishers, can distinguish Rijndael-256 under a specific key relation from a random permutation.

5.1 Boomerang Distinguisher for 7-Round Rijndael-256

The adversary is provided with four oracles and seeks to distinguish whether they correspond to Rijndael-256 encryption and decryption oracles under a related-key relation or to random permutation oracles. The key relation available to the adversary is specified in Table 2, and the boomerang trail derived from this relation is illustrated in Fig. 6. The key relation must satisfy the condition described in Sect. 4.3, and X_0 to X_4 denote Δ_{unf} values that are identical in both directions of ΔK_{AC}^r. Since $\Delta K_{AC}^0(*, 4)$ has the same values in both directions, the same holds for $\Delta K_{AB}^0(*, 4)$.

Table 2. Related-key boomerang difference for Rijndael-256

ΔK^{T}_{AB}					
0	1f 00 00 00 ?? 00 00 00	1	1f 1f 1f 1f 00 00 00 00	2	1f 00 1f 00 00 00 00 00
	1f 00 00 00 ?? 00 00 00		1f 1f 1f 1f 00 00 00 00		1f 00 1f 00 00 00 00 00
	?? 00 00 00 ?? 00 00 00		21 21 21 21 00 00 00 00		21 00 21 00 00 00 00 00
	3e 00 00 00 ?? 01 01 01		3e 3e 3e 3e 01 00 01 00		3e 00 3e 00 01 01 00 00
3	1f 1f 00 00 00 00 00 00	4	1f 00 00 00 00 00 00 00		
	1f 1f 00 00 00 00 00 00		1f 00 00 00 00 00 00 00		
	21 21 00 00 00 00 00 00		21 00 00 00 00 00 00 00		
	3e 3e 00 00 01 00 00 00		3e 00 00 00 01 01 01 01		
ΔK^{T}_{AC}					
0	?? 06 06 06 X_0 X_0 X_0 X_0	1	06 00 06 00 X_0 00 X_0 00	2	06 06 00 00 X_0 X_0 00 00
	?? 06 06 06 X_1 X_1 X_1 X_1		06 00 06 00 X_1 00 X_1 00		06 06 00 00 X_1 X_1 00 00
	?? ?? ?? ?? X_2 X_2 X_2 X_2		?? 00 ?? 00 X_2 00 X_2 00		?? ?? 00 00 X_2 X_2 00 00
	?? 0c 0c 0c X_3 X_4 X_3 X_4		0c 00 0c 00 X_3 bc X_4 00		0c 0c 00 00 X_3 X_4 00 00
3	06 00 00 00 X_0 00 00 00	4	06 06 06 06 00 00 00 00	5	06 00 06 00 00 00 00 00
	06 00 00 00 X_1 00 00 00		06 06 06 06 00 00 00 00		06 00 06 00 00 00 00 00
	?? 00 00 00 X_2 00 00 00		0a 0a 0a 0a 00 00 00 00		0a 00 0a 00 00 00 00 00
	0c 00 00 00 X_3 bc bc bc		0c 0c 0c 0c bc 00 bc 00		0c 00 0c 00 bc bc 00 00
6	06 06 00 00 00 00 00 00	7	06 00 00 00 00 00 00 00		
	06 06 00 00 00 00 00 00		06 00 00 00 00 00 00 00		
	0a 0a 00 00 00 00 00 00		0a 00 00 00 00 00 00 00		
	0c 0c 00 00 bc 00 00 00		0c 00 00 00 bc bc bc bc		

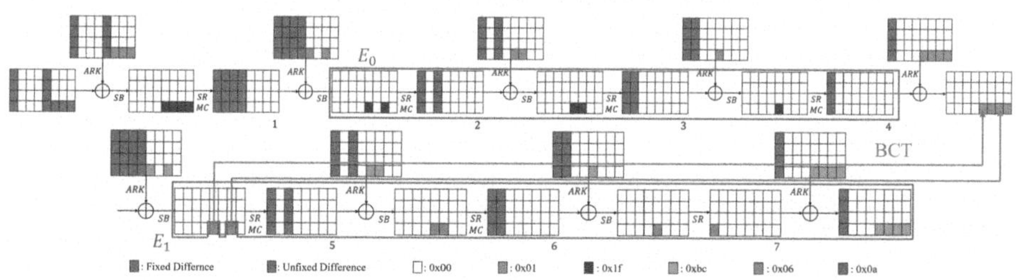

Fig. 6. Boomerang distinguishing trail for Rijndael-256

The adversary employs the following distinguishing strategy.

1. The adversary fixes the 24-byte subset $c_{i,j}$ of the 32-byte state to arbitrary constants, and assigns all possible values `0x00--0xff` to the remaining 8 bytes (denoted as `??` below), thus generating a plaintext set P_1 of size 2^{64}.

$c_{0,0}$	$c_{0,1}$	$c_{0,2}$	$c_{0,3}$	??	$c_{0,5}$	$c_{0,6}$	$c_{0,7}$
$c_{1,0}$	$c_{1,1}$	$c_{1,2}$	$c_{1,3}$	??	$c_{1,5}$	$c_{1,6}$	$c_{1,7}$
??	$c_{2,1}$	$c_{2,2}$	$c_{2,3}$	??	$c_{2,5}$	$c_{2,6}$	$c_{2,7}$
$c_{3,0}$	$c_{3,1}$	$c_{3,2}$	$c_{3,3}$	??	??	??	??

2. In a similar manner, the adversary generates another plaintext set P_2 of the same size, with the structure shown below.

$c_{0,0} \oplus$ 1f	$c_{0,1}$	$c_{0,2}$	$c_{0,3}$	??	$c_{0,5}$	$c_{0,6}$	$c_{0,7}$
$c_{1,0} \oplus$ 1f	$c_{1,1}$	$c_{1,2}$	$c_{1,3}$	??	$c_{1,5}$	$c_{1,6}$	$c_{1,7}$
??	$c_{2,1}$	$c_{2,2}$	$c_{2,3}$	??	$c_{2,5}$	$c_{2,6}$	$c_{2,7}$
$c_{3,0} \oplus$ 3e	$c_{3,1}$	$c_{3,2}$	$c_{3,3}$	??	??	??	??

3. By computing $O^{dec}_{K_C}(O^{enc}_{K_A}(P_1)\oplus\Delta C)$ and $O^{dec}_{K_D}(O^{enc}_{K_B}(P_2)\oplus\Delta C)$, the adversary obtains the sets P_3 and P_4. The value of ΔC is specified as follows:

06	00	00	00	00	00	00	00
06	00	00	00	00	00	00	00
0a	00	00	00	00	00	00	00
0a	00	00	00	bc	bc	bc	bc

4. We filter the quartets (P_1, P_2, P_3, P_4) and retain only those that satisfy the condition.

5. Steps 3 and 4 are repeated with P_1 and P_2 swapped.

6. Steps 1 to 5 are repeated N times.

If any quartets remain after filtering, the adversary concludes that the oracles correspond to Rijndael-256 under the related-key relation. Otherwise, the oracles are regarded as random permutations.

Detailed Analysis

Trail Probability. The probability that a random $\Delta_{\texttt{unf}}$ byte, after passing through SB, satisfies the first-round difference of the boomerang distinguisher is 2^{-8} for each of the 8 bytes, resulting in a total probability of 2^{-64}. In Rounds 2–4 and 6–7, each active S-box propagates a difference with probability 2^{-6}. Accordingly, the forward trail probability is $p = 2^{-6\times5} = 2^{-30}$, and the backward trail probability is $q = 2^{-6\times3} = 2^{-18}$. For the switching probability `P_switch`, all bytes except those at positions $(3,4)$ and $(3,6)$ satisfy the condition with probability 1, while these two positions contribute with probability 6×2^{-8} according to the BCT. Thus, `P_switch` $= (6 \times 2^{-8})^2 \approx 2^{-10.83}$.

Taking all factors into account, the probability is Pr[`right quartet`] $= 2^{-64} \times (2^{-30} \times 2^{-18})^2 \times 2^{-10.83} = 2^{-170.83}$.

Data Complexity Analysis. As $|P_1| = |P_2| = 2^{64}$, a single execution of Steps 1 to 5 produces $2^{64} \times 2^{64} \times 2 = 2^{129}$ quartets. Accordingly, when Steps 1 to 5 are repeated N times, the number of generated quartets is $N \times 2^{129}$. As the probability that a random quartet becomes a `right quartet` is $2^{-170.83}$, the expected number of right quartets is $N \times 2^{129} \times 2^{-170.83}$. To ensure a reliable success probability, we set $N = 2^{43.83}$ so that the expected number of right quartets is four.

Therefore, the overall data complexity amounts to $2|P_1| \times N = 2^{108.83}$ 256-bit blocks.

Filtering Analysis. Among the values generated through the oracles, 24 bytes of $P_3 \oplus P_4$ are 0 or fixed difference bytes, which allows $24 \times 8 = 192$ bits of filtering. For the bytes $(2,0)$, $(3,5)$, $(3,6)$, and $(3,7)$ in $P_1 \oplus P_2$ and $P_3 \oplus P_4$, each must take one of $127 \approx 2^7$ possible values, so each byte contributes 1 bit of filtering. Thus, these four bytes provide $2 \times 4 = 8$ bits of filtering in total. For the bytes $(0,4)$, $(1,4)$, and $(2,4)$ in $P_1 \oplus P_2$, each must also take one of $127 \approx 2^7$ possible values, contributing 1 bit of filtering each. In addition, due to the related-key condition $P_1 \oplus P_2 = P_3 \oplus P_4$, each of these 3 bytes contribute an additional 8-bit filtering. Thus, these 3 bytes contribute a total of $9 \times 3 = 27$ bits.

In total, the filtering enforces 227-bit conditions on the quartets.

Distinguishing Probability. The total number of quartets is $2^{172.83}$. In the related-key oracle, the expected number of right quartets is $\lambda_R = 4$: by Poisson approximation, the probability that at least one exists is $\Pr_{\text{RK}}[\text{survive}] \geq 1 - e^{-4} \approx 0.9817$, where "$\geq$" indicates that the actual probability can be greater when the survival of wrong quartets is also taken into account. By contrast, in the random permutation oracle, the expected number is only $\lambda_{\text{RP}} = 2^{172.83-227} = 2^{-54.17}$. Consequently, $\Pr_{\text{RP}}[\text{survive}] \approx 1 - e^{-\lambda_{\text{RP}}} = 1 - e^{-2^{-54.17}}$, which is negligible.

Therefore, the adversary can effectively distinguish 7-round Rijndael-256 from a random oracle.

5.2 Rectangle Distinguisher for 7-Round Rijndael-256

As described in Sect. 5.1, the adversary is given four related-key oracles. However, in this case, all four are encryption oracles. Table 3 presents the corresponding key relations, and Fig. 7 illustrates the rectangle trail employed for distinguishing. Note that x_0 through x_4 are not guaranteed to take identical values in both directions.

Table 3. Related-key rectangle difference for Rijndael-256

ΔK^{r}_{AB}					
0	1f 1f 1f 1f 00 00 00 00	1	1f 00 1f 00 00 00 00 00	2	1f 1f 00 00 00 00 00 00
	1f 1f 1f 1f 00 00 00 00		1f 00 1f 00 00 00 00 00		1f 1f 00 00 00 00 00 00
	21 21 21 21 00 00 00 00		21 00 21 00 00 00 00 00		21 21 00 00 00 00 00 00
	3e 3e 3e 3e 01 00 01 00		3e 00 3e 00 01 01 00 00		3e 3e 00 00 01 00 00 00
3	1f 00 00 00 00 00 00 00				
	1f 00 00 00 00 00 00 00				
	21 00 00 00 00 00 00 00				
	3e 00 00 00 01 01 01 01				
ΔK^{r}_{AC}					
3	06 06 06 06 00 00 00 00	4	06 00 06 00 00 00 00 00	5	06 06 00 00 00 00 00 00
	06 06 06 06 00 00 00 00		06 00 06 00 00 00 00 00		06 06 00 00 00 00 00 00
	0a 0a 0a 0a 00 00 00 00		0a 00 0a 00 00 00 00 00		0a 0a 00 00 00 00 00 00
	0c 0c 0c 0c bc 00 bc 00		0c 00 0c 00 bc bc 00 00		0c 0c 00 00 bc 00 00 00
6	06 00 00 00 00 00 00 00	7	06 06 06 06 x_1 x_1 x_1 x_1		
	06 00 00 00 00 00 00 00		06 06 06 06 x_2 x_2 x_2 x_2		
	0a 00 00 00 00 00 00 00		x_0 x_0 x_0 x_0 x_3 x_3 x_3 x_3		
	0c 00 00 00 bc bc bc bc		0c 0c 0c 0c x_4 x_4 x_4 x_4		

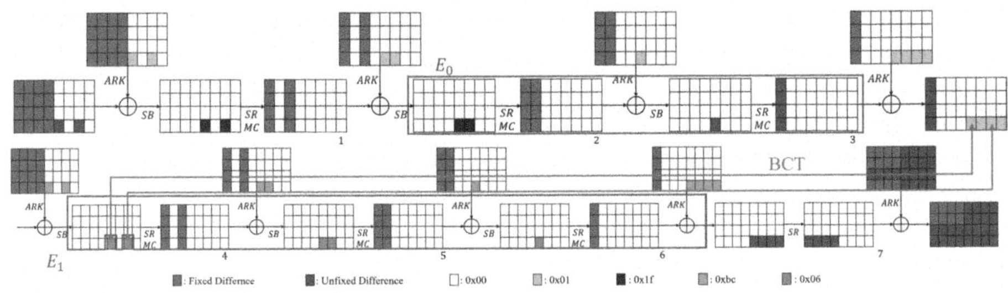

Fig. 7. Rectangle distinguishing trail for Rijndael-256

The adversary employs the following rectangle distinguishing strategy.

1. The adversary collects N independent structures. For each $i \in \{1, \ldots, N\}$, a plaintext set $P_1^{(i)}$ of size 2^{16} is generated by fixing all but 2 bytes to arbitrary

constants (chosen independently for each structure) and enumerating all possible values `0x00--0xff` for the remaining 2 bytes.

$c_{0,0}$	$c_{0,1}$	$c_{0,2}$	$c_{0,3}$	$c_{0,4}$	$c_{0,5}$	$c_{0,6}$	$c_{0,7}$
$c_{1,0}$	$c_{1,1}$	$c_{1,2}$	$c_{1,3}$	$c_{1,4}$	$c_{1,5}$	$c_{1,6}$	$c_{1,7}$
$c_{2,0}$	$c_{2,1}$	$c_{2,2}$	$c_{2,3}$	$c_{2,4}$	$c_{2,5}$	$c_{2,6}$	$c_{2,7}$
$c_{3,0}$	$c_{3,1}$	$c_{3,2}$	$c_{3,3}$	??	$c_{3,5}$	??	$c_{3,7}$

2. For each i, the adversary constructs another plaintext sets $P_2^{(i)}$ of the same size, as shown below.

$c_{0,0} \oplus$ `1f`	$c_{0,1} \oplus$ `1f`	$c_{0,2} \oplus$ `1f`	$c_{0,3} \oplus$ `1f`	$c_{0,4}$	$c_{0,5}$	$c_{0,6}$	$c_{0,7}$
$c_{1,0} \oplus$ `1f`	$c_{1,1} \oplus$ `1f`	$c_{1,2} \oplus$ `1f`	$c_{1,3} \oplus$ `1f`	$c_{1,4}$	$c_{1,5}$	$c_{1,6}$	$c_{1,7}$
$c_{2,0} \oplus$ `21`	$c_{2,1} \oplus$ `21`	$c_{2,2} \oplus$ `21`	$c_{2,3} \oplus$ `21`	$c_{2,4}$	$c_{2,5}$	$c_{2,6}$	$c_{2,7}$
$c_{3,0} \oplus$ `3e`	$c_{3,1} \oplus$ `3e`	$c_{3,2} \oplus$ `3e`	$c_{3,3} \oplus$ `3e`	??	$c_{3,5}$	??	$c_{3,7}$

3. Using the four oracles, the adversary obtains ciphertext sets $C_{x,t}^{(i)} = O_{K_x}^{enc}(P_t^{(i)})$ for $x \in \{A, B, C, D\}$ and $t \in \{1, 2\}$. For each ordered pair of structures (i, j), quartets are constructed as follows:

$$Q_1^{(i,j)} = \{C_{A,1}^{(i)}, C_{B,2}^{(i)}, C_{C,1}^{(j)}, C_{D,2}^{(j)}\}, \qquad Q_2^{(i,j)} = \{C_{A,1}^{(i)}, C_{B,2}^{(i)}, C_{C,2}^{(j)}, C_{D,1}^{(j)}\},$$
$$Q_3^{(i,j)} = \{C_{A,2}^{(i)}, C_{B,1}^{(i)}, C_{C,1}^{(j)}, C_{D,2}^{(j)}\}, \qquad Q_4^{(i,j)} = \{C_{A,2}^{(i)}, C_{B,1}^{(i)}, C_{C,2}^{(j)}, C_{D,1}^{(j)}\}.$$

4. Filtering conditions are applied to both the plaintext and ciphertext components of all quartets, and only those satisfying the conditions are retained.

If a quartet survives filtering, the oracles are regarded as related-key Rijndael-256; otherwise, they are regarded as random permutations.

Detailed Analysis

Trail Probability. The probability of passing the first round is 2^{-16}, as each of the 2 active bytes contributes 2^{-8}. In the related-key rectangle attack, both directions must simultaneously satisfy the first-round condition, resulting in a total probability of 2^{-32}. In the second round, each active S-box propagates a difference with probability 2^{-6} in both directions. In the third round, the two directions must yield identical output differences among 127 possible pairs. According to the DDT of the AES S-box, one pair occurs with probability 2^{-6}, while the remaining 126 pairs each occur with probability 2^{-7}. Accordingly, the RMS probability of E_0 is $\hat{p} = \sqrt{(2^{-6})^{2\times 2}\left[(2^{-6})^2 + 126 \cdot (2^{-7})^2\right]} \approx 2^{-15.5}$. In Rounds 5 and 6, there are three active S-boxes, and in each direction a difference propagates with probability 2^{-6}. Thus, the probability of E_1 is $\hat{q} = (2^{-6})^3 = 2^{-18}$. The switching probability is computed in the same manner as in Subsect. 5.1, yielding $\mathtt{P\_switch} = (6 \times 2^{-8})^2 \approx 2^{-10.83}$.

Taking all factors into account, the probability that a random quartet becomes a `right quartet` is Pr[`right quartet`] $= 2^{-32} \times (2^{-15.5})^2 \times (2^{-18})^2 \times 2^{-10.83} \times 2^{-256} = 2^{-365.83}$.

Data Complexity Analysis. Because each $P_1^{(i)}$ has size 2^{16} for $i \in \{1, \ldots, N\}$, the union of all structures yields $|P_1| = N \times 2^{16}$. For each quartet type $k \in \{1, 2, 3, 4\}$, the total number of quartets obtained over all pairs of structures (i, j) is $|Q_k| = (N \times 2^{16})^2$. Thus, the total number of quartets is $(N \times 2^{16})^2 \times 4 = N^2 \times 2^{66}$. Given that the probability for a random quartet to be a `right quartet` is $2^{-365.83}$, the expected number of right quartets is $N^2 \times 2^{66} \times 2^{-365.83}$. To achieve an expected count of four right quartets to ensure reliable success probability, we set $N = 2^{150.92}$.

Therefore, the overall data complexity amounts to $(2|P_1^{(i)}|) \times N = 2^{167.92}$ 256-bit blocks.

Filtering Analysis. Let $Q = (p_a, p_b, p_c, p_d) \rightarrow (c_a, c_b, c_c, c_d)$ represents an arbitrary quartet obtained from Steps 1 to 3. For the plaintext part, the XORs $p_a \oplus p_b$ and $p_c \oplus p_d$ at byte positions $(3, 4)$ and $(3, 6)$ must each take one of 127 possible values. This yields 4-bit filtering. For the ciphertext part, the XORs $c_a \oplus c_c$ and $c_b \oplus c_d$ contain 8 bytes with fixed differences, contributing 16×8 bits of filtering. Furthermore, the bytes $(2, *_L)$ in both $c_a \oplus c_c$ and $c_b \oplus c_d$ must each take one of $127 \approx 2^7$ values and all equal, yielding 50-bit filtering. Similarly, the bytes $(i, *_R)$ for $i = 0, 1, 2, 3$ satisfy the same constraint; for $i = 2$, filtering follows once $(2,_L)$ is fixed. Finally, the bytes $(3, *_L)$ in $c_a \oplus c_c$ and $c_b \oplus c_d$ must also take one of $127 \approx 2^7$ values, contributing an additional 8 bits.

In total, the filtering results in 390 bits of filtering for the quartets.

Distinguishing Probability. The total number of quartets is $2^{367.83}$. In the related-key oracle setting, the expected number of right quartets is $\lambda_R = 4$. By the Poisson approximation, the probability of having at least one right quartet is $\Pr_{\text{RK}}[\text{survive}] \approx 0.9817$. By contrast, for the random permutation oracle, the expected number of right quartets is only $\lambda_{\text{RP}} = 2^{367.83-390} = 2^{-22.17}$. Thus, $\Pr_{\text{RP}}[\text{survive}] \approx 1 - e^{-2^{-22.17}}$, which is negligible.

Therefore, the adversary can effectively distinguish 7-round Rijndael-256 from a random oracle.

6 Conclusion

In this paper, we analyzed the resistance of Rijndael-256 against related-key attacks. Beyond the enumeration of differential trails, we comprehensively examined the round structure and key schedule of Rijndael-256, and proposed an effective exploration method for constructing effective trails. The proposed procedure integrates trail probabilities, filtering conditions, and key schedule constraints, facilitating the construction of optimal related-key distinguishers through current techniques. Applying this method, we derived the most efficient boomerang and rectangle trails, thereby establishing related-key distinguishers for 7-round Rijndael-256. This work contributes to the evaluation of Rijndael-256 for use in emerging operation modes by offering a comprehensive related-key analysis with respect to boomerang and rectangle attacks.

Acknowledgement. This work was supported by the National Research Foundation of Korea(NRF) grant funded by the Korea government(MSIT) (No. RS-2025-00564126).

A Eight Disturbance Groups in a Rijndael-256 Key State Word

Figure 8 illustrates the eight disturbance groups G_j ($j = 0, \ldots, 7$) within a single word, as described in Property 4.

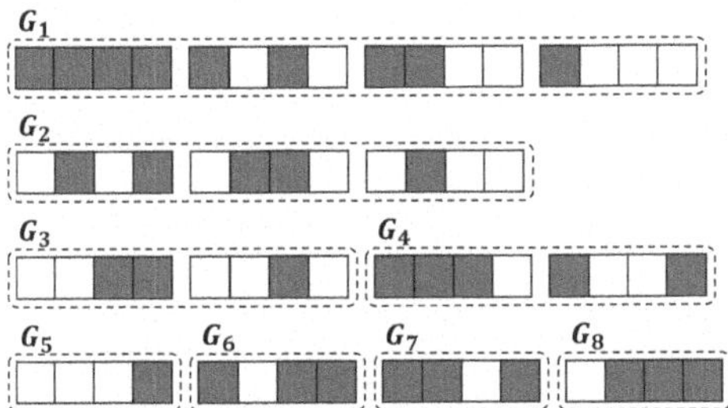

Fig. 8. Illustration of eight initial disturbance groups within a single word

B Final Seven Key Differential Trails

Figure 9 presents the key differential trails corresponding to the seven initial disturbances mentioned in Observation 1. Each element in group G_j is related through the key schedule.

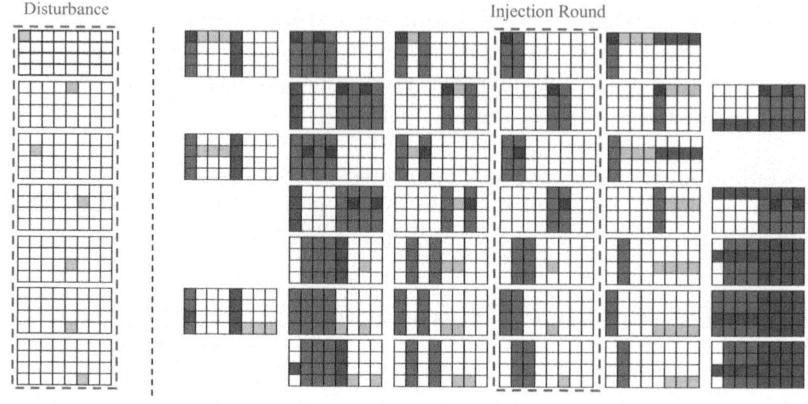

Fig. 9. Illustration of seven key differential trails

References

1. Bertoni, G., et al.: TurboSHAKE. Cryptology ePrint Archive, Report 2023/342 (2023). https://eprint.iacr.org/2023/342
2. Biham, E.: New types of cryptanalytic attacks using related keys. J. Cryptol. **7**(4), 229–246 (1994)
3. Biham, E., Dunkelman, O., Keller, N.: The rectangle attack–rectangling the serpent. In: Advances in Cryptology - EUROCRYPT 2001, LNCS, vol. 2045, pp. 340–357. Springer, Heidelberg (2001). https://doi.org/10.1007/3-540-44987-6_21, https://www.iacr.org/archive/eurocrypt2001/20450338.pdf
4. Biryukov, A., Khovratovich, D.: Related-key cryptanalysis of the full AES-192 and AES-256. In: Matsui, M. (ed.) Advances in Cryptology - ASIACRYPT 2009, LNCS, vol. 5912, pp. 1–18. Springer, Heidelberg (2009). https://doi.org/10.1007/978-3-642-10366-7_1
5. Boura, C., Canteaut, A., Naya-Plasencia, M., Suder, V.: Improved Impossible Differential Attacks on Large-Block Rijndael. In: Advances in Cryptology - ASIACRYPT 2014, LNCS, vol. 8873, pp. 392–410. Springer, Heidelberg (2014). https://doi.org/10.1007/978-3-662-45608-8_21
6. Boura, C., Canteaut, A., Naya-Plasencia, M.: Improving Integral Attacks against Rijndael-256 up to 9 Rounds. In: Selected Areas in Cryptography - SAC 2011, LNCS, vol. 7118, pp. 1–17. Springer, Heidelberg (2012). https://doi.org/10.1007/978-3-642-28496-0_1
7. Cid, C., Huang, J., Peyrin, T., Sasaki, Y., Song, L.: Boomerang connectivity table: a new cryptanalysis tool. In: EUROCRYPT 2018. LNCS, vol. 10821, pp. 683–714. Springer, Heidelberg (2018)
8. Daemen, J., Rijmen, V.: AES Proposal: Rijndael. NIST AES Proposal, Gaithersburg, MD, USA (1999)
9. Dinu, D., Guo, C., Prokop, L., Schilling, R.: Brief Comments on Rijndael-256 and the Standard RISC-V Cryptography Extension. IACR Cryptology ePrint Archive, Paper 2023/1747 (2023). https://eprint.iacr.org/2023/1747
10. Ferguson, N., et al.: The Skein Hash Function Family. Submission to NIST (Round 1 of the SHA-3 Competition) (2008). https://www.schneier.com/academic/skein/

11. Kim, J., Hong, S., Preneel, B., Biham, E., Dunkelman, O., Keller, N.: Related-key boomerang and rectangle attacks: theory and experimental analysis. IEEE Trans. Inf. Theory **58**(7), 4948–4966 (2012). https://doi.org/10.1109/TIT.2012.2191655
12. Kim, J., Kim, G., Hong, S., Lee, S., Hong, D.: The related-key rectangle attack - application to SHACAL-1. In: Information Security and Privacy - ACISP 2004, LNCS, vol. 3108, pp. 123–136. Springer, Heidelberg (2004). https://doi.org/10.1007/978-3-540-27800-9_11
13. Matyas, S., Meyer, C., Oseas, J.: Generating strong one-way functions with cryptographic algorithms. IBM Techn. Disclos. Bull. **27**(10A), 5658–5659 (1985)
14. McGrew, D., et al.: Practical Challenges with AES-GCM and the Need for a New Cipher. NIST Workshop on Block Cipher Modes of Operation (2023). https://csrc.nist.gov/csrc/media/Events/2023/third-workshop-on-block-cipher-modes-of-operation/documents/accepted-papers/Practical%20Challenges%20with%20AES-GCM.pdf
15. Miyaguchi, S., Ohta, K., Iwata, M.: Confirmation that some hash functions are not collision free. In: EUROCRYPT'90, LNCS, vol. 473, pp. 326–343. Springer, Heidelberg (1991). https://doi.org/10.1007/3-540-46877-3_30
16. National Institute of Standards and Technology: Announcing Request for Candidate Algorithm Nominations for the Advanced Encryption Standard (AES). Federal Register **62**(177), 48051–48058 (1997)
17. National Institute of Standards and Technology: NIST Proposes to Standardize a Wider Variant of AES. CSRC News (2024). https://csrc.nist.gov/news/2024/nist-proposes-to-standardize-wider-variant-of-aes
18. Nikolić, I.: Tweaking AES. In: Selected Areas in Cryptography - SAC 2010, LNCS, vol. 6544, pp. 198–210. Springer, Heidelberg (2011). https://doi.org/10.1007/978-3-642-19574-7_14
19. Preneel, B., Govaerts, R., Vandewalle, J.: Hash functions based on block ciphers: a synthetic approach. In: CRYPTO 1993, LNCS, vol. 773, pp. 368–378. Springer, Heidelberg (1994). https://doi.org/10.1007/3-540-48329-2_31
20. Thompson, A., Sönmez Turan, M.: NIST Workshop on the Requirements for an Accordion Cipher Mode 2024: Workshop Report. NIST Interagency Report (NIST IR 8537). National Institute of Standards and Technology, Gaithersburg, MD (2024). https://doi.org/10.6028/NIST.IR.8537
21. Wagner, D.: The boomerang attack. In: Fast Software Encryption - FSE 1999, LNCS, vol. 1636, pp. 156–170. Springer, Heidelberg (1999). https://doi.org/10.1007/3-540-48519-8_12

On the Weak Differential Resistance of MGFN and the Exploration of Variants

Bingqing Li[1,2,3] and Ling Sun[1,2,3,4](✉)

[1] State Key Laboratory of Cryptography and Digital Economy Security, Shandong University, Qingdao, China
[2] State Key Laboratory of Cryptology, P. O. Box 5159, Beijing 100878, China
lingsun@sdu.edu.cn
[3] School of Cyber Science and Technology, Shandong University, Qingdao, China
[4] Quan Cheng Shandong Laboratory, Jinan, China

Abstract. The Generalized Feistel Network (GFN) has long served as a versatile foundation for lightweight block cipher design, with the even-odd shuffle variant offering particularly strong diffusion properties. Recently, MGFN was introduced under Malaysia's National Cryptography Policy, followed by MGFN-P, which replaces the original S-box with that of PRESENT to enhance resistance against differential attacks. In this work, we present a comparative study of MGFN, MGFN-P, and TWINE to reassess the root causes of MGFN's cryptanalytic weaknesses. Our analysis shows that these weaknesses cannot be attributed solely to the low branch number of MGFN's S-box, but arise primarily from the structural permutations used in its design. To investigate whether security can be improved through alternative permutations while fixing the S-box, we evaluate MGFN variants under both nibble-wise and bit-wise permutations. By exploiting equivalence relations, we reduce 40320 nibble-wise candidates to only 22 equivalence classes and identify variants with stronger resistance than MGFN and MGFN-P, though still weaker than TWINE. In the bit-wise setting, exploratory experiments with cyclic shifts and random permutations yield stronger variants, but none match TWINE's robustness. Overall, our results underscore the limitations of MGFN's design and reaffirm the reliability of well-established GFN configurations for lightweight cryptography.

Keywords: Generalized Feistel Network · MGFN · TWINE

1 Introduction

The Generalized Feistel Network (GFN) was first introduced by Zheng *et al.* [21] as a flexible extension of the classical Feistel network [8]. Since then, GFN has attracted sustained attention within the symmetric-key cryptography community [6,7,13,17], owing to its ability to balance efficiency and security through careful adjustment of the shuffle operation. Among these, the even-odd shuffle identified by Suzaki and Minematsu [17] has proven particularly influential.

H. Seo (Ed.): ICISC 2025, LNCS 16487, pp. 456–470, 2026.
https://doi.org/10.1007/978-981-95-8034-7_24

Several lightweight block ciphers, including TWINE [18] and LBlock [20], have adopted GFN-based designs and demonstrated competitive trade-offs between implementation cost and resistance to cryptanalysis.

In alignment with Malaysia's National Cryptography Policy (NCP) and National Cyber Security Policy (NCSP), Shah *et al.* recently proposed MGFN [14], a block cipher that employs a modified form of GFN. Owing to MGFN's weak resistance against differential attacks, Li *et al.* [9] introduced a variant, denoted MGFN-P, which replaces the original S-box with that of PRESENT [5]. The rationale behind this modification was to enhance the cipher's resistance to differential analysis.

Since MGFN is presented as a modification of GFN, its resistance to differential cryptanalysis should, in principle, be comparable to that of other GFN-based ciphers of similar scale, such as TWINE. However, our evaluation reveals a striking discrepancy: both MGFN and MGFN-P exhibit significantly weaker resistance to differential attacks than TWINE.

This finding prompts us to re-examine the conclusion of [9], namely, whether MGFN's relatively weak resistance to differential attacks can indeed be explained solely by its use of an S-box with a branch number of two. To address this question, we constructed hybrid designs by replacing the S-box of TWINE with those of MGFN and PRESENT. Experimental results show that substituting TWINE's S-box with MGFN's produces only negligible deviation in the differential probability bound. These results suggest that MGFN's weakness cannot be attributed solely to the low branch number of its S-box. Rather, its structural design, particularly the choice of permutations, plays a decisive role in undermining its differential resistance.

To assess whether MGFN's resistance can be improved by altering its permutation while keeping the S-box fixed, we analyzed MGFN variants under two different settings: nibble-wise permutations and bit-wise permutations.

- **Nibble-wise setting.** In this case, MGFN variants can be regarded as special instances of GFNs with even-odd shuffles. Leveraging the equivalence conditions for such GFNs established by Cauchois *et al.* [6], we reduced the 40320 possible variants to just 22 equivalence classes and evaluated their differential probability bounds using class representatives. Our results revealed one equivalence class whose members exhibit stronger resistance than both MGFN and MGFN-P, although still falling short of TWINE.
- **Bit-wise setting.** In this case, the candidate space is vastly larger, and the equivalence relation derived for nibble-wise permutations no longer applies. To explore this space, we considered two approaches: (i) restricting permutations to bit-level cyclic shifts, and (ii) generating random bit permutations. We found that the strongest variant generated by a cyclic-shift permutation achieved resistance comparable to that of the best nibble-wise permutation variant, while several variants generated by random permutations outperformed both MGFN and MGFN-P, yet still fell short of the optimal cyclic-shift and nibble-wise constructions.

Taken together, these results demonstrate that although variants stronger than the original MGFN can be identified, none achieve the robustness of TWINE. While it remains possible that unexplored bit-wise permutations could yield substantially stronger resistance, our findings indicate that the modified GFN adopted in MGFN should be employed with caution, and that well-established GFN configurations continue to represent safer design choices.

The remainder of this paper is organized as follows. Section 2 reviews the Generalized Feistel Network, differential cryptanalysis, and the target cipher MGFN along with its variant MGFN-P. Section 3 analyzes the key factors that weaken MGFN's resistance to differential attacks. Section 4 investigates MGFN variants under two different settings. Finally, Sect. 5 concludes the paper.

2 Preliminary

2.1 Generalized Feistel Network

The Generalized Feistel Network (GFN) [17] is a block cipher design paradigm that extends the classical Feistel network [8] to operate on more than two data branches. This generalization provides greater flexibility in balancing security, performance, and implementation cost.

Let k be a positive integer. A single round of a $2k$-branch GFN is defined as a permutation over $(\mathbb{F}_2^m)^{2k}$:

$$(X_0^{r+1}, X_1^{r+1}, \ldots, X_{2k-1}^{r+1}) \leftarrow \pi\left(X_0^r, F_0^r(X_0^r) \oplus X_1^r, \ldots, F_{k-1}^r(X_{2k-2}^r) \oplus X_{2k-1}^r\right),$$

where each $F_i^r : \mathbb{F}_2^m \to \mathbb{F}_2^m$ is a cryptographic keyed function, and $\pi : (\mathbb{F}_2^m)^{2k} \to (\mathbb{F}_2^m)^{2k}$ is a fixed branch permutation (or shuffle), i.e., a reordering of the $2k$ branches. An illustration of the GFN round function is shown in Fig. 1(a).

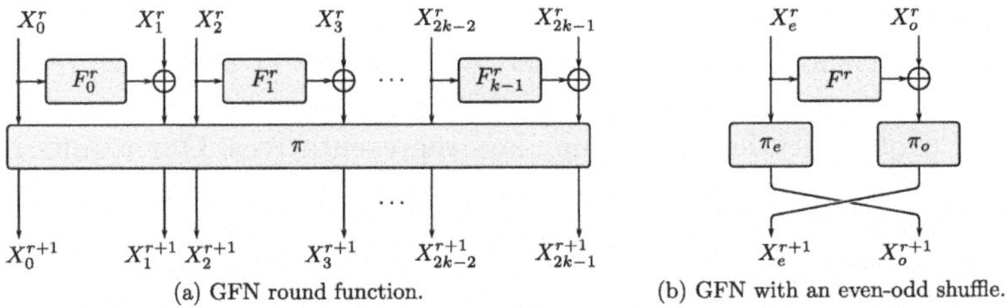

Fig. 1. Two representations of the GFN round function.

The most widely known instance of GFN is the Type-II structure, introduced by Zheng *et al.* [21], in which π is defined as a left cyclic shift by one branch. Since a Type-II GFN with large k exhibits limited diffusion, Suzaki and Minematsu [17] enhanced its diffusion by replacing the cyclic shift with alternative permutations. These permutations were identified through an exhaustive search over all possible

π mappings for k ranging from 2 to 8, evaluating the diffusion properties of the resulting GFN instances. Their results demonstrated that all optimal branch shuffles share a common property: each even-indexed input branch is mapped to an odd-indexed output branch, and vice versa. Such permutations are referred to as *even-odd shuffles*. When a GFN employs an even-odd shuffle, its round function can be expressed as shown in Fig. 1(b), where $X_e^r = X_0^r \| X_2^r \| \cdots \| X_{2k-2}^r$, $X_o^r = X_1^r \| X_3^r \| \cdots \| X_{2k-1}^r$, $F^r = F_0^r \times F_1^r \times \cdots \times F_{k-1}^r$ denotes the parallel application of k keyed functions, and π_e and π_o are k-branch shuffles.

Cauchois *et al.* [6] established conditions under which two $2k$-branch GFNs can be regarded as equivalent. For GFNs with even-odd shuffles, this condition is given below; Derbez and Euler [7] refer to it as the *natural equivalence relation* based on conjugacy.

Proposition 1 (Proposition 1, [6]**).** *Consider the construction in Fig. 1(b), namely a $2k$-branch GFN with even-odd shuffles. Let (π_e, π_o) and (π_e', π_o') denote two pairs of k-branch shuffles. If there exists a k-branch shuffle Q such that*

$$\pi_e' = Q \circ \pi_e \circ Q^{-1}, \quad \pi_o' = Q \circ \pi_o \circ Q^{-1}, \tag{1}$$

then the two GFN instances with even-odd shuffles corresponding to (π_e, π_o) and (π_e', π_o') are equivalent. The only distinction is the presence of additional shuffles applied to the plaintext input and ciphertext output.

One of the optimized 16-branch GFN instances identified by Suzaki and Minematsu [17] was adopted in the design of the block cipher TWINE [18]. Around the same time, the block cipher LBlock [20] was introduced, featuring a round function that can likewise be regarded as an instance of a GFN with even-odd shuffles. More recently, WARP [2] has been proposed as a representative example of a 32-branch GFN with even-odd shuffles.

2.2 Differential Cryptanalysis

Differential cryptanalysis [4] is one of the most powerful and widely studied methods for evaluating the security of symmetric-key primitives, particularly block ciphers. The core idea of differential cryptanalysis is to investigate how an *input difference* propagates through the cipher and influences the resulting *output difference*. A pair of differences $(\Delta_{\text{in}}, \Delta_{\text{out}})$ is called a *differential*, where Δ_{in} denotes the XOR difference applied to the plaintext (or an intermediate state), and Δ_{out} is the corresponding difference observed at the output.

To analyze a multi-round cipher, one typically constructs a *differential trail* (also referred to as a *differential characteristic*) $(\Delta_0, \Delta_1, \ldots, \Delta_R)$, where $\Delta_0 = \Delta_{\text{in}}$, $\Delta_R = \Delta_{\text{out}}$, and Δ_r represents the input difference before round r for all $0 \leqslant r < R$. Such a trail specifies how the input difference evolves round by round through the cipher. The *probability* of a differential characteristic is defined as the product of the round-level transition probabilities:

$$\Pr(\Delta_0, \Delta_1, \ldots, \Delta_R) = \prod_{0 \leqslant r < R} \Pr_{F_{K_r}}(\Delta_r, \Delta_{r+1}),$$

where F_{K_r} is the round function under round key K_r, and $\Pr_{F_{K_r}}(\Delta_r, \Delta_{r+1})$ is the probability that input difference Δ_r leads to output difference Δ_{r+1} through this round function. Since these probabilities are usually very small, it is common to represent them using the differential *weight* $\omega = -\log_2 \Pr(\Delta_0, \Delta_1, \ldots, \Delta_R)$. This logarithmic measure is particularly convenient for evaluating and comparing the resistance of different ciphers against differential attacks.

Searching for differential characteristics is a challenging problem. In recent years, numerous automated search techniques [10–12,15,16] have been developed to address this task. In this work, we adopt the method proposed by Wang *et al.* [19] to evaluate the differential probabilities of different ciphers.

2.3 MGFN and Its Variant MGFN-P

MGFN [14] operates on a 64-bit plaintext P, which is divided into two 32-bit words[1]: P_0 and P_1. The cipher comprises 24 rounds and employs a 128-bit master key, from which subkeys are derived. These subkeys are applied during the pre-whitening, round, and post-whitening stages.

The encryption begins with a pre-whitening step, where each of the two 32-bit words P_0 and P_1 is XORed with the corresponding subkey. The state then enters the round function, which in the r-th round ($0 \leqslant r < 24$) is applied to the first word X_0^r. The round function consists of four sequential layers:

- **AddKey Layer.** The 32-bit input is XORed with the round subkey RK^r.
- **RShift Layer.** The 32-bit input is split into two 16-bit words, which are rotated right by 3 bits and 8 bits, respectively. This permutation over the 32-bit input is denoted as P_R.
- **SBox Layer.** Each 4-bit nibble x is replaced with its corresponding 4-bit value $S_\text{M}(x)$ according to Table 1. The substitution over the entire 32-bit word is denoted as $\overline{S_\text{M}}$.
- **PBox Layer.** The 32-bit word is permuted bit-wise according to the mapping P_M (see Table 2), which is identical to the one used in PICO [3].

Table 1. S-boxes employed in MGFN and PRESENT.

x	0	1	2	3	4	5	6	7	8	9	a	b	c	d	e	f
$S_\text{M}(x)$	7	e	f	0	d	b	8	1	9	3	4	c	2	5	a	6
$S_\text{P}(x)$	c	5	6	b	9	0	a	d	3	e	f	8	4	7	1	2

[1] The description of the round function in this paper differs from that provided in the design document [14]. Whereas the design document presents the MGFN round function as a variant of the 4-branch GFN, we describe it here in terms of its Feistel-structure representation. In Sect. 3, we demonstrate that MGFN can be viewed as a modified GFN with an even-odd shuffle.

The output of the round function is then XORed with X_1^r. After 24 rounds, a post-whitening step is applied, and the ciphertext is obtained by concatenating the two 32-bit words.

Remark 1. Since our analysis does not rely on the pre-whitening, post-whitening, or AddKey layers, we omit a detailed discussion of the MGFN key schedule. For additional details, readers are referred to Shah *et al.* [14].

Table 2. Bit permutation P_M in MGFN.

i	0	1	2	3	4	5	6	7	8	9	10	11	12	13	14	15
$P_M(i)$	4	11	18	7	23	19	2	25	14	26	1	28	20	8	29	0
i	16	17	18	19	20	21	22	23	24	25	26	27	28	29	30	31
$P_M(i)$	31	5	15	21	9	13	24	6	17	12	22	3	16	30	10	27

Li *et al.* [9] examined the resistance of MGFN to differential cryptanalysis and identified a 6-round iterative differential trail with probability 2^{-10}. This directly implies the existence of a full-round trail with probability 2^{-40}, thereby demonstrating the cipher's insecurity. They attributed this weakness to MGFN's S-box, which has a branch number of 2—that is, the minimum sum of the Hamming weights of the input and output differences across all nontrivial differentials. To address this limitation, they proposed a variant, denoted MGFN-P, in which the original MGFN S-box is replaced with the PRESENT S-box S_P [5] (see Table 1), which has a branch number of 3. According to their analysis, this substitution substantially improves the cipher's resistance to differential cryptanalysis. A subsequent search for differential trails in MGFN-P revealed a 4-round iterative differential trail with probability 2^{-10}, from which they inferred the existence of a 24-round trail with probability 2^{-60}. Since this probability is considerably lower than that of MGFN, they concluded that MGFN-P provides stronger security than the original design.

3 On the Weak Differential Resistance of MGFN

In this section, we first provide a precise evaluation of the differential probability bounds of MGFN and MGFN-P. We then conduct a series of comparative experiments to identify the decisive factors that undermine MGFN's resistance to differential attacks.

3.1 Reassessment of MGFN and MGFN-P Differential Properties

The differential probability bounds of MGFN and MGFN-P reported in [9] were obtained through searches for iterative differential trails. To achieve more precise estimates, we reassessed the full-round differential probabilities of both ciphers using the method introduced by Wang *et al.* [19]. The evaluation results, expressed in terms of differential weight, are shown in Fig. 2. Our findings reveal a notable deviation from the bounds reported in [9]. In particular, the best 24-round differential trail in MGFN-P was found to have a probability of 2^{-53}, demonstrating that the 24-round version of MGFN-P still lacks adequate resistance against differential attacks.

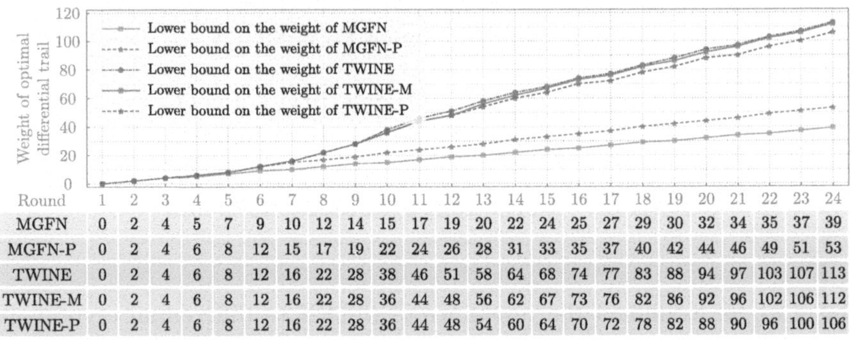

Round	1	2	3	4	5	6	7	8	9	10	11	12	13	14	15	16	17	18	19	20	21	22	23	24
MGFN	0	2	4	5	7	9	10	12	14	15	17	19	20	22	24	25	27	29	30	32	34	35	37	39
MGFN-P	0	2	4	6	8	12	15	17	19	22	24	26	28	31	33	35	37	40	42	44	46	49	51	53
TWINE	0	2	4	6	8	12	16	22	28	38	46	51	58	64	68	74	77	83	88	94	97	103	107	113
TWINE-M	0	2	4	6	8	12	16	22	28	36	44	48	56	62	67	73	76	82	86	92	96	102	106	112
TWINE-P	0	2	4	6	8	12	16	22	28	36	44	48	54	60	64	70	72	78	82	88	90	96	100	106

Fig. 2. Differential weight bounds of MGFN, TWINE, and their variants.

On the other hand, we observe that the round function of MGFN can be abstracted into the structure[2] illustrated in Fig. 3(a). Through an equivalent transformation and a recombination of the permutations used in two adjacent rounds, we obtain the equivalent round function of MGFN, as shown in Fig. 3(b). Consequently, ciphers constructed with either of the two round functions in Fig. 3 are equivalent, differing only in that the plaintext input and ciphertext output are subject to additional bit permutations.

Notably, the algorithmic structure in Fig. 3(b) closely resembles the GFN with an even-odd shuffle shown in Fig. 1(b). Since the designers of MGFN explicitly describe it as a modified GFN, we further compared its differential weight bounds with those of TWINE, a cipher whose round function also employs an even-odd shuffle GFN and shares the same block size and S-box size as MGFN. The differential weight bounds of TWINE are taken from the evaluation results reported in [15,19], as shown in Fig. 2. For 24 rounds, the best differential trail in TWINE has a probability of 2^{-113}. In contrast, both MGFN and MGFN-P exhibit substantially higher upper bounds on their differential probabilities.

This discrepancy raises doubts about the conclusion of [9]—namely, that the weak resistance of MGFN to differential attacks is solely due to its S-box with a branch number of two. To clarify this issue, we designed a set of comparative experiments to identify additional structural factors that may contribute to its limited resistance against differential attacks.

[2] Since the AddKey layer does not influence the search for differential trails in the single-key attack setting, it is omitted throughout the following discussion.

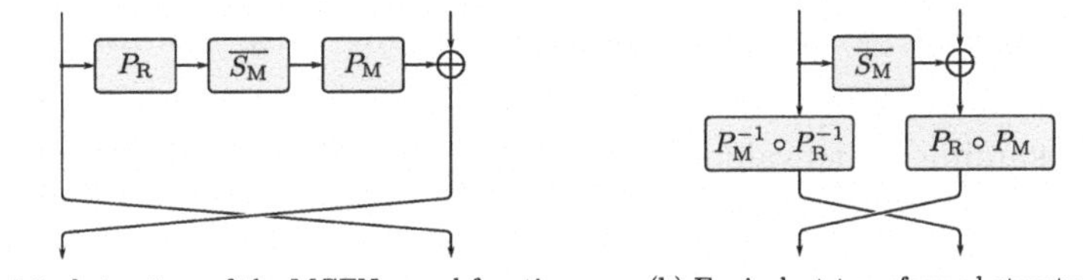

(a) Original structure of the MGFN round function. (b) Equivalent transformed structure.

Fig. 3. Two equivalent representations of the MGFN round function.

3.2 Structural Causes of MGFN's Weak Differential Resistance

We replaced the S-box of TWINE with those of MGFN and PRESENT, denoting the resulting variants as TWINE-M and TWINE-P, respectively. The differential weight bounds of TWINE-M and TWINE-P were then evaluated using the method described in [19]. As shown in Fig. 2, the lower bounds on the trail weights of both TWINE-M and TWINE-P are substantially higher than those observed for MGFN and MGFN-P. Notably, TWINE-M exhibits the closest behavior to the original TWINE, with the deviation in trail weight never exceeding 3. Moreover, the optimal 24-round trail weight of TWINE-M is approximately twice that of MGFN-P. In contrast, despite the PRESENT S-box having a larger branch number, TWINE-P consistently produces noticeably lower trail weights than both TWINE and TWINE-M, with the disparity increasing as the number of rounds grows.

These results suggest that the relatively weak resistance of MGFN to differential attacks cannot be explained solely by its reliance on an S-box with a small branch number. Rather, the structural components of MGFN, particularly the permutations P_R and P_M, play a crucial role in reducing its resistance. Taken together, our findings indicate that structural design choices are the more decisive factor in MGFN's differential weakness.

4 On Variants of MGFN

Building on the analysis in Sect. 3, we observe that the choice of P_R and P_M has a substantial impact on the differential resistance of MGFN. This naturally raises the question of whether alternative selections of P_R and P_M could significantly strengthen MGFN's resistance without modifying its S-box.

It is important to note that, in the equivalent structure shown in Fig. 3(b), P_R and P_M always occur together as a functional composition. Denoting $P_R \circ P_M$ by π_M, we obtain $\pi_M^{-1} = P_M^{-1} \circ P_R^{-1}$. Thus, although MGFN seems to employ two separate 32-bit permutations, its differential resistance ultimately depends on a single 32-bit permutation, π_M.

In the remainder of this section, we analyze MGFN variants under two scenarios—nibble-wise permutations and bit-wise permutations—by considering different selections of π_M.

4.1 Variants of MGFN with π_M as Nibble-Wise Shuffles

When π_M is restricted to a nibble-wise shuffle, there are $8! = 40320$ possible choices. Assuming that evaluating the full-round differential probability bound for each variant requires approximately one minute—though in practice some variants may take longer—testing all 8! possibilities in a single-threaded setting would take about one month. While this runtime is not entirely prohibitive and could be substantially reduced through multithreading, it is worth noting that when π_M is a nibble-wise shuffle, MGFN variants become special instances of GFNs with even-odd shuffles (see Fig. 1(b)). Consequently, the natural equivalence relation defined in Proposition 1 can be used to partition these MGFN variants into equivalence classes. Specifically, we obtain the following proposition.

Proposition 2. *Let π_M and π'_M be nibble-wise shuffles on eight nibbles. If there exists another nibble-wise shuffle Q on eight nibbles such that $\pi'_M = Q \circ \pi_M \circ Q^{-1}$, then the MGFN variants defined by π_M and π'_M are equivalent. The only difference is the presence of additional nibble-wise shuffles applied to the plaintext input and the ciphertext output.*

Under the equivalence relation defined in Proposition 2, the 8! possible MGFN candidates can be partitioned into distinct equivalence classes. Since all variants within the same class share identical cryptographic properties, they also exhibit the same differential probability bounds. Therefore, it suffices to evaluate a single representative from each class. The remaining task is thus to determine the number of equivalence classes and to identify appropriate representatives.

Determining the Number of Equivalence Classes. The equivalence relation defined in Proposition 2 coincides with *conjugacy* in the *symmetric group* $\mathbb{S}_8$, which consists of all permutations of the 8 elements in the set $\{0, 1, \ldots, 7\}$. In group theory, two permutations π_M and π'_M are conjugate if and only if they share the same *cycle type*. The cycle type τ of a permutation is determined by the lengths of the disjoint cycles in its cycle decomposition. For example, in $\mathbb{S}_4$, the permutation $[1, 0, 3, 2]$ decomposes into two disjoint 2-cycles, yielding the cycle type $\tau = \langle \tau_1, \tau_2, \tau_3, \tau_4 \rangle = \langle 0, 2, 0, 0 \rangle$, which indicates that the permutation has τ_i cycles of length i. Similarly, the permutation $[1, 2, 0, 3]$ decomposes into a 3-cycle and a 1-cycle, corresponding to the cycle type $\langle 1, 0, 1, 0 \rangle$. In $\mathbb{S}_4$, the permutations $\pi_1 = [1, 2, 0, 3]$ and $\pi_2 = [0, 2, 3, 1]$ share the same cycle type $\langle 1, 0, 1, 0 \rangle$, and therefore there exists a permutation $Q \in \mathbb{S}_4$ such that $\pi_2 = Q \circ \pi_1 \circ Q^{-1}$. Consequently, the number of equivalence classes of MGFN variants is equal to the number of distinct cycle types $\mathcal{N}_8$ of permutations in $\mathbb{S}_8$.

It is well known that the conjugacy classes of $\mathbb{S}_n$ are in one-to-one correspondence with the *integer partitions* $p(n)$ of n, where a partition of n expresses n as a sum of positive integers, disregarding order. For instance, the integer 4 has five partitions: 4, $3 + 1$, $2 + 2$, $2 + 1 + 1$, and $1 + 1 + 1 + 1$, corresponding to the five conjugacy classes of $\mathbb{S}_4$. By Euler's partition theorem [1], we obtain $\mathcal{N}_8 = p(8) = 22$.

Therefore, among the 8! possible MGFN variants based on nibble-wise permutations π_{M} in $\mathbb{S}_8$, only 22 need to be considered as distinct under the equivalence relation defined in Proposition 2.

Selecting Class Representatives. To select a representative permutation for each equivalence class, we proceed as follows.

1. **Enumerate the Cycle Types:** List all integer partitions of 8, each corresponding to a distinct cycle type.
2. **Construct Canonical Representatives:** For each cycle type, define a canonical permutation according to the following rules.
   - Cycles are ordered by increasing length, and cycles of the same length are ordered by their smallest element.
   - Within each cycle, the smallest element is placed first, followed by the remaining elements in ascending order.

This procedure ensures that each equivalence class is assigned a unique and deterministic representative. The 22 representative permutations, denoted $\pi_{\mathrm{M}}^{(0)}$ through $\pi_{\mathrm{M}}^{(21)}$, are listed in Table 3.

Table 3. 22 representative permutations of π_{M} when restricted to nibble-wise shuffles.

Index	Permutation	Index	Permutation
$\pi_{\mathrm{M}}^{(0)}$	[1, 2, 3, 4, 5, 6, 7, 0]	$\pi_{\mathrm{M}}^{(11)}$	[1, 2, 3, 0, 4, 5, 6, 7]
$\pi_{\mathrm{M}}^{(1)}$	[1, 2, 3, 4, 5, 6, 0, 7]	$\pi_{\mathrm{M}}^{(12)}$	[1, 2, 0, 4, 5, 3, 7, 6]
$\pi_{\mathrm{M}}^{(2)}$	[1, 2, 3, 4, 5, 0, 7, 6]	$\pi_{\mathrm{M}}^{(13)}$	[1, 2, 0, 4, 5, 3, 6, 7]
$\pi_{\mathrm{M}}^{(3)}$	[1, 2, 3, 4, 5, 0, 6, 7]	$\pi_{\mathrm{M}}^{(14)}$	[1, 2, 0, 4, 3, 6, 5, 7]
$\pi_{\mathrm{M}}^{(4)}$	[1, 2, 3, 4, 0, 6, 7, 5]	$\pi_{\mathrm{M}}^{(15)}$	[1, 2, 0, 4, 3, 5, 6, 7]
$\pi_{\mathrm{M}}^{(5)}$	[1, 2, 3, 4, 0, 6, 5, 7]	$\pi_{\mathrm{M}}^{(16)}$	[1, 2, 0, 3, 4, 5, 6, 7]
$\pi_{\mathrm{M}}^{(6)}$	[1, 2, 3, 4, 0, 5, 6, 7]	$\pi_{\mathrm{M}}^{(17)}$	[1, 0, 3, 2, 5, 4, 7, 6]
$\pi_{\mathrm{M}}^{(7)}$	[1, 2, 3, 0, 5, 6, 7, 4]	$\pi_{\mathrm{M}}^{(18)}$	[1, 0, 3, 2, 5, 4, 6, 7]
$\pi_{\mathrm{M}}^{(8)}$	[1, 2, 3, 0, 5, 6, 4, 7]	$\pi_{\mathrm{M}}^{(19)}$	[1, 0, 3, 2, 4, 5, 6, 7]
$\pi_{\mathrm{M}}^{(9)}$	[1, 2, 3, 0, 5, 4, 7, 6]	$\pi_{\mathrm{M}}^{(20)}$	[1, 0, 2, 3, 4, 5, 6, 7]
$\pi_{\mathrm{M}}^{(10)}$	[1, 2, 3, 0, 5, 4, 6, 7]	$\pi_{\mathrm{M}}^{(21)}$	[0, 1, 2, 3, 4, 5, 6, 7]

Differential Properties of the 22 Representative MGFN Variants. We evaluated the differential probability bounds of the MGFN variants associated with the 22 representative permutations listed in Table 3. As shown in Fig. 4, we observed that, with the exception of the MGFN variants using $\pi_{\mathrm{M}}^{(0)}$, $\pi_{\mathrm{M}}^{(4)}$, and $\pi_{\mathrm{M}}^{(7)}$, all other variants, collectively denoted as MGFN($\pi_{\mathrm{M}}^{(*)}$) in Fig. 4, exhibit identical differential probability bounds. In particular, these variants exhibit an upper bound of 2^{-32} for 24 rounds, which is even weaker than that of the original MGFN. In contrast, the variants based on $\pi_{\mathrm{M}}^{(0)}$, $\pi_{\mathrm{M}}^{(4)}$, and $\pi_{\mathrm{M}}^{(7)}$ demonstrate stronger resistance to differential attacks than the original design. Among them, $\pi_{\mathrm{M}}^{(0)}$ offers the highest level of security, lowering the probability of the best 24-round differential trail to 2^{-72}, thereby outperforming the MGFN-P variant introduced in [19]. Nonetheless, none of the MGFN variants corresponding to the 22 representative permutations achieves a differential probability bound comparable to that of TWINE.

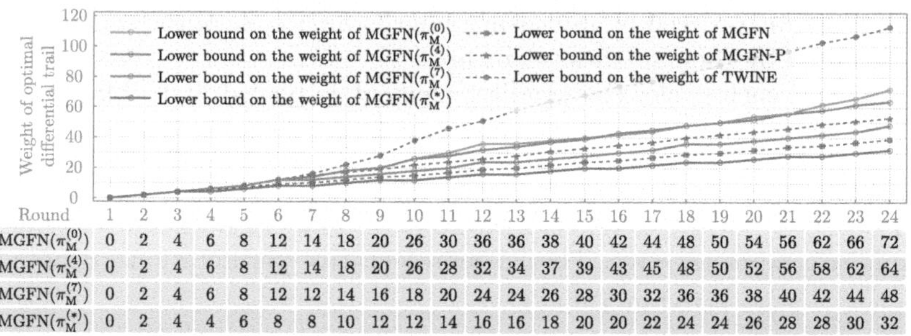

Round	1	2	3	4	5	6	7	8	9	10	11	12	13	14	15	16	17	18	19	20	21	22	23	24
MGFN($\pi_{\mathrm{M}}^{(0)}$)	0	2	4	6	8	12	14	18	20	26	30	36	36	38	40	42	44	48	50	54	56	62	66	72
MGFN($\pi_{\mathrm{M}}^{(4)}$)	0	2	4	6	8	12	14	18	20	26	28	32	34	37	39	43	45	48	50	52	56	58	62	64
MGFN($\pi_{\mathrm{M}}^{(7)}$)	0	2	4	6	8	12	12	14	16	18	20	24	24	26	28	30	32	36	36	38	40	42	44	48
MGFN($\pi_{\mathrm{M}}^{(*)}$)	0	2	4	4	6	8	8	10	12	12	14	16	16	18	20	20	22	24	24	26	28	28	30	32

Fig. 4. Test results of the 22 representative MGFN variants with nibble-wise shuffles.

4.2 Variants of MGFN with π_{M} as Bit Permutations

If π_{M} is defined as a bit permutation, the number of possible MGFN variants increases dramatically to approximately $32! \approx 2^{117.66}$. Unlike nibble-wise shuffles, bit permutations do not commute with the S-box layer, which makes it impossible to establish an equivalence condition analogous to Proposition 2 for partitioning these variants into equivalence classes. An exhaustive search across all 32! possibilities is clearly infeasible. To gain insights under this constraint, we restrict our analysis to two subclasses of bit permutations: (i) π_{M} limited to bit-level cyclic shifts, and (ii) π_{M} selected randomly.

MGFN Variants with π_{M} as Bit-Level Cyclic Shifts. We conducted exhaustive searches of the differential probability bounds for MGFN variants in which π_{M} is restricted to the 31 possible bit-level cyclic shifts. Specifically, $\pi_{\mathrm{M}}^{\lll i}$ denotes a left rotation by i bits for $0 < i < 32$. Note that when $i \bmod 4 \equiv 0$, $\pi_{\mathrm{M}}^{\lll i}$ corresponds to a nibble-wise left rotation. Consequently, the strongest differential resistance among these 31 variants is at least as high as that of the best nibble-wise shuffle variant, MGFN($\pi_{\mathrm{M}}^{(0)}$), which represents a left rotation by one nibble. The results for the 31 variants are summarized in Fig. 5. We observe that the vast majority of these variants provide stronger differential probability bounds than the original MGFN, with several even surpassing both MGFN and

MGFN-P. In particular, the variants MGFN($\pi_{\mathrm{M}}^{\lll 5}$) and MGFN($\pi_{\mathrm{M}}^{\lll 21}$), based on left rotations by 5 and 21 bits respectively, exhibit slightly stronger resistance than MGFN($\pi_{\mathrm{M}}^{(0)}$). Nevertheless, in all cases, the bounds remain substantially weaker than those achieved by TWINE.

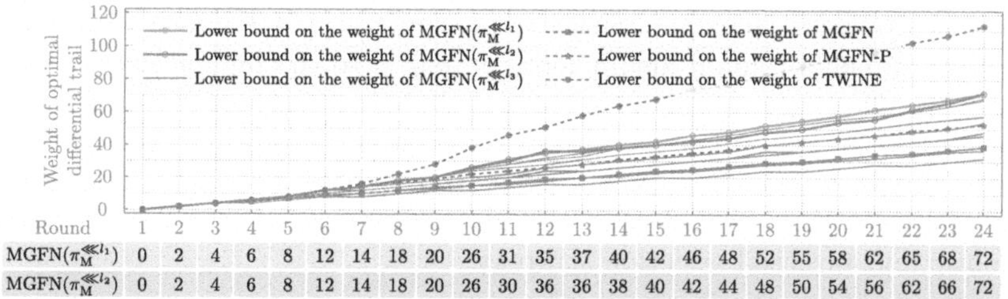

Round	1	2	3	4	5	6	7	8	9	10	11	12	13	14	15	16	17	18	19	20	21	22	23	24
MGFN($\pi_{\mathrm{M}}^{\lll l_1}$)	0	2	4	6	8	12	14	18	20	26	31	35	37	40	42	46	48	52	55	58	62	65	68	72
MGFN($\pi_{\mathrm{M}}^{\lll l_2}$)	0	2	4	6	8	12	14	18	20	26	30	36	36	38	40	42	44	48	50	54	56	62	66	72

Fig. 5. Test results of the 31 MGFN variants with bit-level cyclic shifts. Let L_1, L_2, and L_3 be subsets of the integers from 1 to 31 (inclusive), where $L_1 = \{5, 21\}$, $L_2 = \{4, 12, 20, 28\}$, and L_3 consists of all remaining integers in the range $[1, 31]$ that are not included in L_1 or L_2. Let l_1, l_2, and l_3 denote integers selected from L_1, L_2, and L_3, respectively.

Table 4. Randomly drawn bit permutation $\pi_{\mathrm{M}}^{\$}$.

i	0	1	2	3	4	5	6	7	8	9	10	11	12	13	14	15
$\pi_{\mathrm{M}}^{\$}(i)$	1	6	10	12	18	31	25	2	5	15	29	28	26	24	8	17
i	16	17	18	19	20	21	22	23	24	25	26	27	28	29	30	31
$\pi_{\mathrm{M}}^{\$}(i)$	16	22	4	20	9	7	27	19	11	23	30	3	0	14	13	21

MGFN Variants with π_{M} as Random Bit Permutations. We randomly generated 1000 32-bit permutations and evaluated the corresponding MGFN variants. The results are presented in Fig. 6. A comparison shows that the strongest resistance against differential attacks achieved by these randomly generated permutations is weaker than that of the variant using the nibble-wise shuffle $\pi_{\mathrm{M}}^{(0)}$ as well as the variants using the bit permutations $\pi_{\mathrm{M}}^{\lll 5}$ and $\pi_{\mathrm{M}}^{\lll 21}$. The uniquely selected random bit permutation that achieves the best differential resistance, denoted as $\pi_{\mathrm{M}}^{\$}$, is provided in Table 4 for verification.

Furthermore, although we tested 1000 variants, many of the resulting differential probability bounds were identical. In fact, these bounds fall into 18 distinct patterns. This observation suggests that when π_{M} is defined as a bit permutation, there may also exist an underlying equivalence relation that partitions the set of MGFN variants into equivalence classes. Establishing such a relation would substantially reduce the number of candidate variants requiring security evaluation.

Developing this equivalence framework for MGFN variants—or more generally, for GFN variants with bit-level permutations—thus represents an interesting direction for future research.

Based on the results of this section, we observe that the resistance of MGFN to differential attacks can be substantially enhanced—without modifying its S-box—by selecting suitable nibble-wise shuffles or bit-level cyclic shifts, yielding stronger effects than the S-box replacement in MGFN-P. Nevertheless, these improvements remain insufficient compared to the higher level of security achieved by GFN-based designs such as TWINE. Since our exploration of bit permutations was not exhaustive, we cannot rule out the possibility that certain permutations may yield MGFN variants with differential resistance approaching that of TWINE. However, identifying such permutations would require a more systematic and targeted selection strategy.

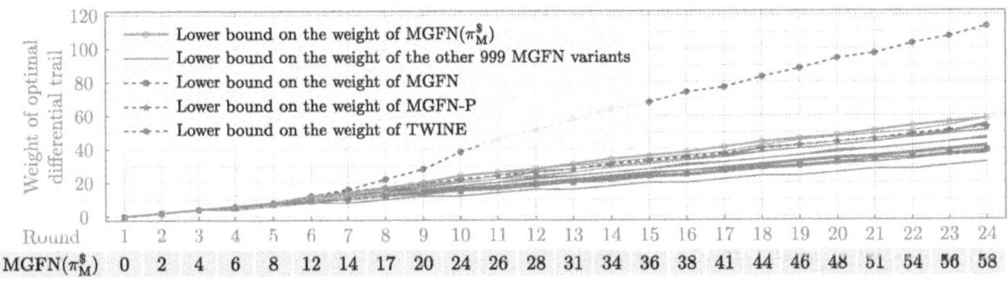

Fig. 6. Test results of the 1000 MGFN variants with random bit permutations.

5 Conclusion

In this paper, we revisited MGFN and its variant MGFN-P within the broader context of modified GFN-based cipher design. Our evaluation shows that MGFN's weakness is not solely due to its S-box, but more fundamentally to the choice of permutations, which critically undermine its resistance to differential attacks. By systematically analyzing MGFN variants under both nibble-wise and bit-wise permutations, we identified improved constructions through equivalence-class reduction and exploratory permutation strategies. Although these variants exhibit stronger resistance than the original MGFN, none achieve the robustness of TWINE, underscoring the importance of carefully established GFN design principles. In conclusion, MGFN serves as a cautionary example of how inappropriate permutation choices can compromise the security of a cipher.

Acknowledgement. The research leading to these results has received funding from the Shan-dong Key Research and Development Program (Grant No. 2024ZLGX05), the National Natural Science Foundation of China (Grant No. 62272273, Grant No. 62032014, Grant No. U2336207), and the National Cryptologic Science Fund of China

(Grant No. 2025NCSF02006). Ling Sun gratefully acknowledges the support by the Program of TaiShan Scholars Special Fund for young scholars (Grant No. tsqn202306043) and Xiaomi Young Talents Program.

References

1. Andrews, G.E.: Number theory. Courier Corporation (1994)
2. Banik, S., et al.: WARP: revisiting GFN for lightweight 128-bit block cipher. In: Dunkelman, O., Jr., M.J.J., O'Flynn, C. (eds.) Selected Areas in Cryptography - SAC 2020 - 27th International Conference, Halifax, NS, Canada (Virtual Event), 21–23 October 2020, Revised Selected Papers. Lecture Notes in Computer Science, vol. 12804, pp. 535–564. Springer (2020). https://doi.org/10.1007/978-3-030-81652-0_21
3. Bansod, G., Pisharoty, N., Patil, A.: PICO: an ultra lightweight and low power encryption design for ubiquitous computing. Def. Sci. J. **66**(3), 259–265 (2016)
4. Biham, E., Shamir, A.: Differential cryptanalysis of DES-like cryptosystems. In: Menezes, A., Vanstone, S.A. (eds.) Advances in Cryptology - CRYPTO '90, 10th Annual International Cryptology Conference, Santa Barbara, California, USA, 11–15 August 1990, Proceedings. Lecture Notes in Computer Science, vol. 537, pp. 2–21. Springer (1990). https://doi.org/10.1007/3-540-38424-3_1
5. Bogdanov, A., et al.: PRESENT: an ultra-lightweight block cipher. In: Paillier, P., Verbauwhede, I. (eds.) Cryptographic Hardware and Embedded Systems - CHES 2007, 9th International Workshop, Vienna, Austria, September 10-13, 2007, Proceedings. Lecture Notes in Computer Science, vol. 4727, pp. 450–466. Springer (2007). https://doi.org/10.1007/978-3-540-74735-2_31
6. Cauchois, V., Gomez, C., Thomas, G.: General diffusion analysis: how to find optimal permutations for generalized type-ii feistel schemes. IACR Trans. Symmetric Cryptol. **2019**(1), 264–301 (2019). https://doi.org/10.13154/TOSC.V2019.I1.264-301
7. Derbez, P., Euler, M.: Equivalence of generalised feistel networks. IACR Trans. Symmetric Cryptol. **2024**(1), 412–440 (2024). https://doi.org/10.46586/TOSC.V2024.I1.412-440
8. Feistel, H., Notz, W.A., Smith, J.L.: Some cryptographic techniques for machine-to-machine data communications. Proc. IEEE **63**(11), 1545–1554 (1975)
9. Li, Y., Bi, X., Xiang, Y., Lin, Y.: Differential analysis and improvement of full-round MGFN based on MILP. Appl. Res. Comput. **41**(3), 911–915 (2024)
10. Liu, Y., Wang, Q., Rijmen, V.: Automatic search of linear trails in ARX with applications to SPECK and Chaskey. In: Manulis, M., Sadeghi, A., Schneider, S.A. (eds.) Applied Cryptography and Network Security - 14th International Conference, ACNS 2016, Guildford, UK, June 19-22, 2016. Proceedings. Lecture Notes in Computer Science, vol. 9696, pp. 485–499. Springer (2016). https://doi.org/10.1007/978-3-319-39555-5_26
11. Mouha, N., Preneel, B.: A proof that the ARX cipher Salsa20 is secure against differential cryptanalysis. IACR Cryptol. ePrint Arch. 328 (2013)
12. Mouha, N., Wang, Q., Gu, D., Preneel, B.: Differential and linear cryptanalysis using mixed-integer linear programming. In: Wu, C., Yung, M., Lin, D. (eds.) Information Security and Cryptology - 7th International Conference, Inscrypt 2011, Beijing, China, November 30 - December 3, 2011. Revised Selected Papers. Lecture Notes in Computer Science, vol. 7537, pp. 57–76. Springer (2011). https://doi.org/10.1007/978-3-642-34704-7_5

13. Nyberg, K.: Generalized feistel networks. In: Kim, K., Matsumoto, T. (eds.) Advances in Cryptology - ASIACRYPT 1996, International Conference on the Theory and Applications of Cryptology and Information Security, Kyongju, Korea, November 3-7, 1996, Proceedings. Lecture Notes in Computer Science, vol. 1163, pp. 91–104. Springer (1996). https://doi.org/10.1007/BFB0034838
14. Shah, I.N.M., Ismail, E.S., Samat, F., Rahman, N.N.A.: Modified generalized Feistel network block cipher for the internet of things. Symmetry **15**(4), 900 (2023). https://doi.org/10.3390/SYM15040900
15. Sun, L., Wang, W., Wang, M.: Accelerating the search of differential and linear characteristics with the SAT method. IACR Trans. Symmetric Cryptol. **2021**(1), 269–315 (2021). https://doi.org/10.46586/TOSC.V2021.I1.269-315
16. Sun, S., Hu, L., Wang, P., Qiao, K., Ma, X., Song, L.: Automatic security evaluation and (related-key) differential characteristic search: application to SIMON, PRESENT, LBlock, DES(L) and other bit-oriented block ciphers. In: Sarkar, P., Iwata, T. (eds.) Advances in Cryptology - ASIACRYPT 2014 - 20th International Conference on the Theory and Application of Cryptology and Information Security, Kaoshiung, Taiwan, R.O.C., December 7-11, 2014. Proceedings, Part I. Lecture Notes in Computer Science, vol. 8873, pp. 158–178. Springer (2014). https://doi.org/10.1007/978-3-662-45611-8_9
17. Suzaki, T., Minematsu, K.: Improving the generalized Feistel. In: Hong, S., Iwata, T. (eds.) Fast Software Encryption, 17th International Workshop, FSE 2010, Seoul, Korea, February 7-10, 2010, Revised Selected Papers. Lecture Notes in Computer Science, vol. 6147, pp. 19–39. Springer (2010). https://doi.org/10.1007/978-3-642-13858-4_2
18. Suzaki, T., Minematsu, K., Morioka, S., Kobayashi, E.: TWINE: a lightweight block cipher for multiple platforms. In: Knudsen, L.R., Wu, H. (eds.) Selected Areas in Cryptography, 19th International Conference, SAC 2012, Windsor, ON, Canada, 15–16 August 2012, Revised Selected Papers. Lecture Notes in Computer Science, vol. 7707, pp. 339–354. Springer (2012). https://doi.org/10.1007/978-3-642-35999-6_22
19. Wang, S., Feng, D., Hu, B., Guan, J., Zhang, K., Shi, T.: New method for combining Matsui's bounding conditions with sequential encoding method. Des. Codes Cryptogr. **91**(11), 3603–3642 (2023). https://doi.org/10.1007/S10623-023-01259-9
20. Wu, W., Zhang, L.: LBlock: a lightweight block cipher. In: López, J., Tsudik, G. (eds.) Applied Cryptography and Network Security - 9th International Conference, ACNS 2011, Nerja, Spain, June 7-10, 2011. Proceedings. Lecture Notes in Computer Science, vol. 6715, pp. 327–344 (2011). https://doi.org/10.1007/978-3-642-21554-4_19
21. Zheng, Y., Matsumoto, T., Imai, H.: On the construction of block ciphers provably secure and not relying on any unproved hypotheses. In: Brassard, G. (ed.) Advances in Cryptology - CRYPTO '89, 9th Annual International Cryptology Conference, Santa Barbara, California, USA, August 20-24, 1989, Proceedings. Lecture Notes in Computer Science, vol. 435, pp. 461–480. Springer (1989). https://doi.org/10.1007/0-387-34805-0_42

New Derivation Rule for Linear Approximations and Its Application to ChaCha

Zhengting Li, Lin Ding(✉), Xinhai Wang, Honglei Wang, and Jiang Wan

Information Engineering University, Zhengzhou 450001, China
dinglin_cipher@163.com

Abstract. ChaCha is an ARX-based stream cipher and has been widely used in practice. In this paper, we propose a new derivation rule for linear approximations of ARX-based ciphers and then apply it to ChaCha. Compared with the previous derivation rules for linear approximations, it can reduce the number of active bits when deriving linear approximations. By combining this new derivation rule with the previous derivation rules in a mixed pattern, we improve the 3.5- and 4-round linear approximations for ChaCha. The original 3.5-round linear approximation presented at EUROCRYPT 2021 has a correlation of 2^{-47}, which was improved to be -2^{-41} recently. This paper further improves it with a better correlation of -2^{-40}. Besides, we enhance the 4-round linear approximation for ChaCha with correlation 2^{-48}, improving the previous result (i.e., -2^{-50}) by a factor of -2^{2}. The new derivation rule for linear approximations is general and can be applied to other ARX-based ciphers.

Keywords: Linear approximation · Differential-linear cryptanalysis · ChaCha · Stream cipher

1 Introduction

Symmetric key primitives play a crucial role in communication networks. Block ciphers and stream ciphers are two types of such primitives. Among them, stream ciphers have been widely used due to their advantages of simple implementation and fast encryption/decryption speed. ChaCha [6] is one of the most famous stream ciphers based on the ARX machinery. ARX is short for **A**ddition, **R**otation and **X**OR. ARX-based designs not only have high efficiency, but also have good security. Due to the carry function of modular addition, the ARX ciphers can reach high algebraic degree after a fewer rounds.

The ChaCha stream cipher as a variant of Salsa [5], was introduced in 2008 to provide better diffusion and higher security to resist against various attacks. Nowadays, this cipher has been deployed in several domains, including protocols(e.g., SSH, Noise, QUIC and TLS), networks(e.g., Lighting Network), oper-

H. Seo (Ed.): ICISC 2025, LNCS 16487, pp. 471–491, 2026.
https://doi.org/10.1007/978-981-95-8034-7_25

ating systems(e.g., Linux, Android and OpenBSD), hardware(e.g., PAx5), software(e.g., Chrome and Safari) and so on. A full List of the usage and deployment of ChaCha refer to [1].

1.1 Related Works

Because of the wide usage and deployment of ChaCha, it is important to analyze its security. Since ChaCha was proposed in 2008, numerous cryptanalytic attacks have been conducted. For ARX-based designs like ChaCha, differential-linear cryptanalysis is a particularly effective method due to it combines the advantages of differential attack [7] and linear attack [21]. The cryptanalytic researches on ChaCha are mainly divided into two categories, i.e. distinguishers and key recovery attacks. Since this paper only makes improvements on the linear approximations, we ignore the key recovery attacks. For the existing key recovery attacks on ChaCha, we refer to [2–4,8,9,12–17,20,22,23,25,26].

At FSE 2017, Choudhuri and Maitra [8] focused on the structure of ChaCha for the first time, and proposed several linear approximations for it. In 2020, Coutinho and Souza [9] presented a new linear approximation that leads to a better distinguisher for 6-round ChaCha with a time/data complexity of $2^{75}/2^{75}$. At EUROCRYPT 2021, they [11] proposed two linear approximations for ARX-based ciphers and gave a 3.5-round linear approximation with correlation 2^{-47}. They used the result proposed in [8] to show that the 4-round linear approximation holds with correlation 2^{-55}, and gave distinguishers for 6- and 7-round ChaCha with complexities less than 2^{51} and 2^{224}, respectively. At ASIACRYPT 2022, Coutinho et al. [10] proposed a new approach to derive linear approximations by viewing the cipher in terms of simpler sub-rounds. They proposed seven lemmas to derive linear approximations and improved a 7-round differential-linear distinguisher by improving its linear part which holds with correlation 2^{-53}. At FSE 2023, Bellini et al. [4] used the MILP tool to search linear approximations automatically. They obtained 4- and 4.5-round linear approximations starting from the multi-bits, which were then used to improve 7- and 7.5-round distinguishers with complexity $2^{166.89}$ and $2^{251.54}$, respectively. At FSE 2024, Xu et al. [26] considered the differential-linear hull to improve the results in [4]. At ISPEC 2025, Li et al. [19] proposed a systematic three-case framework called *Mixdrive* to find linear approximations for ChaCha. They tackled the problem presented in [10] by deriving the linear approximations in a mixed mode.

1.2 Our Contributions

In this paper, we propose a new derivation rule for linear approximations and then apply it to ChaCha. Unlike the previous cases where only the bits with carry are considered, we now take into account the combination of bits with carry and those without carry. Eventually, we find that compared with the previous derivation rules, it leads to better correlation when the rounds increase. The advantage of our new derivation rule is fully confirmed by applying it to the ChaCha stream cipher. Furthermore, the new derivation rule for linear approximations is general and can be applied to other ARX-based ciphers.

By combining this new derivation rule for linear approximations with the previous derivation rules in a mixed pattern, we improve the 3.5- and 4-round linear approximations for ChaCha. We summarize two improved linear approximations for ChaCha in Table 1. For 3.5-round ChaCha, we have obtained an improved linear approximation for ChaCha with correlation -2^{-40}. To the best of our knowledge, the linear approximation is proposed at EUROCRYPT 2021 [11], and improved at ISPEC 2025 [19] with correlation -2^{-41}. For 4-round ChaCha, we have derived an enhanced linear approximation with correlation 2^{-48}. This improves the results presented at EUROCRYPT 2021 [11], ASIACRYPT 2022 [10], as well as the result at ISPEC 2025 [19], which have correlations of 2^{-55}, 2^{-53} and -2^{-50}, respectively. The improved linear approximations for ChaCha demonstrate the effectiveness and correctness of our new derivation rule.

Table 1. Linear approximations for 3.5- and 4-round ChaCha

Rounds	Input	Theoretical correlation	Computational result	Ref.
3.5	$x_{5,0}^{(3.5)}$	2^{-47}	$2^{-42.30}$	[11]
		-2^{-41}	$-2^{-36.98}$	[19]
		-2^{-40}	$-2^{-36.22}$	**This paper**
4	$x_{3,0}^{(3)} \oplus x_{4,0}^{(3)}$	2^{-55}	$2^{-50.42}$	[11]
		2^{-53}	$2^{-47.99}$	[10]
		-2^{-50}	$-2^{-46.00}$	[19]
		2^{-48}	$2^{-44.41}$	**This paper**

Organization of the Paper. In Sect. 2, we give a brief description of ChaCha and review the differential-linear cryptanalysis. In Sect. 3, we review the approaches to derive linear approximations for ChaCha proposed at ASIACRYPT 2022 and ISPEC 2025. In Sect. 4, we list one linear approximation regarding the carry operation, and then introduce a new derivation rule for linear approximations for ChaCha. In Sect. 5, two improved linear approximations are presented. Section 6 concludes this paper.

2 Preliminaries

This section is divided into two parts as follows. In the first part, we give a brief description of ChaCha. After then, we review the differential-linear cryptanalysis which is the most effective cryptanalysis method for ChaCha. For the convenience of description, we list the notations used throughout the paper in Table 2.

Table 2. List of the main notations used throughout the paper.

Notation	Description
X	The state matrix of ChaCha256 consisting of 16 words
$X^{(0)}$	The initial state matrix of ChaCha256
$X^{(r)}$	The state matrix after application of r round functions
$X^{[s]}$	The state matrix after application of s subround functions
$x_i^{(r)}$	The i-th word of the state matrix $X^{(r)}$
$x_{i,j}^{(r)}$	The j-th bit of i-th word of the state matrix $X^{(r)}$
$x_i^{(r)}[j_0, j_1, \ldots, j_t]$	The sum $x_{i,j_0}^{(r)} \oplus x_{i,j_1}^{(r)} \oplus \cdots \oplus x_{i,j_t}^{(r)}$
$x + y$	Addition of x and y modulo 2^{32}
$x \oplus y$	Bitwise XOR of x and y
$x \lll l$	Rotation of x by l bits to the left

2.1 A Brief Description of ChaCha

ChaCha consists of two versions: a 256-bit key version called ChaCha256 and a 128-bit key version called ChaCha128. We only focus on ChaCha256, so in this paper, ChaCha always refers to the 256-bit version. The state of ChaCha is represented as a 4×4 matrix, where the size of each word is 32-bit. The initial state matrix $X^{(0)}$ is initialized from a 256-bit key $k = (k_0, k_1, \cdots, k_7)$, a 96-bit nonce $v = (v_0, v_1, v_2)$, a 32-bit counter t_0, and four 32-bit constants $c_0 = 0x61707865$,$c_1 = 0x3320646e$,$c_2 = 0x79622d32$, and $c_3 = 0x6b206574$. In the subsequent content, we will refer to the nonce and counter words together as *IV*words. The matrix is given as follows.

$$X^{(0)} = \begin{pmatrix} x_0^{(0)} & x_1^{(0)} & x_2^{(0)} & x_3^{(0)} \\ x_4^{(0)} & x_5^{(0)} & x_6^{(0)} & x_7^{(0)} \\ x_8^{(0)} & x_9^{(0)} & x_{10}^{(0)} & x_{11}^{(0)} \\ x_{12}^{(0)} & x_{13}^{(0)} & x_{14}^{(0)} & x_{15}^{(0)} \end{pmatrix} = \begin{pmatrix} c_0 & c_1 & c_2 & c_3 \\ k_0 & k_1 & k_2 & k_3 \\ k_4 & k_5 & k_6 & k_7 \\ t_0 & v_0 & v_1 & v_2 \end{pmatrix}$$

Then, the initial state matrix is updated by the *Round* function, which comprises four simultaneous computations of the *QuarterRound*(*QR*) function. Taking four words $x_a^{(r-1)}, x_b^{(r-1)}, x_c^{(r-1)}, x_d^{(r-1)}$ as inputs and can obtain $x_a^{(r)}, x_b^{(r)}, x_c^{(r)}, x_d^{(r)}$ through *QR* function.

$$x_{a'}^{(r-1)} = x_a^{(r-1)} + x_b^{(r-1)}; \qquad x_{d'}^{(r-1)} = (x_d^{(r-1)} \oplus x_{a'}^{(r-1)}) \lll 16;$$
$$x_{c'}^{(r-1)} = x_c^{(r-1)} + x_{d'}^{(r-1)}; \qquad x_{b'}^{(r-1)} = (x_b^{(r-1)} \oplus x_{c'}^{(r-1)}) \lll 12;$$
$$x_a^{(r)} = x_{a'}^{(r-1)} + x_{b'}^{(r-1)}; \qquad x_d^{(r)} = (x_{d'}^{(r-1)} \oplus x_a^{(r)}) \lll 8;$$
$$x_c^{(r)} = x_{c'}^{(r-1)} + x_d^{(r)}; \qquad x_b^{(r)} = (x_{b'}^{(r-1)} \oplus x_c^{(r)}) \lll 7.$$

Due to the consistency of the overall structure, each QR function can be divided into two *SubRound* (SR) function, i.e., $x^{[s]} = x^{(s/2)}$, shown as follows.

$$x_a^{[s]} = x_a^{[s-1]} + x_b^{[s-1]}; \qquad x_d^{[s]} = (x_d^{[s-1]} \oplus x_a^{[s]}) \lll r_1;$$
$$x_c^{[s]} = x_c^{[s-1]} + x_d^{[s]}; \qquad x_b^{[s]} = (x_b^{[s-1]} \oplus x_c^{[s]}) \lll r_2$$

where $(r_1, r_2) = (16, 12)$ when s is odd, and $(r_1, r_2) = (8, 7)$ when s is even.

There is a difference between odd and even rounds. For odd rounds, the function QR is applied to the four columns $(x_0, x_4, x_8, x_{12}), (x_1, x_5, x_9, x_{13}), (x_2, x_6, x_{10}, x_{14})$ and $(x_3, x_7, x_{11}, x_{15})$. For even rounds, the function QR is applied to the four diagonals $(x_0, x_5, x_{10}, x_{15}), (x_1, x_6, x_{11}, x_{12}), (x_2, x_7, x_8, x_{13})$ and (x_3, x_4, x_9, x_{14}).

The keystream block Z after R-rounds is obtained as the word-wise modular addition of the states $X^{(0)}$ and $X^{(R)}$, i.e., $Z = X^{(0)} + X^{(R)}$, where $X^{(R)}$ is the state matrix after application of R *Round* function.

2.2 Differential-Linear Cryptanalysis

In this section, we describe the technique of differential-linear cryptanalysis used in this paper. At CRYPTO 1994, Langford [18] introduced the idea of differential-linear cryptanalysis. As a combination of differential attack [7] and linear attack [21], it has been widely used in ARX ciphers such as Salsa and ChaCha. Let E be a cipher and can be divided into two parts E_1 and E_2 such that $E = E_2 \circ E_1$(see the left side of Fig. 1). The differential attack is used in the first part, assume that the differential part $\Delta_{in} \xrightarrow{E_1} \Delta_m$ holds with probability $\Pr_{x \in F_2^n}(E_1(x) \oplus E_1(x \oplus \Delta_{in}) = \Delta_m) = p$. The linear attack is used in the second part, let us further assume that the linear part $\Gamma_m \xrightarrow{E_2} \Gamma_{out}$ holds with correlation $\varepsilon_L = \mathbf{Cor}_{x \in F_2^n}[\langle \Gamma_m, x\rangle \oplus \langle \Gamma_{out}, E_2(x)\rangle]$. By assuming this two parts are independent, a differential-linear distinguisher $\Delta_{in} \xrightarrow{E} \Gamma_{out}$ with correlation $p\varepsilon_L^2$ can be obtained. The distinguisher complexity is computed as $O\left(\frac{1}{p^2 \varepsilon_L^4}\right)$.

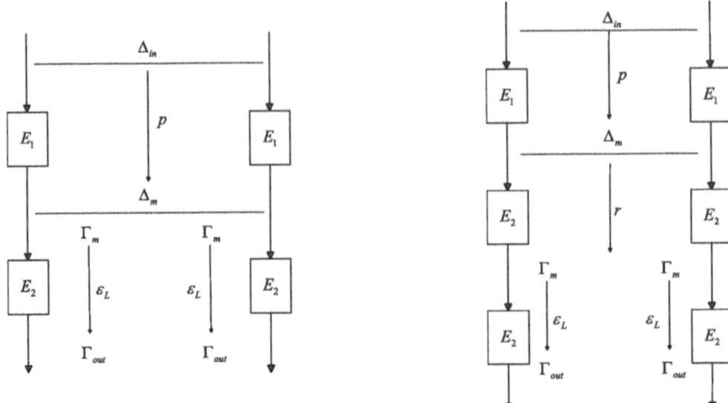

Fig. 1. A classical differential-linear distinguisher (on the left) and a differential-linear distinguisher with an improved structure that mitigates the independence assumption between the top and bottom parts (on the right).

However, when we assume E_1 and E_2 are independent sometimes may lead to overestimates or underestimates the correlation. At CRYPTO 2020, Beierle et al. [3] proposed dividing the cipher into three parts instead of two parts to minimize the error value, i.e., $E = E_2 \circ E_m \circ E_1$(see the right side of Fig. 1). Assume the middle part $\Delta_m \xrightarrow{E_m} \Gamma_m$ holds with correlation $r = \mathbf{Cor}_{x\in\mathcal{S}}[\langle\Gamma_m, E_m(x)\rangle \oplus \langle\Gamma_m, E_m(x \oplus \Delta_m)\rangle]$, where is the set of samples over which the correlation r is computed. Then the correlation can be estimated as $pr\varepsilon_L^2$, so the complexity of differential-linear distinguisher is $O\left(\frac{1}{p^2r^2\varepsilon_L^4}\right)$.

3 A Review on the Previous Derivation Rules for Linear Approximations

In this section, we review the simple linear approximations to the carry function of addition, and the previous derivation rules for linear approximations.

The operations for ChaCha include linear operations (e.g., bitwise XOR and rotation) and non-linear operation (e.g., modulo addition). Let $\Theta(x, y) = (x + y) \oplus (x \oplus y)$ be the carry function of modulo addition $x + y$ and $\Theta_i(x, y)$ is the i-th bit of $\Theta(x, y)$. At EUROCRYPT 2021, Coutinho and Souza introduced two linear approximations for ChaCha, derived using **Theorem 3** from Wallén [24], which are shown as follows:

$$\Pr\left(\Theta_i(x, y) = y_{i-1}\right) = \frac{1}{2}\left(1 + \frac{1}{2}\right), i > 0 \quad (1)$$

$$\Pr\left(\Theta_i(x, y) \oplus \Theta_{i-1}(x, y) = 0\right) = \frac{1}{2}\left(1 + \frac{1}{2}\right), i > 0 \quad (2)$$

Not same as [8], Coutinho et al. [11] considered SR rather than QR. By using the aforementioned linear approximations, they proposed the following five lemmas. Note that the expansions for $x_{b,i}^{[s-1]}$ and $x_{d,i}^{[s-1]}$ are deterministic and the least significant bits of $x_a^{[s-1]}$ and $x_c^{[s-1]}$ do not have carry, i.e. $\Theta_0\left(x_a^{[s-1]}, x_b^{[s-1]}\right) = 0$ and $\Theta_0\left(x_c^{[s-1]}, x_d^{[s]}\right) = 0$. The following two lemmas hold with probability 1.

Lemma 1 (Eqs. 22 and 24 of [10] respectively). *For one active input bit in subround $s-1$ and multiple output bits in subround s, the following linear approximations hold with the probability 1 for the SR with rotation distances r_1 and r_2 when $i > 0$*

$$\begin{aligned} x_{b,i}^{[s-1]} &= x_{b,i+r_2}^{[s]} \oplus x_{c,i}^{[s]} \\ x_{d,i}^{[s-1]} &= x_{a,i}^{[s]} \oplus x_{d,i+r_1}^{[s]} \end{aligned}$$

Lemma 2 (Lemma 4 of [10]). *Consider the SR with rotation distances r_1 and r_2. Then we have that*

$$\begin{aligned} x_{a,0}^{[s-1]} &= x_{a,0}^{[s]} \oplus x_{b,r_2}^{[s]} \oplus x_{c,0}^{[s]} \\ x_{c,0}^{[s-1]} &= x_{c,0}^{[s]} \oplus x_{d,0}^{[s]} \end{aligned}$$

The following three lemmas do not hold with probability 1.

Lemma 3 (Lemma 5 of [10]). *For one active input bit in subround $s-1$ and multiple output bits in subround s, the following linear approximations hold with probability $\frac{1}{2}\left(1+\frac{1}{2}\right)$ for the SR with rotation distances r_1 and r_2 when $i > 0$*

$$\begin{aligned} x_{a,i}^{[s-1]} &= x_{a,i}^{[s]} \oplus x_{b,i+r_2}^{[s]} \oplus x_{c,i}^{[s]} \oplus x_{b,i+r_2-1}^{[s]} \oplus x_{c,i-1}^{[s]} \\ x_{c,i}^{[s-1]} &= x_{c,i}^{[s]} \oplus x_{d,i}^{[s]} \oplus x_{d,i-1}^{[s]} \end{aligned}$$

Lemma 4 (Lemma 7 of [10]). *For two active input bits in subround $s-1$ and multiple output bits in subround s, the following linear approximation hold with probability $\frac{1}{2}\left(1+\frac{1}{2}\right)$ for the SR with rotation distances r_1 and r_2*

$$\begin{aligned} x_{a,i}^{[s-1]} \oplus x_{a,i-1}^{[s-1]} &= x_{a,i}^{[s]} \oplus x_{b,i+r_2}^{[s]} \oplus x_{c,i}^{[s]} \\ x_{c,i}^{[s-1]} \oplus x_{c,i-1}^{[s-1]} &= x_{c,i}^{[s]} \oplus x_{d,i}^{[s]} \end{aligned}$$

Lemma 5 (Lemma 6 of [10]). *For two active input bits in subround $s-1$ and multiple output bits in subround s, the following linear approximation hold with probability $\frac{1}{2}\left(1+\frac{1}{2}\right)$ for the SR with rotation distances r_1 and r_2*

$$\begin{aligned} x_{a,i}^{[s-1]} \oplus x_{a,i-1}^{[s-1]} &= x_{a,i}^{[s]} \oplus x_{b,i+r_2}^{[s]} \oplus x_{c,i}^{[s]} \oplus x_{a,i-1}^{[s]} \oplus x_{b,i+r_2-1}^{[s]} \oplus x_{c,i-1}^{[s]} \\ x_{c,i}^{[s-1]} \oplus x_{c,i-1}^{[s-1]} &= x_{c,i}^{[s]} \oplus x_{d,i}^{[s]} \oplus x_{c,i-1}^{[s]} \oplus x_{d,i-1}^{[s]} \end{aligned}$$

As Coutinho et al. explained, we should comprehensively consider about Lemma 4 and 5 when they expanding the same pair of bits. Intuitively speaking, we should start by deriving the equation on the right side of the equation that has fewer bits. But the truth is that such a choice might not be the best one. After a sufficient number of rounds, certain bits generated by Lemma 5 may be counterbalanced by bits from other lemmas, leading to cancellation. Therefore, the best rules will be the one that results in other bits being canceled. But they did not provide a method for choosing which specific lemma to use for the derivation.

Recently, Li et al. [19] introduced a new framework to tackle this problem. They proposed a new rule to expand the bits $x_{a,i}^{[s-1]}$ and $x_{c,i}^{[s-1]}$ as follows.

Lemma 6 (Lemma 6 of [19]) *For one active input bit in subround $s-1$ and multiple output bits in subround s, the following linear approximations hold with probability $\frac{1}{2}\left(1-\frac{1}{2}\right)$ for the SR with rotation distances r_1 and r_2 when $i>0$*

$$\begin{aligned} x_{a,i}^{[s-1]} &= x_{a,i}^{[s]} \oplus x_{b,i+r_2}^{[s]} \oplus x_{c,i}^{[s]} \oplus x_{a,i-1}^{[s]} \\ x_{c,i}^{[s-1]} &= x_{c,i}^{[s]} \oplus x_{d,i}^{[s]} \oplus x_{c,i-1}^{[s]} \end{aligned}$$

Now, Lemma 3 and Lemma 6 expand the same bits, i.e., $x_{a,i}^{[s-1]}$ and $x_{c,i}^{[s-1]}$, Lemma 4 and Lemma 5 expand the same pair of bits $x_{a,i}^{[s-1]} \oplus x_{a,i-1}^{[s-1]}$ and $x_{c,i}^{[s-1]} \oplus x_{c,i-1}^{[s-1]}$. In their framework, they use these four lemmas in a mixed mode, rather than use them individually, to exhaust all possible options.

4 A New Derivation Rule for Linear Approximations

We find only use the six lemmas above is not enough to obtain the best linear approximations for ChaCha. It is because that the derivation rules for linear approximations are incomplete. By using **Theorem 3** of Wallén [24], we generate one new linear approximation as follows.

$$\Pr\left(\Theta_i\left(x,y\right)=y_{i-h}\right)=\frac{1}{2}\left(1+\frac{1}{2^h}\right), i>0. \tag{3}$$

By using Eq. 3, we can obtain a new derivation rule for linear approximations.

Lemma 7. *For two active input bits in subround $s-1$ and multiple output bits in subround s, the following linear approximation holds with probability $\frac{1}{2}\left(1+\frac{1}{2^h}\right)$ for the SR with rotation distance r_1 when $i \geq 0$ and $h>0$*

$$x_{c,i+r_1+h}^{[s-1]} \oplus x_{d,i}^{[s-1]} = x_{a,i}^{[s]} \oplus x_{c,i+r_1+h}^{[s]} \oplus x_{d,i+r_1+h}^{[s]}$$

Proof. By the SR function of ChaCha, we have $x_{c,i+r_1+h}^{[s-1]} = x_{c,i+r_1+h}^{[s]} \oplus x_{d,i+r_1+h}^{[s]} \oplus \Theta_{i+r_1+h}\left(x_c^{[s-1]}, x_d^{[s]}\right)$ and $x_{d,i}^{[s-1]} = x_{a,i}^{[s]} \oplus x_{d,i+r_1}^{[s]}$, and then

$$\begin{aligned} & x_{c,i+r_1+h}^{[s-1]} \oplus x_{d,i}^{[s-1]} \\ =& x_{c,i+r_1+h}^{[s]} \oplus x_{d,i+r_1+h}^{[s]} \oplus \Theta_{i+r_1+h}\left(x_c^{[s-1]}, x_d^{[s]}\right) \oplus x_{a,i}^{[s]} \oplus x_{d,i+r_1}^{[s]} \end{aligned}$$

Using Eq. 3, we have

$$\Pr\left(\Theta_{i+r_1+h}\left(x_c^{[s-1]}, x_d^{[s]}\right) \oplus x_{d,i+r_1}^{[s]} = 0\right) = \frac{1}{2}\left(1+\frac{1}{2^h}\right)$$

Therefore, $x_{c,i+r_1+h}^{[s-1]} \oplus x_{d,i}^{[s-1]} = x_{a,i}^{[s]} \oplus x_{c,i+r_1+h}^{[s]} \oplus x_{d,i+r_1+h}^{[s]}$ holds with probability $\frac{1}{2}\left(1+\frac{1}{2^h}\right)$. □

Initially, we cannot imagine why Lemma 7 could help us to obtain better linear approximations, compared with the previous derivation rules for linear approximations. When we revisit the selection of bit combinations, it becomes evident that $x_{a,i}^{[s-1]} \oplus x_{b,i}^{[s-1]}$ produces equivalent outcomes as the joint consideration of $x_{a,i}^{[s-1]}$ and $x_{b,i}^{[s-1]}$. A similar phenomenon is observed between $x_{c,i+r_1}^{[s-1]}$ and $x_{d,i}^{[s-1]}$. Consequently, we extended our analysis to encompass a more generalized scenario, i.e., $x_{c,i+r_i+h}^{[s-1]} \oplus x_{d,i}^{[s-1]}$ with $h > 0$. We can obtain $\Pr\left(\Theta_{i+r_1+h}(x_c^{[s-1]}, x_d^{[s]}) = x_{d,i+r_1}^{[s]}\right) = \frac{1}{2}\left(1 + \frac{1}{2^h}\right)$ with $i > 0, h > 0$ by using Eq. 3, and thus $x_{c,i+r_i+h}^{[s-1]} \oplus x_{d,i}^{[s-1]} = x_{c,i+r_i+h}^{[s]} \oplus x_{d,i+r_i+h}^{[s]} \oplus x_{a,i}^{[s]}$ holds with probability $\frac{1}{2}\left(1 + \frac{1}{2^h}\right)$. Compared with the independent derivation of these two bits, the proposed derivation rule reduces the number of active bits by two, i.e. $x_{c,i+r_1+h-1}^{[s]} \oplus x_{d,i+r_1}^{[s]}$ or $x_{d,i+r_1+h-1}^{[s]} \oplus x_{d,i+r_1}^{[s]}$. We know only $x_{a,i}$ and $x_{c,i}$ generate carry, so avoid generating $x_{a,i}$ and $x_{c,i}$ is clearly helpful for improving the correlations of linear approximations. Hence, although Lemma 7 presents a lower correlation, its bit-conservation property prevents the exponential growth of active bits. This strategy will be systematically employed in the subsequent derivation of linear approximations.

5 Improved Linear Approximations for ChaCha

5.1 Improved Linear Approximation for 3.5-Round ChaCha

At EUROCRYPT 2021, Coutinho and Souza [11] presented a linear approximation for 3.5-round ChaCha with correlation 2^{-47}. Now, we will provide an improved linear approximation for 3.5-round ChaCha obtained by our new lemma. The new linear approximation will be given by Lemma 9. Before introducing it, a linear approximation for 2.5-round ChaCha is given by the following lemma, as it will be used in the proof of Lemma 9.

Lemma 8. *The following linear approximation for 2.5-round ChaCha holds with probability* $\frac{1}{2}\left(1 - \frac{1}{2^{10}}\right)$*::*

$$\begin{aligned}
x_{5,0}^{(3.5)} =& x_0^{(6)}[0] \oplus x_2^{(6)}[0,6,7,22,23] \oplus x_3^{(6)}[0,7,8,19,24] \oplus \\
& x_4^{(6)}[7,14,15] \oplus x_5^{(6)}[13] \oplus x_7^{(6)}[7,13,14,19] \oplus x_8^{(6)}[6,7,12] \oplus \\
& x_9^{(6)}[0,8,18,19] \oplus x_{10}^{(6)}[0,6,25,26] \oplus x_{13}^{(6)}[0,30,31] \oplus \\
& x_{14}^{(6)}[0,7,15,19,27] \oplus x_{15}^{(6)}[0,8,26]
\end{aligned}$$

Proof. By Lemma 1 and Lemma 2, we have

$$x_{5,0}^{(3.5)} = x_{5,7}^{(4)} \oplus x_{10,0}^{(4)} = x_{5,19}^{(4.5)} \oplus x_{9,7}^{(4.5)} \oplus x_{10,0}^{(4.5)} \oplus x_{14,0}^{(4.5)}$$

with probability 1.

Next, we expand $x_{9,7}^{(4.5)}$ with Lemma 3 to obtain

$$\begin{aligned} & x_{5,19}^{(4.5)} \oplus x_{9,7}^{(4.5)} \oplus x_{10,0}^{(4.5)} \oplus x_{14,0}^{(4.5)} \\ = & x_2^{(5)}[0] \oplus x_5^{(5)}[26] \oplus x_9^{(5)}[7,19] \oplus x_{10}^{(5)}[0] \oplus x_{13}^{(5)}[6,7] \oplus x_{14}^{(5)}[0,8] \end{aligned}$$

with probability $\frac{1}{2}\left(1+\frac{1}{2}\right)$.

After then, we expand $x_{9,7}^{(5)}$ with Lemma 6 and $x_{9,19}^{(5)} \oplus x_{14,0}^{(5)}$ with Lemma 7 with $h=3$ to get

$$\begin{aligned} & x_2^{(5)}[0] \oplus x_5^{(5)}[26] \oplus x_9^{(5)}[7,19] \oplus x_{10}^{(5)}[0] \oplus x_{13}^{(5)}[6,7] \oplus x_{14}^{(5)}[0,8] \\ = & x_2^{(5.5)}[0,6,7] \oplus x_3^{(5.5)}[0,8] \oplus x_5^{(5.5)}[6] \oplus x_7^{(5.5)}[12] \oplus x_8^{(5.5)}[0] \oplus \\ & x_9^{(5.5)}[6,7,19] \oplus x_{10}^{(5.5)}[0,26] \oplus x_{13}^{(5.5)}[22,23] \oplus x_{14}^{(5.5)}[7,19,24] \oplus x_{15}^{(5.5)}[0] \end{aligned}$$

with probability $\frac{1}{2}\left(1-\frac{1}{2^4}\right)$.

Then, we expand $x_{3,8}^{(5.5)}$ with Lemma 3, $x_9^{(5.5)}[6,7]$ with Lemma 4, $x_2^{(5.5)}[6,7]$ with Lemma 5 and $x_{9,19}^{(5.5)}, x_{10,26}^{(5.5)}$ with Lemma 6 to obtain

$$\begin{aligned} & x_2^{(5.5)}[0,6,7] \oplus x_3^{(5.5)}[0,8] \oplus x_5^{(5.5)}[6] \oplus x_7^{(5.5)}[12] \oplus x_8^{(5.5)}[0] \oplus \\ & x_9^{(5.5)}[6,7,19] \oplus x_{10}^{(5.5)}[0,26] \oplus x_{13}^{(5.5)}[22,23] \oplus x_{14}^{(5.5)}[7,19,24] \oplus x_{15}^{(5.5)}[0] \\ = & x_0^{(6)}[0] \oplus x_2^{(6)}[0,6,7,22,23] \oplus x_3^{(6)}[0,7,8,19,24] \oplus x_4^{(6)}[7,14,15] \oplus x_5^{(6)}[13] \oplus \\ & x_7^{(6)}[7,13,14,19] \oplus x_8^{(6)}[6,7,12] \oplus x_9^{(6)}[0,8,18,19] \oplus x_{10}^{(6)}[0,6,25,26] \oplus \\ & x_{13}^{(6)}[0,30,31] \oplus x_{14}^{(6)}[0,7,15,19,27] \oplus x_{15}^{(6)}[0,8,26] \end{aligned}$$

with probability $\frac{1}{2}\left(1+\frac{1}{2^5}\right)$.

By the Piling-up Lemma, we can combine these linear relations to get Lemma 8 with probability $\frac{1}{2}\left(1-\frac{1}{2^{10}}\right)$. □

Computational Result 1. *The linear approximation of Lemma 8 holds computationally with* $\varepsilon_{\text{Lemma 8}} = -2^{-9.22}$. *This correlation was verified using* 2^{34} *random samples.*

Lemma 9. *The following linear approximation for 3.5-round ChaCha holds with probability* $\frac{1}{2}\left(1-\frac{1}{2^{40}}\right)$*:*

$$\begin{aligned}x_{5,0}^{(3.5)} =& x_0^{(7)}[0,7,12] \oplus x_1^{(7)}[8,14,15,16,19,31]\oplus \\ & x_2^{(7)}[0,3,5,6,11,14,15,16,18,19,27,31]\oplus \\ & x_3^{(7)}[10,16,19,26] \oplus x_4^{(7)}[1,2,7,19,26] \oplus x_5^{(7)}[0,6,7]\oplus \\ & x_6^{(7)}[2,10,19,22,29,30] \oplus x_7^{(7)}[11,19,27,31]\oplus \\ & x_8^{(7)}[15,19,26,27] \oplus x_9^{(7)}[8,13,19,25,31]\oplus \\ & x_{10}^{(7)}[3,7,12,15,26,27] \oplus x_{11}^{(7)}[0,4,8,12,14,20]\oplus \\ & x_{12}^{(7)}[0,12,20] \oplus x_{13}^{(7)}[0,12,13,16,18,19,22,23,24,27]\oplus \\ & x_{14}^{(7)}[2,8,11,13,14,19,23,24,25,26,31] \oplus x_{15}^{(7)}[8,14,18,23]\end{aligned}$$

Proof. We start from the linear approximation of Lemma 8 and expand the linear approximation one more round. Since we are transitioning from round 6 to 7, we have $(a,b,c,d) \in \{(0,4,8,12),(1,5,9,13),(2,6,10,14),(3,7,11,15)\}$. Therefore, we can divide the right-hand side of Lemma 8 into 4 distinct groups:

Group I: $x_0^{(6)}[0], x_4^{(6)}[7,14,15], x_8^{(6)}[6,7,12]$
Group II: $x_5^{(6)}[13], x_9^{(6)}[0,8,18,19], x_{13}^{(6)}[0,30,31]$
Group III: $x_2^{(6)}[0,6,7,22,23], x_{10}^{(6)}[0,6,25,26], x_{14}^{(6)}[0,7,15,19,27]$
Group IV: $x_3^{(6)}[0,7,8,19,24], x_7^{(6)}[7,13,14,19], x_{15}^{(6)}[0,8,26]$

For Group I, we first expand $x_{8,12}^{(6)}$ with Lemma 6 and $x_8^{(6)}[6,7]$ with Lemma 4 to get

$$\begin{aligned}& x_0^{(6)}[0] \oplus x_4^{(6)}[7,14,15] \oplus x_8^{(6)}[6,7,12] \\ =& x_0^{(6.5)}[0] \oplus x_4^{(6.5)}[12,19,26,27] \oplus x_8^{(6.5)}[0,11,12,14,15] \oplus x_{12}^{(6.5)}[7,12]\end{aligned}$$

with probability $\frac{1}{2}\left(1-\frac{1}{2^2}\right)$.

Next, we expand $x_8^{(6.5)}[11,12], x_8^{(6.5)}[14,15]$ with Lemma 4 to obtain

$$\begin{aligned}& x_0^{(6.5)}[0] \oplus x_4^{(6.5)}[12,19,26,27] \oplus x_8^{(6.5)}[0,11,12,14,15] \oplus x_{12}^{(6.5)}[7,12] \\ =& x_0^{(7)}[0,7,12] \oplus x_4^{(7)}[1,2,7,19,26] \oplus x_8^{(7)}[15,19,26,27] \oplus x_{12}^{(7)}[0,12,20]\end{aligned}$$

with probability $\frac{1}{2}\left(1+\frac{1}{2^2}\right)$.

By the Piling-up Lemma, we can combine these linear relations to obtain

$$\begin{aligned}& x_0^{(6)}[0] \oplus x_4^{(6)}[7,14,15] \oplus x_8^{(6)}[6,7,12] \\ =& x_0^{(7)}[0,7,12] \oplus x_4^{(7)}[1,2,7,19,26] \oplus x_8^{(7)}[15,19,26,27] \oplus x_{12}^{(7)}[0,12,20]\end{aligned} \tag{4}$$

with probability $\frac{1}{2}\left(1-\frac{1}{2^4}\right)$.

For Group II, we first expand $x_{9,8}^{(6)}$ with Lemma 6 and $x_9^{(6)}[18,19]$ with Lemma 4 to get

$$\begin{aligned} & x_5^{(6)}[13] \oplus x_9^{(6)}[0,8,18,19] \oplus x_{13}^{(6)}[0,30,31] \\ = & x_1^{(6.5)}[0,30,31] \oplus x_5^{(6.5)}[25] \oplus x_9^{(6.5)}[0,7,8,13,19] \oplus x_{13}^{(6.5)}[0,8,14,15,16,19] \end{aligned}$$

with probability $\frac{1}{2}\left(1-\frac{1}{2^2}\right)$.

Next, we expand $x_1^{(6.5)}[30,31], x_9^{(6.5)}[7,8]$ with Lemma 4 and $x_{9,13}^{(6.5)}, x_{9,19}^{(6.5)}$ with Lemma 3 to obtain

$$\begin{aligned} & x_1^{(6.5)}[0,30,31] \oplus x_5^{(6.5)}[25] \oplus x_9^{(6.5)}[0,7,8,13,19] \oplus x_{13}^{(6.5)}[0,8,14,15,16,19] \\ = & x_1^{(7)}[8,14,15,16,19,31] \oplus x_5^{(7)}[0,6,7] \oplus x_9^{(7)}[8,13,19,25,31] \oplus \\ & x_{13}^{(7)}[0,12,13,16,18,19,22,23,24,27] \end{aligned}$$

with probability $\frac{1}{2}\left(1+\frac{1}{2^4}\right)$.

By the Piling-up Lemma, we can combine these linear relations to obtain

$$\begin{aligned} & x_5^{(6)}[13] \oplus x_9^{(6)}[0,8,18,19] \oplus x_{13}^{(6)}[0,30,31] \\ = & x_1^{(7)}[8,14,15,16,19,31] \oplus x_5^{(7)}[0,6,7] \oplus x_9^{(7)}[8,13,19,25,31] \oplus \\ & x_{13}^{(7)}[0,12,13,16,18,19,22,23,24,27] \end{aligned} \quad (5)$$

with probability $\frac{1}{2}\left(1-\frac{1}{2^6}\right)$.

For Group III, we first expand $x_2^{(6)}[6,7], x_2^{(6)}[22,23], x_{10}^{(6)}[25,26]$ with Lemma 4 and $x_{10,6}^{(6)}$ with Lemma 3 to get

$$\begin{aligned} & x_2^{(6)}[0,6,7,22,23] \oplus x_{10}^{(6)}[0,6,25,26] \oplus x_{14}^{(6)}[0,7,15,19,27] \\ = & x_2^{(6.5)}[15,19,23,27] \oplus x_6^{(6.5)}[3,12,19] \oplus x_{10}^{(6.5)}[6,7,23,26] \oplus \\ & x_{14}^{(6.5)}[0,3,5,6,11,16,23,26,31] \end{aligned}$$

with probability $\frac{1}{2}\left(1+\frac{1}{2^4}\right)$.

Next, we expand $x_{10}^{(6.5)}[6,7]$ with Lemma 4, $x_{2,15}^{(6.5)}, x_{2,19}^{(6.5)}, x_{2,27}^{(6.5)}, x_{10,23}^{(6.5)}$ with Lemma 6 and $x_{2,23}^{(6.5)}, x_{10,23}^{(6.5)}$ with Lemma 3 to obtain

$$\begin{aligned} & x_2^{(6.5)}[15,19,23,27] \oplus x_6^{(6.5)}[3,12,19] \oplus x_{10}^{(6.5)}[6,7,23,26] \oplus \\ & x_{14}^{(6.5)}[0,3,5,6,11,16,23,26,31] \\ = & x_2^{(7)}[0,3,5,6,11,14,15,16,18,19,27,31] \oplus \\ & x_6^{(7)}[2,10,19,22,29,30] \oplus x_{10}^{(7)}[3,7,12,15,26,27] \oplus \\ & x_{14}^{(7)}[2,8,11,13,14,19,23,24,25,26,31] \end{aligned}$$

with probability $\frac{1}{2}\left(1+\frac{1}{2^7}\right)$.

By the Piling-up Lemma, we can combine these linear relations to obtain

$$\begin{aligned} & x_2^{(6)}[0,6,7,22,23] \oplus x_{10}^{(6)}[0,6,25,26] \oplus x_{14}^{(6)}[0,7,15,19,27] \\ = & x_2^{(7)}[0,3,5,6,11,14,15,16,18,19,27,31] \oplus \\ & x_6^{(7)}[2,10,19,22,29,30] \oplus x_{10}^{(7)}[3,7,12,15,26,27] \oplus \\ & x_{14}^{(7)}[2,8,11,13,14,19,23,24,25,26,31] \end{aligned} \tag{6}$$

with probability $\frac{1}{2}\left(1+\frac{1}{2^{11}}\right)$.

For Group IV, we first expand $x_3^{(6)}[7,8]$ with Lemma 4 and $x_{3,19}^{(6)}, x_{3,24}^{(6)}$ with Lemma 6 to get

$$\begin{aligned} & x_3^{(6)}[0,7,8,19,24] \oplus x_7^{(6)}[7,13,14,19] \oplus x_{15}^{(6)}[0,8,26] \\ = & x_3^{(6.5)}[18,19,23,24,26] \oplus x_7^{(6.5)}[4,12,19,20,25,26] \oplus \\ & x_{11}^{(6.5)}[0,7,8,13,14,24] \oplus x_{15}^{(6.5)}[10,16,24] \end{aligned}$$

with probability $\frac{1}{2}\left(1+\frac{1}{2^3}\right)$.

Next, we expand $x_3^{(6.5)}[18,19], x_3^{(6.5)}[23,24], x_{11}^{(6.5)}[7,8], x_{11}^{(6.5)}[13,14]$ with Lemma 4 and $x_{3,26}^{(6.5)}, x_{11,24}^{(6.5)}$ with Lemma 3 to obtain

$$\begin{aligned} & x_3^{(6.5)}[18,19,23,24,26] \oplus x_7^{(6.5)}[4,12,19,20,25,26] \oplus \\ & x_{11}^{(6.5)}[0,7,8,13,14,24] \oplus x_{15}^{(6.5)}[10,16,24] \\ = & x_3^{(7)}[10,16,19,26] \oplus x_7^{(7)}[11,19,27,31] \oplus \\ & x_{11}^{(7)}[0,4,8,12,14,20] \oplus x_{15}^{(7)}[8,14,18,23] \end{aligned}$$

with probability $\frac{1}{2}\left(1+\frac{1}{2^6}\right)$.

By the Piling-up Lemma, we can combine these linear relations to obtain

$$\begin{aligned} & x_3^{(6)}[0,7,8,19,24] \oplus x_7^{(6)}[7,13,14,19] \oplus x_{15}^{(6)}[0,8,26] \\ = & x_3^{(7)}[10,16,19,26] \oplus x_7^{(7)}[11,19,27,31] \oplus \\ & x_{11}^{(7)}[0,4,8,12,14,20] \oplus x_{15}^{(7)}[8,14,18,23] \end{aligned} \tag{7}$$

with probability $\frac{1}{2}\left(1+\frac{1}{2^9}\right)$.

Finally, using the Piling-up Lemma we obtain Lemma 9 by combining the result from Lemma 8 and Eqs. (4)-(7), which leads to a correlation of $-2^{-(10+4+6+11+9)} = -2^{-40}$. □

Computational Result 2. *The linear approximation of Eq.* (4) *holds computationally with* $\varepsilon_{L_0} = -2^{-3.58}$. *This correlation was verified using* 2^{32} *random samples.*

Computational Result 3. *The linear approximation of Eq.* (5) *holds computationally with* $\varepsilon_{L_1} = -2^{-5.17}$. *This correlation was verified using* 2^{32} *random samples.*

Computational Result 4. *The linear approximation of Eq.* (6) *holds computationally with* $\varepsilon_{L_2} = 2^{-10.10}$. *This correlation was verified using* 2^{34} *random samples.*

Computational Result 5. *The linear approximation of Eq.* (7) *holds computationally with* $\varepsilon_{L_3} = 2^{-8.15}$. *This correlation was verified using* 2^{34} *random samples.*

Using the Piling-up Lemma and **Computational Results 1–5**, the linear approximation of Lemma 9 holds computationally with correlation $\varepsilon_{Lemma\ 9} = -2^{-(9.22+3.58+5.17+10.10+8.15)} = -2^{-36.22}$.

5.2 Improved Linear Approximation for 4-Round ChaCha

At EUROCRYPT 2021, Coutinho and Souza [11] presented a linear approximation for 4-round ChaCha with correlation 2^{-55}. Soon after, Coutinho et al. [9] gave an improved linear approximation for 4-round ChaCha with correlation 2^{-53} at ASIACRYPT 2022. Recently, Li et al. [19] proposed a new framework to derive linear approximations and reduced the correlation of linear approximations to -2^{-50} for 4-round ChaCha. Now, we will further improve the linear approximation for 4-round ChaCha by our new lemma. It will be given by Lemma 11. Before introducing this lemma, a linear approximation for 3-round ChaCha is given by the following lemma, as it will be used in the proof of Lemma 11.

Lemma 10. *The following linear approximation for 3-round ChaCha holds with probability* $\frac{1}{2}\left(1 - \frac{1}{2^{10}}\right)$*:*

$$
\begin{aligned}
x_{3,0}^{(3)} \oplus x_{4,0}^{(3)} =& x_0^{(6)}[0,16] \oplus x_1^{(6)}[0,7,12,23] \oplus \\
& x_2^{(6)}[0,7,8,19,24] \oplus x_4^{(6)}[7,13,19] \oplus \\
& x_5^{(6)}[7] \oplus x_6^{(6)}[7,13,14,19] \oplus x_7^{(6)}[6,7,14,15,26] \oplus \\
& x_8^{(6)}[0,7,8,19,31] \oplus x_9^{(6)}[0,6,12,25,26] \oplus x_{10}^{(6)}[0] \oplus \\
& x_{11}^{(6)}[6,7] \oplus x_{12}^{(6)}[0,12,20,31] \oplus \\
& x_{13}^{(6)}[0,15,27] \oplus x_{14}^{(6)}[8,26] \oplus x_{15}^{(6)}[24]
\end{aligned}
$$

Proof. By Lemma 1 and Lemma 2, we directly have

$$
\begin{aligned}
x_{3,0}^{(3)} \oplus x_{4,0}^{(3)} &= x_{3,0}^{(3.5)} \\
&= x_{3,0}^{(4)} \oplus x_{4,7}^{(4)} \oplus x_{9,0}^{(4)} \\
&= x_{3,0}^{(4.5)} \oplus x_{4,19}^{(4.5)} \oplus x_{7,12}^{(4.5)} \oplus x_{8,7}^{(4.5)} \oplus x_{9,0}^{(4.5)} \oplus x_{11,0}^{(4.5)} \oplus x_{13,0}^{(4.5)}
\end{aligned}
$$

with probability 1.

Next, we expand $x_{8,7}^{(4.5)}$ with Lemma 6 to get

$$\begin{aligned}
&x_{3,0}^{(4.5)} \oplus x_{4,19}^{(4.5)} \oplus x_{7,12}^{(4.5)} \oplus x_{8,7}^{(4.5)} \oplus x_{9,0}^{(4.5)} \oplus x_{11,0}^{(4.5)} \oplus x_{13,0}^{(4.5)} \\
=&x_1^{(5)}[0] \oplus x_3^{(5)}[0] \oplus x_4^{(5)}[26] \oplus x_7^{(5)}[7,19] \oplus x_8^{(5)}[6,7,19] \oplus \\
&x_9^{(5)}[0] \oplus x_{11}^{(5)}[12] \oplus x_{12}^{(5)}[7] \oplus x_{13}^{(5)}[0,8] \oplus x_{15}^{(5)}[0]
\end{aligned}$$

with probability $\frac{1}{2}\left(1-\frac{1}{2}\right)$.

For the next subround, we expand $x_8^{(5)}[6,7]$ with Lemma 4, $x_{11,12}^{(5)}$ with Lemma 6 and $x_{8,19}^{(5)} \oplus x_{13,0}^{(5)}$ with Lemma 7 with $h=3$ to obtain

$$\begin{aligned}
&x_1^{(5)}[0] \oplus x_3^{(5)}[0] \oplus x_4^{(5)}[26] \oplus x_7^{(5)}[7,19] \oplus x_8^{(5)}[6,7,19] \oplus \\
&x_9^{(5)}[0] \oplus x_{11}^{(5)}[12] \oplus x_{12}^{(5)}[7] \oplus x_{13}^{(5)}[0,8] \oplus x_{15}^{(5)}[0] \\
=&x_0^{(5.5)}[0] \oplus x_1^{(5.5)}[0,7] \oplus x_2^{(5.5)}[0,8] \oplus x_3^{(5.5)}[0] \oplus \\
&x_4^{(5.5)}[6,12] \oplus x_6^{(5.5)}[12] \oplus x_7^{(5.5)}[19,31] \oplus \\
&x_9^{(5.5)}[26] \oplus x_{11}^{(5.5)}[0,11,12] \oplus x_{12}^{(5.5)}[12,23] \oplus \\
&x_{13}^{(5.5)}[7,19,24] \oplus x_{14}^{(5.5)}[0] \oplus x_{15}^{(5.5)}[16]
\end{aligned}$$

with probability $\frac{1}{2}\left(1-\frac{1}{2^5}\right)$.

Finally, we expand $x_{1,7}^{(5.5)}, x_{2,8}^{(5.5)}$ with Lemma 3, $x_{11}^{(5.5)}[11,12]$ with Lemma 4 and $x_{9,26}^{(5.5)}$ with Lemma 6 to get

$$\begin{aligned}
&x_0^{(5.5)}[0] \oplus x_1^{(5.5)}[0,7] \oplus x_2^{(5.5)}[0,8] \oplus x_3^{(5.5)}[0] \oplus x_4^{(5.5)}[6,12] \oplus \\
&x_6^{(5.5)}[12] \oplus x_7^{(5.5)}[19,31] \oplus x_9^{(5.5)}[26] \oplus x_{11}^{(5.5)}[0,11,12] \oplus \\
&x_{12}^{(5.5)}[12,23] \oplus x_{13}^{(5.5)}[7,19,24] \oplus x_{14}^{(5.5)}[0] \oplus x_{15}^{(5.5)}[16] \\
=&x_0^{(6)}[0,16] \oplus x_1^{(6)}[0,7,12,23] \oplus x_2^{(6)}[0,7,8,19,24] \oplus \\
&x_4^{(6)}[7,13,19] \oplus x_5^{(6)}[7] \oplus x_6^{(6)}[7,13,14,19] \oplus \\
&x_7^{(6)}[6,7,14,15,26] \oplus x_8^{(6)}[0,7,8,19,31] \oplus \\
&x_9^{(6)}[0,6,12,25,26] \oplus x_{10}^{(6)}[0] \oplus x_{11}^{(6)}[6,7] \oplus \\
&x_{12}^{(6)}[0,12,20,31] \oplus x_{13}^{(6)}[0,15,27] \oplus x_{14}^{(6)}[8,26] \oplus x_{15}^{(6)}[24]
\end{aligned}$$

with probability $\frac{1}{2}\left(1-\frac{1}{2^4}\right)$.

By the Piling-up Lemma, we can combine these linear relations to obtain Lemma 10 with probability $\frac{1}{2}\left(1-\frac{1}{2^{10}}\right)$. □

Computational Result 6. *The linear approximation of* Lemma 10 *holds computationally with* $\varepsilon_{\text{Lemma10}} = -2^{-9.16}$. *This correlation was verified using* 2^{34} *random samples.*

Lemma 11. *The following linear approximation for 4-round ChaCha holds with probability* $\frac{1}{2}\left(1+\frac{1}{2^{48}}\right)$*:*

$$\begin{aligned} x_{3,0}^{(3)} \oplus x_{4,0}^{(3)} = & x_0^{(7)}[0,4,7,8,11,12,15,18,19,20,28,30] \oplus \\ & x_1^{(7)}[0,5,7,14,15,16,23,27,31] \oplus x_2^{(7)}[10,19,26] \oplus \\ & x_3^{(7)}[6,7,8,23,24] \oplus x_4^{(7)}[0,3,23,27] \oplus \\ & x_5^{(7)}[2,10,14,22,25,30,31] \oplus x_6^{(7)}[7,11,19,27,31] \oplus \\ & x_7^{(7)}[1,2,13,25,26,31] \oplus x_8^{(7)}[8,13,20,25,28,31] \oplus \\ & x_9^{(7)}[3,7,15,18,24,25,26,27] \oplus x_{10}^{(7)}[0,4,8,12,14,20,23] \oplus \\ & x_{11}^{(7)}[6,15,18,19,24,27] \oplus x_{12}^{(7)}[4,13,23,24,26,27,31] \oplus \\ & x_{13}^{(7)}[2,7,8,13,14,20,22,23,24,26] \oplus x_{14}^{(7)}[0,14,18,24] \oplus \\ & x_{15}^{(7)}[14,16,25,26] \end{aligned}$$

Proof. We start from the linear approximation of Lemma 10 and have $(a,b,c,d) \in \{(0,4,8,12),(1,5,9,13),(2,6,10,14),(3,7,11,15)\}$. Therefore, we can divide the right-hand side of Lemma 10 into 4 distinct groups. Each group will expand from round 6 to 7.

Group I: $x_0^{(6)}[0,16], x_4^{(6)}[7,13,19], x_8^{(6)}[0,7,8,19,31], x_{12}^{(6)}[0,12,20,31]$

Group II: $x_1^{(6)}[0,7,12,23], x_5^{(6)}[7], x_9^{(6)}[0,6,12,25,26], x_{13}^{(6)}[0,15,27]$

Group III: $x_2^{(6)}[0,7,8,19,24], x_6^{(6)}[7,13,14,19], x_{10}^{(6)}[0], x_{14}^{(6)}[8,26]$

Group IV: $x_7^{(6)}[6,7,14,15,26], x_{11}^{(6)}[6,7], x_{15}^{(6)}[24]$

For Group I, we first expand $x_{8,19}^{(6)}$ with Lemma 3, $x_8^{(6)}[7,8]$ with Lemma 5 and $x_{0,16}^{(6)}, x_{8,31}^{(6)}$ with Lemma 6 to obtain

$$\begin{aligned} & x_0^{(6)}[0,16] \oplus x_4^{(6)}[7,13,19] \oplus x_8^{(6)}[0,7,8,19,31] \oplus x_{12}^{(6)}[0,12,20,31] \\ = & x_0^{(6.5)}[12,15,16,20,31] \oplus x_4^{(6.5)}[12,19,25,28,31] \oplus \\ & x_8^{(6.5)}[8,13,16,30,31] \oplus x_{12}^{(6.5)}[0,4,7,8,15,16,18,19,28,31] \end{aligned}$$

with probability $\frac{1}{2}\left(1+\frac{1}{2^4}\right)$.

For the next and final subround, we expand $x_0^{(6.5)}[15,16], x_8^{(6.5)}[30,31]$ with Lemma 4, $x_{0,20}^{(6.5)}, x_{8,8}^{(6.5)}, x_{8,13}^{(6.5)}, x_{8,16}^{(6.5)}$ with Lemma 3 and $x_{0,12}^{(6.5)}, x_{0,31}^{(6.5)}$ with Lemma 6 to get

$$\begin{aligned} & x_0^{(6.5)}[12,15,16,20,31] \oplus x_4^{(6.5)}[12,19,25,28,31] \oplus \\ & x_8^{(6.5)}[8,13,16,30,31] \oplus x_{12}^{(6.5)}[0,4,7,8,15,16,18,19,28,31] \\ = & x_0^{(7)}[0,4,7,8,11,12,15,18,19,20,28,30] \oplus x_4^{(7)}[0,3,23,27] \oplus \\ & x_8^{(7)}[8,13,20,25,28,31] \oplus x_{12}^{(7)}[4,13,23,24,26,27,31] \end{aligned}$$

with probability $\frac{1}{2}\left(1+\frac{1}{2^8}\right)$.

By the Piling-up Lemma, we can combine these linear relations to obtain

$$\begin{aligned} &x_0^{(6)}[0,16] \oplus x_4^{(6)}[7,13,19] \oplus x_8^{(6)}[0,7,8,19,31] \oplus x_{12}^{(6)}[0,12,20,31] \\ =&x_0^{(7)}[0,4,7,8,11,12,15,18,19,20,28,30] \oplus x_4^{(7)}[0,3,23,27] \oplus \\ &x_8^{(7)}[8,13,20,25,28,31] \oplus x_{12}^{(7)}[4,13,23,24,26,27,31] \end{aligned} \tag{8}$$

with probability $\frac{1}{2}\left(1+\frac{1}{2^{12}}\right)$.

For Group II, we first expand $x_9^{(6)}[25,26]$ with Lemma 4, $x_{1,12}^{(6)}, x_{1,23}^{(6)}$ with Lemma 6 and $x_{1,7}^{(6)}, x_{9,6}^{(6)}, x_{9,12}^{(6)}$ with Lemma 3 to obtain

$$\begin{aligned} &x_1^{(6)}[0,7,12,23] \oplus x_5^{(6)}[7] \oplus x_9^{(6)}[0,6,12,25,26] \oplus x_{13}^{(6)}[0,15,27] \\ =&x_1^{(6.5)}[7,11,12,15,22,23,27] \oplus x_5^{(6.5)}[3,12,18,24] \oplus \\ &x_9^{(6.5)}[23,26] \oplus x_{13}^{(6.5)}[0,5,6,12,16,26,31] \end{aligned}$$

with probability $\frac{1}{2}\left(1+\frac{1}{2^6}\right)$.

For the next and final subround, we expand $x_1^{(6.5)}[11,12], x_1^{(6.5)}[22,23]$ with Lemma 4, $x_{1,7}^{(6.5)}, x_{1,15}^{(6.5)}, x_{9,26}^{(6.5)}$ with Lemma 6 and $x_{1,27}^{(6.5)}, x_{9,23}^{(6.5)}$ with Lemma 3 to get

$$\begin{aligned} &x_1^{(6.5)}[7,11,12,15,22,23,27] \oplus x_5^{(6.5)}[3,12,18,24] \oplus \\ &x_9^{(6.5)}[23,26] \oplus x_{13}^{(6.5)}[0,5,6,12,16,26,31] \\ =&x_1^{(7)}[0,5,7,14,15,16,23,27,31] \oplus \\ &x_5^{(7)}[2,10,14,22,25,30,31] \oplus x_9^{(7)}[3,7,15,18,24,25,26,27] \oplus \\ &x_{13}^{(7)}[2,7,8,13,14,20,22,23,24,26] \end{aligned}$$

with probability $\frac{1}{2}\left(1-\frac{1}{2^7}\right)$.

By the Piling-up Lemma, we can combine these linear relations to obtain

$$\begin{aligned} &x_1^{(6)}[0,7,12,23] \oplus x_5^{(6)}[7] \oplus x_9^{(6)}[0,6,12,25,26] \oplus x_{13}^{(6)}[0,15,27] \\ =&x_1^{(7)}[0,5,7,14,15,16,23,27,31] \oplus \\ &x_5^{(7)}[2,10,14,22,25,30,31] \oplus x_9^{(7)}[3,7,15,18,24,25,26,27] \oplus \\ &x_{13}^{(7)}[2,7,8,13,14,20,22,23,24,26] \end{aligned} \tag{9}$$

with probability $\frac{1}{2}\left(1-\frac{1}{2^{13}}\right)$.

For Group III, we expand $x_2^{(6)}[7,8]$ with Lemma 4 and $x_{2,19}^{(6)}, x_{2,24}^{(6)}$ with Lemma 6 to get

$$\begin{aligned} &x_2^{(6)}[0,7,8,19,24] \oplus x_6^{(6)}[7,13,14,19] \oplus x_{10}^{(6)}[0] \oplus x_{14}^{(6)}[8,26] \\ =&x_2^{(6.5)}[0,18,19,23,24,26] \oplus x_6^{(6.5)}[4,12,19,20,25,26] \oplus \\ &x_{10}^{(6.5)}[7,8,13,14,24] \oplus x_{14}^{(6.5)}[0,10,24] \end{aligned}$$

with probability $\frac{1}{2}\left(1+\frac{1}{2^3}\right)$.

For the next and final subround, we expand $x_2^{(6.5)}[18,19], x_2^{(6.5)}[23,24]$, $x_{10}^{(6.5)}[7,8]$, $x_{10}^{(6.5)}[13,14]$ with Lemma 4, $x_{10,24}^{(6.5)}$ with Lemma 6 and $x_{2,26}^{(6.5)}$ with Lemma 3 to obtain

$$\begin{aligned}&x_2^{(6.5)}[0,18,19,23,24,26] \oplus x_6^{(6.5)}[4,12,19,20,25,26] \oplus \\ &x_{10}^{(6.5)}[7,8,13,14,24] \oplus x_{14}^{(6.5)}[0,10,24] \\ =&x_2^{(7)}[10,19,26] \oplus x_6^{(7)}[7,11,19,27,31] \oplus \\ &x_{10}^{(7)}[0,4,8,12,14,20,23] \oplus x_{14}^{(7)}[0,14,18,24]\end{aligned}$$

with probability $\frac{1}{2}\left(1-\frac{1}{2^6}\right)$.

By the Piling-up Lemma, we can combine these linear relations to obtain

$$\begin{aligned}&x_2^{(6)}[0,7,8,19,24] \oplus x_6^{(6)}[7,13,14,19] \oplus x_{10}^{(6)}[0] \oplus x_{14}^{(6)}[8,26] \\ =&x_2^{(7)}[10,19,26] \oplus x_6^{(7)}[7,11,19,27,31] \oplus \\ &x_{10}^{(7)}[0,4,8,12,14,20,23] \oplus x_{14}^{(7)}[0,14,18,24]\end{aligned} \tag{10}$$

with probability $\frac{1}{2}\left(1-\frac{1}{2^9}\right)$.

For Group IV, we first expand $x_{11}^{(6)}[6,7]$ with Lemma 5 to get

$$\begin{aligned}&x_7^{(6)}[6,7,14,15,26] \oplus x_{11}^{(6)}[6,7] \oplus x_{15}^{(6)}[24] \\ =&x_3^{(6.5)}[24] \oplus x_7^{(6.5)}[6,18,19,26,27] \oplus \\ &x_{11}^{(6.5)}[14,15,26] \oplus x_{15}^{(6.5)}[6,7,8]\end{aligned}$$

with probability $\frac{1}{2}\left(1+\frac{1}{2}\right)$.

For the next and final subround, we expand $x_{11}^{(6.5)}[14,15]$ with Lemma 4, $x_{3,24}^{(6.5)}$ with Lemma 6 and $x_{11,26}^{(6.5)}$ with Lemma 3 to obtain

$$\begin{aligned}&x_3^{(6.5)}[24] \oplus x_7^{(6.5)}[6,18,19,26,27] \oplus x_{11}^{(6.5)}[14,15,26] \oplus x_{15}^{(6.5)}[6,7,8] \\ =&x_3^{(7)}[6,7,8,23,24] \oplus x_7^{(7)}[1,2,13,25,26,31] \oplus \\ &x_{11}^{(7)}[6,15,18,19,24,27] \oplus x_{15}^{(7)}[14,16,25,26]\end{aligned}$$

with probability $\frac{1}{2}\left(1-\frac{1}{2^3}\right)$.

By the Piling-up Lemma, we can combine these linear relations to obtain

$$\begin{aligned}&x_7^{(6)}[6,7,14,15,26] \oplus x_{11}^{(6)}[6,7] \oplus x_{15}^{(6)}[24] \\ =&x_3^{(7)}[6,7,8,23,24] \oplus x_7^{(7)}[1,2,13,25,26,31] \oplus \\ &x_{11}^{(7)}[6,15,18,19,24,27] \oplus x_{15}^{(7)}[14,16,25,26]\end{aligned} \tag{11}$$

with probability $\frac{1}{2}\left(1-\frac{1}{2^4}\right)$.

Finally, using the Piling-up Lemma we obtain Lemma 11 by combining the result from Lemma 10 and Eqs. (8)–(11), which leads to a correlation of $2^{-(10+12+13+9+4)} = 2^{-48}$. □

Computational Result 7. *The linear approximation of Eq.* (8) *holds computationally with* $\varepsilon_{L_4} = 2^{-11.66}$. *This correlation was verified using* 2^{34} *random samples.*

Computational Result 8. *The linear approximation of Eq.* (9) *holds computationally with* $\varepsilon_{L_5} = -2^{-11.46}$. *This correlation was verified using* 2^{34} *random samples.*

Computational Result 9. *The linear approximation of Eq.* (10) *holds computationally with* $\varepsilon_{L_6} = -2^{-8.14}$. *This correlation was verified using* 2^{34} *random samples.*

Computational Result 10. *The linear approximation of Eq.* (11) *holds computationally with* $\varepsilon_{L_7} = -2^{-3.99}$. *This correlation was verified using* 2^{32} *random samples.*

Using the Piling-up Lemma and Computational Result 6–10, the linear approximation of Lemma 11 holds computationally with correlation $\varepsilon_{Lemma\ 11} = 2^{-(9.16+11.66+11.46+8.14+3.99)} = 2^{-44.41}$.

6 Conclusions

In this paper, we propose a new derivation rule for linear approximations and then apply it to ChaCha. Unlike the previous cases where only the bits with carry are considered, we now take into account the combination of bits with carry and those without carry. Eventually, we find that compared with the previous derivation rules, it leads to better correlation when the rounds increase. By combining this new derivation rule with the previous derivation rules in a mixed pattern, we improve the 3.5- and 4-round linear approximations for ChaCha. The original 3.5-round linear approximation presented at EUROCRYPT 2021 has a correlation of 2^{-47}, which was improved to be -2^{-41} recently. This paper further improves it with a better correlation of -2^{-40}. Besides, we enhance the 4-round linear approximation for ChaCha with correlation 2^{-48}, improving the previous result (i.e., -2^{-50}) by a factor of -2^2. The advantage of our new derivation rule is fully confirmed by applying it to the ChaCha stream cipher. Furthermore, the new derivation rule for linear approximations is general and can be applied to other ARX-based ciphers. We leave it as a future work.

Acknowledgements. This work was supported by the National Cryptologic Science Fund of China under Grant number 2025NCSF02044 and the National Natural Science Foundation of China under Grant number 62472439.

References

1. ChaCha usage and deployment. https://ianix.com/pub/chacha-deployment.html
2. Aumasson, J.P., Fischer, S., Khazaei, S., Meier, W., Rechberger, C.: New features of Latin dances: analysis of salsa, ChaCha, and rumba. In: Nyberg, K. (eds) FSE 2008. LNCS, vol. 5086, pp. 470–488. Springer, Cham (2008). https://doi.org/10.1007/978-3-540-71039-4_30
3. Beierle, C., Leander, G., Todo, Y.: Improved differential-linear attacks with applications to ARX ciphers. J. Cryptol. **35** (2020). https://doi.org/10.1007/s00145-022-09437-z
4. Bellini, E., Gerault, D., Grados, J., Makarim, R.H., Peyrin, T.: Boosting differential-linear cryptanalysis of ChaCha7 with MILP. IACR Trans. Symmetric Cryptol. **2023**(2), 189–223 (2023). https://doi.org/10.46586/tosc.v2023.i2.189-223
5. Bernstein, D.J.: The Salsa20 family of stream ciphers. In: Robshaw, M., Billet, O. (eds.) New Stream Cipher Designs. LNCS, vol. 4986, pp. 84–97. Springer, Heidelberg (2008). https://doi.org/10.1007/978-3-540-68351-3_8
6. Bernstein, D.J.: ChaCha, a variant of Salsa20. In: Workshop Record of SASC, vol. 8, pp. 3–5 (2008)
7. Biham, E., Shamir, A.: Differential cryptanalysis of des-like cryptosystems. In: Menezes, A.J., Vanstone, S.A. (eds.) CRYPTO 1990. LNCS, vol. 537, pp. 2–21. Springer, Cham (1990). https://doi.org/10.1007/3-540-38424-3_1
8. Choudhuri, A.R., Maitra, S.: Significantly improved multi-bit differentials for reduced round salsa and ChaCha. IACR Trans. Symmetric Cryptol. 261–287 (2017). https://doi.org/10.46586/tosc.v2016.i2.261-287
9. Coutinho, M., Neto, T.C.S.: New multi-bit differentials to improve attacks against ChaCha. IACR Cryptol. ePrint Arch. **2020**, 350 (2020). https://eprint.iacr.org/2020/350
10. Coutinho, M., et al.: Latin dances reloaded: improved cryptanalysis against Salsa and ChaCha, and the proposal of Forró. In: Agrawal, S., Lin, D. (eds.) ASIACRYPT 2022. LNCS, vol. 13791, pp. 256–286. Springer, Cham (2022). https://doi.org/10.1007/978-3-031-22963-3_9
11. Coutinho, M., Souza, T.C.N.: Improved linear approximations to ARX ciphers and attacks against ChaCha. In: Canteaut, A., Standaert, FX. (eds) EUROCRYPT 2021. LNCS, vol. 12696, pp. 711–740. Springer, Cham (2021). https://doi.org/10.1007/978-3-030-77870-5_25
12. Dey, S.: Advancing the idea of probabilistic neutral bits: first key recovery attack on 7.5 round ChaCha. IEEE Trans. Inf. Theory **70**(8), 6091–6106 (2024). https://doi.org/10.1109/TIT.2024.3389874
13. Dey, S., Garai, H.K., Maitra, S.: Cryptanalysis of reduced round ChaCha- new attack and deeper analysis. IACR Trans. Symmetric Cryptol. 89–110 (2023). https://doi.org/10.46586/tosc.v2023.i1.89-110
14. Dey, S., Garai, H.K., Sarkar, S., Sharma, N.K.: Revamped differential-linear cryptanalysis on reduced round ChaCha. In: Dunkelman, O., Dziembowski, S. (eds.) EUROCRYPT 2022. LNCS, vol. 13277, pp. 86–114. Springer, Cham (2022). https://doi.org/10.1007/978-3-031-07082-2_4
15. Dey, S., Garai, H.K., Sarkar, S., Sharma, N.K.: Enhanced differential-linear attacks on reduced round ChaCha. IEEE Trans. Inf. Theory **69**(8), 5318–5336 (2023). https://doi.org/10.1109/TIT.2023.3269790

16. Dey, S., Sarkar, S.: Improved analysis for reduced round salsa and ChaCha. Discret. Appl. Math. **227**, 58–69 (2017). https://doi.org/10.1016/j.dam.2017.04.034
17. Flórez-Gutiérrez, A., Todo, Y.: Improved cryptanalysis of ChaCha: beating PNBs with bit puncturing. In: Fehr, S., Fouque, P.A. (eds.) EUROCRYPT 2025. LNCS, vol. 15601, pp. 427–457. Springer, Cham (2025). https://doi.org/10.1007/978-3-031-91107-1_15
18. Langford, S.K., Hellman, M.E.: Differential-linear cryptanalysis. In: Desmedt, Y.G. (ed.) CRYPTO 1994. LNCS, pp. 17–25. Springer, Heidelberg (1994). https://doi.org/10.1007/3-540-48658-5_3
19. Li, Z., Ding, L., Wang, X., Wan, J.: Mixderive: a new framework of deriving linear approximations and improved differential-linear distinguishers for ChaCha (2025). https://eprint.iacr.org/2025/1670
20. Maitra, S.: Chosen IV cryptanalysis on reduced round ChaCha and salsa. Discret. Appl. Math. **208**, 88–97 (2016). https://doi.org/10.1016/j.dam.2016.02.020
21. Matsui, M., Yamagishi, A.: A new method for known plaintext attack of feal cipher. In: Rueppel, R.A. (ed.) EUROCRYPT 1992. LNCS, vol. 658, pp. 81–91. Springer, Cham (1992). https://doi.org/10.1007/3-540-47555-9_7
22. Miyashita, S., Ito, R., Miyaji, A.: PNB-focused differential cryptanalysis of ChaCha stream cipher. In: Australasian Conference on Information Security and Privacy (2022). https://doi.org/10.1007/978-3-031-22301-3_3
23. Shi, Z., Zhang, B., Feng, D., Wu, W.: Improved key recovery attacks on reduced-round salsa20 and ChaCha. In: Kwon, T., Lee, MK., Kwon, D. (eds.) ICISC 2012. LNCS, vol. 7839, pp. 337–351. Springer, Heidelberg (2012). https://doi.org/10.1007/978-3-642-37682-5_24
24. Wallén, J.: Linear approximations of addition modulo 2^n. In: Johansson, T. (ed.) FSE 2011. LNCS, vol. 2887, pp. 261–273. Springer, Heidelberg (2003). https://doi.org/10.1007/978-3-540-39887-5_20
25. Wang, S., Liu, M., Hou, S., Lin, D.: Moving a step of ChaCha in syncopated rhythm. In: Handschuh, H., Lysyanskaya, A. (eds.) CRYPTO 2023. LNCS, vol. 14083, pp. 273–304. Springer, Cham (2023). https://doi.org/10.1007/978-3-031-38548-3_10
26. Xu, Z., Xu, H., Tan, L., Qi, W.: Differential-linear cryptanalysis of reduced round chaCha. IACR Trans. Symmetric Cryptol. **2024**(2), 166–189 (2024). https://doi.org/10.46586/tosc.v2024.i2.166-189

Advanced Cryptographic Protocols & Signatures

Strong Designated Verifier Signatures with Non-delegatability from CSIDH

Hiroki Minamide[1,2], Keisuke Tanaka[2], and Masayuki Tezuka[2](✉)

[1] National Institute of Technology, Tokyo College, Hachioji, Japan
minamide@tokyo-ct.ac.jp
[2] Institute of Science Tokyo, Tokyo, Japan
keisuke@is.titech.ac.jp, tezuka.m.eab3@m.isct.ac.jp

Abstract. Designated verifier signature allows a signer to designate a verifier who can verify the signature. Strong designated verifier signature (SDVS) enhances privacy by ensuring that the signature itself does not leak information about the signer's identity to anyone other than the designated verifier. Non-delegatability is a property, as it prevents the signer's ability to generate valid signatures from being delegated to others. This property is crucial for SDVS applications such as e-voting.

To date, post-quantum SDVS schemes with non-delegatability have been proposed. These schemes are lattice-based or hash-based schemes. While isogeny-based SDVS schemes have been proposed, none of the existing works provide a proof of non-delegatability.

In this paper, we present the first isogeny-based SDVS scheme with a formal proof of non-delegatability. Our construction uses the quadratic twists of elliptic curves. The security of our scheme is proven under the commutative supersingular isogeny gap Diffie-Hellman assumption and the group action inversion problem assumption in the random oracle model.

Keywords: Strong designated verifier signature · Non-delegatability · Commutative supersingular isogeny Diffie-Hellman · Quadratic twist

1 Introduction

1.1 Background

Designated Verifier Signatures. Designated verifier signature (DVS) introduced by Jakobsson, Sako, and Impagliazzo [17] allows a signer to designate a verifier who can verify the signature. The designated verifier uses its own secret key to verify a signature. Typically, a DVS scheme satisfies unforgeability and non-transferability. Unforgeability guarantees that if a user has neither the signer's nor the designated verifier's secret key, it is computationally infeasible to

A part of this work was supported by JSPS KAKENHI JP24H00071, JST CREST JPMJCR2113, and JST K Program JPMJKP24U2.

H. Seo (Ed.): ICISC 2025, LNCS 16487, pp. 495–509, 2026.
https://doi.org/10.1007/978-981-95-8034-7_26

generate a valid signature for the designated verifier. Non-transferability allows the designated verifier to generate simulated signatures that are indistinguishable from those generated by the signer. Thanks to these properties, DVS has found applications in a variety of privacy-preserving contexts, including deniable authentication [39], e-voting [17], and undeniable signature [9].

Strong Designated Verifier Signatures. Non-transferability guarantees that one cannot distinguish whether a signature was generated by the signer or by the designated verifier. However, this property alone does not prevent a third party from identifying the two potential signers. That is, signatures generated by different signers may still be distinguishable to anyone other than the designated verifier. Saeednia, Kremer, and Markowitch [28] introduced strong designated verifier signatures (SDVS). Laguillaumie and Vergnaud [22] formalized the security notion called privacy of signer's identity for SDVS to enhance the signer's privacy. Privacy of signer's identity ensures that a signature does not reveal the identity of the signer to anyone other than the designated verifier.

Non-delegatability. Lipmaa, Wang, and Bao [23] pointed out a weakness in the informal definition of DVS [17]. A weakness of DVS is that a signer can delegate the ability to generate valid signatures for a specific designated verifier to a third party, without disclosing their secret key. This weakness is undesirable in certain applications of SDVS. For example, we consider the application of SDVS for an e-voting system. A voter is a signer who sends a signed ballot, and an election authority is a verifier that verifies the ballot. If SDVS has this weakness, the signer could delegate their voting capability to a third party, making it impossible to guarantee that a ballot was generated by the real voter. To address such an issue, Lipmaa et al. [23] introduced non-delegatability for DVS. Non-delegatability requires that a valid signature be the proofs of knowledge of either the signer's secret key or the designated verifier's secret key. After the proposal by Lipmaa et al., non-delegatability has become a standard security notion for SDVS.

1.2 Motivation

Post-quantum SDVS with Non-delegatability. Upon until now, there have been a sequence of works for constructing SDVS under various assumptions, including pairing-free group [15,28,35,38,40], pairing-based [1,16,36,37], isogeny [27,33], lattice-based [6,26,41], code-based [2,30], hash-based [34] and generic construction [10,13]. Despite this extensive line of above works on SDVS, there exist only a few post-quantum constructions of SDVS with non-delegatability. To the best of our knowledge, only lattice-based SDVS schemes and [26,41] and a hash-based SDVS scheme [34] were proposed.

Current Open Question. In light of previous works [10,13,27,33], the following question remains open in isogeny-based cryptography:

Is it possible to construct an isogeny-based SDVS with non-delegatability?

1.3 Our Contributions

Contributions. In this paper, we give an affirmative answer to the question. More precisely, we propose an SDVS with non-delegatability from the commutative supersingular isogeny Diffie-Hellman (CSIDH) class group action. The security of our scheme is proven under the group action inversion problem (GAIP) assumption and the commutative supersingular isogeny gap Diffie-Hellman (CSI-GDH) assumption in the random oracle model (ROM) [4].

Comparison in Previous Works. We provide comparisons among our scheme, generic SDVS constructions [10,13], and isogeny-based SDVS constructions [27, 33] in Fig. 1.

Scheme	Assumption	Unf	NT	PSI	ND
[10]	Ring Signature + IND-CPA PKE	✓	✓	✓$^\sharp$	?$^\flat$
[10]	Deniable Authenticated Key Exchange	✓	✓	✓$^\sharp$	?$^\flat$
[13]	IND-CCA KEM + PRF	✓	✓	✓	×
[33] (insecure†)	SS-CDH + SS-DDH + ROM	–†	–†	–†	–†
[27]	MT-GAIP + ROM	✓	✓	✓	?$^\flat$
$\mathsf{SDVS}_{\mathsf{Ours}}$	GAIP + CSI-GDH + ROM	✓	✓	✓	✓

Fig. 1. Comparisons among our scheme, the generic construction, and isogeny-based SDVS schemes in previous works. In the column "Assumption", "IND-CCA KEM" represents an IND-CCA secure key encapsulation mechanism. "PRF" represents a pseudorandom function. "SS-DDH (resp. SS-CDH)" represents the supersingular decisional (resp. computational) Diffie-Hellman assumption. "MT-GAIP" represents the multi-target group action inversion problem assumption. In the column "Unf", ✓ represents that the corresponding scheme satisfies unforgeability. In the column "NT", ✓ represents that the corresponding scheme satisfies non-transferability. In the column "PSI", ✓ represents that the corresponding scheme satisfies the privacy of signer's identity. In the column "ND", ✓ represents that the corresponding scheme satisfies non-delegatability. $\sharp$: [10] proved privacy of signer's identity in a weak security model. $\flat$: [10,27] did not prove non-delegatability for the constructions. $\dagger$: The scheme [33] is insecure. The SS-CDH and SS-DDH assumptions are broken by the attack of Castryck and Decru [7].

There are three generic constructions of SDVS. Two of them were proposed by Feng, Xu, and Chen [10]: one based on a ring signature scheme combined with indistinguishability under chosen-plaintext attacks (IND-CPA) public-key encryption (PKE), and the other based on a deniable authenticated key exchange protocol. However, the privacy of signer's identity of these constructions was proven in a weak security model, where the adversary is not allowed to access the signing oracle or the verification oracle after receiving the challenge signature. Moreover, [10] did not provide a security analysis for non-delegatability.

The generic construction of SDVS proposed by Gong, Au, Xue [13], which is based on the indistinguishability under chosen ciphertext attacks (IND-CCA) secure key encapsulation mechanism (KEM) enables the derivation of several isogeny-based SDVS schemes.[1] However, their generic construction does not satisfy non-delegatability.[2]

There are two isogeny-based SDVS constructions. An isogeny-based SDVS scheme by Sun, Tian, and Wang [33] is insecure. This scheme relies on the supersingular Diffie-Hellman assumption, which was broken by an attack of Castryck and Decru [7].

Renan [27] proposed an isogeny-based SDVS based on a commutative group action and provided a security analysis with respect to unforgeability, non-transferability, and privacy of the signer's identity. However, no security analysis was given for non-delegatability.

Thus, to the best of our knowledge, the existing generic constructions [10,13] and isogeny-based constructions [27,33] either do not satisfy non-delegatability or lack a formal security proof for non-delegatability. Our scheme is the first isogeny-based SDVS scheme with a formal proof of non-delegatability.

1.4 How to Obtain Our Scheme

DH Key Exchange + OR Proof Approach. Huang, Yang, Wong, and Susilo [15] proposed an SDVS scheme with non-delegatability, constructed from the combination of the Diffie-Hellman key exchange and a Σ-protocol for the OR relations.

We outline the idea of their gap Diffie-Hellman (GDH) based SDVS construction [15]. Let $\mathbb{G}$ be a cyclic group of prime order p and g be a generator of $\mathbb{G}$. Let $(\mathrm{pk}_s = g^{x_s}, \mathrm{sk}_s = x_s)$ be a public/secret key of the signer and $(\mathrm{pk}_v = g^{x_v}, \mathrm{sk}_v = x_v)$ be a public/secret key of the verifier. In their scheme, a signature σ is an OR proof derived via the Fiat-Shamir transformation [11] from the Σ-protocol for the OR relation, which proves knowledge of either sk_s or sk_v. To ensure that only the designated verifier can verify the signature, $K = \mathrm{pk}_v^{x_s}$ is included in the hash input when transforming the Σ-protocol to a non-interactive proof. As a result, the only designated verifier can compute $K = \mathrm{pk}_s^{x_v}$ and thus verify the signature. In contrast, any other party (excluding the signer and the designated verifier) cannot compute $K = g^{xy}$ from under the hardness of the CDH problem (more precisely, the hardness of the GDH problem). Therefore any other party cannot verify the signature.

Problem in Abstracting SDVS Scheme [15] from Group Actions. One might expect that their scheme could be directly abstracted using group actions. The GDH assumption can be replace the CSI-GDH assumption, which is the

[1] By applying the Fujisaki-Okamoto transformation [12,14] to a public key encryption scheme such as [3,25], an IND-CCA secure KEM can be obtained. The resulting KEM can be used in the generic construction.

[2] In scheme [13], the signer and the designated verifier share a pseudorandom function (PRF) key K via KEM, and a signature σ on a message m is computed as $\sigma = PRF_K(m)$. Any party to which K is delegated can generate signatures on behalf of the signer, which shows that the scheme does not satisfy non-delegatability.

analog of the GDH assumption in the commutative supersingular isogeny setting. However, the direct abstraction of their scheme is not possible due to the following reason. Their scheme needs the computation $g^z \cdot \mathrm{pk}^c$ where $z, c \in \mathbb{Z}_p$. Let us denote a group action as $* : G \times X \to X$. By using the group action, g^z can be represented as $z * g$ and pk^c as $c * \mathrm{pk}$. However, since both $z * g$ and $c * \mathrm{pk}$ belong to X, there is no way to define an operation between $z * g$ and pk^c. Consequently, we cannot directly abstract their SDVS scheme by group actions.

Our Solution. To obtain an isogeny-based SDVS, we employ the quadratic twist of an elliptic curve, which provides a richer structure than an abstract group action. Recently, Katsumata, Lai, LeGrow, and Qin [18,19] proposed the quadratic twist-based Σ-protocol of the OR relation. By using their Σ-protocol, we address the above problem. We follow the blueprint of the SDVS construction [15], adapting it to the commutative supersingular isogeny Diffie-Hellman (CSIDH) [8] based key exchange protocol and Σ-protocol by Katsumata et al. [18,19]. Consequently, we obtain our SDVS scheme $\mathsf{SDVS}_{\mathsf{Ours}}$.

Our Paper and Concurrent Work. As concurrent work, Khuc et al. [21] proposed isogeny-based SDVS constructions with non-delegatability. The one construction is obtained by modifying the isogeny-based signature scheme CSI-FiSh [5] and security is proven under the GAIP assumption in the ROM. Moreover, they gave the optimized variant of the construction by using the MT-GAIP assumption in the ROM.

1.5 Organization

In Sect. 2, we introduce notation and briefly review the background of elliptic curves. In Sect. 3, we review the definition of SDVS and its security notions. In Sect. 4, we propose our SDVS scheme with non-delegatability and prove the security. Due to page limitations, the security proof has been omitted. Please refer to the full version of this paper [24] for the omitted security proof.

2 Preliminaries

In this section, we introduce notation, briefly review the background of elliptic curves.

2.1 Notation

Let 1^λ be the security parameter. A function $f(\lambda)$ is negligible in λ if $f(\lambda)$ tends to 0 faster than $\frac{1}{\lambda^c}$ for every constant $c > 0$. We write $f(\lambda) = \mathsf{negl}(\lambda)$ to denote that $f(\lambda)$ is a negligible function. We write $f(\lambda) = \mathsf{poly}(\lambda)$ to denote that $f(\lambda)$ is a polynomial function in λ.

For a finite set S, $s \xleftarrow{\$} S$ denotes that an element s is sampled uniformly at random from S, and $\#S$ denotes the number of elements in S. We denote the set of all finite binary strings by $\{0,1\}^*$. For a vector $\mathbf{v}$, $\mathbf{v}[i]$ denotes the

i-th element of $\mathbf{v}$. For an algorithm A, we write $y \leftarrow \mathsf{A}(x)$ to indicate that A outputs y on input x. When explicitly showing that A uses randomness r, we write $y \leftarrow \mathsf{A}(x; r)$. We abbreviate probabilistic polynomial time as PPT.

In this paper, we use standard code-based security games. A game Game_A is a probabilistic experiment in which an adversary A interacts with an implicit challenger C that answers oracle queries issued by A. We denote the output $b \in \{0,1\}$ of the game Game between a challenger and an adversary A as $\mathsf{Game}_\mathsf{A} \Rightarrow b$. We say that A wins the game if $\mathsf{Game}_\mathsf{A} \Rightarrow 1$.

2.2 Elliptic Curves and Hard Homogeneous Spaces

We briefly review the ideal class group action on supersingular elliptic curves, hard homogeneous space, quadratic twist, and computational assumptions.

Prime and Finite Field. Let $p = 4\ell_1 \cdots \ell_n - 1$ be a cryptographically large prime satisfying $p \equiv 3 \pmod 8$, where $\ell_1, \ldots, \ell_n$ are distinct small odd primes. Let $\mathbb{F}_p$ denote the finite field with p elements. All computations in our construction are carried out over $\mathbb{F}_p$. In this work, we consider the parameter setting the same as CSIDH [8]. For instance, the CSIDH-512 parameter set chooses $n = 74$, $\ell_1 = 3$, $\ell_{73} = 373$, and $\ell_{74} = 587$.

Supersingular Montgomery Curves. Let p be a prime that satisfies $p \equiv 3 \pmod 8$ and $p > 5$. We define the set of supersingular elliptic curves of Montgomery type as

$$\mathrm{Ell}_p := \left\{ E_A : y^2 = x^3 + Ax^2 + x \mid A \in \mathbb{F}_p,\ A \neq \pm 2,\ \#E_A(\mathbb{F}_p) = p + 1 \right\}.$$

Here, $\#E_A(\mathbb{F}_p) = p + 1$ means that the equation of E_A has exactly p distinct solutions $(x, y) \in \mathbb{F}_p^2$, together with one distinguished point at infinity. A simple and concrete example of such a curve is $E_0 : y^2 = x^3 + x$.

Group Action. Rather than relying on advanced algebraic geometry, we emphasize a key fact: all curves in Ell_p form a single orbit under the action of the ideal class group $\mathrm{Cl}_p := \mathrm{Cl}(\mathbb{Z}[\sqrt{-p}])$, associated with the quadratic imaginary field $\mathbb{Q}(\sqrt{-p})$. It is known that the group Cl_p is finite, abelian, and has cardinality asymptotically $\#\mathrm{Cl}_p \approx \sqrt{p}$.

$$\mathrm{Cl}_p \times \mathrm{Ell}_p \longrightarrow \mathrm{Ell}_p, \quad ([\mathfrak{a}], E_A) \longmapsto [\mathfrak{a}] * E_A,$$

where $E_A \in \mathrm{Ell}_p$ and $[\mathfrak{a}] \in \mathrm{Cl}_p$. This action is free and transitive:

- **Free:** The action is called free if the condition $[\mathfrak{a}] * E = E$ for some $E \in \mathrm{Ell}_p$ implies that $[\mathfrak{a}]$ is the identity element $[(1)] \in \mathrm{Cl}_p$. In other words, no non-trivial element of Cl_p fixes a point of Ell_p.
- **Transitive:** The action is called transitive if for any two elements $E, E' \in \mathrm{Ell}_p$, there exists a $[\mathfrak{a}] \in \mathrm{Cl}_p$ such that $[\mathfrak{a}] * E = E'$. This means that the entire set Ell_p forms a single orbit under the group action.

Hard Homogeneous Space. The pair $(\mathrm{Cl}_p, \mathrm{Ell}_p)$ is an example of a hard homogeneous space (HHS) [8]. While computing $[\mathfrak{a}] * E_A$ for a given ideal class is efficient, inverting the action, i.e., recovering $[\mathfrak{a}]$ from $(E_A, [\mathfrak{a}] * E_A)$, is conjectured to be hard, forming the basis of security. This inversion problem is called the group action inversion problem (GAIP).

Quadratic Twist. In the CSIDH setting, each supersingular Montgomery curve admits a unique quadratic twist. For a prime $p \equiv 3 \pmod 4$, the quadratic twist of a curve E_A is denoted by $(E_A)^{-1}$ and is explicitly given by

$$(E_A)^{-1} = E_{-A} : y^2 = x^3 - Ax^2 + x.$$

This twist plays a key role in enabling certain optimizations and symmetry arguments. The special curve E_0 is self-dual under this operation.

The following lemma formalizes the natural compatibility of this twist operation with the class group action.

Lemma 1. *Let $[\mathfrak{a}] \in \mathrm{Cl}_p$ be an ideal class and $E_A \in \mathrm{Ell}_p$ a supersingular Montgomery curve. Then:*

$$([\mathfrak{a}] * E_A)^{-1} = [\mathfrak{a}]^{-1} * E_A^{-1} = [\mathfrak{a}]^{-1} * E_{-A}.$$

This lemma states that twisting commutes with the class group action: applying an ideal class and then twisting is equivalent to twisting first and applying the inverse class.

Now, we introduce computational assumptions for the ideal class group action on supersingular elliptic curves.

Definition 1 (CSI-GDH Assumption [18,19]**).** *The commutative supersingular isogeny gap Diffie-Hellman (CSI-GDH) assumption holds on (Cl_p, Ell_p), if for any PPT adversary A,*

$$\mathsf{Adv}_{\mathsf{A}}^{\mathsf{CSI-GDH}}(\lambda) := Pr\left[E' = [\mathfrak{x}\mathfrak{y}] * E : \begin{array}{l} [\mathfrak{x}], [\mathfrak{y}] \xleftarrow{\$} Cl_p, \\ E' \leftarrow \mathsf{A}^{\mathcal{O}^{\mathsf{CSI-DDH}}(\cdot,\cdot,\cdot)}](E, [\mathfrak{x}] * E, [\mathfrak{y}] * E) \end{array}\right]$$

is $negl(\lambda)$ where $\mathcal{O}^{\mathsf{CSI-DDH}}$ is the oracle that takes a tuple $([\mathfrak{a}] * E, [\mathfrak{b}] * E, E')$ and returns 1 if $E' = [\mathfrak{a}\mathfrak{b}] * E$ and 0 otherwise.

Definition 2 (Group Action Inversion Problem Assumption [20]**).** *The group action inversion problem (GAIP) assumption holds on $(\mathrm{Cl}_p, \mathrm{Ell}_p)$, if for any PPT adversary A,*

$$\mathsf{Adv}_{\mathsf{A}}^{\mathsf{GAIP}}(\lambda) := \Pr[E' = [\mathfrak{x}'] * E_0 : [\mathfrak{x}] \xleftarrow{\$} \mathrm{Cl}_p, E' \leftarrow [\mathfrak{x}] * E_0, [\mathfrak{x}'] \leftarrow \mathsf{A}(E_0, E')]$$

is $\mathsf{negl}(\lambda)$.

3 Strong Designated Verifier Signatures

In this section, we review the definition of a strong designated verifier signature (SDVS) scheme and its security notions.

3.1 Syntax

We recall the definition of a SDVS scheme.

Definition 3. *A strong designated verifier signature scheme* SDVS *is a tuple of PPT algorithms* $(\mathsf{KGen}, \mathsf{Sign}, \mathsf{Ver})$.

- $\mathsf{KGen}(1^\lambda)$: *The key generation algorithm takes as input a security parameter* 1^λ. *It outputs a public key* pk *and a secret key* sk.
- $\mathsf{Sign}(\mathrm{sk}_s, \mathrm{pk}_s, \mathrm{pk}_v, m)$: *The signing algorithm takes as input a secret key of a signer* sk_s, *a public key of the signer* pk_s, *a public key of a verifier* pk_v, *and a message* m. *It outputs a signature* σ.
- $\mathsf{Ver}(\mathrm{sk}_v, \mathrm{pk}_s, \mathrm{pk}_v, m, \sigma)$: *The verification algorithm takes as input a secret key of a verifier* sk_v, *a public key of the verifier* pk_v, *a public key of a signer* pk_s, *a message* m, *and a signature* σ. *It outputs a bit* $b \in \{0, 1\}$.

Correctness. We require $\mathsf{SDVS} = (\mathsf{KGen}, \mathsf{Sign}, \mathsf{Ver})$ to satisfy the following correctness. For any $\lambda \in \mathbb{N}$, $(\mathrm{pk}_s, \mathrm{sk}_s) \leftarrow \mathsf{KGen}(1^\lambda)$, $(\mathrm{pk}_v, \mathrm{sk}_v) \leftarrow \mathsf{KGen}(1^\lambda)$, for any $m \in \{0,1\}^*$, and $\sigma \leftarrow \mathsf{Sign}(\mathrm{sk}_s, \mathrm{pk}_s, \mathrm{pk}_v, m)$, $\mathsf{Ver}(\mathrm{sk}_v, \mathrm{pk}_s, \mathrm{pk}_v, m, \sigma) = 1$ holds.

3.2 Security

In this section, we review security notions for a SDVS scheme. First, we introduce the definition of unforgeability. Our definition is obtained by modifying the unforgeability definition in [36] to capture strong unforgeability.

Definition 4 (Strong Unforgeability). *Strong unforgeability of* SDVS *is defined by the following strong unforgeability game* $\mathsf{Game}^{\mathsf{SUF}}_{\mathsf{SDVS},\mathsf{A}}(1^\lambda)$ *between a challenger* C *and an adversary* A.

- C *initializes a list* $L^{\mathsf{Sign}} \leftarrow \{\}$, *runs* $(\mathrm{pk}_s, \mathrm{sk}_s) \leftarrow \mathsf{KGen}(1^\lambda)$, $(\mathrm{pk}_v, \mathrm{sk}_v) \leftarrow \mathsf{KGen}(1^\lambda)$, *and gives* $(\mathrm{pk}_s, \mathrm{pk}_v)$ *to* A.
- A *is allowed to accesses oracles* $\mathcal{O}^{\mathsf{Sign}}(\cdot)$ *and* $\mathcal{O}^{\mathsf{Verify}}(\cdot,\cdot)$ *polynomially many times:*
  - $\mathcal{O}^{\mathsf{Sign}}(\cdot)$: *For a query on* m, *it runs* $\sigma \leftarrow \mathsf{Sign}(\mathrm{sk}_s, \mathrm{pk}_s, \mathrm{pk}_v, m)$, *updates* $L^{\mathsf{Sign}} \leftarrow L^{\mathsf{Sign}} \cup \{(m, \sigma)\}$ *and returns* σ *to* A.
  - $\mathcal{O}^{\mathsf{Verify}}(\cdot,\cdot)$: *For a query on* (m, σ), *it computes* $b \leftarrow \mathsf{Ver}(\mathrm{sk}_v, \mathrm{pk}_s, \mathrm{pk}_v, m, \sigma)$ *and returns* b *to* A.
- *Finally,* A *outputs a forgery* (m^*, σ^*).
- A *wins the game if the following condition holds:*

$$(m^*, \sigma^*) \notin L^{\mathsf{Sign}} \wedge \mathsf{Ver}(\mathrm{sk}_v, \mathrm{pk}_s, \mathrm{pk}_v, m^*, \sigma^*) = 1$$

The advantage of A *is defined as* $\mathsf{Adv}^{\mathsf{SUF}}_{\mathsf{SDVS},\mathsf{A}}(\lambda) := \Pr[\mathsf{Game}^{\mathsf{SUF}}_{\mathsf{SDVS},\mathsf{A}}(1^\lambda) \Rightarrow 1]$. *We say* SDVS *satisfies strongly unforgeability if for any PPT adversary* A, $\mathsf{Adv}^{\mathsf{SUF}}_{\mathsf{SDVS},\mathsf{A}}(\lambda) = \mathsf{negl}(\lambda)$.

Second, we review the definition of non-transferability. This security notion is formalized by [31,32]. We refer to the non-transferability definition in [29].

Definition 5 (Non-Transferability [29]**).** *We say* SDVS *satisfies perfect non-transferability if there exists a PPT simulation algorithm* Sim *such that for any two pairs of keys* $(\mathrm{pk}_s, \mathrm{sk}_s) \leftarrow \mathsf{KGen}(1^\lambda)$ *and* $(\mathrm{pk}_s, \mathrm{sk}_s) \leftarrow \mathsf{KGen}(1^\lambda)$, *and for any message* $m \in \{0,1\}^*$, *the following two random variables are the same distribution:*

$$\{\mathsf{Sign}(\mathrm{sk}_s, \mathrm{pk}_s, \mathrm{pk}_v, m)\} \text{ and } \{\mathsf{Sim}(\mathrm{sk}_v, \mathrm{pk}_s, \mathrm{pk}_v, m)\}.$$

Third, we review the definition of privacy of signer's identity. We refer to the definition of privacy of the signer's identity in [22].

Definition 6 (Privacy of Signer's Identity [22]**).** *Privacy of signer's identity (PSI) of* SDVS *is defined by the following privacy of signer's identity game* $\mathsf{Game}^{\mathsf{PSI}}_{\mathsf{SDVS,A}}(1^\lambda)$ *between a challenger* C *and an adversary* A.

- C *runs* $(\mathrm{pk}_{s_0}, \mathrm{sk}_{s_0}) \leftarrow \mathsf{KGen}(1^\lambda)$, $(\mathrm{pk}_{s_1}, \mathrm{sk}_{s_1}) \leftarrow \mathsf{KGen}(1^\lambda)$, $(\mathrm{pk}_v, \mathrm{sk}_v) \leftarrow \mathsf{KGen}(1^\lambda)$, *and gives* $(\mathrm{pk}_{s_0}, \mathrm{pk}_{s_1}, \mathrm{pk}_v)$ *to* A.
- A *is allowed to access oracles* $\mathcal{O}^{\mathsf{Sign}}(\cdot,\cdot)$ *and* $\mathcal{O}^{\mathsf{Verify}}(\cdot,\cdot,\cdot)$ *polynomially many times:*
  - $\mathcal{O}^{\mathsf{Sign}}(\cdot,\cdot)$: *For a query on* (d, m), *it runs* $\sigma \leftarrow \mathsf{Sign}(\mathrm{sk}_{s_d}, \mathrm{pk}_{s_d}, \mathrm{pk}_v, m)$ *and returns* σ *to* A.
  - $\mathcal{O}^{\mathsf{Verify}}(\cdot,\cdot,\cdot)$: *For a query on* (d, m, σ), *it computes* $\beta \leftarrow \mathsf{Ver}(\mathrm{sk}_v, \mathrm{pk}_{s_d}, \mathrm{pk}_v, m, \sigma)$ *and returns* β *to* A.
- A *sends a challenge* m^* *to* C.
- C *samples a bit* $b \xleftarrow{\$} \{0,1\}$, *and runs* $\sigma^* \leftarrow \mathsf{Sign}(\mathrm{sk}_{s_b}, \mathrm{pk}_{s_b}, \mathrm{pk}_v, m^*)$ *and gives* σ^* *to* A.
- A *is allowed to access oracles* $\mathcal{O}^{\mathsf{Sign}}(\cdot)$ *and* $\mathcal{O}^{\mathsf{Verify}^*}(\cdot,\cdot,\cdot)$ *polynomially many times where* $\mathcal{O}^{\mathsf{Verify}^*}$ *is the restricted oracle* $\mathcal{O}^{\mathsf{Verify}}$ *that queries* (d, m^*, σ^*) *not allowed for* $d \in \{0,1\}$.
- *Finally,* A *outputs a guess* b^*.
- A *wins the game if* $b^* = b$ *holds.*

The advantage of A *is defined as* $\mathsf{Adv}^{\mathsf{PSI}}_{\mathsf{SDVS,A}}(\lambda) := \left|\Pr[\mathsf{Game}^{\mathsf{PSI}}_{\mathsf{SDVS,A}}(1^\lambda) \Rightarrow 1] - \frac{1}{2}\right|$. *We say* SDVS *satisfies privacy of signer's identity if for any PPT adversary* A, $\mathsf{Adv}^{\mathsf{PSI}}_{\mathsf{SDVS,A}}(\lambda) = \mathsf{negl}(\lambda)$.

Finally, we review the definition of non-delegatability. This security is formalized by [23]. We refer to the equivalent non-delegatability definition in [15].

Definition 7 (Non-Delegatability [15]**).** *Let* $\kappa \in [0,1]$ *be the knowledge error and* F *a forger algorithm. Let* F_m *be* F *with* m *as its input, and oracle calls to* F_m *be counted as one step. We say* SDVS *satisfies non-delegatability with knowledge error* κ *if there exists a positive polynomial* $\mathsf{poly}(\lambda)$ *and a probabilistic oracle machine* Ext *such that for every PPT algorithm* F, Ext *satisfies the following condition:*

Let ϵ be the probability that F *on the input $m \in \{0,1\}^*$ produces a valid signature on m. For any two pairs of keys $(\mathrm{pk}_s, \mathrm{sk}_s) \leftarrow \mathsf{KGen}(1^\lambda)$ and $(\mathrm{pk}_s, \mathrm{sk}_s) \leftarrow \mathsf{KGen}(1^\lambda)$, and for any message $m \in \{0,1\}^*$, if $\epsilon > \kappa$, $\mathsf{Ext}^{\mathsf{F}_m}(m)$ produces either sk_s or sk_v in expected polynomial time with probability at least $(\epsilon - \kappa)/\mathsf{poly}(\lambda)$.*

4 Our SDVS Scheme

In this section, we give our SDVS construction and provide security analysis results.

4.1 Our Construction

In this section, we describe our SDVS construction. Let $(p, N, \mathfrak{g}, E_0)$ be the public parameter specified as the underlying prime p, the order N of the ideal class group $\mathrm{Cl}_p \cong \mathbb{Z}_N$, a generator $\mathfrak{g}$, and the Montgomery type elliptic curves $E_0 : y^2 = x^3 + Ax^2 + x$. For a vector $\mathbf{r} \in \mathbb{Z}_N^\lambda$, $\mathbf{c} \in \{\pm 1\}$ and an elliptical curve $E \in \mathrm{Ell}_p$, $[\mathfrak{g}^{\mathbf{r}}] * E$ stands for a vector $([\mathfrak{g}^{\mathbf{r}[1]}] * E, \ldots, [\mathfrak{g}^{\mathbf{r}[\lambda]}] * E)$ and $[\mathfrak{g}^{\mathbf{r}}] * E^{\mathbf{c}}$ stands for a vector $([\mathfrak{g}^{\mathbf{r}[1]}] * E^{\mathbf{c}[1]}, \ldots, [\mathfrak{g}^{\mathbf{r}[\lambda]}] * E^{\mathbf{c}[\lambda]})$. We use $\odot$ to denote the component-wise multiplication of vectors in $\mathbb{R}$. Let $H : \{0,1\}^* \to \{0,1\}^\lambda$ be a hash function. Now, we give our SDVS scheme $\mathsf{SDVS}_{\mathsf{Ours}}$ as follows.

- $\mathsf{KGen}(1^\lambda)$:Sample $x \xleftarrow{\$} \mathbb{Z}_N$, set $(\mathrm{pk}, \mathrm{sk}) \leftarrow ([\mathfrak{g}^x] * E_0, x)$, and return $(\mathrm{pk}, \mathrm{sk})$.
- $\mathsf{Sign}(\mathrm{sk}_s = x_s, \mathrm{pk}_s, \mathrm{pk}_v, m)$: Sample $\mathbf{r}_s, \mathbf{z}_v \xleftarrow{\$} \mathbb{Z}_N^\lambda$, $\mathbf{c}_v \xleftarrow{\$} \{\pm 1\}^\lambda$. set $\mathbf{R}_s \leftarrow [\mathfrak{g}^{\mathbf{r}_s}] * E_0$, $\mathbf{R}_v \leftarrow [\mathfrak{g}^{\mathbf{z}_v}] * \mathrm{pk}_v^{\mathbf{c}_v}$, $K \leftarrow [\mathfrak{g}^{x_s}] * \mathrm{pk}_v$, $\mathbf{c} \leftarrow H(m, K, \mathbf{R}_s, \mathbf{R}_v) \in \{\pm 1\}^\lambda$, $\mathbf{c}_s \leftarrow \mathbf{c} \odot \mathbf{c}_v$, $\mathbf{z}_s \leftarrow \mathbf{r}_s - x_s \cdot \mathbf{c}_s$, and return $\sigma := (\mathbf{c}_s, \mathbf{z}_s, \mathbf{c}_v, \mathbf{z}_v)$
- $\mathsf{Ver}(\mathrm{sk}_v = x_v, \mathrm{pk}_s, \mathrm{pk}_v, m, \sigma = (\mathbf{c}_s, \mathbf{z}_s, \mathbf{c}_v, \mathbf{z}_v))$: Set $\mathbf{R}_s \leftarrow [\mathfrak{g}^{\mathbf{z}_s}] * \mathrm{pk}_s^{\mathbf{c}_s}$, $\mathbf{R}_v \leftarrow [\mathfrak{g}^{\mathbf{z}_v}] * \mathrm{pk}_v^{\mathbf{c}_v}$, $K \leftarrow [\mathfrak{g}^{x_v}] * \mathrm{pk}_s$. If $\mathbf{c}_s \odot \mathbf{c}_v = H(m, K, \mathbf{R}_s, \mathbf{R}_v)$, return 1. Otherwise, return 0.

Correctness: Let $(\mathrm{pk}_s = [\mathfrak{g}^{x_s}] * E_0, \mathrm{sk}_s = x_s) \leftarrow \mathsf{KGen}(1^\lambda)$, $(\mathrm{pk}_v = [\mathfrak{g}^{x_v}] * E_0, \mathrm{sk}_v = x_v) \leftarrow \mathsf{KGen}(1^\lambda)$, and $\sigma = (\mathbf{c}_s, \mathbf{z}_s, \mathbf{c}_v, \mathbf{z}_v) \leftarrow \mathsf{Sign}(\mathrm{sk}_s = x_s, \mathrm{pk}_s, \mathrm{pk}_v, m)$. Then $\mathbf{c} = H(m, K = [\mathfrak{g}^{x_s}] * \mathrm{pk}_v, \mathbf{R}_s = [\mathfrak{g}^{\mathbf{r}_s}] * E_0, \mathbf{R}_v = [\mathfrak{g}^{\mathbf{z}_v}] * \mathrm{pk}_v^{\mathbf{c}_v})$ holds. Since $K = [\mathfrak{g}^{x_s}] * \mathrm{pk}_v = [\mathfrak{g}^{x_v}] * \mathrm{pk}_s$, $\mathbf{R}_s = [\mathfrak{g}^{\mathbf{r}_s}] * E_0 = [\mathfrak{g}^{\mathbf{z}_s - x_s \cdot \mathbf{c}_s}] = [\mathfrak{g}^{\mathbf{z}_s}] * \mathrm{pk}_s^{\mathbf{c}_s}$, and $\mathbf{c} = \mathbf{c}_s \odot \mathbf{c}_v$ hold, $\mathbf{c}_s \odot \mathbf{c}_v = \mathbf{c} = H(m, [\mathfrak{g}^{x_v}] * \mathrm{pk}_s, [\mathfrak{g}^{\mathbf{z}_s}] * \mathrm{pk}_s^{\mathbf{c}_s}, [\mathfrak{g}^{\mathbf{z}_v}] * \mathrm{pk}_v^{\mathbf{c}_v})$ holds. Thus, we see that $\mathsf{SDVS}_{\mathsf{Ours}}$ satisfies correctness.

4.2 Security Analysis

In this section, we provide security analysis results for our scheme. We give the full security proofs in the full version of our paper [24].

Theorem 1. $\mathsf{SDVS}_{\mathsf{Ours}}$ *satisfies perfectly non-transferability.*

Theorem 2. *If the GAIP assumption holds on* $(\mathrm{Cl}_p, \mathrm{Ell}_p)$*,* $\mathsf{SDVS}_{\mathsf{Ours}}$ *satisfies strong unforgeability in the ROM.*

Theorem 3. *If* $\mathsf{SDVS}_{\mathsf{Ours}}$ *satisfies strong unforgeability in the ROM and the CSI-GDH assumption holds on* $(\mathrm{Cl}_p, \mathrm{Ell}_p)$*,* $\mathsf{SDVS}_{\mathsf{Ours}}$ *satisfies privacy of signer's identity in the ROM.*

We give the sketch of the proof Theorem 3. Let A be a PPT adversary for $\mathsf{Game}^{\mathsf{PSI}}_{\mathsf{SDVS}_{\mathsf{Ours}}}$.

First, we introduce the sequence of games $\mathsf{Game}_{0,\mathsf{A}}, \ldots, \mathsf{Game}_{6,\mathsf{A}}$ as follows.

- $\mathsf{Game}_{0,\mathsf{A}}$: The original privacy of signer's identity security game $\mathsf{Game}^{\mathsf{PSI}}_{\mathsf{SDVS}_{\mathsf{Ours}},\mathsf{A}}$ in the ROM with some modification. We introduce a signing list L^{Sign}. For a query on input (d, m) to the signing oracle $\mathcal{O}^{\mathsf{Sign}}$, $\mathcal{O}^{\mathsf{Sign}}$ outputs a signature and records a tuple (d, m, σ) to L^{Sign}. We also introduce the hash table $\mathbb{T}$. These modifications do not change the view of an adversary A.
- $\mathsf{Game}_{1,\mathsf{A}}$: This game is identical to $\mathsf{Game}_{0,\mathsf{A}}$ except that we modify the generation of the signature σ^* for the challenge and the verification oracle $\mathcal{O}^{\mathsf{Ver}}$. For a challenge query on m^*, sample $b \xleftarrow{\$} \{0, 1\}$ and query (b, m^*) the signing oracle $\mathcal{O}^{\mathsf{Sign}}$, obtain a signature σ^* and return σ^*.
  For a query on $(0, m, \sigma)$, search a tuple $(0, m, \sigma)$ from L^{Sign}. If there is tuple in L^{Sign} return 1 and 0 otherwise. For a query on $(1, m, \sigma)$, return $b = \widetilde{\mathsf{Ver}}(\mathrm{sk}_{s_1}, \mathrm{pk}_{s_1}, \mathrm{pk}_v, m, \sigma)$ where $\widetilde{\mathsf{Ver}}$ is the modified algorithm obtained from $\mathsf{Ver}(\mathrm{sk}_v, \mathrm{pk}_{s_1}, \mathrm{pk}_v, m, \sigma)$ by modifying the computation of K from $K = [\mathfrak{g}^{x_v}] * \mathrm{pk}_{s_1}$ to $K = [\mathfrak{g}^{x_{s_1}}] * \mathrm{pk}_v$.
- $\mathsf{Game}_{2,\mathsf{A}}$: This game is identical to $\mathsf{Game}_{1,\mathsf{A}}$ except that we modify the signing oracle $\mathcal{O}^{\mathsf{Sign}}$. For a query on $(0, m, \sigma)$, samples $\mathbf{c}_s, \mathbf{c}_v \xleftarrow{\$} \{\pm 1\}^\lambda$, $\mathbf{z}_s, \mathbf{z}_v \xleftarrow{\$} \mathbb{Z}_N^\lambda$, set $K \leftarrow [\mathfrak{g}^{x_v}] * \mathrm{pk}_{s_0}$, $\mathbf{R}_s \leftarrow [\mathfrak{g}^{\mathbf{z}_s}] * \mathrm{pk}_s^{\mathbf{c}_s}$, $\mathbf{R}_v \leftarrow [\mathfrak{g}^{\mathbf{z}_v}] * \mathrm{pk}_v^{\mathbf{c}_v}$, $\mathbf{c} \leftarrow \mathbf{c}_s \odot \mathbf{c}_v$. If there is $\mathbb{T}[m, K, \mathbf{R}_s, \mathbf{R}_v] \neq \perp$, then abort. Otherwise, update $\mathbb{T}[m, K, \mathbf{R}_s, \mathbf{R}_v] = \mathbf{c}$ and return $\sigma \leftarrow (\mathbf{c}_s, \mathbf{c}_v, \mathbf{z}_s, \mathbf{z}_v)$.
- $\mathsf{Game}_{3,\mathsf{A}}$: This game is identical to $\mathsf{Game}_{2,\mathsf{A}}$ except that we modify the hash oracle $\mathcal{O}^H$ and the signing oracle $\mathcal{O}^{\mathsf{Sign}}$. We modify the $\mathcal{O}^H$ as follows. For a query on $(m, K, \mathbf{R}_s, \mathbf{R}_v)$, check $K = [\mathfrak{g}^{x_v}] * \mathrm{pk}_{s_0}$ by using the CSI-DDH oracle. If $K = [\mathfrak{g}^{x_v}] * \mathrm{pk}_{s_0}$ holds, then abort. Otherwise, behave the same as an ordinary random oracle and output a hash value.
  We modify the $\mathcal{O}^{\mathsf{Sign}}$ as follows. For a query on $(0, m, \sigma)$, samples $\mathbf{c}_s, \mathbf{c}_v \xleftarrow{\$} \{\pm 1\}^\lambda$, $\mathbf{z}_s, \mathbf{z}_v \xleftarrow{\$} \mathbb{Z}_N^\lambda$, set $K \leftarrow \perp_0$, $\mathbf{R}_s \leftarrow [\mathfrak{g}^{\mathbf{z}_s}] * \mathrm{pk}_s^{\mathbf{c}_s}$, $\mathbf{R}_v \leftarrow [\mathfrak{g}^{\mathbf{z}_v^*}] * \mathrm{pk}_v^{\mathbf{c}_v^*}$, $\mathbf{c} \leftarrow \mathbf{c}_s \odot \mathbf{c}_v$. If there is $\mathbb{T}[m, \perp_0, \mathbf{R}_s, \mathbf{R}_v] \neq \perp$, then abort. Otherwise, update $\mathbb{T}[m, \perp_0, \mathbf{R}_s, \mathbf{R}_v] = \mathbf{c}$ and return $\sigma \leftarrow (\mathbf{c}_s, \mathbf{c}_v, \mathbf{z}_s, \mathbf{z}_v)$.
- $\mathsf{Game}_{4,\mathsf{A}}$: This game is identical to $\mathsf{Game}_{3,\mathsf{A}}$ except that we modify the verification oracle $\mathcal{O}^{\mathsf{Ver}}$. For a query on $(1, m, \sigma)$, search a tuple $(1, m, \sigma)$ from L^{Sign}. If there is tuple in L^{Sign} return 1 and 0 otherwise.
- $\mathsf{Game}_{5,\mathsf{A}}$: This game is identical to $\mathsf{Game}_{4,\mathsf{A}}$ except that we modify the signing oracle $\mathcal{O}^{\mathsf{Sign}}$. For a query on $(1, m, \sigma)$, samples $\mathbf{c}_s, \mathbf{c}_v \xleftarrow{\$} \{\pm 1\}^\lambda$, $\mathbf{z}_s, \mathbf{z}_v \xleftarrow{\$} \mathbb{Z}_N^\lambda$, set $K \leftarrow [\mathfrak{g}^{x_v}] * \mathrm{pk}_{s_1}$, $\mathbf{R}_s \leftarrow [\mathfrak{g}^{\mathbf{z}_s}] * \mathrm{pk}_s^{\mathbf{c}_s}$, $\mathbf{R}_v \leftarrow [\mathfrak{g}^{\mathbf{z}_v}] * \mathrm{pk}_v^{\mathbf{c}_v}$, $\mathbf{c} \leftarrow \mathbf{c}_s \odot \mathbf{c}_v$. If there

is $\mathbb{T}[m, K, \mathbf{R}_s, \mathbf{R}_v] \neq \bot$, then abort. Otherwise, update $\mathbb{T}[m, K, \mathbf{R}_s, \mathbf{R}_v] = \mathbf{c}$ and return $\sigma \leftarrow (\mathbf{c}_s, \mathbf{c}_v, \mathbf{z}_s, \mathbf{z}_v)$.

- $\mathsf{Game}_{6,\mathsf{A}}$: This game is identical to $\mathsf{Game}_{5,\mathsf{A}}$ except that we modify the hash oracle $\mathcal{O}^H$ and the signing oracle $\mathcal{O}^{\mathsf{Sign}}$. We modify the $\mathcal{O}^H$ as follows. For a query on $(m, K, \mathbf{R}_s, \mathbf{R}_v)$, check $K = [\mathfrak{g}^{x_v}] * \mathrm{pk}_{s_0}$ by using the CSI-DDH oracle. If $K = [\mathfrak{g}^{x_v}] * \mathrm{pk}_{s_0}$ holds, then abort. Also, check $K = [\mathfrak{g}^{x_v}] * \mathrm{pk}_{s_1}$ by using the CSI-DDH oracle. If $K = [\mathfrak{g}^{x_v}] * \mathrm{pk}_{s_1}$ holds, then abort. Otherwise, behave the same as an ordinary random oracle and output a hash value. We modify the $\mathcal{O}^{\mathsf{Sign}}$ as follows. For a query on $(1, m, \sigma)$, samples $\mathbf{c}_s, \mathbf{c}_v \xleftarrow{\$} \{\pm 1\}^\lambda$, $\mathbf{z}_s, \mathbf{z}_v \xleftarrow{\$} \mathbb{Z}_N^\lambda$, set $K \leftarrow \bot_1$, $\mathbf{R}_s \leftarrow [\mathfrak{g}^{\mathbf{z}_s}] * \mathrm{pk}_s^{\mathbf{c}_s}$, $\mathbf{R}_v \leftarrow [\mathfrak{g}^{\mathbf{z}_v}] * \mathrm{pk}_v^{\mathbf{c}_v}$, $\mathbf{c} \leftarrow \mathbf{c}_s \odot \mathbf{c}_v$. If there is $\mathbb{T}[m, \bot_1, \mathbf{R}_s, \mathbf{R}_v] \neq \bot$, then abort. Otherwise, update $\mathbb{T}[m, \bot_1, \mathbf{R}_s, \mathbf{R}_v] = \mathbf{c}$ and return $\sigma \leftarrow (\mathbf{c}_s, \mathbf{c}_v, \mathbf{z}_s, \mathbf{z}_v)$.

Then, for a sequence of games $\mathsf{Game}_{0,\mathsf{A}}, \ldots, \mathsf{Game}_{6,\mathsf{A}}$, we prove the following lemmas.

Lemma 2. *If the* $\mathsf{SDVS}_{\mathsf{Ours}}$ *satisfies strong unforgeability,*

$$|\Pr[\mathsf{Game}_{0,\mathsf{A}} \Rightarrow 1] - \Pr[\mathsf{Game}_{1,\mathsf{A}} \Rightarrow 1| = \mathsf{negl}(\lambda).$$

Lemma 3.

$$|\Pr[\mathsf{Game}_{1,\mathsf{A}} \Rightarrow 1] - \Pr[\mathsf{Game}_{2,\mathsf{A}} \Rightarrow 1| = \mathsf{negl}(\lambda).$$

Lemma 4. *If the CSI-GDH assumption holds,*

$$|\Pr[\mathsf{Game}_{2,\mathsf{A}} \Rightarrow 1] - \Pr[\mathsf{Game}_{3,\mathsf{A}} \Rightarrow 1| = \mathsf{negl}(\lambda).$$

Lemma 5. *If the* $\mathsf{SDVS}_{\mathsf{Ours}}$ *satisfies strong unforgeability,*

$$|\Pr[\mathsf{Game}_{3,\mathsf{A}} \Rightarrow 1] - \Pr[\mathsf{Game}_{4,\mathsf{A}} \Rightarrow 1| = \mathsf{negl}(\lambda).$$

Lemma 6.

$$|\Pr[\mathsf{Game}_{4,\mathsf{A}} \Rightarrow 1] - \Pr[\mathsf{Game}_{5,\mathsf{A}} \Rightarrow 1| = \mathsf{negl}(\lambda).$$

Lemma 7. *If the CSI-GDH assumption holds,*

$$|\Pr[\mathsf{Game}_{5,\mathsf{A}} \Rightarrow 1] - \Pr[\mathsf{Game}_{6,\mathsf{A}} \Rightarrow 1| = \mathsf{negl}(\lambda).$$

Lemma 8.

$$\Pr[\mathsf{Game}_{6,\mathsf{A}} \Rightarrow 1] = \frac{1}{2}.$$

Finally, we bound $\mathsf{Adv}^{\mathsf{PSI}}_{\mathsf{SDVS},\mathsf{A}}(\lambda)$. From Lemma 2 to Lemma 8, we have

$$\begin{aligned}
&\mathsf{Adv}^{\mathsf{PSI}}_{\mathsf{SDVS},\mathsf{A}}(\lambda)\\
&= \left|\Pr[\mathsf{Game}^{\mathsf{PSI}}_{\mathsf{SDVS},\mathsf{A}}(1^\lambda) \Rightarrow 1] - \frac{1}{2}\right|\\
&= \left|\sum_{i=0}^{5} (\Pr[\mathsf{Game}_{i,\mathsf{A}} \Rightarrow 1] - \Pr[\mathsf{Game}_{i+1,\mathsf{A}} \Rightarrow 1]) - \frac{1}{2}\right|\\
&\leq \sum_{i=0}^{5} |\Pr[\mathsf{Game}_{i,\mathsf{A}} \Rightarrow 1] - \Pr[\mathsf{Game}_{i+1,\mathsf{A}} \Rightarrow 1]| + \left|\Pr[\mathsf{Game}_{6,\mathsf{A}} \Rightarrow 1] - \frac{1}{2}\right|\\
&= \mathsf{negl}(\lambda).
\end{aligned}$$

Theorem 4. *If there is an algorithm* F_m *that generates valid signatures on a message* m *in polynomial time and the probability* ϵ *with at most* Q_H *queries to the random oracle, then* $\mathsf{SDVS}_{\mathsf{Ours}}$ *satisfies non-delegatability with knowledge error* $2^{-\lambda}$ *in the ROM.*

References

1. Asaar, M.R., Salmasizadeh, M.: A novel strong designated verifier signature scheme without random oracles. IACR Cryptol. ePrint Arch. 259 (2012)
2. Assidi, H., Souidi, E.M.: Strong designated verifier signature based on the rank metric. In: WISTP 2019. LNCS, vol. 12024, pp. 85–102. Springer (2019)
3. Basso, A., Maino, L.: Poké: a compact and efficient PKE from higher-dimensional isogenies. In: EUROCRYPT 2025, Part II. LNCS, vol. 15602, pp. 94–123. Springer (2025)
4. Bellare, M., Rogaway, P.: Random oracles are practical: a paradigm for designing efficient protocols. In: ACM CCS 1993, pp. 62–73. ACM (1993)
5. Beullens, W., Kleinjung, T., Vercauteren, F.: CSI-fish: efficient isogeny based signatures through class group computations. In: ASIACRYPT 2019, Part I. LNCS, vol. 11921, pp. 227–247. Springer (2019)
6. Cai, J., Jiang, H., Zhang, P., Zheng, Z., Lyu, G., Xu, Q.: An efficient strong designated verifier signature based on r-sis assumption. IEEE Access **7**, 3938–3947 (2019)
7. Castryck, W., Decru, T.: An efficient key recovery attack on SIDH. In: EUROCRYPT 2023, Part V. LNCS, vol. 14008, pp. 423–447. Springer (2023)
8. Castryck, W., Lange, T., Martindale, C., Panny, L., Renes, J.: CSIDH: an efficient post-quantum commutative group action. In: ASIACRYPT 2018, Part III. LNCS, vol. 11274, pp. 395–427. Springer (2018)
9. Chaum, D., Antwerpen, H.V.: Undeniable signatures. In: CRYPTO 1989. LNCS, vol. 435, pp. 212–216. Springer (1989)
10. Feng, D., Xu, J., Chen, W.: Generic constructions for strong designated verifier signature. J. Inf. Process. Syst. **7**(1), 159–172 (2011)
11. Fiat, A., Shamir, A.: How to prove yourself: practical solutions to identification and signature problems. In: CRYPTO 1986. LNCS, vol. 263, pp. 186–194. Springer (1986)
12. Fujisaki, E., Okamoto, T.: Secure integration of asymmetric and symmetric encryption schemes. In: CRYPTO 1999. LNCS, vol. 1666, pp. 537–554. Springer (1999)
13. Gong, B., Au, M.H., Xue, H.: Constructing strong designated verifier signatures from key encapsulation mechanisms. In: TrustCom/BigDataSE 2019, pp. 586–593. IEEE (2019)
14. Hofheinz, D., Hövelmanns, K., Kiltz, E.: A modular analysis of the Fujisaki-Okamoto transformation. In: TCC 2017, Part I. LNCS, vol. 10677, pp. 341–371. Springer (2017)
15. Huang, Q., Yang, G., Wong, D.S., Susilo, W.: Efficient strong designated verifier signature schemes without random oracle or with non-delegatability. Int. J. Inf. Sec. **10**(6), 373–385 (2011)
16. Huang, X., Susilo, W., Mu, Y., Zhang, F.: Short (identity-based) strong designated verifier signature schemes. In: ISPEC 2006. LNCS, vol. 3903, pp. 214–225. Springer (2006)

17. Jakobsson, M., Sako, K., Impagliazzo, R.: Designated verifier proofs and their applications. In: EUROCRYPT 1996. LNCS, vol. 1070, pp. 143–154. Springer (1996)
18. Katsumata, S., Lai, Y., LeGrow, J.T., Qin, L.: CSI -otter: isogeny-based (partially) blind signatures from the class group action with a twist. In: CRYPTO 2023, Part III. LNCS, vol. 14083, pp. 729–761. Springer (2023)
19. Katsumata, S., Lai, Y., LeGrow, J.T., Qin, L.: CSI-otter: isogeny-based (partially) blind signatures from the class group action with a twist. Des. Codes Cryptogr. **92**(11), 3587–3643 (2024)
20. Kawashima, T., Takashima, K., Aikawa, Y., Takagi, T.: An efficient authenticated key exchange from random self-reducibility on CSIDH. In: ICISC 2020. LNCS, vol. 12593, pp. 58–84. Springer (2020)
21. Khuc, T.X., et al.: Strong designated verifier signatures from isogeny assumptions. In: CANS 2025. LNCS, vol. 16351, pp. 46–69. Springer (2025)
22. Laguillaumie, F., Vergnaud, D.: Designated verifier signatures: anonymity and efficient construction from any bilinear map. In: SCN 2004. LNCS, vol. 3352, pp. 105–119. Springer (2004)
23. Lipmaa, H., Wang, G., Bao, F.: Designated verifier signature schemes: attacks, new security notions and a new construction. In: ICALP 2005. LNCS, vol. 3580, pp. 459–471. Springer (2005)
24. Minamide, H., Tanaka, K., Tezuka, M.: Strong designated verifier signatures with non-delegatability from CSIDH. IACR Cryptol. ePrint Arch. 1673 (2025)
25. Nakagawa, K., Onuki, H.: QFESTA: efficient algorithms and parameters for FESTA using quaternion algebras. In: CRYPTO 2024, Part V. LNCS, vol. 14924, pp. 75–106. Springer (2024)
26. Poddar, S., Mishra, S., Mohanty, T., Srivastava, V., Gangopadhyay, S.: Las-dvs: a post-quantum secure compact strong-designated verifier signature. CoRR, abs/2504.16571 (2025)
27. Renan, F.: A compact post-quantum strong designated verifier signature scheme from isogenies. IACR Cryptol. ePrint Arch. 1335 (2025)
28. Saeednia, S., Kremer, S., Markowitch, O.: An efficient strong designated verifier signature scheme. In: ICISC 2003. LNCS, vol. 2971, pp. 40–54. Springer (2003)
29. Shahandashti, S.F., Safavi-Naini, R.: Construction of universal designated-verifier signatures and identity-based signatures from standard signatures. In: PKC 2008. LNCS, vol. 4939, pp. 121–140. Springer (2008)
30. Shooshtari, M.K., Ahmadian-Attari, M., Aref, M.R.: Provably secure strong designated verifier signature scheme based on coding theory. Int. J. Commun. Syst. **30**(7) (2017)
31. Steinfeld, R., Bull, L., Wang, H., Pieprzyk, J.: Universal designated-verifier signatures. In: ASIACRYPT 2003. LNCS, vol. 2894, pp. 523–542. Springer (2003)
32. Steinfeld, R., Wang, H., Pieprzyk, J.: Efficient extension of standard Schnorr/RSA signatures into universal designated-verifier signatures. In: PKC 2004. LNCS, vol. 2947, pp. 86–100. Springer (2004)
33. Sun, X., Tian, H., Wang, Y.: Toward quantum-resistant strong designated verifier signature from isogenies. In: INCoS 2012, pp. 292–296. IEEE (2012)
34. Thanalakshmi, P., Anitha, R., Anbazhagan, N., Park, C., Joshi, G.P., Seo, C.: A hash-based quantum-resistant designated verifier signature scheme. Mathematics **10**(10), 1642 (2022)
35. Tian, H., Chen, X., Jiang, Z., Du, Y.: Non-delegatable strong designated verifier signature on elliptic curves. In: ICISC 2011. LNCS, vol. 7259, pp. 219–234. Springer (2011)

36. Tian, H., Chen, X., Li, J.: A short non-delegatable strong designated verifier signature. In: ACISP 2012. LNCS, vol. 7372, pp. 261–279. Springer (2012)
37. Tian, H., Jiang, Z., Liu, Y., Wei, B.: A non-delegatable strong designated verifier signature without random oracles. In: INCoS 2012, pp. 237–244. IEEE (2012)
38. Tso, R., Okamoto, T., Okamoto, E.: Practical strong designated verifier signature schemes based on double discrete logarithms. In: CISC 2005. LNCS, vol. 3822, pp. 113–127. Springer (2005)
39. Wang, B., Song, Z.: A non-interactive deniable authentication scheme based on designated verifier proofs. Inf. Sci. **179**(6), 858–865 (2009)
40. Yang, B., Sun, Y., Yu, Y., Xia, Q.: A strong designated verifier signature scheme with secure disavowability. In: INCoS 2012, pp. 286–291. IEEE (2012)
41. Zhang, Y., Susilo, W., Guo, F.: Lattice-based strong designated verifier signature with non-delegatability. Comput. Stand. Interfaces **92**, 103904 (2025)

An Undeniable Signature Scheme Utilizing Module Lattices

Kunal Dey[1], Mansi Goyal[2(✉)], Aditi Kar Gangopadhyay[2], and Bhupendra Singh[3]

[1] Department of Computer Science, University of Calgary, Calgary, AB T2N1N4, Canada
kunal.dey@ucalgary.ca, kunaldey3@gmail.com

[2] Department of Mathematics, Indian Institute of Technology Roorkee, Roorkee 247667, Uttarakhand, India
{mansi,aditi.gangopadhyay}@ma.iitr.ac.in

[3] CAIR, DRDO, Bangalore 560093, Karnataka, India
bhupendra@cair.drdo.in

Abstract. An undeniable signature scheme is a form of digital signature in which the signer maintains control over the verifiability of signatures. In particular, verification can only be performed by an authenticated verifier with the explicit cooperation of the signer. In this work, we present a post-quantum undeniable signature scheme constructed over module lattices. Our construction builds upon the GPV framework and derives its security from the hardness of the SIS and LWE problems. We formally establish that the proposed scheme satisfies all the required security properties. Moreover, this work provides a concrete *implementation* of a lattice-based undeniable signature scheme, evaluated across different parameter sets. The choice of the module-lattice setting over the ring-lattice variant is motivated by the additional flexibility it offers in parameter selection.

Keywords: Digital signature · Lattice-based cryptography · Module lattices · Post-quantum cryptography · LWE problem · SIS problem · Undeniable signature

1 Introduction

A digital signature is a cryptographic mechanism used to authenticate messages. It typically involves three algorithms: one for generating the user's public and secret keys, a signing algorithm, and a verification algorithm. Unlike traditional digital signatures, undeniable signatures require the active involvement of the signer to verify the signature. This concept was first introduced by Chaum and van Antwerpen [7]. Unlike standard digital signatures, which can be verified by anyone with access to the signer's public key, undeniable signatures require an interactive protocol with the signer for verification. This design grants the

H. Seo (Ed.): ICISC 2025, LNCS 16487, pp. 510–532, 2026.
https://doi.org/10.1007/978-981-95-8034-7_27

signer control over who is permitted to verify their signatures, providing an added layer of selective verification. During this protocol, the verifier obtains either an affirmative (confirmation protocol) or a negative response (disavowal protocol), indicating whether the signature was generated by the original signer. The signer is unable to deceive the verifier by making a valid signature appear invalid or an invalid signature appear valid. Given that merely copying a signature does not yield directly verifiable results, undeniable signatures are favored over conventional digital signatures for specific applications such as e-voting, e-cash, etc. Over the years, there has been notable research activity focused on undeniable signature schemes [5,10,15,17,33,43]. These cryptographic schemes are based on number-theoretic problems, such as the discrete logarithm and integer factorization problems, which are vulnerable to quantum attacks due to *Shor's algorithm* [35]. This poses a significant threat to modern cryptographic protocols, as many widely adopted encryption, key exchange, and digital signature schemes could become obsolete with the advent of powerful quantum computers. This urgency underscores the need to transition toward quantum-safe cryptographic methods. Post-quantum cryptography (PQC) evolved to provide quantum-resistant protocols in response to the growing threat of quantum computing. Several candidates for PQC exist, including *Lattice-based cryptography* [30], *Isogeny-based cryptography* [11], *Code-based cryptography* [40], *Hash-based cryptography* [37], *Multivariate cryptography* [12]. Each of these PQC approaches has distinct advantages and disadvantages, making direct comparisons challenging. Numerous post-quantum undeniable signature schemes have been proposed in the literature on PQC. Jao et al. [21] introduced an isogeny-based undeniable signature scheme, and Srikant et al. [36] extended it to a blind signature version. Additionally, there are code-based undeniable signature schemes [1,20]. On the other hand, a lattice-based undeniable signature scheme has been proposed by Rawal et al. [31].

Lattice-based cryptography being one of the most promising candidates in the area of PQC. In 2016, the post-quantum cryptography standardisation initiative was started by the National Institute of Standards and Technology (NIST), aiming to update its cryptographic standards with PQC to safeguard against the threat posed by quantum computers. This project launched a global competition to identify quantum-resistant cryptographic algorithms capable of replacing classical schemes vulnerable to quantum attacks. By 2023, NIST had selected three algorithms for post-quantum digital signatures. The noteworthy aspect is that two of these algorithms are lattice-based: CRYSTALS-Dilithium [13,26] and FALCON [14]. While CRYSTALS-Dilithium employs the Schnorr signature framework [34], FALCON follows the GPV signature framework [18]. Over the years, numerous variants derived from the Schnorr and GPV frameworks have been proposed, resulting in advancements in cryptographic schemes. These include group signatures [19,42], which facilitate anonymous authentication within a group; ring signatures [6,25], which maintain signer anonymity without disclosing the identity of the member who signed a message; and undeniable signatures [31], which require the signer's cooperation for verification.

These innovations highlight the adaptability and potential of lattice-based cryptography in addressing the challenges posed by quantum computing.

The initial preference for lattice-based constructions often centers on ideal lattices and ring settings [27,29,38]. However, module lattices [24] offer a compelling alternative, as schemes based on a module setting are nearly as efficient as their ring-based counterparts while providing additional practical advantages, including computational efficiency and low memory usage [4]. Furthermore, module lattice-based schemes can potentially reduce the sizes of public keys and ciphertexts while ensuring robust security guarantees, making them particularly suitable for constrained environments such as embedded systems or mobile devices. Notably, the NIST-standardized CRYSTALS-Dilithium scheme [13] is based on module lattices, and a recent study [9] introduces a module version of the Falcon signature scheme. In light of these advantages, module lattices are increasingly being viewed as a promising alternative for PQC, potentially offering a more scalable and secure foundation for future cryptographic schemes. Despite the advantages of module lattices, there is a notable absence of undeniable signature schemes based on this framework. Therefore, developing such a protocol presents an intriguing research opportunity.

1.1 Motivation and Our Contribution

An undeniable signature scheme is considered secure if it satisfies two fundamental properties: *existential unforgeability*, which ensures that only the legitimate signer can generate valid signatures, and *invisibility*, which guarantees that an adversary cannot decide whether a given signature is valid. Security additionally requires *completeness*, *soundness*, and *zero-knowledge* for the interactive verification protocols, the *confirmation* and *disavowal* protocols.

Rawal et al. [31] proposed the first lattice-based undeniable signature scheme, instantiated using the GPV framework [18] over ideal lattices. Ideal lattices, typically defined over rings of the form $\mathcal{R}_q = \mathbb{Z}_q[X]/(X^n+1)$, are widely adopted for efficiency, while module lattices [24], represented as $\mathcal{R}_q^d$, strike a balance between ideal and unstructured lattices.

Upon examining the construction of [31], we identified a critical weakness: a dishonest signer can execute the Disavowal protocol on a valid message signature pair with non-negligible probability. This violates the *soundness* requirement of the zero-knowledge property, which guarantees that no dishonest signer can convince an honest verifier to reject a valid message signature pair except with negligible probability. Furthermore, to the best of our knowledge, no prior work has provided a concrete *implementation* of a lattice-based undeniable signature scheme.

The main contributions of this work are as follows:

- In this work, we construct an undeniable signature scheme based on the GPV signature scheme [4,18], adapted to the module lattice setting. Our scheme's security relies on the module-LWE and module-SIS problems. The primary goal of our work is to design a module-based variant of the undeniable signature scheme that provides enhanced flexibility in parameter selection rather than focusing solely on performance.

- Our construction prevents a dishonest signer from running the Disavowal protocol with a valid signature with a non-negligible probability (Theorem 5). The Disavowal and Confirmation protocols of our scheme are influenced by Stern's identification scheme [22,39].
- We leverage the work on trapdoors over module lattices by Bert et al. [4], who implemented lattice trapdoors for various security parameters. Our protocol was implemented in C, and we evaluated the communication and computation costs using the proposed parameters for different security levels.

1.2 Organization of the Paper

The structure of this paper is organized as follows: Sect. 2 outlines the essential preliminaries needed for a comprehensive understanding of our scheme. Section 3 introduces our undeniable signature scheme, which is built on module lattices. Section 4 discusses the security analysis, while Sect. 5 evaluates the communication and computation costs. Lastly, Sect. 6 provides a summary of the key findings.

2 Preliminaries

Notations. Bold lowercase letters (e.g., $\mathbf{a}$, $\mathbf{h}$) are used to denote vectors, while bold uppercase letters (e.g., $\mathbf{U}$, $\mathbf{E}$) represent matrices. The Euclidean norm is denoted by $\|\cdot\|$, and for a matrix $\mathbf{X}$, the norm is defined as $\| \mathbf{X} \| = \max_i \| \mathbf{x}_i \|$, where $\mathbf{x}_i$ is the ith column of $\mathbf{X}$. The norm of a vector in $\mathbb{Z}_q$ is defined as the norm of the corresponding vector over $\mathbb{Z}$ with each entry taken from the set $\{-\lfloor \frac{q}{2} \rfloor, \dots, \lfloor \frac{q}{2} \rfloor\}$. The symbol $\cdot \| \cdot$ represents the concatenation of two entities. $\mathcal{U}(S)$ represents the uniform distribution over the finite set S. $\omega(\cdot)$ denotes the lower bound of the asymptotic growth rate. Let $\mathbf{u}$ and $\mathbf{v}$ be two vectors in $\mathbb{R}^n$. The expression $< \mathbf{u}, \mathbf{v} >$ denotes the standard dot product, defined by $< \mathbf{u}, \mathbf{v} > = \mathbf{u} \cdot \mathbf{v}^T$.

Definition 1. ***Negligible function.*** *A function* $\mathsf{negl} : \mathbb{N} \to \mathbb{R}$ *is considered negligible if it decreases faster than the inverse of any polynomial.*

Definition 2. ***Lattice.*** *Given* m *linearly independent vectors* $\mathbf{p}_1, \mathbf{p}_2, \dots, \mathbf{p}_m \in \mathbb{R}^n$, *the* lattice *generated by these vectors is defined as,*

$$\mathcal{L} = \mathcal{L}(\mathbf{p}_1, \mathbf{p}_2, \dots, \mathbf{p}_m) = \left\{ \sum_{i=1}^{m} x_i \mathbf{p}_i \mid x_i \in \mathbb{Z} \right\}.$$

The set $\{\mathbf{p}_1, \dots, \mathbf{p}_m\}$ *forms a basis for* $\mathcal{L}$. *Here,* m *denotes the rank, and* n *represents the lattice's dimension. When* n *equals* m*, the lattice is referred to as a full-rank lattice. The* dual lattice $\mathcal{L}^*$ *corresponding to* $\mathcal{L}$ *is defined as,*

$$\mathcal{L}^* = \{\mathbf{w} \in span(\mathcal{L}) : \forall \mathbf{v} \in \mathcal{L}, < \mathbf{w}, \mathbf{v} > \in \mathbb{Z}\}.$$

2.1 Gaussian on Lattices [8,18]

Consider a basis $B \subset \mathbb{R}^n$ for an n-dimensional lattice $\mathcal{L}$ (or a full-rank set $S \subset \mathcal{L}$). The Gaussian sampling algorithm randomly selects a lattice vector according to a probability distribution resembling the Gaussian distribution.

Definition 3. ***Gaussian Function on*** $\mathbb{R}^n$. *Let* $\mathcal{L}$ *be an* n*-dimensional lattice,* $\mathbf{c} \in \mathbb{R}^n$*, and* $s > 0$*. A Gaussian function centered at* $\mathbf{c}$ *on* $\mathbb{R}^n$ *is defined as,*

$$\rho_{s,\mathbf{c}}(\mathbf{x}) = \exp\left(\frac{-\pi\|\mathbf{x}-\mathbf{c}\|^2}{s^2}\right), \;\forall\, \mathbf{x} \in \mathbb{R}^n.$$

If $s = 1$ *and* $\mathbf{c} = \mathbf{0}$*, we can eliminate the subscripts* s *and* $\mathbf{c}$*.*

Definition 4. ***Discrete Gaussian Distribution****. Let* $\mathcal{L}$ *be an* n*-dimensional lattice,* $s > 0$ *and* $\mathbf{c} \in \mathbb{R}^n$*. The discrete Gaussian distribution over* $\mathcal{L}$ *is defined as,*

$$D_{\mathcal{L},s,\mathbf{c}}(\mathbf{x}) = \frac{\rho_{s,\mathbf{c}}(\mathbf{x})}{\rho_{s,\mathbf{c}}(\mathcal{L})}, \;\forall\, \mathbf{x} \in \mathcal{L}, \qquad \textit{where } \rho_{s,\mathbf{c}}(\mathcal{L}) = \sum_{\mathbf{y}\in\mathcal{L}} \rho_{s,\mathbf{c}}(\mathbf{y}).$$

2.2 Some Hard Problems in Lattice

1. **The Short Integer Solution Problem** (SIS) [2]: Let we have a matrix $\mathbf{A} \in \mathbb{Z}_q^{m\times n}$, a real number β and an integer q. The problem is to find a non-zero vector $\mathbf{s} \in \mathbb{Z}^n$ such that $\mathbf{A}\mathbf{s} = 0 \mod q$ with $\|\mathbf{s}\| \leq \beta$.
2. **Inhomogeneous Short Integer Solution Problem** (ISIS)**:** This problem is the inhomogeneous version of the SIS problem. Let we have a matrix $\mathbf{A} \in \mathbb{Z}_q^{m\times n}$, an integer q and a real number β and $\mathbf{u} \in \mathbb{Z}_q^m$. The problem is to find a non-zero vector $\mathbf{s} \in \mathbb{Z}^n$ such that $\mathbf{A}\mathbf{s} = \mathbf{u} \mod q$ with $\|\mathbf{s}\| \leq \beta$.
3. **Learning with Error** (LWE) [32]: LWE is a computational problem where secret information is embedded into a system of linear equations, with small errors added to perturb the system.
   Learning with Error (Decisional version): Suppose $\mathcal{E}$ is an error distribution over $\mathbb{Z}_q$ for an integer q and n is a positive integer. Let the probability distribution $\mathcal{X}_{\mathbf{s},\mathcal{E}}$ on $\mathbb{Z}_q^n \times \mathbb{Z}_q$ be defined as,
   - Choose a vector $\mathbf{a}$ from $\mathbb{Z}_q^n$ uniformly, and x according to $\mathcal{E}$, and for $\mathbf{s} \in \mathbb{Z}_q^n$, output $(\mathbf{a}, \mathbf{a}^T\mathbf{s} + x)$.
   The goal of this problem is to distinguish between the distribution $\mathcal{X}_{\mathbf{s},\mathcal{E}}$ for some $\mathbf{s} \in \mathbb{Z}_q^n$ and the uniform distribution of $\mathbb{Z}_q^n \times \mathbb{Z}_q$. Note that all of the above operations are done in $\mathbb{Z}_q$.

2.3 Hard Random Lattices

Let n, m, q be some positive integers, where n is the security parameter and all other variables are functions of n and $\mathbf{A} \in \mathbb{Z}_q^{n\times m}$. We now consider an m-dimensional lattice of full rank defined by $\mathbf{A}$.

$$\mathcal{L}^{\perp}(\mathbf{A}) = \{\mathbf{e} \in \mathbb{Z}^m : \mathbf{A}\mathbf{e} = \mathbf{0} \mod q\}.$$

The set of syndromes is defined as $synd = \{\mathbf{u} = \mathbf{Ae} \mod q : \mathbf{e} \in \mathbb{Z}^m\}$. The set $synd$ is a subset of $\mathbb{Z}_q^n$. It can be shown that $synd \approx \mathbb{Z}^m/\mathcal{L}^\perp(\mathbf{A})$.

The following Lemma 1 from [18] is instrumental in defining a trapdoor function, as discussed in the subsequent subsection. Readers are encouraged to consult [16,18,28] for the essential background on sampling from the discrete Gaussian distribution.

Lemma 1. *Let $m \geq 2n \log q$, where q is a prime number and n is a positive integer. Then, for all $s \geq \omega(\sqrt{\log m})$ and for any but a $2q^{-n}$ fraction of matrices $\mathbf{A} \in \mathbb{Z}_q^{n\times m}$, the following holds:*

1. *There exists a vector $\mathbf{e} \in \{0,1\}^m$ such that $\mathbf{Ae} = \mathbf{u} \mod q$ for every syndrome $\mathbf{u} \in \mathbb{Z}_q^n$.*
2. *The distribution of $\mathbf{u} = \mathbf{Ae} \mod q$ is statistically close to uniform across $\mathbb{Z}_q^n$ for $\mathbf{e} \sim D_{\mathbb{Z}^m,s}$.*
3. *The conditional distribution of $\mathbf{e} \sim D_{\mathbb{Z}^m,s}$, given $\mathbf{u} = \mathbf{Ae} \mod q$, is precisely $\mathbf{t} + D_{\mathcal{L}^\perp(\mathbf{A}),s,-\mathbf{t}}$. This is for a fixed $\mathbf{u} \in \mathbb{Z}_q^n$ and an arbitrary solution $\mathbf{t} \in \mathbb{Z}^m$ to the equation $\mathbf{u} = \mathbf{At} \mod q$.*

2.4 Trapdoor Functions

A *trapdoor function* [18,28,41] refers to a type of mathematical function that is simple to evaluate in one direction but becomes hard to reverse without access to a specific key, known as the *trapdoor*. The trapdoor is typically a secret key that is used to enable efficient computation of the function in the reverse direction. Trapdoor functions play a crucial role in lattice-based cryptography, where they are used to produce a secret key and public key pair for both encryption and digital signature schemes. In a typical lattice-based signature scheme, the signer generates a random lattice and applies a trapdoor function to it to obtain a public key. The trapdoor enables the signer to efficiently generate a secret key that can be used to sign messages. Trapdoor functions with preimage sampling are determined by three PPT algorithms (TrapGen, SampleDom, SamplePre).

- $(a,t) \leftarrow \text{TrapGen}(1^n)$: Given the security parameter this algorithm outputs the pair (a,t), where a is the description of a function $f_a : D_n \to R_n$ and t is a trapdoor for the function f_a.
- $x \leftarrow \text{SampleDom}(1^n)$: Given the security parameter, this algorithm samples x from D_n in such a way that $f_a(x)$ is uniformly distributed over R_n.
- $x \leftarrow \text{SamplePre}(t,y)$: For every $y \in R_n$ this algorithm sample from a conditional distribution of $x \leftarrow$SampleDom(1^n) such that $f_a(x) = y$.

To proceed with construction, we refer to the result by Ajtai [3], which demonstrates a method for sampling an approximately uniform matrix $\mathbf{A} \in \mathbb{Z}_q^{n\times m}$ and simultaneously generating a short, full-rank trapdoor set of lattice vectors $\mathbf{S} \subseteq \mathcal{L}^\perp(\mathbf{A})$.

Proposition 1. *Let q be a prime number, and let m and n be two positive integers such that $m \geq 5n \log q$. Then, there exists a probabilistic polynomial time* (PPT) *algorithm that outputs a matrix $\mathbf{A} \in \mathbb{Z}_q^{n\times m}$ and a full-rank set $\mathbf{T} \subseteq \mathcal{L}^{\perp}(\mathbf{A})$ based on the input security parameter n. The distribution of $\mathbf{A}$ is uniform over $\mathbb{Z}_q^{n\times m}$, and the norm $\|\mathbf{T}\| \leq L = m^{2.5}$.*

Construction of Trapdoor Function Using SIS: Let q, m, and L be as defined in Proposition 1. The collection of trapdoor functions with preimage sampling are determined by a Gaussian parameter $s \geq L \cdot \omega(\sqrt{\log m})$. The construction is described as follows:

1. The pair $(\mathbf{A}, \mathbf{T})$ is selected based on the criteria outlined in the Proposition 1.
2. The matrix $\mathbf{A}$ defines a function $f_{\mathbf{A}}$ such that $f_{\mathbf{A}}(\mathbf{e}) = \mathbf{Ae} \mod q$, where $D_n = \{\mathbf{e} \in \mathbb{Z}^m : \|\mathbf{e}\| \leq s\sqrt{m}\}$ is the domain and $R_n = \mathbb{Z}_q^n$ is the range.
3. Given a tuple $(\mathbf{A}, \mathbf{T}, s, \mathbf{u})$, the task is to find a solution to the equation $\mathbf{At} = \mathbf{u} \mod q$. According to Lemma 1, such a vector $\mathbf{t}$ can be selected. Once this is done, sample $\mathbf{v}$ from the distribution $D_{\mathcal{L}^{\perp}(\mathbf{A}),s,-\mathbf{t}}$ and then produce the solution $\mathbf{e} = \mathbf{t} + \mathbf{v}$.

Theorem 1. *If the* $\mathsf{ISIS}_{q,m,\beta=2s\sqrt{m}}$ *problem is hard, then the construction described above will form a collection of trapdoor functions.*

2.5 The GPV Signature

The GPV signature scheme, introduced by Gentry, Peikert, and Vaikuntanathan [18], is a lattice-based cryptographic signature scheme. It serves as a modified version of the traditional Fiat-Shamir signature scheme and depends on the computational difficulty of the *Short Integer Solution* (SIS) problem in lattice-based cryptography.

Construction: Let $n \in \mathbb{N}$ be a security parameter. A *collision-resistant* hash function $H = H_n : \{0,1\}^* \rightarrow R_n$ has been used to model it as a random oracle. The GPV signature has three algorithms KeyGen, Sign and Verification as discussed below:

- (pk,sk) $\leftarrow$ KeyGen(1^n):
  1. The signer runs the TrapGen algorithm and receives the pair (a, t), where t is its trapdoor and a is the description of the function f_a (see Subsect. 2.4).
  2. Public key pk $= a$ and secret key sk $= t$.
- $(\sigma) \leftarrow$ Sign(sk, msg):
  1. Parse sk $= t$.
  2. The signer computes $H(msg)$.
  3. Generates $\sigma \leftarrow$ SamplePre$(t, H(msg))$.
- $(0/1) \leftarrow$ Verification(msg, a, σ):
  1. Parse pk $= a$.

2. If $\sigma \notin D_n$ output $\perp$.
3. Else computes $f_a(\sigma)$.
4. If $f_a(\sigma) = H(msg)$, output 1 else output 0.

Theorem 2. *Based on the belief that the Short Integer Solution* (SIS) *problem is difficult to solve, the GPV scheme guarantees existential unforgeability against chosen message attacks (EUF-CMA).*

2.6 Undeniable Signature Scheme

In our work, we adhere to the definition of undeniable signatures as outlined in [21,23].

Definition 5. ***Undeniable signature****. An undeniable signature scheme is a tuple of polynomial-time algorithms* (KeyGen, Sign, Confirmation, Disavowal)*. Let $n \in \mathbb{N}$ be a security parameter. This scheme entails interactions between the signer (S) and the verifier (V).*

- $(pk, sk) \leftarrow \mathsf{KeyGen}(1^n)$*: Given the security parameter n as input, the algorithm produces a signing key (secret key) sk and a verification key (public key) pk.*
- $\sigma \leftarrow \mathsf{Sign}(msg, sk)$*: This algorithm takes (msg, sk) as inputs and generates a signature σ.*
- $(0/1) \leftarrow \mathsf{Verification}(\sigma, msg)$*: It consists two subprotocols:*
  1. $(0/1) \leftarrow \mathsf{Confirmation}(\sigma, msg)$*: Through the protocol, the signer S can prove the validity of the signature σ to the verifier V. This interactive process returns 1 if the signature is confirmed as valid; otherwise, it returns 0.*
  2. $(0/1) \leftarrow \mathsf{Disavowal}(\sigma, msg)$*: This protocol is designed to allow a verifier to determine whether a given signature is invalid. The interactive process will return a value of 1 if the signature is determined to be invalid, and 0 if it is valid.*

Security Properties for Undeniable Signature Scheme: The confirmation and disavowal protocols must be complete, sound, and zero-knowledge. The entire protocol should satisfy unforgeability and invisibility. We follow the security properties from [21,31].

- Completeness: If the signature σ is valid, then the probability of a successful confirmation for any message msg with a valid signature σ is 1. Similarly, if σ is found to be invalid, the probability of a successful disavowal is also 1.
- Soundness: In the case where the signer S is acting dishonestly, the probability of a successful confirmation when processing any message msg with an invalid signature σ is negligible. Similarly, if σ is determined to be valid for a dishonest Signer S, the probability of a successful disavowal is also negligible.

- Zero-knowledge: If the signature σ is valid, the verifier gains no knowledge about the secret other than the fact that the statement is true.
- Unforgeability: The notion of unforgeability in the context of an undeniable signature scheme is defined through a game played by a challenger ($\mathcal{C}$) and an adversary ($\mathcal{A}$).
  1. The challenger $\mathcal{C}$ runs the KeyGen algorithm and provides the adversary $\mathcal{A}$ with the verification key pk.
  2. $\mathcal{A}$ is allowed to make adaptive signing oracle queries for messages msg^i, for all $i \in \{1, \ldots, q\}$. For each signing query, $\mathcal{C}$ responds with a signature σ^i computed using the Sign algorithm. Furthermore, $\mathcal{A}$ can access the confirmation/disavowal protocol for each received signature σ^i.
  3. Finally, $\mathcal{A}$ responds with a forge message-signature pair (msg^*, σ^*).
  4. $\mathcal{A}$ wins if (msg^*, σ^*) is valid and msg^* is not equal to the messages queried before in the singing query phase.

  The scheme is considered *existentially unforgeable* under the chosen message attack (EUF-CMA) if the probability that any polynomial-time adversary $\mathcal{A}$ succeeds in the aforementioned scenario is negligible.
- Invisibility: This property can be described by a game between a challenger $\mathcal{C}$ and an adversary $\mathcal{A}$.
  1. The challenger $\mathcal{C}$ runs the KeyGen algorithm and provides the adversary $\mathcal{A}$ with the verification key pk.
  2. $\mathcal{A}$ can issue a series of signing oracle queries for some message msg^i and receives some signature σ^i. $\mathcal{A}$ is allowed to access the confirmation/disavowal oracle for each received signature σ^i.
  3. Eventually, $\mathcal{A}$ selects a message msg^* and forwards it to $\mathcal{C}$.
  4. $\mathcal{C}$ selects $b \in \{0, 1\}$ randomly. For $b = 1$, it computes the *real* signature σ^* for msg^* using the secret key sk. Otherwise, it outputs a fake signature and sets it as σ^* for msg^*.
  5. $\mathcal{A}$ can continue singing oracle queries. Here $\mathcal{A}$ does not have access to the confirmation/Disavowal oracle.
  6. Finally, $\mathcal{A}$ outputs a bit $b' \in \{0, 1\}$.
  7. If $b = b'$, then $\mathcal{A}$ wins.

  The signature scheme attains the *invisibility* property if the probability that any polynomial-time adversary $\mathcal{A}$ succeeds in the previously described game is negligible.

2.7 Module Lattice

A module lattice [4] with a polynomial structure is a type of lattice in which the basis vectors are polynomials with integer coefficients. This lattice naturally arises in the context of polynomial ring extensions, where it is constructed over a polynomial ring. The polynomial rings are defined as $\mathcal{R} = \mathbb{Z}[X]/(X^n + 1)$ and $\mathcal{R}_q = \mathbb{Z}_q[X]/(X^n + 1)$, where q is a prime number and n is an integer power of 2.

Ideal Lattice: Let $\mathcal{R} = \mathbb{Z}[X]/(f)$ be a quotient ring, where f is a degree n irreducible polynomial over $\mathbb{Z}[X]$. Ideal lattices correspond to the ideals of the ring $\mathcal{R}$. Notably, the quotient ring $\mathcal{R}$ is isomorphic to the ring $\mathbb{Z}^n$ with each polynomial mapped to an n-dimensional vector composed of its coefficients. Given an ideal $\mathcal{I}$ of $\mathcal{R}$, the sublattice of $\mathbb{Z}^n$ that corresponds to $\mathcal{I}$ is called an ideal lattice. In short, if B is a basis of an ideal lattice, then $\mathcal{L}(B) \subset \mathbb{Z}^n$.

Module Lattice: Module lattices are sublattices of $\mathcal{R}^k$ for some positive integer k. It is important to note that if $\mathcal{R} = \mathbb{Z}[X]/(X^n + 1)$, then $\mathcal{R}^k$ is isomorphic to $\mathbb{Z}^{kn}$. The module versions of Ring-SIS and Ring-LWE were first presented in [24].

Definition 6. ***Shortest Integer Solution Problem for Module Lattice.*** Module-SIS$_{l,k,q,\gamma}$: *Given a matrix* $\mathbf{A} \in \mathcal{R}_q^{l\times k}$, *an integer* q, *and a real number* γ, *the goal is to find a non-zero vector* $\mathbf{s} \in \mathcal{R}^k$ *such that* $\mathbf{As} = \mathbf{0} \mod q$ *and* $||\mathbf{s}|| \leq \gamma$.

Definition 7. ***Decisional Learning with Errors for Module Lattices.*** Decision Module-LWE$_{l,k,q,\gamma}$: *Consider a matrix* $\mathbf{A} \in \mathcal{R}_q^{l\times k}$, *an integer* q, *and a real number* γ. *Let* $\mathbf{b} = \mathbf{As} + \mathbf{e} \mod q$, *where* $\mathbf{s}$ *is chosen uniformly at random from* $\mathcal{R}^k$ *and* $\mathbf{e}$ *is sampled from the discrete Gaussian distribution* $D_{\mathcal{R}^l,\gamma}$. *The problem is to distinguish between the distribution* $(\mathbf{A}, \mathbf{b})$ *and the uniform distribution over* $\mathcal{R}_q^{l\times k} \times \mathcal{R}_q^l$.

2.8 Building Trapdoor Function for Module Lattice

In this section, we outline the procedure for constructing a trapdoor function on module lattices, based on the works of [4,28]. We recall the representations of k-dimensional q-array lattice $\mathcal{L}^{\perp}(\mathbf{A})$ and its coset $\mathcal{L}^{\mathbf{u}}(\mathbf{A})$ for a matrix $\mathbf{A} \in \mathcal{R}^{l\times k}$ at first.

$$\mathcal{L}^{\perp}(\mathbf{A}) = \{\mathbf{x} \in \mathcal{R}^k : \mathbf{Ax} = \mathbf{0} \mod q\}.$$
$$\mathcal{L}^{\mathbf{u}}(\mathbf{A}) = \{\mathbf{x} \in \mathcal{R}^k : \mathbf{Ax} = \mathbf{u} \mod q\}.$$

Ring G-Lattice: The ring gadget vector is defined by,

$$\mathbf{y}^T = [1 \ \ a \ \ a^2 \ \dots \ a^{m-1}] \in \mathcal{R}_q^{1\times m}, \quad \text{where } m = \lceil \log_a q \rceil.$$

The *Ring G-Lattice* is the q-array lattice,

$$\mathcal{L}^{\perp}(\mathbf{y}^T) = \{\mathbf{x} \in \mathcal{R}^m : \mathbf{y}^T\mathbf{x} = \mathbf{0} \mod q\}.$$

Module G-Lattice: Using the ring gadget vector $\mathbf{y}^T$ we can construct a G-matrix as follows,

$$\mathbf{G} = \mathbf{I}_l \otimes \mathbf{y}^T = \begin{pmatrix} \mathbf{y}^T & & & \\ & \mathbf{y}^T & & \\ & & \ddots & \\ & & & \mathbf{y}^T \end{pmatrix} \in \mathcal{R}_q^{l\times lm}$$

where $\otimes$ is the tensor product between two vectors. The *module G-lattice* is defined by,

$$\mathcal{L}^{\perp}(\mathbf{G}) = \{\mathbf{x} \in \mathcal{R}^{lm} : \mathbf{G}\mathbf{x} = \mathbf{0} \mod q\}.$$

Trapdoor: A trapdoor $\mathbf{T} \in \mathcal{R}^{(k-lm)\times lm}$ for the given matrix $\mathbf{A} \in \mathcal{R}_q^{l\times k}$ can be defined as,

$$\mathbf{A}\left[\frac{\mathbf{T}}{\mathbf{I}_{lm}}\right] = \mathbf{E}\mathbf{G}$$

for some invertible matrix $\mathbf{E} \in \mathcal{R}_q^{l\times l}$, where $k = l(m+2)$. $\mathbf{I}_{lm}$ is the identity matrix of order lm.

Lemma 2. *[4] Let $k = l(m+2)$ with $m = \lceil \log q \rceil$ and q and l be positive integers. From the above algorithm, we have* $\mathsf{MLTrapGen}(\mathbf{E} \in \mathcal{R}_q^{l\times l}, \beta > 0) \rightarrow (\mathbf{A}, \mathbf{T})$. *Then $\mathbf{A}$ is computationally indistinguishable from uniform distribution (over $\mathcal{R}_q^{l\times k}$) based on the hardness assumption of* $\mathsf{Decision\ Module\text{-}LWE}_{l,k,q,\beta}$.

Algorithm 1 $\mathsf{MLTrapGen}(\mathbf{E} \in \mathcal{R}_q^{l\times l}, \beta > 0)$ to generate Trapdoor

1: **function** $\mathsf{MLTrapGen}(\mathbf{E} \in \mathcal{R}_q^{l\times l}, \beta > 0)$
2: $\mathbf{B} \leftarrow \mathcal{U}(\mathcal{R}_q^{l\times l})$ $\triangleright \mathbf{B} \in \mathcal{R}_q^{l\times l}$
3: $\mathbf{B}' \leftarrow [\mathbf{I}_l \mid \mathbf{B}]$ $\triangleright \mathbf{B}' \in \mathcal{R}_q^{l\times 2l}$
4: $\mathbf{T} \leftarrow D_{\mathcal{R}^{2l\times lm},\beta}$ $\triangleright \mathbf{T} \in \mathcal{R}^{2l\times lm}$
5: $\mathbf{A} \leftarrow [\mathbf{B}' \mid \mathbf{E}\mathbf{G} - \mathbf{B}'\mathbf{T}]$ $\triangleright \mathbf{A} \in \mathcal{R}_q^{l\times k}$
6: **return** $(\mathbf{A}, \mathbf{T})$

Algorithm 2 $\mathsf{MLSamplePre}(\mathbf{A}, \mathbf{T}, \mathbf{E}, \mathbf{w} \in \mathcal{R}_q^l, \chi, \alpha)$ for sampling Gaussian preimage

1: **function** $\mathsf{MLSamplePre}(\mathbf{A} \in \mathcal{R}_q^{l\times k}, \mathbf{T} \in \mathcal{R}^{2l\times lm}, \mathbf{E} \in \mathcal{R}_q^{l\times l}, \mathbf{w} \in \mathcal{R}_q^l, \chi, \alpha)$
2: $\mathbf{p} \leftarrow \mathsf{SamplePerturb}(\mathbf{T}, \chi, \alpha)$ $\triangleright \mathbf{p} \in \mathcal{R}^k$
3: $\mathbf{z} \leftarrow \mathbf{E}^{-1}(\mathbf{w} - \mathbf{A}\mathbf{p})$ $\triangleright \mathbf{z} \in \mathcal{R}^l$
4: $\mathbf{d} \leftarrow D_{\mathcal{L}^{\mathbf{z}}(\mathbf{G}),\alpha}$ $\triangleright \mathbf{d} \in \mathcal{R}^{lm}$
5: $\mathbf{u} \leftarrow \mathbf{p} + \left[\frac{\mathbf{T}}{\mathbf{I}}\right]\mathbf{d}$ $\triangleright \mathbf{u} \in \mathcal{R}^k$
6: **return** $\mathbf{u}$

2.9 Gaussian Preimage Sampling

We discuss the Gaussian preimage sampling technique for module lattices, referred to as $\mathsf{MLSamplePre}$ [4]. This sampling technique consists of two underlying algorithms: **G-sampling** and **Perturbation sampling**.

G-Sampling: The primary objective of G-sampling is to take a vector $\mathbf{w} \in \mathcal{R}_q^l$ and output a vector $\mathbf{u} \in \mathcal{R}^k$ from $\mathcal{L}^{\mathbf{w}}(\mathbf{G})$ by following a discrete Gaussian distribution with Gaussian parameter α, where $\mathbf{G}$ is the G-matrix defined in Subsect. 2.8. The construction is detailed in [4,16]. Specifically, let $\mathbf{z} = \mathbf{E}^{-1}\mathbf{w}$. We then sample $\mathbf{d}$ from the discrete Gaussian distribution $D_{\mathcal{L}^{\mathbf{z}}(\mathbf{G}),\alpha}$ and output $\mathbf{u} = \left[\frac{\mathbf{T}}{\mathbf{I}}\right]\mathbf{d}$. However, this process may leak some information about the trapdoor $\mathbf{T}$, which is why the **Perturbation sampling** algorithm has been introduced.

Perturbation Sampling: Perturbation sampling techniques are designed to produce random values that are statistically indistinguishable from truly random values. This means that an observer should be unable to differentiate between the generated values and genuine random values, even with substantial computational power or knowledge of the sampling algorithm. For module lattices [4], perturbation sampling involves drawing a vector from the Gaussian distribution over $\mathcal{R}^k$. We refer to this algorithm as SamplePerturb, which takes the trapdoor $\mathbf{T}$ and two parameters, χ and α, as inputs. It outputs a perturbation vector $\mathbf{p} \in \mathcal{R}^k$ such that when $\mathbf{p}$ is added to $\left[\frac{\mathbf{T}}{\mathbf{I}}\right]\mathbf{d}$, no information about $\mathbf{T}$ can be determined.

Lemma 3. *[4] Let $\mathbf{T} \in \mathcal{R}^{2l\times lm}$ be a trapdoor for the matrix $\mathbf{A} \in \mathcal{R}_q^{l\times k}$ with tag $\mathbf{E} \in \mathcal{R}_q^{l\times l}$, $\mathbf{w} \in \mathcal{R}_q^l$ a target vector, and χ and α Gaussian parameters satisfying the given constraints. Then, SamplePre$(\mathbf{A}, \mathbf{T}, \mathbf{E}, \mathbf{w}, \chi, \alpha)$ outputs a vector whose distribution is statistically close to $D_{\mathcal{L}_q^{\mathbf{w}}(\mathbf{A}),\chi}$.*

3 Proposed Undeniable Signature Scheme on Module Lattice

In this section, we present our proposed undeniable signature scheme based on module lattices. Our approach involves three main algorithms: MLKeyGen, MLSign, and MLVerification. The MLVerification algorithm includes two subprotocols: confirmation and disavowal. The public key-secret key pair (PK, SK) can be generated by the signer using the MLKeyGen algorithm. In the MLSign algorithm, the signer produces a signature σ for a given message msg. During the MLVerification algorithm, the verifier checks the validity of the message-signature pair (msg, σ) using either the confirmation or the disavowal protocol. A detailed explanation of each component is provided below:

Parameters: Let n be a security parameter. $q = poly(n)$ and the size of q is $m = \lceil \log q \rceil$. β, χ, α are Gaussian parameters. t, s, l, k are positive integers with $k = l(m+2)$. We need two cryptographically secure collision-resistance hash functions: $h : \{0,1\}^* \to \mathcal{R}_q^l$ and $h_1 : \{0,1\}^* \to \mathcal{R}_q^{l\times k}$.

- $(\mathsf{PK}, \mathsf{SK}) \leftarrow \mathsf{MLKeyGen}(1^n)$: This randomized key generation algorithm runs by the signer.
  1. The signer runs the MLTrapGen$(\mathbf{I}, \beta)$ algorithm to generate a pair $(\mathbf{A}, \mathbf{T})$, where $\mathbf{A} \in \mathcal{R}_q^{l\times k}$, $\mathbf{T} \in \mathcal{R}^{2l\times lm}$ and $\mathbf{I}$ is the identity matrix of order l.
  2. Chooses $\mathbf{L}$ randomly from $\mathcal{R}_q^{l\times k}$.
  3. Selects $\mathbf{v}$ from $D_{\mathcal{R}^k,\beta}$ and computes $\mathbf{H} = \mathbf{L}\mathbf{v} \mod q$.

  This algorithm outputs the public key and secret key pair of the signer, where the public key $\mathsf{PK} = (\mathbf{A}, \mathbf{L}, \mathbf{H})$ and the secret key $\mathsf{SK} = (\mathbf{T}, \mathbf{v})$.
- $\sigma \leftarrow \mathsf{MLSign}(msg, \mathsf{SK})$: This randomized algorithm generates a signature σ for a given message. This algorithm runs by the signer.
  1. Computes $h_1(msg) = \mathbf{M} \in \mathcal{R}_q^{l\times k}$.
  2. Chooses $\mathbf{r}$ randomly from $\{0,1\}^*$.

3. Calculates $h(\mathbf{H} \parallel \mathbf{r}) = \mathbf{w} \in \mathcal{R}_q^l$.
4. Runs the MLSamplePre algorithm and calculates MLSamplePre$(\mathbf{A}, \mathbf{T}, \mathbf{I}, \mathbf{w}, \chi, \alpha) = \sigma_1$.
5. Generates $\sigma_2 = \mathbf{Mv} \mod q$.

The algorithm outputs a signature $\sigma = (\mathbf{r}, \sigma_1, \sigma_2)$ for the message msg.

- $(0/1) \leftarrow$ MLVerification $(msg, \sigma, \mathsf{PK})$: This verification algorithm involves of two algorithms: the Confirmation and the Disavowal protocol. Before initiating those protocols, the verifier will first verify σ_1 as follows:
  1. Check whether $\|\sigma_1\| \leq t\chi\sqrt{kn}$.
  2. Verifies $\mathbf{A}\sigma_1 = h(\mathbf{H} \parallel r) \mod q$.

  In Confirmation or Disavowal, the verifier only proves the correctness of σ_2. Note that the verifier can compute $\mathbf{M}$ using the message msg respectively.

  Confirmation/Disavowal: This protocol runs between the signer and the verifier as follows:
  1. The signer randomly chooses $\mathbf{e}$ from $\mathcal{R}^k$ and a permutation ϕ over the set $\{1, \ldots, k\}$.
  2. It computes $\mathbf{j} = \mathbf{Me} \mod q$.
  3. Evaluates three commitments $comm_1 = h(\phi||(\mathbf{L} + \mathbf{M})\mathbf{e} \mod q)$, $comm_2 = h(\phi(\mathbf{e}))$ and $comm_3 = h(\phi(\mathbf{v} + \mathbf{e}))$.
  4. The signer outputs $comm_1$, $comm_2$ and $comm_3$ as commitments.
  5. As a challenge the verifier outputs $ch \in \{0, 1, 2\}$.
  6. If $ch = 0$, the signer responses $\phi(\mathbf{v})$ and $\phi(\mathbf{e})$.
     If $ch = 1$, it responses ϕ, $\mathbf{v} + \mathbf{e}$ and $\mathbf{j}$.
     If $ch = 2$, it responses ϕ, $\mathbf{e}$.
  7. The verifier performs the verification as follows:
     i. For $ch = 0$, the verifier first checks if $\|\phi(\mathbf{v})\| \leq \beta$ and verifies the correctness of $comm_2$ and $comm_3$.
     ii. For $ch = 1$, the verifier first checks if the condition $\mathbf{M}(\mathbf{v}+\mathbf{e}) - \mathbf{j} = \sigma_2$ is satisfied. If this condition holds, the verifier proceeds with the following steps:
        - It checks the correctness of $comm_3$.
        - Confirmation: The interaction protocol is termed a Confirmation protocol if $comm_1 = h(\phi||(\mathbf{L} + \mathbf{M})(\mathbf{v} + \mathbf{e}) - \mathbf{H} - \sigma_2 \mod q)$.
        - Disavowal: If $comm_1 \neq h(\phi||(\mathbf{L} + \mathbf{M})(\mathbf{v} + \mathbf{e}) - \mathbf{H} - \sigma_2 \mod q)$, it is referred to as a Disavowal protocol.
     iii. Finally, for $ch = 2$ the verifier checks the validity of $comm_1$ and $comm_2$.

  The verifier outputs 1 after a successful verification; otherwise, it outputs 0.

4 Security

We analyze our proposed scheme's security in this part. We demonstrate that the confirmation and disavowal protocols within our construction are both complete and sound, and uphold zero-knowledge. Additionally, we show that the protocol meets the unforgeability and invisibility criteria.

4.1 Zero-Knowledge Proof of Confirmation and Disavowal Protocol

Theorem 3. *The* confirmation *and* disavowal *protocol in our proposed scheme are complete.*

Proof. Let the signature $\sigma = (\mathbf{r}, \sigma_1, \sigma_2)$ be valid for a message msg. Hence, for any $\mathbf{e} \in \mathcal{R}^k$ and any permutation ϕ over the set $\{1, \ldots, k\}$, the following holds:

- $\mathbf{M}(\mathbf{v} + \mathbf{e}) - \mathbf{j} = \sigma_2$.
- $comm_1 = h(\phi || (\mathbf{L} + \mathbf{M})(\mathbf{v} + \mathbf{e}) - \mathbf{H} - \sigma_2 \mod q) = h(\phi || (\mathbf{L} + \mathbf{M})\mathbf{e} \mod q)$.
- $comm_3 = h(\phi(\mathbf{v} + \mathbf{e})) = h(\phi(\mathbf{v}) + \phi(\mathbf{e}))$.

Therefore, the confirmation protocol executes successfully.

Now, let σ_1 be valid during verification, while σ_2 is invalid for a message msg. Then, for a chosen $\mathbf{e}$ and ϕ, the following holds:

- $\mathbf{M}(\mathbf{v} + \mathbf{e}) - \mathbf{j} = \sigma_2$.
- $comm_1 = h(\phi || (\mathbf{L} + \mathbf{M})(\mathbf{v} + \mathbf{e}) - \mathbf{H} - \sigma_2 \mod q) \neq h(\phi || (\mathbf{L} + \mathbf{M})\mathbf{e} \mod q)$.
- $comm_3 = h(\phi(\mathbf{v} + \mathbf{e})) = h(\phi(\mathbf{v}) + \phi(\mathbf{e}))$.

Therefore, the disavowal protocol executes successfully. □

Theorem 4. *The probability of successfully executing the* confirmation *protocol with an invalid σ_2 is negligible.*

Proof. We consider the scenario where σ_2 is invalid, i.e., $\sigma_2 \neq \mathbf{M}\mathbf{v} \mod q$. For the confirmation protocol to execute successfully, the verifier must validate the responses given by the signer to the corresponding challenges. The signer responds as follows:

1. If $ch = 0$, the signer selects ϕ_1 over the set $\{1, \ldots, k\}$, $\mathbf{e}_1 \in \mathcal{R}^k$ and responses as $\phi_1(\mathbf{v})$ and $\phi_1(\mathbf{e}_1)$.
2. If $ch = 1$, it selects ϕ_2 over $\{1, \ldots, k\}$, $\mathbf{e}_2 \in \mathcal{R}^k$ and responses as ϕ_2, $\mathbf{v} + \mathbf{e}_2$ and $\mathbf{j} = \mathbf{M}\mathbf{e}_2 \mod q$.
3. If $ch = 2$, it selects ϕ_3 over $\{1, \ldots, k\}$, $\mathbf{e}_3 \in \mathcal{R}^k$ and responses as ϕ_3 and $\mathbf{e}_3$.

We consider the following cases based on the challenge ch:

$ch = 0$: In this case, $comm_1 = h(\phi_1 || (\mathbf{L} + \mathbf{M})\mathbf{e}_1 \mod q)$, $comm_2 = h(\phi_1(\mathbf{e}_1))$, and $comm_3 = h(\phi_1(\mathbf{v} + \mathbf{e}_1))$. The verifier checks correctness of $comm_2$, $comm_3$ and verifies $\|\phi_1(\mathbf{v})\| \leq \beta$.

$ch = 1$: In this case, $comm_1 = h(\phi_2 || (\mathbf{L} + \mathbf{M})\mathbf{e}_2 \mod q)$, $comm_2 = h(\phi_2(\mathbf{e}_2))$, and $comm_3 = h(\phi_2(\mathbf{v} + \mathbf{e}_2))$. Here, the verifier checks $comm_1$ and $comm_3$. First, the verifier verifies if $\mathbf{M}(\mathbf{v} + \mathbf{e}_2) - \mathbf{j} = \sigma_2$ holds. Next, the verifier checks $comm_3$, which can also be verified without issue. For $comm_1$, the verifier checks if $h(\phi_2 || (\mathbf{L} + \mathbf{M})(\mathbf{v} + \mathbf{e}_2) - \mathbf{H} - \sigma_2 \mod q)$ equals $comm_1$. However, $(\mathbf{L} + \mathbf{M})(\mathbf{v} + \mathbf{e}_2) - \mathbf{H} - \sigma_2 \mod q = (\mathbf{M} + \mathbf{L})\mathbf{e}_2 + \mathbf{M}\mathbf{v} - \sigma_2 \mod q \neq comm_1$ ($\because \sigma_2 \neq \mathbf{M}\mathbf{v} \mod q$). Thus, in this case, verification fails.

ch = 2: In this case, $comm_1 = h(\phi_3||(\mathbf{L}+\mathbf{M})\mathbf{e}_3 \mod q)$, $comm_2 = h(\phi_3(\mathbf{e}_3))$, and $comm_3 = h(\phi_3(\mathbf{v}+\mathbf{e}_3))$. Here, the verifier checks $comm_1$ and $comm_2$. With the given information, the verifier can compute both $comm_1$ and $comm_2$ correctly.

Hence, for one round, the probability of successfully completing the confirmation protocol with an invalid σ_2 is $\frac{2}{3}$. If the protocol runs for n rounds, the probability becomes $(\frac{2}{3})^n$, which is a negligible function of n. □

Theorem 5. *The probability of successfully executing the* disavowal *protocol is negligible if* σ_2 *is valid.*

Proof. We consider two scenarios: 1) for an honest signer and 2) for a dishonest signer to prove this theorem. Suppose a valid signature σ_2 is generated by an honest signer, i.e., $\sigma_2 = \mathbf{Mv} \mod q$. The verifier's task is to validate σ_2 through interactions with the signer. In the case of an honest signer, the responses are as follows:

1. If *ch* = 0, the signer selects ϕ_1 over $\{1,\ldots,k\}$, $\mathbf{e}_1 \in \mathcal{R}^k$ and responses as $\phi_1(\mathbf{v})$ and $\phi_1(\mathbf{e}_1)$.
2. If *ch* = 1, it selects ϕ_2 over $\{1,\ldots,k\}$, $\mathbf{e}_2 \in \mathcal{R}^k$ and responses as ϕ_2, $\mathbf{v}+\mathbf{e}_2$ and $\mathbf{j} = \mathbf{Me}_2 \mod q$.
3. If *ch* = 2, it selects ϕ_3 over the set $\{1,\ldots,k\}$, $\mathbf{e}_3 \in \mathcal{R}^k$ and responses as ϕ_3 and $\mathbf{e}_3$.

Verifier's Checks:

ch = 0: In this case, $comm_1 = h(\phi_1||(\mathbf{L}+\mathbf{M})\mathbf{e}_1 \mod q)$, $comm_2 = h(\phi_1(\mathbf{e}_1))$ and $comm_3 = h(\phi_1(\mathbf{v}+\mathbf{e}_1))$. The verifier has to check $comm_2$ and $comm_3$ and verify $\|\phi_1(\mathbf{v})\| \leq \beta$.

ch = 1: In this case, $comm_1 = h(\phi_2||(\mathbf{L}+\mathbf{M})\mathbf{e}_2 \mod q)$, $comm_2 = h(\phi_2(\mathbf{e}_2))$ and $comm_3 = h(\phi_2(\mathbf{v}+\mathbf{e}_2))$. The verifier checks if $\mathbf{M}(\mathbf{v}+\mathbf{e}_2) - \mathbf{j} = \sigma_2$. Since σ_2 is valid and the signer is honest, this holds easily. The verifier can check $comm_3$ without issue. To verify $comm_1$, the verifier checks whether $h(\phi_2||(\mathbf{L}+\mathbf{M})(\mathbf{v}+\mathbf{e}_2) - \mathbf{H} - \sigma_2 \mod q)$ equals $comm_1$. Since $\sigma_2 = \mathbf{Mv} \mod q$, this verification is satisfied.

ch = 2: In this case, $comm_1 = h(\phi_3||(\mathbf{L}+\mathbf{M})\mathbf{e}_3 \mod q)$, $comm_2 = h(\phi_3(\mathbf{e}_3))$ and $comm_3 = h(\phi_3(\mathbf{v}+\mathbf{e}_3))$. In this case, the verifier has to check $comm_1$ and $comm_2$. With the given information, the verifier can compute $comm_1$ and $comm_2$ correctly.

Consequently, for an honest signer, the probability of the disavowal protocol running if σ_2 is legitimate is zero.

Now, let us consider a scenario where a dishonest signer possesses a valid signature σ and attempts to run the disavowal protocol. The signer tries to deceive the verifier into believing that the signature σ is invalid. To do this, during the interaction phase, the signer selects a vector $\mathbf{v}'$ randomly from $D_{\mathcal{R}^k,\beta}$ (distinct from the original vector $\mathbf{v}$) and chooses some random vectors to present challenges and their corresponding responses to the verifier.

In the case of $ch = 1$, note that the relation $\mathbf{M}(\mathbf{v}' + \mathbf{e}_2) - \mathbf{j} = \sigma_2$ does not hold because the signer is dishonest, and σ_2 is valid. Therefore, the dishonest signer cannot successfully run the disavowal protocol, even with a valid σ_2. This completes the proof. □

In [31], the verifier directly executes the confirmation or disavowal protocol without any preliminary verification step that ensures the authenticity of the signer. As a result, a dishonest signer who does not possess the secret key can still perform the disavowal protocol with non-negligible probability for a valid signature. In contrast, our scheme introduces an additional verification layer prior to the confirmation or disavowal phase, which prevents a dishonest signer from successfully executing the disavowal protocol on a valid signature.

Theorem 6. *The* confirmation *and* disavowal *protocols attain statistical zero-knowledge properties.*

Proof. We construct a simulator $\mathcal{S}$ that, using public information, generates a simulated transcript to prove the desired property. Initially, $\mathcal{S}$ randomly selects $\overline{ch} \in \{0, 1, 2\}$, representing a prediction of the value that the cheating verifier $\mathcal{CV}$ will not choose before interacting with $\mathcal{CV}$. We will now discuss each possible case.
$\overline{ch} = 0$: $\mathcal{S}$ computes a vector $\mathbf{v}' \in \mathcal{R}^k$ such that $\mathbf{H} + \sigma_2 = (\mathbf{L} + \mathbf{M})\mathbf{v}' \mod q$. Next, it randomly selects a permutation ϕ' from the set $\{1, \ldots, k\}$ and a vector $\mathbf{e}' \in \mathcal{R}^k$. Finally, $\mathcal{S}$ computes $\mathbf{j}' = \mathbf{M}\mathbf{e}' \mod q$. The corresponding commitments are as follows:

- $comm_1' = h(\phi' || (\mathbf{L} + \mathbf{M})\mathbf{e}' \mod q)$
- $comm_2' = h(\phi'(\mathbf{e}'))$
- $comm_3' = h(\phi'(\mathbf{v}' + \mathbf{e}'))$

$\mathcal{S}$ sends all commitments to $\mathcal{CV}$. Then, $\mathcal{CV}$ outputs a challenge $ch \in \{0, 1, 2\}$. The subsequent responses from $\mathcal{S}$ are:

1. For ch =0, $\mathcal{S}$ outputs $\perp$ and aborts.
2. For $ch = 1$, $\mathcal{S}$ outputs $(comm_1', comm_2', comm_3', \phi', \mathbf{v}' + \mathbf{e}', \mathbf{j}')$.
3. For ch =2, $\mathcal{S}$ outputs $(comm_1', comm_2', comm_3', \phi', \mathbf{e}')$.

When $ch = 1$, the real transcript would be $(comm_1, comm_2, comm_3, \phi, \mathbf{v} + \mathbf{e}, \mathbf{j}')$. We assume that $(\phi', \mathbf{e}') = (\phi, \mathbf{v} + \mathbf{e} - \mathbf{v}')$. Therefore $(\mathbf{L} + \mathbf{M})(\mathbf{v} + \mathbf{e} - \mathbf{v}') = (\mathbf{L} + \mathbf{M})\mathbf{e}$ and we can say that, $comm_1' = comm_1$ and $comm_3' = comm_3$. Hence, we can infer that the distributions of the real transcript and the simulated transcript are statistically similar. A similar proof applies for the case when $ch = 2$.

$\overline{ch} = 1$: $\mathcal{S}$ randomly selects a permutation ϕ' from the set $\{1, \ldots, k\}$, along with two vectors $\mathbf{e}'$ and $\mathbf{v}'$ from $\mathcal{R}^k$. The corresponding commitments are:

- $comm_1' = h(\phi' || (\mathbf{L} + \mathbf{M})\mathbf{e}' \mod q)$
- $comm_2' = h(\phi'(\mathbf{e}'))$
- $comm_3' = h(\phi'(\mathbf{v}' + \mathbf{e}'))$

$\mathcal{S}$ sends them to $\mathcal{CV}$. Now $\mathcal{CV}$ outputs $ch \in \{0, 1, 2\}$ as a challenge. The subsequent responses by $\mathcal{S}$ are:

1. For $ch = 0$, $\mathcal{S}$ outputs $(comm'_1, comm'_2, comm'_3, \phi'(\mathbf{v}'), \phi'(\mathbf{e}'))$.
2. For $ch = 1$, $\mathcal{S}$ returns $\perp$ and halts.
3. For $ch = 2$, $\mathcal{S}$ outputs $(comm'_1, comm'_2, comm'_3, \phi', \mathbf{e}')$.

When $ch = 0$, the real transcript would be $(comm_1, comm_2, comm_3, \phi(\mathbf{v}), \phi(\mathbf{e}))$. Let ψ be a permutation over $\{1, \ldots, k\}$ with $\psi(x) = x'$. We set $\phi' = \phi \circ \psi^{-1}$ and $\mathbf{e}' = \psi(\mathbf{e})$. Then we have, $\phi'(\mathbf{e}') = \phi(\mathbf{e})$ and $\phi'(\mathbf{v}') = \phi(\mathbf{v})$. Thus, we can say that the distributions of the real transcript and the simulated transcript are statistically comparable. The case for $ch = 2$ is straightforward.

$\overline{ch} = 2$: We omit the discussion as it can be addressed in a similar manner.

Therefore, we have constructed a simulator $\mathcal{S}$ that can simulate the real transcript with probability $\frac{1}{3} + \mathsf{negl}(n)$. □

Overall Security of Our Proposed Signature Scheme:

Theorem 7. *Our proposed undeniable signature scheme achieves existential unforgeability under a chosen-message attack (EUF-CMA) security in the random oracle model under the hardness of* $\mathsf{Module} - \mathsf{SIS}_{l,k,q,\gamma}$ *and* $\mathsf{Decision\ Module-}\ \mathsf{LWE}_{l,k,q,\beta}$ *where* $\gamma = 2t\chi\sqrt{kn}$.

Proof. We will prove this theorem by contradiction. Suppose there exists an adversary $\mathcal{A}$ that can break the existential unforgeability of the proposed undeniable signature scheme with non-negligible probability. If this is true, then it would imply the ability to solve both the $\mathsf{Decision\ Module} - \mathsf{LWE}_{l,k,q,\beta}$ and $\mathsf{Module} - \mathsf{SIS}_{l,k,q,\gamma}$ problems, where $\gamma = 2t\chi\sqrt{kn}$. The adversary $\mathcal{A}$ is given the public key (PK) and is allowed to make a polynomial number of queries to the hash oracle and the signature oracle before producing a forged message-signature pair.

1. If the pair $(msg, \mathbf{M})$ already exists in the database, the challenger returns the same output value. Otherwise, it generates new output using the hash function and stores it in the database.
2. Whenever $\mathcal{A}$ submits a sign query for a message msg', the challenger first checks if the corresponding signature $\sigma_{msg'}$ is already in the database. If so, the challenger responds with $\sigma_{msg'}$. Otherwise, the signature is generated by executing the MLSign algorithm and returned along with the corresponding signature.

At some point $\mathcal{A}$ outputs a forge signature σ^* for some message msg^*. The challenger parses the signature as $\sigma^* = (r^*, \sigma_1^*, \sigma_2^*)$. Note that in the construction, r^* and σ_1^* are independent of the message. Therefore, two cases can happen:

- r^* and σ_1^* are different from the queried database. This would be a forgery on the standalone GPV signature scheme based on module lattice and it admits *unforgeability* under the hardness of $\mathsf{Module} - \mathsf{SIS}_{l,k,q,\gamma}$ and $\mathsf{Decision\ Module}$ $-\mathsf{LWE}_{l,k,q,\beta}$ (see [4]).

- If r^* and σ_1^* match a previously queried signature, then only σ_2^* has been forged. In this case, $\sigma_2^* = \mathbf{M}^*\mathbf{v}^* \mod q$ for some $\mathbf{v}^*$, where $\mathbf{M}^* = h_1(msg^*)$. The original signature for the message msg^* is $\sigma_2 = \mathbf{M}^*\mathbf{v} \mod q$. Therefore from MLVerification, $(\mathbf{L}+\mathbf{M}^*)\mathbf{e} \mod q = (\mathbf{L}+\mathbf{M}^*)(\mathbf{v}+\mathbf{e}) - \mathbf{H} - \sigma_2^* \mod q$. This implies $\mathbf{M}^*\mathbf{v}^* = \mathbf{M}^*\mathbf{v} \mod q$, where $\|\mathbf{v} - \mathbf{v}^*\| \leq 2t\chi\sqrt{kn}$. Therefore, an attacker can be constructed using $\mathcal{A}$, enabling them to break the security of the inhomogeneous Module-$\mathsf{SIS}_{l,k,q,\gamma}$ on input σ_2^* and $\mathbf{M}^*$.

Therefore our scheme attains *existential unforgeablility* under the chosen message attack under the hardness of Module − $\mathsf{SIS}_{l,k,q,\gamma}$ and Decision Module − $\mathsf{LWE}_{l,k,q,\beta}$ where $\gamma = 2t\chi\sqrt{kn}$. □

Theorem 8. *Our proposed undeniable signature scheme satisfies the* invisibility *property.*

Proof. The signature σ in our proposed scheme consists of three components: $\mathbf{r}$, σ_1, and σ_2. The challenger $\mathcal{C}$ first runs the MLKeyGen algorithm and sends the public key (PK) to the adversary $\mathcal{A}$. The adversary may then submit signing oracle queries for certain messages msg^i and receive the corresponding signatures σ^i. Furthermore, the confirmation and disavowal oracles are accessible to $\mathcal{A}$. Eventually, $\mathcal{A}$ comes with a challenge message msg^*, and the challenger proceeds as follows:

- The value of σ_1 is computed, as in the original undeniable signature scheme, using PK and the specific parameter $\mathbf{T}$ from the secret key (SK).
- A vector $\mathbf{v}'' \neq \mathbf{v}$ is sampled from $D_{\mathcal{R}^k,\beta}$, and $\sigma_2'' = \mathbf{M}^*\mathbf{v}'' \mod q$ is computed, where $\mathbf{M}^* = h_1(msg^*)$.
- A bit $b \in \{0,1\}$ is randomly chosen. If $b = 1$, the actual signature is produced; otherwise, a fake signature is generated.

In this stage, neither the confirmation nor the disavowal oracles are accessible to $\mathcal{A}$. Therefore, while the adversary can verify σ_1, it cannot verify σ_2''. As both σ_2 (in the real signature) and σ_2'' are uniformly distributed, $\mathcal{A}$ is unable to determine whether σ_2'' is valid. As a result, it cannot correctly guess the value of b, ensuring that the proposed signature scheme achieves the *invisibility* property. □

5 Efficiency

This section analyzes the computation and communication costs associated with our proposed scheme. The computed sizes of the signatures, public keys, and secret keys are shown in Table 1. The public key, denoted as PK, consists of three components: $\mathbf{A}$, $\mathbf{L}$, and $\mathbf{H}$. The size of $\mathbf{r}$ is excluded from Table 1 because it can be generated using a random bit generator. We implemented the scheme using the C programming language to evaluate the practical time complexity of our proposed design. The detailed hardware and software specifications for the experimental setup are provided in Table 2. In Table 3, five parameter sets are

Table 1. Sizes (in bits) of the signature, public key, and secret key

Parameter	Size (in bits)
$\mathbf{A}$	$nlk \log q$
$\mathbf{L}$	$nlk \log q$
$\mathbf{H}$	$nl \log q$
PK	$2nlk \log q + nl \log q = nl(2k+1) \log q$
$\mathbf{T}$	$2l^2mn \log(2\beta\sqrt{n2l^2m})$
$\mathbf{v}$	$nl(m+2) \log q$
SK	$2l^2mn \log(2\beta\sqrt{n2l^2m}) + nl(m+2) \log q$
σ_1	$nk \log(2t\chi\sqrt{kn})$
σ_2	$nl \log q$
$\sigma = (\mathbf{r}, \sigma_1, \sigma_2)$	$nl \log q + nk \log(2t\chi\sqrt{kn})$

presented. Set I corresponds to the ring setting, while the remaining sets pertain to the module setting. Parameter sets I and V are adopted from the work of Bert et al. [4]. Parameters I-IV offer 96-bit quantum security, while V provides 128-bit quantum security. The communication costs associated with these parameter sets are detailed in Table 4. The overall performance of our signature scheme, evaluated using the selected parameter sets, is summarized in Table 5.

Table 2. Specific experimental scenarios for the implementation

Language	C
Processor	AMD Ryzen 5
RAM	8 GB
CPU Frequency	2.1 GHz
Number of Cores	4 cores

Table 3. Parameters for implementation

Parameter set	I	II	III	IV	V
q	1073707009	1073707009	1073707009	1073738753	1073738753
m	30	30	30	30	30
n	1024	512	256	256	256
l	1	2	4	4	5
k	32	64	128	128	160
β	7.00	7.00	7.00	7.00	5.55
χ	83832.0	83832.0	83832.0	83832.0	83290.0
α	48.34	48.34	48.34	48.34	54.35
t	12	12	12	12	14

Table 4. Communication cost for different parameter sets

Parameter set	I	II	III	IV	V
$\mathbf{A}$(KB)	124	25	496	496	775
$\mathbf{L}$(KB)	124	25	496	496	775
$\mathbf{H}$(KB)	4	4	4	4	5
PK(KB)	252	54	996	996	1555
$\mathbf{T}$(KB)	240	480	960	960	1500
$\mathbf{v}$(KB)	124	124	124	124	124
SK(KB)	364	604	1084	1084	1624
σ(KB)	106	106	106	106	132.5

Table 5. CPU cycles and Time taken (ms) for MLKeyGen, MLSign, and MLVerification

Parameter Set	Operation	CPU Cycles	Time Taken (ms)
I	MLKeyGen	93410898	44.29
	MLSign	52855509	25.12
	MLVerification	16500015	7.86
II	MLKeyGen	103719840	49.39
	MLSign	72123429	34.35
	MLVerification	1749862	8.31
III	MLKeyGen	229843257	109.45
	MLSign	104722212	49.87
	MLVerification	18750081	8.93
IV	MLKeyGen	200929911	95.21
	MLSign	107095863	51.00
	MLVerification	17185392	8.18
V	MLKeyGen	322669662	153.13
	MLSign	151808391	72.19
	MLVerification	21853188	10.41

6 Conclusion

A post-quantum undeniable signature scheme is presented in this work, based on the hardness of the Module-SIS and Module-LWE problems. To the best of our knowledge, this is the first undeniable signature scheme based on module lattices. We provide comprehensive proofs for all associated security properties, ensuring the robustness of our approach. Furthermore, we have implemented our protocol in C and tested it across various parameter sets. For a 128-bit security level, the time required by our scheme for key generation, signing, and verification is 153.13 ms, 72.19 ms, and 10.41 ms, respectively. These results highlight the practicality of our scheme in real-world applications. Future work will focus on developing more efficient and secure instantiations, supported by a detailed performance evaluation against the ML-DSA benchmark and an exploration of NTT-based optimizations to minimize communication overhead.

Acknowledgement. The financial assistance of Mansi Goyal is supported by a research fellowship from the CSIR, Govt. of India (09/143(1028)/2020-EMR-I). Additionally, this work was supported in part by the ISEA Phase-III Project funded by MeitY, Govt. of India.

References

1. Aguilar-Melchor, C., Bettaieb, S., Gaborit, P., Schrek, J.: A code-based undeniable signature scheme. In: Cryptography and Coding: 14th IMA International Conference, IMACC 2013, Oxford, UK, 17–19 December 2013. Proceedings 14, pp. 99–119. Springer (2013)
2. Ajtai, M.: Generating hard instances of lattice problems. In: Proceedings of the 28th Annual ACM Symposium on Theory of Computing, pp. 99–108. ACM (1996)
3. Ajtai, M.: Generating hard instances of the short basis problem. In: Automata, Languages and Programming: 26th International Colloquium, ICALP'99 Prague, Czech Republic, July 11–15, 1999 Proceedings 26, pp. 1–9. Springer (1999)
4. Bert, P., Eberhart, G., Prabel, L., Roux-Langlois, A., Sabt, M.: Implementation of lattice trapdoors on modules and applications. In: Post-Quantum Cryptography: 12th International Workshop, PQCrypto 2021, Daejeon, South Korea, July 20–22, 2021, Proceedings 12, pp. 195–214. Springer (2021)
5. Boyar, J., Chaum, D., Damgård, I., Pedersen, T.: Convertible undeniable signatures. In: Conference on the Theory and Application of Cryptography, pp. 189–205. Springer (1990)
6. Cayrel, P.L., Lindner, R., Rückert, M., Silva, R.: A lattice-based threshold ring signature scheme. In: Progress in Cryptology–LATINCRYPT 2010: First International Conference on Cryptology and Information Security in Latin America, Puebla, Mexico, August 8-11, 2010, Proceedings 1, pp. 255–272. Springer (2010)
7. Chaum, D., Van Antwerpen, H.: Undeniable signatures. In: Advances in Cryptology–CRYPTO'89 Proceedings 9, pp. 212–216. Springer (1990)
8. Chi, D.P., Choi, J.W., San Kim, J., Kim, T.: Lattice based cryptography for beginners. Cryptology ePrint Archive (2015)
9. Chuengsatiansup, C., Prest, T., Stehlè, D., Wallet, A., Xagawa, K.: ModFalcon: compact signatures based on module-NTRU lattices. In: Proceedings of the 15th ACM Asia Conference on Computer and Communications Security (ASIA CCS 2020), pp. 853–866. ACM, Association for Computing Machinery, New York, NY, USA (2020). https://doi.org/10.1145/3320269.3384758
10. Damgård, I., Pedersen, T.: New convertible undeniable signature schemes. In: International Conference on the Theory and Applications of Cryptographic Techniques, pp. 372–386. Springer (1996)
11. De Feo, L.: Mathematics of isogeny based cryptography. arXiv preprint arXiv:1711.04062, vol. 12 (2017)
12. Ding, J., Yang, B.Y.: Multivariate public key cryptography. Post-quantum cryptography, pp. 193–241 (2009)

13. Ducas, L., et al.: Crystals-Dilithium: a lattice-based digital signature scheme. IACR Transactions on Cryptographic Hardware and Embedded Systems, pp. 238–268 (2018)
14. Fouque, P.A., et al.: Falcon: fast-fourier lattice-based compact signatures over NTRU. Submission to the NIST's Post-Quantum Cryptography Standardization Process, vol. 36, no. 5 (2018)
15. Galbraith, S.D., Mao, W., Paterson, K.G.: RSA-based undeniable signatures for general moduli. In: Topics in Cryptology—CT-RSA 2002: The Cryptographers' Track at the RSA Conference 2002 San Jose, CA, USA, 18–22 February 2002 Proceedings, pp. 200–217. Springer (2002)
16. Genise, N., Micciancio, D.: Faster gaussian sampling for trapdoor lattices with arbitrary modulus. In: Advances in Cryptology–EUROCRYPT 2018: 37th Annual International Conference on the Theory and Applications of Cryptographic Techniques, Tel Aviv, Israel, April 29-May 3, 2018 Proceedings, Part I 37, pp. 174–203. Springer (2018)
17. Gennaro, R., Rabin, T., Krawczyk, H.: RSA-based undeniable signatures. J. Cryptol. **13**, 397–416 (2000)
18. Gentry, C., Peikert, C., Vaikuntanathan, V.: Trapdoors for hard lattices and new cryptographic constructions. In: Proceedings of the Fortieth Annual ACM Symposium on Theory of Computing, pp. 197–206. ACM (2008)
19. Gordon, S.D., Katz, J., Vaikuntanathan, V.: A group signature scheme from lattice assumptions. In: Advances in Cryptology-ASIACRYPT 2010: 16th International Conference on the Theory and Application of Cryptology and Information Security, Singapore, 5–9 December 2010. Proceedings 16, pp. 395–412. Springer (2010)
20. Hua, L., Han, M., Ma, S., Feng, X.: An undeniable signature scheme based on quasi-dyadic codes. In: 2018 IEEE 3rd Advanced Information Technology, Electronic and Automation Control Conference (IAEAC), pp. 2189–2194. IEEE (2018)
21. Jao, D., Soukharev, V.: Isogeny-based quantum-resistant undeniable signatures. In: International Workshop on Post-Quantum Cryptography, pp. 160–179. Springer (2014)
22. Kawachi, A., Tanaka, K., Xagawa, K.: Concurrently secure identification schemes based on the worst-case hardness of lattice problems. In: Advances in Cryptology-ASIACRYPT 2008: 14th International Conference on the Theory and Application of Cryptology and Information Security, Melbourne, Australia, 7–11 December 2008, Proceedings 14, pp. 372–389. Springer (2008)
23. Kurosawa, K., Furukawa, J.: Universally composable undeniable signature. In: Automata, Languages and Programming: 35th International Colloquium, ICALP 2008, Reykjavik, Iceland, 7–11 July 2008, Proceedings, Part II 35, pp. 524–535. Springer (2008)
24. Langlois, A., Stehlé, D.: Worst-case to average-case reductions for module lattices. Des. Codes Crypt. **75**(3), 565–599 (2015)
25. Lu, X., Au, M.H., Zhang, Z.: Raptor: a practical lattice-based (linkable) ring signature. In: Applied Cryptography and Network Security: 17th International Conference, ACNS 2019, Bogota, Colombia, 5–7 June 2019, Proceedings 17, pp. 110–130. Springer (2019)
26. Lyubashevsky, V., et al.: Crystals-Dilithium. Algorithm Specifications and Supporting Documentation (2020)
27. Lyubashevsky, V., Peikert, C., Regev, O.: On ideal lattices and learning with errors over rings. In: Advances in Cryptology–EUROCRYPT 2010: 29th Annual International Conference on the Theory and Applications of Cryptographic Techniques, French Riviera, May 30–June 3, 2010. Proceedings 29, pp. 1–23. Springer (2010)

28. Micciancio, D., Peikert, C.: Trapdoors for lattices: simpler, tighter, faster, smaller. In: Eurocrypt, vol. 7237, pp. 700–718. Springer (2012)
29. Peikert, C., Rosen, A.: Efficient collision-resistant hashing from worst-case assumptions on cyclic lattices. In: Theory of Cryptography: Third Theory of Cryptography Conference, TCC 2006, New York, NY, USA, 4–7 March 2006. Proceedings 3, pp. 145–166. Springer (2006)
30. Ravi, P., Howe, J., Chattopadhyay, A., Bhasin, S.: Lattice-based key-sharing schemes: a survey. ACM Comput. Surv. (CSUR) **54**(1), 1–39 (2021)
31. Rawal, S., Padhye, S., He, D.: Lattice-based undeniable signature scheme. Ann. Telecommun. **77**(3), 119–126 (2022)
32. Regev, O.: On lattices, learning with errors, random linear codes, and cryptography. J. ACM (JACM) **56**(6), 34 (2009)
33. Schuldt, J.C., Matsuura, K.: An efficient convertible undeniable signature scheme with delegatable verification. In: Information Security, Practice and Experience: 6th International Conference, ISPEC 2010, Seoul, Korea, 12–13 May 2010. Proceedings 6, pp. 276–293. Springer (2010)
34. Seurin, Y.: On the exact security of schnorr-type signatures in the random oracle model. In: Advances in Cryptology–EUROCRYPT 2012: 31st Annual International Conference on the Theory and Applications of Cryptographic Techniques, Cambridge, UK, 15–19 April 2012. Proceedings 31, pp. 554–571. Springer (2012)
35. Shor, P.W.: Polynomial-time algorithms for prime factorization and discrete logarithms on a quantum computer. SIAM Rev. **41**(2), 303–332 (1999)
36. Srinath, M.S., Chandrasekaran, V.: Isogeny-based quantum-resistant undeniable blind signature scheme. Cryptology ePrint Archive (2016)
37. Srivastava, V., Baksi, A., Debnath, S.K.: An overview of hash based signatures. Cryptology ePrint Archive (2023)
38. Stehlé, D., Steinfeld, R., Tanaka, K., Xagawa, K.: Efficient public key encryption based on ideal lattices. In: International Conference on the Theory and Application of Cryptology and Information Security, pp. 617–635. Springer (2009)
39. Stern, J.: A new paradigm for public key identification. IEEE Trans. Inf. Theory **42**(6), 1757–1768 (1996)
40. Weger, V., Gassner, N., Rosenthal, J.: A survey on code-based cryptography. arXiv preprint arXiv:2201.07119 (2022)
41. Yao, A.C.: Theory and application of trapdoor functions. In: 23rd Annual Symposium on Foundations of Computer Science (SFCS 1982), pp. 80–91. IEEE (1982)
42. Zhang, L., Zheng, Z., Wang, W.: Survey of lattice-based group signature. In: Proceedings of the First International Forum on Financial Mathematics and Financial Technology, pp. 79–92. Springer (2021)
43. Zhao, W., Ye, D.: Certificateless undeniable signatures from bilinear maps. Inf. Sci. **199**, 204–215 (2012)

A Witness Encryption for Quadratic Arithmetic Programs

Tao-Hsiang Chang[1,2], Yu-Chen Wu[1], Zi-Yuan Liu[3], Jen-Chieh Hsu[1], Raylin Tso[1(✉)], and Masahiro Mambo[2]

[1] Department of Computer Science, National Chengchi University, Taipei, Taiwan
raylin@cs.nccu.edu.tw

[2] School of Electrical, Information and Communication Engineering, Kanazawa University, Kanazawa, Japan

[3] Department of Information Management, National Central University, Taoyuan, Taiwan

Abstract. Witness Encryption (WE) enables encryption under computational problems where decryption requires knowledge of a valid witness to a nondeterministic polynomial-time (NP) statement. While theoretical constructions exist for all NP languages using complex assumptions like multilinear maps, practical schemes remain limited to specialized relations.

We present the first extractable Witness Key Encapsulation Mechanism (WKEM) for Quadratic Arithmetic Programs (QAPs), the mathematical foundation underlying modern zkSNARKs including Groth16. Our construction transforms Groth16's verification equations into an encryption mechanism, enabling practical witness encryption for rich algebraic relations expressible as arithmetic circuits. We prove extractability in the Algebraic Group Model combined with the Random Oracle Model, providing a clean reduction to Groth16's computational knowledge soundness without requiring novel assumptions. Our WKEM composes generically with symmetric encryption to yield a complete extractable WE scheme for QAP relations.

We validate our construction through a complete implementation with practical performance: circuits with 162–150K constraints achieve encryption/decryption in ~20 ms to ~1.7 s. Our approach bridges the gap between WE theory and practice by building on the mature zkSNARK ecosystem while maintaining strong extractability guarantees.

Keywords: Witness Encryption · Witness Key Encapsulation Mechanism · zkSNARK · Quadratic Arithmetic Programs

1 Introduction

Witness Encryption (WE) is a powerful cryptographic primitive introduced by Garg et al. [18] that allows encryption under computational problems. In a

H. Seo (Ed.): ICISC 2025, LNCS 16487, pp. 533–555, 2026.
https://doi.org/10.1007/978-981-95-8034-7_28

WE scheme, anyone can encrypt a message under a statement x from a nondeterministic polynomial-time (NP) language, but only those possessing a valid witness w such that $(x, w) \in R$ can decrypt the message. This enables programmable encryption where decryption conditions can be defined through computational problems. The applications of witness encryption are diverse and compelling. For instance, one can encrypt a message under a Sudoku puzzle such that only those who solve it can decrypt [30], construct time-lock encryption using blockchain timestamps [26], or build broadcast encryption systems with fine-grained access control [14]. Moreover, witness encryption enables applications in contingent payments [7] and decentralized protocols [22]. Many of these compelling witness encryption applications can be naturally expressed as arithmetic circuits compiled to Quadratic Arithmetic Programs [19] (QAPs). QAPs provide the algebraic framework used in the construction of many modern Zero-Knowledge Succinct Non-interactive Arguments of Knowledge (zkSNARKs), most notably in the Groth16 system [23], which has seen widespread deployment. Blockchain conditional payments, threshold-based access control, and privacy-preserving auctions all involve arithmetic constraints that compile directly to QAPs in deployed systems. For instance, encrypting a blockchain transaction under the condition "the total staked amount exceeds 1M tokens" represents exactly the kind of arithmetic relation that QAPs are designed to capture efficiently. This illustrates how real-world policies reduce to structured constraints over numeric variables—precisely the kind of predicates that QAP-based WE can target.

This creates a critical gap in the witness encryption landscape. Current WE constructions fall into two categories: theoretical schemes for all NP languages using complex assumptions like multilinear maps [18] or indistinguishability obfuscation [17] (iO), and practical special-purpose schemes for specific relations. While theoretical constructions target all NP, practical applications predominantly work with arithmetic circuits compiled to QAPs. Current practical WE schemes are not well-suited to QAP-style relations, leaving developers with a trade-off between relying on inefficient general-purpose constructions or settling for narrowly tailored solutions.

From Functionality to Extractability in WE. To understand this gap and the challenge of achieving both practicality and soundness, it helps to trace how WE definitions have evolved. Since its introduction by Garg et al. [18], WE has shifted from merely guaranteeing decryption functionality to ensuring knowledge soundness. Early schemes focused on expressiveness but lacked guarantees that decryption implies witness possession. This motivated stronger correctness notions: Bellare and Hoang [1] proposed adaptive soundness, while Goldwasser et al. [20] introduced extractability for explicit witness recovery. These refinements are crucial in settings like contingent payments [7], time-lock puzzles [26], and smart contracts [22], where witness possession must be provable.

Parallel efforts explored hybrid paradigms for WE, notably witness key encapsulation mechanisms (WKEMs) [9], which adapt the classical key encapsulation mechanism/data encapsulation mechanism (KEM/DEM) separation by allowing a witness to decapsulate an encapsulated key, subsequently used for symmetric encryption. Recent work by Fleischhacker et al. [13] showed that extractable WKEMs suffice to generically build full WE schemes. However, most existing designs treat the witness relation as a black-box NP statement. They offer limited structure, making it difficult to support arithmetic constraints or integrate with modular cryptographic ecosystems. This raises the natural question: can we build WE schemes that target algebraic witness relations, enabling compatibility with real-world systems that already rely on structured proofs, such as those built atop SNARKs?

Advances in SNARK Technologies. The connection between SNARKs and WE was first observed by Goldwasser et al. [20]: SNARK verification equations provide natural relations for WE construction. Foundational work in zero-knowledge [4,21] and succinct proof systems [25,28] laid the groundwork for SNARK development. Extractability, a key security notion in this context, was later formalized by Bitansky et al. [3]. One of the most widely adopted constructions is Groth16 [23], whose three-element proof system has been integrated into systems like Zcash and Tornado Cash. Recent innovations (e.g., zkSTARKs [2], Sonic [27], Marlin [8], and PLONK [16]) explore setup-free, universal, or updatable SNARKs.

Arithmetization maps computational statements to algebraic relations, with QAPs [19] forming the backbone of many zkSNARKs. Security analyses often employ the Algebraic Group Model (AGM) [15], enabling cleaner pairing-based proofs. These advances raise the natural question: can zkSNARK structures like Groth16 be adapted to build practical WE for QAP-based relations?

1.1 Our Contribution

We present an extractable WKEM for QAPs, the mathematical foundation underlying many modern zkSNARKs including the widely-used Groth16 system. Our main contributions are:

- **WKEM for QAPs**: We construct an extractable WKEM allowing encryption under QAP statements and decryption with corresponding witnesses, transforming Groth16's verification equation into an encryption mechanism.
- **Security Analysis in the AGM and ROM**: We prove the extractability of our WKEM using techniques from the AGM combined with the Random Oracle Model (ROM). Our analysis provides a clean reduction to Groth16's computational knowledge soundness (CKS) while modeling the key derivation function as a random oracle, avoiding complex assumptions.
- **Complete Witness Encryption**: Following Fleischhacker et al. [13], we show how our WKEM can be generically composed with symmetric encryption to yield a full extractable WE scheme for QAP relations.
- **Implementation and Evaluation**: We provide a complete Rust implementation with Circom integration, demonstrating practical performance across

circuits ranging from 162 to 150,848 constraints with encryption/decryption times from ∼20 ms to ∼1.7 s.

Our construction provides a practical WE scheme for QAPs, requiring no trusted setup and supporting efficient encryption via pairing-based primitives.

1.2 Organization

The remainder of this paper is organized as follows: Sect. 2 reviews the necessary preliminaries; Sect. 3 presents our proposed WKEM and WE constructions; Sect. 4 provides the security analysis; Sect. 5 presents our implementation, performance evaluation, and comparison with existing witness encryption schemes; and Sect. 6 concludes with future directions.

2 Preliminaries

2.1 Notation

We use the following standard notation. The security parameter is $\lambda \in \mathbb{N}$. A function $\mathsf{negl}(\lambda)$ is *negligible* if $\mathsf{negl}(\lambda) < 1/p(\lambda)$ for all polynomials p and sufficiently large λ. We write $x \leftarrow_{\$} S$ for uniform random sampling from a set S. For bilinear group notation, see Sect. 2.2.

2.2 Pairing

We consider bilinear groups $(p, \mathbb{G}_1, \mathbb{G}_2, \mathbb{G}_T, e, g, h)$ adhering to the same properties and notations as defined by Groth [23]. Here, $\mathbb{G}_1, \mathbb{G}_2, \mathbb{G}_T$ are cyclic groups of prime order p, g and h are generators of $\mathbb{G}_1$ and $\mathbb{G}_2$, respectively, and $e : \mathbb{G}_1 \times \mathbb{G}_2 \to \mathbb{G}_T$ is a non-degenerate bilinear map such that $e(g, h)$ is a generator of $\mathbb{G}_T$. We denote exponentiation in these groups by $[a]_1 := g^a$, $[b]_2 := h^b$, and $[c]_T := e(g, h)^c$, and write $[a]_1 \cdot [b]_2$ for the pairing $e(g^a, h^b)$.

2.3 Quadratic Arithmetic Programs

QAPs are a characterization of the NP complexity class. A QAP is generally reformulated from an arithmetic circuit composed of additive and multiplicative gates over a finite field $\mathbb{F}$. Following [19,23], we consider QAPs that have the following description:

$$Q = (\mathbb{F}, \text{aux}, \ell, \{u_i(X), v_i(X), w_i(X)\}_{i=0}^{m}, t(X)),$$

where $\mathbb{F}$ describes a finite field, aux is some auxiliary information, $1 \leq \ell \leq m$, and the polynomials $u_i(X), v_i(X), w_i(X) \in \mathbb{F}[X]$ have degrees less than n, where n is the degree of $t(X)$. A QAP that has this description defines a binary relation as below:

$$R_Q = \left\{ (\phi, w) \middle| \begin{array}{l} \phi = (a_1, \ldots, a_\ell) \in \mathbb{F}^\ell \\ w = (a_{\ell+1}, \ldots, a_m) \in \mathbb{F}^{m-\ell} \\ \sum_{i=0}^m a_i u_i(X) \cdot \sum_{i=0}^m a_i v_i(X) \equiv \sum_{i=0}^m a_i w_i(X) \bmod t(X) \end{array} \right\},$$

where we set $a_0 = 1$.

2.4 Zero-Knowledge Succinct Non-interactive Argument of Knowledge

zkSNARK refers to a type of argument of knowledge scheme. Note that $\mathcal{R}$ is a relation generator and R is a specific relation it outputs. Traditionally, a simulator formalizes the zero-knowledge property of SNARKs. In our setting, a similar construct is used to define semantic security: we require that a simulator can produce ciphertexts indistinguishable from real ones, even without knowing the plaintext. The definition below captures this formally:

Definition 1 (zkSNARK). *Let $\mathcal{R}$ be a relation generator that given a security parameter λ in unary returns a polynomial time decidable binary relation R, $(\phi, w) \in R$ be pairs of statement and witness, and $\mathcal{R}_\lambda$ be the set of possible relation R the relation generator may output given 1^λ. A zkSNARK is a tuple of algorithms (**Setup**, **Prove**, **Verify**, **Simulator**) defined as follows:*

$(\sigma, \tau) \leftarrow$ **Setup**(R): Given a relation, this algorithm returns a common reference string σ and a simulation trapdoor τ.

$\pi \leftarrow$ **Prove**(R, σ, ϕ, w): Given a relation, a common reference string (CRS) σ, and a pair of statement and witness $(\phi, w) \in R$, this algorithm returns an argument π.

$0/1 \leftarrow$ **Verify**(R, σ, ϕ, π): Given a relation, a common reference string σ, a statement ϕ, and an argument π, this algorithm returns a bit for accept or reject.

$\pi \leftarrow$ **Simulator**(R, τ, ϕ): Given a relation, a simulation trapdoor τ and a statement ϕ, this algorithm returns an argument π.

2.5 Groth16

Groth16 refers to a perfect zkSNARK introduced by Groth [23], which has properties in the previous section and can construct zkSNARKs for QAPs with the form:

$$R = (p, \mathbb{G}_1, \mathbb{G}_2, \mathbb{G}_T, e, g, h, \ell, \{u_i(X), v_i(X), w_i(X)\}_{i=0}^m, t(X))$$

with $|p| = \lambda$. The relation defines a bilinear group and a language of statements $(a_1, ..., a_\ell) \in \mathbb{Z}_p^\ell$ and witnesses $(a_{\ell+1}, ...a_m) \in \mathbb{Z}_p^{m-\ell}$ such that $a_0 = 1$

$$\sum_{i=0}^m a_i u_i(X) \cdot \sum_{i=0}^m a_i v_i(X) = \sum_{i=0}^m a_i w_i(X) + h(X)t(X)$$

for some degree $n-2$ quotient polynomial $h(X)$, where n is the degree of $t(X)$.

Definition 2 (Groth16). *A Groth16 system for a relation R is a tuple of probabilistic polynomial time (PPT) algorithms (**Setup**, **Prove**, **Verify**, **Simulator**) defined as follows:*

$(\sigma, \tau) \leftarrow$ **Setup**(R). Select $\alpha, \beta, \gamma, \delta, x \leftarrow_{\$} \mathbb{Z}_p^*$. Let $\tau = (\alpha, \beta, \gamma, \delta, x)$ and $\sigma = ([\sigma_1]_1, [\sigma_2]_2)$, where

$$\sigma_1 = \begin{pmatrix} \alpha, \beta, \gamma, \delta, \{x^i\}_{i=0}^{n-1}, \left\{\frac{\beta u_i(x)+\alpha v_i(x)+w_i(x)}{\gamma}\right\}_{i=0}^{\ell} \\ \left\{\frac{\beta u_i(x)+\alpha v_i(x)+w_i(x)}{\delta}\right\}_{i=\ell+1}^{m}, \left\{\frac{x^i t(x)}{\delta}\right\}_{i=0}^{n-2} \end{pmatrix}, \sigma_2 = \left(\beta, \gamma, \delta, \{x^i\}_{i=0}^{n-1}\right)$$

$\pi \leftarrow$ **Prove**$(R, \sigma, a_1, ..., a_m)$ Select $r, s \leftarrow_{\$} \mathbb{Z}_p$ and compute $\pi = ([A]_1, [B]_2, [C]_1)$, where

$$A = \alpha + \sum_{i=0}^{m} a_i u_i(x) + r\delta, \quad B = \beta + \sum_{i=0}^{m} a_i v_i(x) + s\delta$$

$$C = \frac{\sum_{i=\ell+1}^{m} a_i(\beta u_i(x) + \alpha v_i(x) + w_i(x)) + h(x)t(x)}{\delta} + As + Br - rs\delta$$

and $h(x)$ is the polynomial that exists when the relation holds and can be computed by the prover.

$0/1 \leftarrow$ **Verify**$(R, \sigma, a_i, ..., a_\ell, \pi)$ Parse $\pi = ([A]_1, [B]_2, [C]_1)$. It returns 1 (accept) if and only if

$$[A]_1 \cdot [B]_2 = [\alpha]_1 \cdot [\beta]_2 + \sum_{i=0}^{\ell} a_i \left[\frac{\beta u_i(x) + \alpha v_i(x) + w_i(x)}{\gamma}\right]_1 \cdot [\gamma]_2 + [C]_1 \cdot [\delta]_2$$

$\pi \leftarrow$ **Simulator**$(R, \tau, a_1, ..., a_\ell)$ Select $A, B \leftarrow_{\$} \mathbb{Z}_p$ and compute a simulated proof $\pi = ([A]_1, [B]_2, [C]_1)$ with

$$C = \frac{AB - \alpha\beta - \sum_{i=0}^{\ell} a_i(\beta u_i(x) + \alpha v_i(x) + w_i(x))}{\delta}$$

Groth16 satisfies several desirable properties, including perfect completeness and perfect zero-knowledge. However, for the purpose of our security analysis, we only rely on its knowledge soundness property, formalized below:

Definition 3 (Computational Knowledge Soundness). *For all non-uniform PPT adversary $\mathcal{A}$, there exists a non-uniform PPT extractor Ext which gets full access to the adversary's state; the following holds:*

$$\Pr\left[\begin{array}{c} (R, z) \leftarrow \mathcal{R}(1^\lambda); (\sigma, \tau) \leftarrow Setup(R); \\ (\phi, \pi) \leftarrow \mathcal{A}(R, z, \sigma); w \leftarrow Ext(R, z, \sigma) : \\ (\phi, w) \notin R \text{ and } Verify(R, \sigma, \phi, \pi) = 1 \end{array}\right] < \mathsf{negl}_{CKS}(\lambda),$$

where $\mathsf{negl}_{CKS}(\lambda)$ *is a negligible function.*

2.6 Symmetric Encryption

Symmetric encryption [24] is a widely known cryptographic primitive. A symmetric encryption scheme for a message space $\mathcal{M}$ is a tuple of PPT algorithms $(\mathbf{KeyGen}, \mathbf{Enc}, \mathbf{Dec})$ defined as follows:

- $k \leftarrow \text{KeyGen}(1^\lambda)$: Given a security parameter λ, and returns a key k.
- $CT \leftarrow \text{Enc}(k, M)$: Given a key and a message, then returns a ciphertext CT.
- $M \leftarrow \text{Dec}(k, CT)$: Given a key and a ciphertext, then returns a message M.

We will require a security notion called indistinguishability against eavesdroppers, abbreviated as *EAV-security* (where EAV stands for eavesdropper, or sometimes eavesdropping attack vulnerability), for the symmetric encryption scheme.

Definition 4 (EAV-Security). *A symmetric encryption scheme (**KeyGen**, **Enc**, **Dec**) is EAV-secure if for any PPT adversary $\mathcal{A}$ the following holds:*

$$\Pr\left[Expt^{EAV}_{SE,\mathcal{A}}(1^\lambda) = 1\right] \leq \frac{1}{2} + \mathsf{negl}(\lambda),$$

where the experiment $Expt^{EAV}_{SE,\mathcal{A}}(1^\lambda)$ is defined as follows.

$$\begin{array}{l}
\underline{\text{Expt}^{\text{EAV}}_{\text{SE},\mathcal{A}}(1^\lambda)} \\
k \leftarrow_{\$} \mathcal{K} \\
(m_0, m_1) \leftarrow \mathcal{A}(1^\lambda) \\
b \leftarrow_{\$} \{0, 1\} \\
ct \leftarrow \text{Enc}(k, m_b) \\
b' \leftarrow \mathcal{A}(ct) \\
\textbf{return} \begin{cases} 1 & \text{if } b' = b \\ 0 & \text{otherwise} \end{cases}
\end{array}$$

2.7 Algebraic Group Model

The AGM is a computational model introduced by Fuchsbauer et al. [15]. In the AGM, any algorithm that outputs a group element must also provide a representation of that element as a linear combination of its input group elements. We adopt the AGM to capture structured adversarial behavior in pairing-based cryptography. In this model, adversaries are restricted to outputting group elements that are algebraic combinations of prior oracle responses. This allows us to extract hidden coefficients from adversarial queries—a key technique in our security reduction for tracking computation on the statement and verifying knowledge of witnesses. Our usage follows the definition adapted from Campanelli et al. [6].

Definition 5 (Algebraic Adversaries). *Let* $\mathsf{bp} = (p, \mathbb{G}_1, \mathbb{G}_2, \mathbb{G}_T, e, g_1, g_2)$ *be a bilinear group and* $[\mathbf{x}]_1 = ([x_1]_1, \dots, [x_n]_1) \in \mathbb{G}_1^n$, $[\mathbf{y}]_2 = ([y_1]_2, \dots, [y_m]_2) \in \mathbb{G}_2^m$, $[\mathbf{z}]_T = ([z_1]_T, \dots, [z_l]_T) \in \mathbb{G}_T^l$. *An algorithm* $\mathcal{A}$ *with input* $[\mathbf{x}]_1, [\mathbf{y}]_2, [\mathbf{z}]_T$ *is called algebraic if in addition to its output*

$$\mathbf{S} = ([S_1]_T, \dots, [S_{l'}]_T) \in \mathbb{G}_T^{l'},$$

$\mathcal{A}$ *also provides a vector*

$$\mathbf{s} = \left((A_{ijk})_{i\in[l'],j\in[n],k\in[m]}, (B_{ij})_{i\in[l'],j\in[l]}\right) \in \mathbb{G}_p^{\zeta} \text{ with } \zeta = l' \cdot (l + n \cdot m)$$

such that $[S_i]_T = \prod_{j=1}^n \prod_{k=1}^m e([x_j]_1, [y_k]_2)^{A_{ijk}} \cdot \prod_{j=1}^l [z_j]_T^{B_{ij}}$ *for* $i \in 1, \dots, l'$.

Remark 1 (AGM for Pairing-Only Adversaries). In our construction, since Encap^H outputs no $\mathbb{G}_T$ element, adversaries receive only $\mathbb{G}_1$ and $\mathbb{G}_2$ elements as input. For such adversaries, Definition 5 simplifies to: when outputting $[S_i]_T$, the adversary must provide coefficients (A_{ijk}) such that

$$[S_i]_T = \prod_{j=1}^{n} \prod_{k=1}^{m} e([x_j]_1, [y_k]_2)^{A_{ijk}}$$

since all B_{ij} are forced to be 0 when no $\mathbb{G}_T$ elements are given as input.

3 Proposed Scheme

3.1 Extractable Witness Key Encapsulation Mechanisms

Our strategy is to first construct an extractable WKEM for QAPs and then show how it can be adapted to a full WE scheme. We follow the work of Fleischhacker et al. [13] to define the notion of an extractable WKEM relative to an indexed family of NP relations.

Definition 6 (Indexed Family of NP Relations). *Let* $\mathcal{I} \subseteq \{0,1\}^*$ *be a set. A set* $\mathcal{F} = \{\mathcal{R}_I\}_{I\in\mathcal{I}}$ *is a family of NP relations with the index set* $\mathcal{I}$ *if for all* $I \in \mathcal{I}$, $\mathcal{R}_I$ *is an NP relation, where* I *means the index of* $\mathcal{R}_I$ *and* $\mathcal{R}_I$ *is the relation identified by* I, *respectively. We denote* $\mathcal{L}_I$ *as the corresponding NP language.*

A WKEM is similar to a traditional KEM, but uses statement-witness pairs from an NP relation instead of public-secret key pairs.

Definition 7 (Witness Key Encapsulation Mechanism). *A WKEM for a key space* $\mathcal{K}$ *and a family of NP relations* $\mathcal{F}$ *is a pair of PPT algorithms WKEM* = (***Encap***, ***Decap***) *as follows:*

$(ct, k) \leftarrow \mathrm{Encap}(I, x)$: Given an index I and a statement x, this algorithm outputs a ciphertext ct and a key $k \in \mathcal{K}$.

$k \leftarrow \text{Decap}(I, w, ct)$: Given an index I, witness w, and a ciphertext ct, this algorithm outputs a key $k \in \mathcal{K}$.

The security properties of a WKEM are correctness and extractability. Correctness ensures that a valid witness allows for decapsulation of the key. Extractability ensures that any adversary who can distinguish a real key from a random one can be used to construct an extractor that finds a valid witness for the statement.

Definition 8 (Correctness of WKEM). *A tuple of algorithms* $(Encap, Decap)$ *is a correct WKEM for a family of NP relations* $\mathcal{F}$ *if for any* $\lambda \in \mathbb{N}$*, any* $\mathcal{R}_I \in \mathcal{F}$*, any* $(x, w) \in \mathcal{R}_I$*, and any* $(ct, k) \leftarrow Encap(I, x)$*, it holds that* $Decap(I, w, ct) = k$*.*

Definition 9 (Extractability of WKEM). *A tuple of algorithms* $(Encap, Decap)$ *is an extractable WKEM for a family of NP relations* $\mathcal{F}$ *if there exists a non-uniform PPT algorithm Ext such that for any non-uniform stateful PPT adversary* $\mathcal{A}$ *and any relation* $\mathcal{R}_I \in \mathcal{F}$ *for which*

$$Pr[Expt^{CPA}_{WKEM,\mathcal{A}}(1^\lambda, I) = 1] \geq \frac{1}{2} + \epsilon(\lambda)$$

for some non-negligible function $\epsilon(\lambda)$*, it holds that*

$$Pr\left[(x, w) \in \mathcal{R}_I : \begin{array}{r} x \leftarrow \mathcal{A}(1^\lambda, I) \\ w \leftarrow Ext^{\mathcal{A}(\cdot,\cdot)}(I, x) \end{array}\right] \geq \delta(\lambda),$$

for some non-negligible function $\delta(\lambda)$*. The experiment* $Expt^{CPA}_{WKEM,\mathcal{A}}(1^\lambda, I)$ *is defined below.*

$\text{Expt}^{\text{CPA}}_{\text{WKEM},\mathcal{A}}(1^\lambda, I)$

$x \leftarrow \mathcal{A}(1^\lambda, I)$

$b \leftarrow_\$ \{0, 1\}$

$(ct, k_0) \leftarrow \text{Encap}(I, x)$

$k_1 \leftarrow_\$ \mathcal{K}$

$b' \leftarrow \mathcal{A}(ct, k_b)$

$$\textbf{return} \begin{cases} 1 & \text{if } b' = b \\ 0 & \text{otherwise} \end{cases}$$

3.2 Construction of the WKEM for QAPs

We construct an extractable WKEM for a family of relations described by QAPs. Let $\mathcal{Q}$ be the set of valid QAPs generated by a relation generator. We define the family of NP relation of valid QAPs as:

$$\mathcal{F}_{\text{QAP}} := \{\mathcal{R}_Q\}_{Q \in \mathcal{Q}},$$

where

$$\mathcal{R}_Q = \left\{ (\{a_i\}_{i=0}^{\ell}, \{a_i\}_{i=\ell+1}^{m}) \;\middle|\; \begin{array}{l} \text{The coefficients satisfy the QAP equation:} \\ \sum_{i=0}^{m} a_i u_i(X) \cdot \sum_{i=0}^{m} a_i v_i(X) \equiv \sum_{i=0}^{m} a_i w_i(X) \bmod t(X) \end{array} \right\}.$$

Here, the statement is the set of public inputs $\{a_i\}_{i=0}^{\ell}$, and the witness is the set of private inputs $\{a_i\}_{i=\ell+1}^{m}$. For notational convenience, we define: $\phi_i(x) := r\beta u_i(x) + r\alpha v_i(x) + r^2 w_i(x)$, where r is a fresh randomness sampled in the Encap^H procedure. The construction uses a hash function $H : \mathbb{G}_T \rightarrow \mathcal{K}$ and the algorithms are as follows:

$\mathsf{Encap}^H(Q, \{a_i\}_{i=0}^{\ell})$

$\alpha, \beta, \delta, r, x \leftarrow_\$ \mathbb{Z}_p^*$

$$\sigma := \left\{ \begin{array}{l} [\alpha]_1, [\beta]_2, [\delta]_2 \\ \{[ru_i(x)]_1\}_{i=0}^{m} \\ \{[rv_i(x)]_2\}_{i=0}^{m} \\ \left\{[\frac{\phi_i(x)}{\delta}]_1\right\}_{i=\ell+1}^{m} \\ \left\{[\frac{r^2 x^i t(x)}{\delta}]_1\right\}_{i=0}^{n-2} \end{array} \right\}$$

$$s := [\alpha]_1 \cdot [\beta]_2 + \sum_{i=0}^{\ell} a_i [\phi_i(x)]_1 \cdot [1]_2$$

$k \leftarrow H(s)$

$ct := (\sigma, \{a_i\}_{i=0}^{\ell})$

return (ct, k)

$\mathsf{Decap}^H(Q, \{a_i\}_{i=\ell+1}^{m}, (\sigma, \{a_i\}_{i=0}^{\ell}))$

$$A := [\alpha]_1 + \sum_{i=0}^{m} a_i [ru_i(x)]_1$$

$$B := [\beta]_2 + \sum_{i=0}^{m} a_i [rv_i(x)]_2$$

$$C := \sum_{i=\ell+1}^{m} a_i [\frac{\phi_i(x)}{\delta}]_1 + [\frac{r^2 h(x) t(x)}{\delta}]_1$$

$s := A \cdot B - C \cdot [\delta]_2$

$k \leftarrow H(s)$

return k

In our construction, the QAP satisfies the constraint $a_0 = 1$ and contains some degree $n-2$ quotient polynomial $h(X)$ (where n is the degree of $t(X)$), which follows Groth16 convention. The intuition behind this construction is as follows. The encryptor provides σ to enable the decryptor to compute the target value s. However, to compute s correctly, the decryptor requires access to the terms $\{[r^2 w_i(x)]_1\}_{i=0}^{\ell}$. Since the randomness r is protected by the discrete logarithm assumption and cannot be extracted from the other provided elements, the decryptor cannot directly compute these terms. Instead, the decryptor must leverage the QAP relation itself: by using both the public statement $\{a_i\}_{i=0}^{\ell}$ and their private witness $\{a_i\}_{i=\ell+1}^{m}$, they can compute the values A, B, and C such that $s = A \cdot B - C \cdot [\delta]_2$. The computation completes successfully only when the QAP condition holds on the statement-witness pair, thereby enforcing access control at the level of arithmetic relations.

3.3 From WKEM to Witness Encryption

Following Fleischhacker et al. [13], the extractable WKEM we just constructed can be generically composed with a symmetric encryption scheme to create a full extractable witness encryption scheme.

Definition 10 (Witness Encryption Scheme). *A WE scheme for a message space $\mathcal{M}$ and a family of NP relations $\mathcal{F}$ is a pair of PPT algorithms WE = (Enc, Dec) as follows:*

$ct \leftarrow \text{Enc}(I, x, m)$: Given an index I, a statement x, and a message $m \in \mathcal{M}$, this algorithm returns a ciphertext ct.

$m/\perp \leftarrow \text{Dec}(I, w, ct)$: Given an index I, a ciphertext ct, and a witness w, this algorithm returns a message $m \in \mathcal{M}$ or an error symbol $\perp$.

Definition 11 (Correctness of WE). *A tuple of algorithms (Enc, Dec) is a correct WE scheme for a family of NP relations $\mathcal{F}$ if for any $\lambda \in \mathbb{N}$, any $\mathcal{R}_I \in \mathcal{F}$, any $m \in \mathcal{M}$, and any $ct \leftarrow Enc(I, x, m)$, it holds that $Dec(I, w, ct) = m$.*

Definition 12 (Extractability of WE). *A tuple of algorithms (Enc, Dec) is an extractable WE scheme for a family of NP relations $\mathcal{F}$ if there exists a PPT algorithm Ext such that for any stateful PPT adversary $\mathcal{A}$ and any relation $\mathcal{R}_I \in \mathcal{F}$ for which*

$$Pr[Expt_{WE,\mathcal{A}}^{CPA}(1^\lambda, I) = 1] \geq \frac{1}{2} + \epsilon(\lambda)$$

for some non-negligible function $\epsilon(\lambda)$, it holds that

$$Pr\left[(x, w) \in \mathcal{R}_I : \begin{array}{r} (x, m_0, m_1) \leftarrow \mathcal{A}(1^\lambda, I) \\ w \leftarrow Ext^{\mathcal{A}(\cdot,\cdot)}(I, x, m_0, m_1) \end{array}\right] \geq \delta(\lambda),$$

for some non-negligible function $\delta(\lambda)$. The experiment $Expt_{WE,\mathcal{A}}^{CPA}(1^\lambda, I)$ is defined below.

$$\begin{array}{l} \underline{\text{Expt}_{\text{WE},\mathcal{A}}^{\text{CPA}}(1^\lambda, I)\qquad\qquad} \\ (x, m_0, m_1) \leftarrow \mathcal{A}(1^\lambda, I) \\ b \leftarrow_\$ \{0, 1\} \\ ct \leftarrow \text{Enc}(I, x, m_b) \\ b' \leftarrow \mathcal{A}(ct) \\ \textbf{return} \begin{cases} 1 & \text{if } b' = b \\ 0 & \text{otherwise} \end{cases} \end{array}$$

Let $(\text{Dec}^{\text{sym}}, \text{Enc}^{\text{sym}})$ be a one-time symmetric encryption scheme. The WE scheme WE is constructed as follows:

$\text{Enc}(I, x, m)$	$\text{Dec}(I, w, (ct_1, ct_2))$
$(ct_1, k) \leftarrow \text{Encap}(I, x)$	$k := \text{Decap}(I, w, ct_1)$
$ct_2 \leftarrow \text{Enc}^{\text{sym}}(k, m)$	$m := \text{Dec}^{\text{sym}}(k, ct_2)$
return (ct_1, ct_2)	**return** m

4 Security Analysis

Security Model. Our security analysis operates in the ROM and the AGM. In the ROM, the hash function $H : G_T \rightarrow \{0,1\}^\lambda$ is modeled as an ideal random function. In the AGM [15], adversaries outputting group elements must provide their algebraic representations (Definition 5). Extractability (Theorem 2) relies on Groth16's CKS (Definition 3).

Theorem 1 (Correctness of WKEM). *The WKEM construction presented in Sect. 3 satisfies correctness as defined in Definition 8. That is, for any $\lambda \in \mathbb{N}$, any $\mathcal{R}_Q \in \mathcal{F}_{QAP}$, any $(\{a_i\}_{i=0}^{\ell}, \{a_i\}_{i=\ell+1}^{m}) \in \mathcal{R}_Q$, and any $(ct, k) \leftarrow Encap^H(Q, \{a_i\}_{i=0}^{\ell})$, it holds that $Decap^H(Q, \{a_i\}_{i=\ell+1}^{m}, ct) = k$.*

Proof. We need to show that for a valid statement-witness pair $(\{a_i\}_{i=0}^{\ell}, \{a_i\}_{i=\ell+1}^{m}) \in \mathcal{R}_Q$, the values s computed in $\text{Encap}^H(\cdot,\cdot)$ and $\text{Decap}^H(\cdot,\cdot)$ are identical.

From Encap: $s_{\text{enc}} = [\alpha]_1 \cdot [\beta]_2 + \sum_{i=0}^{\ell} a_i [r\beta u_i(x) + r\alpha v_i(x) + r^2 w_i(x)]_1 \cdot [1]_2$
From Decap: $s_{\text{dec}} = A \cdot B - C \cdot [\delta]_2$, where

$$A = [\alpha]_1 + \sum_{i=0}^{m} a_i [r u_i(x)]_1, \quad B = [\beta]_2 + \sum_{i=0}^{m} a_i [r v_i(x)]_2$$

$$C = \sum_{i=\ell+1}^{m} a_i [\frac{r\beta u_i(x) + r\alpha v_i(x) + r^2 w_i(x)}{\delta}]_1 + [\frac{r^2 h(x) t(x)}{\delta}]_1$$

Since $(\{a_i\}_{i=0}^{\ell}, \{a_i\}_{i=\ell+1}^{m}) \in \mathcal{R}_Q$, the QAP relation holds:

$$\sum_{i=0}^{m} a_i u_i(x) \cdot \sum_{i=0}^{m} a_i v_i(x) = \sum_{i=0}^{m} a_i w_i(x) + h(x) t(x)$$

Therefore, we expand $A \cdot B$

$$= [\alpha]_1 \cdot [\beta]_2 + \sum_{i=0}^{m} a_i [r\alpha v_i(x)]_T + \sum_{i=0}^{m} a_i [r\beta u_i(x)]_T + [r^2 (\sum_{i=0}^{m} a_i u_i(x)) (\sum_{j=0}^{m} a_j v_j(x))]_T$$

$$= [\alpha]_1 \cdot [\beta]_2 + \sum_{i=0}^{m} a_i [r\alpha v_i(x) + r\beta u_i(x) + r^2 w_i(x)]_T + [r^2\, h(x) t(x)]_T$$

And $C \cdot [\delta]_2 = \sum_{i=\ell+1}^{m} a_i[r\beta u_i(x) + r\alpha v_i(x) + r^2 w_i(x)]_T + [r^2 h(x)t(x)]_T$, thus:

$$\begin{aligned} s_{\text{dec}} &= A \cdot B - C \cdot [\delta]_2 \\ &= [\alpha]_1 \cdot [\beta]_2 + \sum_{i=0}^{\ell} a_i[r\alpha v_i(x) + r\beta u_i(x) + r^2 w_i(x)]_T = s_{\text{enc}} \end{aligned}$$

Since both compute the same s, they produce the same key $k = H(s)$.

All notation and models from the Preliminaries apply; in particular we work in the ROM and AGM and assume Groth16 CKS (Definition 3).

Theorem 2 (Extractability of WKEM). *Let $H : \mathbb{G}_T \to \{0,1\}^\lambda$ be a hash function modeled as a random oracle. In the AGM, if the CKS of Groth16 holds, then the proposed construction is an extractable WKEM for $\mathcal{F}_{QAP}$ as defined in Definition 9.*

Proof. Let $\mathcal{A}$ be a PPT adversary that wins the WKEM extractability experiment of Definition 9 with advantage $\varepsilon(\lambda) = \left|\Pr[b' = b] - \frac{1}{2}\right|$. We build an extractor Ext that outputs a valid witness for Q with probability $\delta(\lambda) \geq \varepsilon(\lambda) \cdot (1 - \mathsf{negl}_{\mathsf{CKS}}(\lambda))$. Roughly:

1. Ext simulates the WKEM experiment and the random oracle;
2. it identifies a target pairing value $\hat{s} \in \mathbb{G}_T$ that the honest encapsulation algorithm would hash to derive the challenge key;
3. if $\mathcal{A}$ ever queries $H(\hat{s})$ (event Good), the AGM provides algebraic coefficients expressing $\hat{s}$ in terms of CRS encodings of the QAP polynomials;
4. from these coefficients we assemble a Groth16 proof π for Q and invoke Groth16 CKS to extract the hidden witness values $\{a_i\}_{i=\ell+1}^{m}$. A standard ROM argument shows $\Pr[\mathsf{Good}] \geq \varepsilon(\lambda)$, yielding the claim.

Extractor Simulation. The extractor Ext receives QAP Q and statement $\{a_i\}_{i=0}^{\ell}$, and operates as follows. It invokes $(\sigma_{\text{Groth16}}, \tau) \leftarrow \text{Setup}(Q)$ to obtain $(\alpha, \beta, \delta, x) \in \tau$, samples $r \leftarrow_{\$} \mathbb{Z}_p$, and constructs σ exactly as in the $\text{Encap}^H(\cdot,\cdot)$ algorithm from Sect. 3.

Ext then computes $\hat{s} = [\alpha]_1 \cdot [\beta]_2 + \sum_{i=0}^{\ell} a_i[r\beta u_i(x) + r\alpha v_i(x) + r^2 w_i(x)]_1 \cdot [1]_2 \in \mathbb{G}_T$. It computes $k_0 \leftarrow H(\hat{s})$, samples $k_1 \leftarrow_{\$} \mathcal{K}$ and samples a challenge bit $b \leftarrow_{\$} \{0,1\}$. It gives $\mathcal{A}$ the challenge ciphertext $ct = (\sigma, \{a_i\}_{i=0}^{\ell})$ and k_b, then answers H queries as follows.

Random Oracle Simulation. Ext maintains a list Γ. On query $s \in \mathbb{G}_T$ from $\mathcal{A}$:

- If $(s, k') \in \Gamma$ return k'.
- Else if $s = \hat{s}$: mark Good, record the AGM algebraic rep for s, set $k' := k_0$, store (s, k') in Γ, return k'.
- Else: sample $k' \leftarrow_{\$} \mathcal{K}$, store (s, k') in Γ, return k'.

Reduction to a Hash Query. Let Good be the event that $\mathcal{A}$ queries $H(\hat{s})$. Conditioned on $\neg$Good, $\mathcal{A}$ never sees $H(\hat{s})$, so its view when $b = 0$ (receiving $k_0 = H(\hat{s})$) is identically distributed to its view when $b = 1$ (receiving a uniform k_1); hence $\Pr[b' = b \mid \neg\mathsf{Good}] = \frac{1}{2}$. Thus $\Pr[b' = b] = (1 - \Pr[\mathsf{Good}])\frac{1}{2} + \Pr[\mathsf{Good}]\Pr[b' = b \mid \mathsf{Good}]$, and therefore $\varepsilon(\lambda) = \left|\Pr[b' = b] - \frac{1}{2}\right| \leq \Pr[\mathsf{Good}]$.

AGM Coefficient Extraction (cond. Good). Since $\mathcal{A}$ operates in the AGM, when it queries $H(s)$ where $s = \hat{s}$, it must provide algebraic representations showing how s was derived from the input group elements.

$\mathcal{A}$'s input (cf. Sect. 3) consists of the following $\mathbb{G}_1$ and $\mathbb{G}_2$ elements only:

$$[\mathcal{X}]_1 = ([\alpha]_1, \{[ru_i(x)]_1\}_{i=0}^m, \{[\frac{\phi_i(x)}{\delta}]_1\}_{i=\ell+1}^m, \{[\frac{r^2x^it(x)}{\delta}]_1\}_{i=0}^{n-2})$$
$$[\mathcal{Y}]_2 = ([\beta]_2, [\delta]_2, \{[rv_i(x)]_2\}_{i=0}^m)$$

where $\phi_i(x) := r\beta u_i(x) + r\alpha v_i(x) + r^2 w_i(x)$.

By the AGM definition (Definition 5 and Remark 1), when $\mathcal{A}$ outputs s such that $s = \hat{s}$, it must also provide a coefficient vector $(\mathcal{A}_{i,j,k})$ such that:

$$s = \prod_j \prod_k e([\mathcal{X}]_1[j], [\mathcal{Y}]_2[k])^{\mathcal{A}_{1,j,k}} \tag{1}$$

where $[\mathcal{X}]_1[j]$ and $[\mathcal{Y}]_2[k]$ denote the j-th and k-th elements of $[\mathcal{X}]_1$ and $[\mathcal{Y}]_2$, respectively. From the coefficient vector $(A_{1,j,k})$, we extract coefficients by identifying which pairings correspond to the Decap^H computation structure. Specifically:

Let $j_\alpha, j_{ru_i}, j_{\phi_k/\delta}, k_\beta, k_{rv_j}, k_\delta$ denote the indices of $[\alpha]_1, [ru_i(x)]_1, [\phi_k(x)/\delta]_1, [\beta]_2, [rv_j(x)]_2, [\delta]_2$, respectively, in the input vectors. Then:

- Coeffs contributing to A: $a_{A,i} := A_{1,j_{ru_i},k_\beta}$ for $i = 0, \ldots, m$
- Coeffs contributing to B: $a_{B,j} := A_{1,j_\alpha,k_{rv_j}}$ for $j = 0, \ldots, m$
- Coeffs contributing to C: $a_{C,k} := A_{1,j_{\phi_k/\delta},k_\delta}$ for $k = \ell+1, \ldots, m$

Having extracted the coefficients from the AGM representation, we now show how these coefficients reveal the algebraic structure needed for Groth16 proof construction.

Algebraic Equation Derivation. The key insight is that if $\mathcal{A}$ successfully computes $s = \hat{s}$, then the AGM coefficients must satisfy a very specific constraint. Since both the left-hand side (AGM representation) and right-hand side (target value) represent the same group element s, we have:

$$\prod_{j=1}^{n_1}\prod_{k=1}^{n_2} e([\mathcal{X}]_1[j], [\mathcal{Y}]_2[k])^{\mathcal{A}_{1,j,k}} = [\alpha]_1 \cdot [\beta]_2 + \sum_{i=0}^{\ell} a_i[r\beta u_i(x) + r\alpha v_i(x) + r^2 w_i(x)]_T \tag{2}$$

This constraint, combined with the linear independence of pairing basis elements $\{e([\mathcal{X}]_1[j], [\mathcal{Y}]_2[k])\}_{j,k}$, forces the coefficients to satisfy specific algebraic relationships. Specifically, the coefficients reveal that the adversary has computed s in the form:

$$s = \Big([\alpha]_1 + \sum_{i=0}^{m} a_{A,i}[ru_i(x)]_1\Big) \cdot \Big([\beta]_2 + \sum_{j=0}^{m} a_{B,j}[rv_j(x)]_2\Big)$$
$$- \Big(\sum_{k=\ell+1}^{m} a_{C,k} \left[\tfrac{r\beta u_k(x) + r\alpha v_k(x) + r^2 w_k(x)}{\delta}\right]_1 + \left[\tfrac{r^2 h(x) t(x)}{\delta}\right]_1 \Big) \cdot [\delta]_2$$

where $\{a_{A,i}\}_{i=0}^m$, $\{a_{B,j}\}_{j=0}^m$, $\{a_{C,k}\}_{k=\ell+1}^m$ are extracted from the AGM coefficients as described in the previous section.

Expanding the right-hand side of (2) using bilinearity and equating with the AGM representation gives:

$$\sum_{i=0}^{m} a_{A,i}[r\beta u_i(x)]_T + \sum_{j=0}^{m} a_{B,j}[r\alpha v_j(x)]_T + \Big[(\sum_{i=0}^{m} a_{A,i} r u_i(x))(\sum_{j=0}^{m} a_{B,j} r v_j(x))\Big]_T$$
$$= \sum_{i=0}^{\ell} a_i [r\beta u_i(x) + r\alpha v_i(x) + r^2 w_i(x)]_T$$
$$+ \sum_{k=\ell+1}^{m} a_{C,k}[r\beta u_k(x) + r\alpha v_k(x) + r^2 w_k(x)]_T + [r^2 h(x) t(x)]_T$$

Collecting $[r\beta u_i(x)]_T$ and $[r\alpha v_i(x)]_T$ terms (noting $r, \alpha, \beta \in \mathbb{Z}_p^*$) yields:

$$\sum_{i=0}^{m} a_{A,i} u_i(x) = \sum_{i=0}^{\ell} a_i u_i(x) + \sum_{i=\ell+1}^{m} a_{C,i} u_i(x), \tag{3}$$

$$\sum_{j=0}^{m} a_{B,j} v_j(x) = \sum_{j=0}^{\ell} a_j v_j(x) + \sum_{j=\ell+1}^{m} a_{C,j} v_j(x), \tag{4}$$

Substituting (3)–(4) above cancels the u- and v-parts and leaves the main relation:

$$\Big[\sum_{i=0}^{m} a_{A,i} u_i(x) \sum_{j=0}^{m} a_{B,j} v_j(x)\Big]_T = \sum_{i=0}^{\ell} a_i [w_i(x)]_T + \sum_{i=\ell+1}^{m} a_{C,i}[w_i(x)]_T + [h(x)t(x)]_T. \tag{5}$$

These derived relationships (3)–(5) allow us to construct a valid Groth16 proof using the extracted coefficients, as we show next.

Why AGM Coefficients Yield Groth16 Proofs. Before proceeding with the construction, we explain why the AGM coefficient extraction directly yields a valid Groth16 proof. This is the crucial insight that makes our reduction work.

Our WKEM construction is designed so that the target value $\hat{s}$ algebraically encodes the same information as a Groth16 verification equation. Specifically:

- The encapsulation computes $\hat{s}$ using the "public" part of the verification equation.
- Successful decapsulation requires computing $s = A \cdot B - C \cdot [\delta]_2$, which is the full verification equation.
- The randomization parameter r ensures this can only be done with knowledge of valid witnesses.

Therefore, any adversary that can distinguish keys in our WKEM must implicitly know how to construct a verifying Groth16 proof, and the AGM makes this knowledge explicit through the coefficient representation.

Groth16 Proof Construction. Using the extracted coefficients, the extractor constructs a Groth16 proof $\pi = ([A']_1, [B']_2, [C']_1)$. The extractor samples $r', s' \leftarrow_{\$} \mathbb{Z}_p$ and constructs:

$$A' = \alpha + \sum_{i=0}^{m} a_{A,i} u_i(x) + r'\delta, \quad B' = \beta + \sum_{i=0}^{m} a_{B,i} v_i(x) + s'\delta$$

$$C' = \frac{\sum_{i=\ell+1}^{m} a_{C,i}(\beta u_i(x) + \alpha v_i(x) + w_i(x)) + h(x)t(x)}{\delta} + s'A' + r'B' - r's'\delta$$

where α, β, δ are the same values from the Groth16 setup used in the WKEM construction.

This proof satisfies the Groth16 verification equation as defined in Definition 2: expanding $[A']_1 \cdot [B']_2$ and applying the coefficient relationships (3), (4), and the main relation (5) ensures the result matches the verification equation's right-hand side, confirming $\mathrm{Verify}(Q, \sigma_{\mathrm{Groth16}}, \{a_i\}_{i=0}^{\ell}, \pi) = 1$.

Knowledge Extraction. From the reduction above we have $\Pr[\mathsf{Good}] \geq \varepsilon(\lambda)$. Conditioned on Good, the AGM parsing recovers $(a_i)_{i=\ell+1}^{m}$ and the constructed π verifies (by the Groth16 equation established above). By Groth16 CKS (Definition 3), any PPT adversary that produces such a verifying proof yields (via the extractor $\mathsf{Ext}_{\mathsf{Groth16}}$) a valid witness except with probability $\mathsf{negl}_{\mathsf{CKS}}(\lambda)$. Therefore

$$\delta(\lambda) \geq \Pr[\mathsf{Good}] \cdot (1 - \mathsf{negl}_{\mathsf{CKS}}(\lambda)) \geq \varepsilon(\lambda) \cdot (1 - \mathsf{negl}_{\mathsf{CKS}}(\lambda)),$$

as required by Definition 9.

Theorem 3. (Fleischhacker et al. [13], Theorem 7). *Let (Enc^{sym}, Dec^{sym}) be algorithms of an EAV-secure symmetric encryption scheme for message space $\mathcal{M}$ and key space $\mathcal{K}$ and $(Encap, Decap)$ be algorithms of an extractable WKEM for a family of NP relations $\mathcal{F}$ and the same key space $\mathcal{K}$ as the symmetric encryption scheme. Then, $WE = (Enc, Dec)$ is an extractable WE scheme for message space $\mathcal{M}$ and the family of NP relations $\mathcal{F}$.*

The proof can be found in [13]. Since Theorem 1 ensures the sound operation of the WKEM, and the symmetric encryption is assumed to be correct, the overall WE construction inherits correctness.

5 Implementation and Comparison

We present a complete implementation of our extractable WKEM for QAPs and evaluate its performance against prior witness encryption schemes.

5.1 Implementation

Core Library. Our implementation provides a Rust library (`zkenc-core`)[1] built on the arkworks ecosystem [10]. The library implements the Encap^H and Decap^H algorithms from Sect. 3 with support for R1CS-to-QAP conversion, BN254 curve operations for Circom compatibility, and Blake3-based key derivation modeled as a random oracle. Each encryption samples fresh randomness $(\alpha, \beta, \delta, r, x) \leftarrow_{\$} \mathbb{Z}_p$, eliminating trusted setup requirements.

Circom Integration. A command-line tool (`zkenc-cli`) enables direct encryption with Circom-compiled circuits [12]. The tool parses Circom's `.r1cs` files and snarkjs's `.wtns` witnesses [11], composes our WKEM with AES-256-GCM following Sect. 3.3, and produces ciphertexts compatible with our JavaScript/WASM bindings (`zkenc-js`) for browser and Node.js environments.

Test Circuits. We validated correctness on four diverse Circom circuits from our benchmark repository[2] spanning different scales and applications: (1) Sudoku verification (9×9 grid, 162 constraints); (2) EdDSA signature verification (8,443 constraints); (3) Merkle tree membership proof (9,307 constraints); (4) Keccak-256 hash computation (150,848 constraints). In the QAP formulation (Sect. 2), the statement $\varphi = (a_1, \ldots, a_\ell)$ consists of public inputs, while the witness $w = (a_{\ell+1}, \ldots, a_m)$ comprises private inputs satisfying the QAP relation.

Table 1 illustrates the decryption requirements for each test circuit, demonstrating the breadth of applications enabled by QAP-based witness encryption. Unlike traditional PKE where decryption requires a secret key, our WE scheme requires knowledge of a valid witness satisfying the public statement.

[1] https://github.com/flyinglimao/zkenc.

[2] https://github.com/flyinglimao/zkenc-benchmark.

Table 1. Application contexts and decryption requirements for test circuits

Circuit	Public Statement (what encryptor specifies)	Witness Required (to decrypt)	Application Scenario
Sudoku	Puzzle cells (81 values: givens + zeros)	Complete solution (81 values)	Encrypt rewards/hints under puzzle; only solvers can claim
EdDSA signature	Message M + public keys PK_1, PK_2, PK_3 (4 values)	Valid signatures $\sigma_1, \sigma_2, \sigma_3$ (6 values)	Multisig-gated access: decrypt only with 3-of-3 signatures
Merkle membership	Merkle root + leaf value (2 values)	Authentication path (85 values: siblings)	Authenticated data release: decrypt if member of committed set
Keccak-256 hash	Preimage hash target h (256 bits)	Preimage x s.t. Keccak$(x) = h$ (256 bits)	Hash-locked secrets: decrypt by revealing hash preimage

Each row demonstrates a different computational predicate: puzzle-solving (Sudoku), threshold signatures (EdDSA), set membership (Merkle), hash preimage (Keccak). The QAP relation enforces that the witness satisfies the public statement, enabling programmable decryption conditions beyond traditional key-based access control.

This demonstrates the expressiveness of QAP-based witness encryption: the same cryptographic primitive supports diverse access control policies: from puzzle-solving (Sudoku) to authentication (signatures) to membership proofs (Merkle trees) to computational hardness (hash inversion). Each application leverages the mature Circom ecosystem, allowing developers to specify access policies as arithmetic circuits rather than ad-hoc cryptographic protocols.

5.2 Performance Evaluation

We benchmarked our implementation on Google Colab with an Intel Xeon CPU @ 2.20 GHz (2 cores, x86_64) and 12 GB RAM, running Linux kernel 6.6.105+. Table 2 reports encryption (Encap), decryption (Decap), and ciphertext (CT) size for all four test circuits. Each circuit was measured over 30 iterations, with timing reported as mean ± standard deviation. The plaintext encrypted in each test is a 32-byte random key (256 bits), which our WKEM encapsulates and then uses to encrypt arbitrary application data via AES-256-GCM.

Table 2. Measured performance of WKEM implementation across various circuits

Circuit	Const.	Pub.	Priv.	Enc. (ms)	Dec. (ms)	CT (KB)
Sudoku 9×9	162	81	81	20.1 ± 27.9	19.8 ± 27.2	121
EdDSA signature	8443	4	6	42.9 ± 6.6	165.3 ± 17.6	5
Merkle membership	9307	2	85	42.0 ± 5.0	189.4 ± 24.9	6
Keccak-256 hash	150848	256	256	1686.5 ± 321.7	1632.2 ± 209.9	395

Const. = constraints; Pub. = public inputs (statement); Priv. = private inputs (witness).
WKEM encrypts a 32-byte key; full WE CT = WKEM CT + AES-GCM(plaintext).

The results demonstrate practical performance across varying scales. Small circuits (Sudoku, 162 constraints) complete in ~20 ms for both encryption and decryption, suitable for interactive applications. Medium circuits (EdDSA and Merkle, ~8–9K constraints) encrypt in ~43 ms and decrypt in ~165–190 ms. The large Keccak circuit (150K constraints) requires ~1.7 s for both operations, still practical for non-interactive use cases. The high variance for Sudoku suggests initial JIT compilation overhead, while larger circuits show more stable timing.

Encryption time correlates primarily with the number of constraints, as Encap must compute $(2m - \ell + n)$ exponentiations in $\mathbb{G}_1$ and $(m + 3)$ in $\mathbb{G}_2$. Decryption time exhibits similar scaling but includes the constant cost of 2 pairings (cf. Table 4). The sublinear relationship between decryption time and constraints (e.g., Keccak has 93× more constraints than Sudoku but only 82× longer decryption) reflects the dominance of witness processing over the fixed pairing overhead.

Ciphertext size exhibits counterintuitive behavior: Sudoku (162 constraints) produces 121 KB, while the 52× larger EdDSA circuit yields only 5 KB. This reflects the ciphertext structure $(2m-\ell+n+1)|\mathbb{G}_1|+(m+3)|\mathbb{G}_2|$, where Sudoku's 81 public inputs inflate the $(2m - \ell)$ prefix term. EdDSA and Merkle have only 4 and 2 public inputs, respectively, resulting in much smaller ciphertexts despite having more constraints. The Keccak circuit with 256 public inputs grows to 395 KB, confirming that ciphertext size depends on both constraint count (m, n) and public input count (ℓ), with substantial compression for circuits minimizing public parameters.

5.3 Comparison with Prior Work

We compare our extractable witness key encapsulation (WKEM) for QAP relations with representative witness-gated/witness encryption (WE) constructions. Table 3 summarizes qualitative features (target language, building block, model, extraction guarantee). Table 4 reports per-ciphertext cost under a uniform counting convention. A full WE instantiation follows from the standard WKEM⇒WE transform (Sect. 3); the extra symmetric ciphertext is omitted from the table for clarity.

Table 3. Landscape of witness-gated encryption primitives (WKEM/WE variants).

Property	Our Work	[13]	[31]	[29]	[6]	[18]
Extractable	✓	✓	×	×	×	×
Target Lang.	QAP	Poly-Commit	All NP	All NP	Func-Commit	Exact Cover
Primitive	zkSNARK	Commitments	Lattice	Lattice	Commitments	MLM
Assumption	CKS (Groth16)	Discrete Log	LWE variant	LWE variant	Function Hiding Commitments	MLM
Model	ROM+AGM	GGM	Standard	Standard	GGM	Idealized
Year	2025	2024	2022	2022	2024	2013

Extractable = knowledge-from-distinguisher witness extractor (Sect. 3.3). Poly-Commit = polynomial commitment (e.g., KZG). Func-Commit = succinct functional commitments. GGM = Generic Group Model. MLM = multilinear map.

Table 4. Per-ciphertext costs (Enc/Dec) and sizes.

Property	Our Work†	[6]	[31]	[29]
Enc. Cost	$\approx (2m - \ell + n)E_{G_1}$ $+(m+3)E_{G_2}$ 1 H	$O(\vert F \vert)$ ops 1 H	$O(w^2 h)$ mat. ops h LWE	$O(wt)$ mat. ops $O(w)$ LWE
Dec. Cost	$\approx (2m - \ell + n)E_{G_1}$ $+(m+1)E_{G_2}$ 2 P, 1 H	1 P 1 H	$O(wh)$ mat. ops ext step	$O(wt)$ mat. ops $O(w)$ LWE
CT Size	$(2m - \ell + n + 1)\ \mathbb{G}_1$ $+(m+3)\ \mathbb{G}_2$	succinct (indep. n)	$O(wh)$ encs	$O(w)$ samples $+O(t)$ aux
Key Feature	**QAP, no setup**	Input-indep. decap	BP-based NP	BP-resilient

Parameters. QAP: m wires, ℓ public, $n = \deg t(X)$. [6]: function size $|F|$ (succinct in n). [31]: BP width w, length h. [29]: width w, program length t. E=exp; P=pairing; H=hash; mat. ops=matrix/LWE ops; encs=lattice encodings; aux=aux public data; BP=branching program. † No reusable CRS (fresh masked SRS per ciphertext).

Expressiveness vs. Specialization. QAPs capture a broad class of relations; our WKEM targets this directly, leveraging mature zkSNARK tooling. Extractable schemes for polynomial and functional commitments [6,13] optimize for narrower languages, trading generality for compactness.

Security and Performance. Our construction provides a knowledge extractor (Theorem 2): any adversary distinguishing real vs. random keys yields a witness. Fleischhacker et al. [13] likewise prove extractable WKEM under discrete log in the GGM. Recent lattice-based WE [29,31] target semantic security (message hiding for false statements) under LWE in the standard model but lack knowledge-from-distinguisher extraction. Campanelli et al. [6] achieve input-independent decapsulation with a single pairing, optimizing for functional commitment openings at the cost of narrower expressiveness. Our per-ciphertext cost is linear in circuit size (m, n) with 2 pairings at decapsulation and no trusted setup. Lattice schemes [29,31] avoid pairings but incur $O(w^2h)$ to $O(wt)$ matrix operations, while Campanelli et al. [6] achieve succinctness independent of input length n.

6 Conclusion

We presented the first extractable witness encryption scheme tailored for QAPs, bridging the gap between WE theory and the mature zkSNARK ecosystem. By repurposing Groth16's verification equations, our construction achieves both expressiveness and practical implementability without introducing complex new assumptions. The security analysis in the AGM reduces cleanly to Groth16's CKS, ensuring strong extractability guarantees while relying on well-established hardness assumptions.

Our implementation demonstrates practical performance: small circuits (162 constraints) complete in ~20 ms, medium circuits (~9K constraints) in ~40–190 ms, and large circuits (150K constraints) in ~1.7 s. Ciphertext sizes range from 5 KB to 395 KB depending on circuit parameters. Our scheme benefits from the extensive optimizations and tooling of zkSNARKs, making QAP-based WE readily deployable for applications such as blockchain-based conditional payments, privacy-preserving auctions, and secure computation protocols.

Future work includes exploring CRS-based variants to reduce ciphertext size. Bowe et al. [5, §6] propose separating Groth16's CRS into reusable and QAP-specific components, which may allow offloading part of the ciphertext to the setup phase.

Acknowledgments. This research was supported by the National Science and Technology Council (NSTC), Taiwan (ROC), under Project Numbers NSTC 114-2634-F-004-002-MBK, NSTC 114-2221-E-004-009-MY3 and NSTC 114-2222-E-008-006-MY2.

References

1. Bellare, M., Hoang, V.T.: Adaptive witness encryption and asymmetric password-based cryptography. In: Public-Key Cryptography–PKC 2015: 18th IACR International Conference on Practice and Theory in Public-Key Cryptography, Gaithersburg, MD, USA, 30 March–1 April 2015, Proceedings 18, pp. 308–331. Springer, Cham (2015)
2. Ben-Sasson, E., Bentov, I., Horesh, Y., Riabzev, M.: Scalable, transparent, and post-quantum secure computational integrity. Cryptology ePrint Archive (2018)
3. Bitansky, N., Canetti, R., Chiesa, A., Tromer, E.: From extractable collision resistance to succinct non-interactive arguments of knowledge, and back again. In: Proceedings of the 3rd Innovations in Theoretical Computer Science Conference, pp. 326–349 (2012)
4. Blum, M., De Santis, A., Micali, S., Persiano, G.: Noninteractive zero-knowledge. SIAM J. Comput. **20**(6), 1084–1118 (1991)

5. Bowe, S., Gabizon, A., Miers, I.: Scalable multi-party computation for zk-SNARK parameters in the random beacon model. Cryptology ePrint Archive, Paper 2017/1050 (2017). https://eprint.iacr.org/2017/1050
6. Campanelli, M., Fiore, D., Khoshakhlagh, H.: Witness encryption for succinct functional commitments and applications. In: Tang, Q., Teague, V. (eds.) Public-Key Cryptography – PKC 2024, pp. 132–167. Springer, Cham (2024). ISBN 978-3-031-57722-2
7. Campanelli, M., Gennaro, R., Goldfeder, S., Nizzardo, L.: Zero-knowledge contingent payments revisited: attacks and payments for services. In: Proceedings of the 2017 ACM SIGSAC Conference on Computer and Communications Security, CCS 2017, pp. 229–243. Association for Computing Machinery, New York, NY, USA (2017). https://doi.org/10.1145/3133956.3134060. ISBN 9781450349468
8. Chiesa, A., Hu, Y., Maller, M., Mishra, P., Vesely, N., Ward, N.: Marlin: preprocessing zksnarks with universal and updatable SRS. In: Advances in Cryptology–EUROCRYPT 2020: 39th Annual International Conference on the Theory and Applications of Cryptographic Techniques, Zagreb, Croatia, 10–14 May 2020, Proceedings, Part I 39, pp. 738–768. Springer, Cham (2020)
9. Choi, G., Vaudenay, S.: Towards witness encryption without multilinear maps: extractable witness encryption for multi-subset sum instances with no small solution to the homogeneous problem. In: International Conference on Information Security and Cryptology, pp. 28–47. Springer, Cham (2021)
10. arkworks contributors: `arkworks` zksnark ecosystem (2022). https://arkworks.rs
11. snarkjs contributors: snarkjs – javascript library for zksnark circuits (2023). https://github.com/iden3/snarkjs. Accessed 30 Oct 2025
12. Contributors, C.: Circom – circuit compiler for zksnarks (2022). https://github.com/iden3/circom. Accessed 30 Oct 2025
13. Fleischhacker, N., Hall-Andersen, M., Simkin, M.: Extractable witness encryption for KZG commitments and efficient laconic OT. Cryptology ePrint Archive (2024)
14. Freitag, C., Waters, B., Wu, D.J.: How to use (plain) witness encryption: registered ABE, flexible broadcast, and more. In: Annual International Cryptology Conference, pp. 498–531. Springer, Cham (2023)
15. Fuchsbauer, G., Kiltz, E., Loss, J.: The algebraic group model and its applications. In: Shacham, H., Boldyreva, A. (eds.) Advances in Cryptology – CRYPTO 2018, pp. 33–62. Springer, Cham (2018). ISBN 978-3-319-96881-0
16. Gabizon, A., Williamson, Z.J., Ciobotaru, O.: Plonk: permutations over Lagrange-bases for oecumenical noninteractive arguments of knowledge. Cryptology ePrint Archive (2019)
17. Garg, S., Gentry, C., Halevi, S., Raykova, M., Sahai, A., Waters, B.: Candidate indistinguishability obfuscation and functional encryption for all circuits. SIAM J. Comput. **45**(3), 882–929 (2016)
18. Garg, S., Gentry, C., Sahai, A., Waters, B.: Witness encryption and its applications. In: Proceedings of the Forty-Fifth Annual ACM Symposium on Theory of Computing, pp. 467–476 (2013)
19. Gennaro, R., Gentry, C., Parno, B., Raykova, M.: Quadratic span programs and succinct NIZKs without PCPs. In: Advances in Cryptology–EUROCRYPT 2013: 32nd Annual International Conference on the Theory and Applications of Cryptographic Techniques, Athens, Greece, 26–30 May 2013. Proceedings 32, pp. 626–645. Springer, Cham (2013)
20. Goldwasser, S., Kalai, Y.T., Popa, R.A., Vaikuntanathan, V., Zeldovich, N.: How to run turing machines on encrypted data. In: Annual Cryptology Conference, pp. 536–553. Springer, Cham (2013)

21. Goldwasser, S., Micali, S., Rackoff, C.: The knowledge complexity of interactive proof-systems. In: Proceedings of the Seventeenth Annual ACM Symposium on Theory of Computing, STOC 1985, pp. 291–304. Association for Computing Machinery, New York, NY, USA (1985). https://doi.org/10.1145/22145.22178. ISBN 0897911512
22. Goyal, R., Goyal, V.: Overcoming cryptographic impossibility results using blockchains. In: Theory of Cryptography Conference, pp. 529–561. Springer, Cham (2017)
23. Groth, J.: On the size of pairing-based non-interactive arguments. In: Advances in Cryptology–EUROCRYPT 2016: 35th Annual International Conference on the Theory and Applications of Cryptographic Techniques, Vienna, Austria, 8–12 May 2016, Proceedings, Part II 35, pp. 305–326. Springer, Cham (2016)
24. Katz, J., Lindell, Y.: Introduction to Modern Cryptography: Principles and Protocols. Chapman and Hall/CRC (2007)
25. Kilian, J.: A note on efficient zero-knowledge proofs and arguments. In: Proceedings of the Twenty-Fourth Annual ACM Symposium on Theory of Computing, pp. 723–732 (1992)
26. Liu, J., Jager, T., Kakvi, S.A., Warinschi, B.: How to build time-lock encryption. Des. Codes Crypt. **86**(11), 2549–2586 (2018)
27. Maller, M., Bowe, S., Kohlweiss, M., Meiklejohn, S.: Sonic: zero-knowledge snarks from linear-size universal and updatable structured reference strings. In: Proceedings of the 2019 ACM SIGSAC Conference on Computer and Communications Security, pp. 2111–2128 (2019)
28. Micali, S.: CS proofs. In: Proceedings 35th Annual Symposium on Foundations of Computer Science, pp. 436–453. IEEE (1994)
29. Tsabary, R.: Candidate witness encryption from lattice techniques. In: Dodis, Y., Shrimpton, T. (eds.) Advances in Cryptology – CRYPTO 2022, pp. 535–559. Springer, Cham (2022). ISBN 978-3-031-15802-5
30. Uberti, G., Luo, K., Cheng, O., Goh, W.: Building usable witness encryption. arXiv preprint arXiv:2112.04581 (2021)
31. Vaikuntanathan, V., Wee, H., Wichs, D.: Witness encryption and null-io from evasive LWE. In: Agrawal, S., Lin, D. (eds.) Advances in Cryptology – ASIACRYPT 2022, pp. 195–221. Springer, Cham (2022). ISBN 978-3-031-22963-3

Author Index

H. Seo (Ed.): ICISC 2025, LNCS 16487, pp. 557–558, 2026.
https://doi.org/10.1007/978-981-95-8034-7

The manufacturer's authorised representative in the EU is Springer Nature Customer Service Centre GmbH, Europaplatz 3, 69115 Heidelberg, Germany. If you have any concerns regarding our products, please contact ProductSafety@springernature.com

Printed and bound by CPI Group (UK) Ltd, Croydon, CR0 4YY
07/07/2026
02160913-0017